The Dawn of the Floating World

1650–1765

Early Ukiyo-e Treasures from the Museum of Fine Arts, Boston

TIMOTHY CLARK
ANNE NISHIMURA MORSE
LOUISE E. VIRGIN
with ALLEN HOCKLEY

Royal Academy of Arts

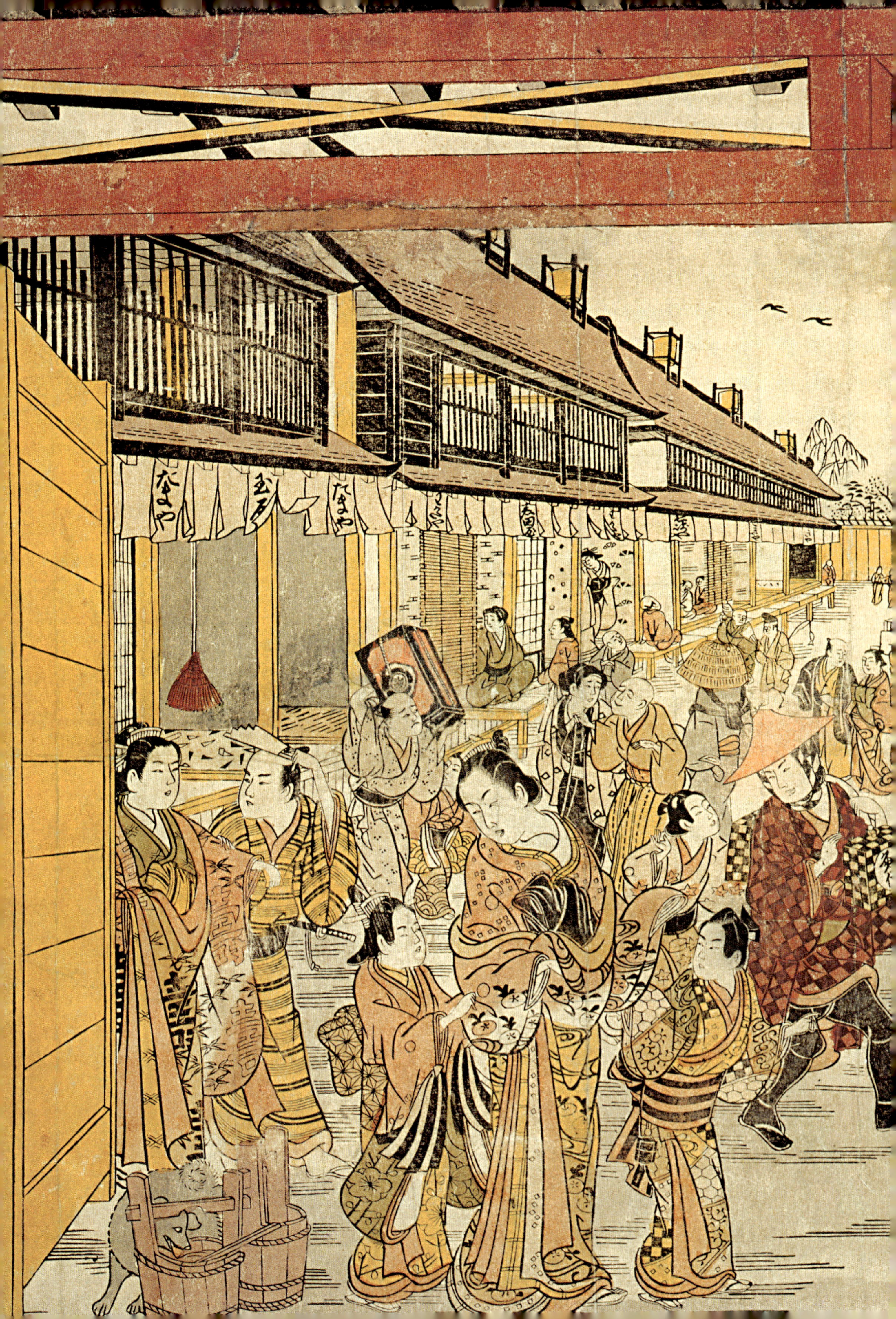

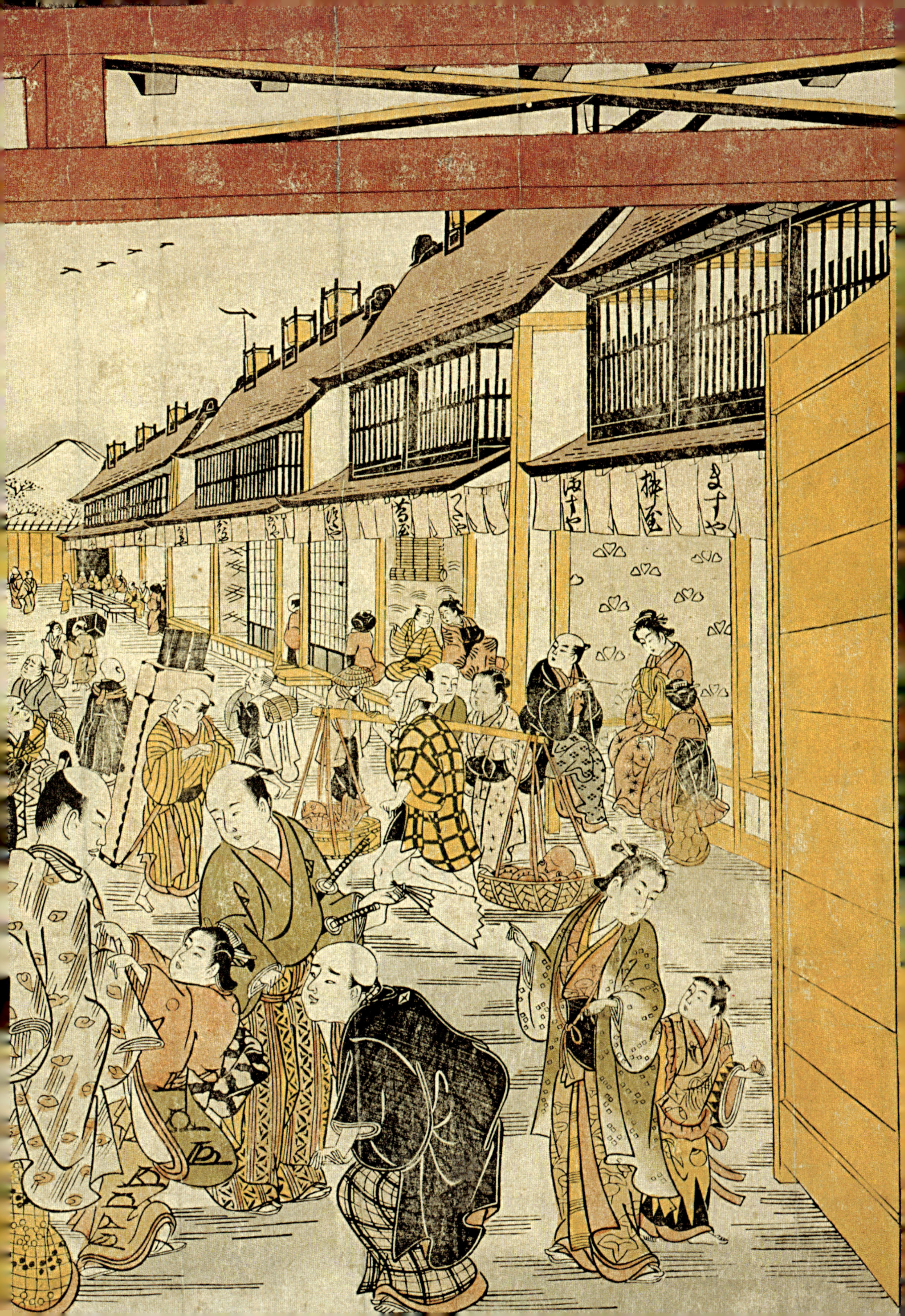
ますや

First published on the occasion of the exhibition 'The Dawn of the Floating World (1650–1765): Early Ukiyo-e Treasures from the Museum of Fine Arts, Boston'

Royal Academy of Arts, London,
24 November 2001 – 17 February 2002

The production of this catalogue was made possible by Fidelity Investments through the Fidelity Foundation

Fidelity Investments

This exhibition is an official Japan 2001 event.

The Royal Academy of Arts is grateful to Her Majesty's Government for agreeing to indemnify this exhibition under the National Heritage Act 1980, and to Resource, The Council for Museums, Archives and Libraries, for its help in arranging the indemnity.

PHOTOGRAPHIC ACKNOWLEDGEMENTS:
All works are reproduced by kind permission of their owners. Special thanks for providing photographs are due to the following institutions:

Aizu Wakamatsu: Fukushima Prefectural Museum of Art, p. 25, fig. 13

Boston: Museum of Fine Arts:
© 2000–01/All Rights Reserved, cover images; all colour plates of works exhibited courtesy Museum of Fine Arts, pp. 12–21, fig. 1–5 and 7–9; p. 23, fig. 11; p. 26, fig. 14; pp. 37–9, fig. 4–6; p. 95, fig.; pp. 35–6, fig. 1–3, courtesy Museum of Fine Arts, Boston

Chicago: Clarence Buckingham Collection, 1925.1845, The Art Institute of Chicago. All Rights Reserved, p. 29, fig. 17

Kyoto: Kyoto National Museum, p. 19, fig. 6

London: by permission of the British Library, p. 22, fig. 10

Tokyo: Shūeisha Ltd., p. 24, fig. 12

Tokyo: Tobacco and Salt Museum, p. 28, fig. 16

Washington: courtesy of the Freer Gallery of Art, Smithsonian Institution, Washington DC: Gift of Charles Lang Freer, F1898.14, p. 27, fig. 15

EXHIBITION CURATORS
Timothy Clark
Anne Nishimura Morse
Louise E. Virgin
with
Norman Rosenthal
MaryAnne Stevens
Cecilia Treves

EXHIBITION ORGANISATION
Royal Academy of Arts, London
Emeline Max
Annie Starkey
Museum of Fine Arts, Boston
Katherine Getchell

CONSERVATION TEAM
Museum of Fine Arts, Boston
Jacki Elgar
Ann Evans
John Robbe
Tanya Uyeda
Joan Wright

PHOTOGRAPHIC AND COPYRIGHT CO-ORDINATION
Royal Academy of Arts, London
Miranda Bennion
Andreja Brulc
Museum of Fine Arts, Boston
Leah Ross
Masaru Shima

CATALOGUE
Royal Academy Publications
David Breuer
Peter Hinton
Fiona McHardy
Peter Sawbridge
Nick Tite

COPY-EDITOR: Michael Foster, with Timothy Clark
DESIGNER: Isambard Thomas
PICTURE RESEARCHER: Celia Dearing
COLOUR ORIGINATION: Bobby Marcuson in association with Field Print & Graphics
TITLE-PAGE CALLIGRAPHY: Nobuyoshi Hamanaka

Printed in Italy by Graphicom srl

British Library Cataloguing-in-Publication Data

A catalogue record for this book is available from the British Library

ISBN 1-903973-03-1 (paperback)
Royal Academy exhibition edition

ISBN 1-903973-00-7 (hardback)
Distributed outside the United States and Canada by Thames & Hudson Ltd, London

ISBN 0-8109-6644-1 (hardback)
Distributed in the United States and Canada by Harry N. Abrams, Inc., New York

Illustration on pp. 2–3 Detail of cat. 109
Illustration on p. 9 Detail of cat. 131
Illustration on pp. 40 1 Detail of cat. 40

Director's Foreword

The Museum of Fine Arts, Boston, is privileged to own one of the world's most extensive collections of ukiyo-e paintings and woodblock prints, works that chronicle the floating world – the demi-monde of theatres and pleasure quarters that was a vibrant part of cultural life in Japan from the 17th to the 19th century. Among these are particularly rare images by artists such as Hishikawa Moronobu, Okumura Masanobu, Torii Kiyonobu I and Suzuki Harunobu who developed an iconography that catered to the tastes of the burgeoning merchant class. Experimenting with new printing techniques, these artists presented works that feature fashionably dressed courtesans or dramatically posed kabuki actors. Early images were rendered with forceful calligraphic outlines and touches of bright hand-colouring. By the mid-18th century they are distinguished by more subtle tonalities and lines made possible by technical advances in colour printing.

'The Dawn of the Floating World' heralds a new era in the history of the Museum's collection. Largely acquired through the efforts of the Boston physician William Sturgis Bigelow (1850–1926) during his residence in Japan in the late 19th century, our holdings number over 55,000 Japanese woodblock prints and 700 ukiyo-e paintings. This exhibition marks the first display of many of these works outside Boston, in fulfilment of our commitment to share our masterpieces with a far wider audience.

In preparation for 'The Dawn of the Floating World', members of our curatorial staff have collaborated with colleagues both in Great Britain and Japan to further knowledge of this area, which is so critical to the development of 'Edo style'. We are, in addition, profoundly grateful to Fidelity Investments, through the Fidelity Foundation, for generously funding conservation of these rare works, which will ensure their preservation for future generations.

The Royal Academy has long been acclaimed for its exhibitions devoted to the works of Katsushika Hokusai and Utagawa Hiroshige. We are delighted to be able to further this tradition and to participate in the United Kingdom's Japan 2001 celebration.

MALCOLM ROGERS
Ann and Graham Gund Director, Museum of Fine Arts, Boston

President's Foreword

'The Dawn of the Floating World' reveals a little-known period of Japanese art. Focusing on the origins of ukiyo-e, it explores its development, from powerful schematic images to full-colour woodblock printing, and describes the rise of a culture concerned with image and style during a fascinating period in the evolution of Edo society. Emblematic of the daily life and literature of the pleasure quarters and entertainment districts of Edo, early ukiyo-e set in motion a wave of image-making that was to shape print production until the end of the Edo period. Painted and printed designs have an intensity that sets them apart from those of later artists of the floating world, such as Utamaro, Hokusai and Hiroshige, and distinguishes them as one of the most accomplished forms of Japanese graphic expression.

The Royal Academy's commitment to Japanese art in recent decades has included the presentation of 'The Great Japan Exhibition' (1981–2) and, more recently, two monographic exhibitions that have highlighted the achievements in woodblock printing of Hokusai and Hiroshige, in 1991–2 and 1997 respectively. The present exhibition recognises that paintings as well as prints and illustrated books are inherently important to any consideration of the development of ukiyo-e. Many of the qualities that we admire in the prints of pioneer, yet little-known, artists, such as Hishikawa Moronobu and Okumura Masanobu, as well as the masters of the Kaigetsudō and Torii schools, represent splendid moments in the history of early ukiyo-e. The paintings and prints are extremely rare. Many of the prints are known only in unique impressions of great fragility and have never been seen in public before. It is a great privilege for the Royal Academy of Arts to host this exhibition, drawn entirely from the world-renowned Asian collections of the Museum of Fine Arts, Boston.

Our greatest debt of gratitude, therefore, is due to the Museum of Fine Arts for making this exhibition possible, and in particular to its director, Malcolm Rogers. This collaboration between our two institutions continues a creative alliance that was established with 'Monet in the Nineties' (1989–90) and consolidated with 'Monet in the Twentieth Century' (1998–9). We are confident that 'The Dawn of the Floating World' will lead to further shared exhibition projects.

At the Museum of Fine Arts, Anne Nishimura Morse and Louise E. Virgin, from the Department of the Art of Asia, Oceania and Africa, have selected the exhibition in close collaboration with Timothy Clark, Assistant Keeper in the Department of Japanese Antiquities at the British Museum. To this expert trio we extend our deepest appreciation for their knowledge, enthusiasm and unstinting commitment to the project. At the Museum of Fine Arts we are also most grateful to Arthur Beale and his staff in the Asian Conservation Studio. Many distinguished scholars have generously assisted with the catalogue that accompanies the exhibition, in particular Mutō Junko.

Funding for this exhibition has come from Fidelity Investments, through the Fidelity Foundation, who have underwritten the production of the superb catalogue, and from the Japan Foundation for the education programme, including a symposium to be held in conjunction with the Sainsbury Institute for the Study of Japanese Arts and Cultures as a fitting conclusion to the exhibition. This exhibition is an official Japan 2001 event, part of a nationwide celebration of the culture and lifestyle of Japan. Just as the floating world defined an ethos of enthusiastic pleasure seeking, it is our sincere hope that this exhibition will reveal to visitors unexplored delights.

PROFESSOR PHILLIP KING CBE
President, Royal Academy of Arts

Acknowledgements

The elucidation of a collection of Japanese art as important and extensive as that of the Museum of Fine Arts, Boston, and a subject as complex and relatively little-studied as early ukiyo-e requires the co-operation of many scholars. The curators of the exhibition, Timothy Clark, Anne Nishimura Morse and Louise E. Virgin, together with the Museum of Fine Arts, Boston, and the Royal Academy of Arts, London, would like to express their thanks to Asano Shūgō, Robert Campbell, John Carpenter, Katie Getchell, Roger Keyes, Kobayashi Tadashi, Mutō Junko, Naitō Masato, Satō Satoru, Timon Screech, Suzuki Jūzō and Tsuji Nobuo. For their outstanding conservation work they extend their appreciation to Joan Wright and Ann Evans, who undertook the preparation of the prints, and to Jacki Elgar and Tanya Uyeda, who remounted the paintings in consultation with Philip Meredith. The Kokuhō Shūri Sōkō-shi Renmei assisted with the conservation of the paintings, while John Robbe has made the art works ready for presentation. At the Museum of Fine Arts they also wish to thank Jennifer Bose, Pat Loiko and Kim Pashko. For their assistance with the catalogue and photography their thanks go to Sylvan Barnet, Rosina Buckland, William Burto, Hayashi Kyōji, Tom Lang, Masubuchi Kyōko, Saravuth Neou, Oka Midori, Leah Ross, Angela Segalla, Shima Masaru, Ellis Tinios, Tung Wu, Uchida Hiromi, Felicia Wivchar and Yamaguchi Keizaburō. Finally, they wish to recognise the debt that they owe to earlier scholars who contributed in important ways to the study of the Boston early ukiyo-e collections: Money Hickman, Donald Jenkins, Robert Treat Paine and David Waterhouse.

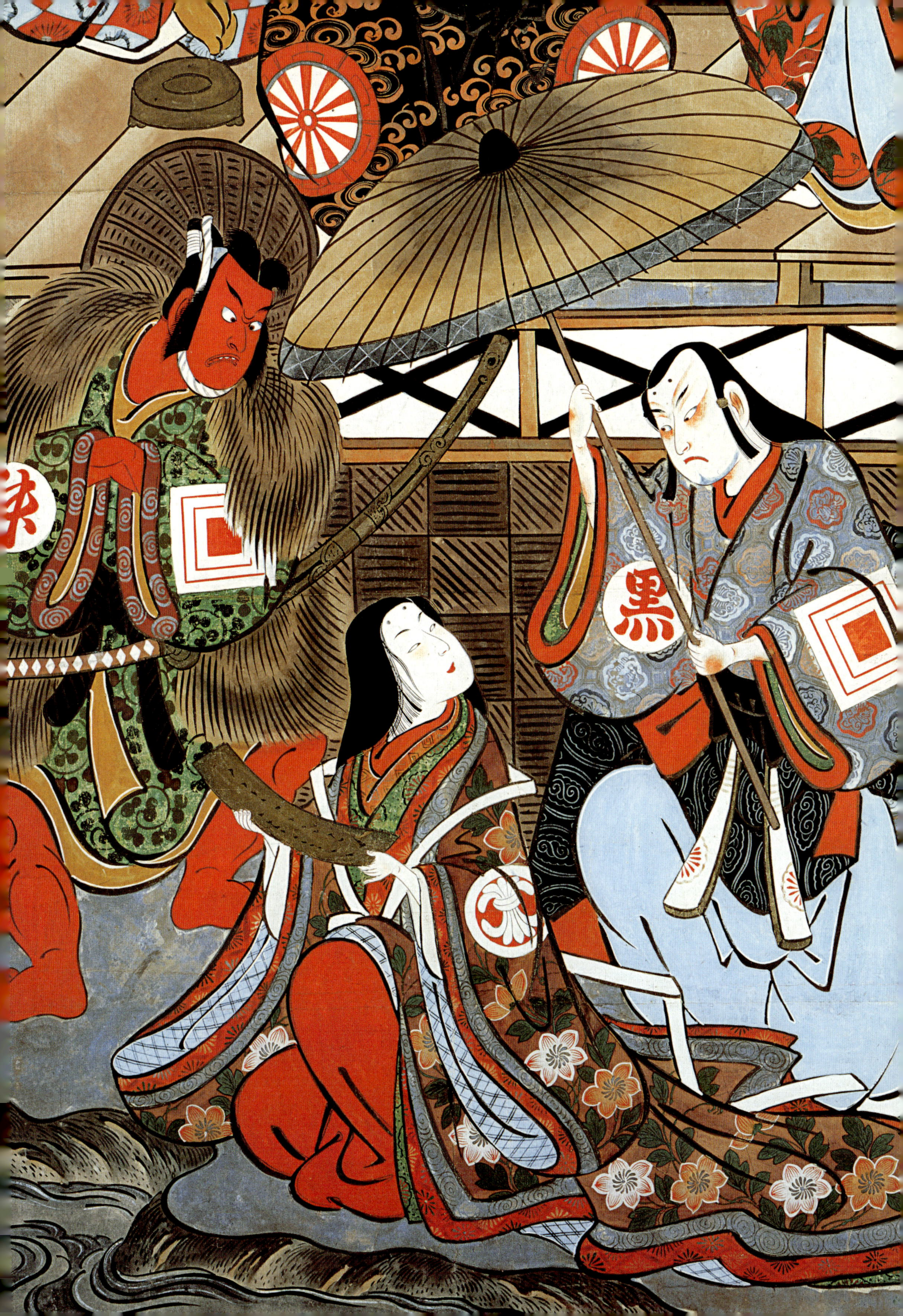
黒

Image and Style in the Floating World

The Origins and Early Development of Ukiyo-e

TIMOTHY CLARK

The great fire of the 18th to 20th days of the first month, 1657, was the worst in the history of Edo (modern Tokyo). The whole area between the castle and the Sumida River was reduced to ashes – almost all the *chōnin* (the 'townsman' class, i.e. merchants and artisans) districts on the low-lying land along the river and many of the daimyo (feudal lord) residences that surrounded the castle to the north, east and south. On the second day the fire spread to Edo Castle itself, destroying everything but the west palace (*nishi-no-maru*), where the fourth Tokugawa shogun, the youthful Ietsuna (1641–80), took refuge. The loss of property and life was terrible: 160 daimyo residences, more than 770 bannermen (*hatamoto*) residences, 350 temples and shrines, 60 bridges, 9000 storehouses, 400 city blocks and more than 100,000 dead.[1]

From the ashes rose a new city and a new urban culture.[2] Since being rebuilt by the first Tokugawa shogun, Ieyasu (1542–1616), as the hub of his new military capital in 1603, Edo Castle had already been remodelled four times, usually as a result of fires.[3] After the Meireki Fire of 1657 (called thus because it took place in the Meireki era [1655–8]) the castle was rebuilt without its central defensive keep – an unnecessary extravagance, it was argued, in an age when the country was secure in its peace. Further urban rearrangement was undertaken: most temples and shrines were moved to the periphery of the city, as was Yoshiwara, the single government-licensed brothel quarter, which had been founded in 1617 and was now exiled from the central Nihonbashi district to open fields on the northern fringes of Edo – henceforth temptation was to be kept at a distance. Overcoming yet another series of fires in the winter of 1682–3 (one set deliberately by a love-sick teenage girl, Oshichi; see cat. 37), the city thrived, servicing the lavish lifestyles of the approximately 250 daimyo and their hundreds of thousands of retainers. The first official census, taken in 1721, listed 501,394 *chōnin* residents and, since there were at least as many of their samurai 'betters',[4] Edo was perhaps the world's largest city at the time.

It was probably within a few years of the Meireki Fire, some time early in the Kanbun era (1661–73), that one Hishikawa Kichibei (*d.* 1694), the eldest son of a family of fabric embroiderers (*nuihaku-shi*), travelled from his native Hoda in nearby Awa Province to seek a new career in Edo as a painter and illustrator.[5] Moronobu, as he had come to call himself by 1678 and as he is known today, at first thought of himself simply as the 'picture master' (*eshi*) Hishikawa Kichibei. That is how he signed the first known work to bear his signature, the printed illustrated book *Buke hyakunin isshu* (*A Warrior 'One Hundred Poems by One Hundred Poets'*) of 1672. From 1678, in addition to the name Moronobu, the artist called himself a 'Yamato picture master' (*Yamato eshi*; see fig. 14). 'Yamato [Japanese] picture' is thought to have been used here in contradistinction to *kanga* (Chinese painting), to the techniques deriving ultimately from the Southern Song dynasty (1127–1279) in China that formed the basis of the style practised by the official Kano school in Japan.[6] By 1680 at the latest, Moronobu was referred to in a preface to one of his illustrated books as a 'floating-world picture master' (*ukiyo eshi*),[7] and a 'floating-world picture' (*ukiyo-e*) is mentioned in another book of this year. The general floating-world ethos had been explained, famously, in the preface to a '*kana* booklet' (*kana-zōshi*) of *c.* 1665, *Ukiyo monogatari* (*A Tale of the Floating World*), by Asai Ryōi (1612?–91), an author active mainly in Kyoto: 'Living only for the moment, turning our full attention to the pleasures of the moon, the snow, the cherry blossoms and the maples, singing songs, drinking wine, and diverting ourselves just in floating, floating, caring not a whit for the poverty staring us in the face, refusing to be disheartened, like a gourd floating along with the river current: This is what we call *ukiyo*.'[8] Here, as Richard Lane has commented, 'for the first time the *Zeitgeist* of the approaching Genroku Era [1688–1704] is embodied in a single word' – *ukiyo*, which was soon being applied as an epithet to a whole range of urban fads and consumer items.

By pairing 'floating world' and 'picture' to produce 'ukiyo-e' a term had finally been found both to describe the recent revolution in image-making and to suggest the unprecedented role that such images played in a wider cultural revolution that was well underway by 1680. The terminology was not yet stable, however. There is evidence from 1690 that Moronobu still preferred to be thought of as a Yamato picture master, rather than merely as a creator of the new, transient, often erotic floating-world pictures.[9] His pupils, referred to in a directory of the early Genroku era as 'masters of preparatory drawings for woodblocks' (*hangi shita-e shi*), implying that they simply designed illustrations for printed books, soon came to be subsumed into the larger category of 'floating-world picture masters' (*ukiyo eshi*).[10]

IMAGE AND STYLE

During the Edo period virtually all aspects of life were defined by a person's place within a finely graded social hierarchy. That status was reflected in the image an individual presented to the world, and the feudal authorities saw fit to issue a constant stream of sumptuary laws that attempted to regulate minutely the behaviour, dress and living conditions of all citizens, applying as much to daimyo and the style of gates they might build for their mansions as to townsmen and the kinds of clothes they might wear.[11] In the absence of warfare or violent class struggle, personal image and style became one of the battlegrounds on which shifting power relations were contested. Edo was a city of spectacle. First and foremost this involved the grand ceremonial played out around the castle between the daimyo and the shogun in accordance with a system, perfected by 1642, of mandatory 'alternate attendance' (*sankin kōtai*) at the shogunal court by the regional lords and their vast samurai retinues. Yet the styles and cultural forms deliberately developed by the townsman class in sharp distinction to those of their feudal 'superiors' were scarcely less significant. Perhaps, therefore, Moronobu was making a point when he called himself a Yamato picture master rather than an exponent of Chinese painting like the members of the Kano school. The floating world represented a conscious flight in terms of behaviour and imagination from the real world of feudal regulation. Barred by birth from participation in high politics and left largely free to make money, the townsman class increasingly sought its own forms of cultural expression predicated on its own system of values. Many samurai also found this flight from reality highly alluring, although their participation as a class was strongly discouraged.

The present publication is full of style and full of images – indeed, full of stylish images. Niceties of style and changes in style meant everything to townsmen and women. You might be a respectable townsman's wife, but there was every chance that you would have seen on the kabuki stage a handsome young man taking the part of a high-ranked courtesan. Indeed, your husband might engage a real courtesan in the Yoshiwara pleasure quarter if he had the funds and inclination. (He might, alternatively, engage the handsome actor.) Little if any social stigma attached to this – your marriage had in any case been arranged primarily to unite two merchant fortunes and produce heirs who would continue the business. The impersonator of women (*onnagata*) in kabuki was encouraged to imitate the styles of real women both on and off the stage,[12] and so influential did the great *onnagata* become in popular culture that real women might in turn imitate their styles of dress and deportment. In other words, mediated by kabuki, a respectable woman might well adopt elements of a courtesan's style. Coiffures, length of *kosode* sleeves, textile patterns, manners of tying the obi – all were subject to increasingly rapid changes of fashion, encouraged by clothing manufacturers, abetted by the publishing industry and to be paid for in cash in what surely marks the beginnings of advanced urban consumerism in Japan.

In the final quarter of the 17th century it suddenly seems to have become important for Edo townsmen to purchase images documenting their own rules and tastes. The medium of the woodblock print was adopted to reproduce imagery of various urban pleasures at a price most could afford. When, from Moronobu onwards, floating-world print artists and painters began signing their works, the purchaser was also buying an example of a named individual's style, which added a layer of 'art style' to the stylishness of the act or clothing depicted. Competition quickly sharpened between designers and between workshops of designers seeking to produce images in distinctive styles. Presumably, ownership of such art works represented an increase in the stylishness of the purchaser as perceived by his or her peers.

We rely almost totally on ukiyo-e paintings, prints and books for information on what Edo society looked like from *c.* 1650 to *c.* 1750: artists of most other schools did not depict the society around them. Early ukiyo-e imagery concentrates on certain subjects, particularly the 'bad places' (*akusho*) – the pleasure quarters and kabuki theatres, which were clearly very enticing – in a vigorous, voracious manner that does not dwell on problematic aspects of society. Much of the imagery in the present volume can be dated exactly, thanks to dates of publication given in books, depictions of unique kabuki performances, known changes in print formats and printing technology, alterations in artists' signatures and publishers' trademarks and, after collation of all the above factors, by reference to a demonstrable historical sequence of changes in fashion. Other issues, gaugeable in less precise terms, suggest themselves for discussion. What role did painted and printed imagery play in the formulation and development of the townsman's stylish self-image? What did townsmen and women see of themselves when looking at paintings and prints? And what part do early ukiyo-e paintings and prints play in our own view of those times?

PLEASURE QUARTERS

The ukiyo-e paintings, prints and books that appeared in the last quarter of the 17th century were quintessential *chōnin* products of the new shogunal capital of Edo in eastern Japan. Yet the types of urban pleasure they depicted had evolved much earlier in the century in the two great cities of the Kamigata region in the west: Kyoto, the ancient Imperial capital, and Osaka, a mercantile city of more recent origin. In 1589 the military dictator Toyotomi Hideyoshi (1536–98) ordered the brothels of Kyoto to be collected in a single licensed quarter, Nijō Yanagi-machi. In 1602 this was moved by the new Tokugawa regime to Rokujō Misuji-machi and in 1640 was finally transferred to a more permanent but remote location, a walled district called Shimabara that had been specially constructed on the south-western fringes of the city. The Osaka pleasure quarter, Shinmachi, was established on the western edge of the city in 1631. Despite periodic attempts to suppress it, unlicensed prostitution continued in numerous locations in all three cities throughout the Edo period.

The first licences to run the quarters were granted to individuals of samurai background. Indeed, the largest number of clients in the early period were samurai and the earliest imagery of the brothel districts took the form of large folding screens painted with hundreds of figures in architectural settings against a gold-leaf background, a type of painting typically done for ruling-class patrons. Modern art historians categorise these screens as 'early modern genre painting' (*kinsei shoki fūzoku-ga*). *Scenes in a House of Pleasure and Pleasure Quarter* (*Teinai yūraku-zu, yūri fūzoku-zu byōbu*; p. 38, fig. 5) shows on the left screen a row of brothels with courtesans either seated in the display windows (*hari-mise*) or parading in the street. Many of their potential clients bear the twin swords of the samurai class. The companion screen, now missing panels at its right and left extremities, focuses on the party rooms at the back of a grand brothel where couples lounge in an interior or stroll in a well-tended garden. The city can be identified as Kyoto, because talismans from Gion Shrine (Kanshin-in) are pasted above one of the brothel entrances on the left screen. The painting has been dated on stylistic grounds to the late Kan'ei era (1624–44) and placed at the end of a sequence of related screens consisting of two pairs of *Amusements at the Dry Riverbed, Shijō* (*Shijō-gawara yūraku-zu byōbu*; see fig. 1).[13] If a real location, rather than a 'brothel utopia', is depicted, then it could be either Rokujō Misuji-machi or Shimabara, depending on the exact date of the painting. Given the absence of artists' signatures on most of the early genre screens, art historians have tended to attribute them to anonymous 'town painters' (*machi-eshi*), whom they generally characterise as drop-outs from the official Kano school who worked for a wealthy

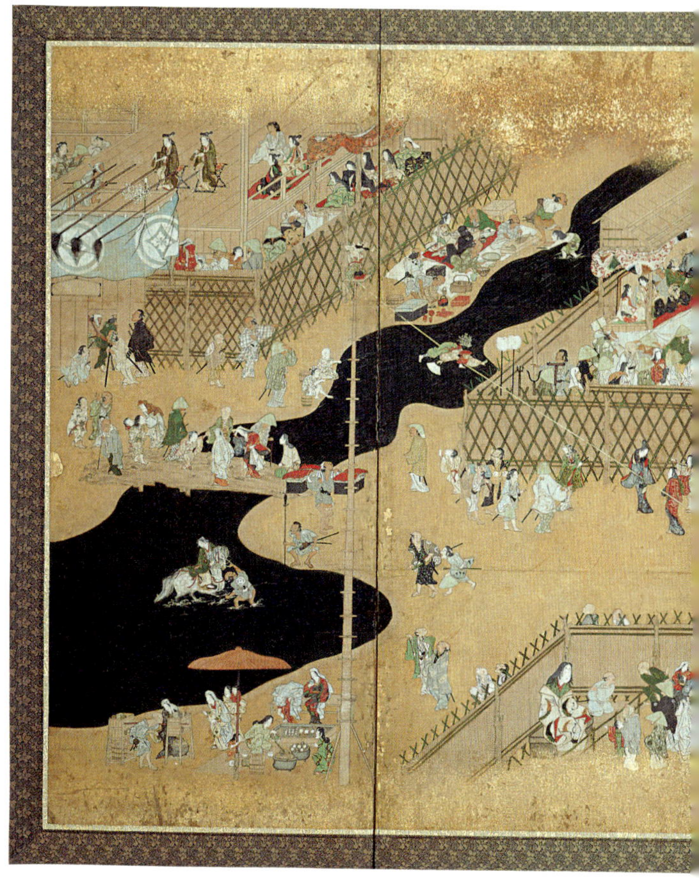

RIGHT SCREEN

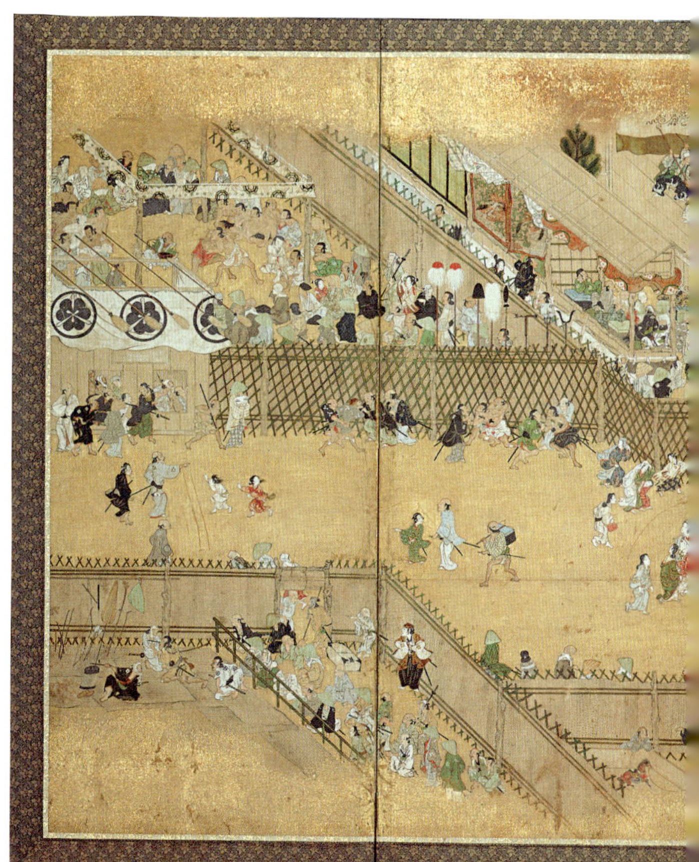

LEFT SCREEN

Fig. 1 ANONYMOUS, *Amusements at the Dry Riverbed, Shijō*, *c.* 1661–73, pair of six-panel folding screens, ink, colour and gold on paper, 104.1 × 290 and 104 × 290 cm, Museum of Fine Arts, Boston, Fenollosa-Weld Collection, 11.4591, 4592

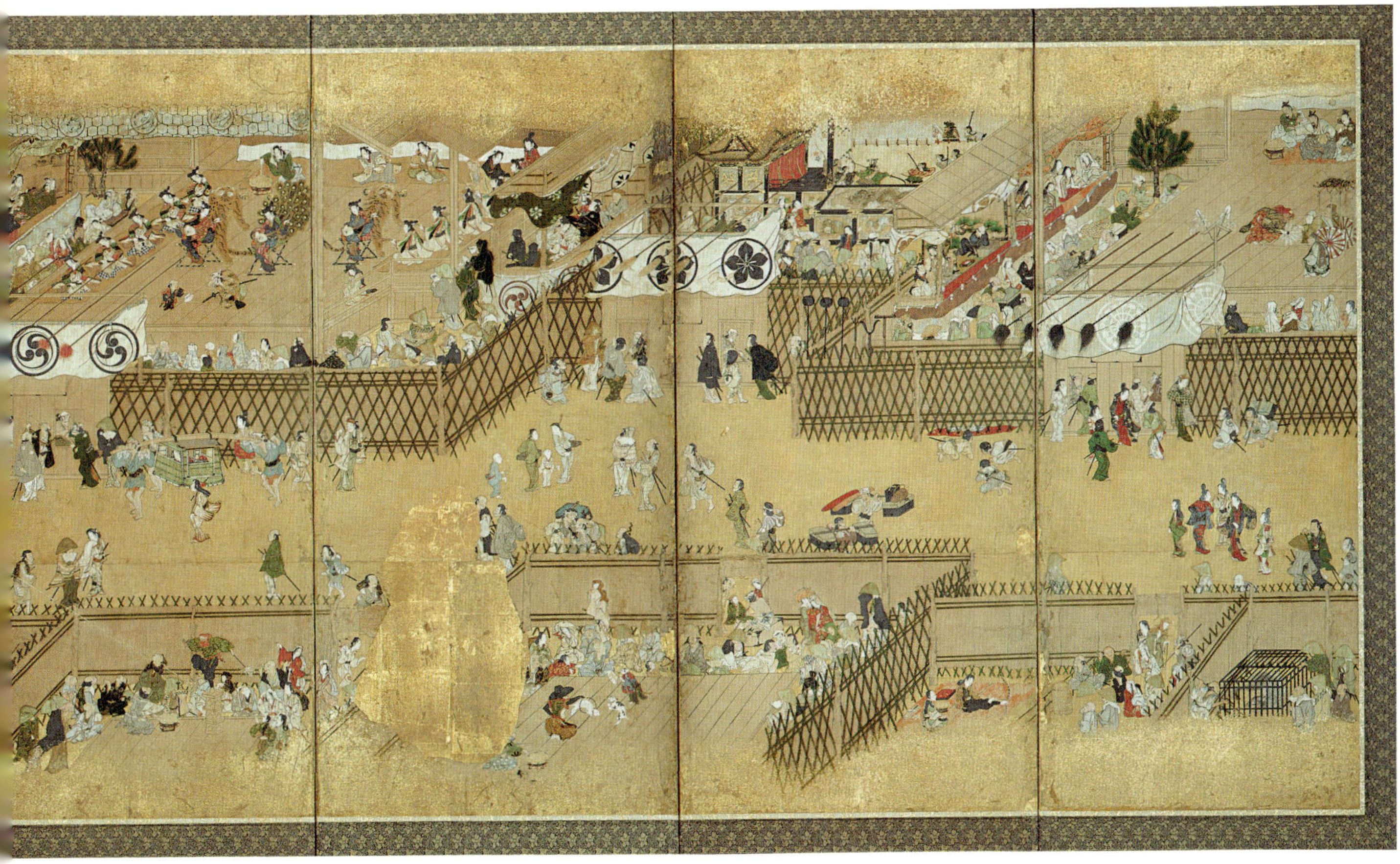

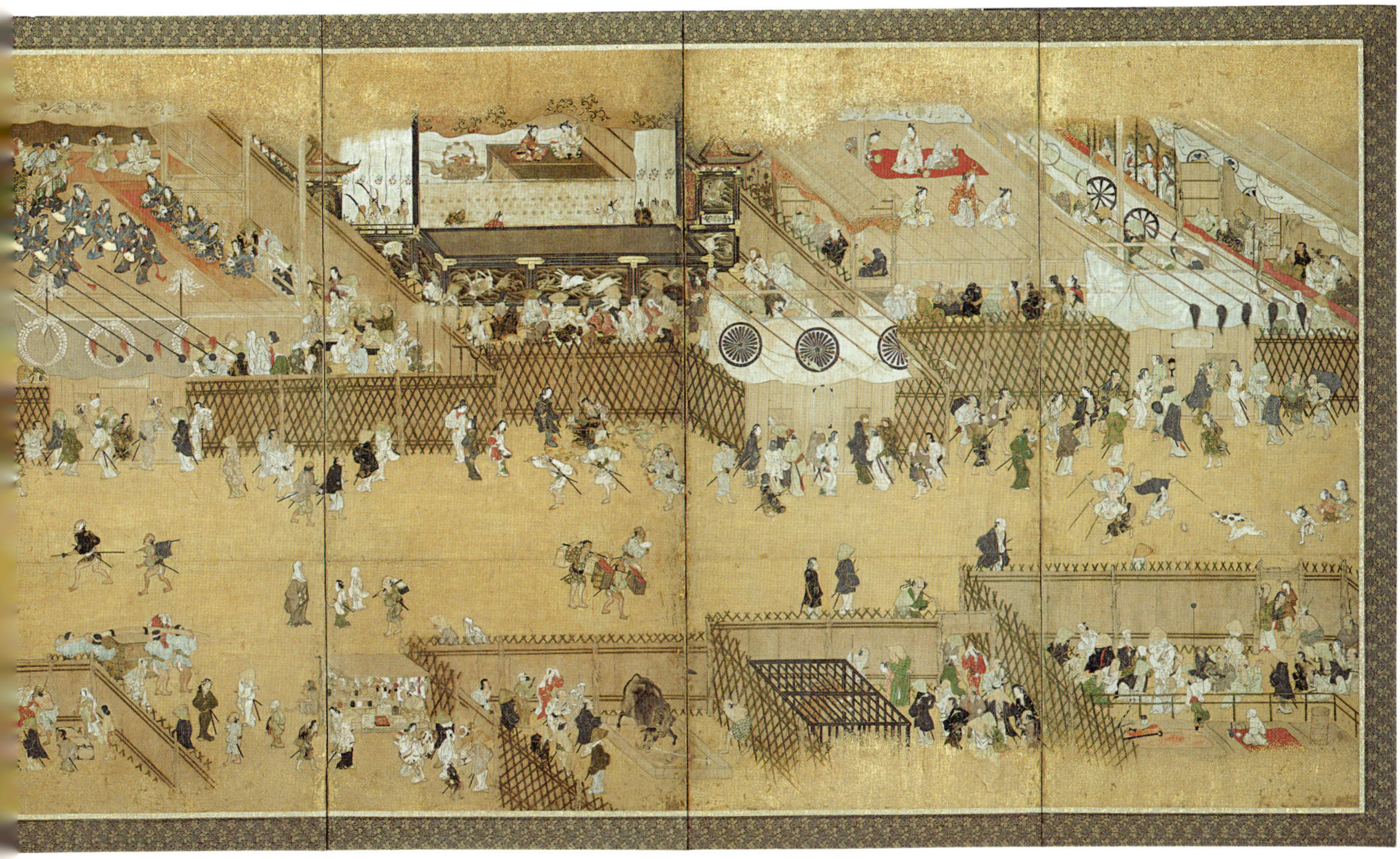

clientele of samurai and, increasingly, merchant patrons in the cities. *Scenes in a House of Pleasure and Pleasure Quarter*, for instance, shows the stylistic influence of Kano Sansetsu (1589–1651) in the painting of the rocks and trees in the brothel garden,[14] and one of the most famous pairs of genre screens, the so-called Sō-ō-ji Screens, which depict a kabuki performance and a luxurious brothel, is thought to have belonged to Okame-no-kata (Sō-ō-in, *d.* 1642), the mother of Tokugawa Yoshinao, daimyo of Owari.[15]

EARLY KABUKI

More egalitarian pleasures, not requiring the patron to engage the exorbitant services of a grand Kyoto courtesan (*tayū*), are shown in *Amusements at the Dry Riverbed, Shijō*.[16] Each summer when the Kamo River dwindled to shallow rivulets, amusements of all kinds were staged in temporary enclosures erected on islands or on the banks at the point where the busy Shijō avenue crossed the river. Such spaces were typically used for kabuki, traditionally held to have originated with performances by a woman called Okuni and her troupe given outside the Kitano Shrine in 1603, during which she mimed and danced the visit of a dandy to a brothel. Cross-dressing and generally outrageous and suggestive behaviour characterised these early shows ('kabuku' as a verb means to behave in a 'tilted', i.e. 'off-kilter', fashion or to dress in a shocking manner) and they were quickly copied by brothel owners at and around the riverbed at Shijō as a showcase for the women in their employ.[17] The worlds of the brothel quarters and kabuki were thus closely connected from the outset. Several competing troupes of 'women's kabuki' (*onna kabuki*) are depicted in the Boston painting, but there are plenty of rival attractions. Nō drama, puppet theatres (*ningyō jōruri*) and *sumō* wrestling are represented along the top of the screens, with rather more ephemeral acrobatic acts and freak shows lined up along the bottom.

Not long after the wild success of their debut in Kyoto, Okuni and her troupe were engaged to perform at Edo Castle in 1607 and, from 1612 to 1615, female kabuki players occasionally appeared before the Imperial court in Kyoto. By 1612 at the latest there were also troupes composed entirely of alluring young men (*wakashu kabuki*) who, like their female counterparts, could be hired as sexual partners. Audiences' infatuation with performers led to riotous behaviour. The authorities reacted with prohibitionary measures, first banning women from the stage (1629), then youths (1642) and eventually suppressing kabuki completely (1652). Ironically, the total ban was announced just after the death of the third Tokugawa shogun, Iemitsu (1604–51), who had been entertained during his final illness by kabuki troupes summoned to Edo Castle.[18] It was lifted only after protracted appeals by theatre owners and the introduction of regulations that profoundly altered the development of kabuki. These reinforced women's absence from the stage and stipulated that impersonators of women shave off their forelocks in the adult male manner. An Edo guidebook of 1662 lamented that the 'appearance of their faces was smooth and like cats with their ears cut off, and they were a sorry sight'.[19] Later *onnagata* were permitted to cover the bald patch with a small piece of purple silk, the 'lad's cap' (*yarō-bōshi*) worn by many impersonators of women in the prints reproduced in this book.

Plays gradually became longer, with more complex plots, as actors strove to showcase more than their immediate sexual allure. By the last two decades of the 17th century, individual actors of great talent had appeared who laid the groundwork for the sophisticated dramatic art that kabuki was to become. In Kamigata, Sakata Tōjūrō (1647–1709) defined the 'soft' (*wagoto*) style of the sympathetic lover, an essentially realistic mode of acting that was to remain at the core of kabuki in Kyoto and Osaka. In Edo, by contrast, Ichikawa Danjūrō I (1660–1704) developed the 'rough' (*aragoto*) style, a more bombastic, fantastic, 'super-hero' acting idiom that appealed more to the male-dominated audiences of what was still in many ways a frontier city.[20]

PUPPET THEATRES AND *JŌRURI*

Puppet plays are in progress immediately adjacent to the kabuki performances in *Amusements at the Dry Riverbed, Shijō*. This neighbourly coexistence continued into the 18th century, as the styles and plays of human and puppet performances constantly cross-influenced one another. The relative paucity of depictions of the puppet theatre in ukiyo-e has tended to obscure its significance within popular culture. In 1979 the great scholar of ukiyo-e, Suzuki Jūzō, published a seminal article in which he pointed out the importance of *jōruri* (puppet theatre, with chanting) as the theme of some early ukiyo-e prints.[21] The styles of *jōruri* prevailing in late 17th-century Edo were those of so-called 'old jōruri' (*ko-jōruri*), particularly that performed by Tosa no Shōjō Tachibana Masakatsu (dates unknown), commonly known as Tosa *jōruri*, which was at its most popular from the Enpō (1673–81) to the Hōei (1704–11) era. Admired by the ruling class, Tosa no Shōjō's *jōruri* was performed in Edo Castle and the mansions of the daimyo, as well as in the public puppet theatres alongside the kabuki playhouses in Sakai-chō and Fukiya-chō in the centre of Edo.[22] A unique book showing the various Edo styles of puppet performance, *Yakusha e-zukushi* (*Pictures of Actors*, *c.* 1685–90), illustrated by Moronobu's pupil Hishikawa Moroshige (active *c.* 1684–1704), includes *'The Tosa no Shōjō Theatre'* (fig. 2). At this time each puppet was relatively small and manipulated by a single puppeteer, rather than by three operators who manipulated a much larger puppet, as became standard after *c.* 1734. Moving away from the bombast of such earlier forms of 'old *jōruri*' as Satsuma *jōruri* and Kinpira *jōruri*, Tosa *jōruri* created more subtle and sophisticated performing styles that in turn influenced Edo kabuki during its formative period, the Genroku era. Most plots were derived from well-known medieval stories, the idea being to rewrite them in an appealing, up-to-date manner. This approach had much in common with the techniques of so-called 'parody pictures' (*mitate-e*), a major genre of early ukiyo-e (see p. 28–9). Tosa *jōruri* reached such a peak of popularity in the early years of the 18th century that the ukiyo-e artist Okumura Masanobu

(1686–1764) designed a series of twelve prints, *Famous Scenes from Japanese Puppet Plays* (*c.* 1705–6), showing imaginary performances by kabuki actors of famous scenes from Tosa *jōruri* puppet plays (cat. 46–57). Puppet theatres are depicted opposite the kabuki playhouses in Masanobu's *Large Perspective Picture of the Theatre District in Sakai-chō and Fukiya-chō* of 1745 (cat. 66).

PLAYWRITING, FICTION AND POETRY

The interdependence of kabuki and puppet theatre is reflected in the career of the leading Kamigata playwright who worked in both genres, Chikamatsu Monzaemon (1653–1725). From his mid-twenties onwards Chikamatsu wrote, in parallel, *jōruri* for the great chanters Uji Kaganojō (1635–1711) and Takemoto Gidayū (1651–1714) and kabuki plays for leading actors, including Sakata Tōjūrō. Chikamatsu's style, particularly in his contemporary-life pieces, was renowned for realism combined with depth of feeling: 'At the touch of his brush even ordinary words gain the power to take our breath away'.[23] Plays by Chikamatsu and others were often rapidly adapted between the two types of theatre and efficiently transmitted from Kamigata to Edo, as kabuki actors regularly toured between the three main cities (see cat. 36, 37). Until about the mid-18th century all the great *onnagata* of the kabuki stage came originally from the Kamigata region.

For both types of theatre, human and puppet, the plays were divided into two categories: contemporary-life (*sewa-mono*) works, which 'engage with contemporary society directly through depictions of an actual incident of the time' (epitomised by the 'love suicide' [*shinjū*] pieces), and history or period (*jidai-mono*) plays, which 'use complex interaction and dialogue with an array of texts from both the Japanese and Chinese traditions to portray contemporary politics. "History"...is a vehicle for a perspective on the present'.[24]

Two other new Kamigata literary forms that contributed crucially to the *chōnin* cultural matrix in the late 17th century should at least be mentioned here, although subjects derived from them are rarely portrayed directly in pictures of the floating world. These were the 'floating-world novels' (*ukiyo-zōshi*) of Ihara Saikaku (1642–93) and the style of *haikai* (*haiku*) poetry developed by his almost exact contemporary Matsuo Bashō (1644–94).

Saikaku had been a prominent *haikai* poet of the Osaka Danrin school before he turned to writing novels. He excelled in Olympian feats of solitary composition ('arrow counting', *yakazu haikai*), which culminated in the staggering 23,500 verses he composed during a single day-and-night sitting in 1684.[25] The new subject matter of Danrin poets shows how firmly their fingers were applied to the pulse of the floating world: 'Birds and flowers and autumn moons were still in evidence, but were obliged to compete for attention with brothel quarters, *daimyō's* concubines, *kabuki* actors, the price of rice, lawsuits, house-rents, pawnshops, bankruptcies'.[26] These were all subjects that Saikaku carried over into his episodic novels, beginning in 1682 with *The Life of an Amorous Man* (*Kōshoku ichidai otoko*), which recounts the *vita amatoria* of its precocious hero, Yonosuke, in the form of one chapter (and many conquests)

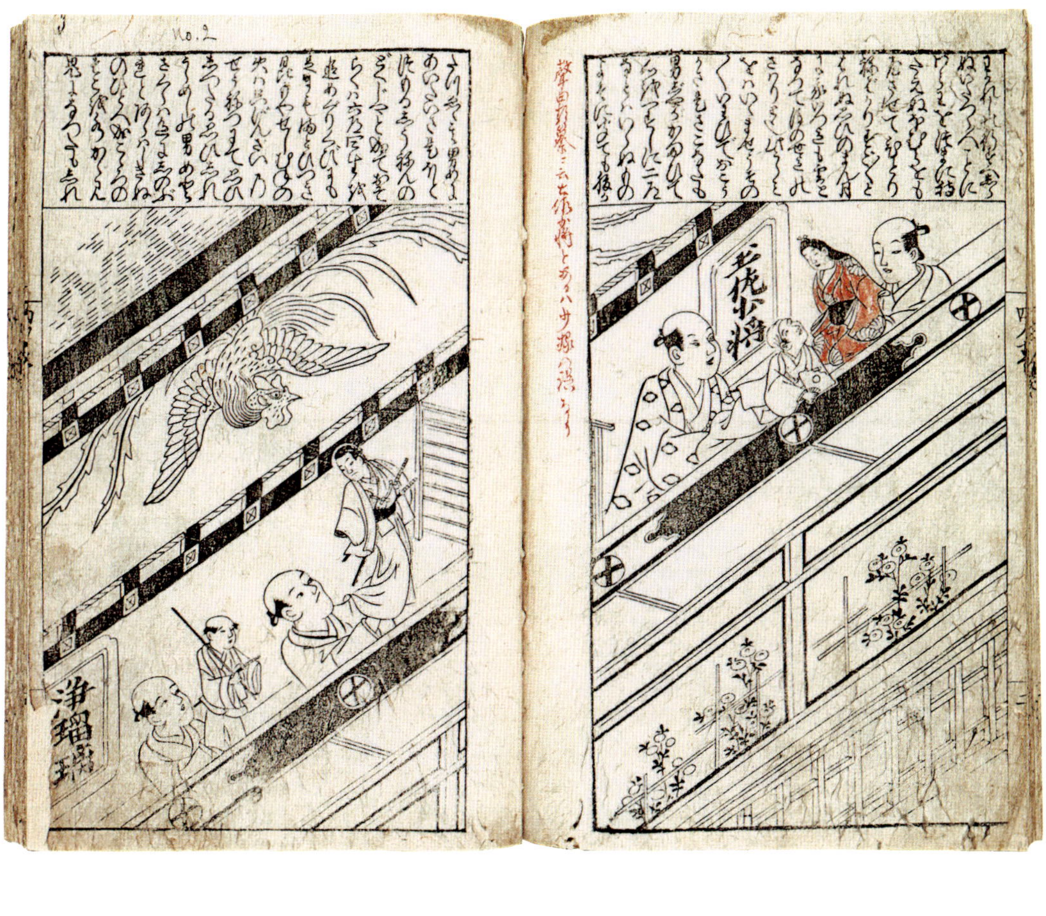

Fig. 2 HISHIKAWA MOROSHIGE, *'The Tosa no Shōjō Theatre'*, from *Yakusha e-zukushi*, *c.* 1685–90, woodblock-illustrated book, 3 vols., 26 × 31 cm, Museum of Fine Arts, Boston, source unknown, 2000.1266

per year of his life from the ages of seven to 60 – a total of 54 chapters that lightly joshed *Tale of Genji* (*Genji monogatari*; see also cat. 111). Explicated in a lively but unemotional style, Saikaku's primary themes were the pursuit of sex and money, the former in the so-called *kōshoku-mono*, erotic but not pornographic stories (like Yonosuke's adventures), the latter in the 'townsman books' (*chōnin-mono*), such as *The Japanese Family Storehouse* (*Nippon eitai-gura*, 1688). The latter opens with an ironic paean to wealth that debunks the Buddhist pieties: 'People tell us that when we die, and vanish in a moment's wisp of smoke, all our gold is less than dross and buys us nothing in the world beyond. It is true enough, and yet – is not what we leave behind of service to our sons and our posterity? And while we live (to take a shorter view) how many of life's desirable things is it not within the power of gold to grant us?'[27]

The first edition of Saikaku's *The Life of an Amorous Man*, issued in Osaka, was illustrated by the author himself. From 1686 onwards his publishers engaged the services of the professional Kamigata illustrator Yoshida Hanbei (*d. c.* 1693?; see cat. 78) for most of Saikaku's remaining novels. In Edo two new editions of *The Life of an Amorous Man*, published in 1684 and 1686 respectively, were illustrated by Moronobu,[28] the second in particular in a much more robust style than the original Kamigata versions, showing to what degree the new ukiyo-e style had gained ground in the eastern capital.

In many ways Bashō's poetic achievement was anathema to floating-world values and, indeed, was accomplished by rejecting much of the stylistic urbanity of the Danrin school, in which he had first studied. A native of Ueno in Iga Province in the Kamigata region, Bashō moved to Edo in 1672. By the early 1680s he had established himself in a small thatched retreat in the soggy Fukagawa district on the far, eastern bank of the Sumida, and the banana tree (*bashō*) planted there by a disciple soon suggested a new name for both the hut (Bashō-an) and its much-revered inhabitant. A verse of *c.* 1681 hints at the mature style of 'solitude and delicacy' that was to revolutionise much subsequent *haikai* poetry:

Bashō nowaki shite	Bashō tree in the storm
tarai ni ame o	a night spent listening to
kiku yo ka na	rain in a basin.[29]

Bashō's main connection with the works included in the present volume is via the influence on Edo *haikai* of his pupil Takarai Kikaku (1661–1707), a poet of a very different temperament who was patronised by daimyo and wealthy Edo merchants. Bashō described the relationship wryly: 'My style favours solitude and is delicate; Kikaku's favours flashiness and is delicate. The delicacy marks him as belonging to my school'.[30] Okumura Masanobu, one of the principal artists represented here, was closely associated with the *haikai* movement in Edo and, perhaps as early as 1707, studied with Tachiba Fukaku (1662–1753),[31] who was in turn strongly influenced by Kikaku. The aesthetic of 'visiting the past to know the new' (*onko chishin*), espoused by Fukaku in the second half of his career (after 1707), in practice entailed parodying the classics[32] in a way linked to the techniques of the *mitate-e* that were to become an important new feature of Masanobu's art (see p. 29). Ichikawa Danjūrō I is said to have studied *haikai* under Shiigamoto Saimaro (1656–1738) when he visited Kyoto in 1693–4, and *hokku* inscriptions appear on many actor prints in the 1750s and 1760s (see cat. 112, 132, 133, 135).

Each of the new performing and literary arts that were developed rapidly under the patronage of a newly wealthy, newly self-confident *chōnin* class during the years leading up to the Genroku era was thus fostered by men of genius who established its salient characteristics at an early stage: Tosa no Shōjō (Tosa *jōruri*), Tōjūrō and Danjūrō (kabuki acting), Chikamatsu (*jōruri* and kabuki playwriting), Saikaku (floating-world novels), Bashō (*haikai*). That individuals could exert such radical influence indicates that control of the new arts had been wrested once and for all from traditional feudal or religious patronage by autocracy and was now sustained by a more diffuse and egalitarian audience, the urban bourgeoisie, as part of a larger, increasingly commercialised market.

GENRE PRECURSORS OF UKIYO-E

Writing in 1718, at the age of 67, the painter Hanabusa Itchō (1652–1724) wistfully recalled the origins of the ukiyo-e style that had become popular in his youth and to which, in spite of his training in the academic Kano school, he had been temperamentally and artistically attracted:

> In recent times a man called Iwasa something-or-other, who was a native of Echizen Province, succeeded in capturing the up-to-date appearances of kabuki and *shirabyōshi* dancers, and people gave him the nickname Ukiyo Matabei [Floating-world Matabei]. After these had been enjoyed in the world for a considerable time, there came to Edo from Awa Province a person called Hishikawa Moronobu, who worked in woodblock and delighted the eye with myriad fashions. Although this was not the way [*michi*] I had studied, I was young and lost my bearings along a shore washed by treacherous waves. At a time when I could not avoid the shame of tears at the morning parting [from a courtesan], thinking to place myself above Iwasa and Hishikawa, I set down the roots of a bad reputation for myself and the thicket of my shame grew rank with weeds.[33]

Itchō's retrospective shame was in large part due to the ignominy he had suffered at the hands of the feudal authorities, who had banished him from Edo to the isolated island of Izu Miyake-jima from 1698 to 1709. The poetic metaphors of this text indicate that, in addition to his activities as a painter with a light and witty touch, and as a *haikai* poet of the Bashō school (he was a close friend of Kikaku), Itchō had led a life as a professional party entertainer (*taiko-mochi*) in the pleasure quarters. Earning a reputation as the 'poisoned insect to the daimyo' (*daimyō no doku-mushi*), he was accused of leading into dissipation some minor nobility relatives of the mother of Shogun Tsunayoshi and this was the cause of his banishment. Itchō's was not the only case of a prominent member of the floating-world elite being made an example of by the authorities (see p. 26).

'Iwasa something-or-other...of Echizen' in Itchō's account refers to Iwasa Matabei (Katsumochi, 1578–1650), the son of the warrior lord Araki Murashige and a major artist who spent most of the first half of his life in Kyoto, before moving to

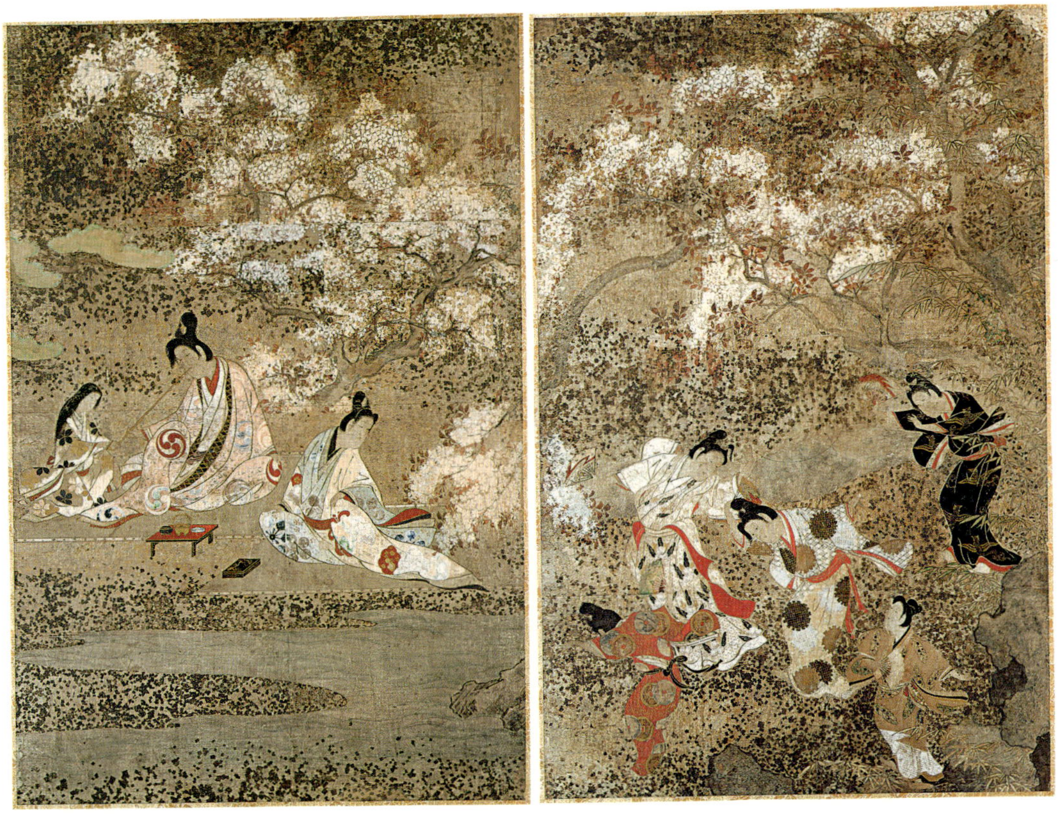

Fig. 3 SCHOOL OF IWASA MATABEI, *Partying Beneath Blossoming Cherry Trees*, *c.* 1624–44, two panels, ink, colour, gold and silver on paper, 116.3 × 78 cm, Museum of Fine Arts, Boston, William Sturgis Bigelow Collection, 11.7737, 7738

Fukui in Echizen *c.* 1616 and thence to Edo by order of the shogunate in 1637. Itchō's implication that Matabei was the founder or a precursor of ukiyo-e is an early reference to a tradition that persisted in the first written histories of ukiyo-e, the lineage of *Ukiyo-e ruikō* manuscripts initiated by Ōta Nanpo (1749–1823) in the 1790s and continued by others in the early 19th century. The claims for considering Matabei the founder of ukiyo-e have been reappraised in a recent monograph on the artist.[34] In this, Sandy Kita argues that Matabei was an important contributor to the *machishu* culture of Momoyama-period Kyoto, which waned with the defeat of the Toyotomi clan by the Tokugawa in the siege of Osaka Castle in 1615. *Machishu* was essentially an egalitarian alliance of court aristocracy and wealthy townsmen, able for a time to resist domination by the new warrior rulers. This unique cultural base sponsored other artistic luminaries in addition to Matabei, including the tea master Sen no Rikyū (1522–91) and the painters Hasegawa Tōhaku (1539–1610) and Tawaraya Sōtatsu (active *c.* 1600–40). Matabei's paintings, with their alternately classical and genre subjects, together constitute a vital link between traditional Yamato-e painting of the court and later *chōnin* ukiyo-e (which suggests another possible reason for Moronobu's insistence that he was a 'Yamato picture master'; see pp. 10–11). In Kita's view, only when Matabei's statement that he was a 'late follower of Tosa Mitsunobu [1434–1525]',[35] the most important medieval courtly painter, is accorded a weight equal to history's claim that Matabei was the founder of ukiyo-e can his crucial transitional role be correctly appreciated.[36]

Matabei's genre paintings, typically scenes of the leisurely pursuit of outdoor pleasures, are thought to date mainly from the second half of his career, after 1623, i.e. from his final years in Fukui and his time in Edo.[37] Tsuji Nobuo has argued for the existence of a Matabei workshop.[38] Certainly, the genre figure style evolved by Matabei and his school, the faces having 'plump cheeks and long chins' (*hōkyō chōi*), exerted a strong influence on genre paintings produced at the time by anonymous town artists of rival lineages. In the Boston collection are two fragments from what were originally sliding-door paintings (*fusuma-e*), *Partying Beneath Blossoming Cherry Trees* (*Ōka yūen zu*; fig. 3), thought to be by a pupil working close to Matabei during his later Fukui period.[39] Although the cut silver-leaf sprinkled over much of the background has tarnished and the paintings are generally not in good condition, contrasting groups of stylish female figures can be distinguished in the two fragments respectively, one dancing boisterously with fans under the cherry tree (including a woman wearing a robe with a bold design of large copper coins), the other seated calmly on mats beneath the blossoms. All have their hair wound into an upright topknot in the *tate-hyōgomage* style, and the studied languor of the seated figures in particular suggests that they may be courtesans.

Another major lineage of early genre painting is represented in the Boston collection, the so-called 'Dancing Courtesans' ('Bugi zu'; fig. 4). The Boston examples are preserved as eleven separate panels, but originally there was probably one more, enabling them to be mounted as a pair of six-panel folding screens. At least six further sets (or fragments of sets) are known that share the same basic characteristics: a single courtesan wearing a beautifully tie-dyed and embroidered *kosode* is shown dancing, sometimes

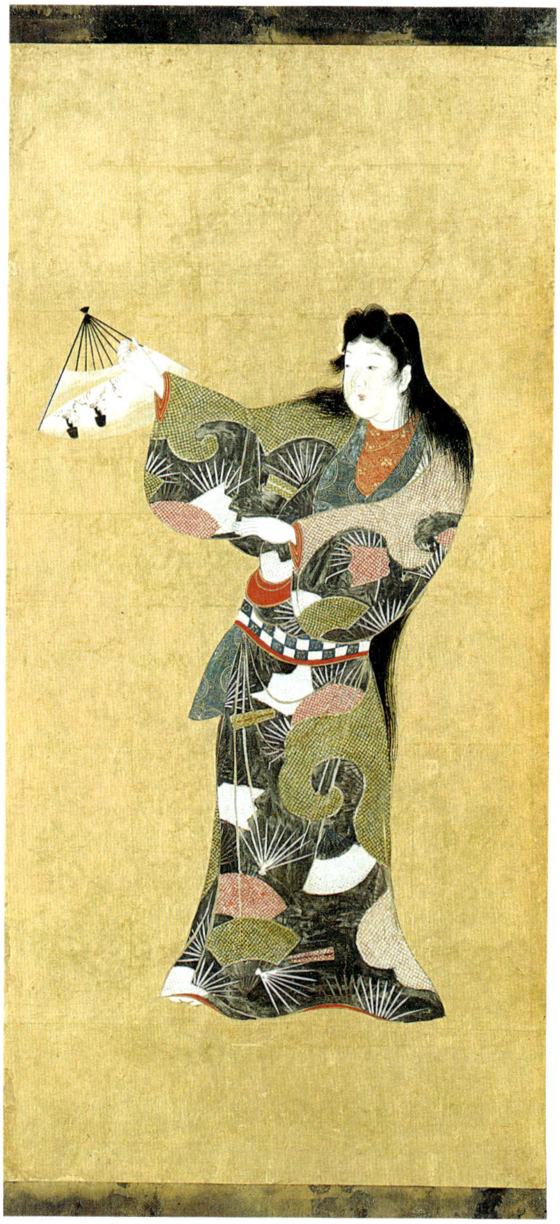

Fig. 4 ANONYMOUS, *Dancing Courtesan*, *c.* 1624–52, one of eleven panels, ink and colour on gold-leafed paper, 75.3 × 37.4 cm, Museum of Fine Arts, Boston, Denman Waldo Ross Collection, 17.1091

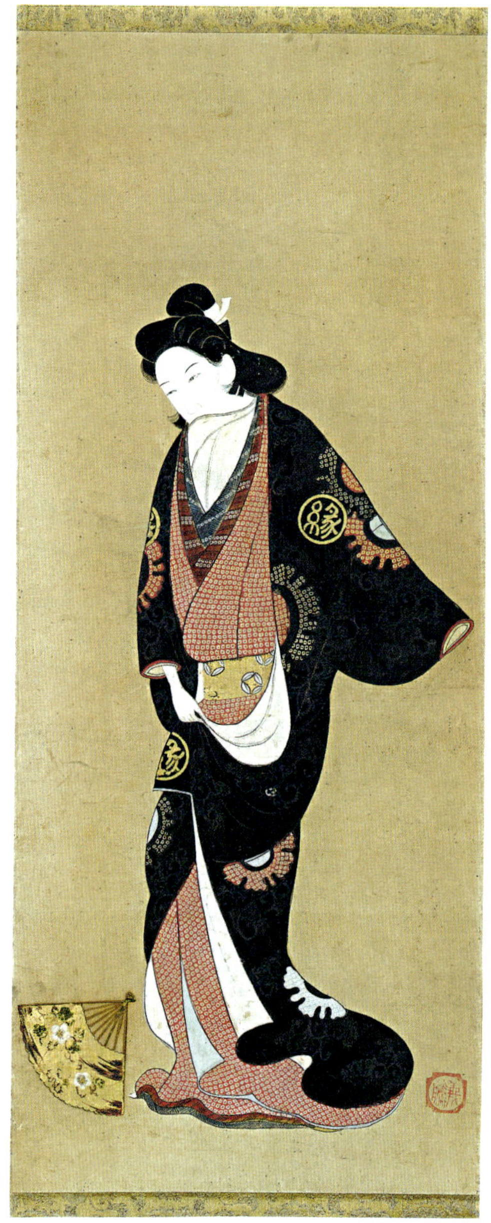

Fig. 5 Seal of YOSHIKATSU, *Standing Courtesan*, *c.* 1661–81, hanging scroll, ink, colour and gold on paper, 81.3 × 33.6 cm, Museum of Fine Arts, Boston, William Sturgis Bigelow Collection, 11.7983

while flourishing a painted fan, against a plain, gold-leaf background. The images have been interpreted as courtesans of the Rokujō Misuji-machi quarter in Kyoto dancing for the appreciation of partying male clients, and the fact that the women are lined up one figure to a panel has even been compared to the 'accumulatory' (*tsukushi*) aesthetic of the 'hawks on perches' (*kayō zu*) and 'horses in their stables' (*umaya zu*) screens painted for military patrons.[40] These works were significant to the evolution of ukiyo-e in several ways. They initiated, for example, the practice of isolating a single female figure against an unpainted background, a trend that was to escalate in the mid-17th century with the production of large numbers of hanging scrolls of single courtesans referred to as the 'Kanbun beauty paintings' (*Kanbun bijin-ga*; see fig. 5) after the era (1661–73) during which most of them were done. The basic formal device can be traced backwards in time to paintings from the medieval period and earlier of Buddhist deities (the subject of a rather different kind of adoration) and forwards to Moronobu's hanging scroll paintings (see cat. 5) and to the bold, large-format ukiyo-e prints of courtesans and kabuki actors that began appearing in the Genroku era (cat. 18, 29).

The second aspect of the 'Dancing Courtesans' that proved significant to the development of ukiyo-e was that they were copied again and again, evincing a desire for repeatable images. In due course, techniques of printing Buddhist texts

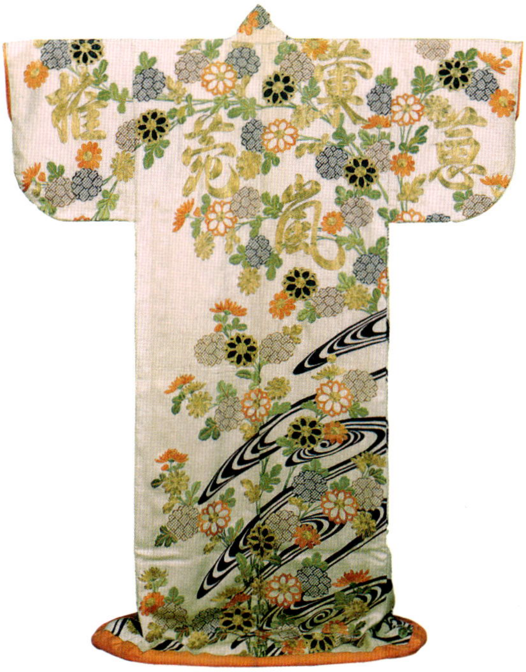

Fig. 6 *Kosode with a Pattern of Chrysanthemums, Flowing Water and Written Characters, c.* 1688–1704, dyed and tie-dyed figured satin-silk (*rinzu*), with embroidery, 166.4 × 133.4 cm, Kyoto National Museum, IK–340

Fig. 7 ANONYMOUS, *'Whose Sleeves?' (Kimonos on a Stand), c.* 1615–44, six-panel folding screen, ink and colour on gold-leafed paper, 167.8 × 321 cm, Museum of Fine Arts, Boston, Gift by Special Contribution, 08.169

from cherrywood blocks that had been in use for almost a millennium were adapted to the new subjects of floating-world imagery, disseminating it more quickly, widely and cheaply. The ukiyo-e illustrated book and print were born.

KOSODE

A further feature of the 'Dancing Courtesans' deserves to be considered at some length: the presentation of the idealised female form (later also male kabuki actors) as a kind of living support for a beautiful robe. The silk *kosode*, luxuriously decorated with combinations of dyeing, embroidery and, sometimes, direct painting, and, beginning in the early 18th century, painted with resists to produce pictorial dyed designs (*yūzen-zome*), was the ultimate signifier of personal style (see fig. 6). One form of screen decoration, a separate category of early 17th-century genre painting, consisted simply of several splendid actual-size *kosode* painted as if thrown over lacquered stands in an apparently casual, but in fact elaborately studied manner (see fig. 7).[41] Enjoyed for their sheer materiality and decorative élan (one imagines that the screens might also be draped with several real *kosode*), the 'whose sleeves?' (*ta-ga-sode*) compositions were also charged with the fragrant, erotic associations of their absent owners. Beyond such direct sensuousness, the fact that the fabric patterns sometimes make obvious reference to famous episodes from classical literature suggests a subsidiary appeal to cultural pretension. One suspects, too, that the implied wearers were the subject of much curiosity and conjecture.

Within the parameters of prevailing sumptuary regulations and of notions of appropriateness with regard to status and profession, the cut of *kosode* might be fairly standard at any given period, but almost everything else could be modified to cater to individual taste: the patterns and designs decorating the fabric(s) along with other accessories, principally sashes, hair ornaments and surcoats (*uchi-kake*), and the manner in which they were combined and worn. Japanese art had no

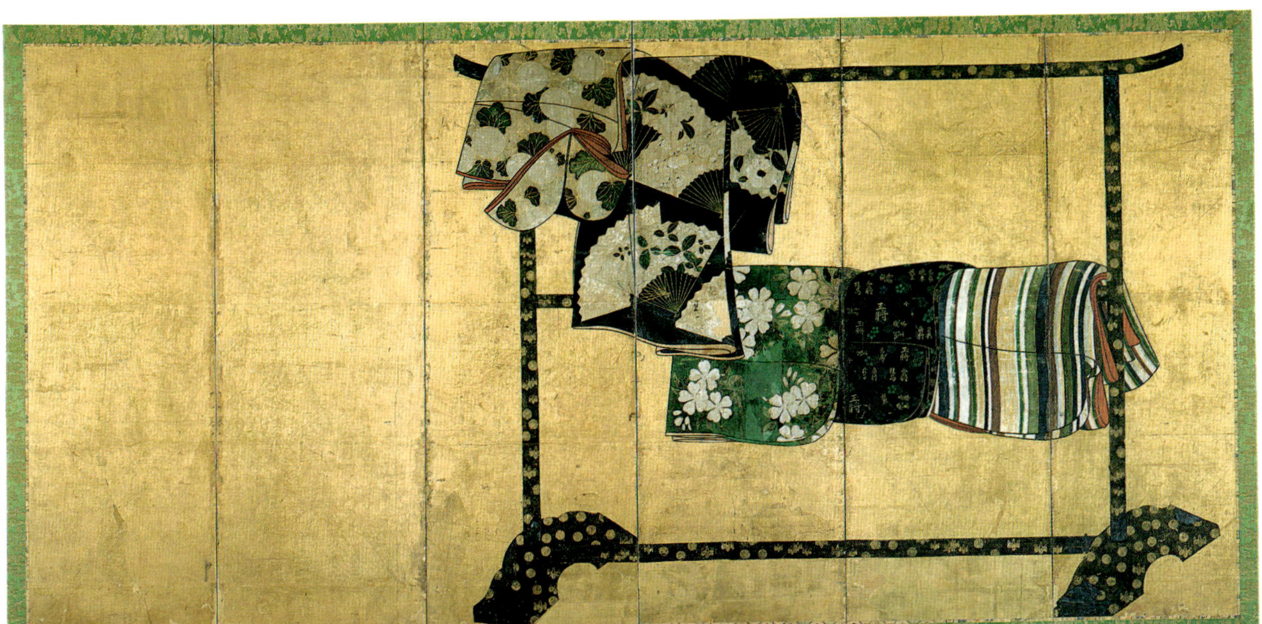

techniques for depicting the play of light on fabric and one wonders whether this absence in representation may have encouraged a compensatory elaboration of dynamic patterning and design, endlessly played out on the simple shape of the *kosode*, as witness the printed pattern books (*hiinagata-bon*) included here (cat. 2, 15, 16, 78, 79). Plant motifs do not merely decorate a *kosode* passively: they appear to be growing on it.

Dress was big business, perhaps the biggest business. Of the succession of large 'department' stores (*ō-dana*) established in Edo, Echigo-ya was notable for pioneering new business methods involving cash sales and lower, fixed prices (see cat. 65). Until the 19th century all these shops sold nothing but *kosode* and related fabrics and accessories.[42] Certain key artists grew up in the fabric and clothing trades. As already noted, Moronobu was the son of a *nuihaku-shi* and designed several *kosode* pattern books (cat. 15, 16), as did the Kyoto ukiyo-e artist Nishikawa Sukenobu (1671–1750; cat. 79). The Ogata brothers Kōrin (1658–1716) and Kenzan (1663–1743), the major figures in the Genroku era revival of the decorative style of Sōtatsu (now called Rinpa – 'Rin school' – from Kōrin's name), were wealthy scions of the Karigane-ya, purveyors of luxurious *kosode* to members of the Kyoto elite from Retired Empress Tōfukumon-in (1607–78) downwards.[43] Such artists clearly possessed an innate sense of how to orchestrate arresting colour and pattern combinations in accordance with the Genroku penchant for bold, all-over designs. And how could ukiyo-e figure painters avoid depicting the very latest and smartest fashions? Up-to-date works of art had to show people wearing up-to-date works of art.

THE WOODBLOCK REVOLUTION

The origins of woodblock printing lie in East Asia, most probably in China. The oldest extant examples, dating to the 8th century, survive in Korea and Japan and were made for ritual Buddhist use, in Japan in the form of the 'million invocations' (*hyakumantō darani*) placed inside small wooden pagodas from 764 to 770. Yet, as Peter Kornicki has been the latest to stress, although printing was known in Japan it did not effect a revolution until almost one thousand years later.[44] Only relatively late, at the beginning of the 17th century, did printing become the principal means of reproducing books for commercial purposes. In that sense, the shift to print is yet one more aspect of the urbanisation of culture that constitutes a main theme of this essay. Printing equipment and wooden type plundered from Korea during Hideyoshi's invasion of that country were presented to Emperor Go-Yōzei in 1593 and used to print *Kobun kōkyō* (*A Classic of Filial Piety*), of which no copies survive. Moveable type was then employed extensively in Japan for about 50 years, chiefly for official publications, but also at some private presses, notably that of Suminokura Soan (1571–1632) at Saga in Kyoto, for the production of the first elegant illustrated editions of Japanese fiction, of classics such as *Tales of Ise* (*Ise monogatari*, 1608). Yet once commercial printing got underway in earnest, publishers found it more convenient to revert to the traditional blockprinting method, which they found better suited to mixing text and image freely on the

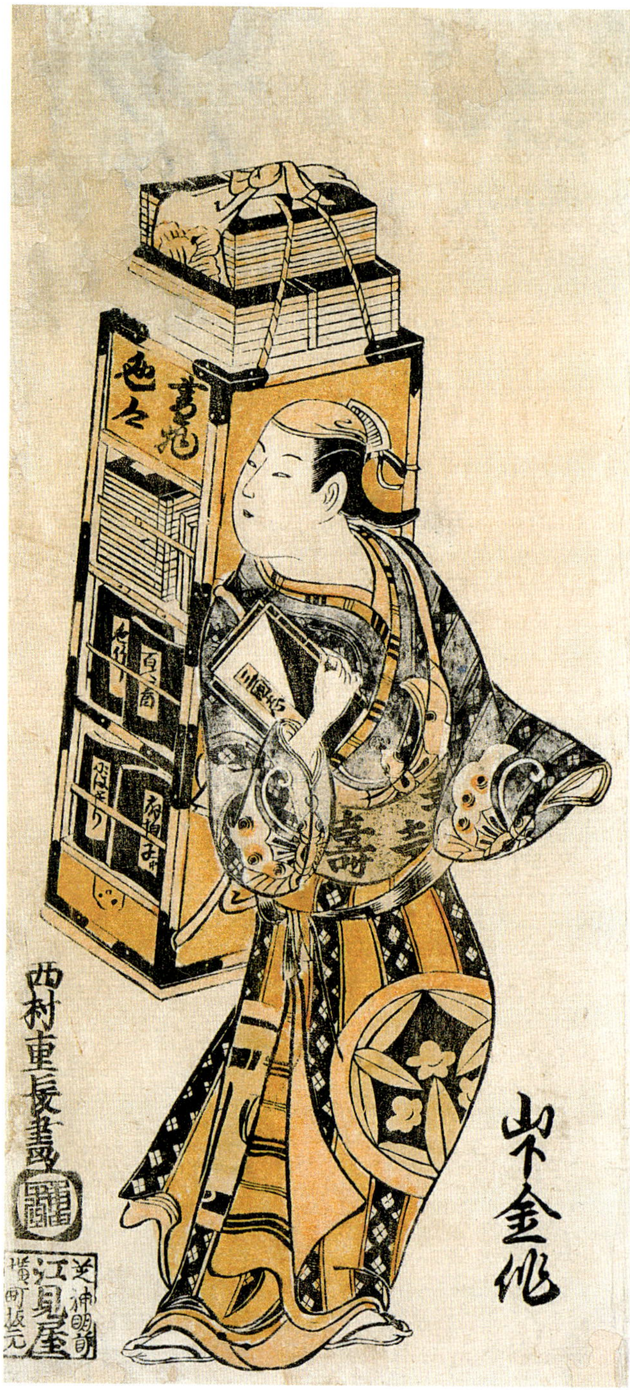

Fig. 8 NISHIMURA SHIGENAGA (*d.* 1756?), *Yamashita Kinsaku I as a Pedlar of Books*, *c.* 1723–9, woodblock, *hosoban*, *urushi-e*, 31.4 × 14.8 cm, Museum of Fine Arts, Boston, William S. and John T. Spaulding Collection, 21.5873

page, reproducing the idiosyncrasies of cursive calligraphy and adding phonetic glosses and other marks to aid reading in the case of texts in Chinese and Sino-Japanese (*kanbun*).[45] 'Kana booklets' (*kana-zōshi*), the name given to easy-to-read printed texts produced from the 1610s to *c.* 1680, before the piquant, more realistic 'floating-world novels' (*ukiyo-zōshi*) of Saikaku came to hold sway, fulfilled a variety of functions in the worlds of entertainment, enlightenment and practical education.[46] The last category included 'courtesan critiques' (*yūjo hyōban-ki*), such as *Mirror of Yoshiwara* (1660; cat. 1), and critiques of kabuki actors (*yarō hyōban-ki*), such as *Yarō mushi* (*Clinging Actors*, 1662), both of which still seem to have been aimed primarily at an upper-class audience, with little explicit mention of the townsmen.[47]

The gap in time between writing and publishing narrowed, so that from the second quarter of the 17th century books were regularly issued in the year they were written. One author has estimated that on average 3000 new titles were printed per year throughout the Edo period, a figure Kornicki describes as probably too low.[48] Best-sellers in the 17th century, increasingly works of prose fiction, would probably have sold from 2000 to 3000 copies,[49] and until the late 18th century fiction readers in Edo were supplied mainly by the great publishers of Kyoto and Osaka.[50] Readership was extended further down the social hierarchy by commercial lending libraries (*kashi-honya*), which used itinerant pedlars to sell and hire out books. Such salesmen were certainly active in Kyoto and Osaka by the late 17th century, in time to cash in on the demand for Saikaku's floating-world novels, and in Edo and other cities not long after.[51] A *hosoban* print by Nishimura Shigenaga (*d.* 1756?) shows the kabuki actor Yamashita Kinsaku in the role of a pedlar (fig. 8) advertising the contents of his backpack as 'lots of different books' (*shomotsu iro-iro*). Although the precise performance has not been identified, the print must date to *c.* 1723–9 and many similar examples exist by other artists. Kinsaku holds a copy of *Romance of the Three Kingdoms* (*Sangoku-shi*), presumably a Japanese translation of the Chinese vernacular novel (see cat. 123), and legible in the display rack behind him are the titles of the classical poetry anthology *Hyakunin isshu* (*One Hundred Poems by One Hundred Poets*; see cat. 13) and of three libretti for practising chanting in various styles: *Iro-take* (cat. 46–57), *Ōgi-byōshi* and *Niotori*.

The many literary genres published in book form in the Edo period, beginning with the Saga editions of *c.* 1599–1610, were nearly always illustrated. Most illustrations were monochrome, but for several decades after *c.* 1615[52] there was a vogue for decorating them in almost all genres of fiction with crude but lively hand-colouring dominated by red lead (*tan*) and green (*roku*)[53] – hence the name 'orange–green books' (*tanroku-bon*). Fig. 9 shows an illustration from an edition of *Soga monogatari* (*Tale of the Soga Brothers*) in the Boston collection, published in 1646. Based on an incident of 1193, this story of the revenge taken by the Soga brothers Jūrō and Gorō on their father's murderer, Kudō Suketsune, was to form the basis of hundreds of kabuki plays (see cat. 33). The *tanroku* vogue seems to have died out by *c.* 1650, but it was no doubt a significant precedent for the hand-colouring of early ukiyo-e prints of the *tan-e* type, which were dominated by the same red lead colour. Indeed, Richard Lane has published unsigned prints dating from the Kanbun era (1661–73) that display a 'proto ukiyo-e' style, classifying them as the work of the Kanbun Master. Some of the prints subsumed in this collective appellation – used for all unsigned prints published in Edo in a floating-world style before signed works by Moronobu and others began to appear during the Enpō era (1673–81) – are embellished in a technique and palette very similar to *tanroku* hand-colouring.[54]

Another type of illustrated publication that must be mentioned here is the 'Kinpira book' (*Kinpira-bon*), which contains the text of a *jōruri* puppet performance along with anonymous illustrations featuring the exploits of a muscular, larger-than-life fictional hero with bulging eyes called Kinpira, son of the warrior Sakata Kintoki. The British Library owns a representative – and rare – example of this genre (fig. 10) that records the certified text (*shōhon*) chanted by Edo Izumi-dayū for the play *Sugawara no shinnō*. Inside the cover it bears

Fig. 9 ANONYMOUS, *Soga monogatari*, published 1646 by Yasuda Jūbei, woodblock-illustrated novel, *tanroku-bon*, 27 × 16.2 cm, Museum of Fine Arts, Boston, Gift of Mrs Jared K. Morse, 2000, 2000.1272.9

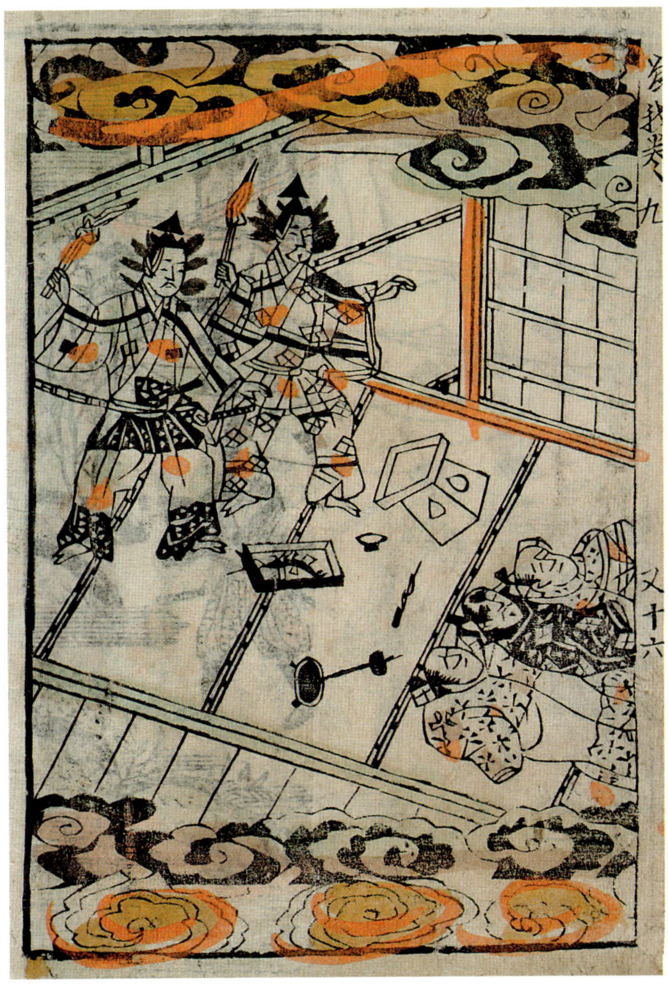

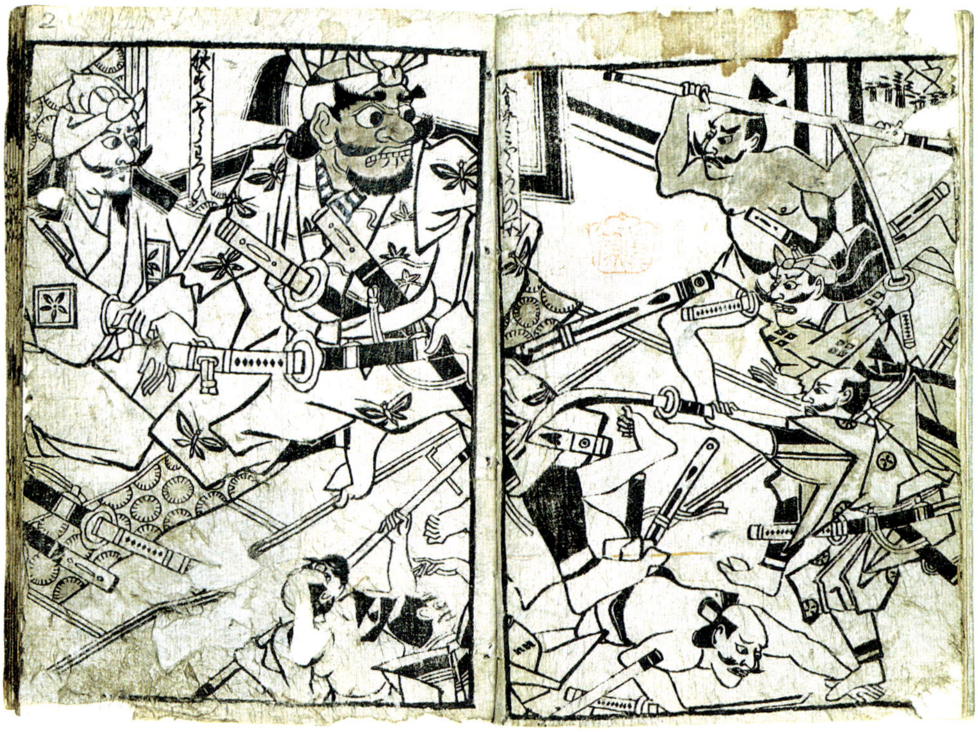

Fig. 10 ANONYMOUS, *Sugawara no shinnō*, published 1650 (?) by Mata'emon of Edo, woodblock-illustrated *jōruri* playbook, slight hand-colouring, 18.3 × 13.1 cm (covers), British Library, London, Oriental and India Office Collections, Or.75.f.23

the manuscript date 'Keian 3' (1650), otherwise uncorroborated, and, after the postscript, the woodblock imprint 'Hibiya Yoko-chō Mata'emon han' (Published by Mata'emon at Hibiya Yoko-chō [Edo]). The bombastic manner of Kinpira *jōruri* was absorbed by later styles of puppet theatre, becoming in turn a vital element in the formation of the *aragoto* style of kabuki acting that was to be perfected at the end of the century by Ichikawa Danjūrō. In the same way, the style of the Kinpira illustrations was absorbed by the paintings and prints of the Torii family artists Kiyonobu I (1664–1729) and Kiyomasu I (active *c.* 1704–18?), the first to search, in the late 1690s and early 1700s respectively, for an idiom suitable to the depiction of Danjūrō's *aragoto* triumphs (see cat. 23).

Ukiyo-e proper was born when the streams of genre painting and woodblock book illustration came together under the guidance of one of those Genroku geniuses who determined the essential characteristics of a new *chōnin* art form: Hishikawa Moronobu.

HISHIKAWA MORONOBU

By 1672, the year of the first four signed and dated works by Moronobu, the new ukiyo-e idiom was firmly established. The works of 1672 are the rather conservative printed illustrations of warrior poets in *Buke hyakunin isshu* and three short sections of painted handscrolls that relate far more closely to the floating-world milieu. One short handscroll depicts a brothel scene in a new style, charged with excitement (Idemitsu Museum of Arts, Tokyo).[55] It includes a snowball fight in the garden and lovemaking in a boudoir. The other two are the earliest of seven handscroll fragments inscribed with dates ranging from 1672 to 1689, collected together as *Illustrated Handscroll of the Northern Quarter [Yoshiwara] and [Kabuki] Theatres* (*Hokurō engeki zukan*, Tokyo National Museum) and showing the approach to the Main Gate (Ōmon-guchi) of Yoshiwara and a scene of encounter between courtesans and clients in the quarter's chief thoroughfare.[56]

During the early part of his career, from the mid-Enpō to the Tenna (1681–4) era, Moronobu concentrated on illustrations for printed 'picture books' (*ehon*). About 60 of these survive and they encompass a wide variety of subjects, some of which the artist was later to use in paintings in all formats (several dozen by him are extant). The subjects included legendary, historical and literary themes from China and Japan, Buddhist deities, genre scenes involving all social classes (including craftsmen), *kosode* pattern books, landscapes and gardens, flowers and animals, warriors and some twenty books of erotica.[57] Increasingly, however, Moronobu's books and paintings came to be dominated by scenes of seasonal pleasures in and around the *chōnin* neighbourhoods of Edo, particularly the kabuki theatres and the Yoshiwara pleasure quarter (see cat. 3, 4) – pleasures that, as the paintings record, were also enjoyed by a number of samurai. Moronobu thus followed in the tradition of earlier genre screens, except that the locus was now the 'bad places' of Edo. As demonstrated by the subjects and their treatment in a number of surviving handscrolls, particularly from late in his career, Moronobu and his pupils became ever more occupied with replicating such scenes to order in various combinations.[58] The chronological display of many of his surviving works staged by the Chiba City Museum of Art in 2000 also made it clear just how much Moronobu's figure style developed, from small figures with faces that are slightly angular around the cheekbones to far more ample types. The distinction between late genre paintings and early ukiyo-e – and the difference is certainly not very great in the case of such hanging scrolls as those of the 'Kanbun Beauties' – surely lies in the extra energetic 'charge' exuded by Moronobu's figures. Whereas the Kanbun Beauties have an air of introspection and coy self-absorption, Moronobu's women come across as self-assured, even assertive. In his famous late painting *Woman Looking Back* (*Mi-kaeri bijin*, Tokyo National Museum) the woman is not paraded for the delectation of the viewer, like the 'Dancing Courtesans' of half a century earlier; rather, she is permitted a considerable degree of self-determination as she deigns to glance back, Moronobu's assured line paying full compliment to her fine figure and exquisite *kosode*. When glances are thrown or exchanged within a painting or print by Moronobu (see fig. 11 and cat. 3, 4), and even more so in works by his presumably younger contemporary Sugimura Jihei (active *c.* 1681–98; see cat. 20), they are invariably flirtatious: people 'cruise' one another in a sexual manner. This is the portrayal of *joie de vivre*, reflecting the fact that *chōnin* are now painting primarily for *chōnin*, for their own kind rather than for military patrons of a different social class.

Moronobu's oeuvre contains a small but historically significant number of single-sheet prints – about 120, less than five per cent of the images contained in his printed oeuvre – almost all issued in sets to be mounted to order as albums or handscrolls. Nearly half these are erotic prints (see fig. 11), issued originally as four sets of twelve designs each, and the fact that some impressions survive from what are clearly contemporary re-cut editions suggests that the blocks, like those of several of Moronobu's illustrated books, had to be replaced following the fires of 1682–3.[59] Moronobu seems to have concentrated more on painting after the Tenna era, leaving the field of book and print design free to his pupils and to Sugimura Jihei. During the first half of the Genroku era, Jihei and others occasionally used grand new print formats: *kakemono-e* (literally, 'hanging scroll pictures', approximately 76 x 23 cm) and *ō-ōban* ('large large sheet', approximately 58 x 32 cm). Richard Lane surmises that Jihei may have designed as many as 50 prints in these large formats,[60] which were adopted just before the turn of the century by Torii Kiyonobu I for actor prints and, in the early 18th century, by Kiyomasu I for actors and courtesans and by the Kaigetsudō school and Okumura Masanobu for images of courtesans.

From the late 17th century in Kamigata, a traditional centre of book publishing, just two sets of twelve horizontal *ōban* prints are known to have survived.[61] In 1702 and 1706 the Kamigata book illustrator Ōmori Yoshikiyo (active *c.* 1702–16) is thought to have designed two folding albums of prints of courtesans and actors – they are both unsigned – modelled respectively on Kiyonobu I's *Illustrated Book of Courtesans* (1700; cat. 25) and *[Painted] Screens in All Directions* (1700; cat. 24).[62] Single-sheet prints remained rare in Kamigata before the mid-18th century. The most accomplished and influential ukiyo-e painter in Kyoto during the first half of the century was Nishikawa Sukenobu (1671–1750; see cat. 80), whose more than 60 printed illustrated books (cat. 79, 81) spread his fame to Edo, where they influenced Okumura Masanobu and Suzuki Harunobu (*d.* 1770) in particular.

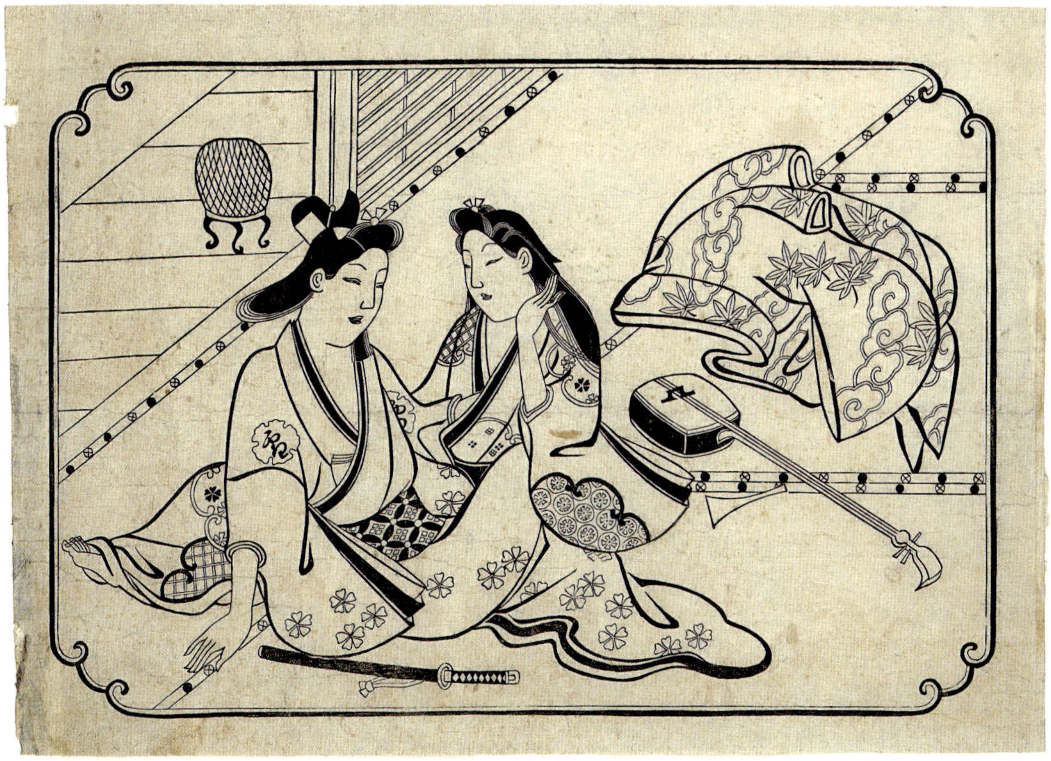

Fig. 11 Attributed to HISHIKAWA MORONOBU, *Young Man Dallying with a Courtesan*, late Enpō era (1673–81), woodblock, *yoko-ōban*, *sumizuri-e*, 26 × 36.8 cm, Museum of Fine Arts, Boston, William S. and John T. Spaulding Collecction, 21.5813

EARLY ACTOR IMAGERY

Genre screens and handscrolls of the first half of the 17th century contain many depictions of kabuki performances, a subject carried over into the representations of Edo kabuki in Moronobu's paintings (see cat. 3) and illustrated books. All surviving theatrical imagery by Moronobu depicts kabuki in the manner of genre scenes, without ever focusing on individual actors. Actor critiques (*yarō hyōban-ki*) came into being in the 1650s and, as already mentioned, initially concentrated on the sexual allure of individual young performers, only occasionally including a generalised portrait in the manner of courtesan critiques (see cat. 1).[63]

Santō Kyōden (1761–1816), an ukiyo-e artist and author who took an interest in its history, described the origins of the single-sheet actor print in his *Kinsei kiseki kō* of 1804, quoting a now lost manuscript entitled *Edo masago* that he dated to the Kan'en era (1747–51): '[Some time] in the Genroku era, at the [Nakamura] Kanzaburō [theatre] in the final part of the performance, Danjūrō took the *aragoto*[64] role of Minister Shō Ki and scored a great hit. Pictures were drawn of him that were called "Minister Shō Ki Danjūrō" and these were sold by hawkers in the streets. ...From that time pictures of other actors were gradually issued'.[65] The play mentioned here has been tentatively identified as *Sankai Nagoya*, performed at the Nakamura Theatre at the New Year, 1697, for which Kiyonobu I is thought to have designed the illustrated playbook (cat. 23). In any event the earliest known dateable single-sheet actor print by Kiyonobu I, a hand-coloured print in the *ō-ōban* format entitled *Sawamura Kodenji as Tsuyu-no-Mae* (Worcester Art Museum, Massachusetts), depicts a performance that took place just over a year later, in the third month of 1698. Exactly two years after that, he issued his first major illustrated book of actor portraits, *[Painted] Screens in all Directions* (cat. 24), which included prints of some three dozen leading actors, beginning with Ichikawa Danjūrō, each depicted on a single page in a characteristic role and accompanied by his name and crest. It has been suggested that the book was put together from single-sheet prints (almost all now lost);[66] certainly, it may be assumed that by this time the actor print was an established genre and that Kiyonobu I played a leading part in making it so. Previously, single-sheet actor prints by Kiyomasu I were held to predate those by Kiyonobu I, because Kiyomasu I's *ō-ōban* print *Gorō Pulling-up Bamboo* (*Take-nuki Gorō*, Tokyo National Museum)[67] seemed to relate to a performance given during the fifth month, 1697. More recently, however, it has been convincingly argued that the print is retrospective, probably done by Kiyomasu I when he first began designing actor prints in earnest in the early Hōei era (1704–11).[68]

The early Torii artists are known to have painted 'picture signboards' (*e-kanban*) for kabuki theatres, though when and how they first did so have been the subject of debate.[69] With most early originals lost, evidence is restricted to written references (in actor critiques and elsewhere), to a few paintings and prints that depict the outsides of theatres (see cat. 66) and to the small printed 'picture title slips' (*e-daisen*) that, from *c.* 1697 onwards, were regularly pasted onto the covers of illustrated playbooks and, drawn with nails in the corners and other fittings suitable for hanging, would seem to copy signboards for specific performances.[70] Painting of a kind similar to that used for theatre signboards was required for votive plaques (*ema*) for shrines, and Kiyonobu I apparently executed a fairly large number of these. Two rare surviving examples surely give a hint as to the appearance of the theatre signboards. The earlier of the two, *Subduing the Demon of Mount Ōe* (*Ōeyama zu*; fig. 13) by Kiyonobu I,[71] is thought to date from *c.* 1711–16, while *The Actor Ichikawa Ebizō II in the 'Arrow-sharpening' Scene* (*Nidai-me Ebizō no ya-no-ne*; fig. 12) by his follower Kiyonobu II (active *c.* 1725–60),[72] is known to have been donated to Saidai-ji Temple, Yamato Province, in the spring of 1754, on the occasion of a display of that temple's treasures in Edo. The second of these plaques, in particular, is a powerful vestige of the grand Torii school manner of painting *aragoto*-style acting, a manner described aptly by later commentators as 'gourd-shaped legs and wriggling worm line' (*hyōtan ashi mimizu-gaki*).[73] One of the earliest painted signboards in the Boston collection dates from 1758 and has been tentatively attributed to Torii Kiyomitsu (cat. 131).[74]

Fig. 12 TORII KIYONOBU II, *The Actor Ichikawa Ebizō II in the 'Arrow-sharpening' Scene*, spring 1754, votive plaque, ink and colour on wood, 178 × 111.4 cm, Saidai-ji Temple, Nara Prefecture

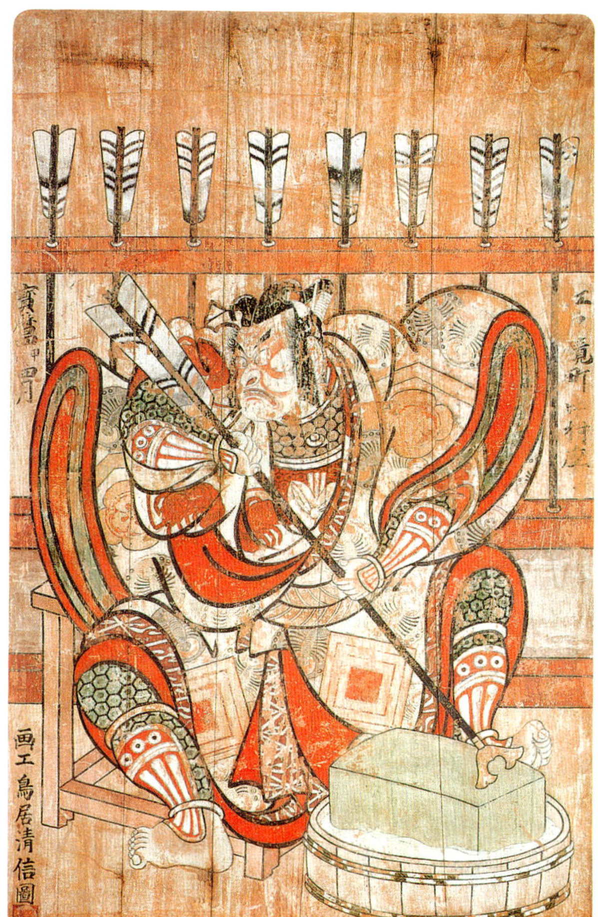

Fig. 13 TORII KIYONOBU I, *Subduing the Demon of Mount Ōe*, *c.* 1711–16, votive plaque, ink and colour on wood, 150 × 222cm, Tamura Shrine, Fukushima Prefecture

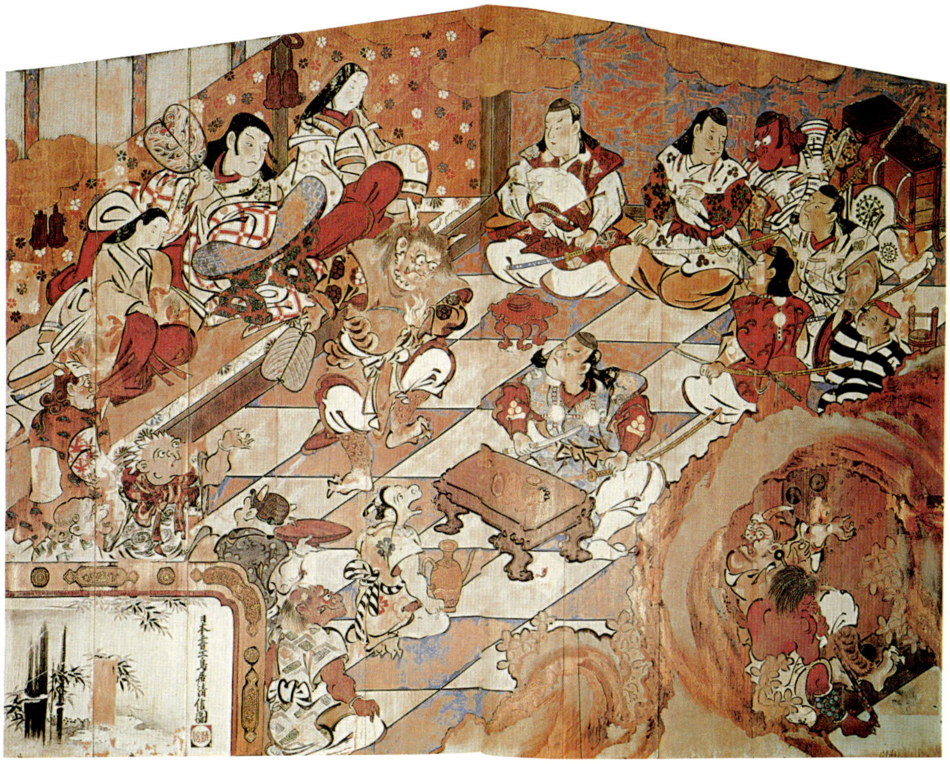

Early *ō-ōban* actor prints with hand-colouring dominated by the brilliant orange *tan* pigment were produced from *c.* 1698 to *c.* 1718 (see cat. 36–8). Their disappearance seems to have coincided with the end of Kiyomasu I's career, though whether he died, retired or ceased working for some other reason has not been established. How such large prints were admired and stored is a mystery. The format might suggest a kind of poor man's hanging scroll painting, yet no surviving examples are mounted in this way.

Several passages in popular *ukiyo-zōshi* provide evidence that images of actors and courtesans – in these cases probably paintings – were appreciated in a libidinous manner. The first of the two examples quoted below occurs in the story of a drunken visit paid by two young men, Koshichi and Shinpachi, to Yoshiwara at New Year:

Koshichi basically did not like sex with women. He swore to himself that, never mind [the courtesans of] Yoshiwara, he would never let himself be touched by any woman, so that he could avoid being reborn 500 times like some useless good-for-nothing. He had Hishikawa paint a likeness of the actor Arashi Kiyosaburō, just down from Osaka, and always hung it by his bed. As if worshipping a holy image, he would pray to it fervently, repeating to himself the *nenbutsu*, with the attendant deities of [the actors] Hayakawa Hatsuse on the left and Tsutsui Kichijūrō on the right, like the [bodhisattvas] Kannon and Seishi.[75]

The second passage reads:

Awakening from a dream of Zen mediation, tempted by a pretty woman, amid the fragrant aromas impregnating her robes, you hang at the altar not the Buddha but a picture of a beauty. Spreading far and wide the female holy of holies, saviour of the world, you violate the tight stiff sect of boys' backsides and, setting out from your hermit's hut, strive to rescue young and old alike for the Way of Women. Is it not a blessed act to hold seventeen days of sermon at the dry riverbed, Shijō, hotbed of homo fun? Tinkle, tinkle [of the monk's bell].[76]

Published in 1708 and 1711 respectively, the books are close in date and share the theme, common at the time, of debating the merits of sex with women versus sex with young men, the second passage appearing especially scandalous in its 'impudent parody of the Buddhist sermon style'.[77] Arashi Kiyosaburō was a great Kamigata *onnagata*, who made a name for himself in Osaka in 1706 in the role of the fire-setting greengrocer's daughter, Oshichi (see cat. 37), which he took on tour to Edo at the New Year 1708. Hatsuse and Kichijūrō were other *onnagata* who performed in Edo (see cat. 55). In connection with a painter the name 'Hishikawa' would at this time be an obvious reference to a follower of Moronobu in the Hishikawa school.

Erotic imagery (*shunga*, 'spring pictures', or *warai-e*, 'pictures for laughing')[78] was an important genre within early ukiyo-e, practised extensively by all major artists from Moronobu onwards, who consistently matched sexual explicitness with a high level of aesthetic beauty in a way encountered only rarely in European art (see cat. 22). Yet the passages quoted above, and others like them, obviously imply that non-explicit images of beautiful young men and women might also be 'worshipped' for arousal. Equally clear is the facetious claim that religion has been usurped by sex or that sex has even become a new *chōnin* religion.

By this time, in the Hōei and Shōtoku eras (1704–16), the market in paintings of courtesans had come to be dominated by the work of Kaigetsudō Ando and his pupils, all working in an identical 'house style' (see cat. 82–6), and they occasionally did paintings of actors as well.[79] One image of an ukiyo-e artist at work, a print by Nishimura Shigenaga from the 1720s (fig. 14), shows a fashionably dressed youth executing a

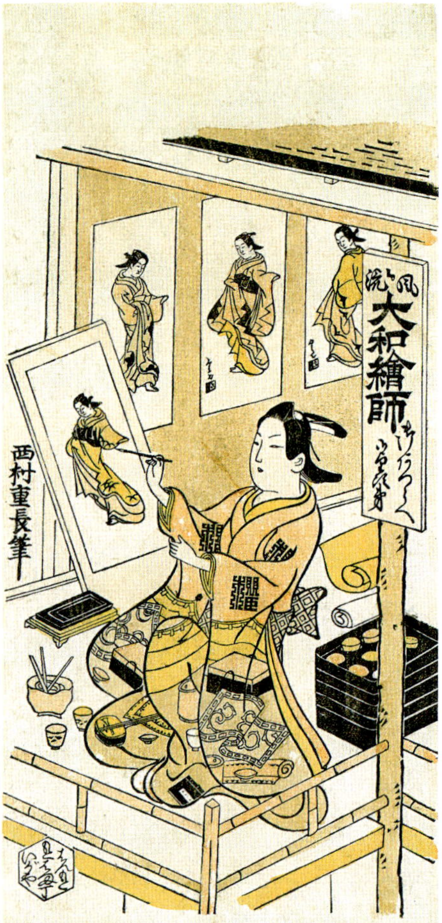

Fig. 14 NISHIMURA SHIGENAGA,
'A Fashionable Yamato Picture Master',
c. 1720–30, woodblock,
hosoban, *beni-e*, 33 × 16.1 cm,
Museum of Fine Arts, Boston,
Denman Waldo Ross
Collection, 06.712

painting of a courtesan at the front of a shop that is open to the street.[80] A triptych of similar paintings (not mounted as hanging scrolls) can be seen behind him and a signboard advertises the artist's services: 'Fūryū Yamato eshi/o-atsurae o-nozomi shidai' (Fashionable Yamato picture master, to order just as you desire).

A succession of great passions and scandals erupted in the world of kabuki during the early years of the 18th century. On the nineteenth day of the second month, 1704, Danjūrō I, the mainstay of Edo kabuki, was stabbed to death while performing on stage. His murderer, a jealous rival actor Ikushima Hanroku, subsequently died under police interrogation. Following one month of mourning, Danjūrō I's 24-year-old son assumed the title Danjūrō II (1688–1758, called Ebizō II after 1735).[81] He proved a more than worthy successor, performing classic *aragoto* roles, including that of Soga no Gorō, in various new guises (he played Gorō more than 50 times), and adding new characters of a more romantic cast, such as Sukeroku, which he first performed in 1713. Images of performances by Danjūrō II dominate the actor prints in the present volume (cat. 11, 34, 60, 89–91, 99, 100, 107).

A second incident occurred almost exactly ten years after Danjūrō's murder. The consequences of this 'Lady Ejima scandal', as it came to be known, were more profound. In the first month of 1714 Lady Ejima, a high-ranking official in the women's quarters at Edo Castle who served the mother of the seventh shogun, Ietsugu, was sent on a proxy pilgrimage to the Tokugawa mortuary temple Zōjō-ji in Shiba. On the return journey she took eleven ladies with her to watch kabuki performances at the Yamamura Theatre, inviting the actors to her box for a drinking party. In the official investigation that ensued it transpired that Lady Ejima had been conducting a secret liaison for nine years with the popular actor Ikushima Shingorō. Punishments were harsh. The shogun's ladies were dispersed under the supervision of various daimyo. Ikushima was banished for eighteen years to the island of Izu Miyake-jima (where the painter Itchō had languished from 1698 to 1709; see p. 16). The Yamamura Theatre was demolished and never rebuilt: henceforth there were to be only three licensed theatres in Edo, the Nakamura, the Ichimura and the Morita. Stringent regulations now governed the construction of theatres, which were permitted only one tier of boxes, no longer discreetly screened with blinds, and the luxuriousness of stage costumes was restricted.[82] For his peripheral involvement in the scandal Kaigetsudō Ando (see cat. 82 and pp. 53–4) was exiled to the island of Izu Ōshima, probably until 1722.[83] Mutō Junko has argued that the three surviving kabuki theatres made a special effort to stage glittering spectacles at the New Year, 1715, so as to demonstrate that business was better than ever. She surmises that at this time a new kind of picture signboard – a large, independent painting – replaced the small pictures above written titles that had previously been hung outside the theatres. Just as an *ema* is a message from man to the gods, so these new, large *e-kanban* were prayerful messages of hope from the theatres to the gods – that henceforth they be allowed to flourish unpunished.[84] Three unusual, large printed playbills (*tsuji-banzuke*) designed by Kiyomasu I in 1715 may reflect the new exterior appearance of the theatres.[85] In addition, a rare hanging scroll painting by Kiyonobu I survives that records the 'Seven Spring Herbs' ('Nana-kusa no dan') scene as performed in the play *Bandō ichi kotobuki Soga* at the Nakamura Theatre at the New Year, 1715 (fig. 15; see also cat. 33).

THE KYŌHŌ REFORMS, CHANGES IN PRINT FORMATS AND TECHNIQUES OF DECORATION

The latest dateable actor print in the *ō-ōban* format seems to have been issued in connection with a performance given during the eleventh month of 1718 to mark the arrival in Edo of the actor Sanogawa Mangiku.[86] Then, from 1719 onwards, the *ō-ōban* format suddenly ceased to be used. Large-format prints did not reappear until the 1740s, when 'wide pillar prints' by Okumura Masanobu and others were published. The standard print format in the intervening decades was the much smaller *hosoban*. What had happened?

The accession in 1716 of the eighth Tokugawa shogun, Yoshimune (1684–1751), ushered in a period of far-reaching reforms, now named the Kyōhō Reforms after the new era (1716–36). Their chief aims were to establish a new legal code and to strengthen the government's economic basis by reforming coinage and increasing tax yields from the land. Beginning in 1721, attempts were made to extend control over merchants by forcing them to form guilds, making it easier to compel them to observe official regulations.[87] The policy was applied to publishers: existing informal associations of booksellers (*honya nakama*) become official organisations, in Kyoto as early as 1716 (approximately 200 firms), in Edo in 1721 (47 firms) and in Osaka in 1723 (24 firms).[88] In addition, regulations were issued in the eleventh month of 1722 that governed the day-to-day activities of the publishing industry. Essentially constituting an enhanced system of censorship, these stipulations have been summarised by Peter Kornicki as follows: 'New books...were acceptable if they were ordinary Confucian, Buddhist, Shintō, medical or *waka* books, but any new books containing obscene matter or divergent views were strictly prohibited, and books dealing with the ancestors and family backgrounds of "people" (i.e., daimyo and ranking members of the Bakufu) with an admixture of falsehood would no longer be tolerated. Of more significance than these prohibitions was the fact that the edict, for the first time, provided for enforcement by requiring all books henceforward to display the real names of the author and the publisher in the colophon and by requiring them to be inspected before being put on sale.'[89]

In many ways the bans repeated existing edicts,[90] but the system of enforcement was new: 'It was thus in the Kyōhō era. . .that the system of internal pre-publication self-censorship by the bookseller's guilds began, for the burden of inspection and enforcement of the law fell squarely on the guilds. Members of the guilds wishing to publish a book were required to submit the manuscript for approval to the duty member acting as censor'.[91] Despite this censorship mechanism, it has been argued that the results of the new regulations were the expansion of a more protected, more monopolistic publishing industry and the blossoming of new areas of scholarship.[92] The edict against erotic books does seem to have been enforced quite strictly for a time. Although such material had often been issued with the name of the artist and publisher given quite openly, for fifteen to twenty years after 1722 no new *shunga* was produced.[93]

The regulations of 1722 did not refer directly to single-sheet prints. Clearly, the edicts were issued too late to explain the sudden disappearance of the *ō-ōban* format. Yet the early years of Yoshimune's rule were marked by frugality campaigns – one commentator observed that 'there is a difference between economy and parsimony...and this is parsimony'[94] – and publishers may have thought it wise to restrict the luxury of prints themselves. One change to prints can definitely be linked to the new regulations: the appearance across the bottom of *hosoban* prints published from 1723 to 1745 (a period almost exactly coextensive with the rule of Shogun

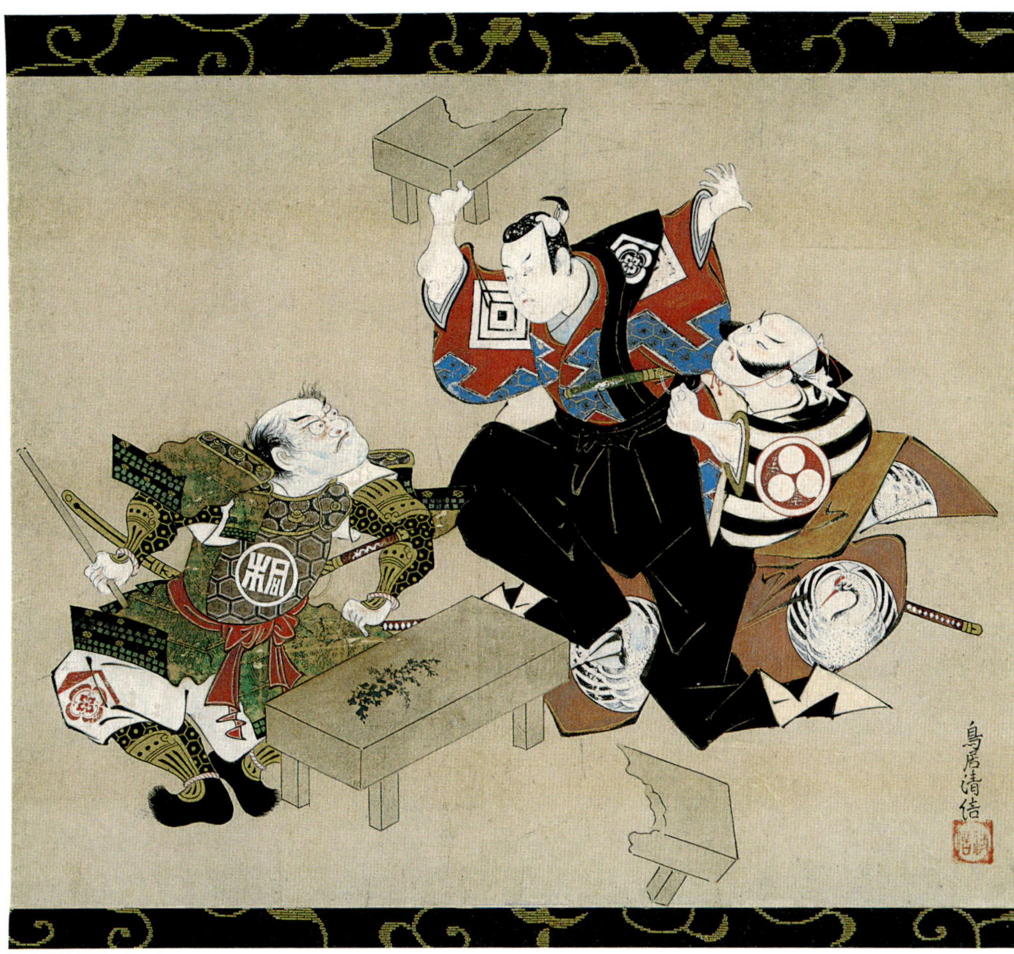

Fig. 15 TORII KIYONOBU I, *Scene of 'Seven Spring Herbs'*, 1715, hanging scroll, ink, colour and gold on paper, 41 × 52.6 cm, Freer Gallery of Art, Smithsonian Institution, Washington DC, Gift of Charles Lang Freer, F1898.14

Yoshimune) of what has been called the 'sash-shaped cartouche' (*obi-gata hyōki*; see, for example, cat. 28).[95] This contained the name of the artist, the name and address of the publisher, his trademark and, sometimes, the term 'wholesaler' (*toiya*) – all elements no doubt adopted from book publishers, who were required by the edicts to print colophons at the end of their volumes. The sash cartouche had two major commercial advantages: the same standard form could quickly be reused from print to print, accelerating a trend towards mass production already apparent in the industry; and the clear naming of the artist and publisher impeded the production of pirate editions.[96] Scholarship, too, has profited from the cartouches: as Mutō Junko has demonstrated, changes in the appearance of the cartouche used by a given firm provide a rough indication of the date of publication of a particular print.

Even before the demise of the *ō-ōban* format, publishers had begun to enliven *hosoban* prints by applying sprinklings of brass filings with glue to certain areas of their designs (see, for example, cat. 27, which dates from the fifth month, 1717). When new, the brass must have sparkled like gold. With the disappearance of large *tan-e* prints, hand-colouring became more detailed, more sophisticated, and was now dominated by a pinker, safflower shade of red (*beni-e*, 'safflower pictures'). Almost simultaneous, there evolved a technique of painting deer glue (*nikawa*) over areas that had been printed matt black, giving them the shiny appearance of black lacquer and extending print terminology by the expression *urushi-e* ('lacquer pictures'). The *beni-e* and *urushi-e* techniques were generally employed together and remained in use at least until the early 1740s (cat. 85 dates from the 11th month, 1742). After *c.* 1742 images printed in two colours – *benizuri-e* (printed safflower red pictures) featuring shades of red and green – began to appear in the small formats (see p. 29), but *beni-e*-style hand-colouring continued to be used throughout the 1740s for large formats, such as 'wide pillar pictures' (*hababiro hashira-e*) (see cat. 69–76, 121–3). The hand-applied colours, mostly vegetable dyes, are prone to fading (see cat. 108, 116), but a good number of the *hosoban* prints from the 1720s and 1730s in the Boston collection survive with remarkably well preserved, pristine colours (for example, cat. 95, 117).

OKUMURA MASANOBU, ARTIST–ENTREPRENEUR

The active career of Okumura Masanobu, from 1701 to the mid-1750s, spans much of the period covered by this volume and his name is associated with the development of many new genres and techniques of printmaking.[97] Masanobu was unusual in that, some time between 1711 and 1719, he established his own publishing firm, Okumura-ya at Tōrishio-chō,[98] which he seems to have handed over to a successor, Okumura-ya Genroku, by 1743.[99] Basing his account on a study of the no less than 58 signatures and 22 publisher's seals used by Masanobu, Aoki Takayuki has summarised the main phases of Okumura-ya's development as follows:

> From its beginnings during the Kyōhō era (1716–36) as a publisher of *sumizuri* prints with hand-colouring, Okumura-ya marketed large quantities of actor prints and also became a seller of illustrated fiction [*e-zōshi*]. The activities of the business were expanded to include prints to be used on folding screens and sliding door panels [see cat. 102, 103], seasonal products, such as pictures of Shō Ki [cat. 76] and Tenjin [cat. 77], and reproductions of old paintings. From the Genbun (1736–41) to the Kanpō era (1741–4), colour printing of the type known as *benizuri-e* became possible and the business was handed over to Genroku. A steady expansion can be seen as new formats and styles were developed, including pillar pictures [cat. 75] and perspective pictures [*uki-e*, cat. 64], and the number of impressions taken was increased.[100]

Masanobu frequently claimed that his works were being pirated (see, for example, the signature of cat. 64) but, since no other artist makes such an accusation, one wonders whether this was a promotional ruse. Certainly, other publishers made bold claims for their products (see the inscriptions on cat. 103, 114, 115). Several innovations associated with Masanobu were of fundamental importance to the development of early ukiyo-e. These new genres were 'parody pictures' (*mitate-e*), initiated *c.* 1704–11, and, as already mentioned, *benizuri-e*, *uki-e* and *hashira-e*, introduced *c.* 1739–44.

'PARODY PICTURES'

'Parody picture' is a convenient but rather free translation of *mitate-e*, a term (and a concept) that in modern times has acquired a meaning different from that current in the 18th century. Both usages have been widely debated in recent years,[101] but no one disputes that a playfully parodic spirit is apparent in many early ukiyo-e images that take a classic theme and rework it in a comic, up-to-date manner. Part parody, part emulation, *mitate* in ukiyo-e was a device for coming to terms with the past while championing the present.

Early genre painting had contained images of people in elegant modern dress acting out themes from Chinese and Japanese classical culture. The most famous example is the so-called Hikone Screen of *c.* 1620–50, in which the figures are engaged in the four elegant pastimes of the Chinese scholar–gentleman: music, chess, calligraphy and painting (*kinki shoga*).[102] At about the same time, literary parodies of the classics were starting to appear – *Ise monogatari* (*Tales of Ise*), for instance, was reworked *c.* 1638–9 as *Nise monogatari* (*Fake Tales*).[103]

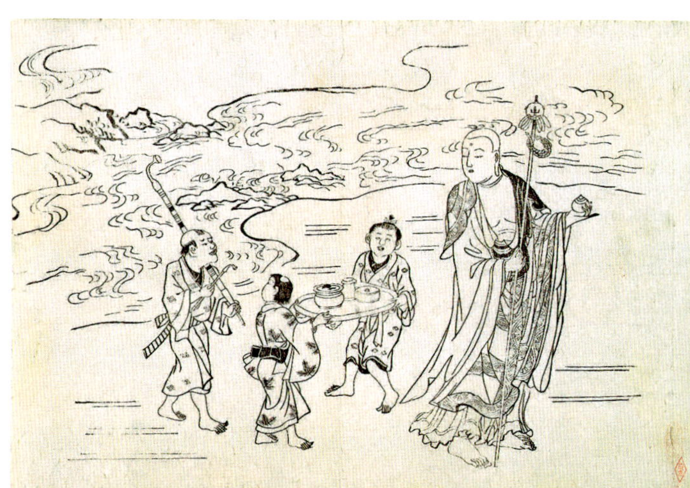

The construction of parallels with the past later becomes explicit in illustrated books by Sugimura Jihei, such as *Genji ukiyo fukusa-e* (*Genji Floating-world Hand-cloth Pictures*) of 1684. Here, images of floating-world pleasures, seemingly painted on a small square hand-cloth (*fukusa*), occupy more than two thirds of each page, while the scenes from *Tale of Genji* with which they are compared are symbolically crammed into a much smaller area. In the past Moronobu was thought not to have designed any parody pictures, but recently an album leaf has been attributed to him in which the bodhisattva Jizō acts out the formal procession of a courtesan accompanied by children carrying a smoking set (fig. 16).[104] Similar 'parody picture' album leaves have been attributed to Jihei.[105]

A wide range of parody subjects is first encountered in folding albums designed by Okumura Masanobu during the Hōei and Shōtoku eras (1704–16). The last systematic study of the surviving sheets from these albums was made in 1929 by Shibui Kiyoshi, who proposed that there were originally fourteen sets, or albums, of twelve designs each.[106] Prints from three of the sets are included in the present volume (cat. 42–5, 46–57, 60, 61). The parodic mechanisms differ slightly in each series, the most complicated being perhaps *Famous Scenes from Japanese Puppet Plays* (cat. 46–57), in which kabuki actors are transplanted to popular scenes from puppet plays. Yet all the sets share many characteristics with Tosa *jōruri*; with the new style of *haikai* poetry that Masanobu was learning from Tachiba Fukaku at about this time (1707 at the latest), which provocatively juxtaposed classical and modern imagery; and with the iconoclastic spirit of the racy *ukiyo-zōshi* novels quoted from above (p. 25), in which paintings of sexy actors are substituted for holy images of the buddha Amida and attendant deities. In the prefatory plate to one of the albums, thought to show Masanobu himself writing on a screen (fig. 17), the artist adopts the voice of a publisher to explain what 'parody pictures' are about. The text may be tentatively translated as follows:

> Pictures of a falcon by Emperor Huizong [of the Northern Song] and Lin Huoqing in the Plum Orchard [a typical Kano school subject] these days are like court caps worn in grand reception rooms [i.e. they are formal and old-fashioned]. Asking him what he thought about such matters, I took out a picture book and showed it to Mr Okumura Masanobu, saying: 'Well, take these pictures by the ancients and turn them quickly into an amusing grab-bag of customs of the floating world'. Straightaway he took up his painting brush and drew, while at his side a [young] man and woman rubbed [the inkstick] to ensure a steady stream of ink. Now, for me to enjoy them alone would be like having a beautiful tree blossom deep in the mountains. Why not be generous and kind, I thought; so I've had them carved on printing blocks.[107]

In essence Masanobu is saying: we do not need the old masters; we have our own ways of drawing things. The range of subjects he selected for parody and the many inventive ways in which he treated them were to serve as models for all subsequent ukiyo-e artists.

COLOUR PRINTING

The earliest known example of a *benizuri-e* is a 'picture calendar' (*e-goyomi*) by Okumura Masanobu, apparently published for the New Year, 1742, in the collection of the Royal Ontario Museum, Toronto.[108] The *kentō* technique used to register the colours was simple. Each cherrywood printing block was cut so that a right-angled ridge of wood (*kagi*) was left in one corner. The sheet of printing paper was inserted into this right-angle and one of its long edges aligned against another, straight ridge (*hikitsuke*) further down the side of the block. The ridges were carved at the same distance from the design on each block so that, provided the blocks did not warp, the colours printed in exactly the right place when an impression was taken by rubbing the back of the sheet with the printer's special pad (*baren*). Accounts written later in the Edo period, collected and described in detail by David Waterhouse, credit the invention of this technique to one Uemura Kichi'emon, a publisher who ran the Emi-ya firm in Shiba, but they give the date as 1744.[109]

Isolated examples of colour printing in Japan survive from the 17th century, in diagrams contained in scientific and technical books, such as *Senmyō-reki*, a volume of 1644 about calendars that appears to have a *kentō* registration mark printed in *tan* in the margin of one page.[110] Colour printing of exquisite refinement was used in China during the late Ming period (1368–1644) for some erotic works[111] and for

Fig. 16 Attributed to HISHIKAWA MORONOBU, *Parody of Courtesan Jizō*, *c.* 1681–4, woodblock, *yoko-ōban*, *sumizuri-e*, 25.7 × 38.2 cm, Tobacco and Salt Museum, Tokyo, 1088-Mukan-I

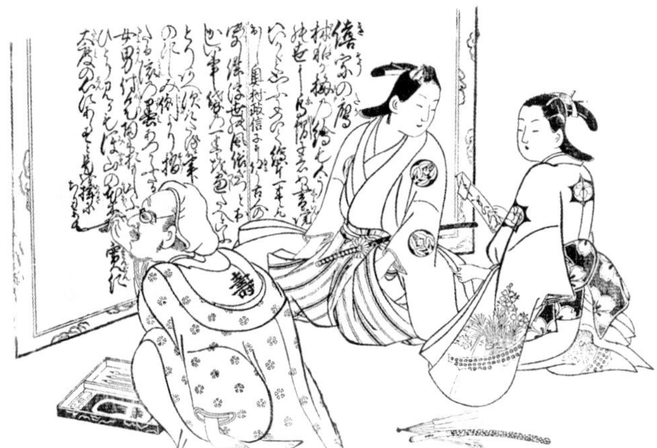

Fig. 17 OKUMURA MASANOBU, *Masanobu Writing a Preface on a Screen*, *c.* 1707–9, from an untitled series of 'parody pictures', woodblock, *yoko-ōban*, *sumizuri-e*, 26.7 × 35.5 cm, The Art Institute of Chicago, Clarence Buckingham Collection, 1925.1845

illustrations in volumes of secular literature, such as the album *Romance of the Western Chamber* (*Xixiang ji*), designed by Min Qiji in 1640, a copy of which is in the Museum für Ostasiatische Kunst, Cologne.[112] The Chinese technique of colour printing, the so-called *tao ban* (or *dou ban*) method,[113] was quite different from the Japanese and it is not clear how widely Chinese colour-printed editions were known in Japan or whether the *tao ban* method was ever attempted there. Two Chinese books, each with some colour-printed illustrations in their original editions, were certainly known in Japan in the 17th century, the painting manuals *Ten Bamboo Studio Calligraphy and Painting Album* (*Shizhuzhai shuhua pu/Jitchikusai gafu*, 1619–33) and *Mustard Seed Garden Painting Manual* (*Jieziyuan huachuan/Kaishien gaden*, 1677–9, 1701). The latter was copied in a two-part Japanese edition (1748, 1753) with multi-coloured printed illustrations of great beauty and refinement, proving that the full-colour woodblock technique had been successfully used in Japan well before Harunobu's 'brocade prints' (*nishiki-e*) of 1765.[114]

Ukiyo-e colour prints in three shades – most often red, green and blue or red, green and yellow – began appearing regularly in the late 1750s (see cat. 112, 132, 133). Cat. 134, issued in the eleventh month of 1762, is printed in red, blue and yellow, with yellow printed over the blue in some areas to produce a fourth colour, green. The drift of developments was therefore clearly towards ever more complex effects of colour printing. However, it would take the sudden injection of patronage from groups of *haikai* poets – notably that led by 'Kyosen', the pen-name of Ōkubo Tadanobu, a high-ranking *hatamoto* in the service of the shogunate – to provide sufficient capital and cultural impetus for Suzuki Harunobu (*d.* 1770) to design their privately printed *e-goyomi* in 1765 and 1766 (see cat. 142). This brought about a rapid switch to full-colour printing for many commercial designs as well.[115]

PERSPECTIVE PICTURES

'Floating pictures' (*uki-e*) or 'sunken pictures' (*kubomi-e*)[116] were the names given to a new genre of ukiyo-e print that appeared *c.* 1739. This consisted of interior or exterior views in which the architectural lines were drawn so as to converge sharply towards a lowered horizon ('converging perspective'), generating a sense of deep spatial recession. Common in European art since at least the early Renaissance, this technique was completely new in Japan. Traditional Japanese painting had tended to tilt the ground plane towards the picture plane, placing distant landscape elements, for example, higher in the picture ('parallel perspective'). A striking feature of the new images – typically, interiors of kabuki theatres during performances or views down a straight street in Edo – was that they often used converging perspective for the main, front part of the composition, while 'reverting' to parallel perspective for the rear part. Although the first securely dateable *uki-e* relate to two kabuki performances given in the spring of 1744,[117] the craze for such views seems to have begun *c.* 1739. In inscriptions on several of Okumura Masanobu's perspective pictures (for instance, cat. 64) he claimed to be the originator of the genre. At any rate, a series by him of six views of famous places in Edo printed on sheets twice the normal *ōban* size (see cat. 65, 66) would appear to have been issued at the New Year, 1745. The following year saw the publication of an illustrated *haikai* anthology, *Haikai tokitsu-kaze*, that put *uki-e* first on a list of 62 items fashionable in Edo at the time – although the accompanying simple line drawing framed in a round window (or telescope?) merely seems to delight in the *repoussoir* effect of distant boats on the sea seen through a round opening and does not use any converging architectural lines.[118] Among others who designed *uki-e* at this time were Torii Kiyotada (see cat. 109) and Nishimura Shigenaga.

In 1720 Shogun Yoshimune's personal interest in science and technology had overcome traditional Tokugawa fears of intellectual pollution from the West: as part of the Kyōhō Reforms, he intervened to lift the ban on the importation of Chinese translations of European books, provided these did not mention Christianity.[119] It is tempting to suggest that this may have resulted in the appearance in Japan of European books on perspective that instigated the vogue for *uki-e*. Yet, as Suzuki Jūzō pointed out some time ago, no early Japanese experiments in perspective show evidence of direct copying from European sources.[120] Another possible transmission route was via Chinese prints that evinced European influence, particularly the popular townscape prints of Suzhou.[121] Until recently, the earliest known dated print of this kind was *View of the Ten Thousand Year Bridge, Suzhou* (*Guzu Wannian-qiao tu*) of 1740,[122] which meant that perspective pictures in China could not be shown to predate the fashion for *uki-e* in Japan. The discovery of a large diptych view of Suzhou dated 1734[123] now makes this a more possible route – except that Chinese prints do not appear to have used compositions with such a rigorous 'vanishing point' system as that seen in many early Japanese perspective pictures.

Uki-e transform our vision of the floating world, literally offering a new perspective on the city of Edo in which figures occupy more plausible interior and exterior spaces. Revived in the late 1760s, perspective prints were to exert a profound long-term influence, informing the landscape vision of both Katsushika Hokusai (1760–1849) and Utagawa Hiroshige (1797–1858).

PILLAR PICTURES

Another print format that Masanobu claimed to have invented (see cat. 75) appeared almost simultaneously with perspective pictures: the 'pillar picture' (*hashira-e*), the earliest securely dateable example of which was issued in 1741.[124] The most convincing explanation for the evolution of this unusual format assumes that two long blocks joined side-by-side to print what is now called the 'wide pillar picture' (*hahahiro hashira-e*) format (adopted by Masanobu at this time) gradually ceased to fit neatly together and had to be separated (several *hahahiro hashira-e* prints by Masanobu included here do indeed show marked evidence of the blocks coming apart about one quarter or one third of the way in from either the left or the right side – see cat. 69, 71, 74). Prints subsequently made from the larger of the two blocks showed most of the figure, but radically cropped down the side where the smaller block had been removed. The aesthetic qualities of this cropping, suggesting movement or a spontaneous glimpse of a grand courtesan or handsome actor, came to be appreciated in their own right, and the classic pillar picture was born – named thus because, apart from the formal alcove (*tokonoma*), where it could be displayed like a hanging scroll painting, the only other place in an interior where it might be hung was the side of a square wooden pillar.[125] Modern art historians have called the earliest examples, designed by Masanobu and his contemporaries in the 1740s, 'wide pillar prints' to distinguish them from the narrower format that seems to have become standard in the late 1750s (see cat. 132, 133).

In typical fashion, once the new format was established, Masanobu seems to have attempted to produce the ultimate example of the genre. Just as in 1745 he designed a set of six perspective views in the unusually large, double-*ōban* format, so, Louise Virgin has suggested, he created at about the same time a triptych of extra-tall *hashira-e* (cat. 75, 126). Daringly cropped figures subsequently seem to have been adopted in ukiyo-e painting.[126]

'PRIMITIVES'?

In Western publications the word 'primitive' has frequently been used to describe ukiyo-e prints (and sometime paintings) from the period prior to 1765.[127] Almost from the outset commentators apologetically qualified the use of the term and questioned its suitability, and it has been completely avoided in the present volume. When was it first applied to early ukiyo-e and what did it connote?

The two most important early writers on ukiyo-e in Britain and the USA, William Anderson (1842–1900) and Ernest Fenollosa (1853–1908) respectively, both lived in Japan for extended periods and appear not to have used the term 'primitive' at all in their writings on early ukiyo-e. Neither do the late 19th-century writers on Japanese art in France, such as Louis Gonse (1846–1921) and Siegfried Bing (1838–1905). This is surprising, particularly in the case of Fenollosa, who compared prints from the 1780s by Torii Kiyonaga (1752–1815), which he regarded as the apogee of the ukiyo-e tradition, to ancient Greek vase painting and canvases by Botticelli and might therefore have been expected to equate previous ukiyo-e with more archaic forms of Western art.[128] The earliest use of the term I have been able to locate occurs in *Geschichte des japanischen Farbenholzschnitts* by Woldemar von Seidlitz (1850–1922), first published in Berlin in 1897, with English and French translations appearing in 1910 and 1911:

> His [Moronobu's] particular glory, however, consists in this, that he brought wood-engraving to such instant perfection that his influence remained predominant throughout the entire period that elapsed until the invention of tone polychrome-printing, that is, of the 'primitives' [*Primitive*] which lasted for two whole generations.
>
> Such 'primitives' are now held in far higher esteem than formerly. We recognise in them not only forerunners, but men of heroic race, who, without being able to claim the highest honours paid to the gods, still exhibit a power, a freshness, and a grace that are hardly met with in the same degree in later times. Despite the imperfections that necessarily attach to their works, despite their lack of external correctness, their limitation to few and generally crude materials and their conventionalism, there clings to their works a charm such as belongs to the works neither of the most brilliant nor of the pronouncedly naturalistic periods. For, in the singleness of their effort to make their drawing as expressive as possible, without regard to any special kind of beauty or truth, these 'primitives' discover a power of idealisation and a stylistic skill which, at a later period and with increased knowledge, are quite unthinkable.[129]

Late 19th-century art-historical usage described as 'primitive' certain artists of the pre- or early Renaissance periods.[130] The term was not intended pejoratively – quite the reverse – and von Seidlitz, when discussing in a more general manner the 'decorative aims ... of Eastern Asiatic art ... in contrast to the naturalistic aims predominating [in Europe] today', finds similarities with 'the art of Egypt and of Greece up to Alexandrine times, in the Roman and Gothic periods up to the discovery of perspective in Italy and the invention of oil painting in Flanders at the beginning of the fifteenth century'.[131]

The extended passage quoted above clearly implies that Moronobu is a 'primitive' because his prints – not his paintings, which are excluded from the equation – were created before the adoption of polychrome printing. Yet von Seidlitz grants that Moronobu's works exhibit 'instant [technical?] perfection'. Von Seidlitz's second paragraph apparently contradicts this by stating that, although the medium is 'generally crude', it is charming in its conventionalism when compared to the relative naturalism of later periods (the analogy is no doubt between pre-Renaissance and Renaissance approaches to form). The origins of the term 'primitive' as applied to early ukiyo-e prints, and the confusion surrounding its use, would not appear to have been elucidated by any later critic of Japanese art, and it is a perhaps a measure of the rather sequestered nature of ukiyo-e scholarship that the word could remain current until the 1980s.

The succession of new decoration techniques, the new formats and genres that constantly followed one another throughout the history of ukiyo-e reflect the intense competition between artists and between publishers in a world driven by the desire to stimulate and satisfy rapacious consumer appetites. The analogies previously drawn by historians in many disciplines to the human life cycle of birth, maturity and decay, from which the terms 'primitive' and 'decadent' derive, were seductive: it is hard not to view the technical proficiency of Harunobu's delicate full-colour *nishiki-e* as anything other than an improvement on what went before. Technically more complex they certainly are – but artistically and culturally more significant? Clear-cut judgements are not possible here, and it is not desirable that they should be. As has been remarked: 'In some respects the history of art is comparable with that of literature. There is continuity and change in both, progressive improvement in neither....only in its use for scientific illustration does printmaking have a progressive history, like technology'.[132] No primitives, no decadents.

Notes

1 Kuroki 1987, pp. 880–1.

2 For a wide-ranging introduction to popular culture of the Edo period, see Shively 1991, pp. 706–69.

3 Gerhart 1999, p. 154, n. 55.

4 Iwata 1992, p. 270.

5 Kobayashi Tadashi, 'Hishikawa Moronobu to sono gagyō', in Chiba 2000, p. 7.

6 See the comments by Satō Satoru, 'Hishikawa ehon no sho-mondai', in Chiba 2000, p. 18.

7 The term first appears in the preface by Ankei to Moronobu's illustrated book *Yamato musha-e* (*Pictures of Japanese Warriors*, 1680 or earlier). Ibid.

8 First translated in Lane 1957, pp. 671–2, and quoted here in the slightly altered version of the translation in Shively 1991, p. 730.

9 In the 1690 edition of the Edo guidebook *Edo sōganoko meisho taizen* the printing block seems to have been altered to change Moronobu's title from *ukiyo-eshi* to *Yamato-eshi*. Satō (note 6), p. 19.

10 The change from *hangi shita-e shi* to *ukiyo eshi* with respect to Moronobu's pupils Moroshige, Ryūsen and Moronaga, and the more independent Sugimura Jihei, seems to have occurred between two editions of the guidebook *Edo zukan kōmoku*, both possibly issued during 1689. Satō (note 6) and Satō 1991, p. 43.

11 Coaldrake 1981; Shively 1964–5. Laws of 1683, for example, exhorted *chōnin* to wear only 'ordinary silk, pongee, cotton and ramie'. Shively 1964–5, p. 126.

12 The first great Kamigata *onnagata*, Yoshizawa Ayame (1673–1729), declared, for example, that the '*onnagata* should continue to have the feelings of an *onnagata* even when in the dressing room'. Dunn and Torigoe 1969, pp. 61–2.

13 The version of *Amusements at the Dry Riverbed, Shijō* in the Dōmoto family collection has been dated to the early Kan'ei era, that in the Seikadō Bunko Art Museum, Tokyo, to the mid-Kan'ei era. Boston 2000, vol. 1, nos. 1–2 (commentary by Tsuji Nobuo).

14 Ibid.

15 *Kinsei fūzoku*, pp. 9–41, fig. 1–21.

16 Although the style and certain details of the Boston *Amusements* screens have led some commentators to date them as late as the Kanbun era (1661–74), they certainly look back in their subject matter and treatment to two depictions of the same theme from the early to mid Kan'ei era (1624–44). See note 13 and Shinoda 1991, pp. 37–43.

17 Shively 1991, pp. 749–61, from which much of my account of early kabuki is derived.

18 Ibid., p. 752.

19 Asai Ryōi, *Edo meisho-ki* (1662), quoted in Shively 1955, p. 333.

20 For detailed accounts of the careers of Tōjūrō and Danjūrō, see Kominz 1997, pp. 34–180.

21 Suzuki Jūzō, 'Ukiyo-e shoki hanga no seisaku shisei', in *Ukiyo-e shūka*, vol. 4, pp. 230–5.

22 My account of Tosa *jōruri* derives from Torii 1989, esp. preface, pp. 1–2, and main text, pp. 1–16.

23 Hozumi Ikan, *Naniwa miyage* (1738), quoted in Gerstle 2001, p. 4.

24 Gerstle 2001, p. 2.

25 Saikaku 1969, intro., p. xix.

26 Ibid.

27 Ibid., p. 13; also quoted in Keene 1976, p. 200.

28 Hillier 1987, vol. 1, p. 107.

29 Keene 1976, p. 78.

30 Ibid., p. 125.

31 Masanobu is known to have used the *haikai* name Baiō from at least as early as 1707, suggesting he may then already have been a pupil of Fukaku (also known as Sen'ō). Aoki 1999, p. 25.

32 Suzuki Katsutada, in *Nihon koten*, s.v. 'Fukaku'.

33 This inscription is appended to the handscroll painting *Illustrated Tale of Nagoya Sanza* (*Nagoya Sanza emaki*, Toyama Kinenkan, Saitama Prefecture) and, although not in Itchō's authentic hand, is thought to be a faithful copy of a text by him. Kobayashi 1988, pp. 21–2, fig. 21.

34 Kita 1999.

35 The signature used by Matabei on his late set of votive paintings *Thirty-Six Poet Immortals* (*Sanjū-rokkasen zu hengaku*, Senba Tōshō-gū, Kawagoe, 1640) was 'Eshi Tosa Mitsunobu matsuryū Iwasa Matabei-no-jō Katsumochi'. 'Matsuryū' can be interpreted as meaning simply 'a late(r) follower', somewhat undercutting the dramatic tone of the 'The Last Tosa' in the title of Kita's book.

36 The playwright Chikamatsu did an unwitting disservice to ukiyo-e scholarship when, in the play *Keisei hangonko* of 1705, he named a fictional character Ukiyo Matahei (Matabei) – a poor artist of Ōtsu folk paintings with a stutter. The identities of 'Ōtsu Matabei' and Iwasa Matabei have been regularly confused or conflated ever since. Welch 1994; McArthur 1999.

37 Kobayashi 1982, pp. 136–8.

38 Tsuji 1987, pp. 66–8.

39 Boston 2000, vol. 1, nos. 22–3 (commentary by Tsuji Nobuo). Tsuji draws attention to the similarities in style, technique and condition between the two Boston paintings and another work of the Matabei school (Tsuji 1987, no. 87) and suggests that they both may come from the same *fusuma-e*.

40 Orii 2000, pp. 5–18.

41 Boston 2000, vol. 1, no. 7 (commentary by Kobayashi Tadashi). For more on *ta-ga-sode* paintings, see Los Angeles 1992 and Tokyo 1994.

42 Nishizaka 1992. Nishizaka lists the department stores in the three cities and, where possible, gives their dates of opening. Those in Edo were: Ōmura Shiroki-ya (1662), Mitsui Echigo-ya (1673), Iwagi Masuya (1702), Shimomura Daimaru (1742), Itō Matsuzaka-ya (1768), Shimada Ebisu-ya (date unknown). Ibid., p. 182.

43 For the Karigane-ya, see Wilson 1991, pp. 40–9, and, for Rinpa, Yamane et al. 1998.

44 Kornicki 1998, pp. 20–6, 112–14.

45 Ibid., pp. 129–36.

46 The classic study of *kana-zōshi* is Lane 1957.

47 Kornicki 1998, p. 697.

48 Ibid., p. 140.

49 Ibid., p. 137.

50 Ibid., p. 139.

51 Ibid., pp. 265, 391–8.

52 Hillier 1987, vol. 1, pp. 63–8.

53 Other colours, including yellow, brown and purple, were sometimes added.

54 For example, Lane 1978, p. 39, fig. 20.

55 Chiba 2000, no. 6.

56 Ibid., no. 5. It has long been debated, inconclusively, whether this handscroll was assembled by Moronobu himself from a collection of dated fragments from different stages in his career or by the group of *kyōka* poets, led by Ōta Nanpo, himself a keen historian of ukiyo-e, whose inscriptions were appended to the scroll in the early 19th century.

57 Estimate by Asano Shūgō, 'Hishikawa Moronobu no hanga', in Chiba 2000, p. 202.

58 For example, ibid., nos. 10–12.

59 Ibid. pp. 202, 205. Satō Satoru was the first to comment in detail on the re-cut editions of Moronobu's books. Satō 1986. See also idem, in Chiba 2000, pp. 21–3.

60 Lane 1981, p. 6, where he suggests the average sizes for the *kakemono-e* and *ō-ōban* formats and encourages consistency in the use of the terms.

61 An erotic set dated 1680, attributed to Shimomura Shichirobei (active *c.* 1673–88) and issued by the Osaka publisher Ise-ya Ichirobei; and an anonymous set dated 1683 showing horse-riding stunts by Koreans, issued by the Kyoto publisher Kawachi-ya Rihei. Chiba 2000, p. 207 and nn. 7, 8.

62 Suwa 1994, pp. 21–30.

63 Lane 1957, pp. 694–7.

64 The text reads 'arasono', but this is thought to be a mistake for 'aragoto'.

65 Quoted in Mutō 1996, pp. 106–7.

66 Mutō 1994, pp. 5–12.

67 *Genshoku ukiyo-e*, vol. 6, p. 9 (frontispiece).

68 Mutō 1992, pp. 28–9.

69 Mutō 1996; Akama 1994.

70 Mutō 1996, p. 107.

71 *Nikuhitsu ukiyo-e*, vol. 5, no. 2 (commentary by Yamaguchi Keizaburō)

72 Ibid., no. 7.

73 *Genshoku ukiyo-e*, vol. 6, p. 36. The expression 'gourd-shaped legs' appeared in Shikitei Sanba, *Gejō suigen maku no soto* (1806). Kobayashi and Ōkubo 1994, p. 55.

74 Boston 2000, vol. 2, no. 94 (commentary by Asano Shūgō).

75 *Yakei tomo-jamisen* (*Male and Female Prostitutes Play the Shamisen Together*) by Hōjō Dansui (1663–1711), published New Year 1708; repr. in *Edo jidai*, p. 317. The passage is referred to by Timon Screech, who makes it clear that the paintings were being used as a stimulus to masturbation. Screech 1999, pp. 18, 21.

76 Andō Jishō, preface to *Keisei kin-tanki* (*Courtesans Forbidden to Lose Temper*) by Ejima Kiseki (1666–1735), 1711; repr. in *Nihon koten bungaku*, p. 154; trans. also quoted in Clark 2000, p. 40.

77 Hibbett 1959, p. 57.

78 Screech 1999, p. 14, comments that *warai-e* had the secondary meaning of 'masturbation picture'.

79 For example, Ando's *The Actor Sakata Oginojō Performing a Dance* (*Sakata Oginojō no mai-sugata*, Cleveland Museum of Art), reproduced in *Nikuhitsu ukiyo-e*, vol. 2, no. 33 (commentary by Kobayashi Tadashi).

80 *Ukiyo-e shūka*, vol. 1, no. 135 (commentary by Money Hickman). A similar illustration by Okumura Masanobu, from the book *Ehon fūga nana Komachi* (*Picture Book: Elegant 'Seven Komachis'*, 1740s), shows Moronobu's granddaughter Osan (otherwise unknown) at work on a painting of a courtesan. Asano 1984, pp. 25–6, and London 1992, pp. 11–12, fig. 5, which also includes a discussion of ukiyo-e painting technique.

81 Kominz 1997, pp. 99–100.

82 Shively 1955, pp. 348–50.

83 Kobayashi 1996a, p. 54.

84 Mutō 1996, pp. 107–8.

85 Mutō 1992, pp. 21–2, nos. 32–4. *Ukiyo-e shūka*, vol. 4, no. 23 (Art Institute of Chicago) includes a large reproduction of the *tsuji-banzuke* for the Ichimura Theatre.

86 *Sanogawa Mangiku as Sanada, Daughter of a Thread-shop Owner* (*Sanogawa Mangiku no itoya musume Sanada*), reproduced in *Ukiyo-e shūka*, vol. 4, no. 18 (Art Institute of Chicago; commentary by Suzuki Jūzō). That this print is signed 'Kiyomasu hitsu' may be significant, since it has been conjectured that the appearance of the characters 'hitsu' or 'zu' after the name signals the change from the work of the artist Kiyomasu I (active *c.* 1704–18) to Kiyomasu II (1706–63). Mutō 1992, p. 28. Certainly, something out of the ordinary was happening at the beginning of 1718, when two, perhaps three, large-format prints were issued with a Kiyonobu signature followed by a Kiyomasu seal (cat. 37, 38). One theory is that Kiyomasu I may have died around this time, leaving the designs to be completed by Kiyonobu I.

87 Tsuji Tatsuya, in Hall 1991, pp. 425–77, esp. 445–56.

88 Nakano 1993, pp. 48–57.

89 Kornicki 1998, pp. 337–8. The texts of the edicts are printed in Japanese in Nakano 1993, pp. 52–3.

90 Kornicki 1998, pp. 334–5. The text of edicts issued in the fifth month of 1673 and the fourth month of 1684 have survived. Along with that dating from the seventh month of 1721, they are partly translated in Lane 1963.

91 Kornicki 1998, p. 338.

92 Nakano 1993, pp. 48–57.

93 Asano 1999, p. 40.

94 Muro Kyūsō (1658–1734), quoted by Tsuji, in Hall 1991, p. 445.

95 Mutō 1997, pp. 3–20.

96 Ibid., pp. 17–18.

97 For an excellent survey of Masanobu's career, see Vergez 1983.

98 Aoki 1999, p.21.

99 Ibid., pp. 22–3.

100 Ibid., p. 23.

101 Suwa 1996, pp. 28–33; Clark 1997.

102 Washington 1998, no. 233 (commentary by John T. Carpenter).

103 Shinoda 1995, esp. chap. 1.

104 Chiba 2000, no. 98.

105 *Hizō ukiyo-e*, vol. 3, nos. 173–4 (commentary by Asano Shūgō).

106 Shibui 1929.

107 Parts of the syntax remain unclear to me, but the text seems to read: 'Kisō no taka Rinna ga ume no e mo ima no yo ni eboshi kinu shoin wa ikaga to omou ni tsuite ehon ikkan tori-dashi Okumura Masanobu-shi ni nani zo inishie-bito no utsushi-e ukiyo no fūzoku zatto okashii koto-bukuro no ikkan o tsukushi-tabe to iu toriaezu toritaru fude no nijimi soba yori suritaru nagare no sumi atsukōtaru nyonan kakaretari sate mo omoshirō hitori miru mo miyama no kaboku...kanjin taido no shin ni arazu to kore o azusa ni chirihame'. An alternative, abbreviated translation is given in Chicago 1955, p. 121, Masanobu no. 14.

108 Toronto 1975, no. 33, first identified as a calendar print for 1742 by Roger Keyes. Masanobu himself used the term *benizuri-e* in an inscription on one of his prints issued in 1747. Mutō 1999, p. 7.

109 Waterhouse 1964, pp. 14–20.

110 Hillier 1987, esp. vol. 1, chap. 5 and p. 76, colour pl. 10.

111 Van Gulik 1951. Lane 1985 publishes an erotic illustrated book by Moronobu, *Fūryū zetchō zu*, *c.* 1686, that is a direct adaptation of a Chinese erotic work of 1606, *Fengliu quechang tu*.

112 Dittrich 1977.

113 Tschichold 1972, pp. 41–4; Tsien 1985, pp. 277–87.

114 Hillier 1987, vol. 1, chap. 15.

115 Waterhouse 1981, pp. 1–6; Tokyo 1996, esp. pp. 14–22, Hara Fumihiko, 'Ōkubo Kyosen to Abe Sakei'.

116 In his *Esora-goto* of 1802 Ishino Hiromichi recorded that an early viewer said such images should be called 'sunken pictures' (*kubomi-e*), because they appeared sunken rather than floating. Kishi 1994a, n. 3. The present account of *uki-e* derives from Kishi's article.

117 Suzuki 1975.

118 I am grateful to Henry Smith for sharing with me a copy of this rare image.

119 Hall 1991, p. 455.

120 Suzuki 1975.

121 Lee 1977.

122 Nara 1972, no. 25.

123 Aoki 2000, esp. fig. 5.

124 Mutō 1999, p. 7, mentioning an actor *hashira-e* by Masanobu dateable to 1741.

125 Pins 1982, esp. pp. 29–32.

126 See, for example, Asano 1987, p. 64, fig. 90.

127 See the titles of the first great exhibition of early ukiyo-e prints, held at the Musée de Arts Décoratifs, Paris, in 1909; of the first volume documenting the collection of the Art Institute of Chicago, published in 1955; of the 1971 exhibition at the same institution, organised by Donald Jenkins, of items from collections worldwide; and of the exhibition in 1980 of works from the James Michener Collection at the Honolulu Academy of Arts. Paris 1909; Chicago 1955; Chicago 1971; Honolulu 1980.

128 Fenollosa 1912, vol. 2, p. 195. This book was written by Fenollosa in 1906 and published posthumously.

129 Von Seidlitz 1910, p. 62.

130 '[P]ainters, particularly of the Netherlandish and Italian Schools, working before *c.* 1500 – i.e., Netherlandish painters of the late 14th and all the 15th centuries, and all Italian painters between Giotto and Raphael'. Murray 1972, p. 342, s.v. 'Primitive'.

131 Von Seidlitz 1910, p. 3.

132 Honour and Fleming 1982, pp. 12, 11. See also London 1992, p. 27, and Clark 1992.

The Early Ukiyo-e Collection at the Museum of Fine Arts, Boston

ANNE NISHIMURA MORSE

In 1905, following the completion of a survey of the collection of Japanese art at the Museum of Fine Arts in Boston, Okakura Kakuzō (1862–1913), the celebrated author of *The Book of Tea* and adviser to the Department of Chinese and Japanese Art, declared that the Museum had 'the largest single collection in the world. In wealth of masterpieces it is second only to the Imperial Japanese collections of Nara and Kioto [*sic*]. In certain schools of Tokugawa painting it is unrivaled anywhere.'[1] Since then collections in Japan have increased in size, but the Boston Museum continues to possess the premier collection of Japanese art outside Japan in terms of both quality and quantity.

For a Western collection largely formed during the late 19th century, the Boston holdings are unusual in that they encompass Buddhist painting and sculpture from the Nara period (710–94), ink painting from the 15th century and ceramics for the tea ceremony from the 16th to the 19th century. The collection also includes types of object more generally acquired by institutions in Europe and the United States at that time. The ukiyo-e images so beloved of British and French collectors have an important place in Boston, represented by more than 55,000 prints and 700 paintings. Preparations for the current exhibition have confirmed that the Museum is unique in the strength of its holdings of early ukiyo-e, both painted and printed – a testament to the foresight and unusual interests of a small group of Boston collectors.

JAPAN AND THE WEST

When the United States naval fleet under the command of Commodore Matthew Perry (1794–1858) sailed into the waters off the Izu Peninsula in 1853, Japan was abruptly forced into direct contact with the West. For over 200 years Japan's military rulers had pursued a strict policy of semi-isolation so as to protect their nation from foreign domination and to ensure strict order at home. Foreigners were barred from entering the country, except at a trading outpost reserved for the Dutch on the island of Dejima in Nagasaki harbour. Although the West had shown interest in Japanese culture, and the Japanese had been curious about Europe, knowledge was largely limited to things that interested the Dutch trader intermediaries.

Begrudgingly, the Japanese government established diplomatic and commercial relations with the USA in 1854; treaties with Britain were concluded in 1858. In the years that immediately followed, Westerners, particularly Europeans, were eager to acquire the bronzes, porcelains and lacquers that had been the staples of the Dutch trade as furnishings for their homes. As early as 1862 Sir Rutherford Alcock (1809–97), the first British Consul General in Japan, helped arrange for Japanese art to be displayed at the International Exhibition in London. Largely drawn from his own collection and therefore reflecting his personal tastes, the over 600 items encompassed not only the standard curios but also a selection of 19th-century prints and woodblock-printed books.[2]
In Paris, shops in the rue Vivienne, such as La Porte Chinoise and A l'Empire Chinois, tried to keep pace with the demand for 'things Japanese'. At about the time of the 1867 Exposition Universelle, at which the Japanese display included items contributed by the Tokugawa shogunate and the Tosa and Satsuma domains, devotees established a secret organisation, the Société du Jing-lar, which was dedicated to the study of Japanese art. The artists Félix Bracquemond (1833–1914) and Jules Jacquemart (1837–80), and critics Philippe Burty (1830–90) and Zacharie Astruc (1833–1907), were among its members.

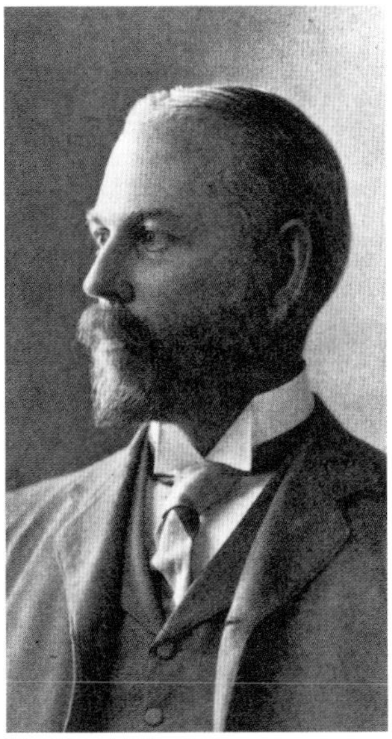

Fig. 1 Ernest Francisco Fenollosa

Despite the success of this initial foray into the West, the Tokugawa leaders faced mounting criticism at home for their 'capitulation' to foreigners. Under the leadership of dissenting military clans, a 'revolution' was staged in 1868 that reinstated the Emperor as the chief political authority in the land. However, realising that Japan could ensure its sovereignty only by emulating the West, the new government, headed by Emperor Meiji (*reg.* 1868–1912), charted a rather radical course of change for the country. Japan's image abroad was to be carefully managed and a whirlwind programme of study of foreign institutions implemented. An Italian, Edoardo Chiossone (1832–98), was employed to advise the Japanese Ministry of Finance on the printing of Western-style banknotes; Josiah Conder (1852–1920) from Britain was commissioned to design European-style public buildings; the German Ottmar von Mohl (1846–1922) was contracted to provide instruction in court etiquette and dress; and the Americans Edward Sylvester Morse (1838–1925) and Ernest Francisco Fenollosa (1853–1908; fig. 1) were employed to teach zoology and philosophy respectively at Tokyo University.

EDWARD SYLVESTER MORSE AND ERNEST FRANCISCO FENOLLOSA

Morse and Fenollosa, like most Americans, had first encountered the art of Japan at the Centennial Exposition of 1876 in Philadelphia. There the Japanese government staged their most ambitious display to date in order to impress on the world that Japan was the leading purveyor of objects evincing high technical virtuosity. Captivated by the works on display, which had been selected primarily to cater to Western tastes, Fenollosa noted: 'The Japanese exhibit is a mine of wonders. Bronzes of the most exquisite workmanship and immense in size, in the shape of animals, men, dragons, temples, vases, etc.'[3] Within five years Fenollosa's tastes in Japanese art, like Morse's, were to undergo a substantive transformation. By that time both men had taken up residence in Japan.

When Morse departed for Japan in 1877 he set out in search of brachiopods, not art. A zoologist by training, he was soon invited to lecture on Darwin's theory of evolution at the Imperial University (now Tokyo University) and established there a department and a museum of natural history. On one of his daily morning walks, prescribed by a physician to strengthen his ailing back, Morse chanced upon a small dish in the shape of a shell. So fascinated was he by this object that he began studying ceramics under the tutelage of the antiquarian Ninagawa Noritane (1835–83), learning to classify works not only by sight but also by touch. Soon Morse was avidly seeking out examples of both historical ceramics (primarily stonewares) and contemporary pieces from every kiln then in operation. His collection grew to 5000 items, acquired by the Museum of Fine Arts by subscription in 1892. Morse accepted an appointment at the Museum as Keeper of Japanese Pottery, a post he retained until his death in 1925. During his tenure, he published *Catalogue of Japanese Pottery*, a description of all the objects in his collection.

Fenollosa, recently graduated from Harvard University, went to Japan in 1878 to deliver lectures on the philosophical treatises of Immanuel Kant, Georg Wilhelm Friedrich Hegel and Herbert Spencer at the Imperial University. Embarrassed by the discovery that paintings he had purchased in a Kyoto curio shop were virtually worthless, Fenollosa sought instruction from some of the leading Japanese connoisseurs of the day. Sumiyoshi Hirokata and Kano Eitoku Tatsunobu, the respective hereditary leaders of the great academic painting schools of the Edo period, the Tosa/Sumiyoshi and the Kano schools, imparted not only tips on connoisseurship but also a respect for the history and lineages of Japanese painting. By 1880 Fenollosa had purchased one of the best-known works in the Boston Museum's collection, the *Matsushima* screen by the Rinpa master Ōgata Kōrin, and by 1884 he had become president of the Kangakai, a society devoted to establishing the authenticity of paintings. Fenollosa attained such high standing in the Japanese art world that he was appointed Imperial Commissioner of Fine Arts from 1886 to 1890. In the latter year he became Curator of Japanese Art at the Boston Museum, a post he held until 1896.

Morse and Fenollosa acquired an understanding of Japanese art as it was appreciated by the Japanese in the 19th century and this is what distinguishes the Boston collection from the holdings of other Western institutions. Many Europeans of the time admired Japanese art purely as a source of decorative design. In his *Art and Art Industries in Japan* of 1878, for example, Alcock wrote: 'Of high Art, such as has been cultivated in Europe since the dark ages, the Japanese have known nothing. But the range of true artistic work in its application to industrial purposes in Japan is very wide, and more varied than anywhere in Europe.'[4] Conversely, Fenollosa, in particular, recognised that Japan's was a long artistic tradition and the equal of those of Western nations. In forming his collection of over 1000 paintings, later purchased by Charles Goddard Weld (1857–1911) and bequeathed to the Museum in 1911, Fenollosa sought to acquire works that would

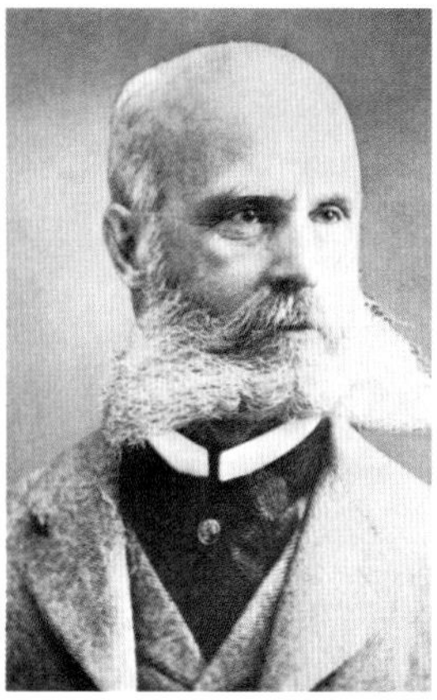

Fig. 2 William Sturgis Bigelow

Fig. 3 William Sturgis Bigelow and Ernest Francisco Fenollosa, photographed in Japan *c.* 1883

relay the history of Japanese art to the Western world. He shared this aim with William Sturgis Bigelow (1850–1926; fig. 2), the greatest benefactor of the Japanese collection at the Boston Museum.

WILLIAM STURGIS BIGELOW

Inspired by lectures delivered by Morse during one of his periodic visits to New England, Bigelow, the scion of a prominent Boston family, decided to experience Japan for himself. In 1882 he took up residence in Tokyo and did not return to the US permanently until 1889. During this period Bigelow, who was an extremely wealthy man, made the acquaintance of Fenollosa (fig. 3) and became a leading supporter of the arts in Japan, providing impoverished artists with financial assistance and underwriting conservation work on treasures in some of the temples in the Nara region. He also collected voraciously, acquiring important Buddhist statues, close to 4000 paintings and approximately 50,000 prints and drawings. Bigelow's collection contained works from almost all periods and schools and, beginning in 1911, came to the Museum virtually in its entirety.

In a letter written in Japan in 1883 Bigelow told a close Boston friend of his admiration for Fenollosa's knowledge of Japanese art: 'He is a genius, & the Jap[anese] themselves say, the best critic in Japan. I have certainly never met a man anywhere who knew a school of art so well as he knows Jap[anese] painting and painters for the last 1200 years.' Bigelow claimed that he bought 'next to nothing but pictures now, that under F[enollosa]'s direction'.[5] A comparison of the two men's collections and an examination of Fenollosa's writings reveal that Bigelow was being far too modest. Although the two men did collaborate on the purchase of many paintings, the Museum's collection of ukiyo-e paintings and prints is primarily the result of Bigelow's own tastes and interests.

In 1884 Fenollosa published in *The Japan Weekly Mail* his well-known review of *L'Art Japonais*, written by the French critic Louis Gonse in 1883 to accompany an exhibition of Japanese art he had organised in Paris. In the essay Fenollosa took exception to many of Gonse's characterisations of painters ranging from the 9th to the 19th century, but particularly those of the Edo period. Of the Utagawa artists and of Katsukawa Shunshō, Katsushika Hokusai and Andō Hiroshige, lavishly praised by Gonse, Fenollosa said:

> Their works are despised, not because the subjects are vulgar, but because their form of painting is vulgar. Clever, undoubtedly they may often be in externals; however it may appear in their engravings, in their paintings their conception, touch, and general technique are without refinement or depth. It may be difficult to specify in words to the inexperienced just in what this vulgarity consists....No European would think of mistaking the saloon lounger with his pomade and diamonds, and showy clothes, for a gentleman....So in the case of Hokusai and the Ukiyoe we miss all that indefinable something which is implied in the word 'taste'.[6]

What particularly galled Fenollosa was that Gonse had dared to elevate ukiyo-e artists above the masters so esteemed by contemporary Japanese connoisseurs. Fenollosa did not mince words: 'But after all has been said about the Ukiyoe artists, the truth remains that they are hardly worthy, with the exception of the first Miyagawa, to be ranked among Japan's masters of painting'.[7]

Fenollosa was later to revise this opinion substantially, but while 'advising' Bigelow in Japan he continued to denigrate ukiyo-e. Hence, the collection that came to the Museum via Weld contained only a few ukiyo-e paintings, among them the Kanbun-era screens *Amusements at the Dry Riverbed, Shijō* (pp. 12–13, fig. 1), the *Amusements* (*Yūraku zukan*) handscroll by Miyagawa Chōshun and the *Procession of a Courtesan* attributed to Hishikawa Moronobu (cat. 5). All three conformed in one way or another to Fenollosa's notion of artistic orthodoxy. In contrast, Bigelow acquired more than 450 ukiyo-e paintings and an encyclopaedic collection of woodblock prints.

Bigelow's enthusiasm for ukiyo-e probably derived from his exposure to the genre in France before he made the acquaintance of established connoisseurs in Japan. After

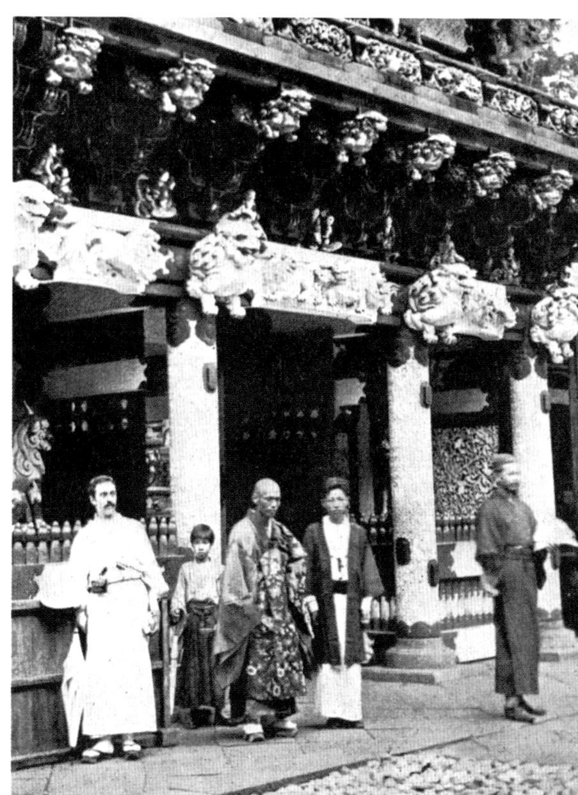

graduating from Harvard Medical School, he travelled to Vienna in 1876 and then to Paris in order to study bacteriology with Louis Pasteur. He soon discovered that a physician's career was not for him; but his years in Europe brought him into contact with dealers in prints and the decorative arts. A sticker on a book by Katsushika Isai, a pupil of Hokusai, that Bigelow bought at this time indicates that he frequented A l'Empire Chinois. Nevertheless, the archival record suggests that he acquired no paintings and few prints at this time. His purchases mostly consisted of textiles, *netsuke*, lacquers and other decorative items, which he placed on loan at the Museum immediately on returning from Europe in 1879.

Thus, although Bigelow's interest in ukiyo-e was developed in Europe, his acquisitions were made primarily in Japan. Their provenance remains obscure. The scant correspondence in the Museum archives does not contain data concerning the dealers from whom he bought his paintings and prints. Only in the case of drawings by Katsushika Hokusai do we possess information of this kind: in a brief passage in an exhibition catalogue devoted to the work of that artist Fenollosa mentions that Bigelow obtained drawings by him from one of his students, Hokusen, just before the latter died in 1885. Bigelow himself wrote to General Caleb Loring, Director of the Museum, about the formation of the print collection:

> Do not suppose that I have never answered your letter of last summer that I did not get it, or did not make a note of it. On the contrary, it caused me a great deal of meditation and cost me a good deal of money, with the result that I think the M.F.A. has now got a series of prints that illustrate pretty much all that is worth illustration in the history of block-printing in Japan. I have not gone myself to the very depths – the roughest and earliest and cussedest looking things – for the reason that they don't seem worth diving after, for the most part. But I have pretty well covered the ground where there seemed to be any artistic merit in the things printed, and have done the 'Nishikiye' or 'color print' business [illegible] indeed, from beginning to end.[8]

Although Bigelow states here that he had not secured some of the earliest prints, he generally attempted to amass an encyclopaedic collection – an approach very much in consonance with that of Fenollosa in his acquisition of paintings (with the notable exceptions of ukiyo-e and literati works). Legends abound suggesting that Bigelow collected art in such quantities that he did not study his purchases, but the number of Bigelow prints in the present exhibition, some of them unique impressions, and the quality of the paintings indicate that he must have had a superb eye.

EARLY UKIYO-E

Although others in the West enthusiastically acquired Japanese prints, in Bigelow's day few people were aware of the aesthetic appeal and the history of early ukiyo-e. Collectors generally focused on ukiyo-e of the late 18th and the 19th century. There were other exceptions in addition to Bigelow – the Englishman William Anderson (1842–1900), for example, collected paintings and prints (later acquired by the British Museum) while Director of the Naval Medical College in Tokyo from 1873 to 1880 – but it is a striking fact that many of the first exhibitions to include early ukiyo-e took place at the Boston Museum. Thus, in 1894 (ironically, during Fenollosa's period as curator) the Museum presented *Japanese Engravings: Old Prints in Color, Collected by S. Bing, Paris* and *Exhibition of Japanese Paintings and Metalwork.*

The first exhibition, which provided a survey of Japanese printmaking, was organised by Siegfried Bing, the Paris dealer associated with the development of Art Nouveau. It included 23 early ukiyo-e images. In the catalogue Bing wrote: 'We now know that the pages which caused so much astonishment and delight only disclosed comparatively recent examples of Japanese engraving, and did but present the most vulgar side of the art. But, such as they were, these foretastes of a superior art which the Japanese still retained appeared to be of extreme rarity, and for several years barely sufficed to supply a few collections.'[9] In its historical survey of Japanese painting the second exhibition, consisting of items from the Shirasu Collection in Tokyo, represented ukiyo-e only by early works, including items attributed to Miyagawa Chōshun and Nishimura Shigenaga. In the catalogue Fenollosa praised the paintings for being 'not unlike the best Kano and Tosa work'.

The Boston Museum featured examples of early ukiyo-e in its galleries. One reason was the interest in this art shown by another Boston collector – Denman Waldo Ross (1853–1935; fig. 4), a Museum trustee and professor of design theory at Harvard University. Ross, who eventually donated over 6000 objects to the Department of Chinese and Japanese Art, found that the early images resonated with his own ideas on design. In such paintings as the *Scenes in a House of Pleasure and Pleasure Quarter* screens from the Kan'ei era (1624–44; fig. 5) he encountered the same colour harmonies of saturated reds, blues and greens that he treasured in Byzantine and early Italian painting, while in the early ukiyo-e prints he discovered a mathematical order much to his taste. An inveterate traveller, Ross made frequent visits to Europe. In addition to Western paintings and decorative objects, he acquired Asian works from such dealers as Marcel Bing and Dikran Kelekian in Paris and Yamanaka and Company in London. At home, in the Boston store of the Japanese print dealer Kobayashi Bunshichi, Ross purchased *kosode* pattern books (*hiinagata-bon*) and picture books (*ehon*) by a number of artists, among them Okumura Masanobu.

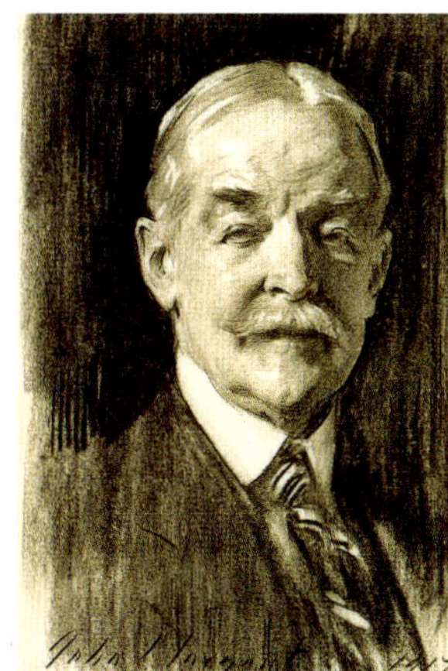

Fig. 4 Denman Waldo Ross, portrait by JOHN SINGER SARGENT, 1917, charcoal and white chalk on paper, 62.9 × 47.9 cm, Museum of Fine Arts, Boston, Gift of the Committee on the Museum, 1917, 17.3175

In the first years of the 20th century, before he visited Japan, Ross gave some of his 17th and early 18th-century works to the Museum. In 1908 these were displayed in an exhibition that explored the art of Hishikawa Moronobu, the Torii school and Okumura Masanobu. This predated by one year the celebrated show *Estampes Japonaises Primitives*, held at the Musée des Arts Décoratifs in Paris.

RESEARCH

By the first decades of the 20th century the character and extent of the Boston ukiyo-e painting collection had been more or less fixed. The Japanese print collection, however, attained even greater stature when two native Bostonians, the brothers William S. and John T. Spaulding, presented the Museum with 6495 works in 1921. Largely acquired through their agent – the architect Frank Lloyd Wright during his time overseeing the construction of his Imperial Hotel in Tokyo – and supplemented with key purchases from connoisseurs such as Fenollosa, Bing, Baron Sumitomo Kichizaemon and Frederick Gookin, the collection is remarkable for the unparalleled quality of its impressions and their state of preservation. Among the approximately 350 early ukiyo-e prints are a number of unique impressions of designs by Torii Kiyonobu and Torii Kiyomasu.

Wishing to ensure that their prints remained in pristine condition, the Spauldings stipulated that the works never be displayed, not even at the Museum. Rather, they were to be made available to scholars for study and publication, a commitment the Museum still honours. Generations of staff members have devoted themselves to studying these prints. Under Robert Treat Paine, Jr. (1900–65), who joined the Museum in 1932 and became Curator in 1962, the Museum undertook detailed research into its early ukiyo-e. Paine made extensive notes on items throughout the collection and published three ground-breaking articles on the prints of Okumura Masanobu – studies of the pillar prints (fig. 6), the bird-and-flower subjects and the 'Courtesans of the Three Cities' theme[10]. Following Paine's untimely death, Money Hickman (*b.* 1928), former Research Fellow for Japanese art,

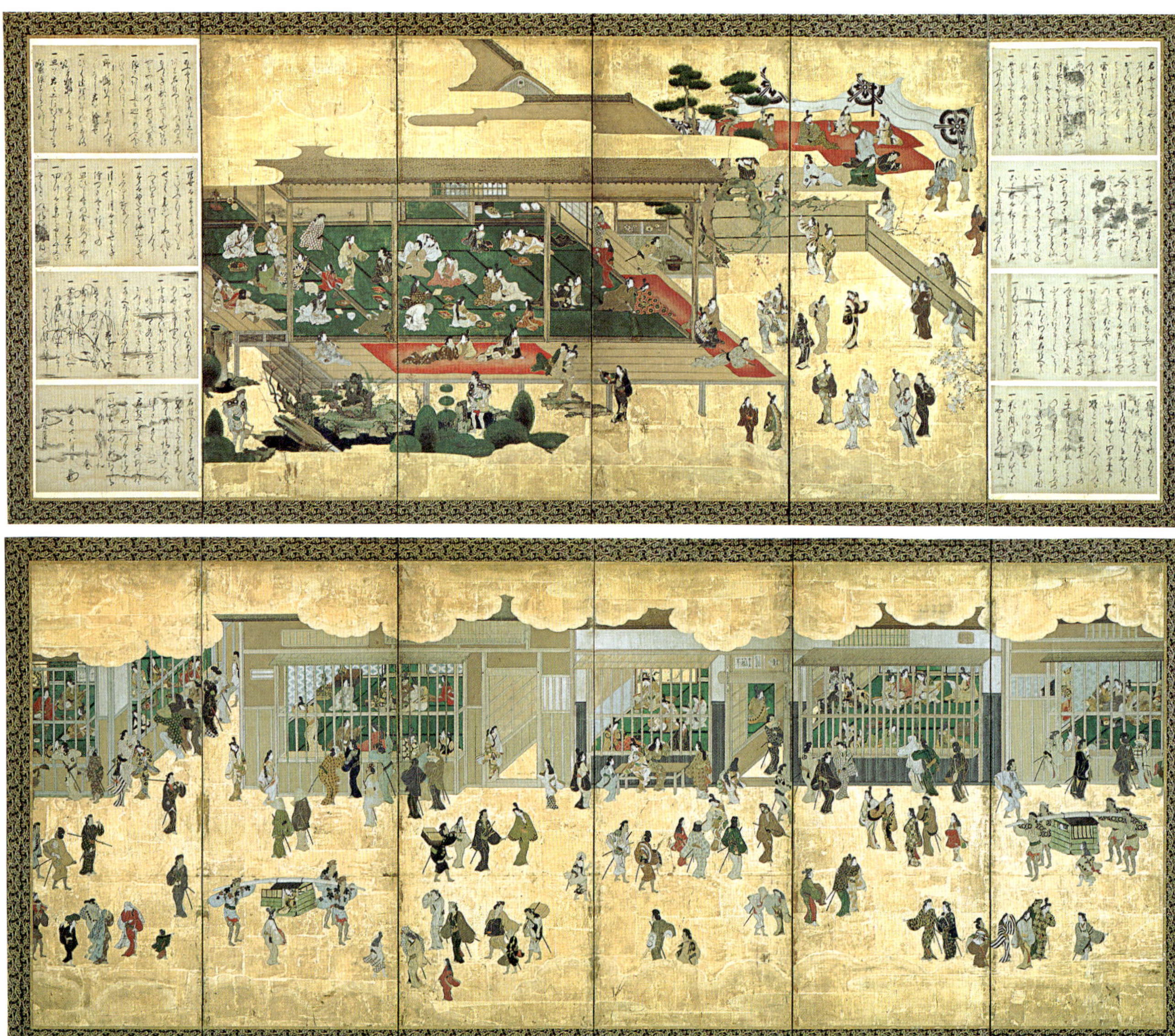

Fig. 6 Cover of vol. 57, no. 308, of the *Bulletin* issued by the Museum of Fine Arts, Boston, 1959, featuring Okumura Masanobu's *Sanogawa Ichimatsu I as Kichisaburō*, 1742, from the William S. and John T. Spaulding Collection, 21.5754

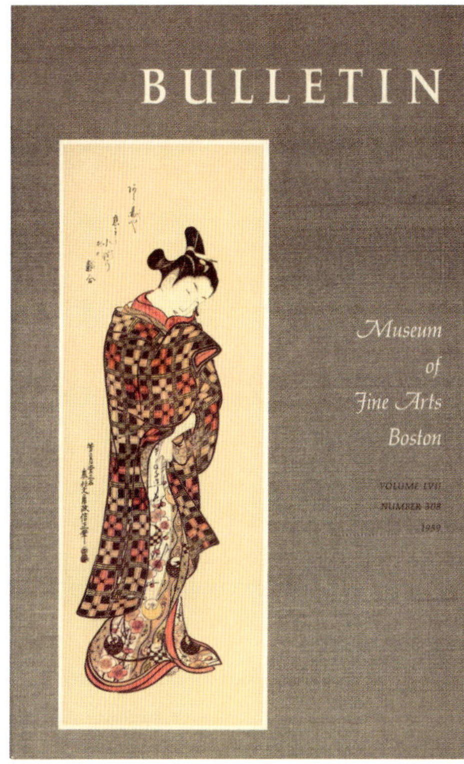

Fig. 5 ANONYMOUS, *Scenes in a House of Pleasure* (above) *and Pleasure Quarter* (below), late Kan'ei era (1624–44), pair of six-panel folding screens, ink and colour on gold-leafed paper, 104.3 × 58.2 cm and 104.6 × 273.6 cm, Museum of Fine Arts, Boston, Denman Waldo Ross Collection, 06.286, 06.287

contributed a thorough examination of Hishikawa Moronobu's *Scenes from the Nakamura Kabuki Theatre and the Yoshiwara Pleasure Quarter* (cat. 3, 4) and an introduction in Japanese to selected prints from the 17th and 18th centuries.[11]

The magnitude of the collection makes it impossible for one person to produce a comprehensive study of it. For the last five years, therefore, curators from the Museum have undertaken a complete re-evaluation of the ukiyo-e painting collection in collaboration with a team of specialists from Japan, headed by Tsuji Nobuo of Tama Women's University and consisting of Kobayashi Tadashi of Gakushūin University, Asano Shūgō of the Chiba City Museum of Art and Naitō Masato of the Idemitsu Museum of Arts, and with Timothy Clark of the British Museum. The current exhibition offers the public an unprecedented opportunity to see a select group of the Museum's early ukiyo-e, including paintings, prints and woodblock-printed books. It confirms the collection's standing as one of the finest of such objects in the world. The challenge now facing the Museum is to investigate its holdings of prints from later periods, in order to increase knowledge of and familiarity with the artistic heritage of Japan.

Notes

1 Chalfin 1904, p. 66.

2 London 1991, p. 19.

3 Quoted in Fischer 1992, pp. 4–5.

4 Rutherford Alcock, *Art and Art Industries in Japan* (1878), quoted in Cortazzi 1991, p. 62.

5 Bigelow to Henry Cabot Lodge, 30 September 1883. Murakata 1971, pp. 67–8. The present discussion of Bigelow is based on the author's account in Boston 2000, vol. 1.

6 Fenollosa 1884, p. 42.

7 Ibid., p. 44.

8 Bigelow to Loring, 1 March 1889. Archives, Museum of Fine Arts, Boston. A copy of the letter from Loring to Bigelow unfortunately no longer exists.

9 Boston 1894, p. 9.

10 Paine 1959, 1963, 1963a.

11 Hickmann 1978; *Ukiyo-e shūka*, vol 1.

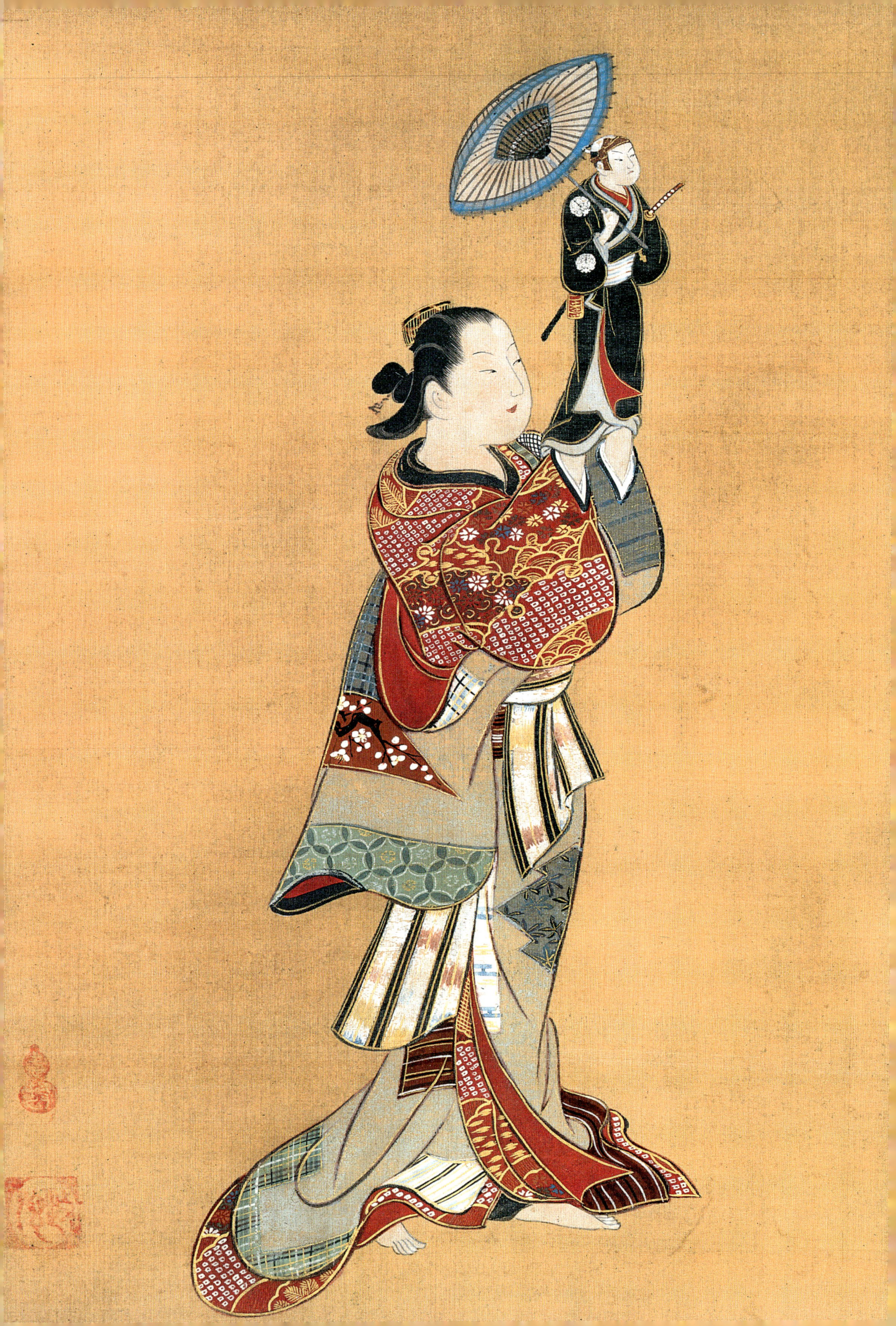

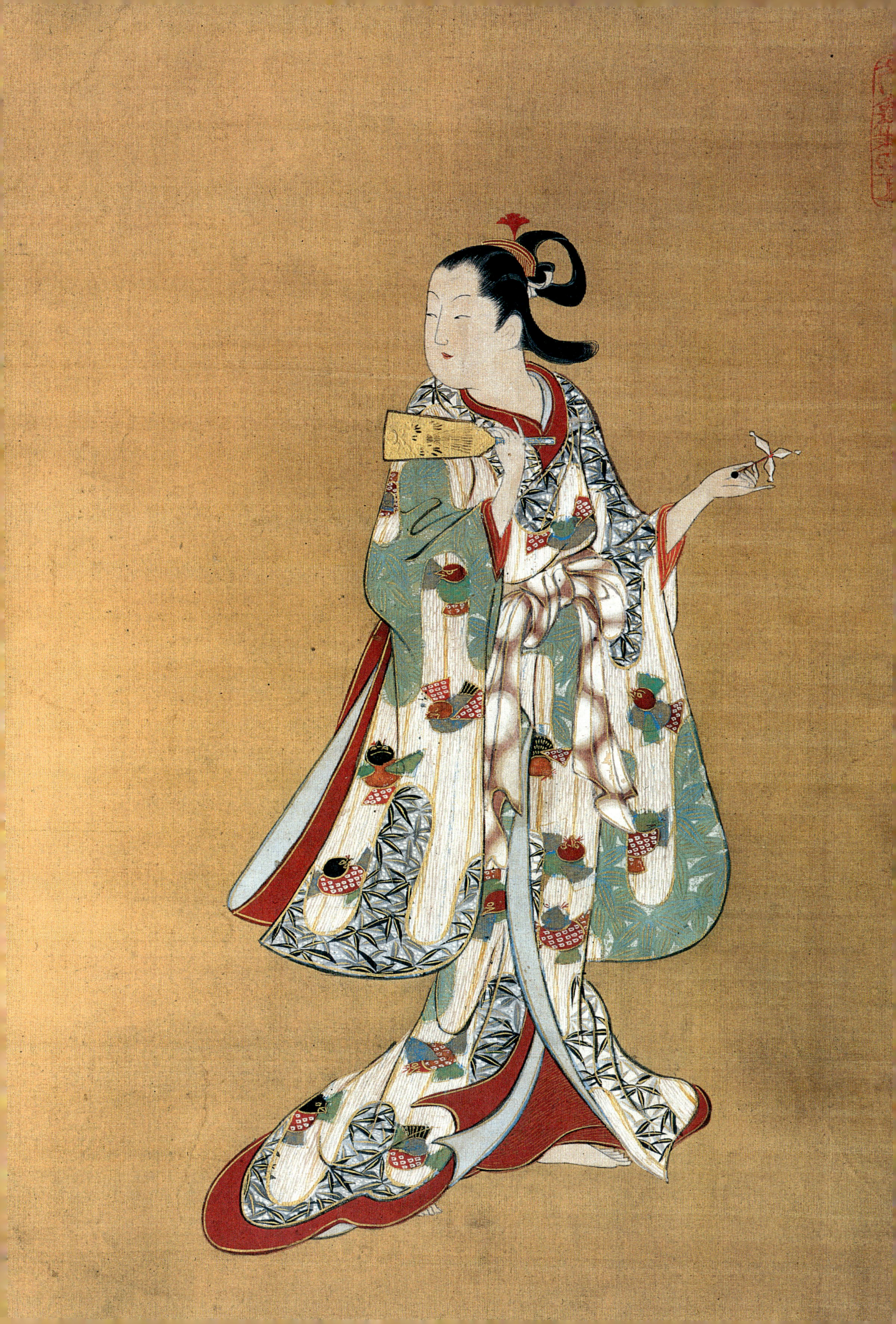

Editorial Note

General

Japanese terms and names are transliterated in accordance with the Hepburn system of Romanisation. Terms used regularly throughout the volume are explained in the Glossary.

In pre-modern Japan people were considered to be one at birth, their age increasing by one year at every New Year. In the present volume such 'traditional' ages have been modified wherever possible to reflect modern practice, generally by subtracting one year.

With the exception of kabuki plays and actor critiques, the titles of which are particularly rich in wordplay, English translations of the titles of literary works are given along with the original Japanese wherever possible. The English appears first in the case of works particularly well known in translation – for example, *Tale of Genji* (*Genji monogatari*).

Bibliographical references are cited throughout in abbreviated form. Full details will be found in the Bibliography.

Biographies of the Artists

The biographies are arranged in the order in which the artists appear in the catalogue section. Individuals in the Edo period used different names depending on social context. The main types of name used by artists were: clan name (*sei/kabane*), denoting affiliation with a large aristocratic clan; art surname (*gasei*), generally the name of a sub-school (Torii, for instance); common name (*tsūshō*), a simple personal name often derived from official or military titles, including names ending in 'uemon' or 'saemon'; *gō*, a pen or art name, changed periodically and often used in conjunction with other names.

Catalogue

Works are arranged by artist, broadly in the chronological sequence of their careers, though pupils are sometimes grouped together after their teacher. Each artist's work is presented by medium – paintings followed by printed books and single-sheet prints – and chronologically within these groups.
An alphabetical list of artists will be found on the page facing this Note.

Catalogue information is arranged as follows:

ARTIST'S NAME OR ATTRIBUTION; TITLE OF WORK
Titles are given in English, followed by a Japanese title in parentheses if the work has an original title in that language. Quotation marks around a title indicate that it appears in this form in the work itself. Where applicable, series titles are likewise given in translation and, in parentheses, in Japanese.

DATE Most albums and books are dated to the month and year in their colophons. The dates given for other works are estimates. Scholars often date with reference to the eras into which Japanese history is divided. In the interests of readability, the dates given for a work or for an artist's period of activity in the present volume have generally been extrapolated from those of the eras. '1704–16', for example, means that a work is judged to have been created in either the Hōei (1704–11) or the Shōtoku (1711–16) era. A list of eras will be found on page 44. Dates are generally given in accordance with the Japanese lunar calendar, which is explained in note 3 to the commentary on cat. 113.
They sometimes appear in the form year/month/day. '1679/3/6', for instance, refers to the sixth day of the third lunar month in the year 1679.

SIGNATURES AND SEALS Wherever possible, artists', publishers' and block-cutters' signatures and seals are transcribed in quotation marks as they appear in the work, followed where necessary by an English translation in parentheses.

MEDIA The descriptions of media use standard Japanese terminology where applicable. These terms are explained in the Glossary.

DIMENSIONS The Japanese names for the standard formats in which books and prints were generally issued appear before dimensions given in centimetres, height before width.
The Japanese terms are explained in the Glossary.

REFERENCES References to additional reproductions of a work appear under the heading 'reproduced'. Other copies of a book, or other impressions of a print, are listed under 'other copy(ies) / other impression(s)', with their location (where known) followed wherever possible by bibliographical references in parentheses.

OWNERS All works are in the collection of the Museum of Fine Arts, Boston. 'Source unknown' indicates that the acquisition source and date are not preserved in the Museum's records. In all other cases this information is given in the line preceding the acquisition number.

AUTHORS' INITIALS
AH= Allen Hockley
ANM= Anne Nishimura Morse
LEV= Louise E. Virgin
TTC= Timothy Clark

The Artists

Chronology

COMPILED BY ALFRED HAFT

Eras (1596–1772)

Keichō	1596–1615
Genna	1615–24
Kan'ei	1624–44
Shōhō	1644–8
Keian	1648–52
Jōō	1652–5
Meireki	1655–8
Manji	1658–61
Kanbun	1661–73
Enpō	1673–81
Tenna	1681–4
Jōkyō	1684–8
Genroku	1688–1704
Hōei	1704–11
Shōtoku	1711–16
Kyōhō	1716–36
Genbun	1736–41
Kanpō	1741–4
Enkyō	1744–8
Kan'en	1748–51
Hōreki	1751–64
Meiwa	1764–72

Periods of rule of the first to tenth Tokugawa shoguns (1603–1786)

Ieyasu	1603–5
Hidetada	1605–22
Iemitsu	1622–51
Ietsuna	1651–80
Tsunayoshi	1680–1709
Ienobu	1709–12
Ietsugu	1713–16
Yoshimune	1716–45
Ieshige	1745–60
Ieharu	1760–86

GOVERNMENT AND SOCIETY

1603
Appointment of Tokugawa Ieyasu as shogun initiates the Tokugawa shogunate; major expansion of the city of Edo begins

1605
Shogun Ieyasu retires in favour of Hidetada

1615
Toyotomi Hideyori commits suicide after Osaka Castle falls to the Tokugawa armies; promulgation of regulations governing warrior and courtier conduct

1623
Shogun Hidetada retires in favour of Iemitsu; English trading post at Hirado closed

1635
Foreign ships and trade restricted to the port of Nagasaki; Japanese forbidden to travel abroad

1637–8
Rebellion of farmers and Christians at Shimabara suppressed by the shogunate

1639
Japan limits foreign trade to the Chinese and the Dutch

1641
Full ban on Christianity; Japanese are required to register with Buddhist temples

1642
System of compulsory 'alternate attendance' (*sankin kōtai*) by daimyo at the shogunal court developed in its final form

1650
Construction of the Kannon Hall at Asakusa Temple begins

1651
Shogun Iemitsu dies after nearly 30 years of rule

1654
Completion of the Tamagawa Aqueduct, providing Edo with its main source of fresh water

1657
The Meireki Fire destroys Edo, including the main keep and central buildings of Edo Castle; government distributes emergency relief funds

1659
The Ming priest Inyuan establishes Manpuku-ji, head temple of the Ōbaku branch of Zen Buddhism in Japan

1660
Construction of Ryōgoku Bridge across the Sumida River, enabling Edo to expand eastwards

1663
Revision of the *Buke shohatto* (rules governing warrior conduct) prohibits warriors from committing ritual suicide on the death of their lord (*junshi*); formation of an official messenger service between the three major cities of Edo, Kyoto and Osaka

ARTS AND LETTERS

1608
Publication of the Saga Press edition of *Tales of Ise* (*Ise monogatari*), the first woodblock-printed edition of a work of secular literature to contain illustrations

1615
Anonymous printed news sheets (*kawara-ban*) circulate for the first time, following the fall of Osaka Castle

1622
Remodelling of Edo Castle, probably including extensive sliding-door paintings (*fusuma-e*) by Kano Tan'yū

1630
Hayashi Razan establishes a Confucian academy at Ueno Shinobu-ga-oka; 32 Chinese books by Matteo Ricci and others, some relating to Christianity, are banned

1636
Establishment of Kōyō-zan Library in Edo Castle

1640
Completion of *Legends of the Founding of Tōshō-gū* (*Tōshō-gū engi emaki*) with text by the monk Tenkai and paintings by Tan'yū

1647
Death of the tea master and garden designer Kobori Enshū

1655
The doctor Itasaka Bokusai opens his private Asakusa Bunko Library

1657
The potter Nonomura Ninsei active in Kyoto

1660
Sakaida Kakiemon perfects procedures for making porcelain decorated with overglaze enamels

1665
Asai Ryōi publishes *Ukiyo monogatari* (*A Tale of the Floating World*)

1666
Publication of the twenty-volume *Kinmō zui* (*Illustrations and Definitions to Train the Untutored*)

YOSHIWARA AND KABUKI

1603
First kabuki performances, by Okuni at Kitano Shrine, Kyoto

1617
Establishment of the Yoshiwara pleasure quarter in Edo

1629
Ban on women's kabuki (*jorō kabuki*)

1642
Ban on young men's kabuki (*wakashu kabuki*); publication of the first Yoshiwara courtesan critique, *Azuma monogatari.*

1650
Nakamura Kanzaburō performs kabuki dance at Edo Castle

1652
Ban on all kabuki

1653
Mature men's kabuki (*yarō kabuki*) authorised

1656
Yoshiwara instructed to move to a site north-west of Asakusa Temple; publication of early actor critique *Yakusha no uwasa*

1659
Business begins to pick up at Shin Yoshiwara; death of the legendary courtesan Takao

1664
Introduction of the *hikimaku* curtain and scenery in theatres

1665
Closure of 70 teahouses around Edo and reassignment of 500 waitresses to Yoshiwara

1666
Introduction of the *hanamichi* walkway in kabuki theatres

GOVERNMENT AND SOCIETY

1669
Standardisation of weights and measures in Edo and Kyoto

1670
Publication of the first official map of Edo, the basis of all maps of the city until the Meiji period (1868–1912)

1671
Kawamura Zuiken establishes an eastern shipping route from Edo to northern Honshū, and the following year a western route from Osaka to towns along the Sea of Japan coast

1673
Mitsui Takatoshi opens Echigo-ya drapery and haberdashery shops in Kyoto and Edo; a British merchant ship arrives at Nagasaki requesting permission to trade, but is turned away

1675
The government distributes rice to famine victims in central Japan

1679
The official number of neighbourhoods in Edo reaches 808, the figure used even late in the Edo period when referring to the entire city

1682
Yaoya Oshichi, a greengrocer's daughter, lays a fire that destroys much of central Edo

1687
Shogun Tsunayoshi issues an edict calling for 'kindness to living things', particularly dogs; the streets of Edo are soon overrun with dogs, necessitating the establishment of kennels and veterinary clinics

1688
Reform of Edo's prison system

1690
The German doctor Engelbert Kaempfer takes up position of physician to the Dutch trading post at Dejima, Nagasaki

1693
Construction of Shin-ōhashi Bridge across the Sumida River, connecting Fukagawa with Edo; population of Edo passes the 800,000 mark

1698
Construction of Eitai-bashi Bridge across the Sumida River; Tsunayoshi orders devaluation of the currency

1700
Depletion of government gold and silver reserves leads to the limiting of Nagasaki trade to eight Chinese ships and five Dutch a year

1701
Asano Naganori, lord of Akō, wounds Kira Yoshinaka in Edo Castle and is ordered to commit ritual suicide

1702
46 men led by the Akō retainer Ōishi Kuranosuke avenge the death of their master by assassinating Kira (the 'Chūshingura Incident')

1703
The 47 Loyal Retainers (Chūshingura) are permitted to commit ritual suicide

ARTS AND LETTERS

1670
Completion of *Honchō tsugan*, an official history of Japan

1674
Death of the painter Kano Tan'yū

1680
Matsuo Bashō takes up residence at Fukagawa; publication of a revised and expanded edition of the 15th-century dictionary *Setsuyō-shū*, now containing more than 30,000 entries

1682
Ihara Saikaku publishes his first novel, *The Life of an Amorous Man* (*Kōshoku ichidai otoko*), inaugurating the fiction genre known as *ukiyo-zōshi*

1686
Saikaku publishes *The Life of an Amorous Woman* (*Kōshoku ichidai onna*)

1689
Bashō departs on the journey that will form the basis of his poetic narrative *Oku no hosomichi* (*Narrow Roads to the Far North*)

1693
Kano Einō publishes *Honchō gashi*, a history of painting in Japan focusing on the development of the Kano school

1701
The painter Ogata Kōrin granted the honorary title *hokkyō* ('Bridge of the Law')

1704
Kōrin begins five years of residence in Edo

YOSHIWARA AND KABUKI

1673
Ichikawa Danjūrō I develops the *aragoto* style of acting; the *kaomise* performance becomes a kabuki institution

1676
Fire destroys Yoshiwara

1683
300 illegal prostitutes arrested and sent to work in Yoshiwara for five years without pay

1693
Daimyo and *hatamoto* (bannermen) banned from visiting Yoshiwara

1697
First performance of *Shibaraku*, starring Ichikawa Danjūrō I

1700
Around this time Yoshiwara courtesans begin to dress in pure white for the Hassaku festival (1st day of the 8th month); purple head coverings become popular

1703
First performance of Chikamatsu Monzaemon's love-suicide play *Sonezaki shinjū*

1704
Murder of Danjūrō I by a fellow actor

GOVERNMENT AND SOCIETY

1707
Mount Fuji erupts twice, scattering ash, sand and rock over the entire Kantō region; sand and ash continue to rain down on Edo for several months

1709
Repeal of Tsunayoshi's 'kindness to living things' edict

1715
Further devaluation of the currency; annual limit on Nagasaki trade altered to 30 Chinese ships and two Dutch

1716
Tokugawa Yoshimune is appointed shogun; institution of the Kyōhō Reforms

1717
Formation of fire-fighting units in daimyo residential areas of Edo

1720
Formation of 47 fire-watch divisions (*iroha-gumi*) in commoner neighbourhoods; permission is granted for the importation of Chinese translations of Western books, other than those dealing with Christianity

1721
First nationwide population census, subsequently carried out every few years; nationwide survey of farm land; government complaint boxes set up outside Hyōjōsho Gate; garden of medicinal plants established at Koishikawa

1722
Institution of censorship system in which publications require advance authorisation from the magistrate's office; ban on erotic books

1723
Punishments instituted for attempted love suicides and for publications or theatrical performances treating the subject

1724
New sumptuary laws instituted

ARTS AND LETTERS

1708
The scholar Kaibara Ekken publishes a catalogue of Japanese medicinal plants

1709
The painter Hanabusa Itchō permitted to return from twelve years of exile on the island of Izu Miyake-jima

1715
Arai Hakuseki writes *Seiyō kibun* (*A Report on the Occident*) after interviewing the priest Sidotti in Edo

1721
Hayashi Moriatsu publishes *Gasan*, a painting manual and compendium of Kano school subjects

1727
Ogyū Sorai publishes *Seidan* (*Political Essays*)

1728
Kada no Azumamaro petitions the shogunate to establish a 'school of national learning'

1729
Ishida Baigan begins propounding the doctrines of the Shingaku movement; Dazai Shundai completes his *Keizai-roku*, a widely read work on political economy

1730
Ichikawa Danjūrō II publishes *Chichi no on*, a *haikai* anthology in memory of his father that includes early examples of multi-colour woodblock printing and illustrations by Ogawa Haritsu and Hanabusa Ippō

1731
Ogata Kenzan moves his kiln permanently to Edo; the Chinese painter Shen (*Jap.* Shin) Nanpin arrives in Nagasaki and teaches the most recent styles of Qing academic painting

YOSHIWARA AND KABUKI

1709
Actors in Edo permitted to perform only within the designated theatre areas, Kobiki-chō and Sakai-chō

1710
Devotional image of a young actor and a young woman, painted in ukiyo-e style, presented to the Mikawa Nodamura Shrine

1713
First performance of *Sukeroku, Yukari no Edo-zakura*, starring Ichikawa Danjūrō II

1714
Closure of the Yamamura Theatre following the Lady Ejima scandal; the Nakamura, Ichimura and Morita continue as the Three Theatres of Edo

1724
The Three Theatres construct roofs

1728
In the summer, lanterns are hung in Yoshiwara to commemorate the third anniversary of the death of the courtesan Tamagiku, inaugurating the quarter's famous lantern festival

1729
First performance of the Soga play *Ya-no-ne*, starring Ichikawa Danjūrō II

1731
Population of Yoshiwara reaches 8960

GOVERNMENT AND SOCIETY

1732
Famine in central and western Japan

1733
Rocketing rice prices lead to the first attack on a rice merchant's storehouse in Edo

1734
The government authorises daimyo to use troops to suppress farmers' revolts

1735
Aoki Kon'yō promotes cultivation of the sweet potato to relieve famine; bumper rice harvest in Kantō region

1737
Cherry trees planted at Asukayama and the grounds opened as a public recreation area

1739
Russian ships sighted off the coast north of Edo; the government strengthens coastal defences

c. 1740
Ichimatsu chequerboard pattern for textiles, first worn by the actor Sanogawa Ichimatsu, becomes popular

1742
Heavy rains lead to severe flooding of the Sumida and other rivers throughout central Japan and to poor harvests

1746
As a means of tightening government control, land in Edo previously administered by temples and shrines is brought under management of the city magistrates; number of Edo neighbourhoods officially reaches 1678; Nagasaki trade limited to ten Chinese ships and two Dutch

1750
Laws instituted strictly prohibiting farmers from leaving the land, forming organisations or submitting petitions

1756
In order to stabilise rice prices, the government bans speculative purchasing by rice merchants

1759
First experiments in sugar production

1761
Daimyo instructed to keep a small proportion of the annual harvest in store in case of famine

1763
Popularity of the Rokō hairstyle (named after the poetry name of the actor Segawa Kikunojō II)

1765
The physician Taki Yasumoto granted land in central Edo to construct a hospital

ARTS AND LETTERS

1737
Kamo no Mabuchi arrives in Edo to promote the study of ancient texts, particularly *Manyō-shū*

c. 1740
Ike no Taiga begins studying Chinese literati painting

1748
Chinese painting manual *The Mustard Seed Garden* published in a Japanese edition

1752
Hiraga Gennai travels to Nagasaki to train in Dutch studies

1757
Gennai organises an exhibition of rare objects at Yushima Tenjin Shrine in Edo (and publishes a catalogue of such items in 1763)

1759
Maruyama Okyō experiments with Western-style perspective in landscape views

1764
Motoori Norinaga begins writing *Kojiki-den*, the first detailed study of Japan's earliest written history

1765
Karai Senryū publishes first edition of *Haifū yanagi-daru*, a collection of short comic verses (*senryū*) submitted to poetry competitions

YOSHIWARA AND KABUKI

1732
Around this time, the Niwaka Festival becomes an annual Yoshiwara event

1735
Daimyo and *hatamoto* again banned from visiting Yoshiwara; perfection of the *hanamichi*

1741
Sakakibara Masamine, lord of Himeji, forced to resign following an affair with the Yoshiwara courtesan Takao; first planting of cherry trees along Nakano-chō

1746
Population of Yoshiwara reaches 12,584; first performance of the puppet play *Sugawara denju tenarai kagami*

1748
First performance of the puppet play *Kana-dehon Chūshingura*, depicting the 1702 vendetta of the 47 Loyal Retainers

1750
Around this time, female geisha appear in Yoshiwara

1758
The revolving stage is developed by a playwright in Osaka

1762
Premier of the *nagauta* dance-drama *Sagi musume*; the revolving stage introduced to Edo

1765
Around this time, the language of Yoshiwara comes to seem distinct enough to warrant publication of dictionaries and glossaries

Biographies of the Artists

COMPILED BY TIMOTHY CLARK

Hishikawa Moronobu (*d.* 1694)

cat. 3–16

Common name: Kichibei; *gō:* Yūchiku. The first major figure in the establishment of the ukiyo-e school and style. Eldest son of a family of fabric decorators and embroiderers (*nuihaku-shi*) at Hoda in Awa Province. By the early Kanbun era (1661–73) he had moved to Edo, where he studied and assimilated such traditional styles as those of the Kano and Tosa schools and was influenced by the earlier Tosa and genre painter Iwasa Matabei (see p. 17). Moronobu founded a new, independent idiom that featured bold, stylish figures and he was described as both a 'Yamato picture master' (*Yamato eshi*) and a 'floating-world picture master' (*ukiyo eshi*). His earliest dated work is the illustrated book *Buke hyakunin isshu* (*A Warrior 'One Hundred Poems by One Hundred Poets'*), published at the New Year, 1672 (signed 'eshi Hishikawa Kichibei'). Two of seven painting fragments mounted as *Illustrated Handscroll of the Northern Quarter [Yoshiwara] and Theatres* (*Hokurō oyobi engeki zukan*, Tokyo National Museum) are dated 1672 (the latest is dated 1689). Otherwise, no dated works before 1677 have survived. Moronobu's total oeuvre is estimated at about 60 picture books, 20 of them erotic, 120 single-sheet prints (mostly issued in sets mounted in albums or as handscrolls), illustrations for some 100 books of fiction and non-fiction[1] and several dozen paintings in all formats. The peak of his picture book production occurred from the mid-Enpō (1673–81) to the Tenna (1681–4) era, and of single-sheet prints from the late Enpō to the Tenna era. Thereafter he devoted himself mainly to painting. The subject matter of his picture books and paintings ranges widely, including legendary, historical and literary themes from China and Japan, Buddhist subjects, genre scenes (among them scenes of craftsmen), *kosode* pattern books, landscapes and gardens, birds and flowers, animals, warriors and erotica. Increasingly, both books and paintings came to be dominated by scenes of seasonal pleasures in and around the townsmen-dominated neighbourhoods of Edo, particularly the kabuki theatres and Yoshiwara, which were the focus of the new 'floating world' culture. Representative of this development are the four pairs of screens of kabuki, Yoshiwara and Ueno cherry-viewing subjects, including cat. 3 and 4, that survive from the early Genroku era (1688–1704), late in Moronobu's career,[2] and the painted handscrolls – and hanging scrolls with scenes extracted from handscrolls – on these themes. The publishing history of Moronobu's picture books (and hence any assessment of the evolution of his figure style based on them) is complicated by the existence of many re-cut editions, issued after the fires in Edo in the winter of 1682–3, during which the original blocks had probably been destroyed, and by the absence in some cases of the original editions from which these re-cut versions must have been made.[3] The study of paintings by and attributed to Moronobu is beset by problems concerning the differentiation of authentic items from works by his school, the consensus being that some workshop pieces were authorised with his signature.[4] Recently, three important painted works have been rediscovered: an album, *Birds and Flowers and Courtly Scenes* (*Kachō fūzoku gajō*, Price Collection, Los Angeles), done by Moronobu himself in the Edo Kano style; a pair of handscrolls dated 1685, *Ghosts and Monsters* (*Henge zukan*, Museum of Fine Arts, Boston, 21.262–3), by Moronobu and five named pupils;[5] and a fragment of a painted erotic handscroll (Museum of Fine Arts, Boston, 09.254).[6] These shed new light on the range of his painting and on the activities of his workshop. Moronobu's stylistic example dominated the work of his younger ukiyo-e contemporaries, such as Sugimura Jihei (cat. 19, 20), his contemporaries in Kamigata, including Yoshida Hanbei (cat. 78), and his immediate pupils and followers, among them Ishikawa Ryūsen, Hishikawa Morofusa, Hishikawa Morohira (cat. 17) and Hishikawa (Furuyama) Moroshige. After Moronobu's death, in 1694, the influence of the Hishikawa school seems to have waned quickly: it was the painters Miyagawa Chōshun (cat. 87, 88) and Hanabusa Itchō (see p. 16) who further developed his style.

1 These estimates are given by Asano Shūgō in Chiba 2000, p. 202. See ibid., pp. 209–17, for a catalogue of Moronobu's single-sheet prints by Asano, and, for the most detailed bibliography of Moronobu's picture books, Matsudaira 1988.

2 The others are in the Tokyo National Museum, the Freer Gallery of Art, Washington DC, and the Suntory Museum of Art, Tokyo.

3 Satō 1991. See also the expanded list of titles thought to have been affected by the fire given by Satō in Chiba 2000, p. 22.

4 For lists of major paintings by Moronobu, see Kobayashi Tadashi, in *Nikuhitsu ukiyo-e*, vol. 2, pp. 129–30, and Asano Shūgō, in *Hizō ukiyo-e*, vol. 1, pp. 26–7.

5 Chiba 2000, nos. 17, 18. The latter is also reproduced in Boston 2002, vol. 1, no. 44 (commentary by Tsuji Nobuo).

6 Boston 2001, no. 3 (commentary by Asano Shūgō), where the painting is attributed to 'Moronobu school' ('Moronobu-ha').

LITERATURE: Miyatake 1909; Lane 1973–6; *Nikuhitsu ukiyo-e*, vol. 2; Matsudaira 1988; Satō 1991; Lane 1995; Kobayashi 1996a; Chiba 2000; Uchida 2000; Asano 2001

Hishikawa Morohira (active *c.* 1688–1711)

cat. 17

Ukiyo-e painter, presumed to be a pupil of Moronobu (cat. 3–16). Roughly a dozen works by him are known: hanging scroll paintings of beautiful women; a pair of six-panel folding screens, *Scenes of Entertainment in Spring and Autumn* (*Shunjū yūraku zu*, Idemitsu Museum of Arts, Tokyo);[1] and a painted erotic handscroll (British Museum, London).[2] His figure style shows similarities with that of Miyagawa Chōshun (cat. 87, 88), who may have regarded himself as a Hishikawa follower.

1 Tokyo 1988, no. 16 (commentary by Naitō Masato).

2 London 1992, no. 11.

LITERATURE: *Genshoku ukiyo-e*, vol. 2, p. 97

Sugimura Jihei (active *c.* 1681–98)

cat. 19, 20

Nephew of Sugimura Kudayū, the adoptive father of Sugimura Kihei, one of the 47 loyal retainers of the Akō fief involved in the famous Chūshingura vendetta of 1703. Lived in Tōriabura-chō, Edo. Early book illustrator and ukiyo-e print artist, particularly active in the fields of erotica (*shunga*), puppet theatre playbooks (*jōruri-bon*) and erotic novels (*kōshoku-bon*). His earliest signed works are *Ukiyo raku-asobi* (1681), an erotic picture book on literary and historical themes, and *Hyakunin isshu kigin-shō* (fourth month, 1681), portraits of 100 famous classical poets with their poems. Active at the same time as Moronobu (cat. 3–16) in the 1680s, in a style sometimes more dynamic and flamboyant. He came to dominate the decade of the 1690s after Moronobu largely retired from designing picture books and single-sheet prints. Seven signed books by Jihei are known and an equal number of albums or series of erotic *ōban* prints listed by Richard Lane,[1] who also attributes over 60 unsigned works to him.[2] Lane suggests that, in addition, as many as 50 large prints in the *kakemono-e* and *ō-ōban* formats are by Jihei, probably dating from the first half of the Genroku era (1688–1704).[3] These occasionally have *tan-e*-style or similar hand-colouring and are thought to have served as cheaper alternatives to hanging scroll paintings. They are never signed in the conventional manner, neither do they bear publisher's marks; yet the names 'Sugimura' and/or 'Jihei' are sometimes hidden in the pattern on a robe.

1 Lane 1995, nos. 14, 15, 50–5.

2 Lane 1980, pp. 2–7.

3 Lane 1981.

LITERATURE: Shibui 1926–8; Hillier 1959; Shibui and Kikuchi 1964; Horioka 1974; Lane 1980; Lane 1981

Torii Kiyonobu I (1664–1729)

cat. 21–8

Common name: Shōbei. Ukiyo-e painter and print artist. Founder of the Torii school, specialising in depictions of kabuki in theatre signboards (*e-kanban*), hanging scrolls, single-sheet prints and illustrated playbooks (*e-iri kyōgen-bon*). Also designed prints of beautiful women and erotica. Said to be the son of the Osaka actor of female roles Torii Kiyomoto and to have moved to Edo in 1687 with his father, living in Naniwa-chō.[1] A 'floating-world novel' (*ukiyo-zōshi*) of this year, *Iro no some-ginu*, contains the signature 'Yamato eshi Shōbei ga' (Drawn by Yamato picture master Shōbei), but it seems doubtful that this is Torii Shōbei Kiyonobu. The earliest signed works generally accepted as by Kiyonobu I are two popular novels, *Kōshoku daifuku-chō* and *Honchō nijūshi-kō*, both published in 1697 (the latter signed 'Eshi Torii Shōbei' [Picture master Shōbei]). Unsigned illustrated playbooks from the same year, notably *Sankai Nagoya* (cat. 23) and *Tsuwamono kongen Soga*, have also been attributed to him. He is thought to have designed many of the approximately 60 illustrated playbooks published before 1711. In 1700 he issued two trendsetting books of illustrations of actors and courtesans, *[Painted] Screens in All Directions* (cat. 24) and *Illustrated Book of Courtesans* (cat. 25), both published by Hangi-ya Shichirobei at Izumi-chō, with whom he seems to have had a close association. The performances depicted in the former volume include some from the eleventh month of 1695, suggesting that Kiyonobu I was already active by then.[2] The erotic handscroll included here (cat. 22), recently rediscovered, is a spectacular example of Kiyonobu I's painted erotica,[3] and at least eight surviving printed erotic albums are either by or attributed to him.[4] Kiyonobu I was the originator of single-sheet prints of actors, which captured the new bravura 'rough' (*aragoto*) acting style of Edo in bold imagery notable for ample figures limned with fluid, rounded outlines. This undoubtedly reflected the painting style of Kiyonobu I's theatre signboards (which are no longer extant) and was later characterised as 'gourd-shaped legs and wriggling worm line' ('hyōtan ashi mimizu-gaki'). The earliest surviving single-sheet actor print signed by Kiyonobu I ('Wa [Yamato] gakō Torii Shōbei' [Yamato painting artisan Torii Shōbei]), in the *ō-ōban* format, is *Sawamura Kodenji as Tsuyu-no-Mae* (Worcester Art Museum, Massachusetts), which relates to a performance from the third month of 1698. Recent research has suggested that Torii Kiyomasu I did not start producing such large-format prints until the Hōei era (1704–10).[5] From the beginning of the Kyōhō era (1716–36), Kiyonobu I, like other artists, designed in the *hosoban* format – primarily, it is surmised, to facilitate greater productivity. Kiyonobu I is said to have died in 1729. Kiyonobu II (cat. 89–93) may have taken over from him *c.* 1725, but the extant works do not permit the precise date to be established – perhaps publishers deliberately obscured the change so as to ensure the continuity of the Kiyonobu 'brand name'.[6] A handful of paintings of beautiful women or actors signed by or attributed to Kiyonobu I have been preserved (p. 27, fig. 15)[7] and there is an impressive votive plaque (p. 25, fig. 13),[8] which must give some idea of what his theatre signboards were like.

1 Kaneko Ban'u, *Torii ga keifu kō*, written in the late Meiji period (1868–1912).

2 Mutō 1994, p. 10.

3 Boston 2001, no. 1 (commentary by Asano Shūgō).

4 Lane 1995, nos. 16–19, 57–60.

5 Mutō 1992, pp. 28–9.

6 Mutō 1997, p. 5.

7 For three examples in the Boston Museum, see Boston 2000, vol. 2, nos. 85–7 (commentaries by Asano Shūgō).

8 *Nikuhitsu ukiyo-e*, vol. 5, no. 2 (commentary by Yamaguchi Keizaburō).

LITERATURE: Inoue 1923; Honolulu 1977; *Genshoku ukiyo-e*, vols. 2 and 6; *Nikuhitsu ukiyo-e*, vol. 5; Mutō 1992; Mutō 1994; Mutō 1997

Torii Kiyomasu I (active *c.* 1704–18?)

cat. 29–38

Early ukiyo-e print artist and painter. No primary evidence concerning his identity, dates and period of activity exists beyond the works signed by him. It has been variously suggested that he was the brother, son or pupil of Torii Kiyonobu I (cat. 21–8) or that he established a separate lineage within the Torii school. Famous large-format print designs by him, including *Gorō Pulling up Bamboo* (*Take-nuki Gorō*, Tokyo National Museum), though probably recording a kabuki performance given from the fifth month of 1697 on, are now thought to have been issued in the Hōei era (1704–11).[1] No signed illustrated books or erotica by Kiyomasu I are known and only one painting has been attributed to him.[2] He designed single-sheet prints with a wide range of subjects, including beautiful women, genre scenes, birds and flowers, warriors and kabuki actors. The most extensive listing of his theatrical prints totals 56 designs.[3] Though some of these have been dated *c.* 1708, most fall within the Shōtoku era (1711–16). Around 1715 Kiyomasu I did several series of horizontal *sumizuri-e* prints showing complete stage scenes relating to *jōruri* or to *jōruri* scenes within kabuki, apparently a new genre of theatrical print (see cat. 33, 34). Beginning in 1719, works signed 'Kiyomasu' bear different signatures ('Torii Kiyomasu hitsu' and 'Torii Kiyomasu zu') and show a different style, suggesting that they are by Kiyomasu II (cat. 94–102). Indeed, no print by Kiyomasu I can be shown to postdate 1718; hence, it is thought that he ceased working or died at this time. No satisfactory explanation has been offered for two works (cat. 37, 38) bearing Kiyonobu I signatures and Kiyomasu I seals, but it has been tentatively suggested that Kiyonobu I completed the signature after the putative death of Kiyomasu I.[4]

1 Mutō 1992, pp. 28–9.

2 A handscroll entitled *Illustrated Poetry Contest on the Theme of Insects* (*Mushi no uta-awase emaki*, Minneapolis Institute of Arts), which bears a 'Kiyomasu' seal. *Nikuhitsu ukiyo-e*, vol. 5, no. 3.

3 Mutō 1992, pp. 11–28.

4 Most of the information given here derives from Mutō 1992.

LITERATURE: Inoue 1923; Honolulu 1977; *Genshoku ukiyo-e*, vols. 2 and 6; Mutō 1992

Okumura Masanobu (1686–1764)

cat. 39–77

Common name: Genpachi (Genpachirō); *gō*: Shinmyō (from 1707), Baiō (from 1707), Hōgetsudō (from Genbun era, 1736–41), Tanchōsai and Bunkaku (both from Enkyō era [?], 1744–8). Ukiyo-e painter, print artist and innovative print publisher, also author and illustrator early in his career.[1] Studied *haikai* poetry under Tachiba (Shōgetsudō) Fukaku (Sen'ō, 1662–1753). Said to have been influenced by the work of Moronobu (cat. 3–16) and Kiyonobu I (cat. 21–8), and his earliest dated work is a copy of Kiyonobu I's *Illustrated Book of Courtesans* of 1700 (cat. 25), published by Kurihara Chōemon in the eighth month of 1701. From 1703 to 1711 he designed illustrations for at least 22 *ukiyo-zōshi* novels and puppet theatre playbooks, notably three works also written by him that parodied *Tale of Genji*.[2] In the Hōei and Shōtoku eras (1704–16) Masanobu designed *ō-ōban* prints of beautiful women, horizontal *ōban sumizuri-e* 'parody pictures' (*mitate-e*) and actor prints, and *hosoban tan-e* actor prints – all influenced by the prevailing Torii and Kaigetsudō school styles. Masanobu's later actor prints concentrate on female roles, leaving leading male parts to the Torii artists. The most complete listing of sets of *sumizuri-e* by Masanobu contains fourteen items, each of which probably originally comprised twelve designs and was sold as a folding album.[3] These established the range of subjects and treatments for *mitate-e* by many later 18th-century artists. From 1718 Masanobu produced *hosoban beni-e* for various publishers and, by the following year at the latest, was publishing designs himself under the Okumura-ya imprint from premises located at Tōrishio-chō (subsequently adopting as his trademark a gourd-shaped publisher's seal). The *beni-e* often used the new decorative technique of painting deer glue (*nikawa*) over areas of black to produce a sheen resembling black lacquer (*urushi-e*, 'lacquer pictures'). Masanobu credited himself with many other innovations in technique, format and style made in ukiyo-e printmaking during the second quarter of the 18th century, but, as with his frequent claims that his 'genuine' works were being pirated, it is hard to judge to what extent this was advertising hyperbole. Certainly, from the early 1740s he was very active in two new important print genres: 'pillar pictures' (*hashira-e*) and perspective pictures (*uki-e*, 'floating pictures'). The earliest *benizuri-e* (two-colour prints, generally in red and green) known by him is a picture calendar (*e-goyomi*) of 1742.[4] From *c.* 1750 he also used the new, larger *ōban* print format. Other innovations with which he may have been connected were triptychs of *hosoban* prints and so-called 'stone print pictures' (*ishizuri-e*) – woodblock prints featuring white outlines in reserve against black backgrounds, like a stone rubbing. His erotic masterpiece in the print medium is the album of hand-coloured *ōban* designs *Neya no hinagata*, which is generally dated to the Genbun (1736–41) or Kanpō (1741–4) era.[5] In the early 1740s Masanobu may have handed over the running of his publishing business to a successor, Okumura-ya Genroku, and seems to have ceased artistic activity altogether during the later Hōreki era (1751–64), perhaps after 1756.

More than 30 paintings by Masanobu have been published, mainly of courtesans but including a few of actors. His most notable erotic work in this medium is the handscroll given the title *Neya no iro-goromo* (Museum of Fine Arts, Boston, 09.241),[6] dated to the Shōtoku era. Several paintings treat or parody *jōruri* themes encountered in his printed *mitate-e*, including the meeting between Princess Shokushi and Fujiwara no Teika at the latter's villa at Mount Ogura, and Matsukaze, Murasame and Yukihira at Suma. Also of note is the half-size, six-panel folding screen *Performance at the Nakamura Theatre* (*Nakamura-za kabuki shibai byōbu*, Idemitsu Museum of Arts, Tokyo), which was painted in the seventh month of 1731 and records that year's New Year performance at the Nakamura Theatre.[7]

1 Most of the information given here derives from Mutō 1999 and Aoki 1999.

2 Vergez 1983, p. 33. The works in question are *Wakakusa Genji monogatari* (1707), *Hinazuru Genji monogatari* (1708) and *Kōhaku Genji monogatari* (1709).

3 Shibui 1929; Paine 1959, 1963, 1963a.

4 Toronto 1975, no. 33, also reproduced in Aoki 1999, fig. 8.

5 Kobayashi 1995, pp. 8, 18–29.

6 Boston 2001, no. 2 (commentary by Kobayashi Tadashi).

7 Tokyo 1988, no. 68 (commentary by Naitō Masato).

LITERATURE: Miyatake 1910; Shibui 1929; Paine 1959, 1963, 1963a; *Nikuhitsu ukiyo-e*, vol. 3; *Genshoku ukiyo-e*, vols. 2 and 6; Vergez 1983; Mutō 1999; Aoki 1999; Satō 2001

Yoshida Hanbei (*d. c.* 1693?)

cat. 78

Main illustrator in the ukiyo-e style in Kamigata in the last quarter of the 18th century. His signed and dated works, mainly illustrations for such *ukiyo-zōshi* novels by Ihara Saikaku as *Life of an Amorous Woman* (*Kōshoku ichidai onna*, 1686) and *Great Mirror of Manly Love* (*Nanshoku ō-kagami*, 1687), cluster in the Jōkyō era (1684–8). He was prolific in most other genres of popular illustration, including *jōruri-bon*, *kyōgen-bon*, *kana-zōshi*, gazetteers and erotic books such as *Uruoi-gusa* (*c.* 1680) and *Genji on-iro-asobi* (1681). Many of these are unsigned. The earliest work sometimes attributed to Hanbei is the *kana-zōshi Yamato nijū-shi kō*, published in 1665; his last dated works are from 1693, and it is thought he died around this time.[1] His illustrations are generally less bold than those of his great contemporary in Edo, Hishikawa Moronobu (cat. 3–16), with large figures used only occasionally in the erotic works. Nevertheless, his sure grasp of multiple-figure composition in complex settings did much to raise the level of Kamigata illustration.

Hanbei's biography is obscure, based on the semi-fictionalised account of an illustrator 'Hanbei' that appears in *Shison Daikoku-bashira*, an *ukiyo-zōshi* of 1709. According to this, he first lived at the end of Ōmiya-dōri in Kyoto and was in service to a workshop of painters. After marrying the widow of a certain 'town painter' (*machi-eshi*), he soon achieved success with his printed illustrations, moving to a shop in Teramachi-dōri, where he attracted many pupils. A Kyoto guidebook of 1692, *Yorozu kaimono chōhō-ki*, gave his address as 'behind the [Yasaka Shrine] lodgings at Shijō' ('Shijō o-tabi no ushiro'). His style was continued, presumably immediately after his death, by 'Genzaburō the lacquer decorator' ('Maki-eshi Genzaburō') and, later, by Ōmori Yoshikiyo and Kawashima Nobukiyo.

1 *Nihon koten*, vol. 6, s.v. 'Yoshida Hanbei'.

LITERATURE: Mizutani 1935, pp. 116–30; *Nihon koten*, vol. 6, s.v. 'Yoshida Hanbei'; Hillier 1987, vol. 1, pp. 100–9; Lane 1995, pp. 141–4

Nishikawa Sukenobu (1671–1750)

cat. 79–81

Common name: Uemon; *gō*: Bunkadō, Jitokusai, Jitokusō, Hōshiken (?); court title: Ukyō. Lived at Yanagi-no-banba Ayakōji-kudaru, Kyoto. The most accomplished and influential ukiyo-e painter in Kyoto during the first half of the 18th century. The more than 60 printed books illustrated by him spread his fame to Edo, where Masanobu (cat. 39–77) and Suzuki Harunobu (cat. 140–2), in particular, were influenced by him. Sukenobu's ancestors had been doctors in Ōtsu; in the generation of his father, Sukeharu, the family moved to Kyoto. Sukenobu was in service to the aristocratic Saionji family during the lifetime of Lord Saionji Munesue (1683–1756), by whom he was granted the title Ukyō, often incorporated in his signature. He is said to have studied with Kano Einō (1631–97), third-generation head of the Kyoto Kano school, and Sukenobu's essay 'Gahō saishiki-hō' (Methods of Painting and Applying Colours), included in volume ten of *Ehon Yamato hiji* of 1742, was doubtless composed in emulation of Einō's famous history of painting, *Honchō gashi* (*A History of Painting in Japan*, 1678). It is possible that Sukenobu also studied with Tosa Mitsusuke (1675–1710). The writer Saitō Gesshin, in his *Zōho ukiyo-e ruikō* (1844), considered that he combined the best elements of the Kano and Tosa schools. Although Sukenobu's first dated work was an *ukiyo-zōshi* novel published in 1708, (*Honchō*) *Kokon kannin-ki*, there exists a group of unsigned works dating to before 1700 that can be confidently attributed to him on stylistic grounds.[1] From *c.* 1700 to the 1730s Sukenobu worked as the principal artist of Hachimonji-ya, the most prominent publishing house in Kyoto in the early 18th century. It is likely that the illustrations in the epoch-making actor critique *Yakusha kuchi-jamisen*, issued by Hachimonji-ya in 1699, belong among his earliest works. During this early period Sukenobu also designed two important multi-volume *hiinagata-bon* for the same publisher (see cat. 79). Images of beautiful women from all classes in Kyoto came to occupy a major place in Sukenobu's mature oeuvre, most notably in the two-volume illustrated book *Hyakunin jorō shina-sadame* (*One Hundred Women Classified According to their Rank*), published by Hachimonji-ya in 1723. Other important subjects in Sukenobu's illustrated books include moralising and educational themes (*kyōkun kyōiku*), generalised and regional genre scenes (*ippan fūzoku, chiiki fūzoku*), warrior pictures (*musha-e*) and episodes from classical literature and history (*koten bungaku, rekishi koji*).[2] Sukenobu's large numbers of paintings generally show single figures or groups of women in poses similar to those in his illustrated books. In his treatise on painting the artist stresses the importance of correct anatomy in the drawing of figures. He clothes these figures in the luxurious *kosode* seen in the *hiinagata* pattern books, decorated with Yūzen dyeing techniques and worn with a wide brocade obi woven in the Nishijin district of Kyoto. Sukenobu was an important creator of erotic imagery (*shunga*), both in printed albums (none of which survives with its original title) and in painted albums and handscrolls. A fragment of a large-scale erotic handscroll, showing the final four erotic couplings in what was probably originally a sequence of twelve, is in the Boston collection (09.255).[3] Sukenobu's last dated painting is the votive panel (*ema*) *Hunter Catching a Fox* (*Tsuri-gitsune zu*) at the Yasaka Shrine, Kyoto, which gives his age as '74 years' and was donated in the fifth month of 1744.[4]

1 Matsudaira 1981.

2 Ibid., p. 61.

3 Boston 2001, no. 6 (commentary by Kobayashi Tadashi).

4 *Nikuhitsu ukiyo-e*, vol. 9, no. 4 (commentary by Akai Tatsurō)

LITERATURE: Miyatake 1911; Matsudaira 1977; Matsudaira 1981; *Nikuhitsu ukiyo-e*, vol. 9; *Genshoku ukiyo-e*, vol. 2, p. 61, and vol. 6, pp. 130–3; Matsudaira 1988

Kaigetsudō Ando (active *c.* 1704–36)
Kaigetsudō Anchi (active *c.* 1704–16)
Kaigetsudō Doshin (active *c.* 1704–16)
Kaigetsudō Dohan (active *c.* 1704–16)

cat. 82–6

The art name Ando may have been read as Yasunobu in the artist's day.[1] Family name: Okazawa (or Okazaki); common name: Dewa-ya Genshichi; *gō*: Kan'unshi. Lived in Asakusa Suwa-chō. Implicated in the Lady Ejima scandal through his acquaintance with the merchant Tsuga-ya Zenroku of the same neighbourhood and, as a result, banished in 1714 to the island of Izu Ōshima. Seems to have been pardoned, and returned to Edo in 1722. Thought to be the same person as both Kaigetsudō Jōsen, whose illustrations and *hokku* appear in the *haikai* anthology *Futako-yama* (1730), and Kaigetsudō Shisui, whose illustrations are included in another anthology, *Kura no atsumari* (1732).[2]

Several dozen of Ando's hanging scroll paintings of Yoshiwara courtesans survive. These are generally uniform in style: a grand, single figure standing against a plain background, the body frequently jutting forward at the waist; a bold, calligraphic outline to the drapery, which contrasts with the more delicate treatment of the large, schematic face; striking plant and floral motifs on the drapery executed in brilliant but somewhat coarse pigments. The signature on these paintings is always headed 'Yamato giga' (Light-hearted Yamato painting). The uniformity of Ando's style must have facilitated mass-production of his works, which were presumably sold from the Kaigetsudō shop in Asakusa, not far from Yoshiwara, and the style was replicated in an almost indistinguishable manner by his pupils Anchi, Dohan, Doshin, Doshu, Doshū and Dochi, all of whom generally prefaced their names with 'Yamato giga Kaigetsu matsuyō' (Light-hearted Yamato painting by the Kaigetsu follower). Anchi, the only pupil to share the 'An' character of his teacher's name and to use independent *gō* – Chōyōdō and

Onsetsu are known – is thought to have been the senior pupil. The close-knit nature of the workshop is suggested by the fact that an Ando seal sometimes appears on paintings signed by one of the pupils.

No woodblock prints have survived by Ando, but a total of 23 are known by three of his pupils, all *sumizuri-e* in the vertical *ō-ōban* format, which imitate closely the style of Ando's paintings. Some exist only in one impression, indicating that the subsequent attrition of the prints has been very high. Each of the three pupils seems to have established a relationship with a particular publisher: Anchi (six prints issued by Maruya at Ōdenma nichō-me Higashiyoko-chō, one by Iga-ya at Hama-chō, one publisher unknown); Dohan (eleven issued by Iga-ya at Hama-chō, one publisher unknown); Doshin (three issued by Nakaya at Tōriabura-chō).[3] There are similarities between some of the publisher's marks found on these prints and those on prints by Torii Kiyomasu I and others dateable *c.* 1704–16, suggesting that the influential Kaigetsudō style must already have been fully established by the Hōei era (1704–11).[4] It is harder to ascertain when the Kaigetsudō workshop ceased to be active. One painting by Ando that must have been done during his exile, *Ebisu and Daikoku,* survives on the island of Izu Nii-jima.[5] Kobayashi Tadashi has tentatively suggested that the painting *Courtesan Playing with a Cat* (*Bijin aibyō zu,* Ujiie Collection, Kamakura), the background of which is more elaborately developed in ink washes and which displays more delicate outlines and patterns, may be representative of Ando's style after his return to Edo.[6] Another painting, *Shōtoku Taishi,* bears the same Kaigetsudō Jōsen signature as appears in the *haikai* anthologies of 1730 and 1732.[7] Elements of the Kaigetsudō idiom continued to be a strong presence in the works of a succession of ukiyo-e painters active until the mid-18th century, including Matsuno Chikanobu, Takizawa Shigenobu, Baiōken Eishun and Tōsendō Rifū.

In addition to his paintings of Yoshiwara courtesans, Ando depicted a number of subjects in a variety of formats, notably several horizontal hanging scrolls of warrior themes and the handscroll *Miscellaneous Subjects* (*Zatsuga-kan,* Museum of Fine Arts, Boston).[8] A painted erotic handscroll by Anchi, *Courtesans and their Clients* (*Yūjo to kyaku zu,* formerly Azabu Museum of Arts and Crafts, Tokyo), is also known.[9]

1 Kobayashi 1996a, p. 51.

2 Narazaki Muneshige and Hanasaki Kazuo, cited in Asano 1987, p. 42.

3 Ibid., p. 47.

4 Ibid., p. 49.

5 Tsuji et al. 1968, fig. 18.

6 Kobayashi 1996a, p. 55.

7 Asano 1994, p. 24, fig. 1.

8 Boston 2000, vol. 1, no. 55. See also the list of paintings in note 1 of the commentary to cat. 83.

9 *Nikuhitsu ukiyo-e taikan,* vol. 6, no. 20 (commentary by Kawaguchi Akiyo).

LITERATURE: Lane 1959; Tsuji et al. 1968, pp. 36–46; Kobayashi 1982a; Asano 1987, pp. 42–9; Asano 1994, pp. 24–8; Kobayashi 1996a, pp. 51–6

Miyagawa Chōshun (1682–1752)

cat. 87, 88

Common name: Chōzaemon; *gō*: Shunkyokudō. According to one account, came from Miyagawa village in Owari Province. Lived in Edo first at Ryōgoku Hirokoji, later at Shiba Shinbori-chō. Birth date based on the age, 62, given in a self-portrait dated 1742 (now lost).[1] Pre-eminent ukiyo-e painter in Edo in the first half of the 18th century and progenitor of the Miyagawa–Katsumiyagawa–Katsukawa–Katsushika line that was to form the mainstream of ukiyo-e painting until the end of the Edo period. Like Kaigetsudō Ando (cat. 82), Chōshun did not design any woodblock prints or illustrated books; dates of publication with which to establish a chronology of his work are thus not available. His many paintings – hanging scrolls of single courtesans, handscrolls of seasonal genre scenes or scenes in the kabuki and puppet theatres – have been tentatively grouped into early, middle and late periods based on the degree of stylistic influence of Hishikawa Moronobu (cat. 3–16) and on the form of Chōshun's signature and seals. A number of depictions by Chōshun of characters and scenes from classical literature have survived, some rendered in up-to-date dress in the manner of 'parody pictures' (*mitate-e*).

Ōta Nanpo (1749–1823) recorded the existence of a now lost votive painting by Chōshun showing amusements of women, presented to the Kannon Temple at Ichiba, Sagami Province, in the fourth month of 1706.[2] Early extant works show the strong thematic and stylistic influence of Moronobu: sometimes whole groups of figures are borrowed with little or no modification. An early handscroll of homosexual erotic scenes bears the signature 'Hishikawa Chōshun hitsu' and the seals 'Chōshun no in' and 'Hishikawa-uji in',[3] demonstrating that, even if Chōshun were too young to have studied directly with Moronobu, he saw himself as a pupil within the lineage of the Hishikawa school. A relatively early large hanging scroll, *Kabuki Female Impersonator* (*Onnagata zu,* Art Gallery of New South Wales, Sydney), may depict the actor Yoshizawa Ayame, who worked in Edo from 1713/11 for only one year.[4] The famous handscroll *Genre Scenes* (*Fūzoku zukan,* Tokyo National Museum), thought to date from the period of Chōshun's early maturity at the beginning of the Kyōhō era (1716–36), shows female dancers invited to perform in a feudal mansion in the presence of a high-ranking samurai lady. The figures are larger and more densely grouped than usual and the quality of the pigments impeccable, making it likely that the handscroll was commissioned to record an actual performance, possibly in a daimyo household. Several screen paintings are known: a full-size pair, *Partying Beneath the Cherry, Pleasure Boats on the Sumida River* (*Ōka yūkyō, Bokutei shūyū zu byōbu,* private collection, Japan), has fresh seal impressions, suggesting a relatively early date;[5] a single half-size, six-panel folding screen, *Genre Scenes in Yoshiwara* (*Yoshiwara fūzoku-zu byōbu,* Museum of Fine Arts, Boston), although unsigned, is firmly attributed to Chōshun during the first half of his career.[6]

In 1750 or 1751 Chōshun was invited with his pupils to participate in repair work at the Tokugawa mausoleum at

Nikkō, the Nikkō Tōshō-gū, under the supervision of Kano Shunga, head of the Inari-bashi branch of the academic Kano school. A dispute over payment culminated in Chōshun being beaten, bound and ejected from Shunga's mansion. In a revenge attack led by Chōsuke, Chōshun's son and his pupil Miyagawa Isshō (1689–1779), Shunga and several of his followers were killed or wounded.[7] Chōshun himself is thought to have died in the eleventh month of 1752. At about this time Isshō was banished to the island of Izu Nii-jima, where he stayed, unpardoned, until his death aged 91 some 27 years later.[8] The Kano school participants in the dispute were also severely punished: Shunga's son Shunchō was banished to the island of Hachijō-jima and the Inari-bashi line abolished. Miyagawa Chōki (active *c.* 1716–44), Chōshun's other talented pupil, seems to have died before the incident, and leadership of the Miyagawa school, renamed Katsumiyagawa, then Katsukawa, subsequently passed to Miyagawa Shunsui (active *c.* 1741–72).

1 This annotated self-portrait is known only in the form of a copy reproduced in *Kaiga sōshi*, vol. 15, June 1888. See *Nikuhitsu ukiyo-e*, vol. 3, p. 126 (text by Kobayashi Tadashi).

2 Ōta Nanpo, *Chōfu nikki* (1809), referred to by Saitō Gesshin in *Zōho ukiyo-e ruikō* (1844). *Nikuhitsu ukiyo-e*, vol. 3, p. 127.

3 Lane 1979, no. 35.

4 Kobayashi 1986, pp. 3–4, frontispiece.

5 *Nikuhitsu ukiyo-e*, vol. 3, nos. 12–13 (commentary by Tanaka Tatsuya). See also the comments by Kobayashi Tadashi, ibid., p. 128.

6 Boston 2000, vol. 2, no. 10 (commentary by Kobayashi Tadashi); Morse 2000.

7 The most comprehensive account of the incident is given by Kobayashi Tadashi, in *Nikuhitsu ukiyo-e*, vol. 3, pp. 129–31. Slightly differing, abbreviated accounts are also found in Asano 1987, p. 54, and Kobayashi 1996a, p. 57.

8 Tsuji et al. 1968, pp. 45–6.

LITERATURE: *Nikuhitsu ukiyo-e*, vol. 3, pp. 124–33; Asano 1987, pp. 50–61; Kobayashi 1996a, pp. 56–61

Torii Kiyonobu II (active *c.* 1725–60)

cat. 89–93

See also the biography of Kiyonobu I (pp. 50–1). Kiyonobu II is the name given by convention to all prints signed 'Kiyonobu' that post-date Kiyonobu I's supposed retirement *c.* 1725[1] and his death in 1729. Establishing the identities and dates of activity of all early Torii artists other than Kiyonobu I (cat. 21–8) has proved problematical. This is because the Torii family lineage, *Torii ga keifu kō*, was not written down until the late Meiji period (1868–1912) and is thought to have been based in part on the study of inscriptions on the Torii family gravestone (originally at Hōjō-ji, Asakusa, but subsequently moved), the contents of which are open to widely differing interpretation.[2] Howard Link has suggested that several different artists may have been responsible for the prints now conventionally ascribed to Kiyonobu II[3] and states that there exist actor prints signed Kiyonobu that are dateable to as late as 1760 and illustrated theatre programmes by him for the years 1755, 1757 and 1758.[4]

Well over 100 prints bearing a Kiyonobu signature have survived from the period 1725–60.[5] They are almost exclusively actor prints in the *hosoban* format, decorated with *beni-e*-style hand-colouring until the early 1740s, thereafter printed in safflower pink and green (*benizuri-e*). Mutō Junko has noted particularly close connections with the publishers Nakajima-ya and Murata-ya.[6] Commentators seem agreed that the diminutive figure style of these prints has little of the power of works by first-generation Torii artists, but there exists a magnificent votive plaque by Kiyonobu II (p. 25, fig. 12), which was donated to Saidai-ji Temple, Nara Prefecture, on the occasion of a display of the temple's treasures in Edo in the spring of 1754.

1 The most recently suggested date of transition from Kiyonobu I and Kiyonobu II. Mutō 1997, p. 5.

2 Inoue 1923, pp. 13–26. Inoue posits the existence of an 'elder brother of Kiyonobu II' and identifies the latter with an individual mentioned on the gravestone who died in 1752. The same author tries to match the people named in the grave inscriptions with some of the Torii school artists. Ibid., p. 27.

3 Link valiantly examined all the conflicting evidence and arguments. Honolulu 1977, esp. pp. 19–29 and notes on pp. 36–41. He summarised his findings in the biographies of early Torii artists in *Genshoku ukiyo-e*, vol. 2, to which my own summary is heavily indebted.

4 *Genshoku ukiyo-e*, vol. 2, p. 28.

5 Mutō 1997, p. 6, gives a provisional figure of 145.

6 Ibid., p. 7.

LITERATURE: Inoue 1923; Honolulu 1977 and 1980; *Genshoku ukiyo-e*, vol. 2, p. 28, and vol. 6, pp. 50–3; Mutō 1997

Torii Kiyomasu II (1706?–1763?)

cat. 94–101, 103–7

See also the biography of Torii Kiyonobu II (this page). As with Kiyonobu II, the attribution Kiyomasu II is conventionally applied to all works signed 'Kiyomasu' that date from after the putative retirement or death of Kiyomasu I. Most recent scholarship conjectures that this may have occurred in 1718.[1] Certainly, from 1719 works signed 'Kiyomasu' have different signatures ('Torii Kiyomasu hitsu', 'Torii Kiyomasu zu' – Brush of / Drawn by Torii Kiyomasu) and a different style. On the other hand, if the birth date 1706 is correct, this would mean that Kiyomasu II was only twelve or thirteen when the change from one generation to the next took place. This date, and that of Kiyomasu II's death given above, derive from the Torii family lineage, *Torii ga keifu kō*, first written down in the late Meiji period (1868–1912), and from a grave that was situated apart from that of the main branch of the family, headed by Kiyonobu I.[2] *Torii ga keifu kō* also stated that Kiyomasu II married in 1724 and that in his later years he moved from Naniwa-chō to Sumiyoshi-chō, yet the same manuscript refers to only one artist with the name Kiyomasu (whom it describes as the second-generation head of the whole Torii family) and does not distinguish between two generations. In 1923 Inoue Kazuo surmised that Kiyomasu II married the daughter of Kiyonobu I and established a separate branch of the Torii family, but this has not been substantiated.

Preliminary findings suggest that Kiyomasu II may have been an even more prolific designer of *hosoban* prints than Kiyonobu II, first in the *tane-e* and *urushi-e* techniques, subsequently in that of the *benizuri-e*.[3] He seems to have had special links with the publishers Iga-ya (a relationship continued from the time of Kiyomasu I) and Urokogata-ya, whose forceful entry into the market for single-sheet prints *c.* 1728 may, in turn, have been facilitated by this connection with Kiyomasu II.[4] Howard Link suggests that the artist's period of activity continued until *c.* 1760.[5] The range of subject matter in his work is wider than Kiyonobu II's and includes so-called 'needle-box pictures' (*haribako-e*, prints intended to be cut out and stuck on needle boxes or screens) and *hosoban* prints on themes drawn from classical literature (see cat. 103–6), along with rudimentary landscapes, bird-and-flower and animal subjects (see cat. 101). The figure style is bolder and livelier than that of Kiyonobu II. Several instances are known of two-colour actor prints by Kiyomasu II designed *c.* 1750 in the *ōban* format (see cat. 107).[6]

1 Mutō 1992, p. 28.

2 Inoue 1923, p. 27.

3 Mutō 1997, p. 6, identifies 186 items in comparison to Kiyonobu II's 145.

4 Mutō 1997, p. 7.

5 *Genshoku ukiyo-e*, vol. 2, p. 30.

6 Two further examples are reproduced in *Genshoku ukiyo-e*, vol. 6, p. 57.

LITERATURE: Inoue 1923; Honolulu 1977 and 1980; *Genshoku ukiyo-e*, vol. 2, p. 30, and vol. 6, pp. 54–7; Mutō 1997

Torii Kiyotada (active *c.* 1716–51)

cat. 108, 109

Thought to be a pupil of Kiyonobu I (cat. 21–8). Known for a small number of *beni-e* and *urushi-e hosoban* prints that combine the Torii and Okumura Masanobu styles. Mutō Junko has identified thirteen actor prints, eight of them published by Izumi-ya.[1] Kiyotada also designed perspective pictures (*uki-e*), notably three extra-large examples (cat. 109) published by Urokogata-ya.[2]

1 Mutō 1997, p. 6.

2 Kishi 1994a, p. 84, n. 10.

LITERATURE: Honolulu 1977, p. 32, and 1980, pp. 76–9; *Genshoku ukiyo-e*, vol. 2, p. 26

Tanaka Masunobu (active *c.* 1741–8)

cat. 110

Gō: Sanseidō. Well known for perspective pictures (*uki-e*) on a wide range of subjects, but he also apparently designed one *hosoban* print of the actor Utagawa Shirogorō (who used this name from 1742 to 1749), a calendar picture for 1745 and *hosoban* portraits of poets in the *ishizuri-e* technique. A single painting by him, *Courtesan and Kamuro* (*Tayū to kamuro*; signed 'Yamato gakō Sanseidō Masunobu hitsu' [From the brush of Yamato painting artisan Sanseidō Masunobu]), is also recorded. He may be the same person as (Zenshinsai?) Masunobu, whose signature is found on Harunobu-style prints and paintings from the Meiwa (1764–72) and early An'ei (1772–81) eras.

LITERATURE: Honolulu 1980, pp. 145–6; *Genshoku ukiyo-e*, vol. 2, pp. 94–5

Torii Kiyoshige (active *c.* 1716–64)

cat. 111, 112

Gō: Seichōken (according to Inoue Kazuo).[1] Born in Edo, lived in Koami-chō. Thought to be a pupil of Kiyonobu I (cat. 21–8). Mutō Junko has identified 41 actor prints by him that date from 1723 (or 1728) to 1763 and has divided these into four groups: standard *hosoban*, *c.* 1723–37; pillar pictures and other formats, *c.* 1742–9; prints with *hokku* inscriptions, *c.* 1751–63; standard *hosoban*, *c.* 1748–53. She has also demonstrated that certain actor portraits, particularly the male lead and villain roles that were Kiyoshige's speciality, show the beginnings of drawing faces as real likenesses (*nigao-e*). There are also a few warrior prints, illustrations for *kuro-hon* and *ao-hon*, and a small number of paintings of actors and beautiful women.[2] A votive painting by him of the kabuki scene 'Armour-pulling' (*Kusazuri-biki*) is dated 1730.[3]

1 Yura 1979, p. 103.

2 For example, London 1992, no. 43.

3 Analysed in detail in Hayashi 1986 and Tokyo 1986.

LITERATURE: Honolulu 1980, pp. 69–75; *Genshoku ukiyo-e*, vol. 2, p. 26; Mutō 1999a

Hanekawa Chinchō (1679?–1754)

cat. 113

Clan name (*honsei*): Manaka; common name: Ōta Bengorō; *gō*: Genshin (Motonobu), Chūshin (Okinobu), Kaijōsai, Sandō. Native of Kawaguchi village, Saitama-gun, Musashi Province. Pupil of Kiyonobu I (cat. 21–8). Active *c.* 1711–36, Chinchō was a member of the samurai class and drew only occasionally. About ten prints by him are known in the *sumizuri-e* and *tan-e* techniques. He was more prolific as an illustrator of courtesan and actor critiques and of *aka-hon*. He may be the same person as Hanekawa Wagen (Kazumoto), who designed a small number of actor prints and calendar pictures in the Kyōhō era (1716–36) and used a similar form of handwritten seal (*kaō*).

LITERATURE: Chicago 1955, pp. 64–7; Yura 1979, pp. 84–5; Honolulu 1980, pp. 86–7; *Genshoku ukiyo-e*, vol. 2, p. 69

Okumura Toshinobu (active *c.* 1716–51)

cat. 114–18

Gō: Kakugetsudō, Bunzen. Pupil of Okumura Masanobu (cat. 39–77). In the Kyōhō and Genbun eras (1716–41) a prolific and accomplished designer of *beni-e* and *urushi-e* for a number of publishers in addition to Masanobu's Okumura-ya. Created many designs of street pedlars and of actors playing such pedlars. In his actor prints he generally concentrated on *wagoto* roles and love scenes, leaving depictions of *aragoto* parts to Torii artists. Only one *benizuri-e* by him has survived from the early 1740s,[1] but his signature on the illustrations in an *ao-hon* published in 1749, *Hōsō-yoke*, indicates that he was still alive at the end of the decade.

1 Chicago 1955, p. 182, Toshinobu no. 23.

LITERATURE: *Genshoku ukiyo-e*, vol. 2, p. 73, and vol. 6, pp. 66–9

Nishimura Shigenaga (*d.* 1756?)

cat. 102

Gō: Eikadō (later Senkadō), Hyakuju. One version of *Ukiyo-e ruikō* says that he was a land owner (*ji-nushi*) at Tōriabura-chō who later moved to Kanda, where he ran a bookshop.[1] Began his artistic activity in the Kyōhō era (1716–36) and was a rival to the Okumura school, whose designs he sometimes imitated. Known for works with a wide variety of subjects – actors, landscapes, birds and flowers, animals, classical literature (see cat. 102), Tosa *jōruri*, Buddhist images – and in many genres and formats – *hosoban*, *haribako-e* ('pictures [to paste on] needle boxes'), perspective pictures (*uki-e*), pillar pictures (*hashira-e*). Devised *hosoban* triptychs showing women of different classes and bearing titles such as *Style of a Servant in a Samurai Mansion* (*O-yashiki fū*). Sometimes said to be the originator of *ishizuri-e* ('stone print pictures') – woodblock prints featuring white outlines in reserve against black backgrounds, like stone rubbings. Wrote *aka-hon* and *kuro-hon* and the illustrated gazetteer *Ehon Edo-miyage* (1753). Influenced Ishikawa Toyonobu (cat. 121–8) and Suzuki Harunobu (cat. 140–2), who are sometimes described as his pupils.

1 Yura 1979, p. 92.

LITERATURE: Chicago 1955, pp. 187–98; Paine 1963; Honolulu 1980, pp. 153–67; *Genshoku ukiyo-e*, vol. 2, p. 47, and vol. 6, pp. 70–3

Nishimura Shigenobu (active *c.* 1729–39)

cat. 119, 120

Gō: Magosaburō. Thought to be a pupil of Nishimura Shigenaga (cat. 102). More than 30 *hosoban* actor, beautiful women and warrior prints by him in the *beni-e* and *urushi-e* techniques are known. Stylistically, they are closest to Shigenaga, but also recall the Okumura school. The theory that Nishimura Shigenobu was a name used by Ishikawa Toyonobu (cat. 121–8) early in his career[1] is based on the stylistic proximity of late prints by Shigenobu to works by Toyonobu, but has not been proved conclusively. During this period the name Shigenobu also occurs on works signed 'Hirose Shigenobu' and 'Tsunekawa Shigenobu'. These are considered to be different artists.[2]

1 Inoue 1920.

2 *Genshoku ukiyo-e*, vol. 2, pp. 47, 118.

LITERATURE: Inoue 1920; Honolulu 1980, pp. 168–72; *Genshoku ukiyo-e*, vol. 2, p. 47

Ishikawa Toyonobu (1711–85)

cat. 121–8

Gō: Tanjōdō, Shūha. Married into a family that ran the Nukaya inn at Kodenma-chō sanchō-me and took their hereditary common name, Shichibei. Father of the scholar and *kyōka* poet Ishikawa Masamochi (1753–1830). Said to be a pupil of Nishimura Shigenaga (cat. 102). For the theory that Nishimura Shigenobu was an early name used by Ishikawa Toyonobu, see the biography of Nishimura Shigenobu (on p. 57). Active from about the Kanpō (1741–4) to the An'ei (1772–81) era. Perhaps the most skilled artist designing in the *benizuri-e* technique in the *hosoban*, (undivided) *hosoban* triptych and, later, *ōban* formats. Also designed a considerable number of prints in the wide pillar picture and the ordinary pillar picture formats,[1] sometimes featuring eroticised images of partly undressed beautiful women (the so-called 'risqué pictures', *abuna-e*). A small number of paintings by him have survived from the Hōreki (1751–64) to the An'ei era, including *Courtesan with Child Attendants* (*Yūjo to kamuro zu*) in the Boston Collection.[2] After the Meiwa era (1764–72) Toyonobu designed very few prints. He was the most important designer of illustrated books in Edo in the Hōreki era, notably of contemporary genre scenes illustrating proverbs.

1 Pins 1982, nos. 44–76, reproduces 34 pillar prints.

2 Boston 2000, vol. 2, no. 19 (commentary by Naitō Masato).

LITERATURE: Inoue 1920; Chicago 1955, pp. 199–229 (combined with Shigenobu); Honolulu 1980, pp. 173–98; *Genshoku ukiyo-e*, vol. 2, p. 76, and vol. 6, pp. 74–9; Hillier 1987, vol. 1, pp. 250–7

Torii Kiyohiro (*d.* 1776?)

cat. 129, 130

Common name:Shichinosuke. One manuscript version of *Ukiyo-e ruikō* apparently states that he died young, of measles, in 1776,[1] but no corroboration of this has been found. Said variously to have been a pupil of Torii Kiyomitsu (cat. 131–6), Kiyomasu II (cat. 94–102) or Kiyonobu II (cat. 89–93), and to have lived at Sakai-chō.[2] Active during the Hōreki era (1751–64) as a designer of delicate *benizuri-e* much influenced by Kiyomitsu and Ishikawa Toyonobu (cat. 121–8) and including fine examples of *abuna-e* (risqué pictures). For a while he seems to have competed with Kiyoshige (cat. 111, 112) in the production of portraits of actors with *hokku* inscriptions, published by Maruya.[3]

1 Yura 1979, p. 103.

2 Honolulu 1980, p. 199.

3 Mutō 1999a, pp. 85–6.

LITERATURE: Chicago 1955, pp. 231–42; Honolulu 1980, pp. 199–213; *Genshoku ukiyo-e*, vol. 2, p. 29, and vol. 6, pp. 84–6

Torii Kiyomitsu (1735–85)

cat. 132–6

Common name: Kamejirō. In the Torii family genealogy he is described as the third-generation head of the Torii school. Inoue Kazuo (1923) suggested he was the second son of Torii Kiyomasu II (cat. 94–102). His earliest known work is a *kuro-hon*, *Taimen no biwa* of 1747. In the later 1750s he suddenly became much more active in the field of single-sheet actor prints. Until the appearance of the *nigao-e* actor likenesses by Katsukawa Shunshō (*d.* 1792) and Ippitsusai Bunchō (active *c.* 1755–90) in the late 1760s, Kiyomitsu was the dominant and most prolific designer of actor prints. At least 48 pillar pictures by him are known, mainly *benizuri-e* and including a considerable number of *abuna-e* (risqué pictures).[1] Three of these are also known in versions by Kiyohiro (see cat. 133). He continued to produce *nishiki-e* single-sheet prints until the late 1770s, generally following innovations by other artists. During this period Kiyomitsu is thought to have concentrated on illustrated kabuki signboards (cat. 131, dating from 1758, has been tentatively attributed to him), playbills and illustrations for popular literature. His pupil Torii Kiyonaga (1752–1815) became the fourth-generation head of the Torii school.

1 Pins 1982, nos. 77–123.

LITERATURE: Inoue 1923; Chicago 1955, pp. 243–73; Honolulu 1980, pp. 214–45; *Genshoku ukiyo-e*, vol. 2, p. 30, and vol. 6, pp. 80–3

Kawamata Tsunemasa (active *c.* 1716–64)

cat. 137–9

Gō: Chōsetsusai. Ukiyo-e painter. Nothing is known about Tsunemasa's life. Several dozen hanging scroll paintings of beautiful women by him have survived, in which the women often act out scenes from the classical literature and lore of China and Japan in the manner of parody pictures (*mitate-e*; see cat. 137–9). The fashions worn by his delicate figures suggest that he worked mainly from the Kanpō (1741–4) to the Kan'en (1748–51) era, although some sources describe him as active as far back as the end of the Kyōhō era (1716–36) and as late as the Hōreki era (1751–64). Two single six-panel folding screens by him are recorded, *Admiring the Cherry at Gion Shrine* (*Gion kanka zu*, collection unknown) and scenes in Yoshiwara and on the Sumida River (collection unknown),[1] which suggest that he was familiar with both Kyoto and Edo. The images on a pair of six-panel folding screens, *Customs of Women in the Twelve Months* (*Fujo fūzoku jūni-ka-getsu zu byōbu*, collection unknown), include depictions of several places in Edo in the background.[2] The influence of the Kyoto artist Nishikawa Sukenobu (cat. 79–81) has been detected, and in many ways Tsunemasa must have served as an exemplar to Suzuki Harunobu (cat. 140–2).

A tentative lineage for the 'Kawamata school' painters Tsuneyuki, Tsunemasa and Tsunetoki was first proposed by Fujikake Shizuya[3] and is apparently borne out by changes in the fashions depicted in their works. A handscroll entitled *Genre Scenes* (*Fūzoku zukan*), documented as by Tsuneyuki, gave his age as 65 and bore the date 1741 on the box, suggesting that this artist was born in 1677. *Gajō yōryaku* (1832) records that he was a native of Niigata and studied with Kano Tsunenobu (1636–1713), a possible link reflected in his relatively grand and ample figure style. Very few paintings by Tsunetoki are known. Similar in style and date to Tsunemasa's, they may indicate that he was a fellow pupil of Tsuneyuki, rather than a student of Tsunemasa. There is mention of another Kawamata artist, Tsunetaka.[4]

1 Both described by Narazaki Muneshige, 'Kawamata, Nishimura, Ishikawa no shoha to zappai', in *Nikuhitsu ukiyo-e*, vol. 3, pp. 139–40.

2 Asano 1987, no. 108.

3 Fujikake 1943, vol. 2, p. 84.

4 Boston 2000, vol. 2, no. 71, pp. 189–90 (commentary by Naitō Masato).

LITERATURE: *Nikuhitsu ukiyo-e*, vol. 3

Suzuki Harunobu (*d.* 1770)

cat. 140–2

Clan name (*honsei*): Hozumi; common name: Jirōbei (or Jihei); *gō*: Shikojin, Chōeiken. Lived at Kanda Shirakabe-chō. Thought to have been born *c.* 1725.[1] Died fifteenth (fourteenth?) day of the sixth month, 1770.[2] Said to be a pupil of Nishimura Shigenaga or, according to one theory, of Nishikawa Sukenobu.[3] His 'brocade pictures' (*nishiki-e*) of 1765 were mainly responsible for the shift to full-colour printing. Their delicate figure style and aesthetic sense dominated ukiyo-e from 1765 until his death five years later. The most extensive list of Harunobu's single-sheet prints, published in 1979, totals 843 works. A more recent article gives a figure of approximately 120 for his *benizuri-e* and *mizu-e* prints of 1760–5, 37 of them actor prints.[4] Some 100 'picture calendars' (*e-goyomi*) printed in full colour, principally by Harunobu, but including examples by minor artists, are known from 1765 and approximately 50 from 1766.[5] After 1765 most of the full-colour prints are in the *chūban* and pillar picture formats. Some seventeen illustrated books by Harunobu are known,[6] notably the colour-printed collection of images of Yoshiwara courtesans, *Ehon seirō bijin-awase* (*Picture Book: Contest of Yoshiwara Beauties*, 5 vols., 1770), published in the month the artist died. He produced several important erotic works, among them the trend-setting adventures of a homunculus called Mane'emon: *Fūryū enshoku Mane'emon* (*Elegant Erotic Mane'emon*, 2 vols., 1770).[7] The recent rediscovery of a signed painting by Harunobu, *Spring Outing on the Banks of the Sumida River* (*Sumida kahan shun'yū zu*), in the collection of the Museum of Fine Arts, Boston (11.7355),[8] has confirmed that he was active as a painter.

The key impetus to the commercial exploitation of full-colour printing came from groups of *haikai* poets who privately commissioned Harunobu, and his rival, the apothecary Komatsu-ya Hyakki (Shōshōken), to design picture calendars for them to exchange at parties in 1765 and early 1766. The leading groups were headed by the bannermen (*hatamoto*) Ōkubo Jinshirō Tadanobu (pen-name Kyosen) and Abe Hachinojō Masahiro (Sakei). Their literary and antiquarian interests were reflected in their playful ideas for 'parody picture' (*mitate-e*)[9] subjects, which Harunobu worked up into finished designs for them – notably in the famous series *Zashiki hakkei* (*Eight Parlour Views*), commissioned by Kyosen. When the fad for *e-goyomi* parties came to an end, Harunobu developed his own ideas for parody pictures, drawing on a rich variety of pictorial and literary sources, including earlier book illustrations by Sukenobu (cat. 79–81) and Tachibana Morikuni (1679–1748) and such classical poetry anthologies as *Wakan rōei shū* (*Japanese and Chinese Poems to Sing*). A fairly large number of Harunobu's brocade pictures fêted the beauty of celebrated young women-about-town, among them Kasamori Osen and Yanagiya Ofuji, who were also lionised in the new genres of popular literature that burgeoned during the relatively liberal regime of Senior Councillor Tanuma Okitsugu (1719–88). Harunobu lived in the same neighbourhood as the unconventional scholar, author and scientist Hiraga Gennai (1728–79), with whom he seems to have been well acquainted. It has been surmised that he may have belonged to Gennai's circle of homosexual friends.[10]

Harunobu's style was much imitated, particularly by Shiba Kōkan (1747–1818), who seems to have produced prints with forged Harunobu signatures in the months immediately after the master's sudden death,[11] and by his leading pupil, Isoda Koryūsai (Harushige, 1735–90).[12]

1 Kobayashi 1985, p. 23.

2 Ibid.

3 Hayashi 1964, pp. 37–54.

4 Takizawa 1998.

5 The estimate given in Waterhouse 1981, p. 3. See also the detailed listing of picture calendars in *Genshoku ukiyo-e*, vol. 3, pp. 112–18.

6 Nakada 1950, pp. 80–3.

7 Kobayashi 1995, pp. 30–43.

8 Boston 2000, vol. 2, no. 37.

9 There has been much debate about whether the original term for such pictures might not have been *yatsushi-e*. Iwata 1993 and Clark 1997.

10 Waterhouse 1981, pp. 3–4.

11 Waterhouse 1991.

12 Hockley n.d.

LITERATURE: Yoshida 1942; Hayashi 1964; Waterhouse 1964; Kobayashi 1970; Philadelphia 1970; Keyes 1972; Waterhouse 1981; *Ukiyo-e shūka*, vol. 4 and suppl. vols. 1, 2; *Genshoku ukiyo-e*, vol. 2, p. 82, and vol. 6, pp. 90–113; Kobayashi 1985; Hillier 1987, vol. 1, pp. 317–29; Tanabe 1990; Waterhouse 1991; Tokyo 1996; Takizawa 1998; Hockley n.d.

1

Anonymous

Mirror of Yoshiwara (Yoshiwara kagami)

'Manji 2' (1659) handwritten on damaged page, correct date probably 9th month, 1660

PUBLISHER: 'Urokogata-ya'

woodblock-printed book, *fukuro-toji, sumizuri*, 1 vol., 38 sheets numbered 1–38, originally 28 illus. (26th torn off and missing), 18.5 × 13.4 cm (covers)

REPRODUCED: Hillier 1987, vol. 1, pp. 83–4, fig. 35

2000.1250

According to one contemporary source, the recently rebuilt Yoshiwara, Edo's pleasure quarter (see cat. 4), became lively in 1659. Visitors enjoyed music and sake, and numerous women (and young men) competed for their favours. Fancying themselves connoisseurs, men from all classes purchased courtesan directories (*yūjo hyōban-ki*).[1]

The present directory was modelled on *Ne-monogatari* (*Bed Tales*), a guide to the Shimabara pleasure quarter in Kyoto published in 1656.[2] *Mirror of Yoshiwara* included a simple map of Yoshiwara showing the location of the large entrance gate, the central street Nakano-chō and six side streets.[3] It also provided a detailed account of the locations of teahouses (*chaya*), houses of assignation (*ageya*) and brothels, as well as listings of second-rank courtesans (*kōshi* [-*jorō*]) and lower-class prostitutes (*hashi* [-*jorō*]). The book's primary selling point was illustrations of 28 top-ranking courtesans (*tayū*) of Yoshiwara along with discussion of their special talents and ways of interacting with clients.[4]

Karasaki, the courtesan shown here, was known for her skills in calligraphy, reciting poetry and letter writing. She worked at an establishment run by Hikozaemon on Shin-machi. Her name brings to mind 'Night Rain at Karasaki', a motif belonging to the classical painting and poetry subject 'The Eight Views of Ōmi'. The unknown artist alludes to the famous pine tree at Karasaki by decorating the courtesan's outer garment with a pine tree pattern. The poem, entitled 'Love Letters' (*koi no tamazusa*), incorporates the courtesan's name in the first two lines and suggests that the feelings expressed in her missives may be as fleeting as dew:

Kono yo kara	Karasaki's love letters,
saki no yo kakete	like sparkling drops of dew,
fuku kaze no	are carried off and scattered
tsurete zo otosu	by the winds that sweep
tsuyu no tamazusa	as from this world into the next.[5]

The courtesans are drawn with even lines and set against plain backgrounds. Reclining or seated, they all wear the same fashionable knotted and looped *hyōgo-mage* hairstyle. The charming 'Kyoto-style' elegance of these figures is closest in spirit to anonymous paintings from the Kanbun era (1661–73) of courtesans with poems likening them to portraits of classical poets. Such paintings, as well as unsigned single-sheet illustrations of couples in intimate encounters, used to be indiscriminately attributed to Moronobu. Now they are generally thought to be by the 'Kanbun Master', an artist (or artists) who inspired Moronobu.[6] The Kanbun Master is also believed to have illustrated the erotic book *Yoshiwara makura* (*Yoshiwara Pillow*), published in Edo in the eighth month of 1660. This work, which is another type of courtesan critique, shows courtesans and clients in simple indoor settings and in varied lovemaking positions.[7] LEV

1 Seigle 1993, pp. 55, 58–9.

2 *Kokusho sō-mokuroku*, vol. 6, p. 445, vol. 7, p. 918; *Nihon koten*, p. 1299; Gerstle 1989, p. 18. *Ne-monogatari* is discussed in Shibui 1927, pp. 27, 61, and reproduced in Tenri 1973, pp. 77–126, and *Kisho fukuseikai*, vol. 25. pp. 121–73. Parts of it, especially the critiques, were copied in *Mirror of Yoshiwara*, but the names of the courtesans were changed and portraits with poems added. The text on the damaged last page of the Boston copy of *Mirror of Yoshiwara* has been repaired and touched up with *sumi*. The missing paper tears may have misled someone to leave out a stroke and retouch the date as Manji 2 (1659) instead of Manji 3 (1660). Shibui's copy is dated 1660 and recorded as a 'shinpan' (new edition). Shibui 1927, pp. 5, 36; Tenri 1973, pp. 303–4. Another copy produced with re-cut blocks and a wave design added below the figures is dated 1661. Christie's 1988, p. 153, no. 98.

3 The map gives the side streets as Edo-chō, Ageya-chō and Kyō-machi to the west, and Ni-chōme, Sumi-chō and Shin-machi to the east.

4 The first courtesan depicted is the famous Takao (II or III) from Miura-ya. It is generally believed that Takao II, courted by Lord Date Tsunamune (dates unknown), died of illness at the age of nineteen in early December 1659. Seigle 1993, pp. 58–61, 248–9; Gerstle 1989, p. 15.

5 Trans. in consultation with John Carpenter.

6 Lane 1962, fig. 8; Lane 1978, pp. 37–41, fig. 15; Christie's 1998, pp. 32–3, no. 11. See also the later, similarly painted courtesans in New York 1986, pp. 176–9; *Kisho fukuseikai*, vol. 27, pp. 1–106 (facsimile reproduction of *Nure-botoke*, 3 vols., fourth month, 1671); and *Nihon koten*, p. 969. *Mirror of Yoshiwara*, like many unsigned works, was previously attributed to Moronobu. *Ukiyo-e jiten*, vol. 3, p. 426; Shibui 1927, pp. 5, 36.

7 Lane 1978, pp. 36–7, fig. 18; Hillier 1987, vol. 1, pp. 83–4, fig. 33, 34

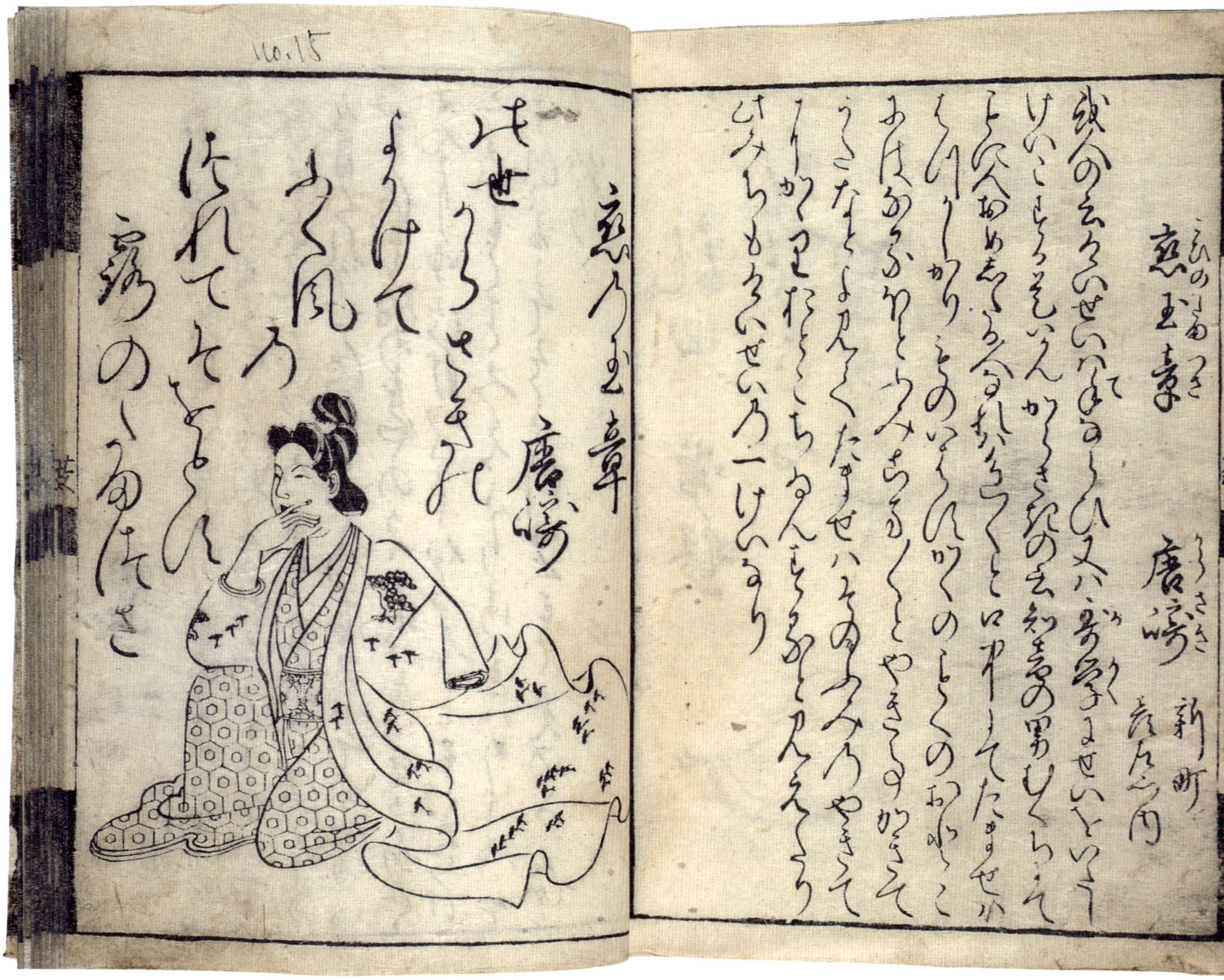

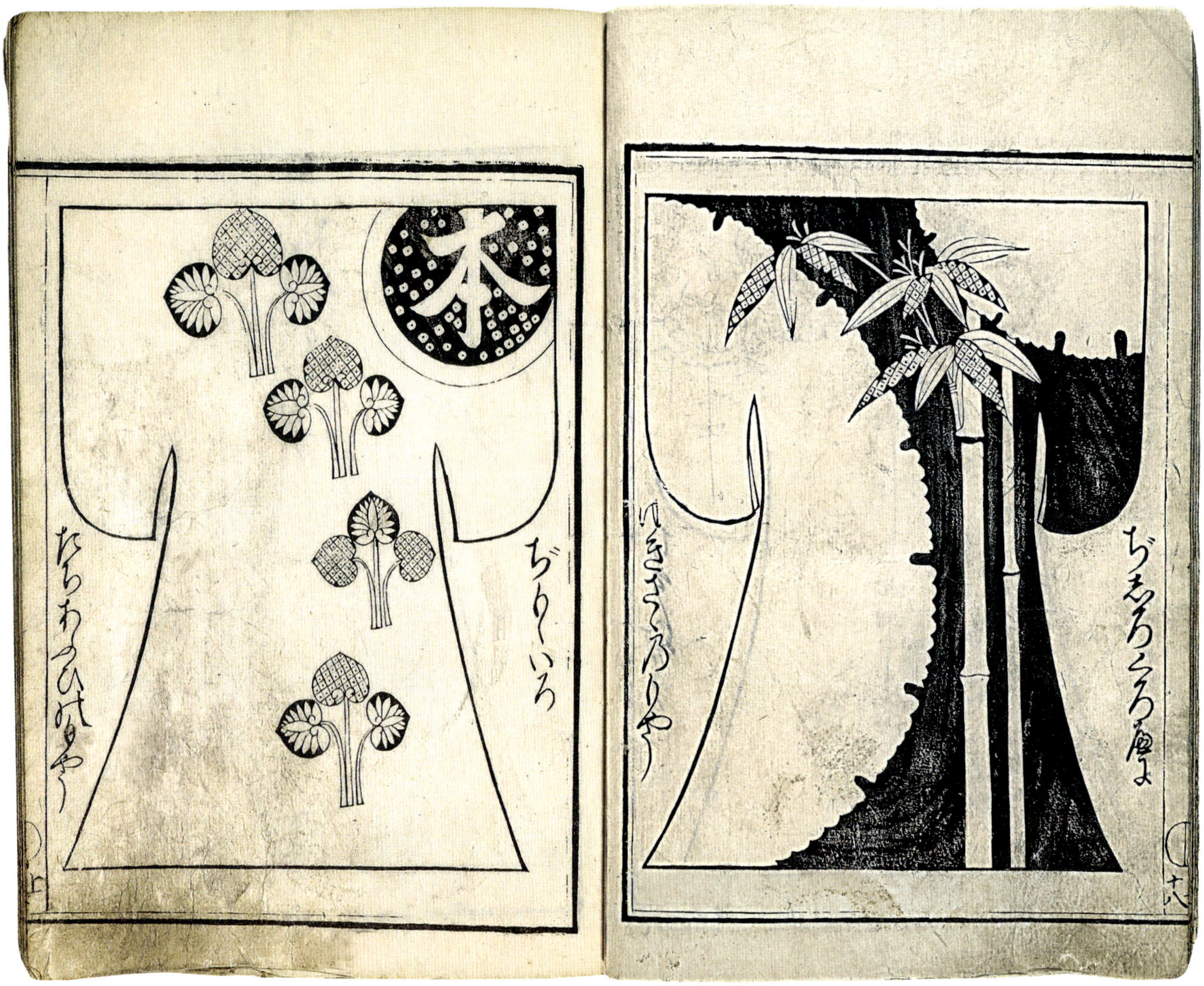

2

Anonymous

A New Selection of Kosode Patterns (Shinsen o-hiinagata)

7th month, 1666

PUBLISHER: 'Yamada Ichirōbei'

woodblock-printed book, *fukuro-toji, sumizuri*, vol. 1 of 2, vol.1 preface numbered, sheets numbered 1–50, 18.2 × 12.5 cm (covers)

source unknown, 2000

2000.1258

1 The 1667 edition was published in two volumes with 200 images. The earlier, Boston version exists in only one volume. Kenneth Gardner notes that a few changes were made to the text for the second edition. London 1993, p. 669.

2 Reproduced in Tokyo 1999, no. 005.

With the emergence of a wealthy and sophisticated merchant class in the mid to late 17th century, fashion increasingly became a statement of their confident stylishness. The publication of *A New Selection of Kosode Patterns*, in the original edition of 1666 shown here and in another from the following year with limited colour printing, made available for the first time designs that could be readily copied by textile makers for clients eager to have 'the latest'.[1]

Each page of the book illustrates a basic outline of the back of a *kosode*, which in its simplicity provided the textile artist with an unbroken plane on which to create inventive designs. Notes along the right and left margins give information about the colour of the fabric ground and the techniques of ornamentation. Most of the designs follow the Kanbun style popular at the time the book was published. This style, which has continued to be admired by textile connoisseurs, generally features strikingly bold forms that extend across the shoulders and down one side of the back. Tie-dyeing (*shibori*) and embroidery are used to delineate the design against the lighter ground colour; in the pattern book small-dotted circles and diamonds meticulously replicate the tie-dyeing technique.

A *kosode* of similar design with tie-dyed decoration on yellow figured satin dating to the 1660s is preserved in the collection of the National Museum of Japanese History in Chiba Prefecture.[2] As on the right-hand page of *A New Selection of Kosode Patterns* illustrated here, it is divided into three zones. One consists of a large snowflake with crenellated edges along the neck and upper right sleeve, while another, larger snowflake extends across the left sleeve and left side of the back. Bands of bamboo emerge between the two. The craftsman who executed the design in textile filled the entire area with stalks and leaves in tie-dye, rather than using *shibori* just for the leaves as suggested by the pattern book. ANM

3, 4

Hishikawa Moronobu

Scenes from the Nakamura Kabuki Theatre and the Yoshiwara Pleasure Quarter

c. 1684–94

ARTIST'S SEALS: 'Hishikawa', 'Moronobu'

pair of six-panel folding screens, ink and colour on gold-leafed paper, 139.8 × 355.2 cm (each)

REPRODUCED: Kobayashi 1977; Takeda 1977, nos. 87, 88; Hickman 1978; Boston 2000, vol. 1, nos. 38–9; Tsuji 2000

Gift of Oliver Peabody, 1879

79.468, 79.469

After achieving political hegemony in 1615, the Tokugawa shogunate moved the seat of political authority from Kyoto, the tradition-bound capital, which remained the home of the Emperor, to the backwater town of Edo. In the succeeding decades Edo was transformed physically by the construction of vast complexes to house the military clans kept in enforced attendance and by the growth of a large urban infrastructure to service them. However, during the first half of the 17th century Kyoto remained the cultural centre of Japan.

In 1657 a conflagration known as the Meireki Fire, which started at Honmyō-ji Temple in Hongō district, reduced more than two-thirds of Edo to ashes. Rebuilding began almost immediately, but government supervision enforced some strict rezoning. Among the groups affected were the proprietors and inhabitants of the theatres and the pleasure quarters, which had previously been scattered around the city. Under the new regulations the theatres were moved to a single district in the adjoining neighbourhoods of Sakai-chō and Kobiki-chō. Shin-Yoshiwara (New Yoshiwara), as the rebuilt brothel district came to be known, was given an officially sanctioned area in the marshy plains in the north of the city.

Hishikawa Moronobu was a native of Awa Province, modern-day Chiba Prefecture. It is not clear when he moved to Edo, but he became one of the first artists to develop an iconography for the rebuilt city – an iconography that captured the increasingly confident spirit and sophistication of the thriving metropolis. Some elements of this iconography Moronobu took from pre-conflagration works that provided panoramic visions of Edo, such as *Famous Scenic Places and Amusements in Edo* (*Edo meisho yūraku zu byōbu*; Hosomi Museum, Kyoto) and *Famous Scenic Places in Edo* (*Edo meisho zu byōbu*; Idemitsu Museum of Arts, Tokyo).[1] However, in *Edo suzume* (*Sparrow of Edo*) of 1677 the artist provided new vignettes of daimyo processions outside Edo Castle, the fish market at Nihonbashi, the bamboo yards at Yotsuya and the fireworks at Ryōgoku Bridge. He also explored the two *akusho*, the 'bad places' – the worlds of the theatre and the brothels. In this and other woodblock-printed books dating to the 1670s, such as *Yoshiwara ō-zassho* (*Great Miscellany of Yoshiwara*) of 1675, *A Guide to Love in Yoshiwara* (cat. 11) of 1678 and *Kokon yakusha monogatari* (*Actors Past and Present*) of the same year, we can see his gradual development of a visual vocabulary to describe different establishments and the people of all classes who frequented them.

In *Genre Scenes in Yoshiwara* (*Yoshiwara fūzoku zukan*), a handscroll now in the Manno Art Museum, Osaka, that is dated by Asano Shūgō to the Enpō (1673–81) or Tenna (1681–4) era,[2] the artist combined various elements to provide a view of Yoshiwara, moving right to left, from the outskirts, through the Ōmon-guchi (Main Gate), along the chief thoroughfare, Nakano-chō, and into the luxurious interior of a high-class house of assignation (*ageya*). In the Boston works, which probably date to before 1690, he attempted an even

1 Okano 1999.

2 Chiba 2000, p. 50.

3 Kobayashi, in Boston 2000, vol. 1, nos. 38–9, transcribes the programme named on these signs as 'Nogai no Hinazuru', 'Musashi no Kuni, Sumidagawa' and 'Ō-odori' on one, 'Jūni-dan no Honbushi', 'Taiheikoku Genji no Kado-ide' and 'Kangen no Ō-yose' on the other.

4 Reproduced in Kyoto 1991, no. 60.

5 Chiba 2000, p. 38.

6 Boston 2000, vol. 2, no. 10; Morse 2000.

more ambitious composition. Here, the main avenue dominates the expanse of the left screen (cat. 4), but additional areas of interest – the interior of a house of assignation and lower-level brothels – are arranged in the upper sections, set off by bands of gold clouds. Several details contribute a strong narrative element to the composition – the highest-ranked courtesans promenading with their attendants along the main street in the early evening on their way to the *ageya*; the men gathering to gawk at these almost unattainable visions of feminine charm; and the inhabitants of the latticed brothels displayed to those in search of entertainment as well as sexual adventure.

In the right-hand screen (cat. 3) Moronobu presents three views of the Nakamura Theatre. The lower left corner, framed by a massive pine tree, depicts the bustle of activity at the entrance, with a barker standing on a raised platform and motioning to the passers-by to attend the day's performances of group dances and war epics detailed on the vertical signs behind him.[3] The right is dominated by the wooden stage, on which a festive procession of actors in male and female roles wends its way rhythmically towards a seated shamisen-player. Shaded from view by bamboo blinds, upper-class women watch the performance from their well-appointed box, while less privileged members of the audience sit on the ground. In the upper left corner Moronobu illustrates the activities backstage, with one actor preparing to don a wig for a female role and another receiving assistance with lacing his armour.

Moronobu must have adapted the representation of the Nakamura's main stage from earlier woodblock book illustrations, such as *Kyō warabe* (*Kyoto Child*) of 1658,[4] which includes a scene in a kabuki theatre in the Shijō-gawara area of Kyoto. In this Kyoto guidebook the artist offers a similar view, while a retinue of four dancers parades across the wooden floor. Moronobu was to develop the juxtaposition of stage and entrance found in the Boston screen in at least two other works – *Genre Scenes of the Nakamura Theatre* (*Kabuki zu byōbu*) in the Tokyo National Museum, which has been dated by Asano to 1692–3, and *Cherry Blossom Viewing at Ueno and Kabuki Theatre* (*Ueno hanami Kabuki zu byōbu*) in the Suntory Museum, Tokyo, which he dates to 1693–4.[5]

During the late 17th and early 18th century Moronobu's vision of the theatres and brothels had a profound influence on members of the Hishikawa school. Morohira, for example, in his *Pastimes in Spring and Autumn* (*Shunjū yūraku zu byōbu*; Idemitsu Museum of Arts, Tokyo), which dates to the Genroku era (1688–1704), borrows freely from Moronobu's depictions of Yoshiwara. Okumura Masanobu and Miyagawa Chōshun also turned to Moronobu's works for inspiration during the early stages of their careers, in paintings such as the pair of hanging scrolls *Scenes in Yoshiwara* (*Yoshiwara fūzoku*; Manno Art Museum, Osaka), dating to the first half of the Kyōhō era (1716–36), and Boston's six-panel screen *Genre Scenes in Yoshiwara* (*Yoshiwara fūzoku-zu byōbu*), dating from the Hōei (1704–11) to the early Kyōhō era.[6] ANM

cat. 3

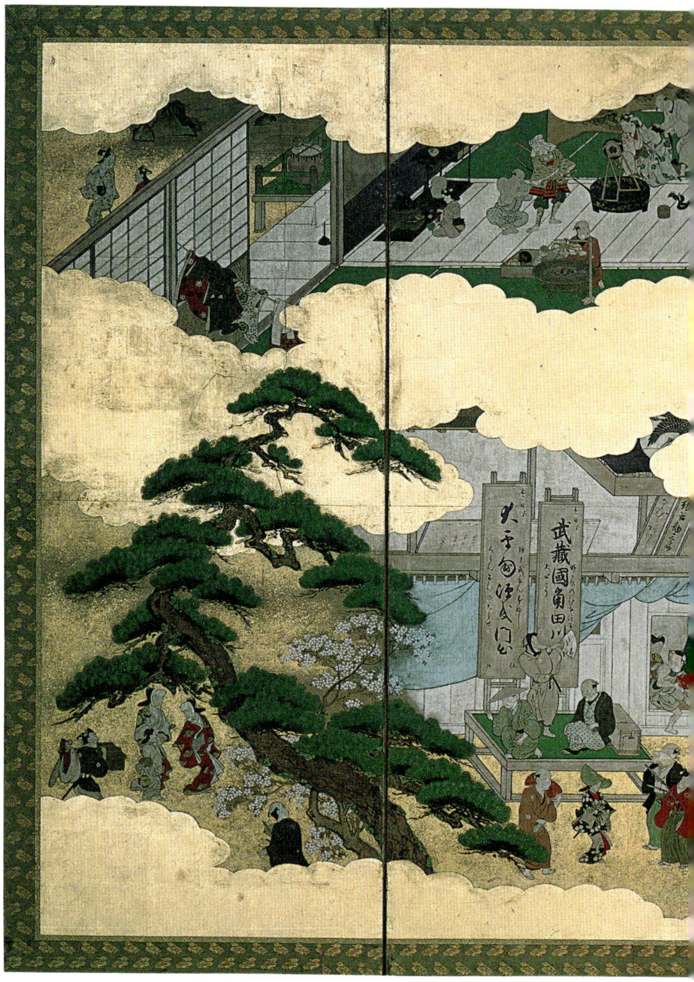

cat. 4

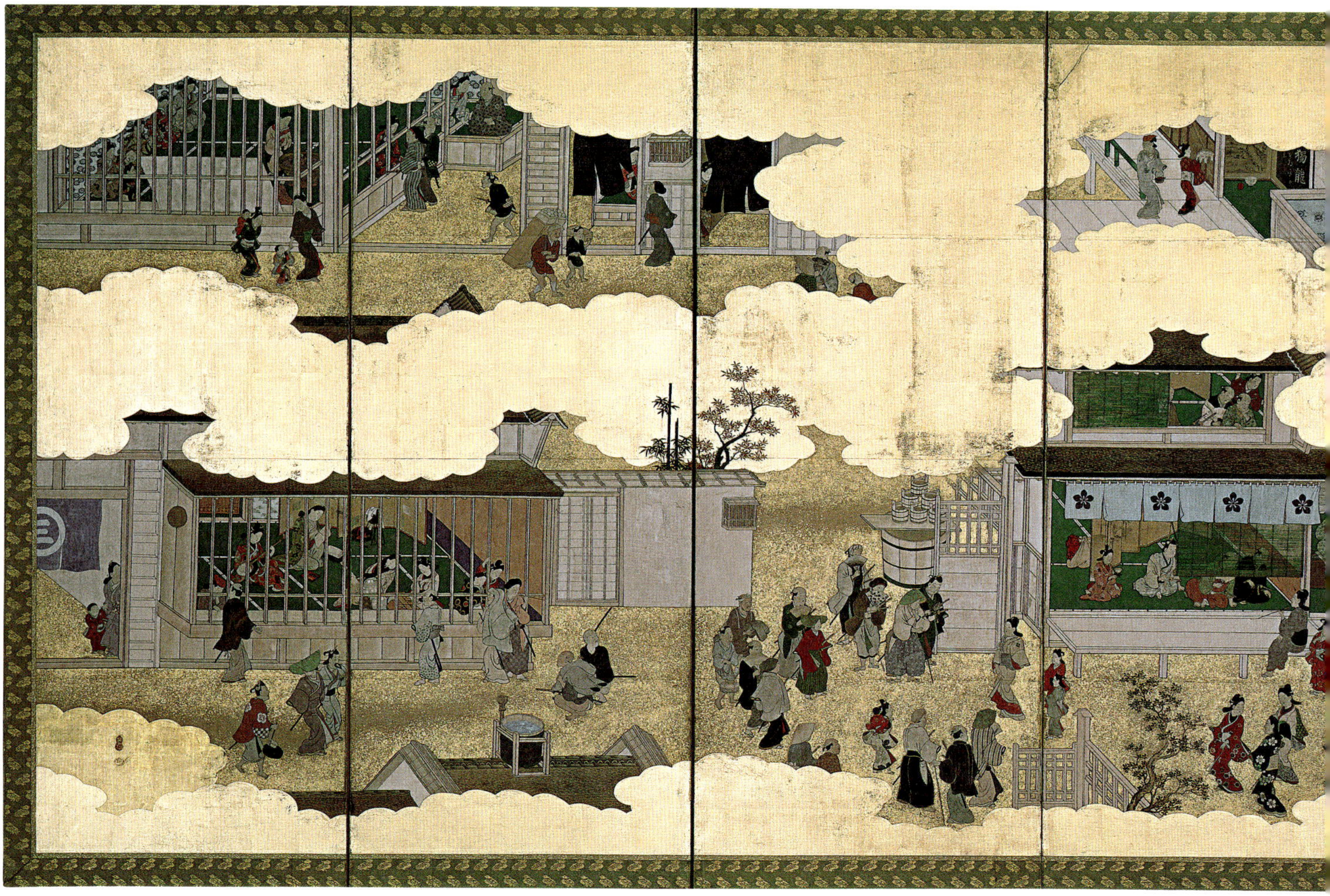

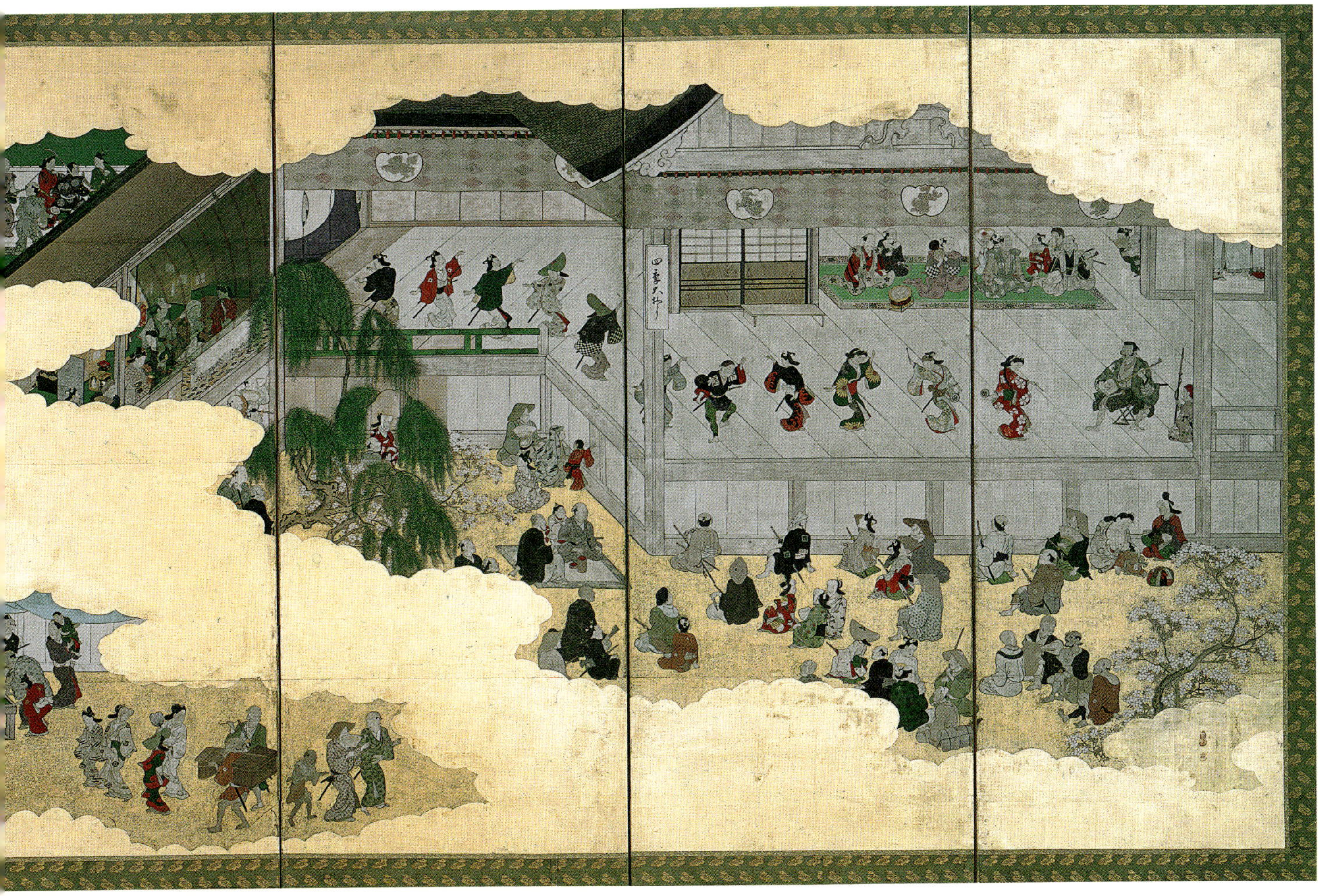

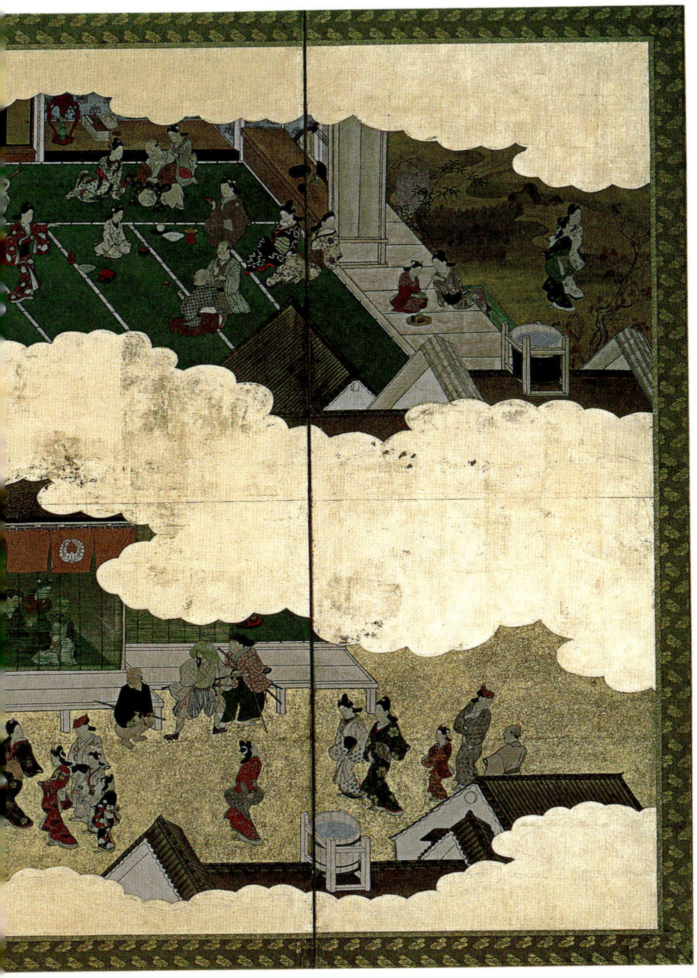

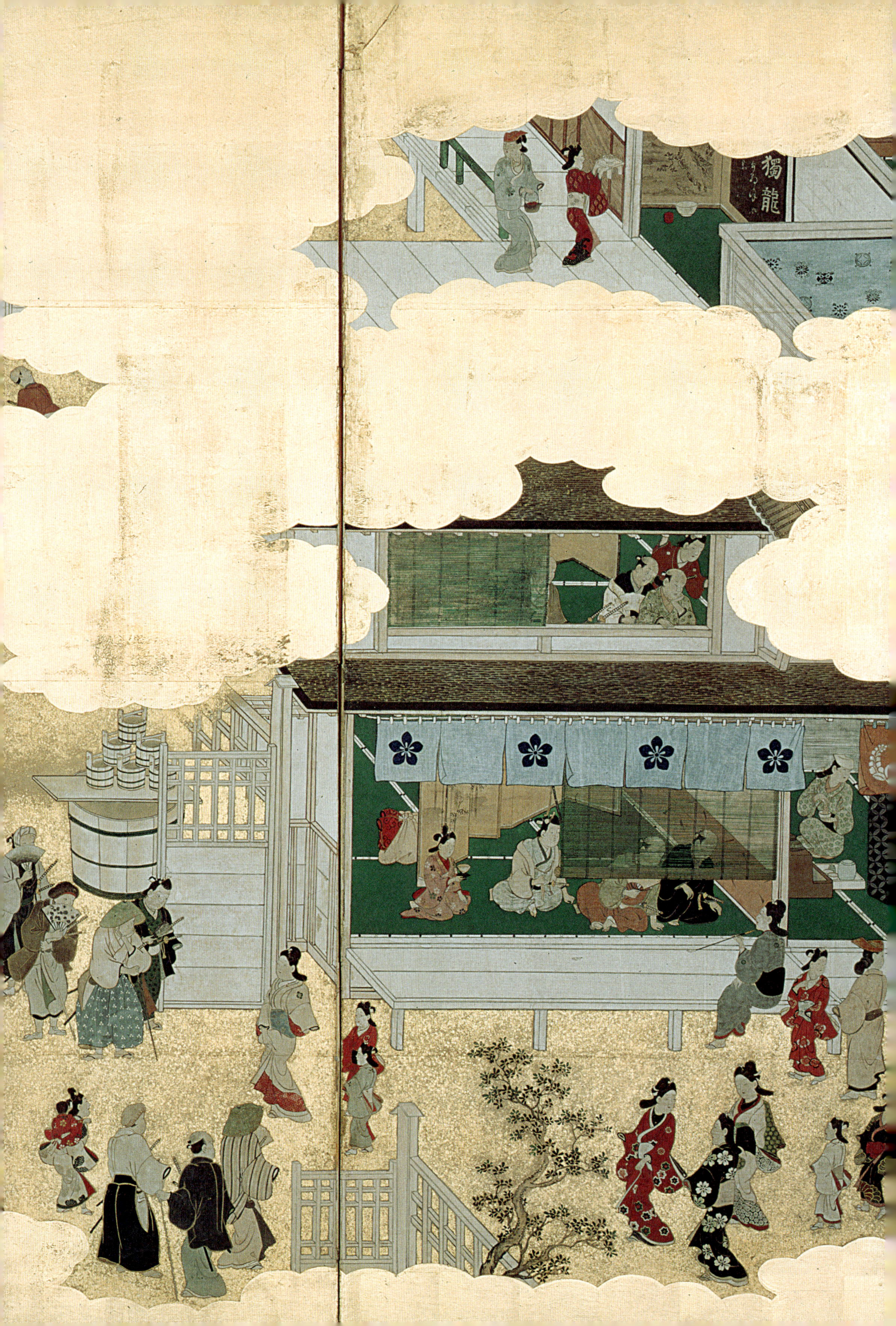
獨龍

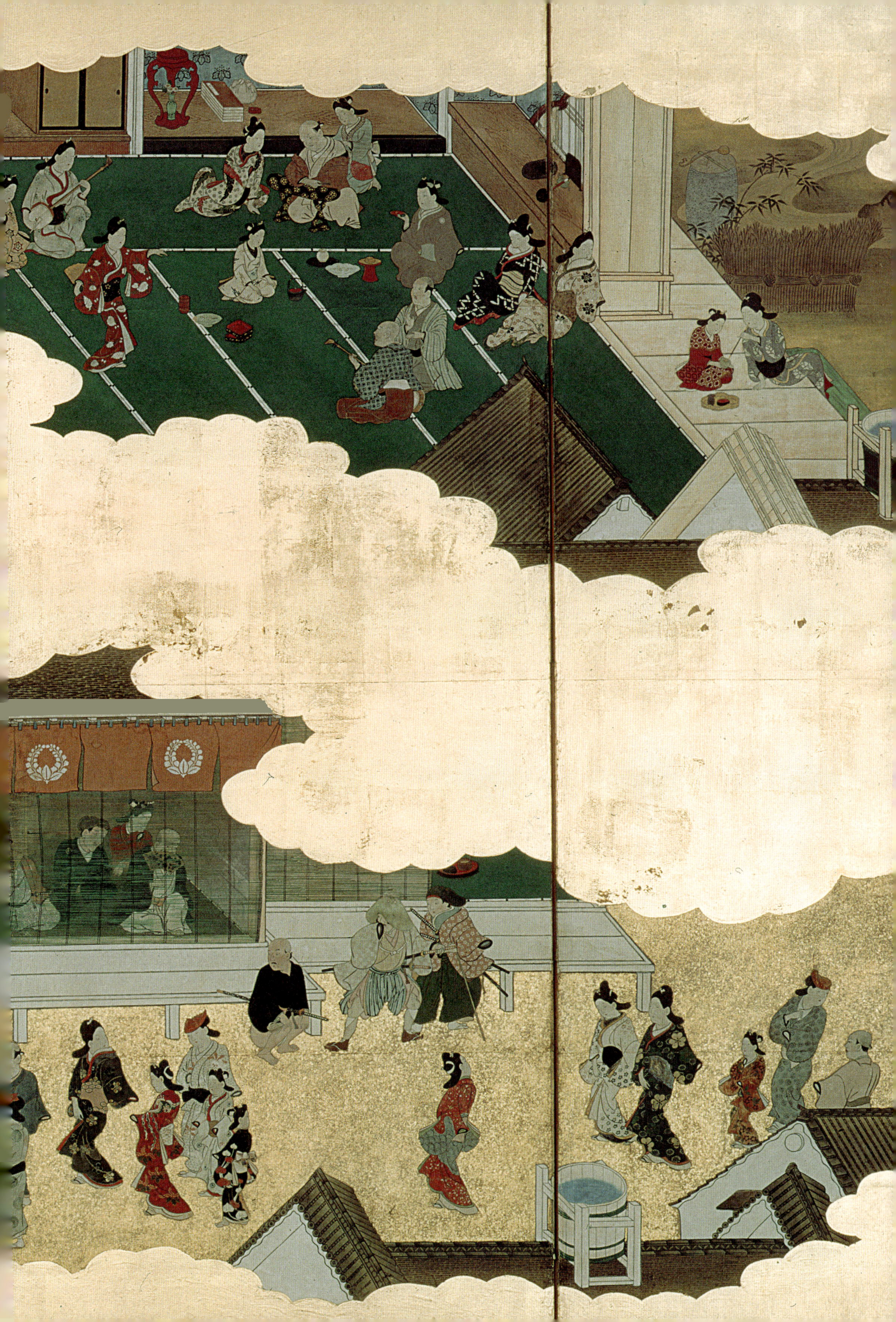

5

Attributed to Hishikawa Moronobu

Procession of a Courtesan

c. 1681–4

hanging scroll, ink, colour, gold and silver on silk, 80 × 39.3 cm

REPRODUCED: Boston 2000, vol. 1, no. 45
Chiba 2000, no. 23

Fenollosa-Weld Collection, 1911

11.4618

Parading through the streets of Yoshiwara with her entourage, an unidentified courtesan (*tayū*) makes her way from her brothel to a house of assignation (*ageya*), where a client awaits her. The maple tree in the background ablaze with colour suggests that it is mid-autumn, when it is said that the courtesans of Edo could be seen in the brothel district in their most ostentatious clothes.[1] Pulling her collar up around her neck as a shield against the cold, the courtesan is clothed in a luxurious red figured-twill robe embellished with floral roundels embroidered with silver and gold.[2] An extremely fashionable obi, hand-painted in ink with scenes from classical literature, completes the ensemble.

Evening processions of courtesans to houses of assignation were a great attraction for visitors to pleasure districts. Generally, the *tayū* would be accompanied by one or two young female attendants, a matron (*yarite*) and a male employee from the brothel. In this painting, however, the artist has limited the retinue to the latter two. The porter strains under the weight of an immense chest that will have contained a minimum of three silk-covered quilts.[3] He is transporting the bedding required for the evening, since the *ageya* that has summoned the courtesan was most likely not usually frequented by her.[4]

Although this composition does not bear a signature or seal, it has been attributed to Hishikawa Moronobu on the basis of the figure style.[5] The placid, measured walk of the courtesan with her right hand gently lifting the hem of her skirts and her left hand tucked into her sleeve is a pose found in numerous works by Moronobu; in many cases only the details of the hairstyles and the ornamentation of the robes differ.[6] One such work, a signed hanging scroll in a private collection, even includes a maple tree in autumn foliage with similar ink shading used for the trunk.[7] ANM

1 Saikaku 1984, p. 190.

2 Asano Shūgō, in his commentary in Boston 2000, vol. 1, p. 180, draws attention to the collar motif.

3 As noted by Ihara Saikaku in his novel *The Life of an Amorous Woman* (*Kōshoku ichidai onna*), in which a courtesan says of herself after being demoted: 'From that day on I had no retinue of courtesans, I slept on two layers of bedding instead of three'. Quoted in Hibbett 1959, p. 181.

4 Asano remarks that the chrysanthemum motif on the chest is the crest of an unidentified courtesan. He points out that the crest appears on another chest in the handscroll *Genre Scenes in Yoshiwara* (*Yoshiwara fūzoku zukan*) attributed to Hishikawa Moronobu in the Manno Art Museum, Osaka. Boston 2000, vol. 1, p. 180.

5 Ibid.

6 See, for example the hanging scrolls *Standing Beauty* (*Tachi bijin zu*, *c.* 1690) and *Woman in a Furisode* (*Furisode bijin zu*, 2nd half of 17th century, Nara Prefectural Museum), reproduced respectively in Christie's 1998, no. 17, and Tokyo 1994a, no. 13.

7 *Woman Standing Underneath a Tree with Autumn Foliage* (*Kōyō shita tachi bijin zu*, late 17th century), reproduced in Tokyo 1994a, no. 15.

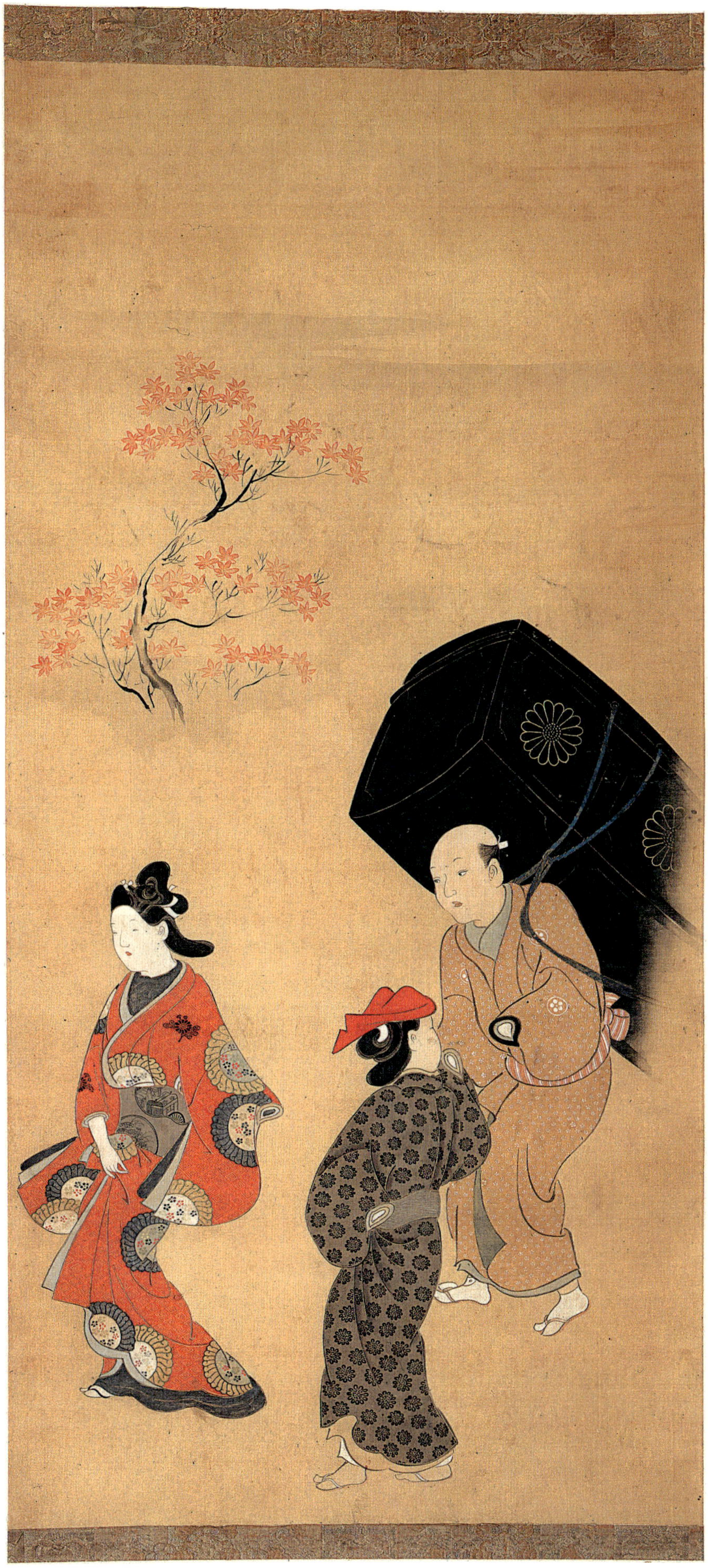

6

Anonymous (Hishikawa school)

Genre Scenes in Edo in the Four Seasons

c. 1684–1704

handscroll, ink, colour, gold and silver on silk, 34.4 × 859.5 cm

REPRODUCED: Boston 2000, vol. 1, no. 43

William Sturgis Bigelow Collection, 1911

11.7619

1 Reizei 1996, pp. 4–7.

2 Boston 2000, vol. 1, p. 178 (commentary by Kobayashi Tadashi).

3 Saikaku 1963, p. 190.

4 Kobayashi 1996a.

Beginning in the Heian period (794–1185), Japanese artists, inspired by *waka* poetry, developed a rich visual vocabulary of flora and fauna to evoke the four seasons (*shiki*) in large-scale screen paintings. In later centuries, influenced by Chinese examples, they also chronicled the main farming and agricultural events of the year, which Confucians believed to be crucial to the moral order of society.[1]

Throughout his career Hishikawa Moronobu looked to his surroundings – the flourishing urban environment of Edo – to provide him with material for detailed depictions of the events that marked the passing of the year.[2] Some, such as *Nenjū gyōji no zu* (*Illustrated Annual Events*, 1680) and *Tsukinami no asobi* (*Amusements of Each Month*, 1691), were published in simple woodblock-printed books. Others, including *Illustrated Genre Scenes of the Twelve Months* (*Jūni-ka-getsu fūzoku zukan*) in the Seikadō Bunko Art Museum, Tokyo, a handscroll executed in ink and colour on silk, assumed a more luxurious form. In his works of this type certain set scenes are repeated to ensure recognition of the time suggested and to ease rapid production.

The present scroll shows six individual scenes relating to events during the four seasons. It opens with a section showing retainers paying their formal respects to their lord at the New Year. Pine seedlings and sprays of bamboo – traditional seasonal decorations – are arranged on either side of the entrance to the residential compound. To their left young women engage in a game of battledore and shuttlecock, and boys play with toy bows and arrows. This scene is a variant of that found in *Nenjū gyōji no zu*, in which a noticeably older feudal lord receives obeisance from his men.

Spring is represented by an outing to view cherry blossoms. Curtains and a folding screen are brought out to create a temporary enclosure for a

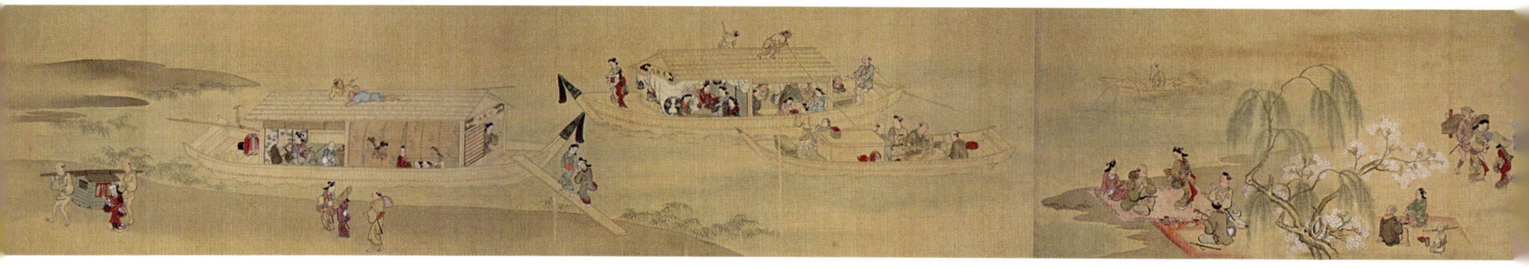

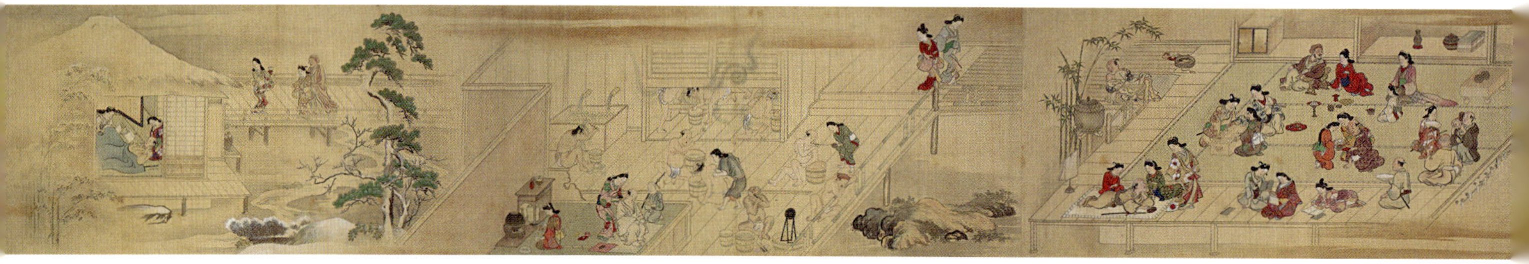

courtesan and her retinue, who enjoy the sounds of a shamisen being played by a blind musician. Attendants struggle to assist a tipsy patron. Again, the basic iconographical elements of this scene can be found in later screens, including *Cherry Blossom Viewing at Ueno* (*Ueno hanami zu byōbu*) in the Boston collection (11.4617), which bears a Moronobu seal. There, the courtesan, who strikes a similar pose with her knee bent, is the focal point of the fifth panel, while the drunken patron is separated from the group and occupies the third panel.

The following kitchen and bathhouse scenes provide an insider's view of Yoshiwara. While Moronobu used the vignette of cooks engaged in filleting fish extensively in other works – such as the Manno Art Museum handscroll *Genre Scenes in Yoshiwara* (*Yoshiwara fūzoku zukan*), dating to the Enpō or the Tenna era, and the well-known print series *Yoshiwara no tei* (*The Appearance of Yoshiwara*), also dating to the early 1680s – the bath scene is more unusual. After clambering in and out of the bath in the steamy room at the rear, the men are administered to by female attendants (detail, pp. 74–5). The image resonates with a fictitious description of the baths by the 17th-century novelist Ihara Saikaku: 'When the customer leaves the bath, one places a tobacco tray next to him and gives him an infusion. He cuts a remarkably fine figure as he sits there, being cooled by a fan, on which is executed the copy of a painting by Yūzen. Then one sits by his back, applies a new plaster to the scar left by his moxa burn and smoothes down his rumpled sidelocks.'[3]

The present scroll bears no signature or seal. Its adoption of the established seasonal motifs suggests, however, that it was painted by a member of the Hishikawa school. Kobayashi Tadashi has suggested that, since seals functioned as trademarks, unattributed scrolls of this type were commissioned by members of the aristocracy.[4] ANM

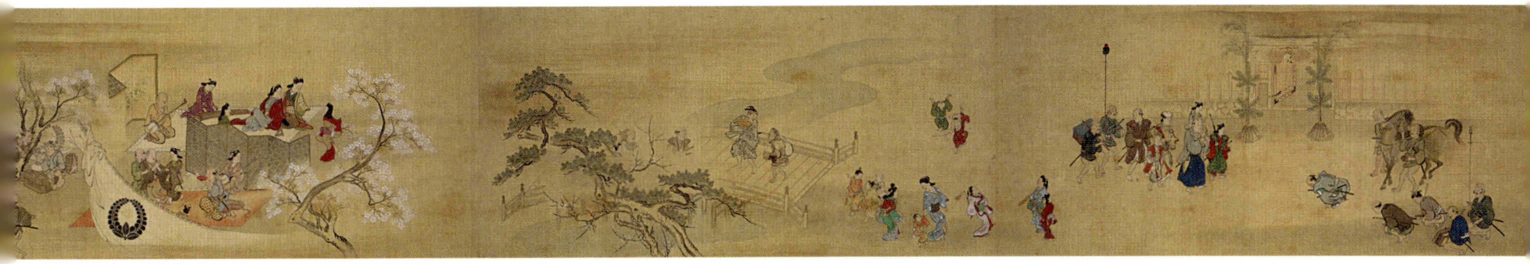

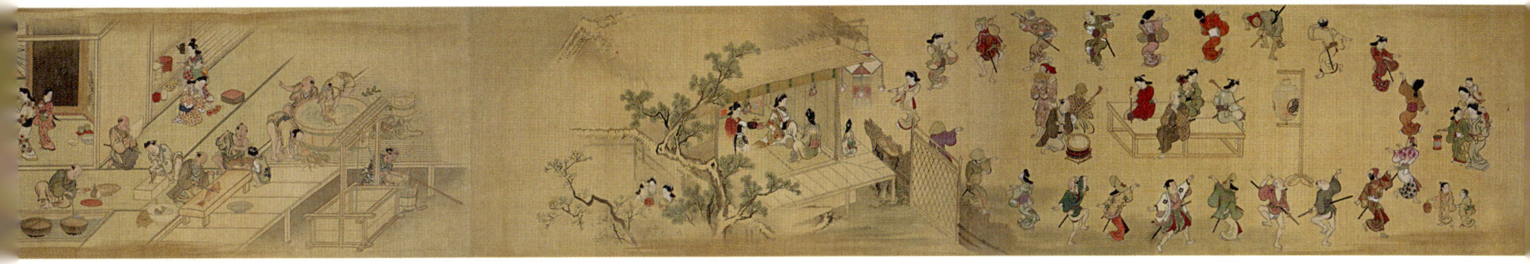

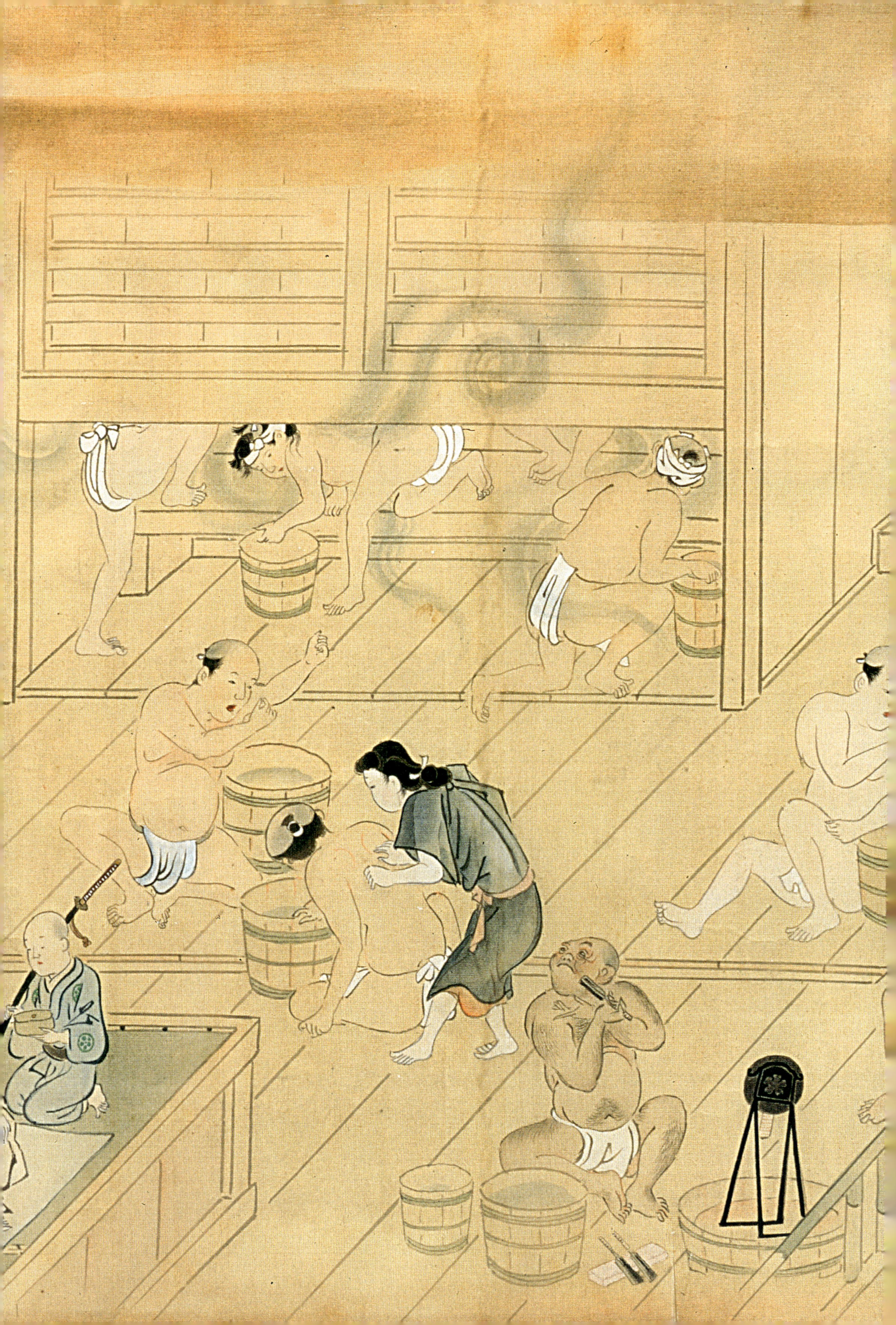

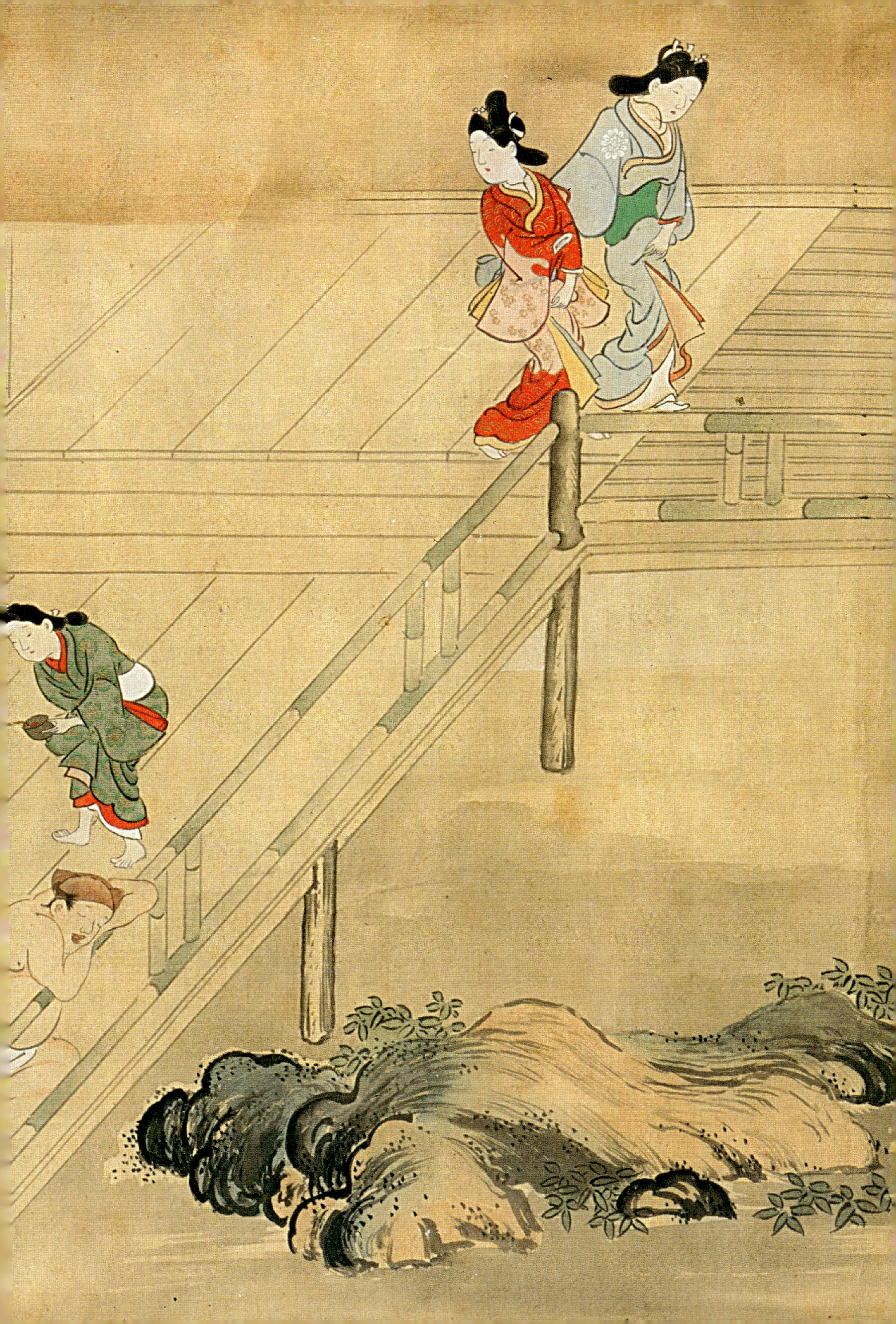

7–10

Hishikawa Moronobu

From the series *The Sake-drinking Boy* (*Shuten-dōji*)

c. 1680

PUBLISHER: 'Ōdenma-chō san-chōme Urokogata-ya Sanzaemon' (Urokogata-ya Sanzaemon at Ōdenma-chō san-chōme)

woodblock, 4 from a set of 19 (?) sheets, horizontal *ōban*, *sumizuri-e*, slight hand-colouring

William Sturgis Bigelow Collection, 1911

11.13417, 11.13420, 11.13423, 11.13424

The Sake-drinking Boy (*Shuten-dōji*) was one of the most popular *otogi-zōshi* tales of the medieval and early Edo periods. It tells how Minamoto no Yorimitsu (Raikō) was commanded by the Emperor to subdue a demon that had been abducting young women from the capital. Enlisting the protection of the deities of three famous shrines, Yorimitsu set out with his Four Retainers (Shitennō) and the warrior Hirai Yasumasa, all disguised as mountain priests (*yamabushi*). Assisted by the deities and directed by a young woman ominously washing a blood-stained robe in a stream, the warriors eventually arrive at the mountain castle of Shuten-dōji, who takes the form of a large temple acolyte (*dōji*) partial to sake. At a banquet during which they must eat flesh the warriors serve poisoned sake, incapacitating Shuten-dōji and his demon followers. Donning their armour, the warriors gain access to where the drunken Shuten-dōji is sleeping and slay him. Releasing the surviving women and escorting them back to the capital, they parade the severed head of Shuten-dōji and are rewarded by the Emperor. This story was often depicted by artists of the Kano school in handscrolls combining paintings and texts, notably the version by Kano Motonobu of *c.* 1522 (Suntory Museum, Tokyo).[1] Depending on whether Shuten-dōji's lair is located on Mount Ōe or Mount Ibuki, the versions of the story divide into two main lineages.

The present prints, unsigned but firmly attributed to Moronobu, come from what is thought to be a set of nineteen that relate to a version of the Shuten-dōji legend adapted for *jōruri*, the puppet stage.[2] Such a version is recorded as having been performed with chanting by Tosa no Shōjō (active *c.* 1673–1711; see pp. 14–15) in a puppet theatre in Sakai-chō in the fourth month, 1680, and it seems possible that Moronobu's prints were issued at about this time.[3] The *jōruri* version added the related Rashōmon tale to the beginning of the *otogi-zōshi* story outlined above. This tells how the warrior Watanabe no Tsuna, one of Yorimitsu's Shitennō, severed the arm of a demon who was haunting the Rashōmon Gate in the capital. Moronobu's set of prints includes scenes from this legend. The most complete known set is that in the Tokyo National Museum, which consists of eighteen sheets. Asano Shūgō has recently suggested an order for these based on the plot of the story and on the printed numbers visible in the bottom right margin of some impressions of certain designs. The impression of the final sheet in the Chiba City Museum of Art bears the number nineteen printed at the bottom right. Asano suggests that the missing design appeared at the beginning of the *jōruri* and showed a banquet scene at Yorimitsu's mansion involving the Shitennō and Hirai Yasumasa. The Boston set contains all three known scenes from the Rashōmon story and fourteen of the sixteen Shuten-dōji episodes.[4]

Moronobu returned to the Shuten-dōji theme in three painted handscrolls, *Subjugation of the Demon of Mount Ōe* (*Ōeyama oni taiji emaki*; Fujita Art Museum), dated 1692,[5] a key work for the study of his late painting style. TTC

1 Sakakibara 1984, pp. 7–26, 33–56. For a detailed account in English of the theme in painting, see Phillips 1996.

2 Much of this account derives from the commentary written by Asano Shūgō in Chiba 2000, nos. 66–83.

3 Torii 1972–7, vol. 2, pp. 284–304, 591–4.

4 See Chiba 2000, pp. 202–8, for a discussion of Moronobu's sets of prints.

5 Chiba 2000, no. 14 (commentary by Matsuo Tomoko). The handscrolls depict the *otogi-zōshi*, not the *jōruri* version of the story and can be more directly linked to Kano school prototypes.

7

Yorimitsu Pays his Respects to Shuten-dōji (No. 10)

27.3 × 34 cm

REPRODUCED: *Ukiyo-e shūka*, vol. 1, no. 58

OTHER IMPRESSIONS: Tokyo National Museum (Chiba 2000, no. 74); MOA Museum of Art, Atami

1911.13417

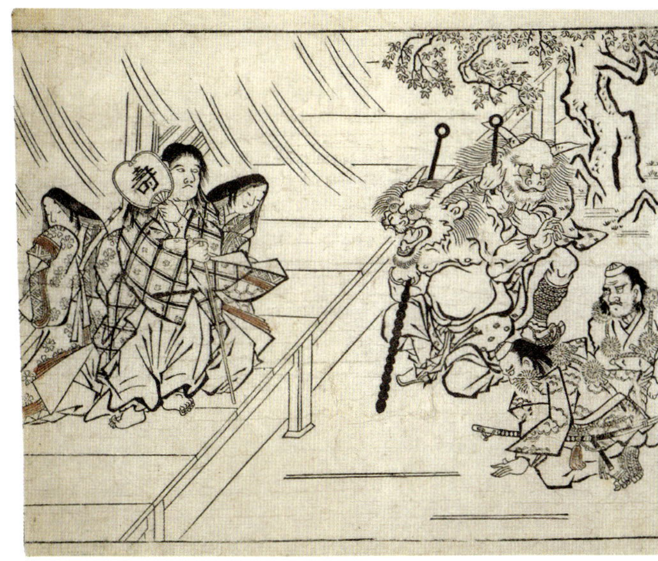

8

Yorimitsu and his Retainers Decapitate Shuten-dōji (No. 13?)

27.2 × 34.6 cm

REPRODUCED: *Ukiyo-e shūka*, vol. 1, no. 59

OTHER IMPRESSIONS: Tokyo National Museum (Chiba 2000, no. 77); MOA Museum of Art, Atami

1911.13420

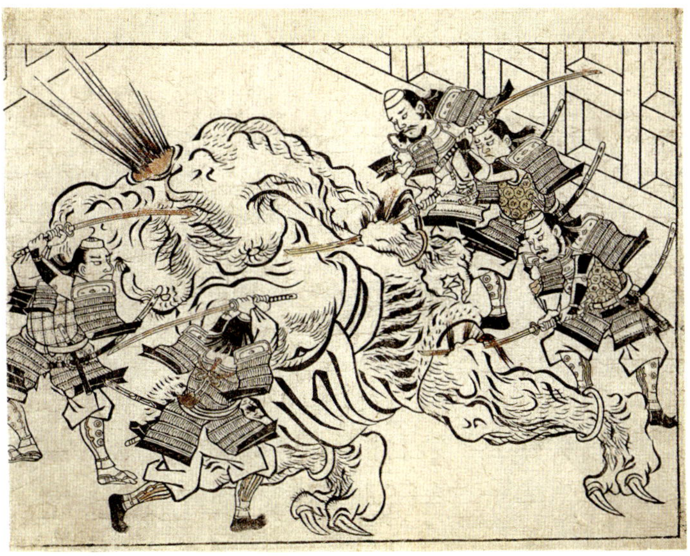

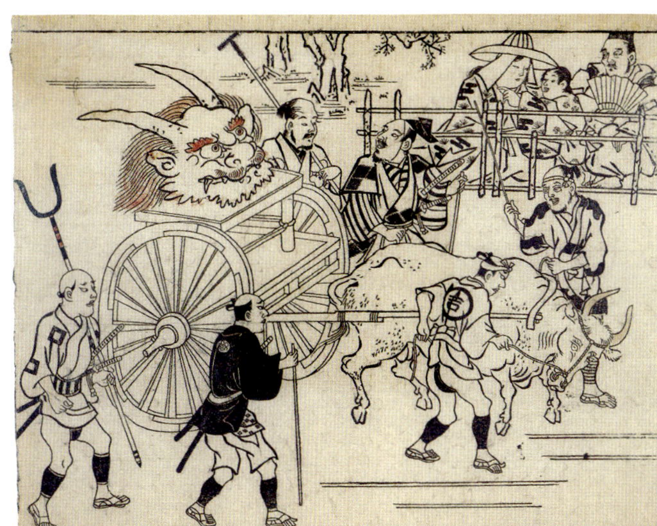

9

The Head of Shuten-dōji Paraded on an Ox-drawn Cart (No. 17?)

27.3 × 36.3 cm

OTHER IMPRESSIONS: Tokyo National Museum (Chiba 2000, no. 81); MOA Museum of Art, Atami

1911.13423

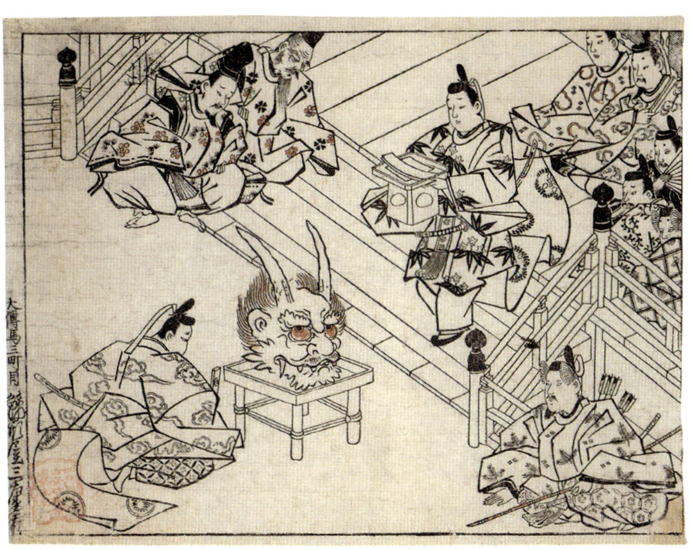

10

Yorimitsu Rewarded for Presenting Shuten-dōji's Head to the Emperor (No. 19)

27.3 × 36 cm

OTHER IMPRESSIONS: British Museum, London; Tokyo National Museum (Chiba 2000, no. 83); Chiba City Museum of Art (ibid., no. 84)

1911.13424

11

Attributed to Hishikawa Moronobu

A Guide to Love in Yoshiwara (*Yoshiwara koi no michi-biki*)

3rd month, 1678

PUBLISHER: 'Tōriabura-chō Hon-toiya kaihan' (Published by Hon-toiya at Tōriabura-chō)

woodblock-printed book, *fukuro-toji, sumizuri,* 1 vol., hand-colouring, 28 × 16.8 cm (covers)

OTHER COPIES: British Library, London (Chiba 2000, no. 107); Bibliothèque Nationale, Paris; National Diet Library, Tokyo; Yokoyama Shigeru (Suzuki 1979a; Matsudaira 1988, no. 3)

Gift of William S. and John T. Spaulding, 2000

2000.1257

A picture book of customs relating to Yoshiwara, the government-licensed pleasure quarter rebuilt on the northern outskirts of Edo after the Meireki Fire of 1657 (see cat. 4). A single-page preface is followed by twenty double-page genre illustrations, each with text above its cusped gable-shaped upper edge and, at the top of the page, a row of six crests thought to be those of leading courtesans. The book concludes with a single-page postscript and colophon. After nine illustrations showing the various routes to Yoshiwara and the modes of transport involved, we arrive in the tenth at Ōmon-guchi, the Main Gate of the quarter. The remaining ten illustrations show different ranks of brothel – *tsubone, sancha, kōshi, ageya* – and the customs of pleasure-seeking associated with each of them. The Boston copy is incomplete – it lacks the preface and three double-page illustrations – and some of the illustrations have been rearranged.[1] The Ōmon-guchi illustration, shown here, depicts courtesans and patrons (mainly samurai) in the central street of the quarter with a teahouse behind.

This publication was clearly intended as a companion to the picture book of theatre customs *Kokon yakusha monogatari* (*Tales of Actors Past and Present*) issued by the same publisher in the same month.[2] Neither volume has an artist's signature, but there is a strong concordance in terms of subject, composition and figure style between the Yoshiwara book and signed painted works of this period by Moronobu, such as the handscroll *Genre Scenes in Yoshiwara* (*Yoshiwara fūzoku zukan*; Manno Art Museum, Osaka) and the set of prints *Yoshiwara no tei* (*The Appearance of Yoshiwara, c.* 1681–4). This has led most scholars to regard these twin volumes as key works in the development of Moronobu's art.[3] TTC

1 The missing illustrations are: *Ryōgoku Bridge* (1v/2r); the right half of *Clients Going to the Pleasure Quarter on Horseback* (3v) and the left half of *Kinryūzan* (7r; the remaining halves of these two illustrations have been combined as the second double-page illustration); and *Kitchen in the Ageya* (17v/18r). The order of the two *sancha* illustrations has been reversed.

2 An incomplete copy of *Kokon yakusha monogatari*, missing the first 16 *chō*, is in the Boston collection and is mentioned in Matsudaira 1988, p. 17.

3 A dissenting voice has been raised by Satō Satoru, who identifies slight stylistic differences and warns against over-hasty attribution to Moronobu himself. Satō 1992, p. 14, and Chiba 2000, p. 17.

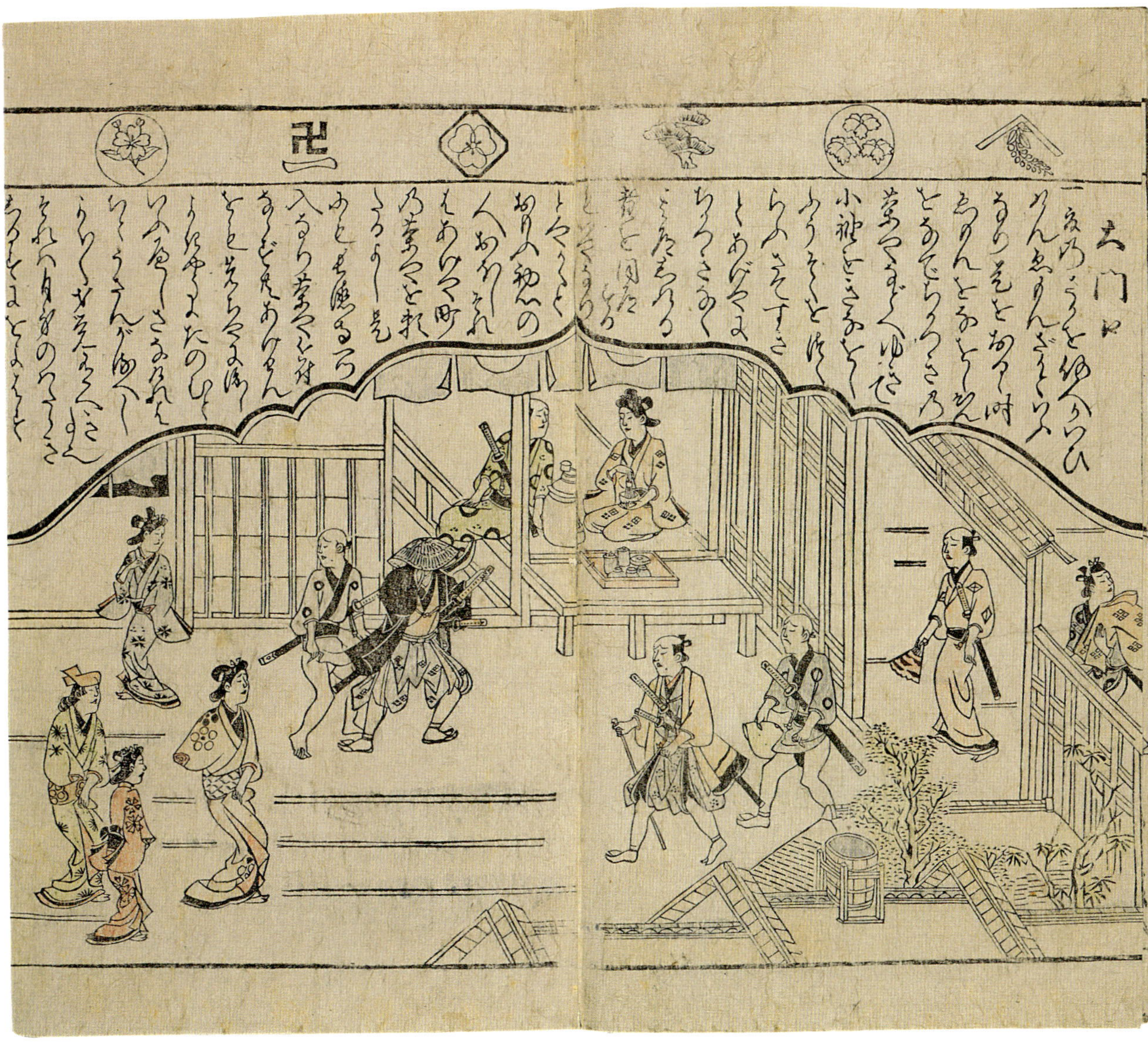

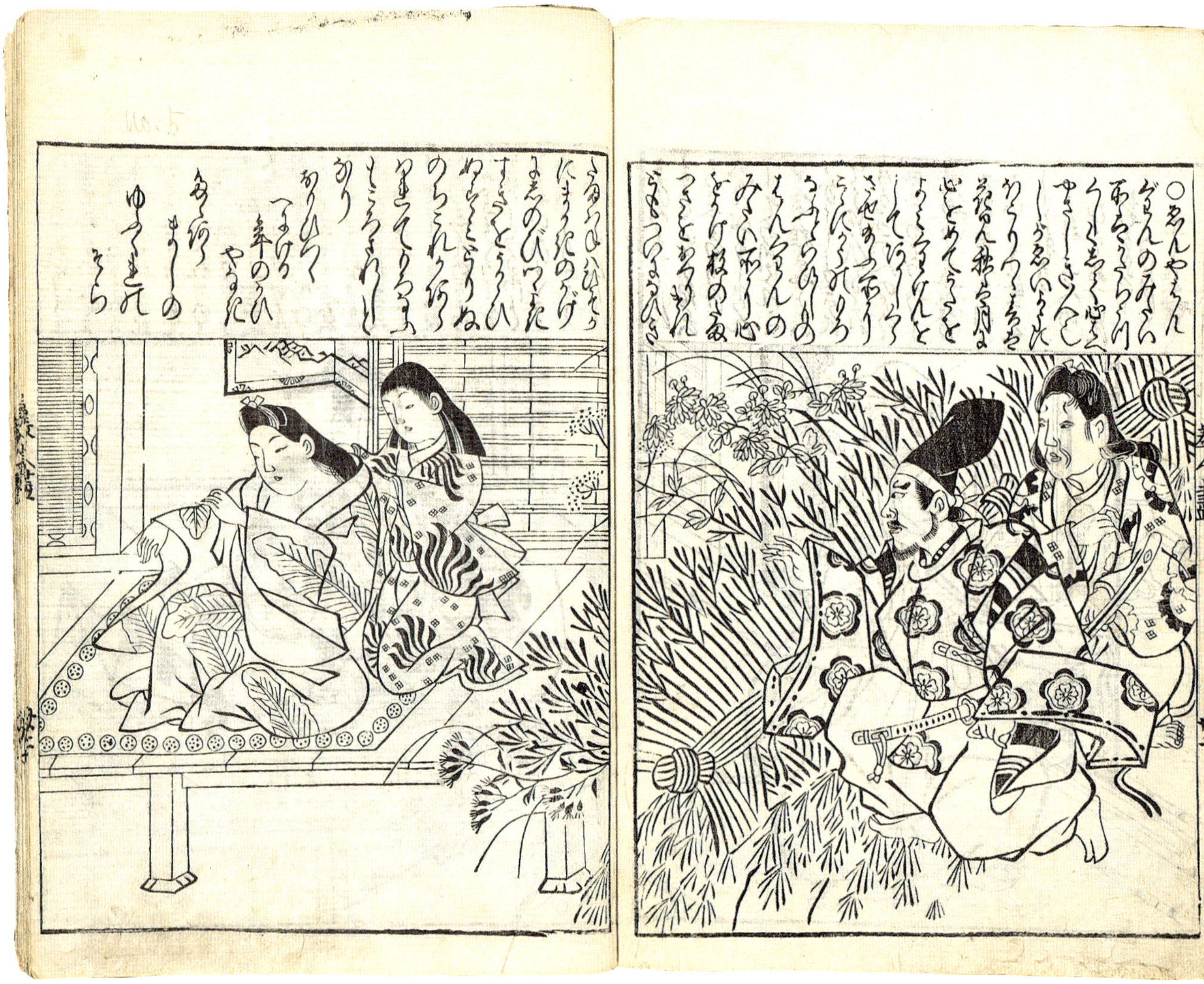

12

Hishikawa Moronobu

Pictures of Beautiful Women of Every Variety (New Edition) (*[Shinpan] Bijin-e zukushi*)

5th month, 1683

ARTIST'S SIGNATURE: 'Yamato eshi Hishikawa Kichibei hitsu' (Brush of the Yamato picture master Hishikawa Kichibei)

PUBLISHER: 'Edo Ōdenma san-chōme Urokogata-ya' (Urokogata-ya at Ōdenma san-chōme in Edo)

woodblock-printed book, *fukuro-toji, sumizuri,* 3 vols., vol. 1 sheets numbered 1–13, vol. 2 14–26, vol. 3 27–40, 39 double-page illus. (13 in each vol.), 27 × 18.6 cm (covers)

OTHER COPIES: British Museum, London (London 1980, p. 47, no. 9); New York Public Library (New York 1978, pp. 86 and 89, no. 336)

2000.1249

Moronobu's most important and original contribution to the history of Japanese book illustration was the 'picture books' (*ehon*) he developed to appeal to the pleasure-loving and increasingly literate citizens of Edo. *Pictures of Beautiful Women of Every Variety*, a work representative of Moronobu's mature style, features beautiful women in scenes drawn from a variety of tales.[1] The first three double-page illustrations present stories of Chinese origin; the rest are derived from Japanese history and classics. Brief accounts of these, often enhanced by poems, are included above the scenes.

The illustration shown here (vol. 3, 31v/32r) shows Kō no Moronao (*d.* 1351), accompanied by an elderly attendant, watching the wife of the military governor Enya Hangan. The text refers to a story, familiar from *Chronicle of the Great Peace* (*Taihei-ki*),[2] in which the arrogant warrior Moronao, serving as chief executive officer to Shogun Ashikaga Takauji (1305–58), lusted after Enya's wife. The text above the illustration mentions how the beautiful and tender-hearted woman enjoyed her prosperity by viewing flowers in spring and the moon in autumn, as well as by composing poems and making music. The love-smitten Moronao sent her many letters, but she valiantly refused to yield to his desires. Frustrated in his longing, he therefore secretly watched for an opportune moment to ravage her.

The poem by Emperor Go-Toba (1180–1239) quoted in the text is no. 1033 in *New Collection of Ancient and Modern Japanese Poems* (*Shin kokin waka-shū*). It relates to the episode depicted by expressing the feelings of unrequited love experienced by a man who waits every day for a lover who never arrives:

Omoitsutsu	Still harbouring love
heni-keru toshi no	as the years pass me by,
kai ya naki	all to no avail, it seems –
tada aramashi no	for all I can hope to see
yūgure no sora	is the evening sky alone.[3]

Moronobu's illustrations were inspired by classical sources, but he often adjusted the pictorial vocabulary to spice the tales with fashionable and erotic nuances. The brushwood fence, autumn flowers and warrior's costume, for example, are elements found in traditional Tosa school paintings of episodes from *Tale of Genji* (*Genji monogatari*). However, the artist's use of lively line work to render the figures in expressive poses and dress them in boldly patterned clothes imbues the illustration with a stylish, contemporary flair. Moronao is depicted stretching his hand towards the object of his desire. The woman, who has just finished taking a bath, is seated on a floor covering similar to those often used by courtesans in erotic pictures (*shunga*) and is putting on a light cotton robe (*yukata*) with a fashionable design of torn plantain leaves.[4] LEV

1 The book is reproduced in *Nihon fūzoku zue*, vol. 1. The first blocks made for the books are believed to have been destroyed in a fire in December 1682. New blocks were cut without altering the contents. Tokyo 1998, p. 200.

2 *Kodansha Encyclopedia*, vol. 7, pp. 274–5; vol. 4, pp. 274–5. *Chronicle of the Great Peace* was completed *c.* 1370–1.

3 Trans. in consultation with John Carpenter.

4 In *Illustrated Book of Courtesans* (cat. 25) the courtesan Naniwa wears a *furisode* with a plantain and cloud design. See also the costume of one of the elephant attendants in cat. 101.

13

Hishikawa Moronobu

Commentary on One Hundred Poems by One Hundred Poets, with Explanatory Pictures (*Hyakunin isshu zōsan-shō*)

1st month, 1678

ARTIST'S SIGNATURE: 'Bushū Gōjō no kagu Yamato eshi Hishikawa Kichibei Moronobu' (The Yamato picture master Hishikawa Kichibei Moronobu long residing below Edo Castle in Musashi Province)

PUBLISHER: 'Ōdenma-chō san-chōme Urokogata-ya shinpan' (New edition by Urokogata-ya at Ōdenma-chō san-chōme)

woodblock-printed book, *fukuro-toji, sumizuri*, 3 vols., vol. 1 numbered 1–19, 1 double-page *tobira-e*, 24 poet illus., vol. 2 numbered 20–44, 48 poet illus., vol. 3 numbered 45–59, 28 poet illus., hand-colouring in light colours, 27.2 × 19 cm (covers)

OTHER COPIES: British Library, London (London 1993, pp. 490–1, nos. 443–4); Kyūshū University (Kyūshū Bunka Kenkyūjo); Tōhoku University (Kano Bunko); Miyagi-ken Toshokan (Date Bunko); Kumagaya Shiritsu Toshokan; Art Institute of Chicago (Chicago 1931, pp. 102–4); Atomi Gakuen Tanki Daigaku Toshokan (Mostow 1996)

source unknown, 2000

2000.1252

Moronobu often called himself a *yamato eshi*, stating that he was an artist of the courtly Yamato-e tradition. Shortly before developing the genre of 'picture books' (*ehon*), which introduced classical tales in digested form, including *Pictures of Beautiful Women of Every Variety* (1683; cat. 12), he illustrated a few edifying publications of classical Japanese prose and poetry with explanatory comments (cat. 14 is another). The illustrations provided by Moronobu for the present example, containing the set of 100 *waka* selected by Fujiwara Teika (1162–1241), were conservative in conception. Moronobu respectfully relied on the Tosa-style poet portraits (*kasen-e*) included in the pioneering, early 17th-century *One Hundred Poems by One Hundred Poets* (*Hyakunin isshu*),[1] a Saga book (see cat. 14) that in turn was based on a long painting tradition originating in the Kamakura period (1185–1333).

As a modern artist, Moronobu was intent on arousing the interest of ordinary townsmen. He therefore conceived a visually stimulating layout and made slight adjustments to his models in order to express the character of the poets and clarify the meaning of their poems. In his image of Kisen Hōshi (seen here on the right), for example, he noted that Kisen's poem contained a phrase with a pivot syllable *u* alluding to 'a bitter / grievous world' ('yo o u') and expressed the monk's world-weariness by drawing his collar higher and adding wrinkles to his forehead. Depicting Kisen in a compact, seated pose, Moronobu showed him dressed in ample robes that suggest a tired, withering body underneath. Similarly, when portraying the poet Ono no Komachi (on the left), who in her poem laments her vanishing beauty, Moronobu had her hold the fan in front of her face instead of in her hand near the floor as in the Saga illustration.

The 100 poets are each introduced with a short biography and sometimes with an abbreviated lineage. The last sheets of the third volume list the poets according to their official rank and social position. Each of the 100 *waka* poems is accompanied by explanatory headnotes derived from a commentary by the learned warrior Hosokawa Fujitaka (Yūsai; 1534–1610),[2] as revised and supplemented by his student Nakanoin Michikatsu (1556–1610), a member of the Saga art community.

Catering to a late 17th-century fashion, Moronobu devoted part of each page to images of the poems (*uta-e*).[3] Moronobu's 'poem-picture' of Kisen's *waka* shows the monk meditating in a retreat in the Uji mountains near the Uji River. The image alludes to the second meaning of the pivotal syllable *u*, which literally implies 'weariness' or 'grief': 'uji-yama to / hito wa iu nari' (I hear people call it Uji, hill / of one weary of the world).[4] Moronobu pictured the melancholy Ono no Komachi leaning on an armrest gazing at cherry blossoms just past full bloom in a garden. They are about to be succeeded by the new green leaves. LEV

1 Mori 1981, pp. 80–3. The poet portraits with corresponding poems from the Saga-bon copy in Atomi Gakuen Tanki Daigaku Toshokan are reproduced in Mostow 1996. According to Mostow, the copy in the Tōyō Bunko is reproduced in Shimazu 1969.

2 Yūsai's commentary, first recorded as 'Yūsai shō' in 1596, was based on lectures by Sanjōnishi no Saneki (1511–79). Several woodblock editions of the commentary were issued, starting in 1631. The text in Moronobu's book is written in a mixture of Chinese characters and *kana* script (*hiragana-majiri*).

3 By the third quarter of the 17th century Edo-based Kano school artists, such as Kano Tan'yū (1602–74), were producing *uta-e* related to the poems for patrons of the samurai class. Furthermore, catalogues from 1671, 1675 and 1691 record editions of *One Hundred Poems by One Hundred Poets* featuring explanatory pictures 'setting out the heart of the poems in pictures'. Moronobu's work is the earliest extant example. Mostow 1996, pp. 97–8.

4 Ibid., pp. 165–6.

5 Ibid., pp. 168–70, and, for a discussion of the numerous possible English translations of Komachi's poem, pp. 58–86.

6 Ibid.

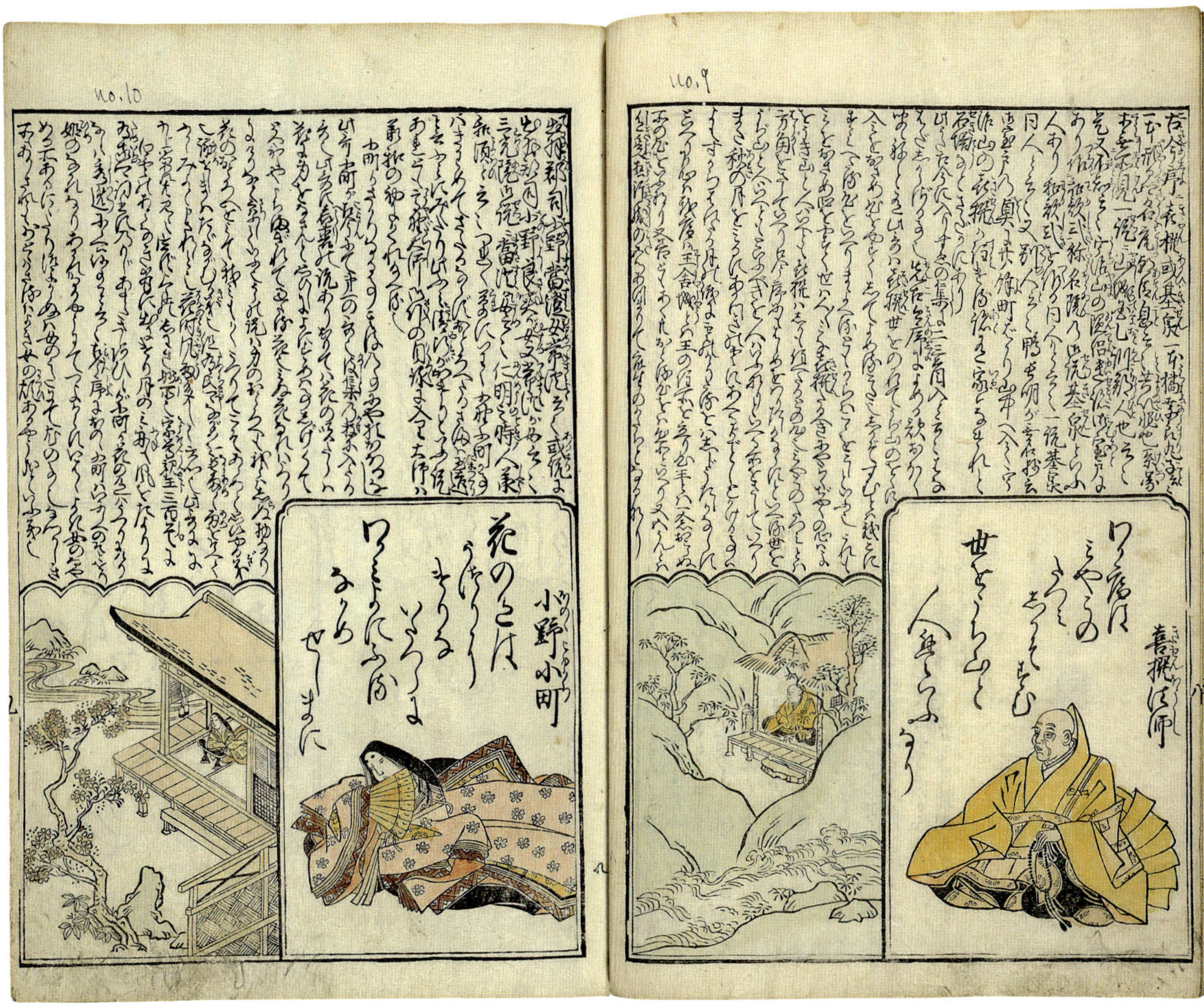

Hana no iro wa
utsurinikeri na
itazura ni
waga mi yo ni furu
nagameseshi ma ni

The colour of the flowers
has faded indeed
in vain
have I passed through the world
while gazing at the falling rains.[5]

ONO NO KOMACHI, active *c.* 833–50; poem no. 9

Waga io wa
Miyako no tatsumi
shika zo sumu
yo o Uji-yama to
hito wa iu nari

My hut is to
the capital's south-east
and thus I live.
People call it 'Uji, hill
of one weary of the world'.[6]

KISEN HŌSHI, mid-9th century; poem no. 8

14
Hishikawa Moronobu
Tales of Ise with Headnotes (*Ise Monogatari tōsho shō*)

3rd month, 1679

ARTIST'S SIGNATURE: 'Hishikawa Kichibei'

PUBLISHER: 'Matsue'

woodblock-printed book, *fukuro-toji*, *sumizuri*, originally 2 or 3 *satsu*, rebound as 1 vol., part one 22 sheets, numbered 1–23 (8 and 9 combined), 2 *tobira-e*, 12 illus., parts two and three 28 sheets, numbered 1–28, 1 *tobira-e*, 15 illus., 27.5 × 19.5 cm (covers)

OTHER COPIES: British Library, London (London 1993, pp. 323–4); Art Institute of Chicago (Chicago 1931, pp. 95–6)

William Sturgis Bigelow Collection, 2000

2000.1253

Moronobu's *Tales of Ise with Headnotes* can be appreciated best in the context of the book-publishing industry and its efforts to disseminate classic native prose and poetry to townsmen during the 17th century. Printed books and movable type looted from Korea in 1593 by Hideyoshi's generals stimulated the development of Japanese book publishing. Emperors Go-Yōzei and Go-Mizuno'o first issued 'Imperial editions' (*Keichō chokuhan*) using a wooden movable type font. In the early 17th century financial sponsorship by political leaders, including Tokugawa Ieyasu (1542–1616), and private and commercial publishers rapidly established a flourishing publishing industry, first in Kamigata and then in Edo. From *c.* 1620 publishers began to revive block printing, since this made it easier to reproduce quickly a variety of calligraphic styles and to issue new editions of popular books. By the mid-17th century they had stopped using 'old movable printing type' (*ko-katsuji*).

Most volumes printed between 1594 and 1621 were Chinese classics, medical books or dictionaries. However, it was the de luxe, privately published 'Saga-bon' (Saga press books; also called Soan-bon or Kōetsu-bon) of Japanese classics that heralded the most significant developments. These early movable type books were produced collaboratively in the art community at Saga, near Kyoto, by the calligrapher, potter and tea master Hon'ami Kōetsu (1558–1637), who acted as designer, and his student, the wealthy, cultivated merchant Suminokura Soan (1571–1632), who supervised the printing. Published in 1608, the Saga *Tales of Ise* (*Ise monogatari*), a poetic narrative (*uta-monogatari*) thought to have been composed in the 10th century by an unknown courtier, proved to be extremely influential. The two-volume book was not only the earliest printed version of the Ise tales, but also the first illustrated secular Japanese publication.[1]

The text of the Saga *Tales of Ise* was based on the definitive early compilation by the poet Fujiwara no Teika (1162–1241) and collated by the courtier–scholar Nakanoin Michikatsu (1556–1610). Elegant and easily read calligraphy (believed to be by Kōetsu) was reproduced with fonts of movable type consisting not only of Chinese characters, but also of native *kana*. The illustrations similarly crystallised traditional Nara-e and Tosa-e style paintings into monochrome woodblock-printed scenes rendered with clear outlines, stylised clouds and characters depicted in the 'dash-for-an-eye, hook-for-a-nose' (*hikime kagibana*) convention and seen in roofless rooms from a high view point (*fukinuki yatai*). Initially issued for the enjoyment of a small circle of contemporary connoisseurs, the Saga *Tales of Ise* eventually reached a wider public, being reprinted at least nine times by *c.* 1630.[2]

Tales of Ise, which includes 125 narrative episodes with 209 poems, recounts the love affairs and poetic reflections of 'a man of old', believed to have been modelled on the courtier–poet Ariwara no Narihira (*c.* 825–80).[3] Increased familiarity with the text of the Saga-bon helped establish the images both as

1 For reproductions of all the illustrations and captions, see Strauss and Bronze 1979, pp. 11–60. Other early illustrated (as opposed to decorated) Saga press publications were *One Hundred Poems by One Hundred Poets* (mentioned in cat. 13), *The Thirty-six Poet Immortals* (*Sanjū-rokkasen*) and *The Twenty-four Paragons of Filial Piety* (*Nijūshi-kō*).

2 For further information about Saga-bon, and especially the *Tales of Ise*, see Rumpf 1932; Katagiri 1996, pp. 171–76; Hillier 1987, pp. 41–50; London 1993, pp. 313–17; Chicago 1931, pp. 14–17; Kornicki 1998, pp. 131–2; Kawase 1932, pp. 23–41, nos. 7–27; Nagata 1989; and Philadelphia 2000, pp. 56–60, 176, no. 38.

3 Narihira's legendary status was due to the inclusion of his passionate verses in the early 10th-century *Collection of Ancient and Modern Japanese Poems* (*Kokin waka-shū*) and to his status as one of the Thirty-six Poet Immortals. For a discussion of Narihira's identification as the 'hero' of *Tales of Ise*, see Bowring 1992.

4 Reproduced in Yoshida 1984, pp. 38–9. For in-depth studies of the history of *Tales of Ise* illustrations, see Sayre 1979 and Itō 1984.

5 Nakamachi 2000, pp. 55–82; Shinoda 1995, pp. 7–35.

6 McCullough 1968, p. 71. See cat. 136 for another depiction of this scene.

7 The Saga-bon 'Journey to the East' illustration is reproduced in Hillier 1987, p. 45, fig. 9.

8 Chicago 1931, pp. 95–6; London 1993, pp. 323–4.

visual symbols for the episodes and as models for later woodblock-printed illustrations of the classic. Subsequent 17th-century commercial editions of *Tales of Ise*, such as a *tanroku-bon* from the Kanei era (1624–44)[4] and Moronobu's *Tales of Ise with Headnotes*, still respectfully copied and/or slightly refashioned the codified scenes. Subsequent familiarity with *Tales of Ise* inspired 18th and 19th-century ukiyo-e artists to draw parody pictures of the scenes.[5]

One of the most popular episodes in *Tales of Ise* is no. 9, 'Journey to the East' (*Azuma-kudari*), which tells of Narihira's 'exile' from Kyoto. The image representing this episode shows the courtier and a few attendants passing Mount Fuji on their journey eastwards. Narihira, on horseback, pauses to look at the mountain and to recite a poem expressing his amazement that its peak is still covered with snow in the fifth month, i.e. late June/early July:

Toki shiranu	Fuji is a mountain
yama wa Fuji no ne	that knows no seasons.
itsu tote ka	What time does it take this for,
ka-no-ko madara ni	that it should be dappled
yuki no fururan	with fallen snow?[6]

As already noted, Moronobu's illustrations in *Tales of Ise with Headnotes*, complementing the tales themselves and the scholarly commentary that appears above the text and illustrations, show a respectful indebtedness to the iconic Saga book images. His 'Journey to the East' illustration, for example, similarly shows Mount Fuji rising 'as tall as twenty Mount Hieis piled on top of one another and shaped like a salt-cone' from a cloudy, mountainous landscape in the Yamato-e style. Furthermore, Narihira's clothes are depicted with similar patterns and the horse is also shown decorated with tassels.[7]

Closer inspection, however, reveals Moronobu's scene to be somewhat more descriptive than its Saga counterpart, to be more concerned, in ukiyo-e fashion, with the figures and their gestures. The Saga illustration shows the comparatively large figure of Narihira as a mysterious courtier, seen from the back as he gazes at Mount Fuji in the distance. Moronobu, on the other hand, depicts the same courtier awkwardly twisting his body towards the viewer as he turns to look at the peak in amazement. Moronobu shows three, instead of two, attendants and eliminates the conventionalised clouds in the foreground to reveal the legs of the walking figures and the horse.

Moronobu's *Tales of Ise with Headnotes* also differs from the Saga publication in the number of its illustrations: a selection of 27 famous scenes as against 48 in the earlier book.[8] On the other hand, Moronobu includes original introductory illustrations (*tobira-e*) evoking settings pervaded by classical aesthetics. The Boston copy has two such extra illustrations in part one: one is believed to show Ariwara no Narihira at his desk; the other depicts noblewomen, perhaps including Lady Ise (*c.* 875 – *c.* 938). The single introductory illustration in part two shows deer in an autumn landscape. LEV

さしうつぶきのよめりしひ
あづまえびすかれてあらばゞ
まことみえし意ときこし
○さればよし　さりけり
○あひ見てハ心ひとつを
かはしまの水のながれてたえじとぞ
[illegible]
[illegible]
[illegible]
○[illegible]
[illegible]
女のもとへいひやればおもひ
○秋の夜のちよを一夜に
[illegible]
[illegible]
[illegible]
二十三 昔田舎わたらひ
常に田舎わたらひしける
[illegible]
○此女　まことの娘
○となりの男　ありひとし
○つゝゐつゝ　[illegible]

てありけれど。男ハこの女をこそえめとおもふ。女ハ此男
をとおもひつゝ。おやのあはすれどもきかでなんありける。さてこ
のとなりのおとこのもとよりかくなん
つゝ井つのゐづゝにかけしまろがたけすぎにけらしないもみざるまに
返し
くらべこしふりわけがみもかたすぎぬきみならずしてたれかあぐべき
などいひ〱て。つゐにほいのごとくあひにけり。さて年
ごろふるほどに。女おやなくたよりなくなるまゝに
もろともにいふかひなくてあらんやはとて。かうちの国
たかやすのこほりに。いきかよふ所いできにけり。さりけれど。このもとの
女あしとおもへるけしきもなくて。いだしやりければ。男
こと心ありてかゝるにやあらんとおもひうたがひて
ざいのなかにかくれゐて。かうちへいぬるかほにて

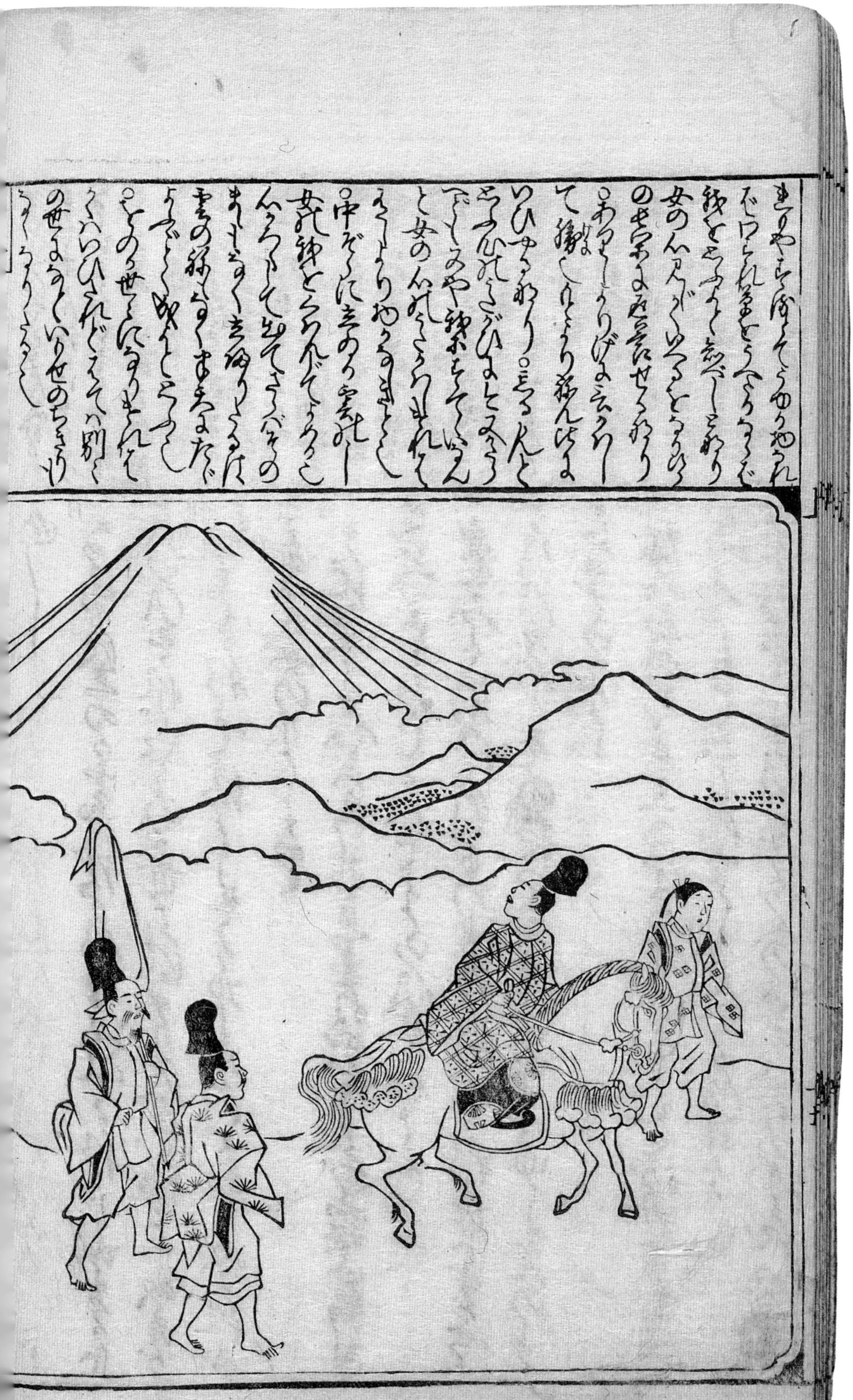

15

Hishikawa Moronobu

Kosode in a Full-length Mirror (*Kosode no sugatami*)

3rd month, 1682

ARTIST'S SIGNATURE: 'Yamato eshi Hishikawa kore [o] egaku' (This was painted by the Yamato picture master Hishikawa)

PUBLISHER: 'Ōdenma-chō san-chōme Urokogata-ya' (Urokogata-ya at Ōdenma-chō san-chōme)

woodblock-printed book, *fukuro-toji*, *sumizuri*, 1 vol., incomplete, 15 sheets (numbered but some pages out of order), 21.2 × 15.2 cm (covers)

OTHER COPY: Tokyo University of Arts and Music; Tenri University Library; Pulverer Collection, Cologne (Chiba 2000, no. 131)

Gift of Mrs Jared K. Morse, 2000

2000.1260

1 Nagasaki 1992, p. 96.

2 Ibid.

Born into a family of textile embroiderers, Hishikawa Moronobu paid close attention to the garments worn by the figures in his paintings and prints. He also produced a small number of woodblock-printed *kosode* pattern books. On the left-hand pages of *Kosode in a Full-length Mirror* Moronobu presents the individual designs in the standard, simplified form of the back of a robe as a foil for the sumptuous graphic textile designs in demand by fashion-conscious Edo consumers. The text extending across each double-page spread discusses at great length the motifs and the various dyeing and embroidery techniques required in the creation of each robe.

Moronobu includes images of women and young men – contemporary idealised fashion models – on the right-hand pages of the book. The textile historian Nagasaki Iwao has pointed out that by adding these figures Moronobu adopts the scheme pioneered by the slightly earlier artist of *On hiinagata manjo shū* (*Kosode Book: Collection of Ten Thousand Women*).[1] The preface to that volume states that the intention of such pictures was to ensure 'that the customer [could] choose [a design] that suit[ed] her own appearance'.[2] In *Kosode in a Full-length Mirror*, though, the models seem to have been included more for visual than practical reasons, for the robes on the figures bear little relation to those on the facing pages. ANM

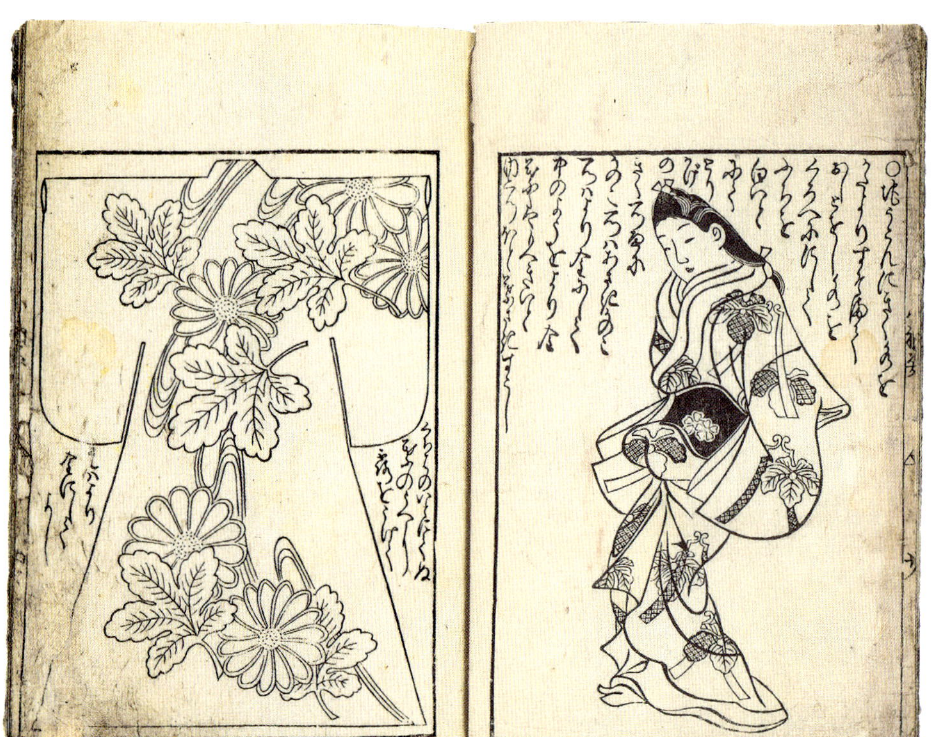

16

Attributed to Hishikawa Moronobu

Mirror of Patterns of the Four Seasons for Various Occasions (*Shiki moyō shorei e-kagami*)

c. 1681–4

woodblock-printed book, *fukuro-toji*, *sumizuri*, 1 of 3 vols., incomplete, 13 unnumbered sheets, 18.4 × 14 cm (covers)

OTHER COPIES: Mitsui Bunko (Osaka 1998, no. 250); Tokyo National Museum; Urushiyama Matashirō Collection

source unknown, 2000

2000.1259

From the time of the publication of the first woodblock-printed pattern book (*hiinagata-bon*) in 1666, fashionable women turned to such compendia for information on the textile designs then in vogue. The three-volume *Mirror of Patterns of the Four Seasons for Various Occasions* (the Boston Museum has only one volume) provides both information about the rules of decorum for women and illustrations of individual robes. Though unsigned, the work has been attributed to Hishikawa Moronobu. On facing pages the artist has presented individual *kosode* on lacquer clothes-stands. Such racks were used not just for hanging up garments, but also for displaying them as decorative objects.

The two designs illustrated here embody an interplay between word and image. On the robe on the right, two large snowflakes and a pattern of hail arranged across the shoulders and back dominate the composition. A sinuous line of Japanese phonetic characters for the word 'arare' (hail), extending from the middle right down to the border of *asa-no-ha* patterns, makes explicit the wintry subject. Similarly, the Chinese characters reading 'Noda' are incorporated into the wisteria patterns, in reference to the famous flowers of Noda in Osaka, which are also described in the inscription on the right.

The illustrations in the book describe the techniques used to decorate the textiles. The artist carefully details the dappled tie-dyed surface of the snowflakes and the characters, for instance, and in the inscriptions he makes clear that the *kosode* would also have been embroidered. ANM

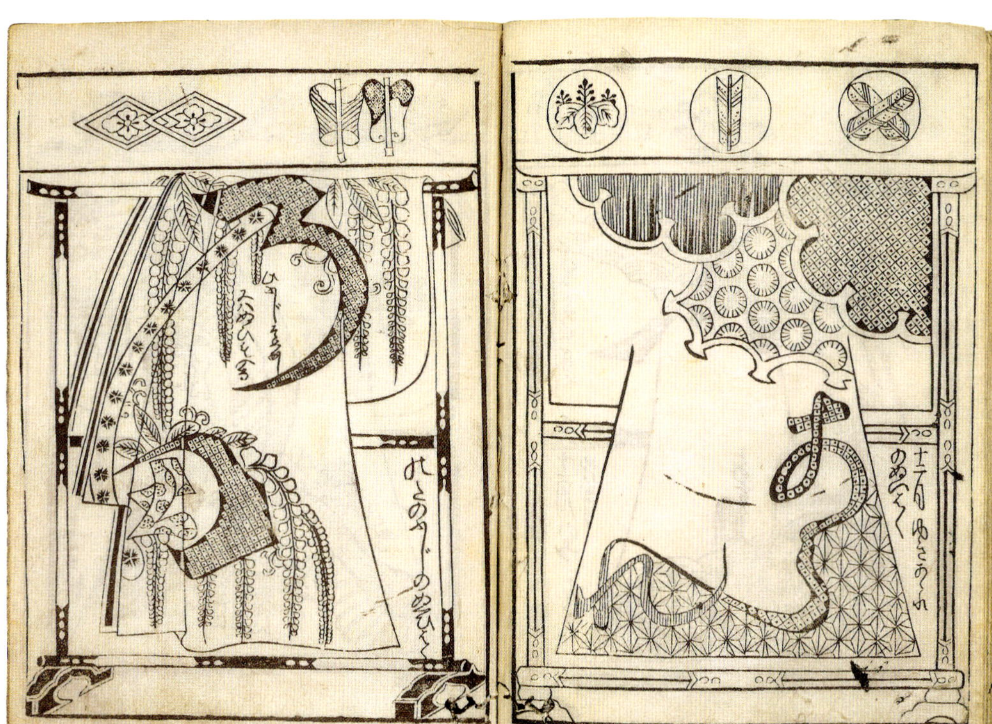

17

Hishikawa Morohira

Street Performers Presenting the Lion Dance

c. 1688–1711

ARTIST'S SIGNATURE:
'Yamato-e Hishikawa Morohira hitsu'
(Yamato picture by Hishikawa Morohira)

ARTIST'S SEAL: 'Hishikawa'

hanging scroll, ink, colour and gold on silk,
25.9 × 38.2 cm

REPRODUCED: Boston 2000, vol. 1, no. 48

William Sturgis Bigelow Collection, 1911

11.7621

Lunging forward and rasping a wooden stick (*sasara*) with a strip of bamboo, a man in the lower centre of this lively painting extemporaneously creates a sacred space and draws the red lion-masked figure into a dance. Musical accompaniment is provided by a small band of drummers and a flautist, who circle around the pair. On the far right stands a man bearing a halberd festooned with strips of white paper and wearing a mask with a dark complexion, long nose and beard. Representing Sarutahiko no Mikoto, a Shintō god, this figure will have led the way and expelled evil spirits by stamping on the ground.

The lion dance was introduced from China to Japan during the 8th century as part of theatrical performances with masks given at Buddhist temples (*gigaku*). It was soon incorporated into native Shintō ceremonies as part of the entertainment provided for the gods (*kagura*). Over the centuries the dance also came to be performed in the street by travelling troupes that drew small crowds wherever they went. The 17th-century writer Ihara Saikaku described one such group in his novel *Five Women who Loved Love* (*Kōshoku gonin onna*), noting: 'the girls were fascinated by it and abandoned all their other amusements to crowd around, applaud and cry for encore after encore, lest the entertainment stop too soon'.[1]

The dance is the subject of a small number of early ukiyo-e paintings and prints by Hishikawa Moronobu and Sugimura Jihei.[2] In these the artists capture the interaction of the troupe with townspeople attracted to the performance. By contrast, in the present composition Hishikawa Morohira isolates the figures on a neutral ground so that it is the movements of the dancer and the musicians that create the rhythms of visual interest. ANM

1 Saikaku 1956, p. 57.

2 Sugimura Jihei, *Lion Dance*, *c.* 1685, *ōban yoko-e*, Portland Art Museum, Oregon, reproduced in Chicago, p. 1971, p. 43. Hishikawa Moronobu, *The Northern Quarter and the Kabuki Stage* (*Hokurō oyobi engeki zukan*), 1672–89, handscroll, Tokyo National Museum, and *Artisans of Various Trades* (*Shokunin zukushi zukan*), *c.* 1684–94, set of two handscrolls, British Museum, London, reproduced in Chiba 2000, nos. 5, 13.

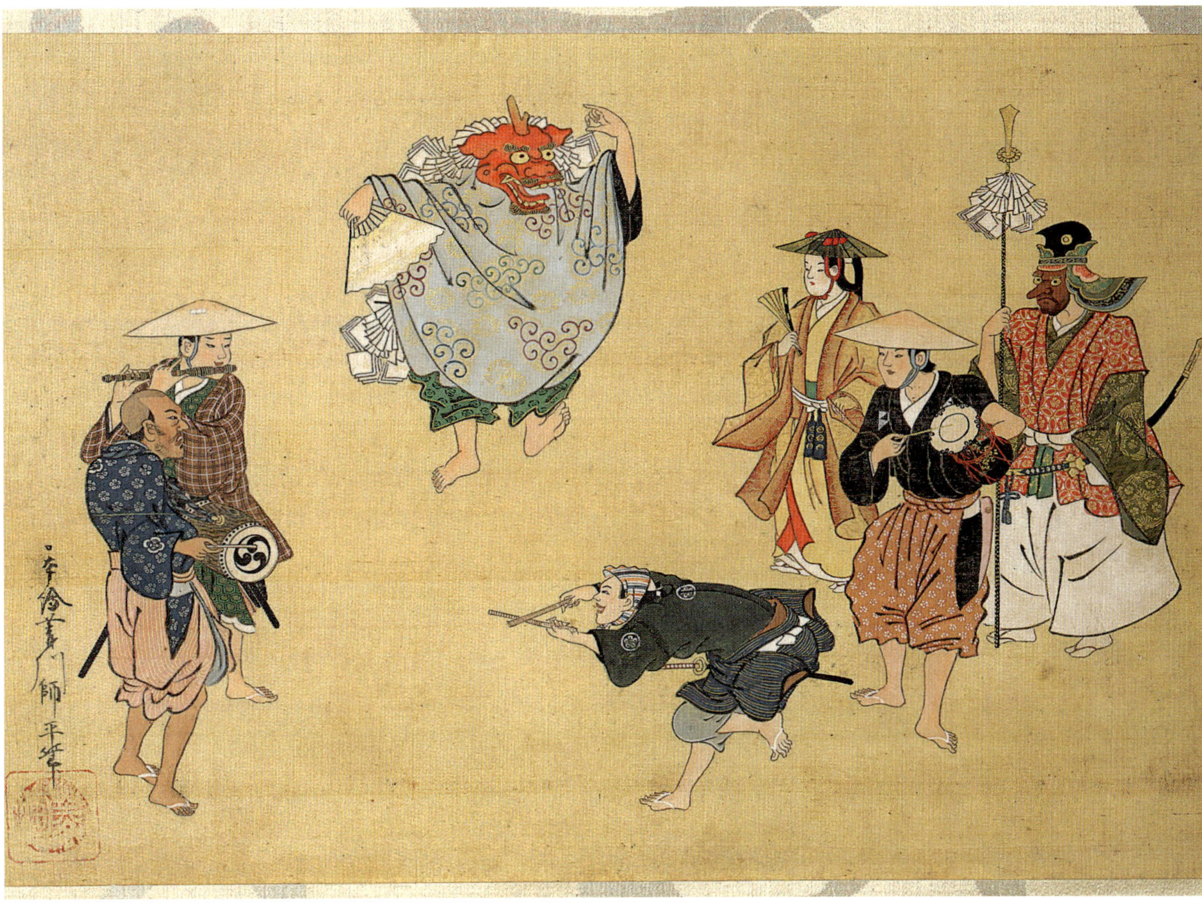

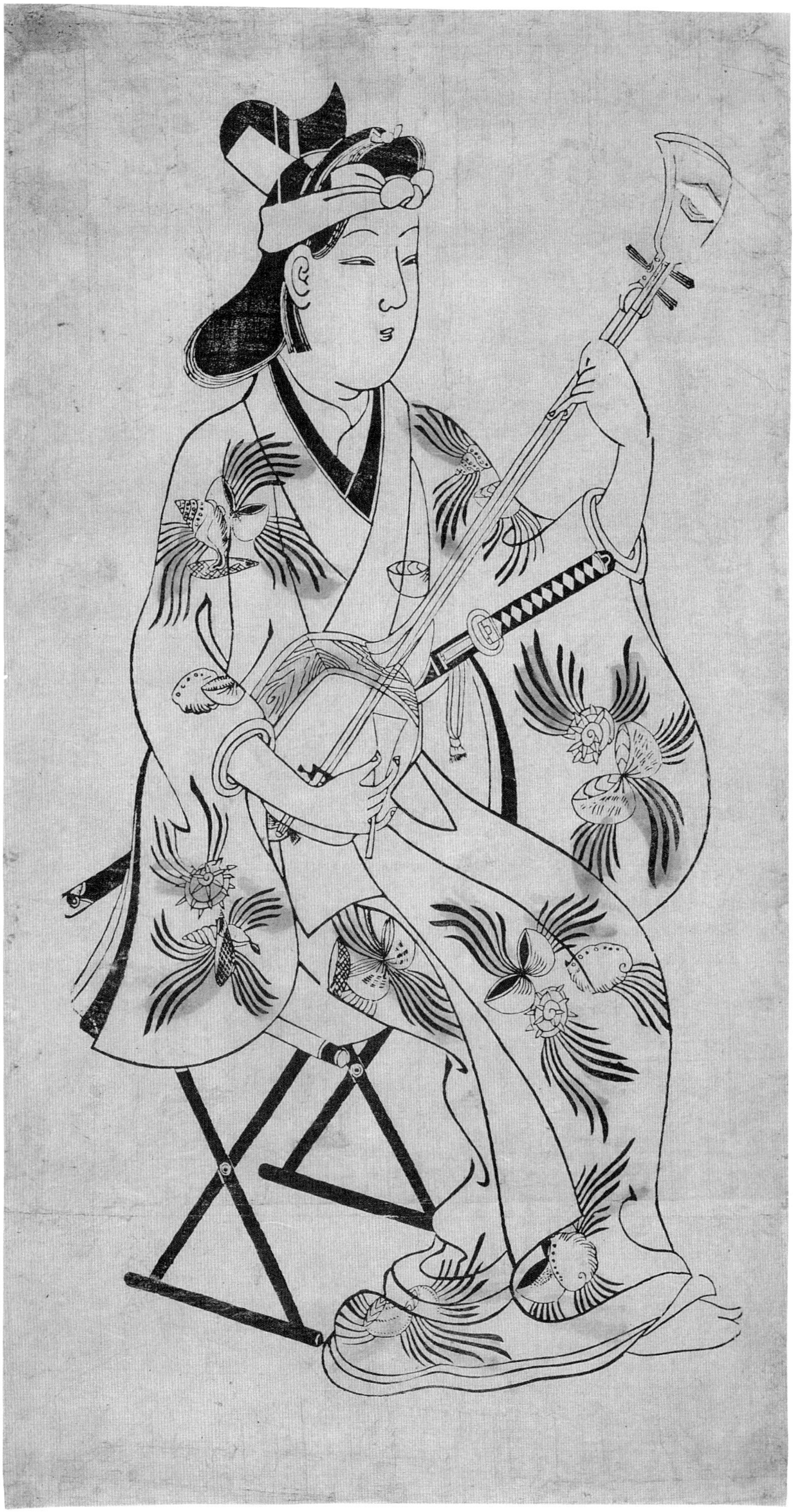

18

Anonymous (Hishikawa school)

Young Kabuki Actor Playing the Shamisen

1680s or 1690s

woodblock, *ō-ōban, tanroku-e*, 58.7 × 31.6 cm

REPRODUCED: Michener 1959, p. 26; Lane 1978, p. 43, fig. 25; Lane 1981, p. 28, fig. 1; *Ukiyo-e shūka*, vol. 1, no. 53

William Sturgis Bigelow Collection, 1911

11.13156

1 Lane 1978, p. 43, fig. 25; idem 1981, p. 28, fig. 1.

2 Lane 1981a, p. 5.

3 Ibid., p. 42, fig. 6.

4 Conversation with Asano Shūgō. Asano suggested that the manner of drawing the double eyelid is closest to the work of Hishikawa Moroshige, but that the print is not by him.

A young kabuki actor is seated on a folding stool, playing the shamisen. The bold pattern of seashells and wrack on his *furisode* has been enlivened with simple *tanroku* (red-lead and green) hand-colouring. Although the costume and most of the hairstyle is feminine, the shaved top of the head, just visible behind the forelock, indicates that the actor is a man. The scarf knotted around the forehead tells us that he is a young trainee kabuki actor (*iro-ko*) of an age at which his acting speciality had not yet been decided and he might be expected to work as a male prostitute in one of the theatre teahouses. Normally, a shamisen-player would perform kneeling on the floor, so perhaps we should imagine him as one of a row of identically clad young men seated onstage to provide an alluring musical accompaniment to some lively dance sequence. The hexagonal crest on the 'lobster tail' (*ebio*) of the shamisen is damaged, so the emblem inside, which might have provided a clue to the player's identity, has been obliterated.

The dating of this print has presented difficulties. Richard Lane has linked it stylistically to the 'Kanbun Master', the collective name he gives to Moronobu's anonymous predecessors working in the Kanbun era (1661–73) – most of them before 1672, the year of the first signed work by Moronobu – and has dated it to the early 1670s. He admits, however, that it is a 'borderline work' that could be by either the Kanbun Master or Moronobu.[1] Since there are no dated signed works by Moronobu from 1672 to 1677, and because Moronobu is thought to have settled in Edo by the beginning of the Kanbun era at the latest, it is most likely that there are early unsigned works by him in existence that fall within the Kanbun Master attribution. In his 1981 article on prints by Sugimura Jihei and others in the grand *ō-ōban* format – that of the present work – Lane observes that 'the fashion for these larger prints seems to date largely from about the time of Moronobu's retirement, the late 1680s'.[2] Lane reproduces another unsigned print, *Young Man Walking* (*Yūho wakashu*), which he attributes to the Moronobu school and dates to the mid-1690s.[3] To the present writer, *Young Man Walking* looks highly similar in style to the Boston *Young Kabuki Actor Playing the Shamisen*. Although the *tanroku* colouring is reminiscent of early 17th-century illustrated novels, the attribution to the Hishikawa school proposed here is accompanied by a provisional, relatively imprecise dating to the 1680s or 1690s.[4] TTC

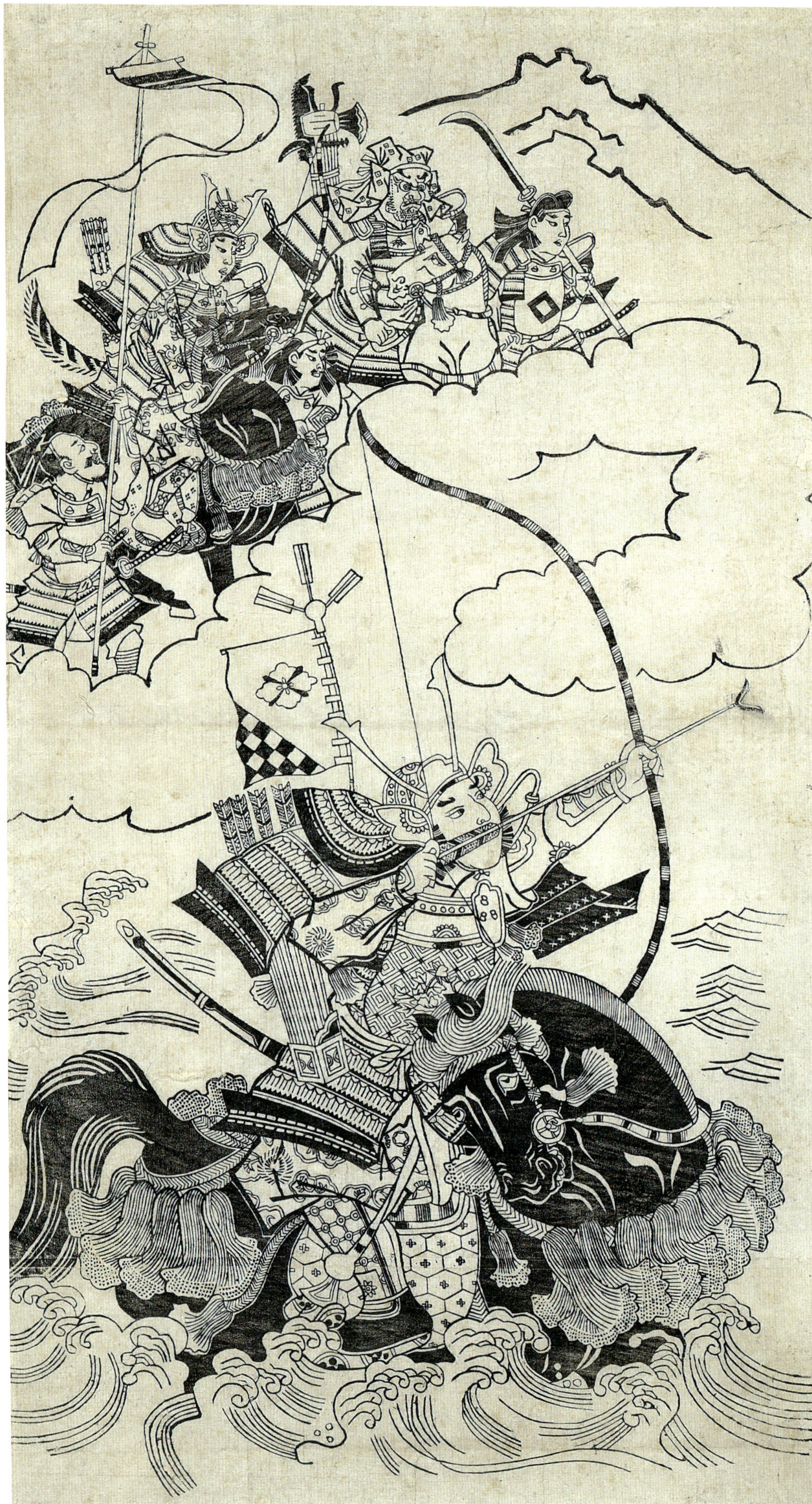

19

Attributed to Sugimura Jihei

Nasu no Yoichi Drawing his Bow

1680s or 1690s

woodblock, *ō-ōban, sumizuri-e,* 55.9 × 30.9 cm

REPRODUCED: Horioka 1974, p. 19, fig. 39; Lane 1981a, fig. 2; *Ukiyo-e shūka,* vol. 1, no. 61

Asiatic Curator's Fund, 1955

55.380

1 *Nihon denki,* pp. 668–9, s.v. 'Nasu no Yoichi'. Lane 1981a, pp. 4–5, does not accept that the print forms a dipytych with the Boston work reproduced below.

2 Ross Collection. Works from this collection are not available for loan.

3 Chicago 1955, Moronobu no. 13.

4 Lane 1957a, p. 350.

5 *Ukiyo-e shūka,* vol. 4, no. 74 (commentary by Suzuki Jūzō).

6 Lane 1981a, p. 5.

7 Torii 1972–7, vol. 3, p. 511. The present print is unlikely to have been produced as early as 1678.

This is probably the left sheet of a large-format diptych depicting the renowned feat of archery performed by the Minamoto warrior Nasu no Yoichi at the battle of Yashima in 1185.[1] As recounted in volume eleven of the war chronicle *Tale of the Heike* (*Heike monogatari*), the youthful Yoichi vowed to break his bow and commit ritual suicide if he failed to hit a fan hoisted provocatively on a ship of the opposing Taira fleet, anchored far offshore, from his position on the shore. Watching from behind are the Minamoto general Yoshitsune (left), who ordered Yoichi to accept the challenge, and Yoshitsune's loyal henchman, the warrior monk Benkei (right). An impression of the right-hand sheet, with hand-colouring in orange, yellow, pink and grey, also in the Boston Museum (reproduced this page),[2] shows the eighteen or nineteen-year-old Lady Tamamushi signalling the challenge with her fan from the prow of the Taira ship, watched by a Taira warrior and (perhaps) the young Emperor Antoku. *Tale of the Heike* described the target fan as having the gold disc of the sun on a red background. Yoichi's arrow shattered the rivet, and fragments of the fan sinking into the waves symbolised the impending doom of the Taira army.

The attribution of the right sheet of the diptych to Moronobu was still upheld in the Chicago 'Primitives' catalogue of 1955.[3] Richard Lane was the first to suggest, in 1957, that the work was 'probably by Sugimura Jihei' and dated from *c.* 1692–5.[4] Suzuki Jūzō, writing in 1979, agreed that the use of angular lines for the drapery is consistent with Jihei's style,[5] and the attribution is now generally accepted. Another distinctive stylistic feature is the curved, bushy eyebrows of the warriors, not found in other works firmly attributed to this artist. The difference in scale between the figures of Yoichi and Lady Tamamushi may have been intended to suggest the distance of the Taira ship from the shore.

The date of the print is hard to pinpoint. Lane has suggested that the vogue for large prints in the *ō-ōban* format did not begin until the late 1680s, when Moronobu had all but ceased to produce prints.[6] If not a straightforward warrior print, then the present work may relate to a *jōruri* version of the story chanted for the puppet theatre. It is recorded that Tosa no Shōjō performed a five-act play entitled *Yashima* in Edo in the first month of 1678, but it is not known if this included a scene of shooting at a fan.[7] TTC

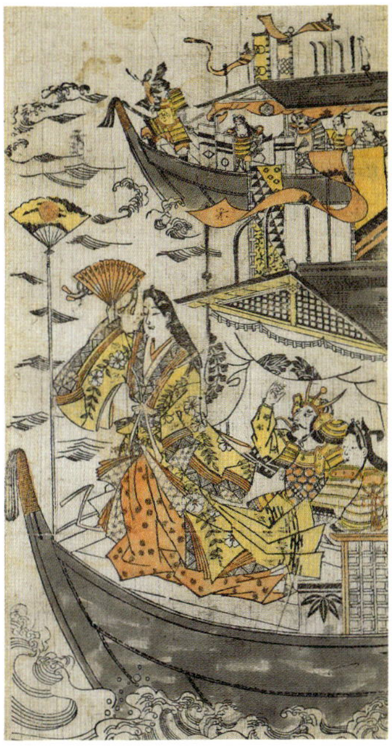

Lady Tamamushi Challenging the Minamato, Museum of Fine Arts, Boston, Denman Waldo Ross Collection, 06.360.

20

Attributed to Sugimura Jihei

Amusements of Warriors on the Eve of Battle
(Ikusa kado-ide no tawamure)

1687 (or later edition)

PUBLISHER: 'Masuya Hei'emon'

woodblock-printed book, *fukuro-toji*, *sumizuri*, 1 vol., slight hand-colouring, 26.2 × 17.8 cm (covers)

OTHER COPY: Shibui Kiyoshi Collection (Lane 1980, pp. 4, 32–7)

source unknown, 2000

2000.1256

An erotic picture book containing imagined scenes of lovemaking involving famous warriors from history on the eve of battle. A two-page preface (unsigned) is followed by one single-page illustration, 22 numbered double-page illustrations and a single-page postscript and colophon. The top quarter of each double page is occupied by a text that begins with the name of a famous warrior, starting with Kiso Yoshinaka. The page shown here depicts Oguri Hangan Masakiyo making love with the courtesan Terute-no-hime. The preface repeats the ancient belief in the efficacy of erotic images in inducing a martial spirit. 'Pillow pictures' (*makura-e*) should be placed at the ready in the warrior's armour chest. They will put him in such a spirited frame of mind that his subsequent renown on the battlefield will ensure that his and his descendants' glory and prosperity are everlasting. All this is explained with a fair degree of facetiousness, directed primarily at an urban audience of pleasure-seekers bold enough to make fun of their military betters. There also seems to be a suggestion that viewing pictures of horse-backed warriors wielding their bows on the field of battle would strengthen the resolve of the purchaser and ensure his own future fame and honour.

The covers of the Boston copy have been replaced and there is no slip bearing the title: that given here is printed at the beginning of the preface. Shibui Kiyoshi offered an alternative title, *Raku no uwamori* (*Pleasure in Excess of Pleasure*).[1] He also cited a much more complete colophon, from a copy he recorded as in the 'Ōta family collection'. This gave the publication date as New Year 1687 and named two publishers, Hyōshi-ya Shichiemon of Ōdenma-chō san-chōme and Masuya Hei'emon. The date and the name of the first publisher have thus been cut from the colophon of the Boston volume, which must therefore be regarded as a later edition. On the other hand, the phrase 'Raku no uwamori' appears at the beginning of the postscript and Shubui may simply have adopted it as a suitable title. Although the artist's name is not given, all authorities seem to agree on an attribution on the basis of style to Sugimura Jihei. TTC

1 Shibui 1954, p. 104, quoted in Horioka 1974, p. 25; reproduced ibid., p. 25, fig. 60, 61.

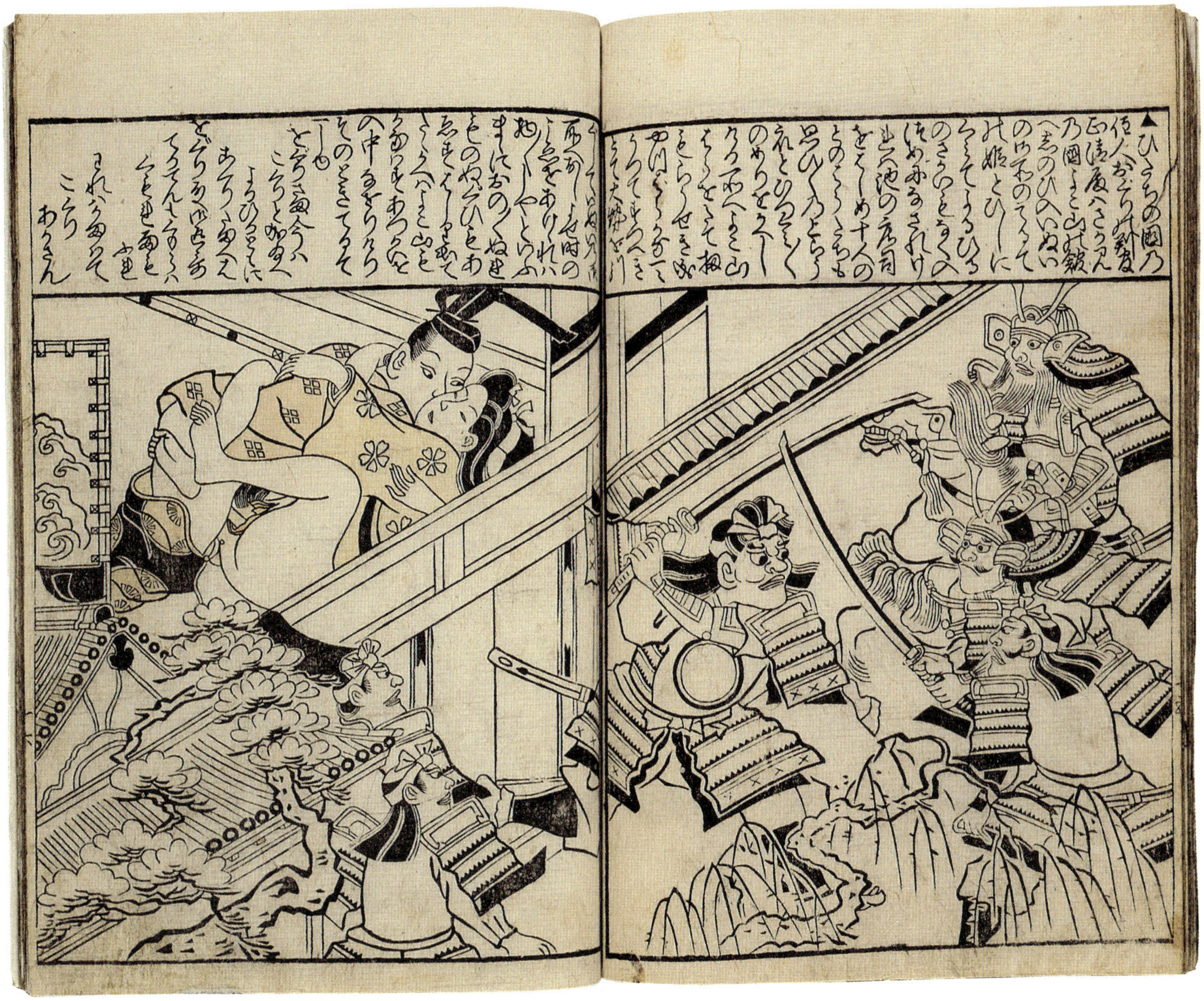

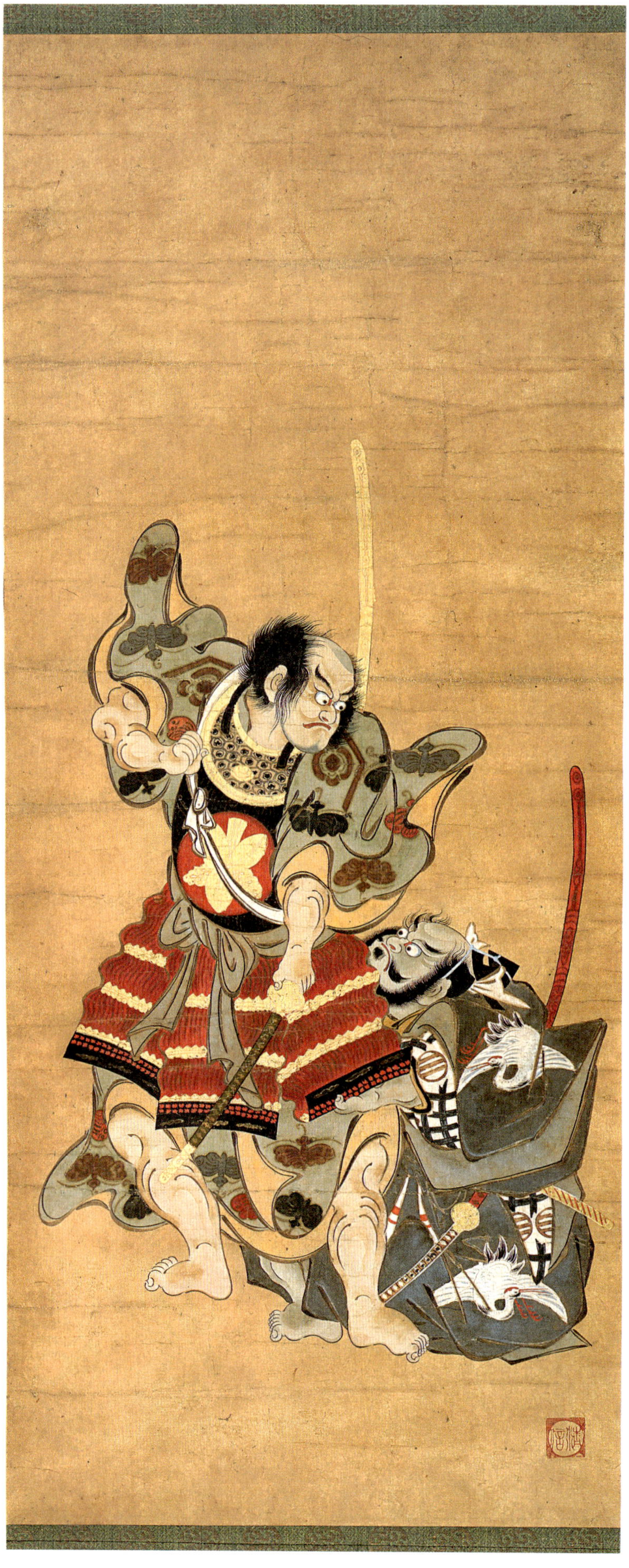

21
Torii Kiyonobu I
Armour-tugging Scene

c. 1716–29

ARTIST'S SEAL: 'Kiyonobu'

hanging scroll, ink, colour and gold on paper, 80.1 × 34.3 cm

REPRODUCED: Boston 2000, vol. 2, no. 87

William Sturgis Bigelow Collection, 1911

11.7538

1 Kominz 1995, fig. 24.

2 Honolulu 1980, p. 43.

3 Asano Shūgō, in Boston 2000, vol. 2, p. 182.

4 Kannon-ji, Nako, Chiba Prefecture, reproduced in Noguchi 1933, no. 34.

From the early 15th century the historic vendetta of the Soga brothers against Kudō Suketsune, a principal adviser to the powerful Shogun Minamoto Yoritomo, inspired numerous nō and kabuki plays. The determination of the youths – Jūrō Sukenari (1172–93) and Gorō Tokimune (1174–93) – in avenging the death of their father appealed to a society that was ruled by military leaders and that valued the Confucian ideal of filial devotion. Over time the events of 1193, when the brothers burst in on a shogunal hunting party at the foot of Mount Fuji and murdered Kudō, became embellished with fictional exploits of the brothers and their companions. In these, Gorō became the archetypal rash strong man, Jūrō the ever-thoughtful lover.

The 'armour-tugging scene', the subject of this painting, was a dramatic highlight of many Soga plays. Gorō, dressed in red laced armour and characteristic butterfly-ornamented under-robes, charges to the rescue of his elder brother. Kobayashi Saburō Yoshihide (known as Asahina), a sympathetic warrior noted for his tremendous strength, attempts to restrain the impetuous youth by grabbing his protective skirt (*kusazuri*).

Ichikawa Danjūrō I (1660–1704), considered the leading actor of heroic parts during the late 17th century, was closely identified with the role of Gorō. His interpretation of Gorō's valiant adventures in the flamboyant style known as *aragoto*, which emphasised highly expressive movement and loud foot-stamping, inspired a woodblock-printed book attributed by some scholars to Torii Kiyonobu: *Tsuwamono kongen Soga* (*The Origin of the Soga Warrior*), dated 1697, in which the violent actions and the strength of the men are depicted by a number of distinctive artistic devices.[1] These include interlocking gazes from bulging eyes, billowing sleeves in 'wriggling worm lines' (*mimizu-gaki*) and rippling muscles on the calves of the actors' 'gourd-shaped legs' (*hyōtan ashi*). These features were adopted by other Torii artists in subsequent portrayals of the armour-tugging scene, as in the 1715 playbill for a production of *Bandō ichi kotobuki Soga* at the Nakamura Theatre and a single-sheet print by Torii Kiyomasu I commemorating the same performance (cat. 33).[2]

Unsigned, the present painting has been attributed to Kiyonobu on the basis of its seal.[3] Compared to printed versions of this subject and to a 1725 painting of Gorō and Asahina attributed to Kiyonobu I,[4] the tension between the two principals is muted; the lines of the robes and legs are conventional. This subdued treatment may be due to the fact that the artist did not refer to specific actors or a specific performance: the image contains Gorō's and Asahina's family crests but no actors' crests. The composition thus represents a generic view of a famous theatrical episode. Curiously, however, the facial features of Gorō resemble those of the actor Ogawa Zengorō as Kudō no Suketsune, the villain of the Soga story, as he appears in another picture by Kiyonobu I, in the Freer Gallery of Art, Washington DC (p. 27, fig. 15). ANM

22

Torii Kiyonobu I

Erotic Contest of Flowers

c. 1704–11

ARTIST'S SIGNATURE: 'Eshi Torii Kiyonobu zu' (Drawn by the picture master Torii Kiyonobu)

ARTIST'S SEAL: 'Kiyonobu'

handscroll, ink, colour, gold and silver on paper, 36.2 × 520 cm

REPRODUCED: Boston 2001, suppl. no. 1

William Sturgis Bigelow Collection, 1909

Res. 09.234

Although it has long been recognised that most leading ukiyo-e artists produced erotic paintings and prints (*shunga*), until fairly recently these images were omitted from exhibitions owing to prudish sensibilities in the West and censorship laws in Japan. Research conducted in preparation for the recent publication of the Boston Museum's holdings of Japanese erotic painting (part of a larger study of ukiyo-e painting) has revealed the significance of these long-closeted works, which were acquired by William Sturgis Bigelow in Japan in 1909.[1] *Erotic Contest of Flowers* by Torii Kiyonobu has been acclaimed not only as the most important erotic scroll produced by the founder of the Torii school, but also as one of the finest examples of the entire genre.[2] It is being shown in public for the first time at the present exhibition.

In creating *shunga*, artists favoured formats that invited private viewing – handscrolls, albums and woodblock-printed books. While there has been much academic debate as to their audience and purpose, these works could not have failed to be a powerful source of fantasy in the tightly controlled society of Edo Japan.[3] From the 1680s Hishikawa Moronobu and Sugimura Jihei produced many series of album prints of this kind; Richard Lane estimates that these made up at least two-thirds of Jihei's oeuvre.[4] Japanese novels of the 17th century suggest that Moronobu, too, was well known for his erotica. The central character of *The Life of an Amorous Woman* (*Kōshoku ichidai onna*) remarks: 'For a warrior's household is bound by the strictest rules, and the women who dwell there never so much as set their eyes on a man, not to speak of enjoying the scent of a loincloth. One day, as I was examining a fascinating depiction by Hishikawa of an erotic scene, I was stirred despite myself to the most intense excitement. I sought, then, to quench my amorous flames.'[5]

Asano Shūgō has established that Kiyonobu must have designed approximately 100 erotic prints, which were originally sold in sets of eight to twelve. All are executed in ink in the horizontal *ōban* (*yoko-ōban*) or *chūban* (*yoko-chūban*) format; some were later hand-coloured. The most celebrated of the complete series is *Neya byōbu* (*Screens of the Bedchamber*), which was published by

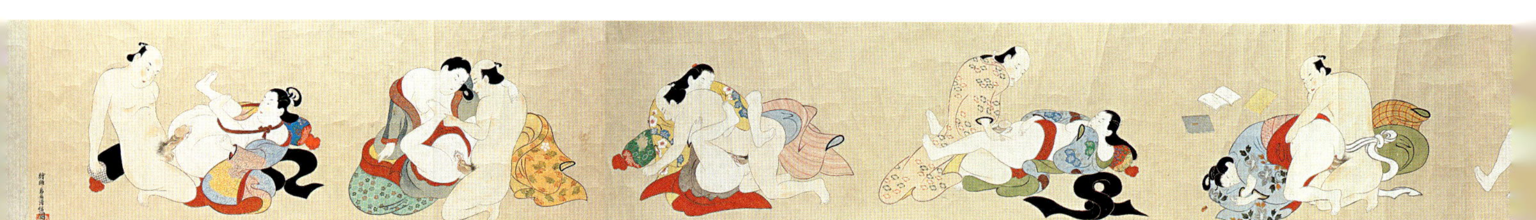

1 Boston 2001, suppl.

2 The author is indebted to the entry by Asano Shūgō in Boston 2001, p. 136–7, and to personal conversations with Asano in May 2001.

3 Timon Screech has declared that *shunga* functioned as auto-erotic stimuli for a predominately male population. Screech 1999. Allen Hockley, questioning whether that was their sole purpose, believed that they may also have been viewed communally. Hockley 2000.

4 Lane 1978, p. 52.

5 Saikaku 1963, p. 135.

6 Asano 1995, p. 123.

7 Asano has established that the opening scene is missing, since the original scroll consisted of six sheets of paper with two scenes on each. Boston 2001, p. 136.

8 Lane 1978, p. 59.

9 *Ryōashi kakae*, reproduced in *Ukiyo-e* 95, Oct. 1983, n.p. The cover of this issue of *Ukiyo-e* features a detail of a painting nearly identical to the fifth section of the Boston scroll, in which a woman with dishevelled hair engages energetically with her reclining partner.

Takeda Chō'emon in 1711. These prints include humorous parodies of certain festival rituals and of incidents in kabuki plays. For example, the well-known 'armour-tugging scene' from the tale of the Soga Brothers (see cat. 21) has been transformed into a 'valorous penis-pulling scene'.[6]

Erotic Contest of Flowers shows eleven spirited visions of lovemaking from what was originally a scroll of twelve images.[7] In each scene the individual couples with their attendants and bedding are isolated against the undecorated paper and their horizontal positions and the rhythm of the colours lead the viewer through the handscroll. Comparison with the artist's printed *shunga* suggests that Kiyonobu adopted the same compositional arrangements in his woodblock albums, allotting one couple to each sheet. There are many corollaries between the handscroll and the prints. The young samurai shown in union with a woman lost in ecstasy in the second section of the scroll, for example, is virtually a simplified mirror image of the couple in a print dated by Lane to the early 1710s.[8] Or again, the pair of lovers in the last section of the scroll, the man supporting his hips on a pillow in order to gain easier access to the exposed charms of the recumbent woman, closely resembles a couple in an unsigned print published as the work of Kiyonobu.[9] The latter differs from the scroll image only in the man's hairstyle, the detailing of the textiles and the absence of a cord binding the women's neck and leg.

Despite the similarities between painted and printed compositions, the works themselves are quite different. In the prints, with their limited palette, Kiyonobu had to exploit strong contrasts of light and dark to evoke moods. The handscroll, on the other hand, offers a veritable explosion of colour, which seems to energise the lovemaking. The juxtaposition of clear, warm reds with the whites of the exposed bodies, and the touches of red for the genitals, contribute to the eroticism of the images. The lustrous black of the hair and the silver in areas of the clothing heighten the vibrancy of the painting, while the use of a flat white for the bodies of the women and of a flesh tone for those of the men adds an element of contrast. ANM

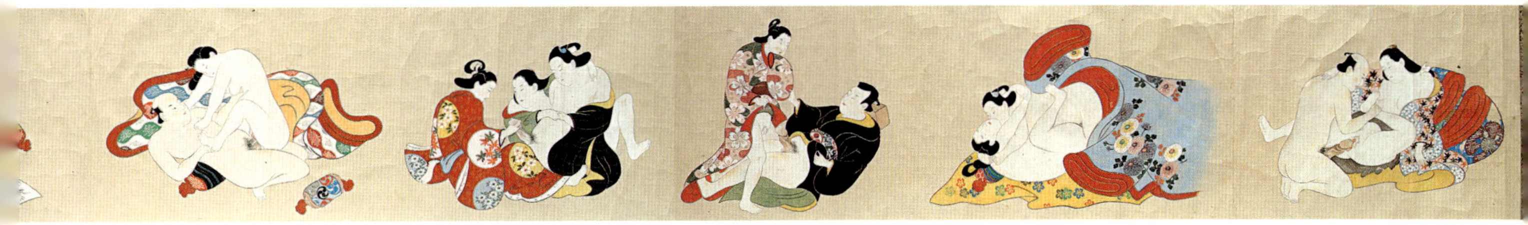

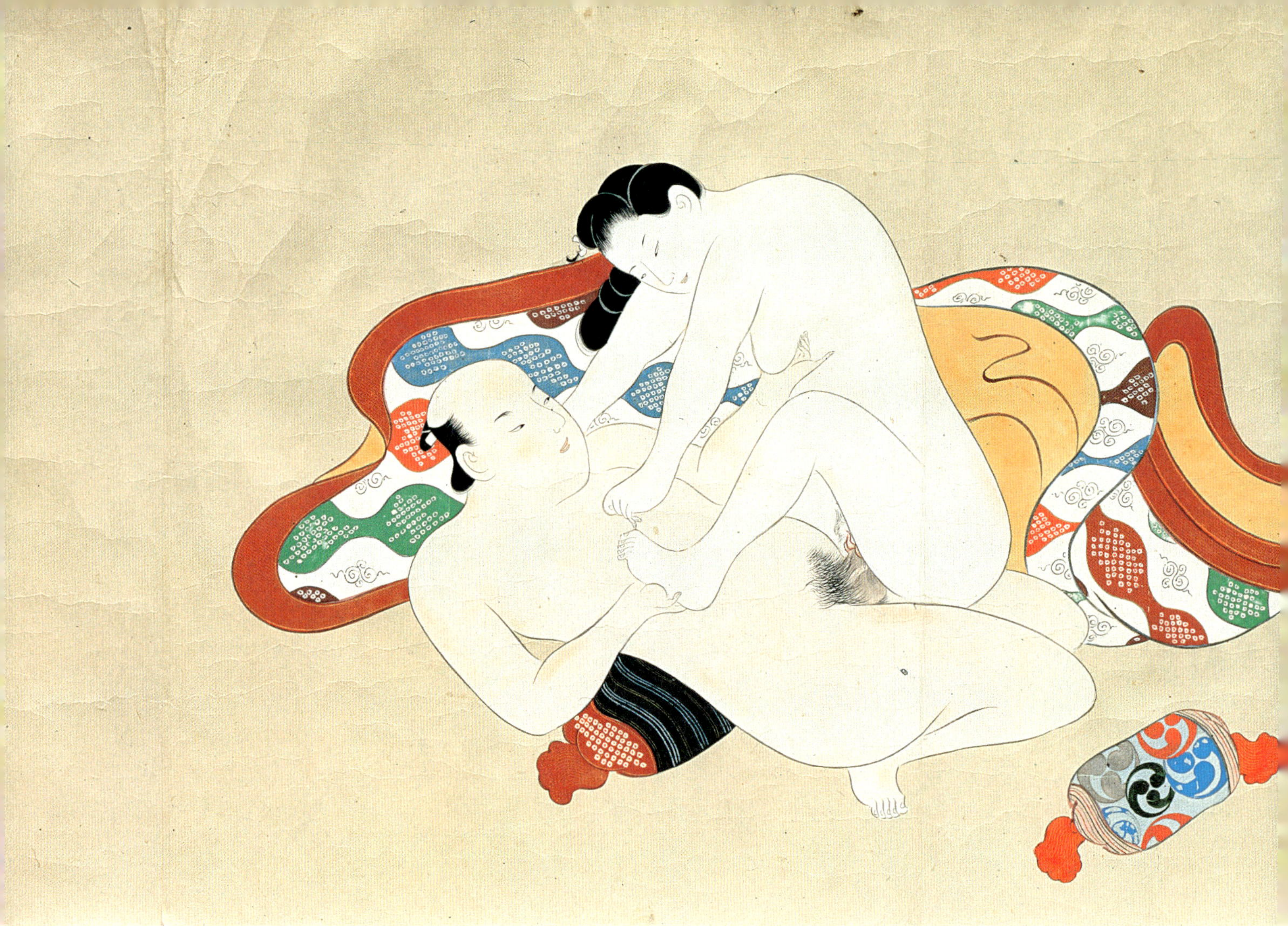

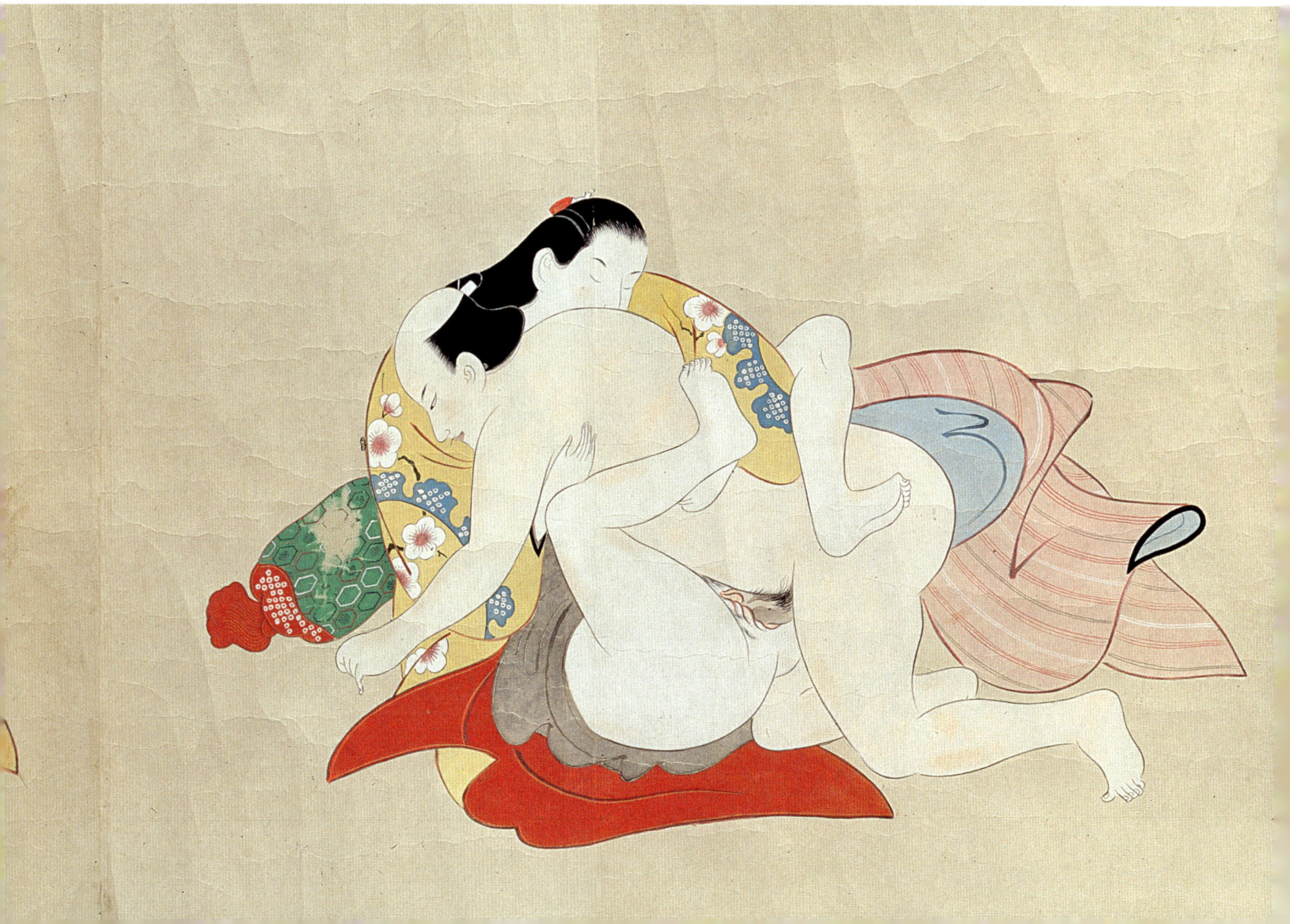

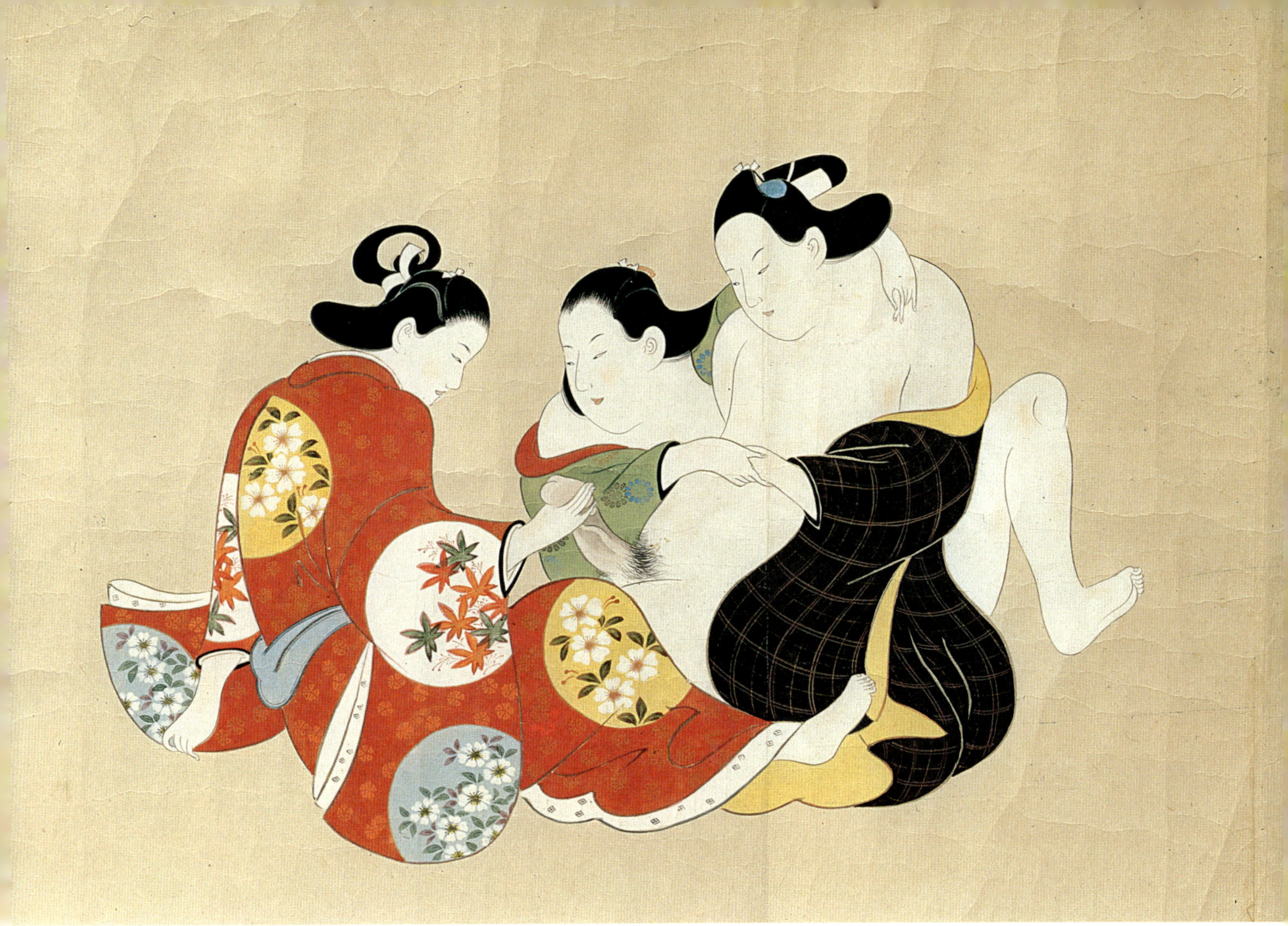

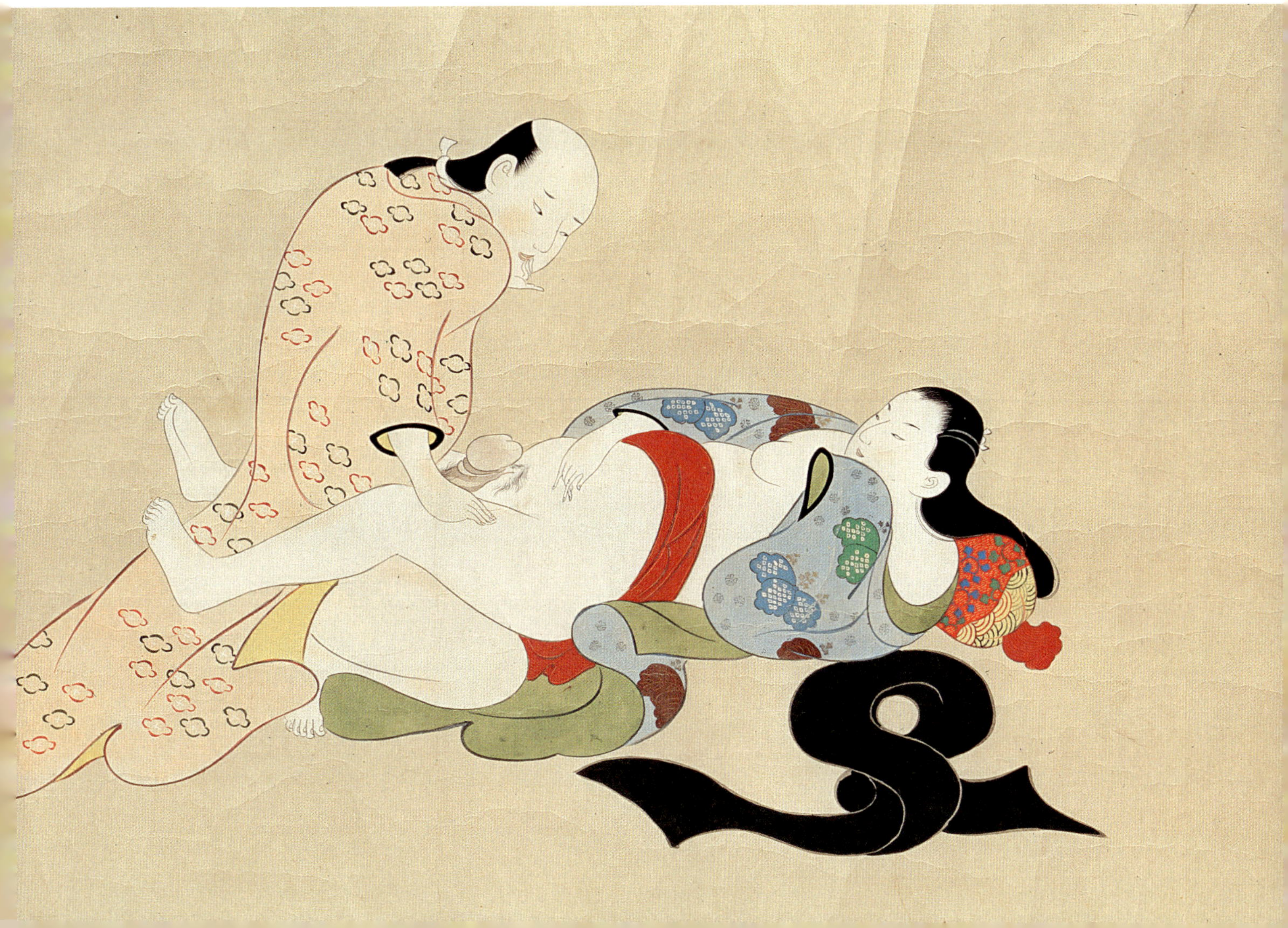

23

Attributed to Torii Kiyonobu I
Sankai Nagoya

2nd month, 1697

PUBLISHER:
'Sakai-chō Higashiyoko-chō Kaifu-ya'
(Kaifu-ya at Sakai-chō Higashiyoko-chō)

woodblock, illustrated kabuki playbook (*e-iri kyōgen-bon*), *fukuro-toji*, *sumizuri*, 2 vols., 22.5 × 15.9 cm (covers)

OTHER COPY: Tokyo University of Fine Arts (Tokyo 1977, no. 96)

Gift of Mrs K. Jared Morse, 2000

2000.1254

The book records the performance of the previous month, New Year, 1697, at the Nakamura Theatre, a programme entitled *Sankai Nagoya*, and is significant from a number of perspectives. The play starred Ichikawa Danjūrō I, in the very process of establishing the Edo *aragoto* style of acting with new plays written partly by himself.[1] With co-author Nakamura Myōseki Kiyosaburō, Danjūrō proudly announces in the postscript that it is a new venture to publish exact transcripts of lines from the play from all four parts of the programme. For this new departure a new artist was clearly needed and, although unsigned, the six very lively illustrations share a sufficient number of stylistic characteristics with *Screens in All Directions* (cat. 24) of 1700 to be attributed confidently to Torii Kiyonobu I at the earliest stage of his career.[2] From this book and the slightly later *Tsuwamono kongen Soga* (*The Origin of the Soga Warrior*, fifth month, 1697) onwards, many of the approximately 60 illustrated playbooks of this type published in Edo up to 1711 are thought to be by Kiyonobu I.[3]

The story was a version of the rivalry of Nagoya Sanzaburō and Fuwa Banzemon for the affections of the courtesan Katsuragi. Danjūrō played the role of Fuwa Banzaemon. The page shown here is the last of the six illustrations, depicting the fourth part of the programme. Nagoya Sanzaburō (played by Murayama Shirōji) and Katsuragi (Ogino Sawanojō) are happily united in the top right corner, while Danjūrō has taken on the guise of the Chinese demon-quelling hero Shō Ki (see cat. 76) to defeat the evil Dazainojō (Yamanaka Heikurō), who is portrayed as a horned demon riding a three-headed black ox (lower left).

The Boston copy has replacement covers bearing the handwritten title *Sankai Nagoya*. The original printed title slip on the cover is accompanied by a square 'picture title slip' (*e-daisen*) showing Danjūrō as Shō Ki. An account published by Santō Kyōden in 1804 says that pictures of Danjūrō as Shō Ki were sold in the streets and that this gradually led to a vogue for prints of other actors. (In fact, the earliest known dateable single-sheet print of an actor by Kiyonobu I records a performance during the third month, 1698.) Mutō Junko has pointed out that the cover picture is apparently drawn with a frame and metal fittings, suggesting it copies a painted signboard or votive plaque.[4] Sixteen-ninety-seven was clearly a formative year for all kinds of imagery associated with Edo kabuki and the artist taking the lead in that process was Kiyonobu I.

The play *Sankai Nagoya* is said to have included the first-ever performance of the 'Shibaraku' (Stop One Moment!) scene,[5] although this was not apparently depicted among the six illustrations in the book. The full name of the play recorded on the title page is *(Ehō otoko ikioi mume-ga-yado) Sankai Nagoya*.[6] TTC

1 Kominz 1997, p. 64, fig. 11, 13.

2 Akama 1994, p. 8; Mutō 1996, pp. 106–7. All six illustrations are reproduced in Tokyo 1977, pp. 82–3, no. 96.

3 Mutō 1997, p. 4.

4 Ibid., pp. 106–7.

5 *Kabuki nenpyō*, vol. 1, p. 204.

6 The 'third assignation' (*sankai*) of the title refers to the third formal meeting with a high-ranked Yoshiwara courtesan required before a client could hope to become intimate with her.

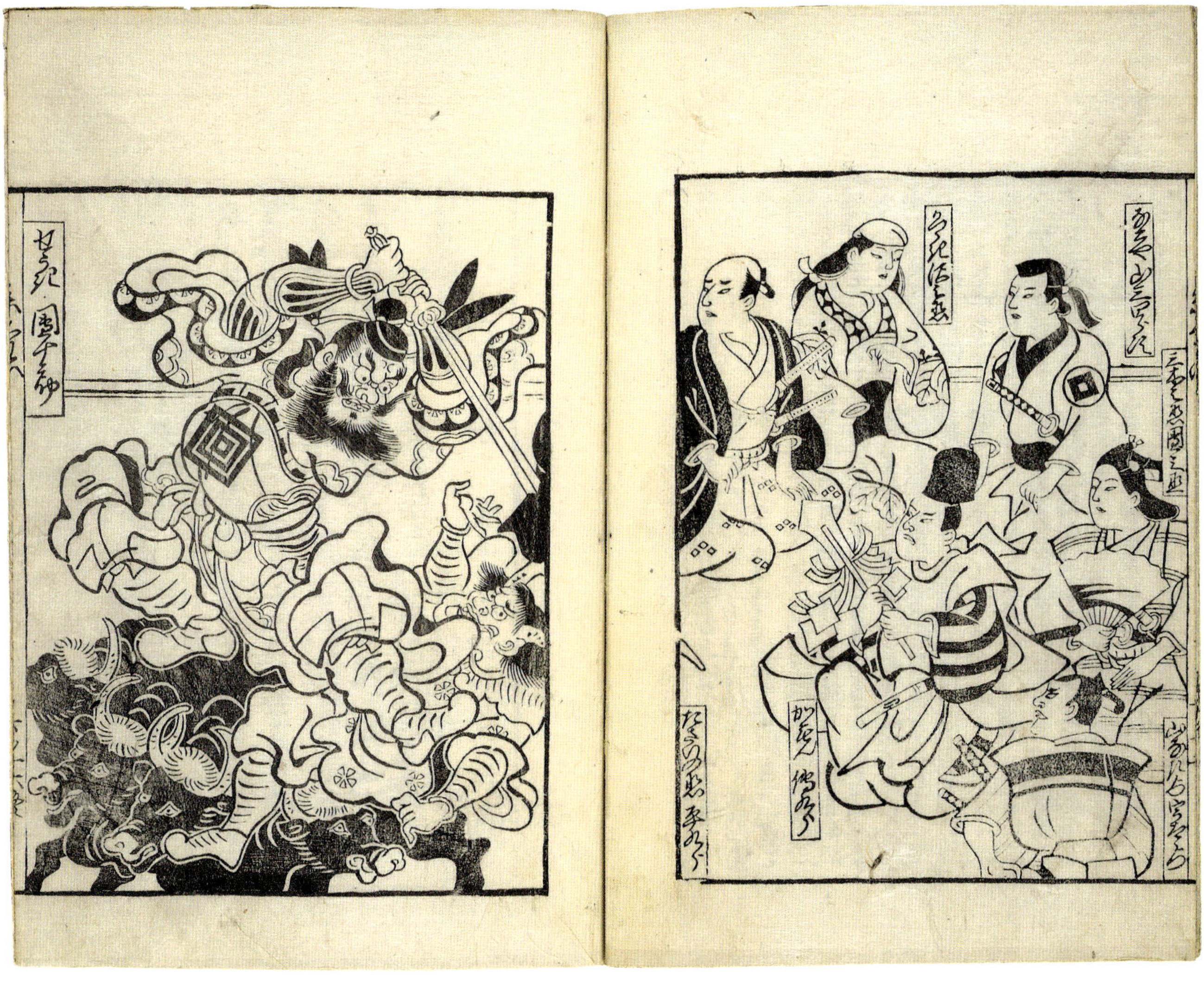

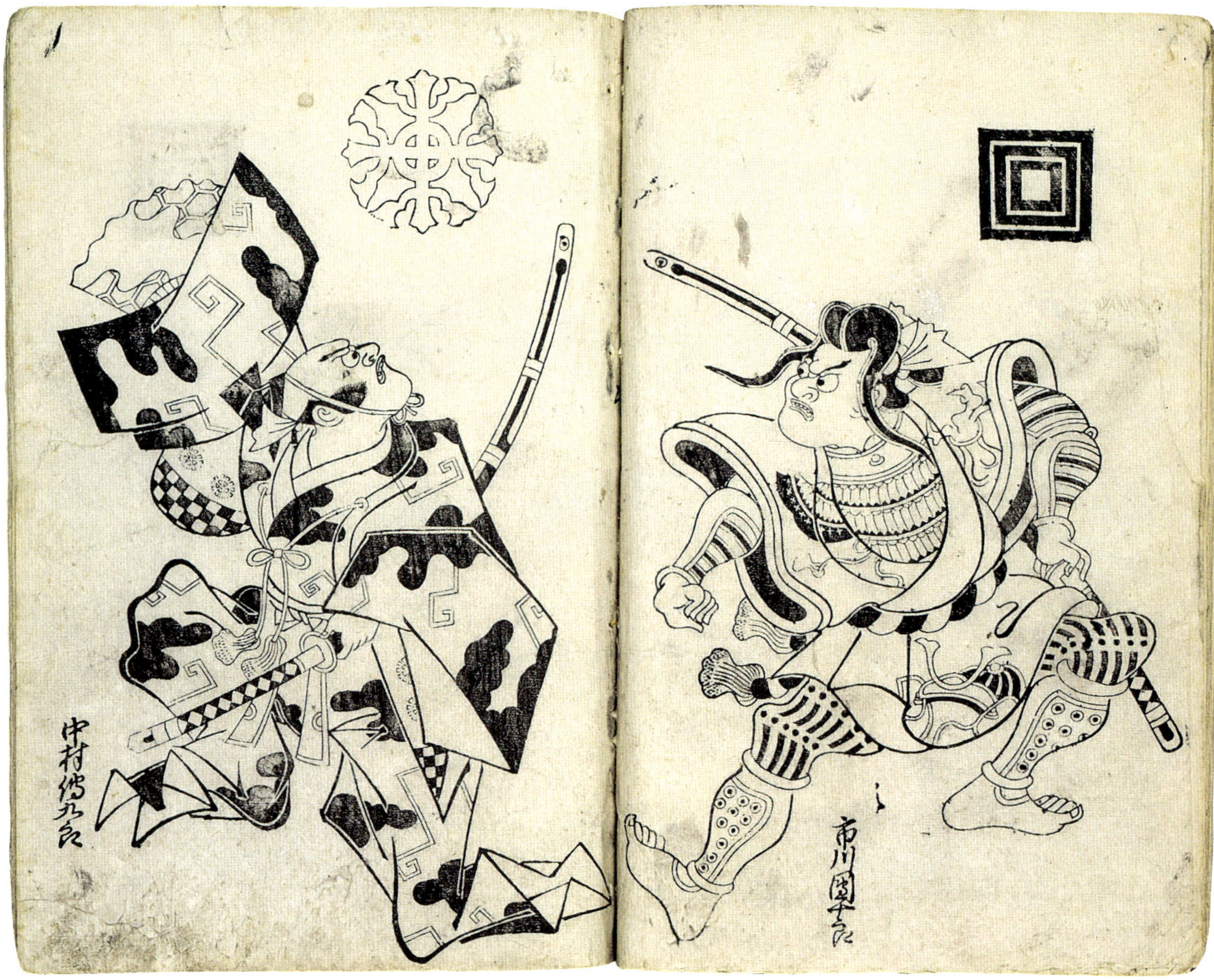

24

Torii Kiyonobu I

Elegant Picture Book: (Painted) Screens in All Directions ([Fūryū ehon] Shihō byōbu)

3rd month, 1700

ARTIST'S SIGNATURE: 'Yamato gakō Torii Shōbei Kiyonobu zu' (Drawn by the Yamato painting artisan Torii Shōbei Kiyonobu)

PUBLISHER: 'Hangi-ya Shichirobei'

woodblock-printed book, *fukuro-toji*, *sumizuri*, 2 vols. bound as 1, 27 × 18.8 cm (covers)

OTHER COPIES: Hiraki Ukiyo-e Museum, Yokohama (2)

Gift of Mrs Jared K. Morse, 2000

2000.1255

This is the most important early printed picture book of kabuki actors, fundamental to the establishment by Kiyonobu I of the Torii school and style.[1] The title is sometimes read as *Yomo byōbu*, but Suzuki Jūzō has cited a publication of 1810 that gives the reading *Shihō byōbu*, adopted here.[2] The most complete copy of the book contains 43 single-page *sumizuri-e* illustrations of leading actors – some illustrated twice – covering the period from the eleventh month, 1695, to publication in the third month, 1700. As Mutō Junko points out, the book is heavily retrospective: by 1700 seven of the actors depicted had returned to Kansai, one had retired, another had died.[3] Each actor is named, his crest appears above him and he is shown in a role for which he was well known. The book aims to present the comprehensive range of acting and role types, showing the actors in quintessential costumes and poses. Mutō argues that the illustrations may well have been reused from published single-sheet prints, serving as a compendium of Kiyonobu I designs, and gives one concrete example of this. She also lists two prints signed by Kiyonobu I and eleven unsigned designs that share certain formal characteristics and can be dated to this period. Signed works by the artist are known from 1697 and this publication of 1700 is another important landmark in the development of the increasingly influential Torii style.

The two volumes of the original publication have been bound together as one in the Boston copy, from which two single pages are missing: the recto and verso of sheet no. 10, which show Ōtani Hiroemon and Matsumoto Koshirō respectively. After a preface of two single pages, the actors are depicted in the following order, followed by a single-page postscript:[4] (original volume one) 1. Ichikawa Danjūrō (sheet 2); 2. Kishida Kosaiji; 3. Nakamura Denkurō (sheet 3); 4. Nakamura Kanzaburō; 5. Mizuki Tatsunosuke (sheet 4); 6. Nakamura Shichisaburō; 7. Nakamura Heikurō (sheet 5); 8. Ogino Sawanojō; 9. Katsuyama Matagorō (sheet 6); 10. Ikushima Daikichi; 11. Murayama Shirōji (sheet 7); 12. Shinomiya Heihachi; 13. Suzuki Hei'emon (sheet 8); 14. Nishikawa Okanosuke; 15. Kamon Rokusaburō (sheet 9); 16. Shinozuka Shōmatsu; 17. [Ōtani Hiroemon] (sheet 10 – missing); 18. [Matsumoto Koshirō] (missing); 19. Saruwaka Sanzaemon (sheet 11); 20. Shinomiya Genpachi; (original volume two) 1. Mizuki Tatsunosuke (sheet 1); 2. Ichikawa Danjūrō; 3. Nakamura Denkurō (sheet 2, illustrated); 4. Yamanaka Heikurō; 5. Kishida Kogenji (sheet 3); 6. Ikushima Shingorō; 7. Sawamura Kodenji (sheet 4); 8. Sodeoka Masanosuke; 9. Yoshikawa Tamon (sheet 5); 10. Saikoku Hyōgorō (name missing); 11. Uemura Kichisaburō (sheet 6); 12. Mizuki Somenosuke; 13. Ichikawa Dannojō (sheet 7); 14. Yokoyama Rokurōji; 15. Tomizawa Hanzaburō (sheet 8); 16. Matsumoto Hyōzō; 17. Sodeoka Muranosuke (sheet 9); 18. Wakamura Sawanosuke; 19. Akita Hikoshirō (sheet 10); 20. Nishimura Yaheiji; 21. Yamashita Kosaisaburō (sheet 11); 22. Kiriyama Masanosuke; 23. Sodesaki Karyū (sheet 12). TTC

1 The contents and significance have been discussed in detail in an article by Mutō Junko, on which this commentary largely relies. Mutō 1994.

2 The *gōkan* illustrated novel *Ito-zakura Honchō bunsui*, with text by Santō Kyōden and illustrations by Torii Kiyomine. Suzuki 1979a, vol. 3, commentary. Cited in Mutō 1994, p. 5, n. 3.

3 Mutō 1994, p. 8.

4 Mutō 1994, pp. 9–10, collates the surviving copies, including that in Boston.

25

Torii Kiyonobu I

Illustrated Book of Courtesans or *Picture Album of Courtesans* (*Keisei ehon* or *Shōgi gachō*)

4th month, 1700

ARTIST'S SIGNATURE: 'Yamato gakō Torii Shōbei Kiyonobu zu' (Drawn by the Yamato painting artisan Torii Shōbei Kiyonobu)

ARTIST'S SEAL: 'Kiyonobu'

PUBLISHER: 'Izumi-chō Hangi-ya Shichirobei han' (Published by Hangi-ya Shichirobei at Izumi-chō)

woodblock-printed book, *sumizuri*, album of 21 separately mounted book pages with 20 illus. and 1 dated colophon, hand-colouring, later mounted as *orihon* with covers in cloth, total size 33 × 447.9 cm, pages 32.5 × 22 cm (each), images approx. 27 × 18 cm

OTHER COPY: Art Institute of Chicago (Chicago 1931, p. 116)

William Sturgis Bigelow Collection, 1911

11.30230–50

In 1700 Kiyonobu I decorated two picture books published by Hangi-ya Shichirobei with full-figure illustrations of the most glamorous people in the *ukiyo* world of Edo: *Screens in All Directions* (cat. 24) and *Illustrated Book of Courtesans*. The latter presents top-ranking courtesans from the Yoshiwara pleasure quarter dressed in elegantly patterned *kosode* and *furisode* and standing or sitting in charming poses while pursuing everyday activities.

Two rare first edition copies of *Illustrated Book of Courtesans* are in American museums, one in the Boston Museum, the other in the Ryerson Collection at the Art Institute of Chicago. Neither of these retains its original title slip, but the title *Keisei ehon* is recorded, in *kana*, in a later book.[1] The title also translates as *Pictures of Castle-breakers*, a reference to the power of courtesans, whose beauty distracts men to such an extent that they forget to defend their castle against the enemy. In Sino-Japanese the Chinese characters used to write *Keisei ehon* read 'Shōgi gachō' (Picture Album of Courtesans).

Both first edition copies have been rebound as folding albums and both open with an illustration of the Main Gate of Yoshiwara. The Boston copy includes nineteen portraits of courtesans, the Chicago eighteen. Each is identified by her name (with the exception of Kodayū, to the right of the figure) and by her crest, but the portraits are organised randomly and differently in the two albums.[2] The courtesans Asagiri and Kodayū are missing from the Chicago copy, Hatsuse from that in Boston.[3] This indicates that both copies are incomplete and that, in its original format, *Illustrated Book of Courtesans* probably contained twenty or more illustrations.

The Boston courtesans are painted with vibrant opaque and transparent colours consonant with those in Kiyonobu's masterpiece, the painted handscroll *Erotic Contest of Flowers* (*c.* 1704–11; cat. 22). The careful and tasteful application of these colours suggests that the Boston *Illustrated Book of Courtesans* may have been produced to commission for a connoisseur. Since the chemical composition of the pigments used here and in the handscroll is similar, nothing stands in the way of dating the hand-colouring to the early 1700s.[4] The wear visible in the lower corners of the illustrations[5] is consistent with the pages being turned in the original book format. What appear to be binding holes can be seen down the edges of some pages. On the evidence of wormholes and other damage, it is likely that many pages were originally arranged in a different order.

Like *Screens in All Directions*, *Illustrated Book of Courtesans* was an instant success and had a catalytic impact on early 18th-century printmaking. Several publications with similar illustrations were soon issued in Edo and Kyoto. Copies of these 'copy-cat' editions are unfortunately as rare as their models and often incomplete. In the sixth month, 1701, the Edo publisher Kurihara Chōemon issued a pirated, unsigned version of *Illustrated Book of Courtesans*. His re-cut portraits, generally faithful to the originals, included minor

1 *Sunkin zattetsu* (*A Compilation of Miscellaneous Brocades*, *c.* 1800). Chicago 1931, p. 116.

2 In the Boston copy they appear in the following order: Asagiri, Kaoru, Masatsune, Ukihashi, Naniwa, Umegae, Miyoshi, Hanamurasaki, Matsukaze, Wakoku, Komurasaki, Kogenda, Kasuma (Kazuma), Takao, Hanasaki, Kodayū, Usugumo, Emon, Ikuyo. The order in the Chicago copy is given in Chicago 1931, pp. 116–17.

3 Ibid., where Hatsuse is listed as 'Hatsugoe'. According to Tenri 1983, p. 19, 'Hatsuse' is the correct reading. Hatsuse is reproduced in Jenkins 1972, p. vi, fig. 2. Hanasaki, Usugumo, Kasuma, Hanamurasaki and Ikuyo from the Chicago copy are reproduced in Hillier 1987, fig. 88, 90, 124, Kaoru in Chicago 1931, pl. III.

4 According to the Analytical Laboratory of the Boston Museum, the pigments include malachite, indigo and smalt.

5 See especially the hem of Hanamurasaki's *kosode*.

6 Kurihara's pirated publication is reproduced in facsimile in *Kisho fukuseikai*, vol. 28, pp. 1–22. Kurihara's book was first called *Meigi jūhachi kō* (*Eighteen Famous Courtesans*), but was later renamed *Shōgi gachō* (*Picture Album of Courtesans*). Honolulu 1980, pp. 89–90. The illustrations are ordered differently from both the Boston and the Chicago copy of *Illustrated Book of Courtesans* and, in contrast to those two books, do not include Hatsuse and Hanasaki. The addition of *nadeshiko* (pinks) to the picture of Ukihashi may have been influenced by an image in *Nure-botoke* (3 vols., fourth month, 1671), reproduced in *Kisho fukuseikai*, vol. 27, p. 80.

changes and details were added to enliven a few of the relatively plain designs – a rectangular pot of wild pinks (*nadeshiko*), for example, was placed on the ground in front of Ukihashi of the Tsutaya pleasure house.[6] Two months later Kurihara issued another publication with similar content. Variously known by the hand-inscribed titles *Genroku tayū awase-kagami* (*Courtesans of the Genroku Era in Paired Hand Mirrors*) and *Hokkaku bigichō* (*Beautiful Courtesans of the Northern Quarter*), this is the first signed and dated work by Okumura Masanobu (1686–1764), an artist who went on to promote numerous printmaking innovations during the first half of the 18th century.[7] Masanobu subsequently illustrated two further such publications.[8] His courtesans are indebted to Kiyonobu, but include original compositions, experimental re-workings of poses and gestures, livelier line work and greater detail.

Another artist influenced by *Illustrated Book of Courtesans* was Ōmori Yoshikiyo of Kyoto (active *c.* 1702–16). This is especially noticeable in his album *Rambling Wisteria* (*Midare fuji*, *c.* 1702–5), in which many of the courtesans and the objects they use (armrest, pipe and tobacco tray, bench) are identical to those seen in Kiyonobu's illustrations.[9]

In the period *c.* 1695–1700, before publishing images of actors in the book *Screens in All Directions*, Shichirobei had issued a number of larger and smaller single-sheet, full-figure prints of kabuki players.[10] It was thus only logical that he should have produced single-sheet prints of Yoshiwara courtesans in addition to *Illustrated Book of Courtesans*. The two books may even have been de luxe compilations of single images. The monumental, simplified and self-contained figures in *Illustrated Book of Courtesans* certainly seem to have influenced the development of courtesan prints during the first fifteen years of the 18th century. One of the most popular designs in *Illustrated Book of Courtesans* was that depicting Masatsune of the Miura-ya, identified by the crest consisting of an uprooted iris (*nebiki kakitsubata*). The courtesan, drawn with bold, curved lines, is shown adjusting her comb with both hands as she sits on a bench (p. 113). This charming figure was not only the model for Yoshikiyo's courtesan Sango in *Midare fuji*;[11] it was also copied (and provided with a more detailed *furisode* pattern) by the publisher Nakaya, who transformed it into a *kakemono-e* design. Two impressions of Masatsune in this format, hand-coloured with *tan*, are in the Art Institute of Chicago and the Otto Reise Collection respectively. Both bear the mark of the publisher and can be dated *c.* 1700–10 on stylistic grounds.[12]

In the eighth month, 1711, at a time when Kiyomasu I, Masanobu and the Kaigetsudō school artists are believed to have begun producing large-format prints of courtesans, the publisher Takeda Chōemon issued a volume that reproduced designs from Masanobu's books of 1701–2.[13] Takeda's book may have encouraged and/or capitalised on the renewed interest in courtesan prints evident in the 1710s. LEV

7 The copy in the Honolulu Academy of Arts bears the handwritten title *Hokkaku bigichō* (*Beautiful Courtesans of the Northern Quarter*). Honolulu 1980, p. 89. Two sheets from a German private collection depicting the courtesans Ausaka and Teika are reproduced in New York 1991a, pp. 52–5. These leaves had come, via the Henri Vever Collection, from a book in the Drukker Collection bearing the handwritten title *Genroku tayū awase-kagami* (*Courtesans of the Genroku Era in Paired Hand Mirrors*) and originally containing sixteen courtesans. Kodayū is reproduced in Hillier 1987, fig. 89. Masanobu's new design for Masatsune is reproduced in Inoue 1929, fig. 2. With the exception of the most famous – Komurasaki, Usugumo, Takao and Masatsune – the courtesans in Masanobu's publication are given names different from those in Kiyonobu's *Illustrated Book of Courtesans*.

8 The first, *Yūjo no zō* (*Figures of Courtesans*), was published by Odera (or Kodera) Chōbei in the first month, 1702. Machida 1987, fig. 300.1–5, reproduces some illustrations from a copy in a private collection. The second (title unknown) was issued by Odera in the fifth month, 1702. Vergez 1983, fig. 1. Several pages from a copy of this second book are in the Pasadena Art Museum (formerly part of the Frank Lloyd Wright Collection). Honolulu 1980, p. 90.

9 Jenkins 1972, pp. vi–vii. When Jenkins wrote his article the illustrations were assumed to be from *Shidare yanagi* (*Weeping Willow*). The 'i-ro-ha' numbered pages in the Chicago copy are now believed to be from *Midare fuji*.

10 They include early dated and signed prints by Kiyonobu I in the *kakemono-e* format (Chicago 1955, p. 37, no. 10; Honolulu 1977, p. 5, no. 2) and smaller actor prints attributed to Kiyonobu I (Chicago 1955, p. 30, no. 2; p. 35, no. 6; p. 36, no. 7; p. 38, no. 12).

11 Jenkins 1972, p. vi.

12 Chicago 1955, p. 40, no. 16; Hempel 1997, no. 1. The Art Institute of Chicago also possesses a later, weaker, unsigned copy of this *kakemono-e* design without a publisher's mark. Chicago 1955, p. 137, no. 57.

13 One copy of this work, containing twenty courtesans and bearing the handwritten title *Okumura Masanobu yūjo no zō* (*Figures of Courtesans by Okumura Masanobu*), is discussed and reproduced in Tenri 1983, pp. 18–20, 387–409. The Boston Museum owns a similar, untitled publication dated 1711 and containing sixteen courtesans. Exceptionally, the depictions of Ukihashi and Masatsune in this work are based not on Masanobu's but on those in Kurihara's unsigned publication from the sixth month, 1701. The order of the courtesans is different in both publications.

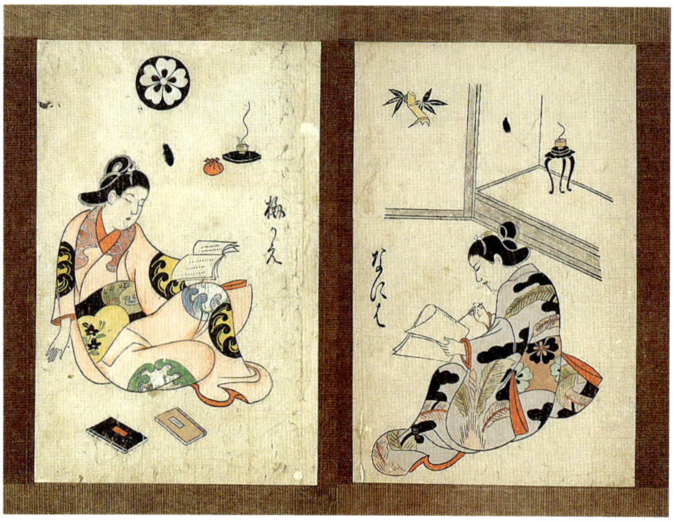

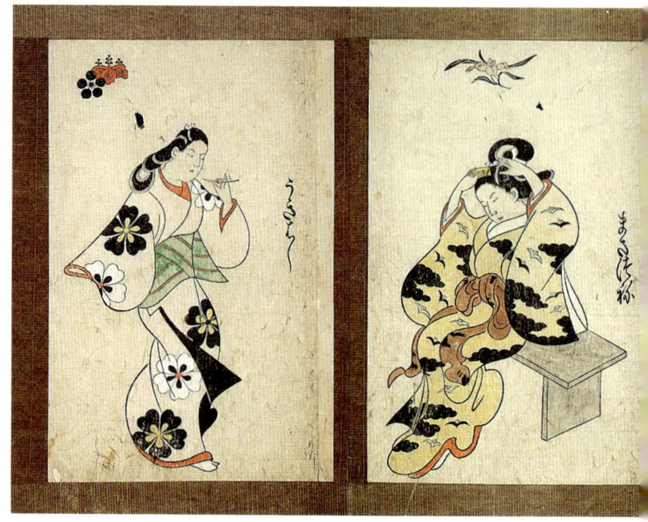

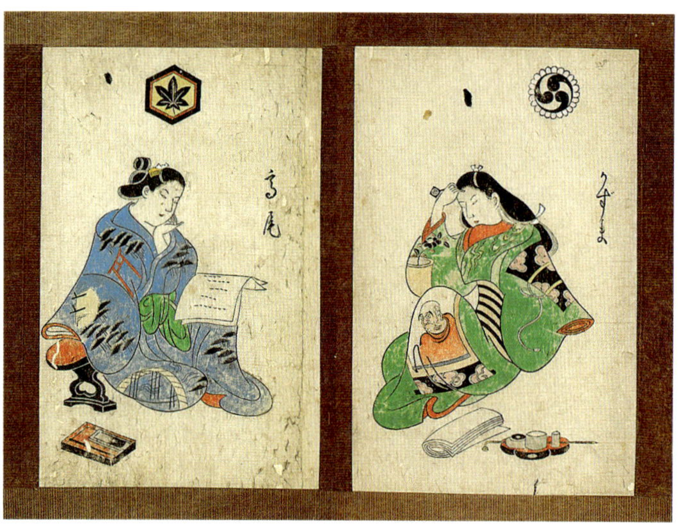

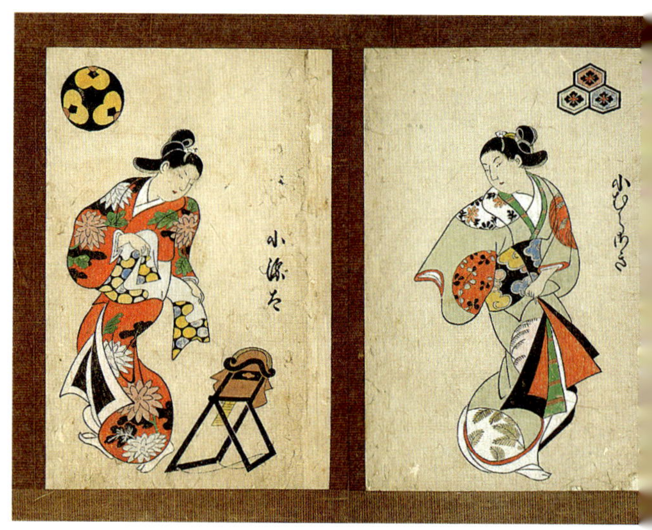

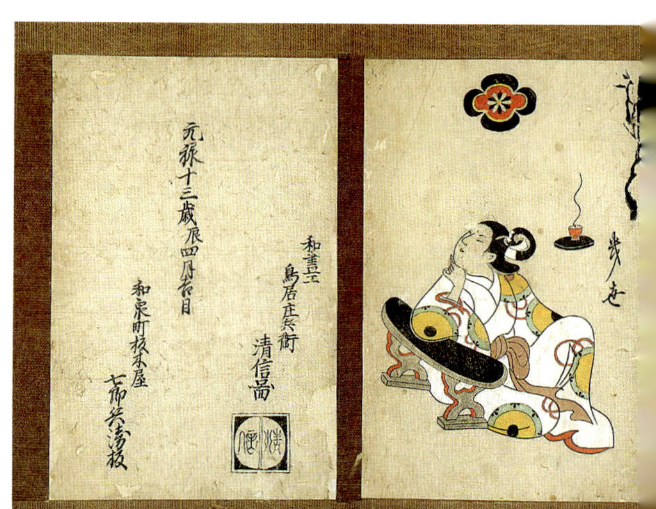
和画工 鳥居庄兵衛 清信画
元禄十三歳辰四月吉日
和泉町板木屋 七郎兵衛板

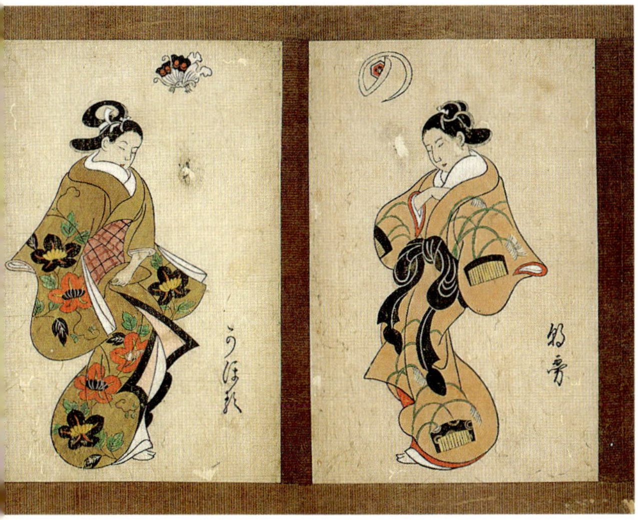

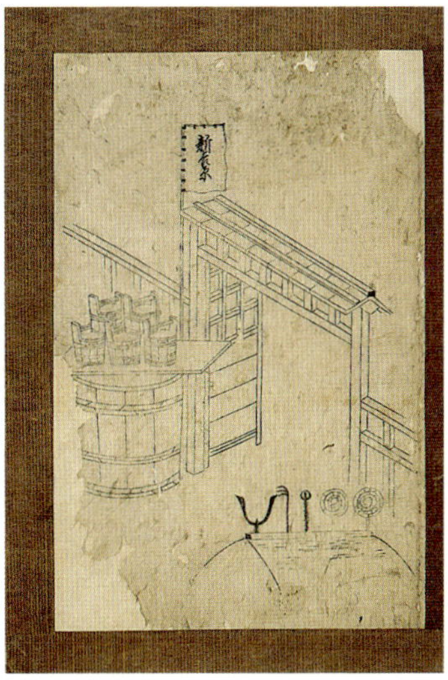

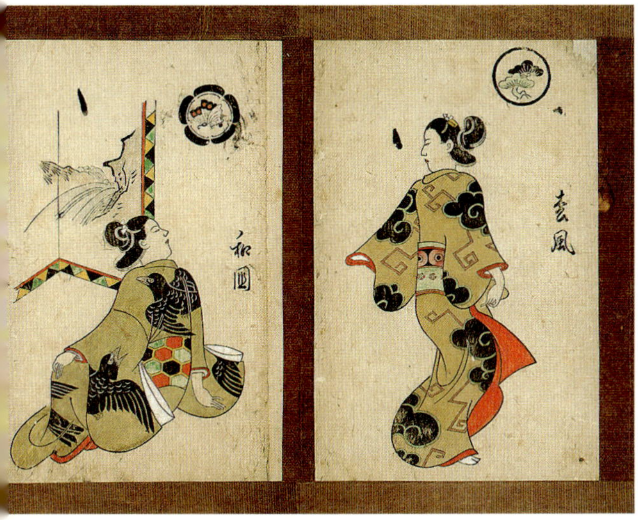

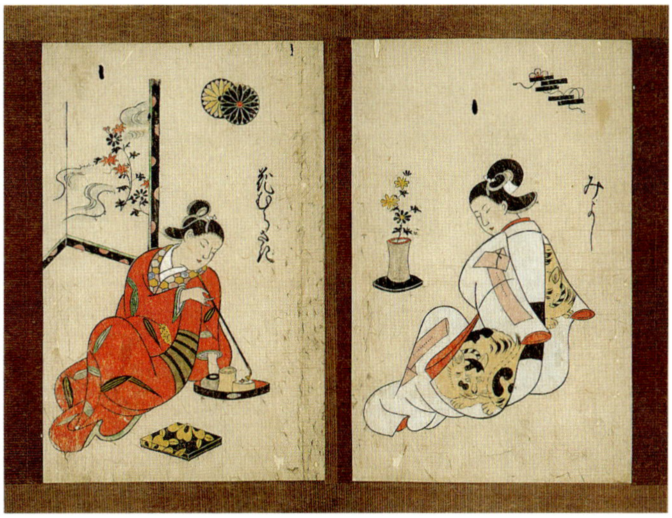

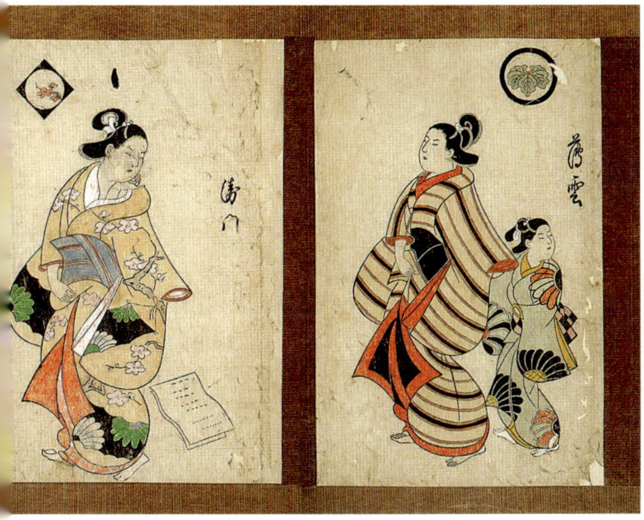

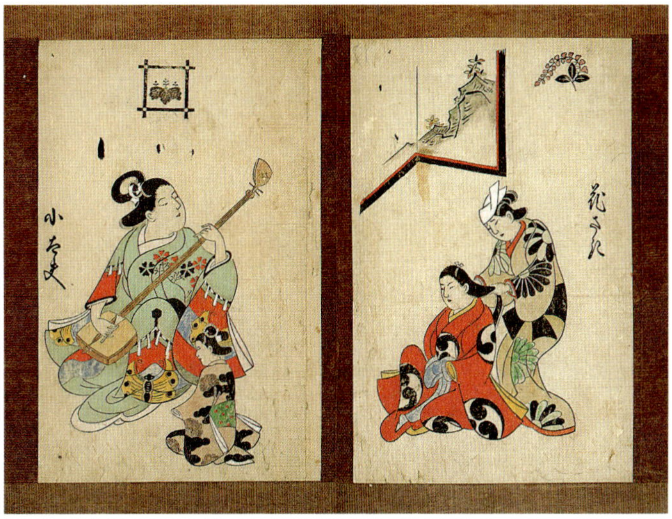

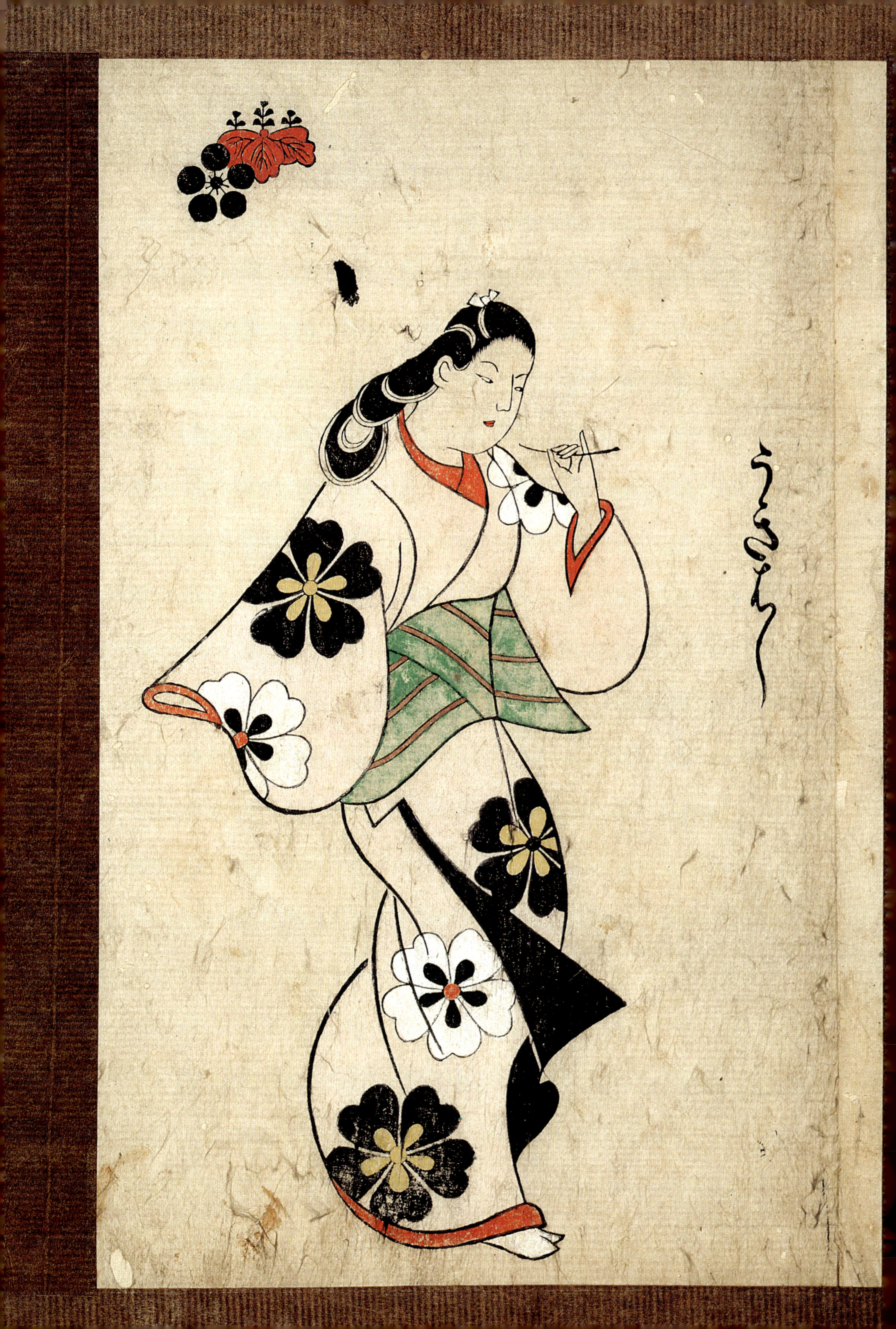

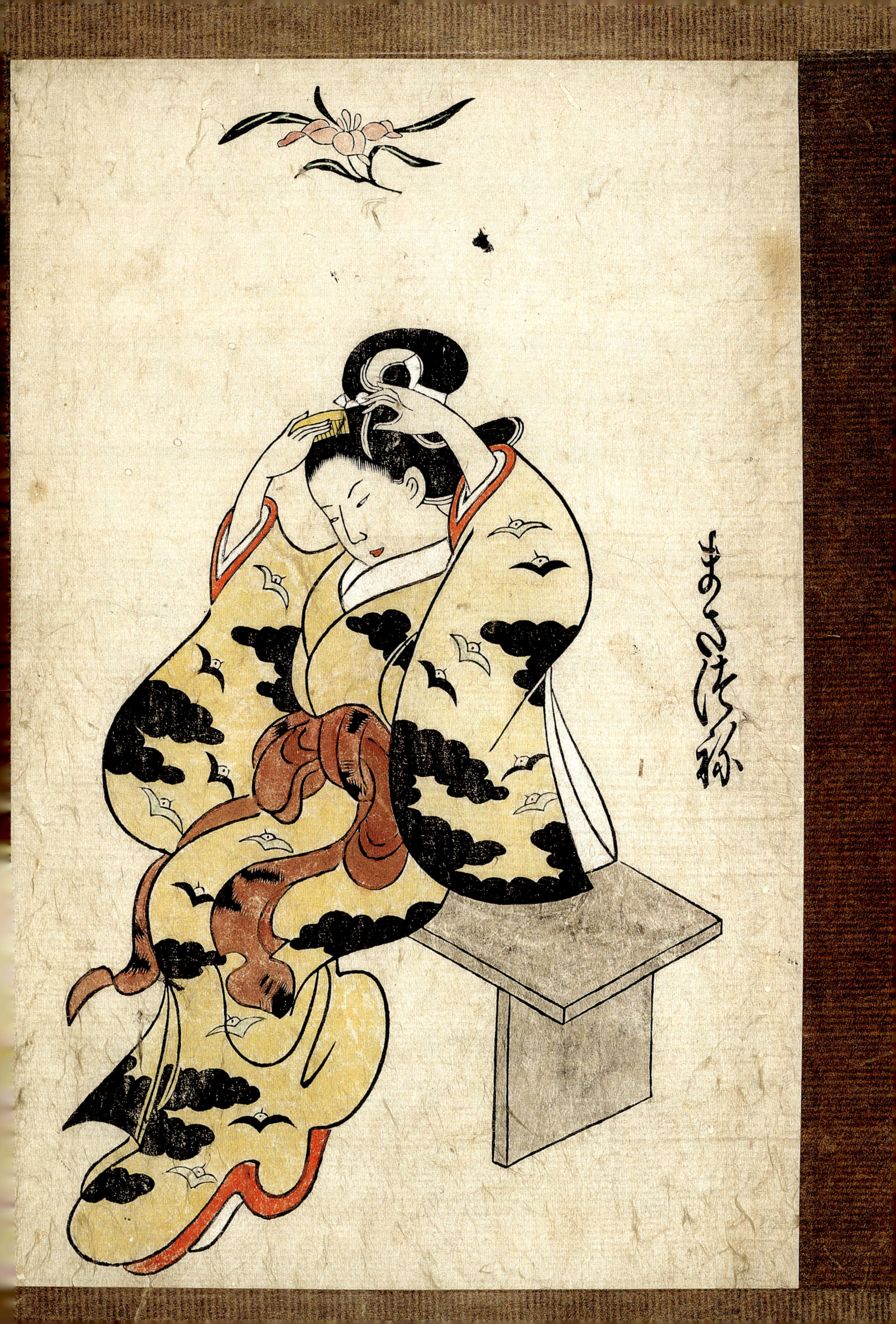

26

Torii Kiyonobu I

'The Female Groom: Teika's Journey'
(Onna mumakata Teika no michiyuki)

10th month, 1702 (?)

ARTIST'S SIGNATURE: 'Torii Kiyonobu'

ARTIST'S SEAL: 'Kiyonobu'

PUBLISHER: 'Hangi-ya kongen e-dokoro Shichirobei' (Picture shop of Shichirobei, originator of Hangi-ya [literally, 'woodblock shop'])

woodblock, horizontal *ō-ōban, sumizuri-e* with slight hand-colouring, 30.5 × 55.3 cm

Gift of Nathan Chaikin by exchange, 1967

67.653

1 Torii 1989, p. 364.

2 Private communication.

3 *Hizō ukiyo-e*, vol. 6 (Musée Guimet, Paris), no. 24 (commentary by Asano Shūgō).

4 Hillier 1970, vol. 1, pp. 50–1, no. 24, where the print is attributed to Kiyomasu I.

The title indicates that this depicts 'Teika's journey', a scene originally from Act IV of the popular Tosa *jōruri* puppet play *Teika*. The character Nowake no Tsubone, who is secretly in love with the poet Fujiwara no Teika, disguises herself as a horseman and leads Teika's horse on his journey to Fujikawa in the eastern provinces. The story develops into a 'new' version of *Dōjō-ji* as, tricked and left behind by Teika, Nowake turns herself into a giant snake to cross the Ōi River (see also cat. 50).[1] Here Nowake's attire is perfectly feminine, however – which explains the title, 'The Female Groom'. Nakamura Gentarō appears as Nowake (right), Ikushima Shingorō as Teika (on horseback, centre) and Nakamura Denkurō as the character Gotō Saemon (left). The title is written prominently down the right side; above this is the turret curtain of the Ichimura Theatre. Surviving records of performances do not include a play of this name; nor is this line-up of actors known to have appeared together at the Ichimura. Hence the print probably either represents a 'dream line-up' (*mitate*), with popular actors imagined in this combination, or formed part of advance publicity for a performance that never took place.

Mutō Junko has suggested the following possibility.[2] Nakamura Denkurō was actor–manager of the Nakamura Theatre, so he did not often appear at other theatres. Yet he did perform at the Ichimura for the year-long season from 1701/11. Nakamura Gentarō made his first appearance in the actor critiques as a promising young actor of female leads from 1702/11, performing at the Ichimura together with Ikushima Shingorō. The print may have been produced around the tenth month, 1702, as advance publicity, perhaps even as an inducement to Nakamura Denkurō to stay on at the Ichimura Theatre for another season. (In the event he returned to the Nakamura.)

The landscape includes names of some of the famous spots described to Teika on his journey by the horseman: (from right to left) 'Karasaki no matsu' (Karasaki Pine), 'Shiga-ura' (Shiga Bay), 'Hiei-zan' (Mount Hiei), 'Mii-dera' (Mii Temple), 'Sakamoto Sannō' (Sakamoto Sannō Shrine). A narrow, vertical section cut out towards the far left has removed part of the final place name, perhaps 'Semimaru [waraya no toko?]' (Thatched Hut of Semimaru).

A horizontal *ō-ōban* print by Kiyomasu I illustrates a performance entitled *Ukare-mumakata Teika no michiyuki*, staged at the Yamamura Theatre in the eleventh month, 1710.[3] Although the actors appearing on that occasion were different, the poses are remarkably similar and Kiyomasu I must have referred to Kiyonobu I's design. Also related is an unsigned vertical *ō-ōban* print in the early Torii style (Minneapolis Institute of Arts), in which the three main characters do not have actor's crests and which has some of the same place names in the background landscape.[4] The absence of actors' crests suggests perhaps that the Minneapolis print relates to Tosa *jōruri* rather than to kabuki.

Kiyonobu I appears to have had a particularly close relationship with the publisher Hangi-ya Shichirobei (see also cat. 24, 25). TTC

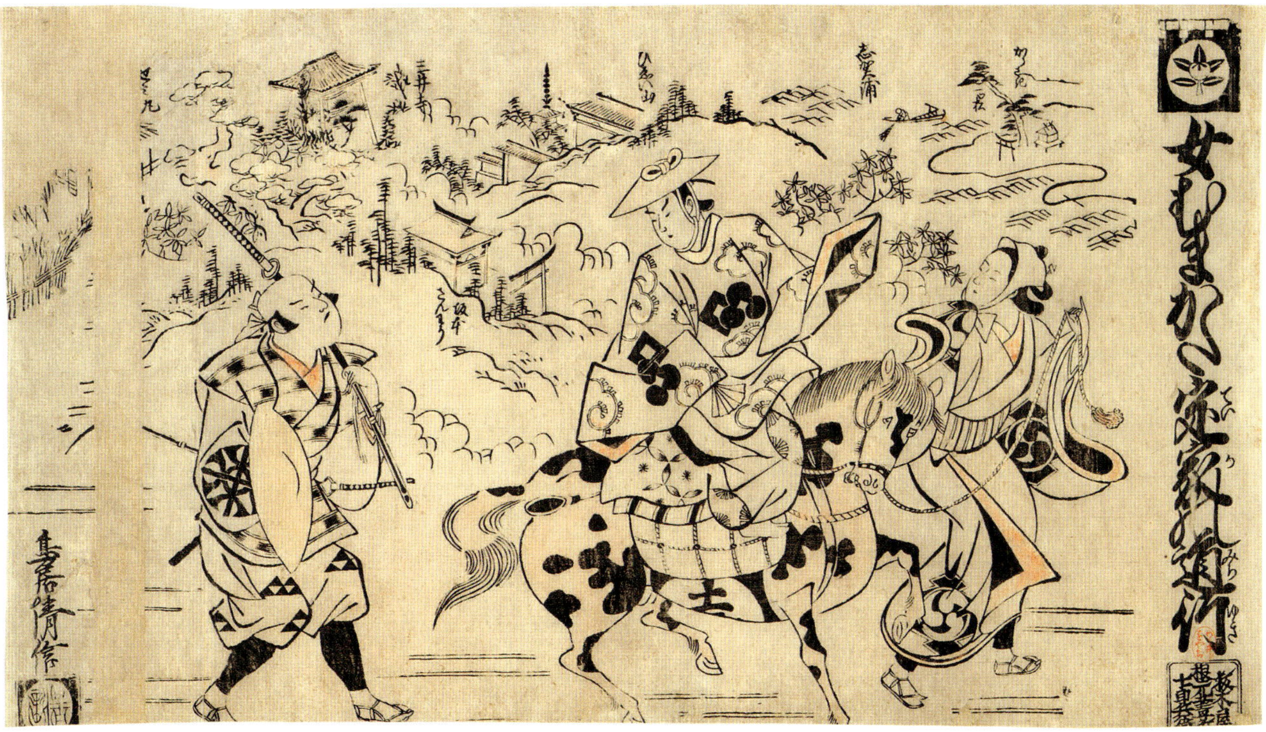

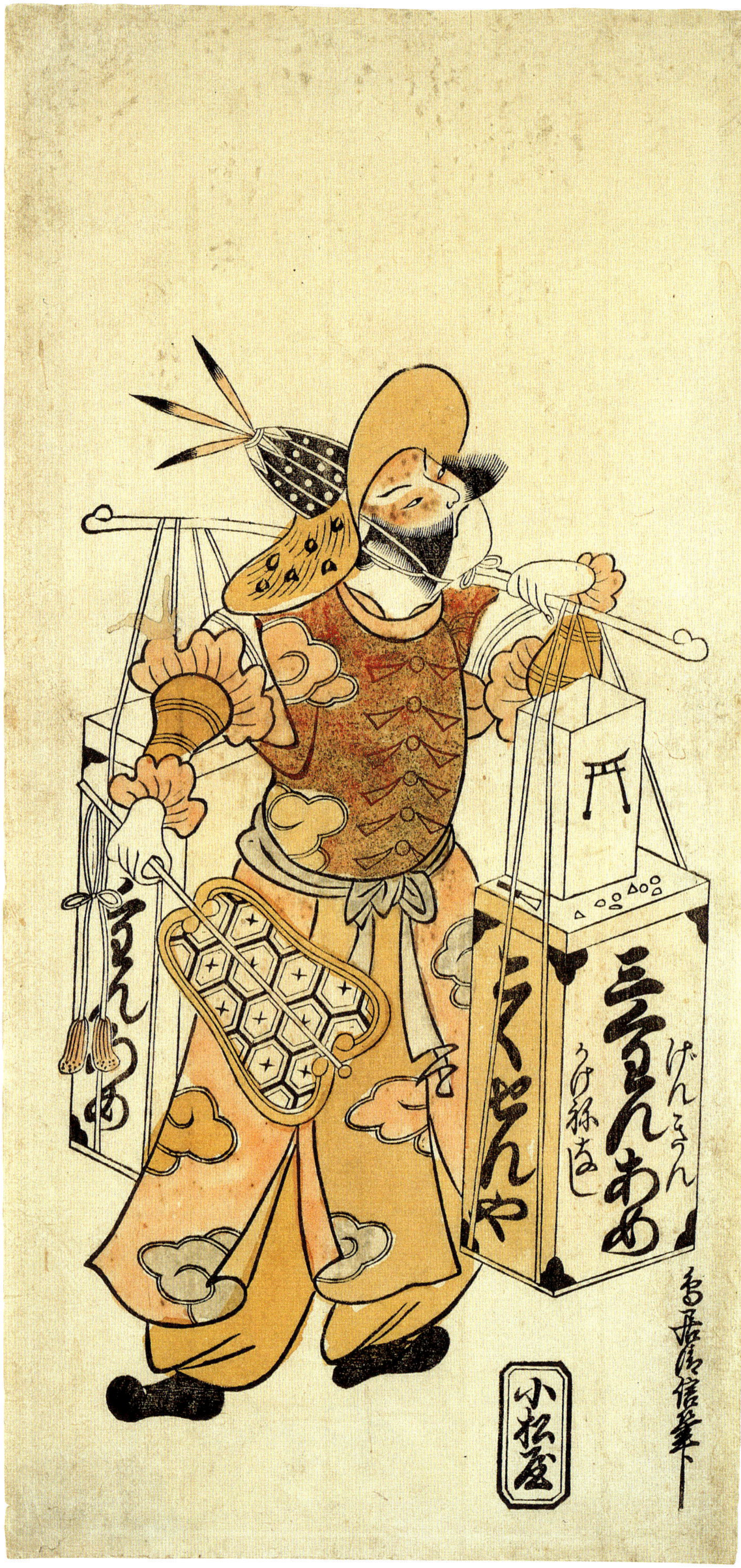
小松屋

27

Torii Kiyonobu I

The Actor Ōtani Hiroji [?] as a Candy-seller

5th month, 1717 (?)

ARTIST'S SIGNATURE: 'Torii Kiyonobu hitsu' (Brush of Torii Kiyonobu)

PUBLISHER: 'Komatsu-ya'

woodblock, *hosoban, beni-e* with brass filings, 33.1 × 16.4 cm

William Sturgis Bigelow Collection, 1911

11.13165

From the late Hōei (1704–11) to the early Kyōhō (1716–36) era Ichikawa Danjūrō II had a string of hits performing as various types of street pedlar, each time selling a different product: moxa (*mogusa*, 1709/1; cat. 60), fans (1714/7, cat. 30), patent medicine (*uirō*, 1718/1) and so on. The popularity of such scenes was due partly to the fast, tongue-twisting sales patter that the actor delivered on each occasion. Here, unusually, there is no actor's crest on the costume. The general demeanour and characteristic bristling whiskers (*kama-hige*, 'scythe-shaped whiskers') suggest not Danjūrō II, but Ōtani Hiroji as the performer of another role of this type, selling *sankan* candy, dressed in exotic pseudo-Korean costume.[1] The trade name on the carrying-cases is Kokusen-ya, accompanied by such standard business slogans as 'cash [only]' (*genkin*) and 'set prices' (*kake-ne nashi*) (see also cat. 65).

Sankan was a type of candy popular in Edo from about the Enpō era (1673–81), the recipe for which was said to have been devised by a Chinese, one San Guan (Sankan).[2] The role of the *sankan* candy-seller had apparently been created by Tosa-dayū II (active from the late Hōei era) and incorporated by him in the puppet play *Taimen Soga*, in which Oniō and Dansaburō, retainers of the Soga brothers, both took on the guise of candy-sellers.[3] The business name of the pedlar on this print, Kokusen-ya, suggests *Kokusen-ya kassen*, a famous Chikamatsu play of which rival versions were performed at the three Edo theatres in the fifth month, 1717. The actor critique *Yakusha sanpuku-tsui*, published at the New Year, 1718, mentions that the version given at the Ichimura Theatre inserted the Coxinga story into a variant of the Soga plot and that Ōtani Hiroji scored a great hit as Watōnai (eclipsing Danjūrō II, who played the roles of Soga no Gorō and Watōnai at the Nakamura Theatre). In part three 'he [Hiroji] took the role of an old-fashioned seller of *sankan* candy, Kokusen-ya, and his sinister voice effects ['nitta nita-nita no kowairo'], set to rhythm, were a great hit throughout Edo'.[4]

The print is delicately hand-coloured in shades of orange, pink and blue. Brass filings have been sprinkled over the breast of the exotic jacket. TTC

1 Mutō Junko has kindly suggested this identification (private communication).

2 Satō Satoru (private communication).

3 Torii 1989, pp. 8–9, 182.

4 *Kabuki hyōban-ki I*, vol. 6, p. 561; *Kabuki nenpyō*, vol. 1, p. 473.

28
Torii Kiyonobu I
The Actor Yamashita Kinsaku as Naniwazu

11th month, 1723

ARTIST'S SIGNATURE: 'Gakō Torii Kiyonobu hitsu hon-toiya' (Brush of artist Torii Kiyonobu, book wholesaler)

PUBLISHER: 'Hasegawa-chō Ōmiya Kuhei hanmoto' (Ōmiya Kuhei, publisher at Hasegawa-chō) with publisher's mark

woodblock, *hosoban, beni-e, urushi-e,* brass filings, 30.1 × 15.8 cm

REPRODUCED: *Ukiyo-e shūka,* vol. 1, no. 73

William Sturgis Bigelow Collection, 1911

11.13167

1 Hattori 1983, p. 327, s.v. 'Hachi-no-ki mono'.

2 *Ukiyo-e shūka,* vol. 1, no. 73; Mutō 1997, p. 3.

3 Mutō 1997, esp. pp. 17–19.

The inscription reads: 'A female version of "The Potted Trees", Yamashita Kinsaku down from Osaka' ('Onna hachi-no-ki / Osaka-kudari Yamashita Kinsaku'). Kinsaku appears in the role of Naniwazu, wife of Sano no Genzaemon in the play *Hachi-no-ki mi-gyōsho,* performed at the Nakamura Theatre in the eleventh month, 1723. The story was adapted from the nō play *Hachi-no-ki* (*The Potted Trees*) and performed in both puppet and kabuki versions.

Saimyō-ji Nyūdō Tokiyori travels around the country disguised as an itinerant monk in order secretly to survey the disposition of military forces. At Sano in Kōzuke Province he seeks shelter from heavy snow at a humble dwelling, where the impoverished owner, Sano no Genzaemon Tsuneyo, feeds him and chops down his prized potted trees to make a fire. After Tokiyori returns to Kamakura, Genzaemon is rewarded for this demonstration of loyalty in the face of adversity. By the end of the 17th century a variant of the story had been devised in which Tokiyori is met not by Genzaemon, but by his wife – the 'Female Version of "The Potted Trees"' (*Onna hachi-no-ki*).[1]

As has been pointed out, the print matches the description in an actor critique of the following year, which mentions how Kinsaku wore two branches of plum like a pair of swords and imitated the swaggering walk (*roppō*) of the Osaka actor Arashi San'emon.[2] Kinsaku's *kosode* is decorated with an auspicious pattern of cranes, pine and long-tailed turtle (*mino-game*). The brocade bag hanging from the severed pine branch contains fragrant incense (*nioi-bukuro*) and was worn by women inside the breast of a robe. The use of the 'sash-shaped cartouche' (*obi-gata hyōki*) along the bottom of the print, containing the artist's signature and the publisher's name, address and trademark, seems to have begun in this year and continued until *c.* 1745. Mutō Junko has linked this to a government edict of 1722/11 – part of the Kyōhō Reforms (see pp. 26–7) – which created a wholesale guild of illustrated popular fiction (*e-zōshi toiya*) and required all printed books to include the name of the author and publisher in a special colophon, and she has suggested that print publishers voluntarily followed the same practice. The cartouche could easily be reused from design to design and thus facilitated trends towards mass-production, already evident in the print publishing industry.[3] TTC

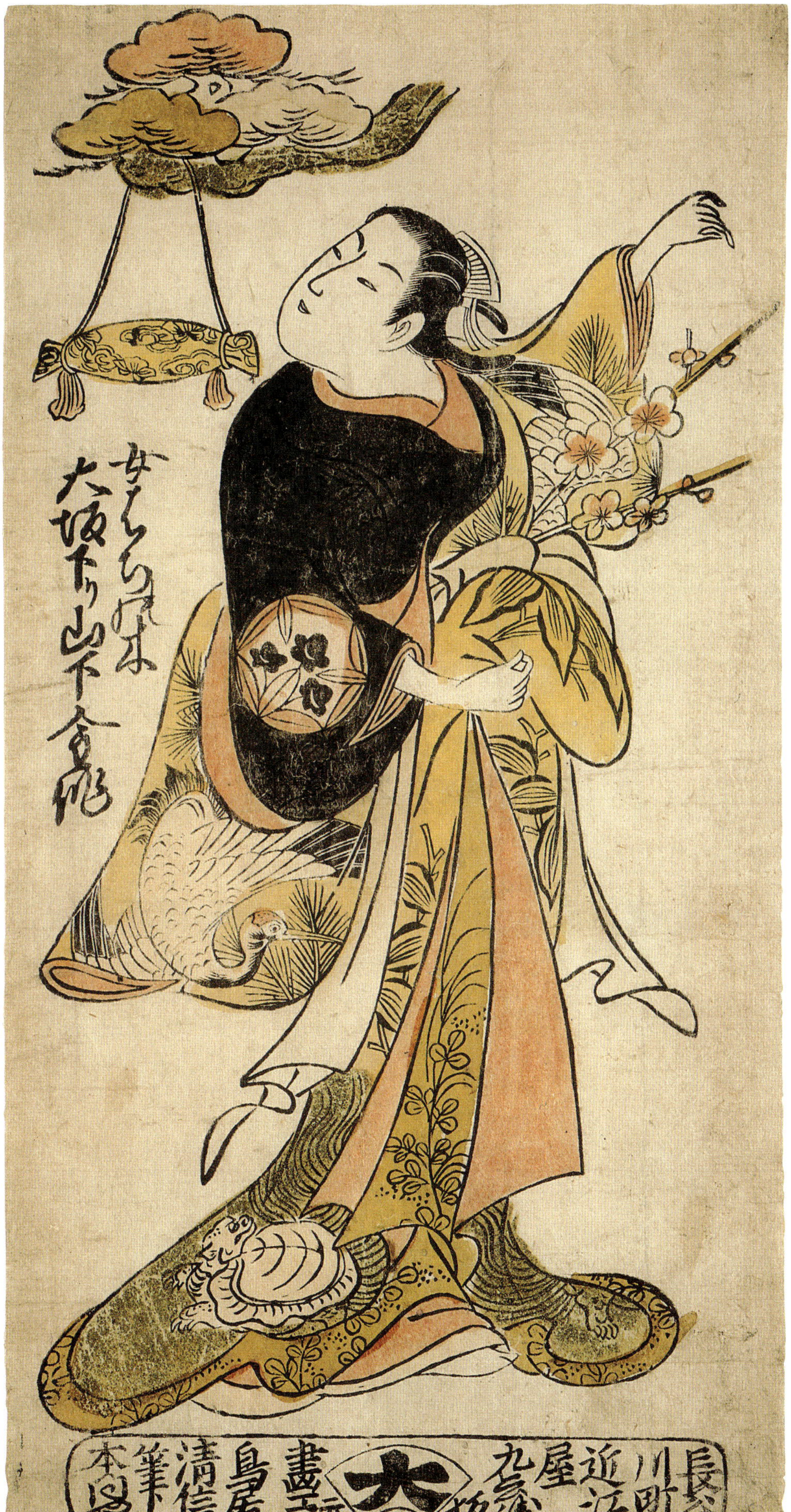
大坂下り山下金作
長谷川町
近江屋
鳥居清信
筆

29

Torii Kiyomasu I

Standing Courtesan

c. 11th month, 1705 – 1707

ARTIST'S SIGNATURE: 'Torii-uji Kiyomasu zu' (Picture by Kiyomasu of the Torii family)

ARTIST'S SEAL: 'Kiyomasu'

PUBLISHER: 'Motohama-chō Iga-ya hanmoto' (Iga-ya, publisher at Motohama-chō)

woodblock, *ō-ōban, sumizuri-e*, 56 × 26.4 cm

William Sturgis Bigelow Collection, 1911

11.13253

1 In general, the most famous actor to use a crest is suggested in each case. Particular doubt is indicated by a question-mark after the name. I am grateful to Mutō Junko for her assistance with the identifications.

2 Mutō 1992, nos. 1–4.

3 Tenri 1983, pp. 392, 398.

A courtesan is shown drawing up her surcoat (*uchikake*) in preparation for taking a step forward, filling the large sheet with her statuesque presence. The pose, with stomach pushed slightly forward and gaze tilted downwards, is coquettish. A similar pose is repeated with minor variations in many grand paintings and prints by rivals of the Kaigetsudō school (see cat. 82–6) and in prints by Okumura Masanobu in the same *ō-ōban* format (cat. 62). Along with the face and delicate hand, the most striking feature of the image is the pattern of decorative roundels amid trailing branches of willow on the *uchikake*. These roundels provide all-important clues to the date of the print.

The roundels contain ten crests used by leading kabuki actors of the day who specialised in roles categorised as *onnagata* (female), *kasha-gata* (older female) and *wakashu-gata* (delicate young male, i.e. relatively 'feminine'). Identification of the actors is complicated by the fact that several different performers – particularly those of the same acting 'family' – may have used the same crest at the same time. The following identifications are thus tentative (wherever possible, the dates during which the actor was active on the Edo stage in one of these three types of role are given after his name and speciality):[1] (right side, from top) 1. Takashima Onoe (?) (*onnagata*, 1704/11–1705); 2. Nakamura Gentarō (*onnagata*, 1702/11– ?); 3. Yoshioka Motome II (*wakashu-gata*, 1706/1–1708); (left, from top) 4. Nakayama Manzaburō (?) (*onnagata*, 1703–6); 5. Tsutsui Kichijūrō (*onnagata*, 1704/11–?); 6. Yasuda Kichirōji (?) (*kasha-gata*, 1707–?); 7. Hayakawa Hatsuse (*onnagata*, 1700/11–?); 8. Ogino Yaegiri (*onnagata*, 1705/11–1707); 9. Sakata Oginojō (*onnagata*, 1704–?); 10. Tsugawa Handayū (*onnagata*, 1698–1707).

Assuming that the print was issued while, or shortly after, these actors were active on the Edo stage (would a self-respecting courtesan wear a pattern that was *passé*?), its date can be narrowed down to *c.* 1705/11–1707. Four theatre-related prints by Kiyomasu I with the same, unusual 'Torii-uji Kiyomasu zu' signature have been identified by Mutō Junko and dated to around the Hōei era (1704–11), making them the artist's earliest securely dateable works.[2] The date of 1705/11–1707 for the present print, proposed here for the first time, therefore accords well with the other examples.

The maple-leaf crest that adorns the end of the woman's hairpin was used by several courtesans of the period – most famously by Takao, as featured in Kiyonobu I's *Illustrated Book of Courtesans* (1700; cat. 25). In Masanobu's version of this book from the following year a maple-leaf crest was also used by Ōkura and Kokura.[3] TTC

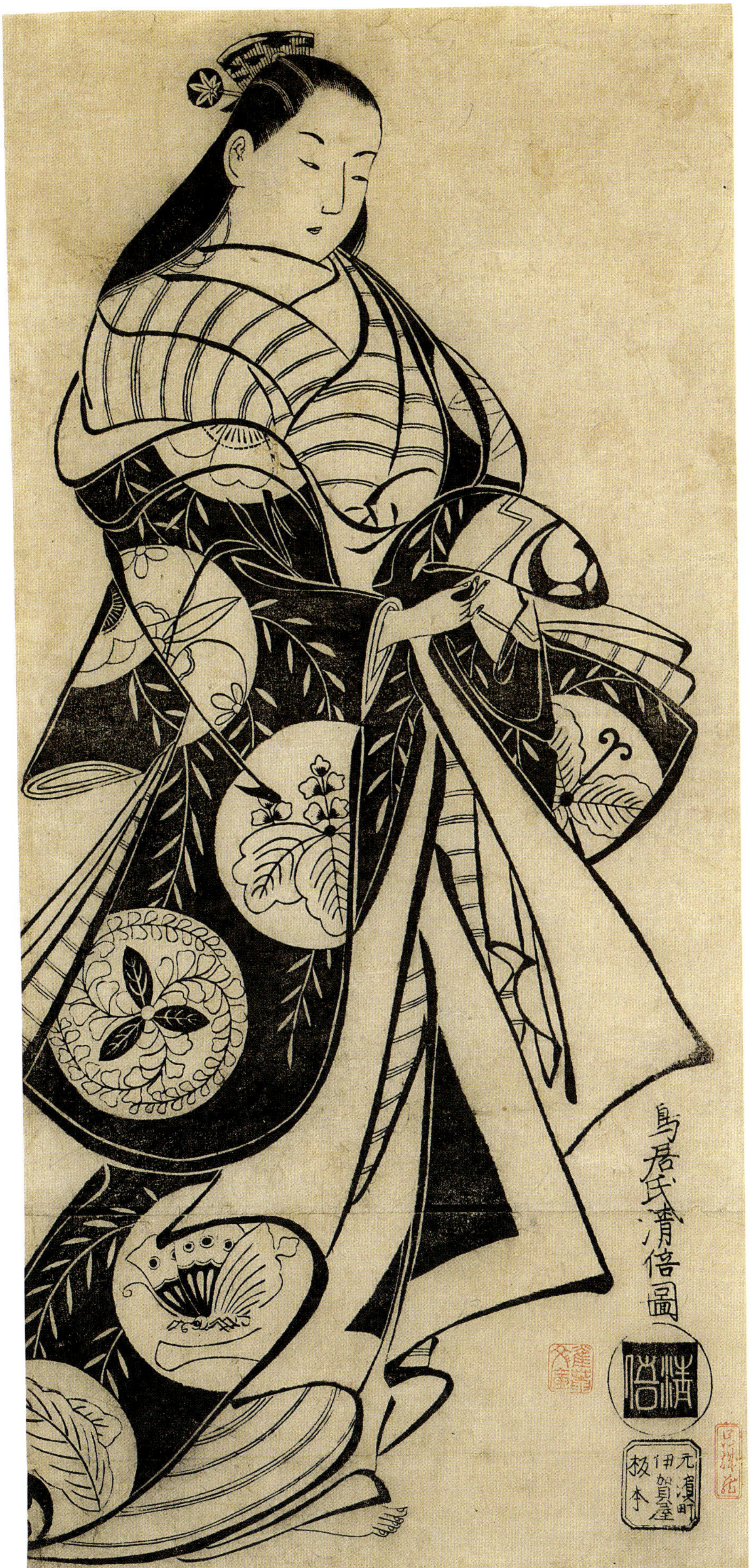
鳥居氏清倍圖
清倍
元濱町
伊賀屋
板本

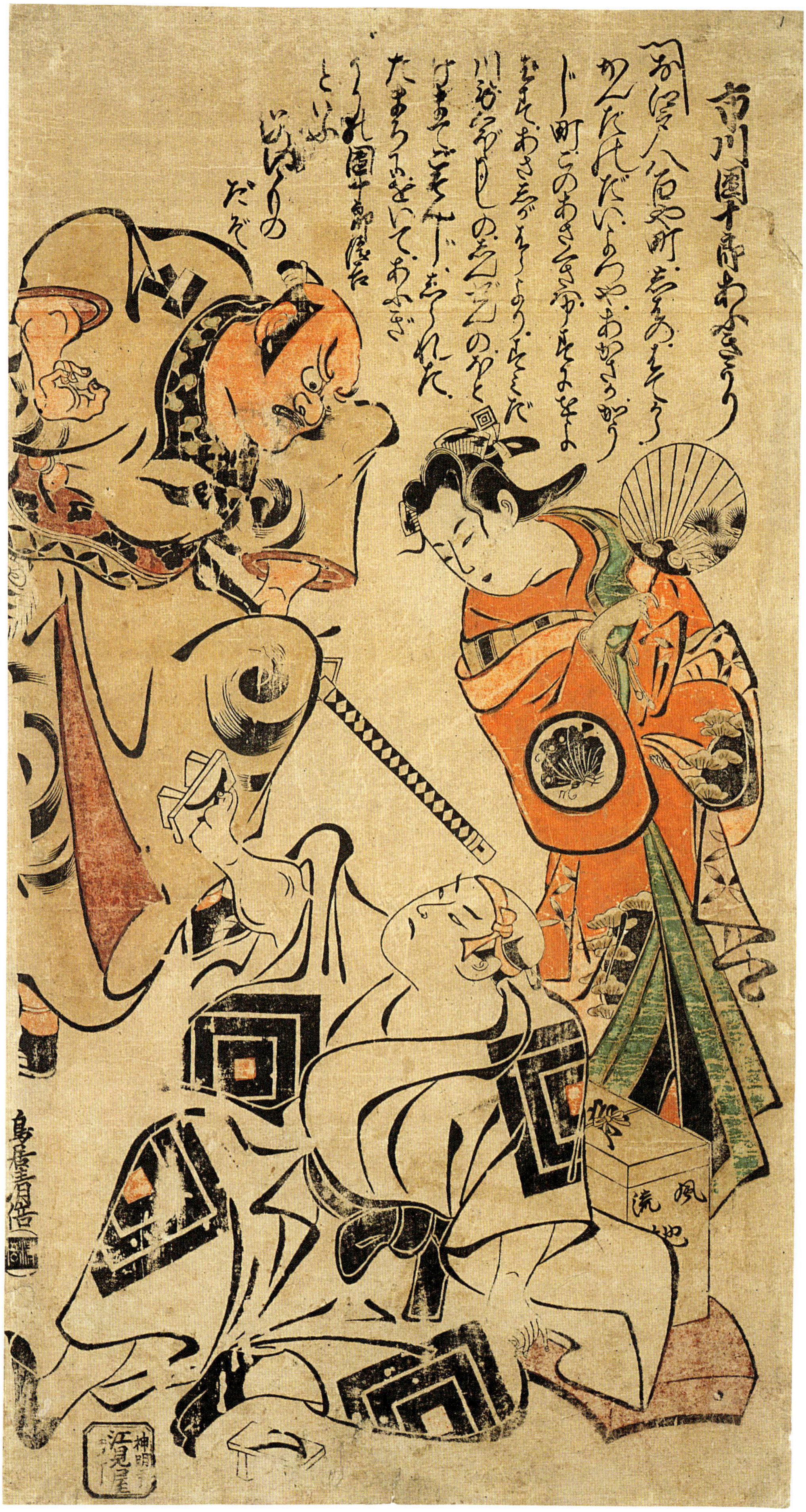
鳥居清倍
神明 江見屋

30

Torii Kiyomasu I

'Ichikawa Danjūrō as a Fan-seller' (*Ichikawa Danjūrō ōgi-uri*)

7th month, 1714 (or later edition)

ARTIST'S SIGNATURE: 'Torii Kiyomasu'

ARTIST'S SEAL: 'Kiyomasu'

PUBLISHER: 'Shinmei-mae Emi-ya . . .' (Emi-ya, at Shinmei-mae . . .)

woodblock, *ō-ōban*, hand-colouring (*tan-e*), 53 × 28.8 cm

OTHER IMPRESSIONS: (*Ukiyo-e taisei*, vol. 2, no. 56; this edn); formerly Yamamoto Hatsujirō Collection (Higuchi 1977, Kiyomasu I no. 12; this edn), Musée Guimet, Paris (*Hizō ukiyo-e*, vol. 6, BW no. 11; re-cut edn?); (Mutō 1992, no. 27; second re-cut edn?)

William Sturgis Bigelow Collection, 1911

11.13254

Ichikawa Danjūrō II appeared as Seikichi the fan-seller (seated, centre) in the third part of the play *Kinkazan ōtomo no matori*, performed at the Morita Theatre in the seventh month, 1714. His character Kanemichi had assumed this as a lowly disguise. Sanjō Kantarō II (right) apparently takes the role of a courtesan and Ōnishi Moriemon (left) is in a villainous guise, though further details of the scene are not known. The inscriptions on the carrying-case on the ground behind Danjūrō II read 'fūryū ji[gami]' (elegant fan papers) and 'ōgi' (folding fan). Itinerant pedlars of folding fans were generally handsome young men who were also known to sell sexual favours. Danjūrō II brandishes one of his wooden clogs ready for a fight; in the text above he introduces himself in lines doubtless delivered thunderingly. They tell of his renown in every corner of the city, listing the neighbourhoods where many of his admirers will also have lived: 'In the 800-odd neighbourhoods of fair Edo, from the fringes of Shiba to the heights of Kanda, in Yotsuya, Akasaka, Kōjimachi, not to mention, of course, here in Asakusa; from Asashi-ga-hara to the Buddhas of Mokubō-ji Temple on the Sumida River, I am the renowned seller of fans in Tamachi, that youth by the name of Danjūrō Seikichi.'[1]

This impression seems to have been printed from a damaged block, with a large split, for instance, passing through Danjūrō II's knee. Above the signature the edge of the block has broken off, removing most of Moriemon's foot. Although the hand-colouring has the red lead (*tan*) and yellow typical of the early 18th century, such extensive damage to the block would seem to militate against the impression having been taken as part of the original edition. The impression reproduced in *Ukiyo-e taisei* in 1931 appears to have been printed from the same block before it was quite so badly damaged. Two other published impressions seem to have been taken from two different re-cut blocks, perhaps made relatively recently.[2] It may be that no early impression has survived of this powerful design. TTC

1 'O-Edo happyaku-ya-chō Shiba no hate kara Kanda no dai Yotsuya Akasaka Kōjimachi kono Asakusa wa mōsu ni oyobazu Asashi-ga-hara yori Sumida-gawa Mokubō-ji no shinzen no hotoke made go-zonji shirareta Tamachi ni oite ōgi-uri no Danjūrō Seikichi to iu wakamono da zo.'

2 *Hizō ukiyo-e*, vol. 6, BW no. 11 (Musée Guimet, Paris); Mutō 1992, no. 27.

31

Torii Kiyomasu I

Courtesan Reading a Poem

c. 1715

ARTIST'S SIGNATURE: 'Torii Kiyomasu'

ARTIST'S SEAL: 'Kiyomasu'

PUBLISHER: 'Motohama-chō Iga-ya hanmoto' (Iga-ya, publisher at Motohama-chō)

woodblock, *ō-ōban*, hand-colouring (*tan-e*), 53.3 × 32.6 cm (two joined sheets, edges torn and trimmed)

REPRODUCED: Chicago 1971, p. 65, no. 70; *Ukiyo-e shūka*, vol. 1, p. 84, no. 17

Gift of Miss Ellen Starkey Bates, 1928

28.198

1 Trans. in consultation with John Carpenter.

Kiyomasu I was primarily known for his actor prints, but during the period *c.* 1704–18, like his contemporaries Masanobu, Kiyonobu and the Kaigetsudō school masters, he also produced prints of courtesans suitable for mounting as *kakemono* images. The artists, aware of and influenced by each other's works, all designed tall figures with fluid line work, in similar poses and hairstyles and with a comparable fall and sweep of skirts.

In this print by Kiyomasu the courtesan's long hair falls loosely over her shoulder and is held in place by a tortoise-shell comb. Her robe is decorated with bamboo-and-snow, zigzag and plum-blossom designs, enlivened by bright and partly oxidised *tan* (red lead), combining to make this one of Kiyomasu's most memorable works. There is a playful and visually striking repetition of S-curves in the stance of the woman and the long sheet of inscribed paper she holds. The *hokku* reads:

Tsuki no koro	Just when the moon is full
uttoshi keredo	plum blossoms by the window
mado no ume	may get in the way, but ...[1]

The cursive calligraphy on the scroll boldly accents the first and last characters of the verse – 'moon' (*tsuki*) and 'plum' (*ume*) – thereby drawing further attention to the poetic dilemma concerning which is more impressive and suggesting that their beauty is mutually enhanced when viewed together. The obscuring clouds and the plum blossoms of the courtesan's robes similarly complement each other and harmonise with the imagery of the poem. LEV

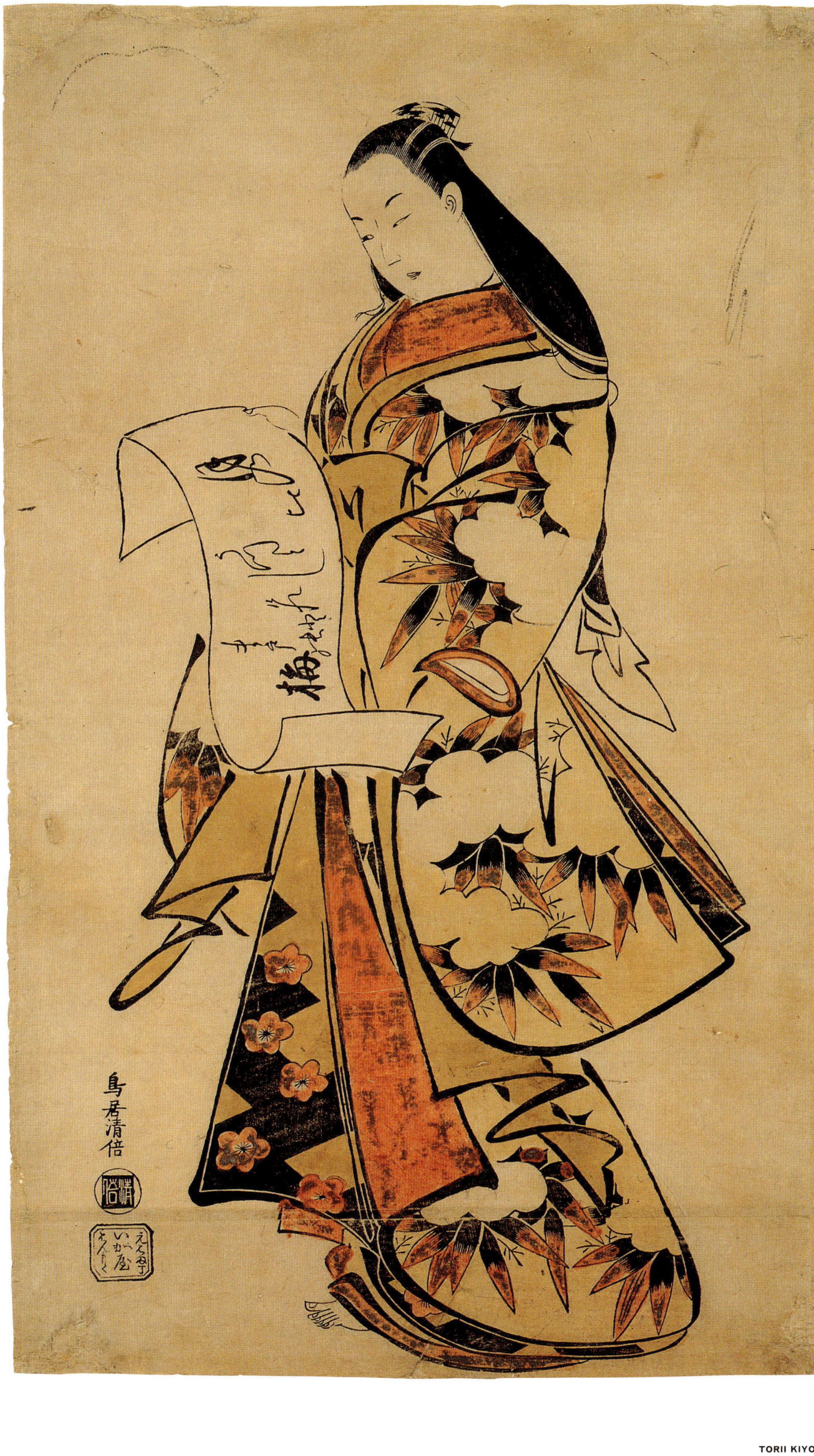
鳥居清倍

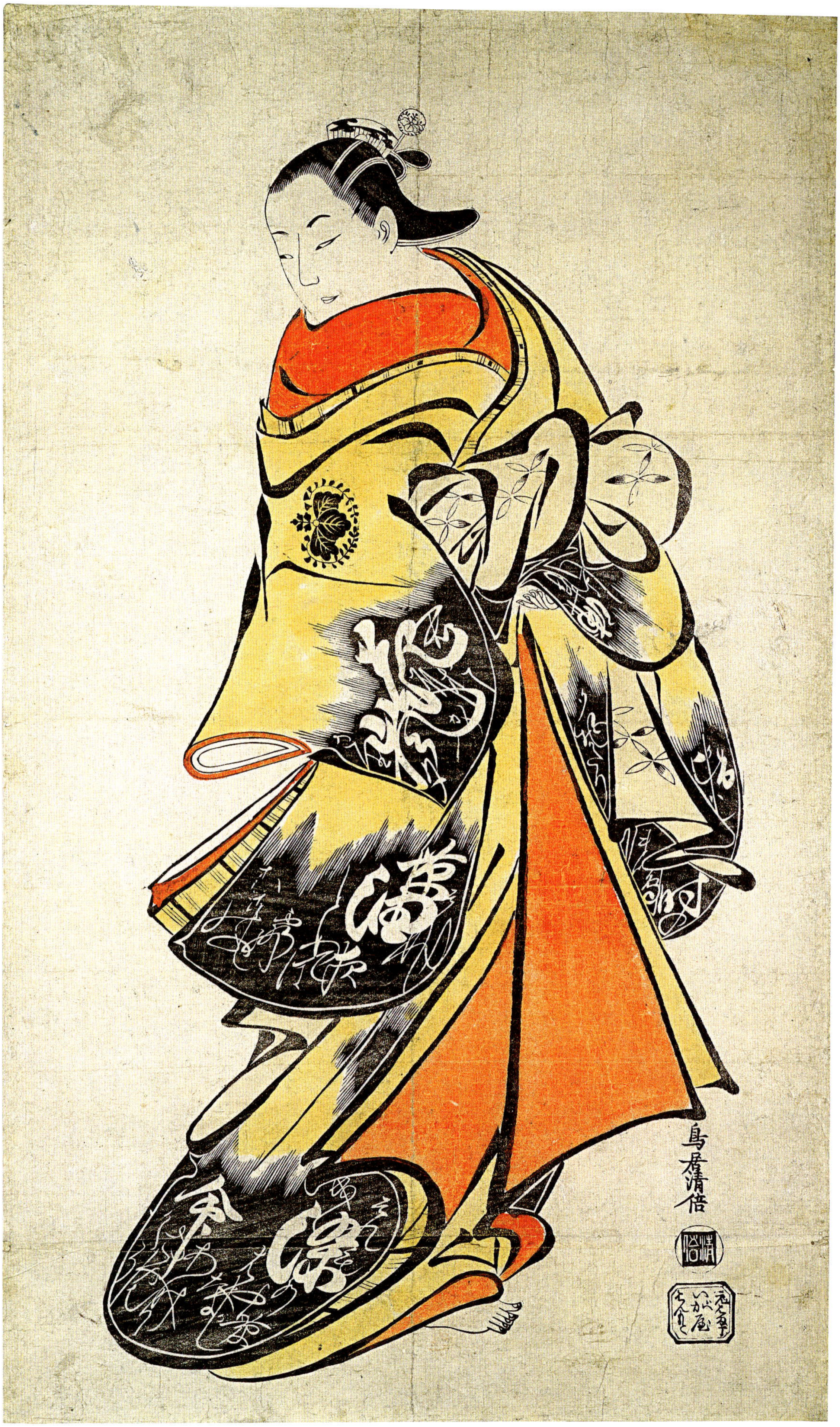
鳥居清倍

32

Torii Kiyomasu I

The Actor Fujimura Handayū II as Ōiso no Tora

1st month, 1715 (?)

ARTIST'S SIGNATURE: 'Torii Kiyomasu'

ARTIST'S SEAL: 'Kiyomasu'

PUBLISHER: 'Motohama-chō Iga-ya hanmoto' (Iga-ya, publisher at Motohama-chō)

woodblock, *ō-ōban, tan-e*, 53 × 32.3 cm

REPRODUCED: *Ukiyo-e shūka*, vol. 1, no. 8

OTHER IMPRESSION: Art Institute of Chicago (*Ukiyo-e shūka*, vol. 4, no. 88)

Special Funds, 1954

54.216

The crest on the sleeve and hairpin, consisting of a paulownia (*kiri*) leaf with flowers stretched around it to meet at the bottom, identifies the actor as Fujimura Handayū II. Handayū II arrived in Edo from Kyoto at the end of 1706 and was to remain there as a mainstay of female roles until his death in 1745. He was particularly noted for his portrayal of female warriors.

Here, it is thought that Handayū II is depicted in the role of the courtesan Tora from Ōiso, the lover of Soga no Jūrō. The most prominent occasion on which he played Tora was at the New Year of 1715, in the play *Bandō ichi kotobuki Soga* at the Nakamura Theatre.[1] At this time the three surviving Edo theatres went all out to revive their fortunes after the trauma of the Lady Ejima scandal and the forced closure of the Yamamura Theatre (see p. 26). Handayū II appeared opposite Katsuyama Matagorō as Jūrō, and the play was a great success, continuing until the seventh month. Other scenes from the same day's performance appear in other works included here (cat. 33, 34; p. 27, fig. 15). Since Soga plays were performed at every New Year, however, Handayū II will have played Tora on other occasions and it may be that this print is not linked to a specific performance.

With her arms pulled inside her robes and flashing a seductive glance back over her shoulder, Tora wears a *furisode* with a striking design of scattered cursive writing that may have been resist-dyed onto the cloth. Certain *kanji* stand out against a background of smaller *kana* written in tangled epistolary style: they are suggestive, poetic words, such as 'flower-storm' (*hana-arashi*), when petals are scattered by a strong breeze, 'love' (*nure*), 'infatuation' (*some*) and 'umbrella' (*kasa*) – for sheltering lovers. Brilliant orange hand-colouring for the under-robe is juxtaposed with yellow on the *furisode* – the classic combination for so-called 'red-lead pictures' (*tan-e*). The pose was one frequently used by contemporary Kaigetsudō artists (see cat. 83–6). TTC

1 Other times when Handayū played Tora at the Nakamura Theatre include New Year, 1720, but by that date Kiyomasu I had ceased to design prints and the *ō-ōban* format was no longer in use. Mutō 1992, p. 19, no. 25.

33
Torii Kiyomasu I
'Seven Spring Herbs' (*Nana-kusa*)

1715–16

ARTIST'S SIGNATURE: 'Torii Kiyomasu'

ARTIST'S SEAL: 'Kiyomasu'

PUBLISHER: 'Motohama-chō Iga-ya hanmoto' (Iga-ya, publisher at Motohama-chō)

woodblock, horizontal *ōban*, *sumizuri-e*, 27.5 × 44.8 cm

REPRODUCED: Mutō 1996, fig. 2

William Sturgis Bigelow Collection, 1911

11.13324

The New Year play at the Nakamura Theatre in 1715 was *Bandō ichi kotobuki Soga*. The first part of the performance contained an 'Argument [over the] Seven Herbs' ('Nana-kusa no tsume-ai'). Ichikawa Danjūrō II as Soga no Gorō (right) brandishes a smashed cutting board in typical *aragoto* fashion. He is restrained by Tomizawa Hanzaburō as Asahina (centre) from striking Ogawa Zengorō as Kudō Suketsune (left), the villain. On the cutting board in front of Kudō are the 'seven herbs of spring' (*nana-kusa*), typically made into soup for the New Year celebrations. A splendid hanging scroll painting by Kiyonobu I (p. 27, fig. 15) shows exactly the same climactic moment, except that the positions of Gorō and Asahina are reversed.[1] The play was an unprecedented success, largely owing to Danjūrō II's appearance in the novel guise of a mendicant monk (*komosō*; see cat. 34). According to a critique of the following New Year, it ran for a staggering seven months and ten days, with Danjūrō II adding an extra Narukami scene from the 28th day of the fifth month onwards.[2]

The print comes from a group of six (possibly seven) horizontal *ōban sumizuri-e* that share certain characteristics: the form of the signature and seal, the form of the publisher's mark and a title cartouche with a double outline (see also cat. 34). Mutō Junko has pointed out that these prints depict either *jōruri* scenes or kabuki dances with *jōruri* accompaniment and suggests that they were planned as a series.[3] They depict performances staged from the New Year of 1715 to the second month of 1716 and could thus have been issued separately during that period or together at the later date. TTC

1 An unusual, large playbill by Kiyomasu I includes an abbreviated version of this composition. Mutō 1992, no. 32.

2 *Yakusha gan-hodoki*, published at the New Year, 1716. *Kabuki hyōban-ki I*, vol. 6, p. 50. Also quoted in Mutō 1992, p. 23.

3 Mutō 1992, pp. 23–4, 28, nos. 38–42.

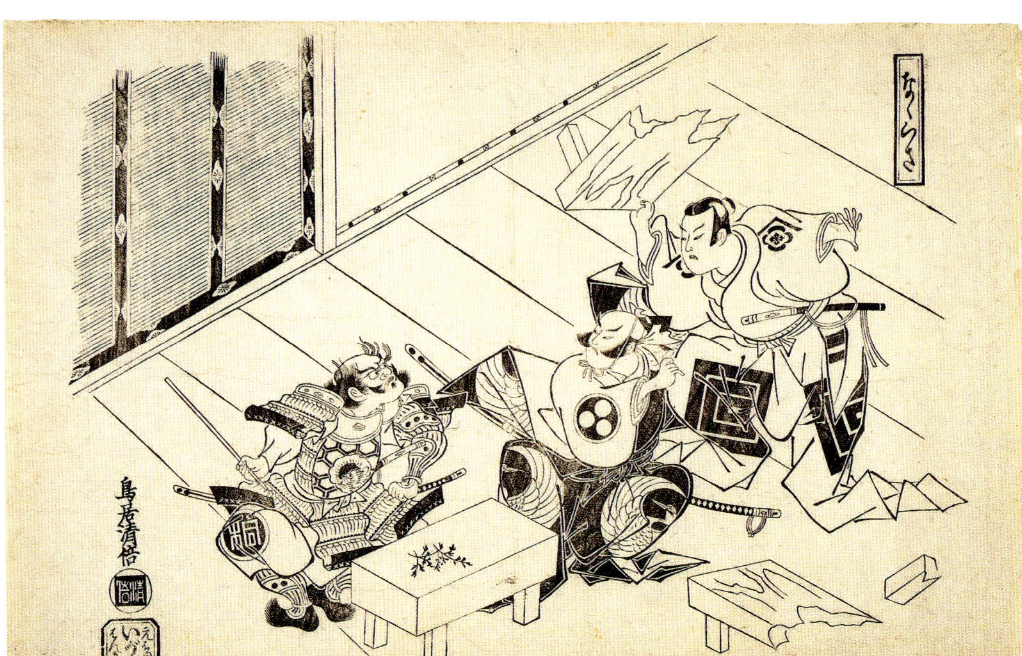

34
Torii Kiyomasu I
'Mendicant Monk Made out of Characters' *(Monji komosō)*

1715–16

ARTIST'S SIGNATURE: 'Torii Kiyomasu'

ARTIST'S SEAL: 'Kiyomasu'

PUBLISHER: 'Motohama-chō Iga-ya hanmoto' (Iga-ya, publisher at Motohama-chō)

woodblock, horizontal *ōban, sumizuri-e,* 28.9 × 39.8 cm

OTHER IMPRESSION: Art Institute of Chicago (Chicago 1955, pp. 53–4, Kiyomasu I no. 12)

Gift of Mrs Jared K. Morse, 1953

53. 2925

This print comes from the same series as cat. 33 and relates to the same day's performance. The play at the Nakamura Theatre in the New Year, 1715, was *Bandō ichi kotobuki Soga.* In the second part of the performance Ichikawa Danjūrō II reinterpreted the customary *aragoto* role of Soga no Gorō in a more delicate guise, as a foppish mendicant monk (*komosō* or *komusō*), building on the success of his dandyish hero Sukeroku of 1713. The role of Gorō's lover, the courtesan Kewaizaka no Shōshō, was taken on this occasion by Nakamura Takesaburō. Another horizontal *ōban sumizuri-e* print by Kiyomasu I depicts the two actors in a similar setting to the present image, but Danjūrō II is drawn as a normal human figure, rather than made up of written phonetic characters (*kana*) as he is here.[1] An abbreviated version of the scene appears in the top left corner of the large *tsuji-banzuke* playbill specially designed by Kiyomasu I for the occasion.[2] Gorō's monk's robes are formed from the characters *ya-tsu-tsu-shi* (*yattsushi,* more commonly *yatsushi*), which in the context of kabuki means a high-born character who has adopted a lowly disguise. One stoke of the *ya* graph has become the bamboo flute (*shakuhachi*) customarily played by *komosō,* and this emerges from beneath the sedge hat worn by such mendicants to hide their identity.

The success of the play led to a craze for everything to do with *komosō* and they appeared as designs in illustrated novels and on tobacco pouches, game boards, children's toys and fans. A complaint was made by the association of *komosō,* which had to be resolved by negotiation. The performances were not interrupted.[3] TTC

1 Art Institute of Chicago, 25.1720; Chicago 1955, pp. 53–4, Kiyomasu I no. 11.

2 Mutō 1992, no. 32.

3 *Kabuki nenpyō,* vol. 1, pp. 447–8.

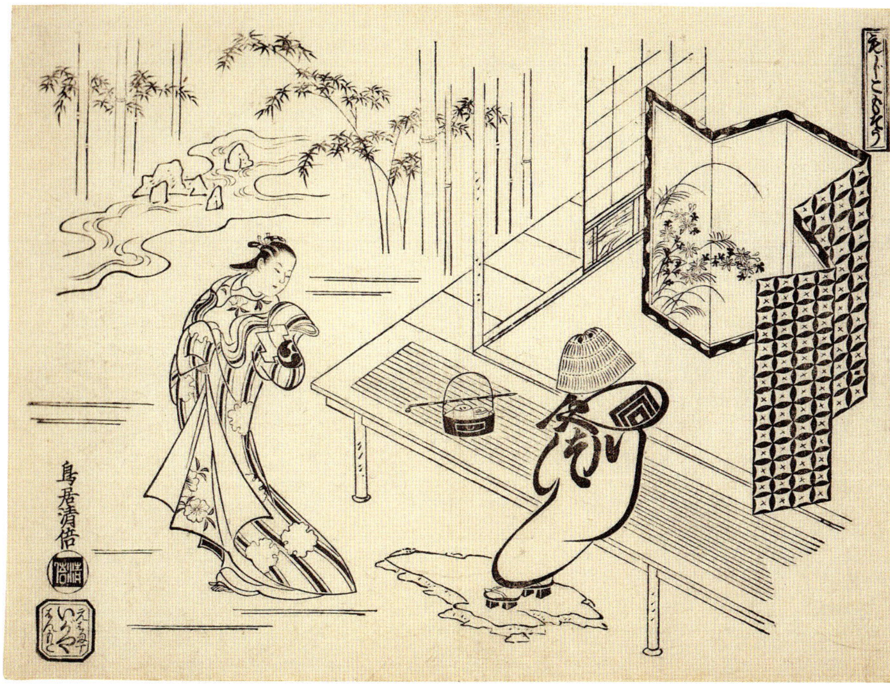

35

Torii Kiyomasu I

'Nakamura Senya, Come Down from Shijō, Kyoto' *(Kyō Shijō kudari Nakamura Senya)*

11th month, 1716

ARTIST'S SIGNATURE: 'Torii Kiyomasu'

ARTIST'S SEAL: 'Kiyomasu'

PUBLISHER: 'Yushima Tenjin, Komatsu-ya, Onna-zaka no shita' (Komatsu-ya, bottom of Onna-zaka Hill, Yushima Tenjin)

woodblock, *ō-ōban, tan-e*, 53.8 × 32.1

REPRODUCED: *Ukiyo-e shūka*, vol. 1, no. 19

OTHER IMPRESSIONS: Metropolitan Museum of Art, New York (Paris 1909, no. 73, pl. 19); Honolulu Academy of Arts, Michener Collection (Honolulu 1977, cover illus.); (Higuchi 1977, no. 28, pl. 26)

John Ware Willard Fund, 1945

45.831

In the eleventh month of 1716 a celebrated actor of female roles, Nakamura Senya, arrived in Edo from Kyoto and immediately caused something of a sensation. His first part was Tokonatsu, wife of Higuchi Jirō, in the play *Mitsu-tomoe katoku-biraki* at the Nakamura Theatre. The inscription next to the name on this print reads 'come down from Shijō, Kyoto', and it may be that Senya is shown here in the role of Tokonatsu. *Yakusha iro-janoyu*, a critique published at the following New Year, described how Senya was preceded onto the stage by two actors of aged female roles (*kasha-gata*) and three who acted female servants (*koshimoto*), all dressed in fabric dyed with the 'Senya' pattern. (This pattern was also used for the door superintendents' jackets and the doormen's scarves and seems to have consisted of bold tie-dyed dots against a purple background.) Carrying an umbrella and wearing a *kosode* with sleeves of modest length and a purple head-kerchief, Senya knelt respectfully on the stage and began a speech of self-introduction: 'I was previously known as Kiriyama Masanosuke [the name he had used on his first visit to Edo in the early 1690s] and I have come here as a new bride to enter my husband's family.'[1]

This is one of Kiyomasu I's most finely composed designs, Senya flourishing the umbrella with impeccable aplomb and throwing back a smiling glance while moving forward sedately on high clogs. The actor has shrugged off one sleeve of an outer-robe patterned with scattered fans to reveal his personal crest – a single gingko leaf within a circle. The plum blossom is in perfect accord with a play staged in the eleventh month, as this was the opening-of-the-season (*kaomise*) performance, considered the kabuki theatre's 'New Year'.

Another impression, in the Michener Collection at the Honolulu Academy of Arts, has darker hand-colouring, applied in more detail to the fans on the actor's kimono, and an additional pink used on the head-cloth and tree trunk. TTC

1 *Kabuki nenpyō*, vol. 1, pp. 465–6; *Kabuki hyōban-ki I*, vol. 6, pp. 336–7; also quoted in Mutō 1992, p. 26.

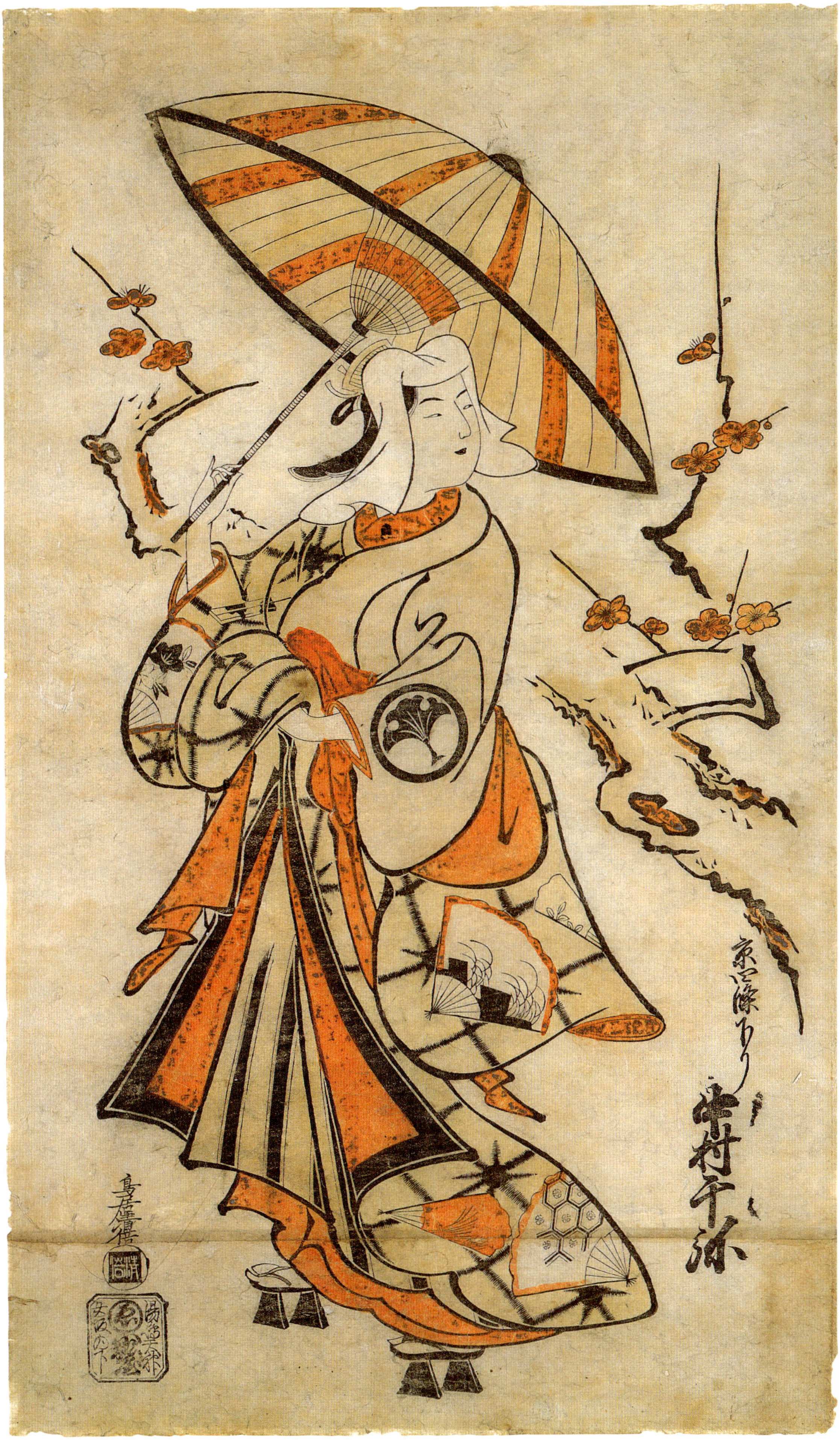
中村千弥
鳥居清倍

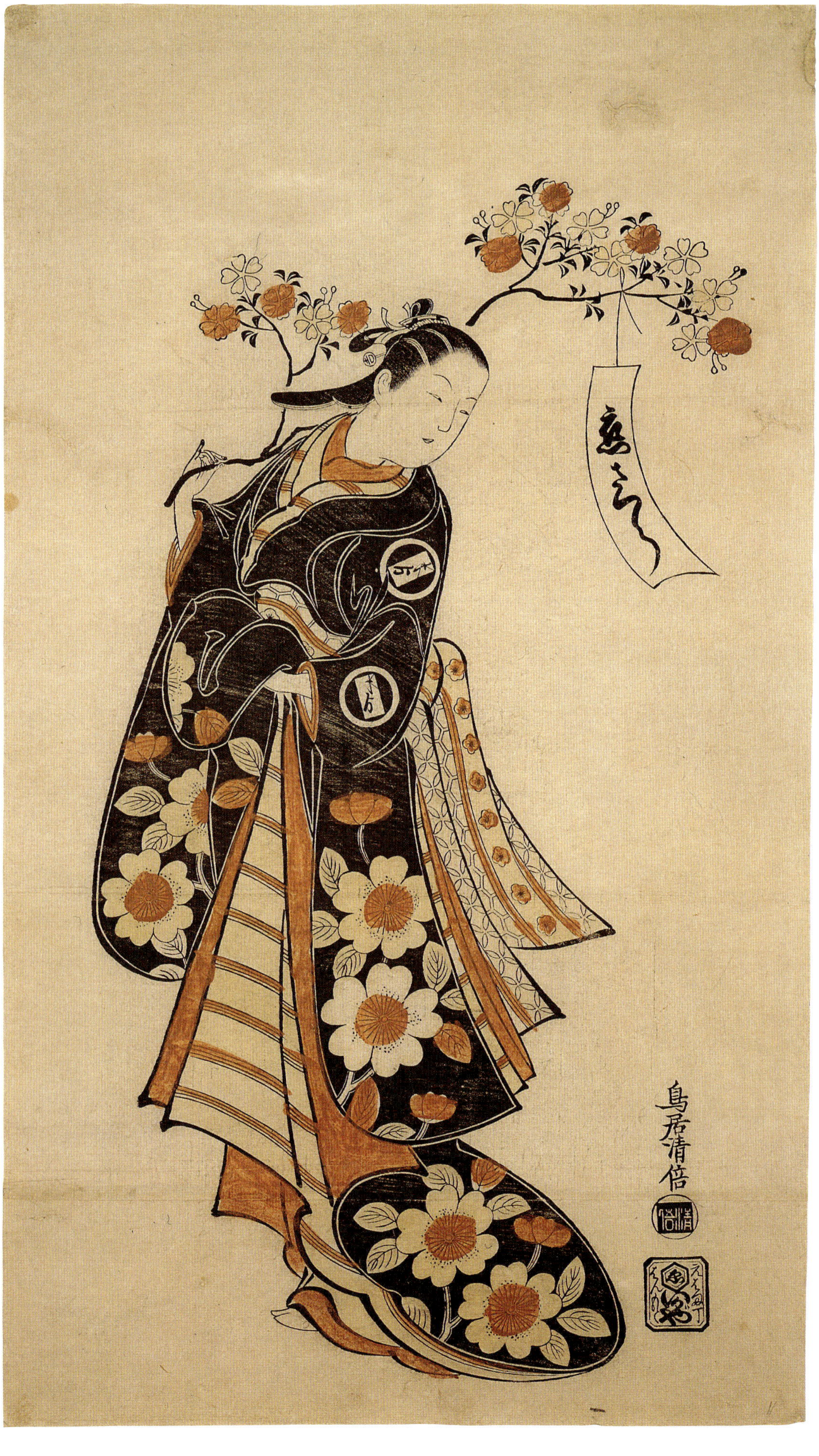
鳥居清倍

36
Torii Kiyomasu I
The Actor Sanjō Kantarō II [?] as Yaoya Oshichi

1st month, 1718

ARTIST'S SIGNATURE: 'Torii Kiyomasu'

ARTIST'S SEAL: 'Kiyomasu'

PUBLISHER: 'Motohama-chō Iga-ya hanmoto' (Iga-ya, publisher at Motohama-chō)

woodblock, *ō-ōban, tan-e*, 55.6 × 32.4 cm

REPRODUCED: Gentles 1964, no. 30; Chicago 1971, no. 85; Higuchi 1977, no. 40, pl. 27; *Ukiyo-e shūka*, vol. 1, no. 70

Julia Bradford Huntingdon James Fund, 1902

02.845

1 Chicago 1955, p. 62, Kiyomasu I no. 22.

The actor's *furisode*, in a style typically worn by teenage girls, is decorated with a bold floral pattern. The cherry branch has a label attached that reads 'love cherry' (*koi-zakura*). This alludes perhaps to the fate of Oshichi, the greengrocer's daughter who, like the cherry, will fall at the height of her beauty, condemned to death for laying a fire in order to be with her lover Kichisaburō (see cat. 37). The role is identified by the crest – a folded love letter – on the sleeve of the *furisode*. This was the personal crest of the Kansai actor Arashi Kiyosaburō, who created the kabuki role of Oshichi in Osaka in 1706 and performed it no less than three times, to great acclaim, at the Nakamura Theatre in Edo in 1708 and 1709. The young actor Sanjō Kantarō II revived the role in the play *Nana-kusa fukuju Soga* at the Ichimura Theatre at the New Year, 1718, to commemorate the seventh anniversary of Kiyosaburō's death.

Two fundamental questions relating to this design remain unresolved: which actor is depicted and when was the print issued? The Art Institute of Chicago possesses a print in quite similar style that shows an impersonator of women holding a libretto, the cover of which reads 'Yaoya Oshichi / Shinjū Edo-zakura / Handayū-bushi' (Oshichi the Greengrocer's Daughter / Love-suicide 'Edo Cherry' / Handayū-style Chanting), with the publisher's name Komatsu-ya.[1] The Chicago print bears the signature 'Torii Kiyonobu' and the seal 'Kiyomasu' and was published by Komatsu-ya. The actor has on his *furisode* both the folded love letter crest (for the role of Oshichi) and a crest consisting of a butterfly in a circle – the crest of Kantarō II. Thus there can be little doubt that the Chicago print was issued at the time of Kantarō II's performance at the New Year, 1718, on the same occasion as cat. 37 (see that commentary for discussion of the problem surrounding the combination of the Kiyonobu signature and the Kiyomasu seal).

The robes of the figure in the Boston print do not bear any of Kantarō II's personal crests, only the love letter crest of Kiyosaburō, twice. Yet the style of the print and the form of the publisher's mark indicate a date later than Kiyosaburō's visit to Edo in 1708–9. If the print was indeed issued in conjunction with the performance by Kantarō II in 1718, it may simply evoke the memory of his great predecessor, who first brought the role to Edo. TTC

37

Torii Kiyomasu I or Torii Kiyonobu I

The Actors Sanjō Kantarō II as Oshichi and Ichimura Takenojō IV as Kichisaburō

1st month, 1718

ARTIST'S SIGNATURE: 'Torii Kiyonobu'

ARTIST'S SEAL: 'Kiyomasu'

PUBLISHER: 'Yushima Tenjin, Komatsu-ya, Onna-zaka no shita' (Komatsu-ya, bottom of Onna-zaka Hill, Yushima Tenjin)

woodblock, *ō-ōban, tan-e*, 55.5 × 32 cm

REPRODUCED: Chicago 1971, no. 61; Higuchi 1977, no. 41, pl. 27; *Ukiyo-e shūka*, vol. 1, no. 16

Julia Bradford Huntingdon James Fund, 1902

02.847

The tragic story of the affair between the greengrocer's daughter Oshichi of Honjo in Edo and the temple page Kichisaburō was based on an actual incident of 1683, when a teenage girl was condemned to death for starting a fire as a pretext to be with her lover. Made popular through Saikaku's novel *Five Women who Loved Love* (*Kōshoku gonin onna*) and by street balladeers (*uta-zaimon*), the tale was first adapted for the kabuki stage in Osaka in 1706. At these performances the role of Oshichi was created to great acclaim by the actor Arashi Kiyosaburō, who later took it to Edo and performed it no less than three times at the Nakamura Theatre – at the New Year, 1708, and in the third month and the autumn of 1709 – before returning to Kamigata. The play was also adapted in various versions for the puppet theatre.[1]

The performance recorded here, *Nana-kusa fukuju Soga*, given at the Ichimura Theatre at the New Year, 1718, was a revival staged to commemorate the seventh anniversary of Kiyosaburō's death. Oshichi was played on that occasion by Sanjō Kantarō II, fifteen or sixteen at the time and thus about the same age as the original greengrocer's daughter. It was from this performance onwards that Kiyosaburō's crest, a folded love letter inside a circle (seen here on Kantarō II's sleeve), was adopted as the standard crest for the role of Oshichi. Kichisaburō was played by Ichimura Takenojō IV, who was barely twenty, so the duo must have been a convincing pair of teenage lovers. The crests associated with the two roles also appear on the umbrella.

An appealing shyness is apparent in Oshichi's gesture of hesitation, raising her sleeve to her chin, as Kichisaburō, his adolescent forelock still unshaved above his forehead,[2] invites her to shelter from the summer shower in a thatched pavilion. This delicacy of sentiment, expressed with fluid lines, and the powerful hand-colouring in bright orange *tan* (red lead) and yellow make this design outstanding among the many splendid early examples in the *ō-ōban* format.

The identity of the artist responsible for this print and two others that bear a Kiyonobu signature but a Kiyomasu seal has long been a mystery. Two of the prints can be related to performances at the New Year, 1718, and, if by Kiyomasu I, would be his latest known works.[3] This has lead to the suggestion that Kiyomasu I died around this time and that the works were finished by Kiyonobu I. The third print (cat. 38), apparently relating to a performance given during the eleventh month, 1715, would seem to contradict this theory. To account for this discrepancy, Mutō Junko has suggested that cat. 38 may have been re-issued in 1718, while the actor Ichimura Tamagashiwa was still in Edo, with the signature altered to reflect the fact that Kiyomasu I had died.[4] TTC

1 Hattori 1983, p. 81, s.v. 'Oshichi Kichisa mono'.

2 The hairstyle of an adolescent male, this would be shaved off after the ceremony of attaining manhood (*genpuku*) in mid-teens.

3 Cat. 31 and Mutō 1992, no. 55.

4 Mutō 1992, pp. 31–2.

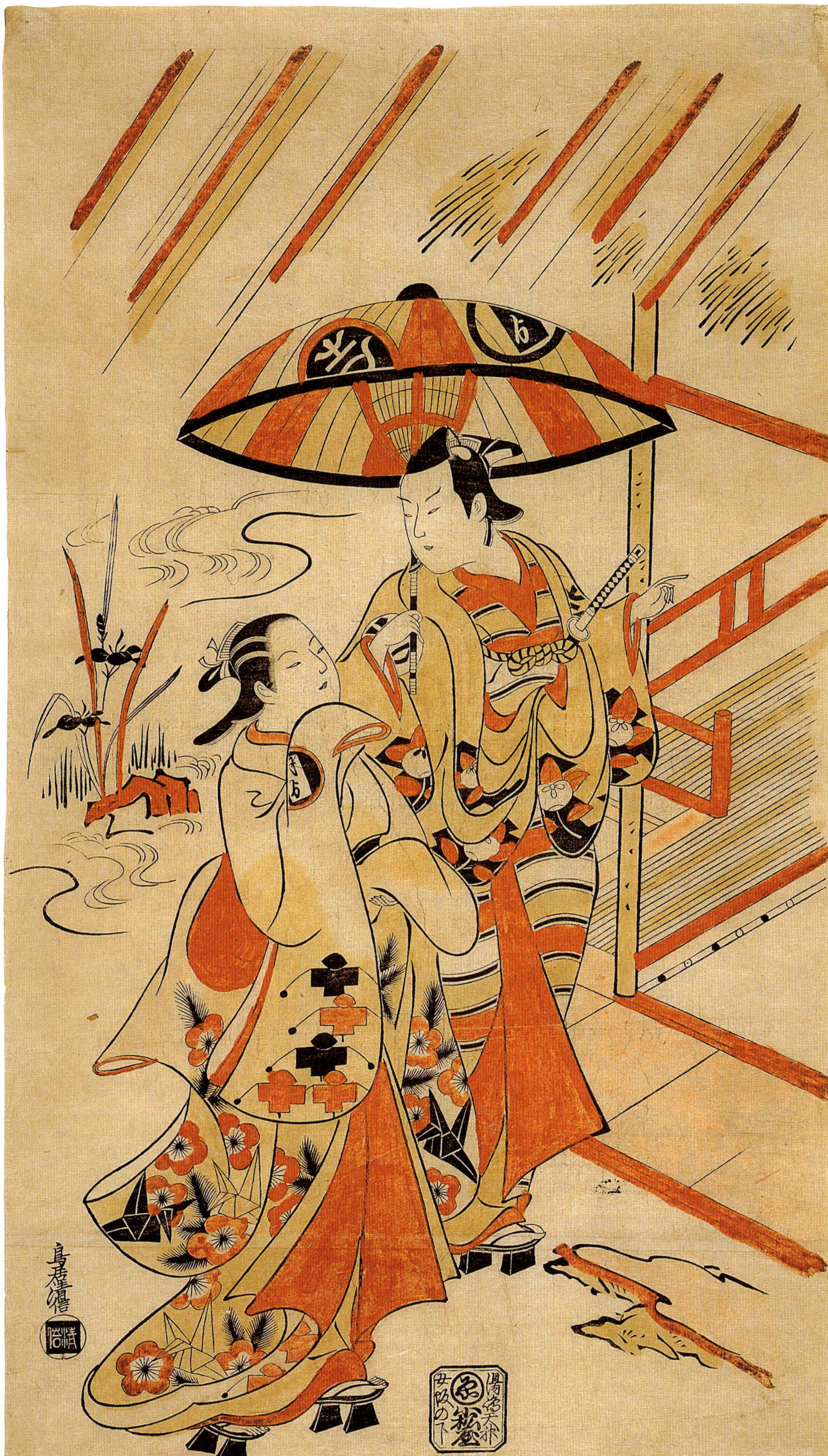

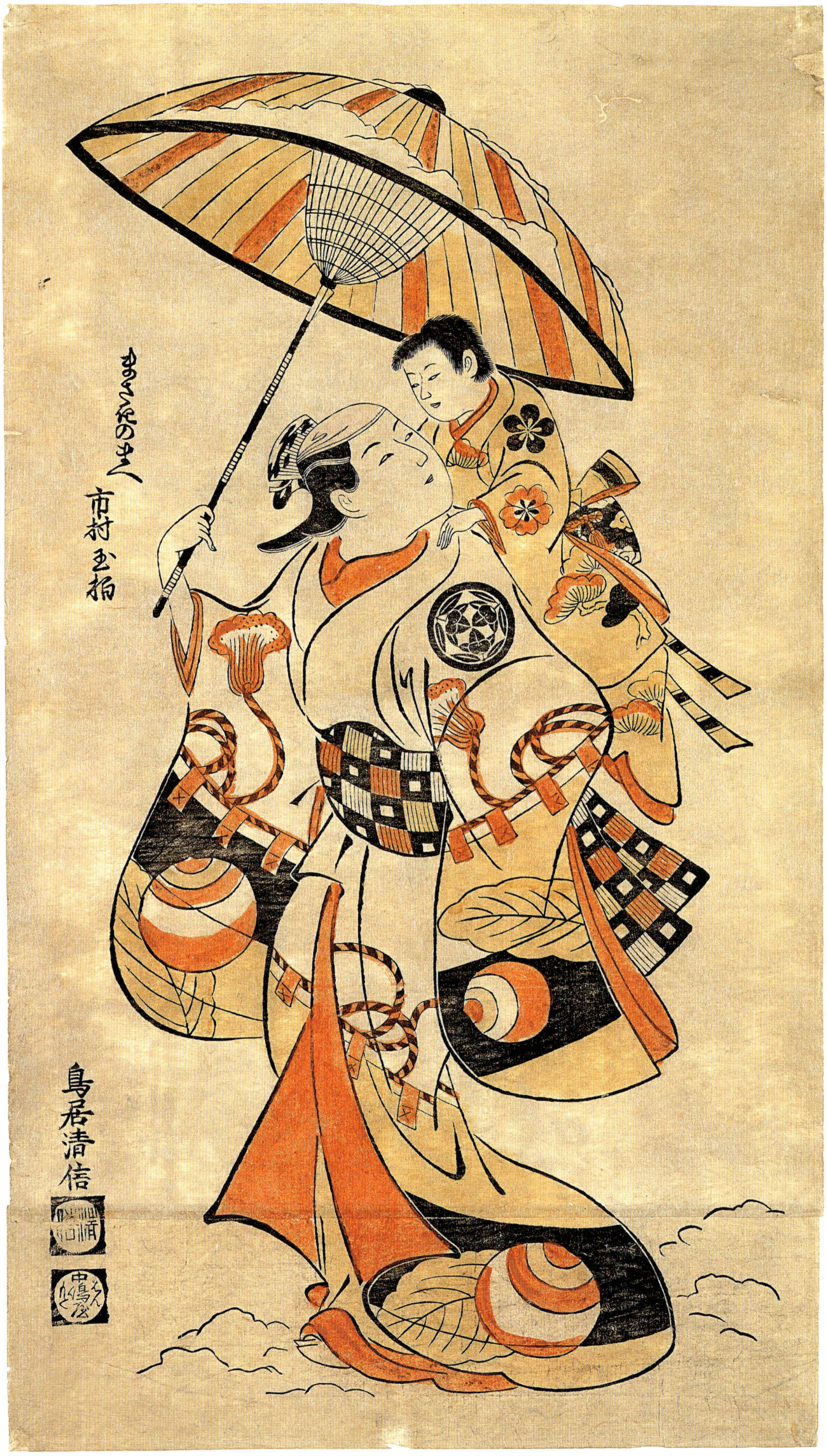
市村玉柏
鳥居清信

38

Torii Kiyomasu I or Torii Kiyonobu I

The Actor Ichimura Tamagashiwa as Masaki-no-Mae

11th month, 1715 (or 1718?)

ARTIST'S SIGNATURE: 'Torii Kiyonobu' (?)

ARTIST'S SEAL: 'Kiyonobu' (or 'Kiyomasu'?)

PUBLISHER: 'Hanmoto Nakajima-ya' (Nakajima-ya, publisher)

woodblock, *ō-ōban, tan-e*, 56.4 × 32.5 cm

REPRODUCED: *Ukiyo-e shūka*, vol. 1, no. 18

Julia Bradford Huntingdon James Fund, 1902

02.848

1 *Yakusha sanpuku-tsui*, published at the New Year, 1718.

2 Mutō 1992, pp. 31–2; *Kabuki nenpyō*, vol. 1, p. 491.

The inscription confirms that Ichimura Tamagashiwa appears here as Lady Masaki-no-Mae, the first role he played after arriving in Edo from Kyoto in the eleventh month, 1715. The play was *Banzei onna hachi-no-ki* at the Ichimura Theatre. A grand print like this may well have been issued to celebrate the arrival of such a celebrity, who excelled in female warrior roles and love scenes in historical plays. By the end of his three-year stay actor critiques were ranking Tamagashiwa joint first with Asao Jūjirō among Edo's impersonators of women.[1]

The actor walks in the snow, shielding with an umbrella the tiny child he carries piggyback. The crest on the robe of the child actor has not been identified. Tamagashiwa's crest consists of three mandarin oranges and leaves inside a circle and the design on his *furisode* evidently alludes to his name – jewels (*tama*) and oak (*kashiwa*) leaves on a striped curtain. He looks back tenderly at the child.

The signature and seal of this print have caused some difficulties. The seal has not printed properly over the join between the two sheets of paper and is hard to decipher at the point that would determine whether it reads 'Kiyonobu' or 'Kiyomasu'. Also, a (handwritten?) line has been added to the signature, apparently to change it from 'Kiyonobu' to 'Kiyomasu'. There are two other, unambiguous instances of prints with a Kiyonobu signature and a Kiyomasu seal (cat. 37 is one). These both date from 1718, probably the final year of Kiyomasu I's career, and a theory has been advanced suggesting that Kiyomasu I died at this time and that the designs were finished by Kiyonobu. Mutō Junko has further developed an ingenious theory to explain why the present print, apparently connected to a performance of three years earlier, would have required alteration in the same way. It may be that a print originally issued to celebrate his arrival in 1715 was re-issued (with the signature changed) to mark the reprise of the role by Tamagashiwa in the play *Oki-miyage onna hachi-no-ki* at the Ichimura Theatre in the autumn of 1718, his farewell performance before returning to Kamigata.[2] TTC

39
Okumura Masanobu
Ono no Komachi Washing the Manuscript

c. 1711–36

ARTIST'S SIGNATURE: 'Okumura Masanobu zu' (Drawn by Okumura Masanobu)

ARTIST'S SEAL: 'Masanobu'

hanging scroll, ink, colour, gold and silver on paper, 38 × 55.8 cm

REPRODUCED: Tokyo 1983, no. 70; Boston 2000, vol. 1, no. 77

William Sturgis Bigelow Collection, 1911

11.7604

Arrayed in traditional aristocratic garments that are luxuriously embellished with peony motifs in gold pigmented impasto (*moriage*) and with scrolling floral vines in silver and gold, the poet Ono no Komachi is seated before a black lacquer basin. A celebrated 9th-century literary figure whose poems were included in the Imperial anthology *Collection of Ancient and Modern Japanese Poems* (*Kokin waka-shū*), she became the subject of many legends. This painting recounts the plot of *Sōshi-arai Komachi*, a well-known play written for the nō theatre – the official theatre of Japan's military elite. The fictional account centres on the invitation of the writer to engage with the courtier Ōtomo no Kuronushi in an Imperial poetry contest. Fearing that he would be unable to win, Kuronushi resorted to trickery. He eavesdropped on Komachi as she penned her contribution the evening before the competition and then inscribed a copy in *Collection of Ten Thousand Leaves* (*Man'yō-shū*), a famous 8th-century anthology. The following day, when Komachi presented her poem, her antagonist pointed to the earlier collection and accused her of plagiarism. The poetess responded by washing the manuscript; the recent addition immediately dissolved. Komachi's reputation was restored and she was declared the winner of the contest.

The mode of depicting the poetess is inspired by 17th-century interpretations of women of the Heian period (794–1185). The Tosa school, hereditary painters to the aristocracy, presented numerous images of classical female literary figures.[1] Ukiyo-e artists such as Hishikawa Moronobu also adopted the figure style with its full, rounded faces, as seen in the illustration of the Komachi tale on the first pages of Moronobu's *Yamato-e zukushi* (*Collection of Japanese-style Paintings*) of 1680. Despite his adherence to these conventions of portraying feminine beauty, Okumura Masanobu injected some contemporary stylishness into the painting: the wave-roundel pattern and colouring of the robes of the young attendant would have been much admired by any woman of the Genroku era (1688–1704). In a later *benizuri* print of the same subject, dating to the 1750s and now in a private collection, Masanobu also began to transform Komachi's facial features in accordance with changing ideals of comeliness.[2] ANM

1 Examples include Tosa Mitsuoki (1617–91), *Ise*, hanging scroll, private collection, and Tosa Mitsunari (1646–1710), *Murasaki Shikibu, Suma and Akashi*, set of three hanging scrolls, Ishiyama-dera, Shiga Prefecture; reproduced in Tokyo 1999a, nos. 20, 24.

2 Reproduced in *Genshoku ukiyo-e*, vol. 6, p. 64.

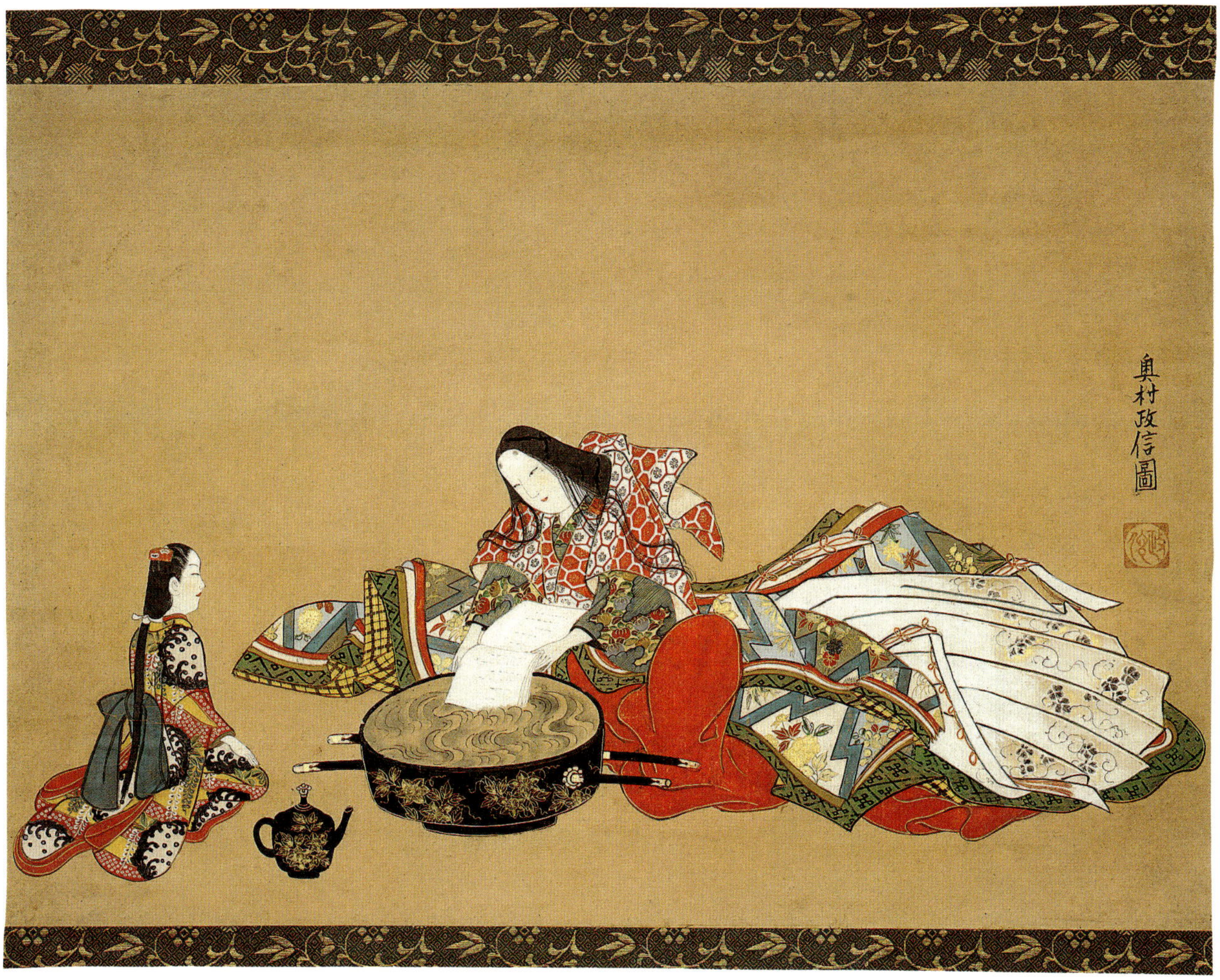
奥村政信圖

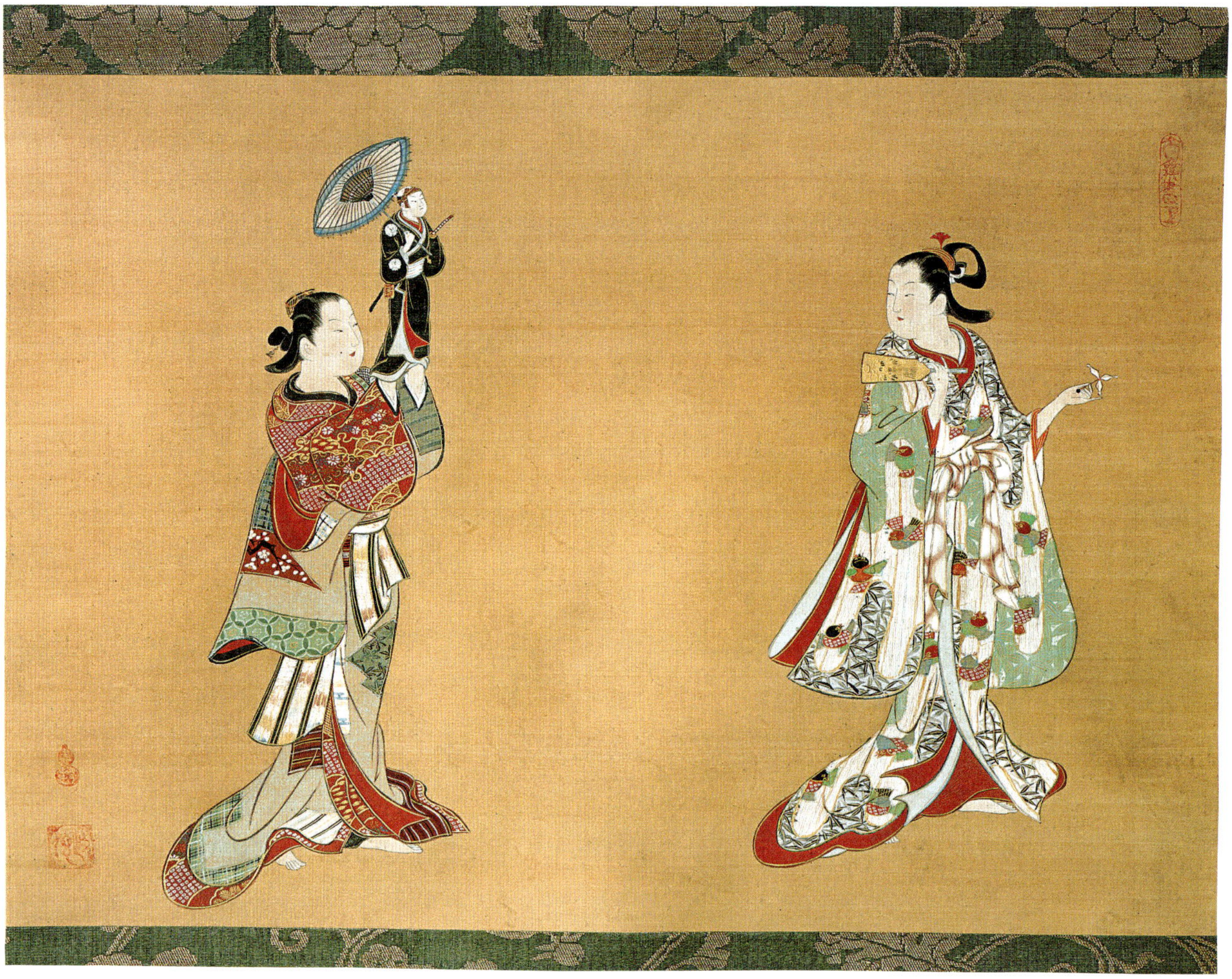

40
Okumura Masanobu
Two Courtesans with a Puppet

c. 1716

ARTIST'S SEALS: 'Yamato gakō' (Yamato painting artisan), 'Okumura', 'Masanobu'

hanging scroll, ink, colour, gold and silver on silk, 36.7 × 54.1 cm

REPRODUCED: Boston 2000, vol. 1, no. 79

William Sturgis Bigelow Collection, 1911

11.7605

Elegantly attired in layered robes ornamented with embroidery, stencilling, tie-dyeing and other intricate techniques, two courtesans celebrate the coming of the New Year. The young woman on the right holds a feathered shuttlecock and a luxuriously decorated battledore – implements for a game that has been played in Japan at the New Year since the 15th century. Her companion manipulates a puppet modelled on the popular actor Ichikawa Danjūrō II (1688–1758) in the role of Soga no Gorō disguising himself as Sukeroku, the dandy who frequented the pleasure districts in order to see his beloved Agemaki.[1]

From the end of the 17th century plays detailing the martial prowess and romantic exploits of the two Soga brothers Gorō and Jūrō became part of the annual programme at the kabuki theatres in Edo during the first months of each year (see cat. 33). Ichikawa Danjūrō II assumed the role of Sukeroku three times during his career. In 1713, in the first of these performances, *Hana-yakata aigo-zakura*, he adopted the bravura *aragoto* style developed by his father. Three years later, in another Sukeroku role, in *Shikirei yawaragi Soga*, and in 1749, in *Sukeroku kuroha no ie-zakura*, he defined his own style, giving the character a gentler, more *wagoto* interpretation.[2]

Sporting Sukeroku's characteristic headband, black kimono with peony crests, bull's-eye umbrella and sword, Danjūrō II was the subject of a wide pillar print by Okumura Masanobu.[3] An allusion in the inscription on the print indicates that the portrait dates from around the time of his last performance.[4] Comparison of this depiction with that of the puppet reveals the close attention that Masanobu has paid in the doll to the individual features of the actor, particularly his sharply upturned eyebrows, full nose and narrow eyes. However, Asano Shūgō believes that the figure style of the two courtesans points to a date around the 1716 performance.[5] Indeed, the dark umber of the puppet's headband and the inclusion of an umbrella indicate that the doll is a conflated portrait of two performances – that of 1713, in which Danjūrō II wore an orange rather than a purple headband, and that of 1716, during which he dramatically appeared on the raised walkway (*hanamichi*) carrying an open umbrella for the first time.[6] ANM

1 Boston 2000, vol. 1, pp. 192–3 (commentary by Asano Shūgō).

2 Kominz 1995, pp. 219–21.

3 Tokyo 1960–3, vol. 1, no. 267; Honolulu 1980, p. 117.

4 Noting that that the poem reads 'Wakayagite / ebira no ume ya / nido no kake', Howard Link points out the puns on the name of the actor and on the plum branch in a quiver – the emblem of the villain in the drama. Honolulu 1980, p. 117.

5 Boston 2000, vol. 1, pp. 192–3.

6 Iizuka 1926, pp. 706–8.

41

Attributed to Okumura Masanobu

The Courtesan Takao and the Actor Ikushima Daikichi I

c. 1705

woodblock, horizontal *ōban*, *sumizuri-e*, 25.7 × 37.1 cm

William Sturgis Bigelow Collection, 1911

11.13180

1 There were many generations of courtesans called Takao at the Miura-ya pleasure house in Yoshiwara and their dates have not all been established. References to studies of Takao are given in Seigle 1993, p. 248, n. 10. Takao is also included in *Mirror of Yoshiwara* and *Album of Courtesans* (cat. 1, 25).

2 The Shimada coiffure (worn by teahouse girls in Shimada on the Tōkaidō Road) became popular in the 1680s among courtesans and unmarried women of approximately 17 to 30 years of age. There were several variations of the hairstyle.

3 The portrait of Daikichi in *Screens in All Directions*, published in 1700 (cat. 24), mistakenly shows Daikichi's old crest. Mutō 1994, p. 6. Daikichi was involved in a liaison with a female attendant of the lord of Owari, for which he was imprisoned in 1706. Two months later he was released on payment of a heavy fine, but is said to have become insane and died in the fourth month, 1706.

4 The *hibachi* was brought out for winter use on the first 'wild boar day' of the tenth month; a festival celebrated in Yoshiwara to ward off fire (*hibuse*) took place on the eighth day of the eleventh month. *Tachibana* or *mikan* were then scattered about in the gardens of the brothels and searched for by children. De Becker 1971, p. 227. *Tachibana* is known as an auspicious evergreen; its flowers, fruit and leaves are not ruined by frost.

This unsigned *sumizuri* masterpiece is believed to be an early work by Okumura Masanobu and was probably part of a series of prints. Designed with calligraphic yet descriptive line work, it shows the influence of Kiyonobu I's style. The young actor Ikushima Daikichi I (*d.* 1706) and the courtesan Takao[1] with her girl assistant (*kamuro*) – both with Shimada hairstyles[2] – are depicted seated around an iron charcoal brazier (*hibachi*) decorated with three goblin-like legs. Daikichi, who started performing youthful female roles in late 1697, is depicted as if on a visit to the Miura-ya pleasure house in Yoshiwara to learn about Takao's skills. Daikichi can be identified by the crest consisting of three black triangles on his sleeve, which he used from 1699.[3] The maple-leaf crest similarly identifies Takao.

There is a sense of intimacy between the two figures. Daikichi looks at Takao and rests his elbow in her lap. He holds a sake cup in his right hand and leans on a set of fire tongs (*hibashi*) with his left. Takao has pulled in her left arm from the sleeve and touches her neck in a charming gesture. She playfully reaches to grab the fire-irons from the actor with her right hand. In the background, behind the actor, is a serving stand with fruits, probably mandarin oranges (*tachibana*); one such fruit has fallen into the *hibachi*, next to the smouldering charcoal. The brazier, mandarin oranges and the pine seedling pattern on Takao's *kosode* are details that indicate the winter season.[4] LEV

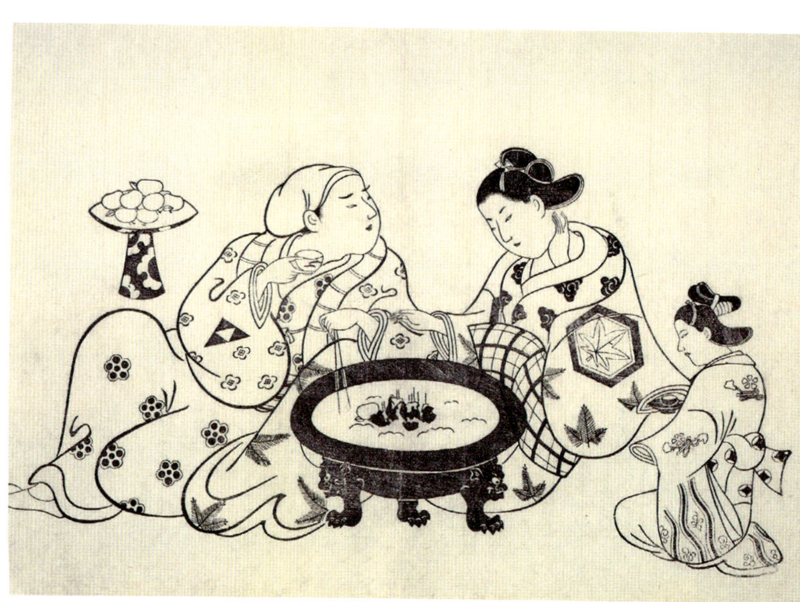

42–5
Okumura Masanobu
From the series *Customs of the Pleasure Quarters in the Twelve Months (Yūri fūzoku jūni-ka-getsu)*

1706 (last sheet dated 1st month, 1706)

ARTIST'S SIGNATURE (last sheet): 'Yamato eshi Okumura Masanobu kore o zu su' (Drawn by the Yamato picture master Okumura Masanobu)

ARTIST'S SEAL (last sheet): 'Masanobu'

PUBLISHER (last sheet): 'Kurihara Chōemon han' (Published by Kurihara Chōemon)

woodblock, from a series of 12, horizontal *ōban*, *sumizuri-e*

William Sturgis Bigelow Collection, 1911

11.13373–6

The Boston Museum possesses eight prints from this rare, untitled series, which Masanobu designed when he was only twenty years old and still greatly influenced by the style of Kiyonobu I.[1] With very few lines and details, each charged with meaning, Masanobu evokes scenes of leisure and entertainment in the Yoshiwara pleasure quarter in a masterly way.

In the print for the eighth month (cat. 42) a courtesan has opened the sliding doors (*fusuma*) to a veranda in order to cool off and enjoy a view of the full, harvest moon of the mid-eighth month, which is seen emerging from behind the clouds.[2] A handsome man, probably a pedlar, has opened a portable case inscribed with the shop name Mikawa-ya. He is about to serve the delighted, but shy, courtesan a tray with a bowl of shaved ice (*kezuri-hi*, now called *kaki-gōri*) and condiments. A similar tray, with a bowl, condiments and chopsticks, remains inside the box along with a small pitcher containing sweet syrup (*amazura*). The visitor is perhaps hoping to spend some time viewing the moon with the courtesan and, judging by the fact that his knee rests upon her hem, it seems likely that he will.

The courtesan is dressed in a striped *kosode*, while her visitor wears a *kosode* patterned with folk toys called *yajirōbei* or *mamezō*, sold by pedlars at shrines and temple festivals. *Yajirōbei* were usually made of wood and paper and were provided with two identical balancing weights (often *mame*, beans).[3]

The print representing the ninth month (cat. 43) shows a man, perhaps a professional male entertainer (*taiko-mochi*), with Daruma crests on his under-robe, dancing with a broom accompanied by a courtesan playing the shamisen.[4] The man is performing the 'spear dance' (*yari-odori*), a well-known pantomimic warrior's dance. In 1691 the *yari-odori* gave rise to a craze among both men and women in Edo when it was transformed into an athletic woman's dance by the *onnagata* kabuki actor Mizuki Tatsunosuke (1673–1745). In book illustrations, prints and paintings Kiyonobu I depicted Tatsunosuke, and the actor Tsutsui Kichijūrō (*d.* 1727), performing the dance with spears adorned with plumes.[5] Even Takarai Kikaku (1661–1707), a prominent student of the famous *haikai* master Matsuo Bashō, wrote verses about the dance: 'Everybody dances with spears, nay, with broom or duster – the joy of house-cleaning!'[6]

The season, autumn, is indicated by a wooden stand (*sanbō*) bearing a pair of sacred sake bottles (*heishi*) with decorative paper offerings (*kazari-gami*). Such items were placed in the *tokonoma* alcove to celebrate the Moon-viewing Festival (*O-tsukimi*), traditionally held on the thirteenth day of the ninth month. To distinguish it from moon viewing during the previous month, the ninth month was called the month of 'later moon viewing' (*ato-no-tsukimi*). One of the most popular activities during moon-viewing parties was to recite and compose *waka* or *hokku*.

1 The months represented in the Boston prints are numbers five to twelve. An impression of the design for the sixth month (Pulverer Collection, Cologne) is reproduced in Cologne 1991, pp. 114–15, fig. 1–4.

2 Moon viewing took place from the fourteenth to the sixteenth day of the eighth month.

3 The popularity of the *yajirōbei* pattern is evident from robes worn in three prints included here (cat. 37, 63, 124) and from the hairpins depicted in two further prints (cat. 69, 73).

4 *Taiko-mochi* are discussed in Seigle 1993, pp. 117–19.

5 Kominz 1997, pp. 185–6. Tatsunosuke is shown performing the spear dance in Kiyonobu's *Screens in All Directions* (1700; cat. 24). Honolulu 1977, p. 20, fig. 6. An unsigned painting of Tatsunosuke is reproduced in Tokyo 1988, p. 241, no. 30. See also a *tan-e* print attributed to Kiyonobu showing Tsutsui Kichijūrō performing the dance in the eleventh month, 1704; reproduced in Noguchi 1933, pp. 51–2, no. 30; *Ukiyo-e taikei*, vol. 1, fig. 95; and Machida 1987, p. 224, fig. 225.

6 Noguchi 1933, p. 52.

7 Nagasaki 1992, pp. 101–2; Mostow 1996, pp. 115–22.

8 Trans. Mostow 1996, pp. 119, 155–7.

9 Chicago 1955, pp. 121–2, 124, nos. 15, 16, 18, 23, 24.

10 Ibid., pp. 155, 157.

The *kosode* worn by the courtesan is decorated with calligraphic drawings of poets (*moji-kasen*), a playful artistic exercise that was popularised by textile patterns, book illustrations and prints from the Genroku to the Kyōhō era (1688–1736; see cat. 113). The male entertainer's outer robe is decorated with a stylish design of deer and maple leaves – a motif often found in poems about autumn. Many fashionable late 17th to early 18th-century *kosode* patterns allude to *tanka* in the popular anthology *One Hundred Poems by One Hundred Poets* (*Hyakunin isshu*).[7] Perhaps the textile design here refers to poem no. 5, by Senior Assistant Minister Sarumaru:

Okuyama ni	*When I hear the voice*
momiji fumiwake	*of the stag crying for its mate*
naku shika no	*stepping through the fallen leaves*
koe kiku toki zo	*deep in the mountains – then is the time*
aki wa kanashiki	*that autumn is the saddest.*[8]

Several designs by Masanobu in books and prints, including his playful *mitate* series provisionally titled *Ukiyo-e Fantasies* by Helen Gunsaulus,[9] showed courtesans interacting with or entertaining the Seven Lucky Gods (*Shichi-fukujin*). As is evident from prints of Yoshiwara, courtesans and their clients sometimes played games in which they enacted the roles of these gods.[10] The courtesan in the print for the tenth month (cat. 44) is playing the role of the god of wealth, success and abundant harvests, Daikoku. She holds up a knotted love letter (*musubi-bumi* or *musubi-jō*), shaped rather like Daikoku's wish-fulfilling mallet (*kozuchi*), and wears a hat reminiscent of his rounded cap. Enthroned on two pillows – an allusion to Daikoku's supply of rice sacks – the courtesan wears a *kosode* tied onto her shoulder in a manner suggesting the treasure sack carried by Daikoku. The *kosode* is lavishly decorated with symbolic 'treasure things' (*takara-mono*), traditionally said to be piled on the gods' treasure ship (*takara-bune*) when it arrives at New Year. Clearly visible in the pattern are Daikoku's mallet, which when shaken or struck against an object produces money, as well as the hat and cloak of invisibility (*kakure-gasa, kakure-mino*) used by all the gods to do good deeds and avoid evildoers. Included in the pattern are also a treasure chest key (*kagi*) and the wish-granting jewel *hōju no tama*.

The visitor enacts the role of Ebisu, wearing the god's tall hat (*kazaori-eboshi*) with the stylish addition of a matching tobacco purse to indicate his fishing basket. The shamisen with its broken string resembles Ebisu's fishing rod, and the bedding – on which the client is seated – is arranged to suggest a flat rock surrounded by water. Ebisu's legendary love of fishing caused him to become the god of bountiful catches and commerce. He also came to be associated with honest and successful business ventures, especially when paired with Daikoku. Ebisu was believed to be deaf and thus unable to hear

43

Ninth Month (*Ku-gatsu no tei*)

25.9 × 36.4 cm

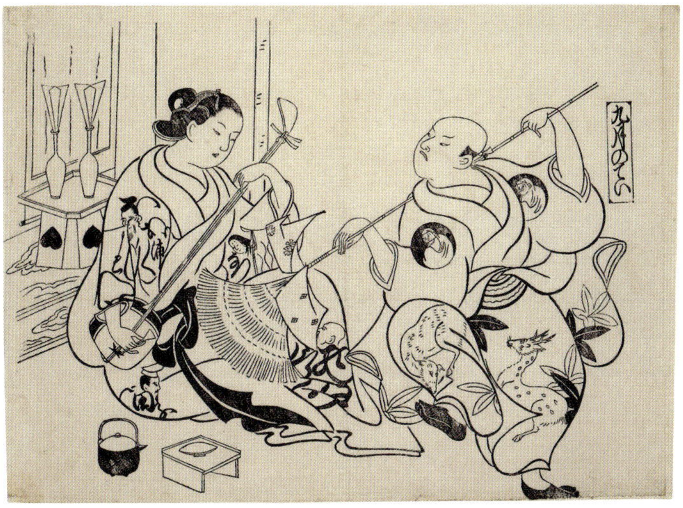

42

Eighth Month (*Hachi-gatsu no tei*)

25.8 × 36.6 cm

OTHER IMPRESSION: Österreichisches Museum für angewandte Kunst, Vienna (*Genshoku ukiyo-e*, vol. 3, p. 75, no. 305)

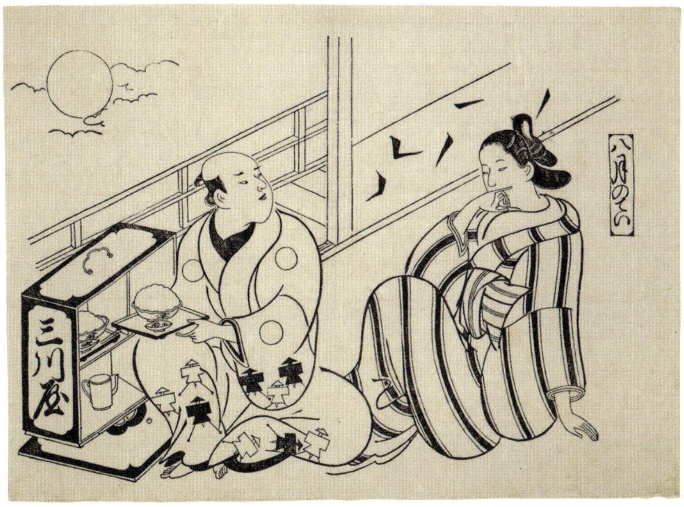

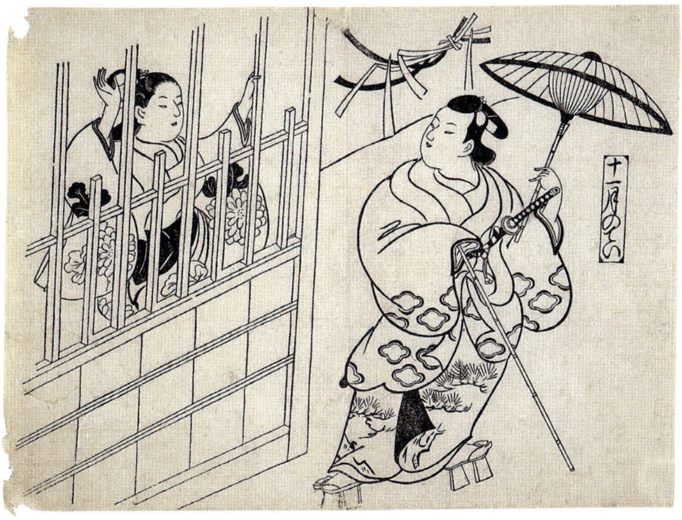

45

Eleventh Month (*Jūichi-gatsu no tei*)

26.4 × 36 cm

REPRODUCED: Lane 1978, p. 65, fig. 52

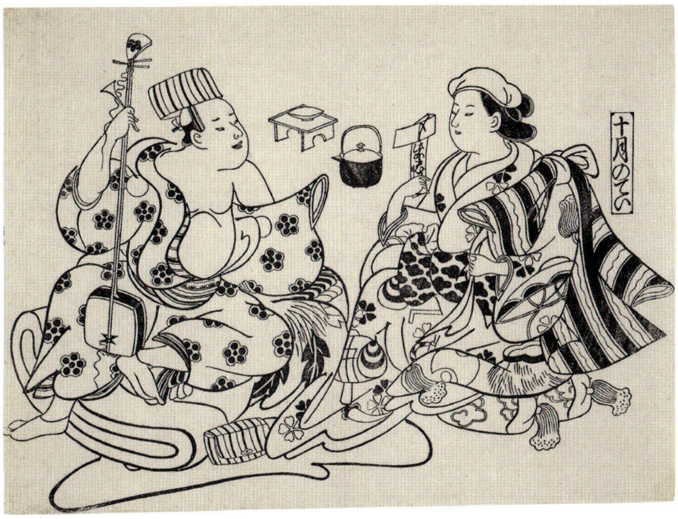

44

Tenth Month (*Jū-gatsu no tei*)

27.2 × 36 cm

11 *Kōshi* (*-jorō*) were courtesans ranked second, after *tayū*, and sat on display in latticed parlours.

12 Takemura 1991, pp. 268–9.

13 Leiter 1997, p. 184. See, for example, a print by Kiyomasu II of Ichikawa Danjūrō II as Sukeroku and Nakamura Takesaburō as Agemaki. Honolulu 1980, p. 47.

the summons to tour Izumo with the other gods in October (*kami-na-zuki* or *kannazuki*, 'month without gods'). When he was left behind each year Ebisu was honoured with a special festival, usually held on the twentieth day of the tenth month.

In the scene representing the eleventh month (cat. 45) a courtesan stands behind a latticed partition waving to a gallant young man bearing a sword. The courtesan, perhaps a *kōshi(jorō)*,[11] is dressed in a *kosode* patterned with chrysanthemums. The young man stops to look back at her, striking a dashing, theatrical pose, feet spread wide. The attraction is mutual. The design of a bundle of dried abalone strips (*tabane noshi*)[12] on the split doorway curtain (*noren*) in the background further implies an auspicious bond between them. To convey a sense of the cold, damp air, the man is shown dressed in several layers of garments. The fashionable short coat is decorated with a classical medallion design, its position above the pine motif of the *kosode* suggesting the shape of drifting rain clouds.

Holding an umbrella and wearing high *geta*, the young man exemplifies the type of dashing, stylish townsman (*machi yakko*) who was soon to inspire the creation of 'chivalrous commoner' (*otokodate*) roles in the kabuki theatre. One such swaggering townsman, Sukeroku, and his courtesan mistress, Agemaki, committed suicide at a temple in Osaka (perhaps *c.* 1673). In 1713 and 1716 Edo audiences saw plays about their romance and tragic fate, with the talented kabuki actor Ichikawa Danjūrō II (1689–1758) performing the role of Sukeroku in a blend of rough (*aragoto*) and gentle (*wagoto*) acting styles.[13]
LEV

46–57
Okumura Masanobu
The series *Famous Scenes from Japanese Puppet Plays* (*Yamato irotake*)

c. 1705–6 (or 1708?)

ARTIST'S SIGNATURE (last sheet): 'Yamato eshi Okumura Masanobu zu' (Drawn by the Yamato picture master Okumura Masanobu)

ARTIST'S SEAL: 'Masanobu'

PUBLISHER (last sheet): 'Nihonbashi Kawaseishi-chō Yamaguchi-ya, shorin Sudō Gonbei' (Yamaguchi-ya, at Kawaseishi-chō, Nihonbashi, the publisher Sudō Gonbei)

woodblock, set of 12 album leaves, horizontal *ōban, sumizuri-e*

OTHER IMPRESSIONS: (Shibui 1929, pp. 7–12, B-1–12); Art Institute of Chicago (Chicago 1955, pp. 117–20, Masanobu nos. 2–13)

William Sturgis Bigelow Collection, 1911

1 Suzuki 1979, pp. 230–2.

2 Torii 1989, pp. 1–2.

3 Torii 1972–7, vol. 3, pp. 520–6

4 Suzuki 1979, pp. 230–2.

5 Torii 1996, p. 642. I am grateful to Mutō Junko for drawing my attention to this article.

6 Mutō Junko (private communication).

7 Mutō Junko (private communication).

8 Mutō 1999, p. 3.

As first pointed out by Suzuki Jūzō, this series of twelve prints (probably originally intended to be mounted in an album) features imaginary combinations of leading kabuki actors in well-known scenes from the puppet theatre. Suzuki demonstrates that quite a number of early ukiyo-e prints relate to the puppet theatre (and to the *jōruri* chanting that accompanied it) rather than to kabuki, as later became exclusively the case.[1] From the Enpō (1673–81) to the Hōei (1704–11) era, the most popular style of *jōruri* in Edo was that of Tosa no Shōjō Tachibana Masakatsu (dates unknown), performed in Edo Castle and the mansions of feudal lords as well as in the puppet theatres.[2] During the late Jōkyō (1684–8) to early Genroku (1688–1704) eras, Tosa no Shōjō issued collections of the famous *jōruri* scenes performed by him (*danmono-shū*) that were given the generic title *Irotake*. Other similar anthologies often have the words *irotake* or *rankyoku* in their titles,[3] and Masanobu's title *Yamato irotake* takes its lead from these. The illustrations in Tosa *jōruri* playbooks can be shown to have influenced the style of certain early Torii school prints and, via these, Masanobu's early work.[4] The large number of *danmono-shū* collections known with 1708 as their date of publication has led to a theory that Tosa no Shōjō may have retired that year and many collections been issued to mark the event.[5] It is just possible that the present series of prints was published at that time.[6]

Even though the strong influence of *jōruri* and the puppet theatre is evident throughout, certain designs (for instance, cat. 48, 49, 51) show the actors in roles that they had performed on the kabuki stage. In two cases (cat. 47, 55) the actors actually appeared together around this time, although in different roles. Perhaps the series is best regarded as a hybrid of *jōruri* and kabuki. The rounded, ample, confident figure style derives ultimately from the illustrations of Torii Kiyonobu I, but demonstrates that the parvenu Masanobu, still in his early twenties, had already achieved maturity as an artist.

Two full sets of *Yamato iro-take* are known, one each in the Boston Museum and the Art Institute of Chicago. For some reason, the address of the publisher Yamaguchi-ya that appears on the last sheet of the Chicago set (Nihonbashi Minami Itchō-me Yamaguchi-ya) differs from that given on the corresponding Boston print; just this section of the block must have been re-cut.[7] The set reproduced in Shibui 1929 (series B, present location unknown) has the same publisher's address as the Chicago set.

46
The illustration prefacing the series shows puppeteers taking puppets out of their storage box. Each puppet has the crest of a leading kabuki actor on its costume and is dressed for the type of role in which that actor specialised. The series appears to have been issued *c.* 1705–6[8] and the puppets/actors have been tentatively identified as follows (some crests were used by more than one

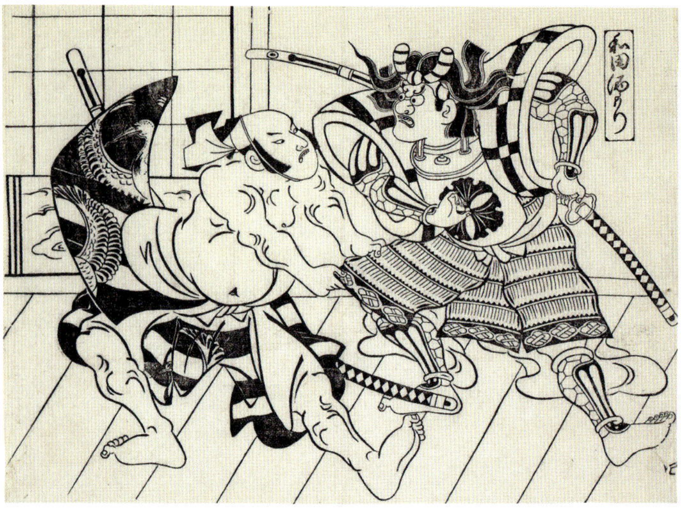

49
'Wada's Banquet, no. 4' (*Wada sakamori, yon*)
26.1 × 36.9 cm 11.13191

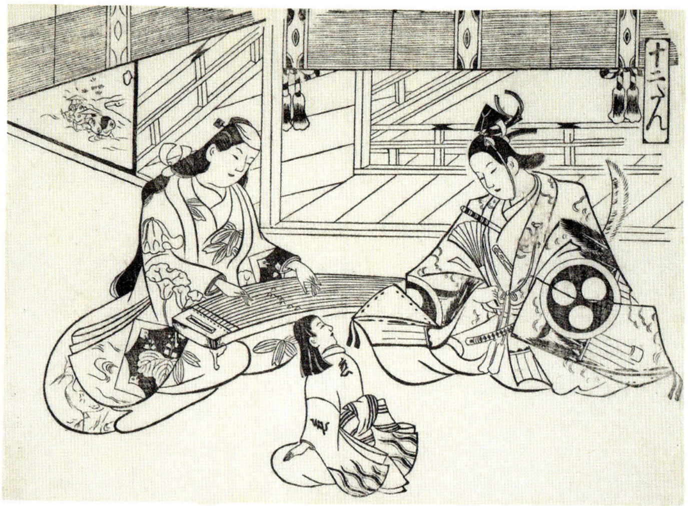

48
'Tale of Ushiwaka and Princess Jōruri' (*Jūni-dan*)
26.2 × 36.8 cm 11.13186

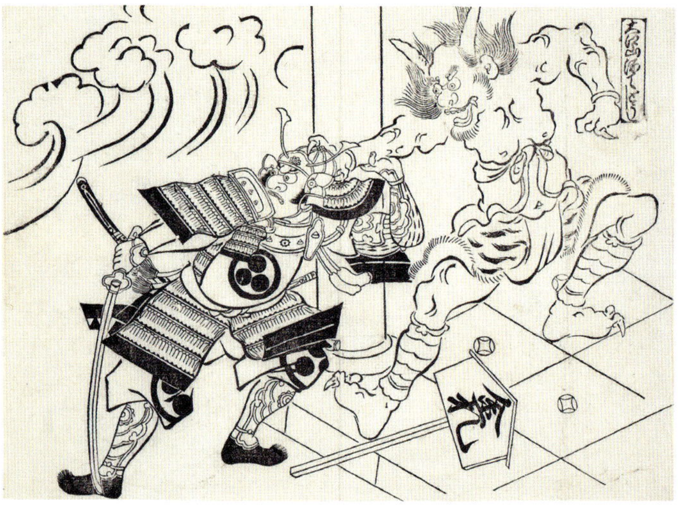

53
'The Shuten-dōji of Mount Ōe' (*Ōe Shuten-dōji*)
26.2 × 36.9 cm 11.13190

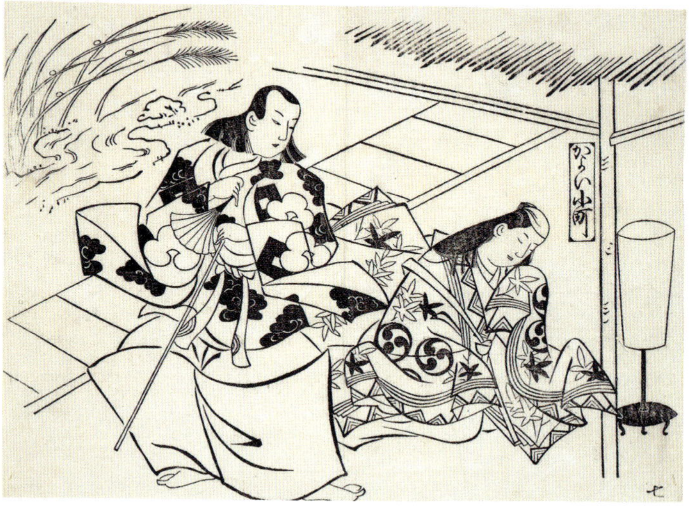

52
'Courting Komachi, no. 7' (*Kayoi Komachi, nana*)
26.2 × 36.8 cm 11.13186

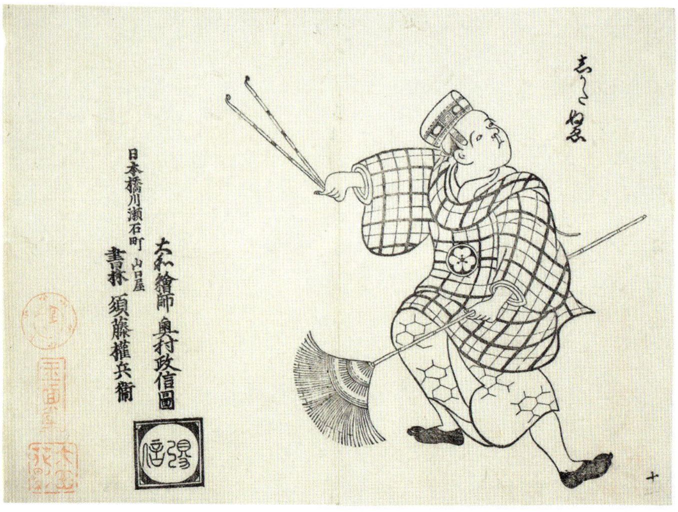

57
'Can't be Helped, no. 12' (*Shikata nue, jūni*)
26.1 × 36.8 cm 11.13192

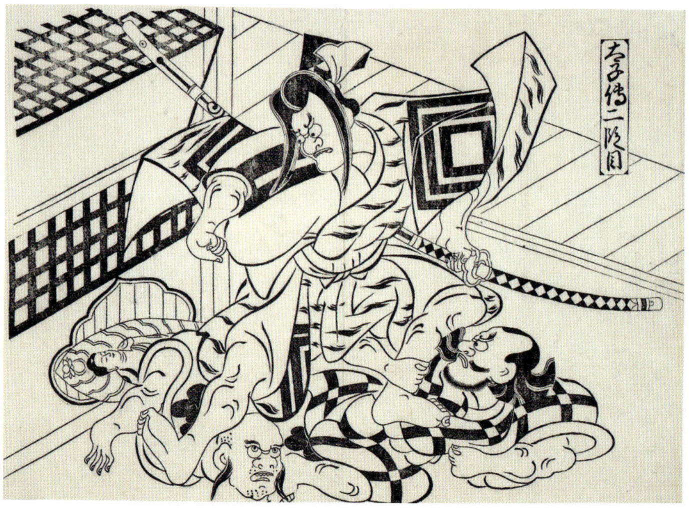

56
'Life of Taishi: Act II' (*Taishi-den nidan-me*)
26.1 × 36.8 cm 11.13181

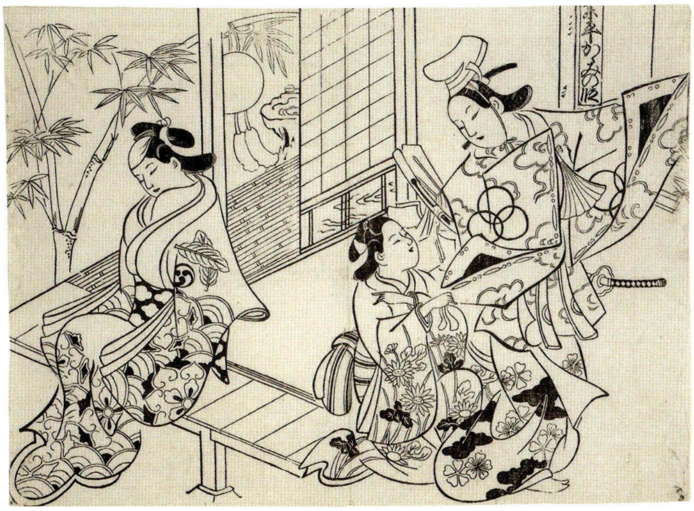

47
'Narihira: The Mirror Scene' (*Narihira kagami no dan*)
26.1 × 36.8 cm 11.13185

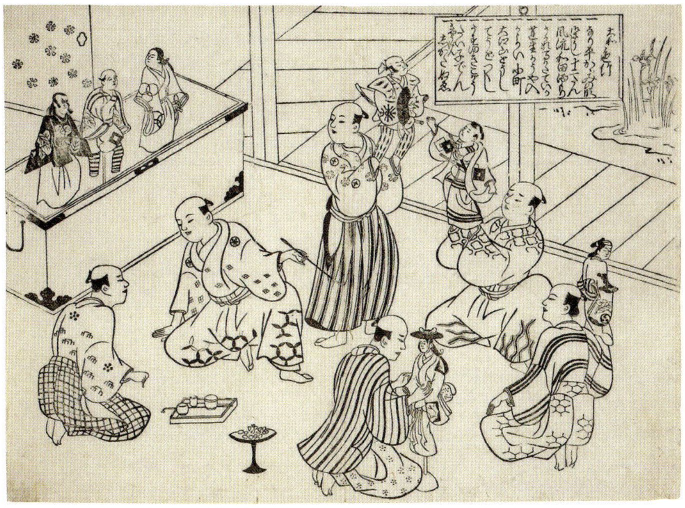

46
Scene in the Dressing Room of a Puppet Theatre (table of contents)
26.1 × 36.8 cm 11.13184

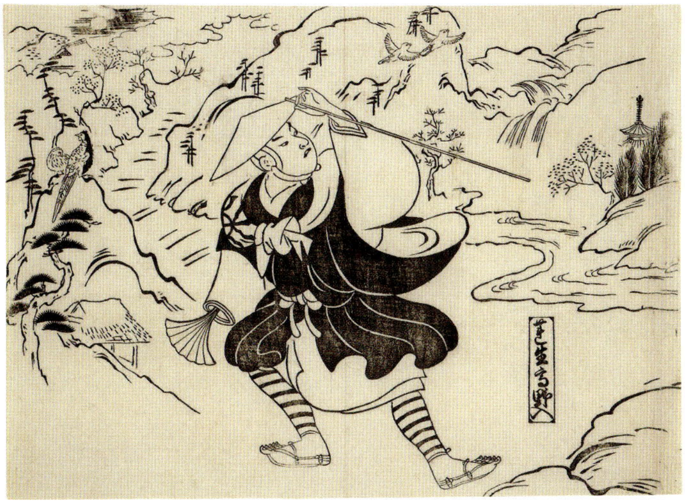

51
'Renshō Going to Mount Kōya' (*Renshō Kōya-iri*)
26.2 × 36.8 cm 11.13188

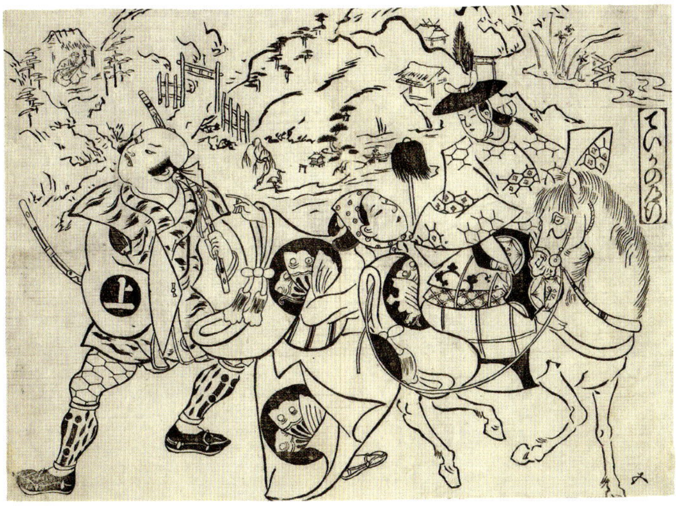

50
'Teika's Journey, no. 5' (*Teika no michiyuki, go*)
26.2 × 36.8 cm 11.13187

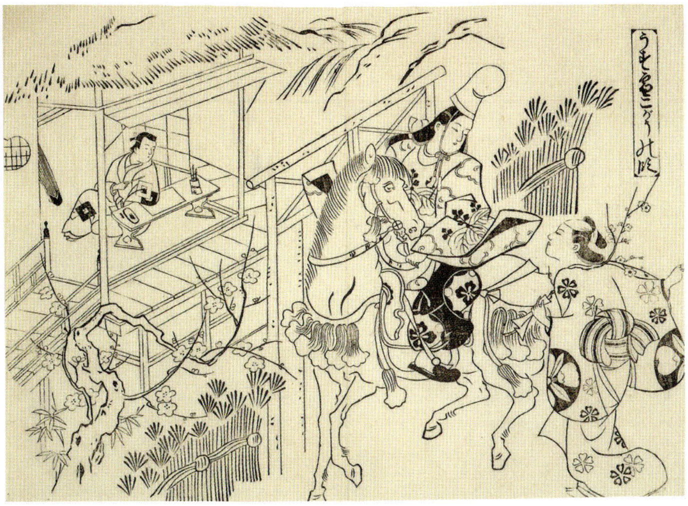

55
'Usuyuki, The Kogō Scene' (*Usuyuki Kogō no dan*)
26.1 × 36.8 cm 11.13183

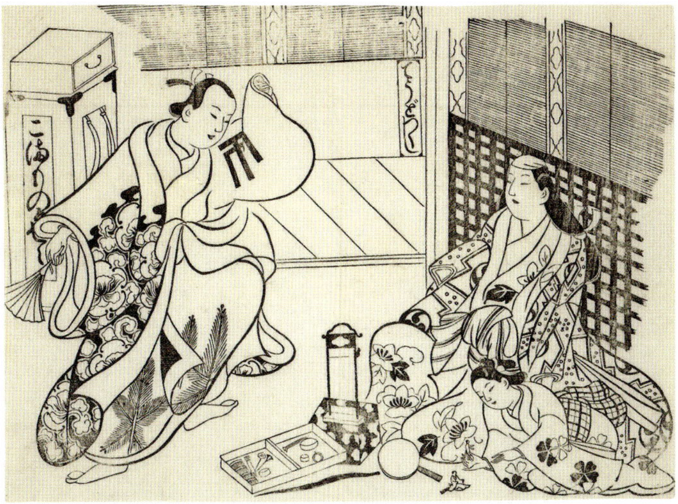

54
'All Kinds of Household Accessories' (*Chōdo-zukushi*)
26.2 × 36.9 cm 11.13182

9 I am grateful to Mutō Junko for assistance with these identifications and those of the actors in the other prints in the series.

10 These titles are taken from Torii 1972–7, vol. 3, pp. 396–545.

individual, in which case an alternative identification is sometimes suggested): (from top left, clockwise, with their acting speciality) 1. Yamanaka Heikurō (*jitsu-aku*); 2. Saikoku Hyōgorō (*d.* 1705/12/9) or Saikoku Hyōsuke (both *dōke-gata*); 3. Nakagawa Hanzaburō (active in Edo until 1705/4, *wakashu-gata*); 4. Nakamura Denkurō (*tachi-yaku*); 5. Nakamura Shichisaburō or Nakamura Shinsaburō (active from 1705) (both *tachi-yaku*); 6. Tsugawa Handayū (*wakaonna-gata*); 7. Dekishima Daisuke [or Dekishima Kozarashi or Kishida Kogenji] (all three *wakaonna-gata*).[9]

In the top right corner of the prefatory design appears a list of the scenes to follow. These correspond, with minor differences, to the titles that appear on the prints. The scenes are sometimes given their popular titles, as listed, for example, in the *danmono-shū* collections. For reference, the formal title of the play and the number of the act are added in parentheses in the following list if they differ from the print inscription:[10] 2. *Narihira kagami no dan* (*Azuma Narihira iro Komachi,* Act V); 3. *Go-sōshi jūni-dan* (*Genji jūni-dan*); 4. *Fūryū Wada sakamori*; 5. *Ukare muma-kata Teika* (*Teika,* Act IV); 6. *Renshō Kōya-iri* (*Genpei tsuwamono-zoroe,* Act III); 7. *Kayoi-Komachi* (*Azuma Narihira iro Komachi,* Act III); 8. *Ōeyama-dōji* (*Shuten-dōji,* Act I); 9. *Chōdo-zukushi* (*Shioya Bunshō monogatari,* Act V); 10. *Usuyuki Kogō* (*Usuyuki,* Act III); 11. *Taishi den*; 12. *Kyōgen Shikata-nue.*

47

This is apparently a scene from Act V of *Azuma Narihira iro Komachi.* Tsugawa Handayū as Komachi (left) is seated lost in thought on the veranda, while Nakagawa Hanzaburō as Narihira (right) performs a dance. A maid tugs at his sleeve. A mirror hangs on the bamboo in the garden. The two actors performed together at the Ichimura Theatre from 1703–4.

48

A scene from *Genji jūni-dan,* the tale of Ushiwaka (the future warrior hero Minamoto no Yoshitsune) and Princess Jōruri, with Mizuki Tominosuke as Ushiwaka (right) and Dekishima Daisuke (?) playing the koto as Jōruri-gozen (left). Three different *wakaonna-gata* actors used the same crest at the time, but Dekishima Daisuke would seem to be the most likely identification of the actor depicted here, as he played Princess Jōruri opposite Tominosuke's Ushiwaka in the play *Jūni-dan himitsu no maki* at the Morita Theatre in the seventh month, 1705.

49

This shows the 'armour-tugging' (*kusazuri-biki*) at the banquet of Wada Yoshimori as performed by Matsumoto Koshirō as Soga no Gorō (right) and Nakamura Denkurō (?) as Asahina no Saburō (left) in the play *Fūryū Wada sakamori* (see also cat. 21). No actor's crest is drawn on the robes of Asahina,

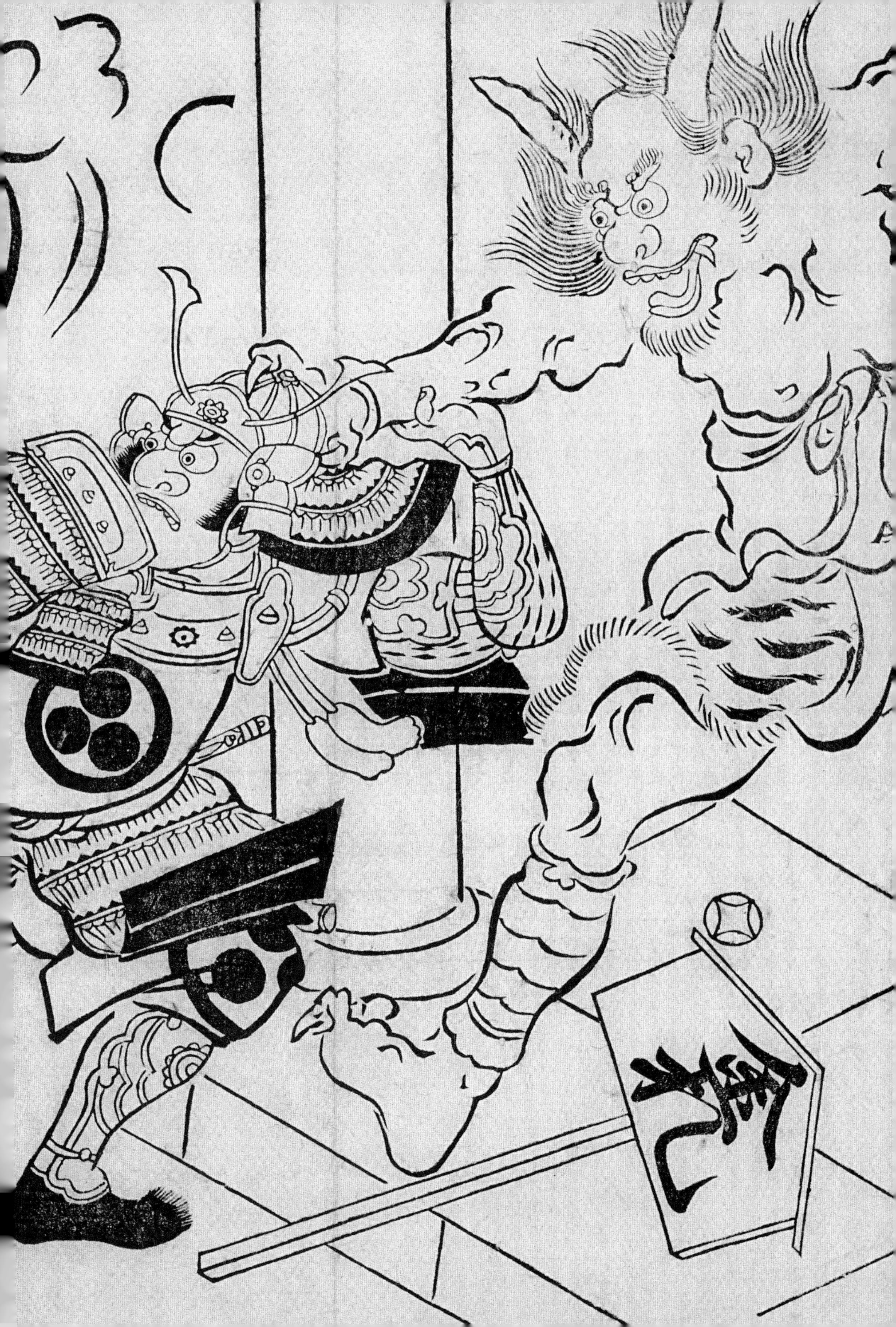

11 Torii 1989, p. 364.
12 Ibid., p. 156.
13 Nojima 1988, p. 465.
14 Torii 1989, p. 300.

but this role was a speciality of Nakamura Denkurō and the face is similar to the portrait of him in cat. 51. The two actors appeared in these parts in the New Year play at the Nakamura Theatre in 1705 and 1706.

50

In this scene from Act IV of *Teika* Nowake no Tsubone, who secretly loves Teika, disguises herself as a horseman and leads Teika's horse on his journey to Fujikawa in the eastern provinces. The story develops into a 'new' version of *Dōjō-ji* as, tricked and left behind by Teika, Nowake turns herself into a giant snake to cross the Ōi River (see also cat. 26).[11] Here Teika on horseback is played as a female role, and the actor has a crest on his trousers possibly identifiable as that of Iwai Tatsusaburō, who specialised in young female roles (*wakaonna-gata*). His last known performance was at the Morita Theatre at the New Year, 1705. The actor playing Nowake (centre) may be Sakata Oginojō, although this actor's butterfly crest should more correctly have a line under it. Oginojō performed at the Ichimura Theatre from the New Year, 1705, and later appeared as Nowake in a kabuki version of *Teika* given at the Yamamura Theatre in the eleventh month, 1710. The actor playing Gotō Saemon (left), with a crest consisting of the character *ue*, is Nakamura Denkurō, who appeared in male lead (*tachi-yaku*) roles at the Nakamura Theatre at this time.

51

The scene comes from Act III of *Genpei tsuwamono-zoroe*. The warrior Kumagae, taking holy orders in remorse at having killed the youth Atsumori in battle, becomes the monk Renshō and sets out for a life of religious austerity on Mount Kōya.[12] Here Renshō is played by Nakamura Denkurō I, praised in an actor critique of 1694 for his *michiyuki* roles (travel scenes, mimicked with dancing), such as Kumagae/Renshō, performed to *jōruri* accompaniment.[13]

52

A scene from Act III of *Azuma Narihira iro Komachi*. Ono no Komachi leaves the mansion of Ōtomo no Kuronushi in secret. She loses her way and asks for lodgings from an old man. In the middle of the night the man takes the form of the deceased Fukakusa no Shōshō, who laments that Komachi made him pay court for 100 nights (see cat. 105).[14] Here Mizuki Takejūrō plays Ono no Komachi (right) and Ikushima Shingorō the ghost of Fukakusa no Shōshō (left). Takejūrō first performed in Edo at the Nakamura Theatre in the eleventh month, 1704.

53

A scene from Act III of *Shuten-dōji* (*The Sake-drinking Boy*). The warrior Watanabe no Tsuna battles with a demon that has been haunting the

15 Torii 1989, pp. 224–7.

16 Torii 1972–7, vol. 3, pp. 89–91.

Rashōmon Gate in Kyoto. The story then develops from this Rashōmon legend into that of the flesh-eating, sake-drinking ogre Shuten-dōji of Mount Ōe, who takes the form of a giant boy dressed as a temple acolyte. This tale was the subject of Moronobu's nineteen prints of some twenty years earlier (cat. 7–10), itself thought to be influenced by puppet performances with *jōruri* chanting. Masanobu's composition is quite similar to Moronobu's, except that the latter had included Watanabe no Tsuna's horse. The stylised gusts of clouds, in particular, are drawn in an almost identical manner. The crest on the armour has been identified elsewhere in this publication (cat. 61) as that of Tomizawa Hanzaburō, who performed at the Ichimura Theatre for two years from 1704/11.

54

The scene comes from Act V of *Shioya Bunshō monogatari*, the puppet play version of the medieval tale *Bunshō no sōshi*. Bunshō was a humble salt manufacturer who managed to acquire great wealth through his industry. Middle Captain Toshimichi, son of the Regent, disguises himself as an itinerant seller of household accessories in order to gain entry into Bunshō's mansion and pay court to his daughter Renge-no-Mae. In the scene depicted here he dances and describes in detail the many wares that he has brought, to the delight of Renge-no-Mae and her attendant.[15]

The inscription on the pack of goods at the rear reads 'komamono iro-iro' (lots of cosmetic articles). The actors depicted are Nakamura Gentarō as Renge-no-Mae (right) and Katsuyama Matagorō as Middle Captain Toshimichi disguised as the pedlar (left). The two actors did not appear together in any performances during the Hōei era (1704–11).

55

Usuyuki monogatari was a best-seller of the early Edo period in the *kana-zōshi* genre. In its adaptation for the puppet stage it told the tale of the love of Sonobe no Uemon Kiyoharu for the Lady Usuyuki Gozen. In this scene Usuyuki disguises herself in male court costume, with *eboshi* cap and *kariginu* robes, and rides on horseback deep into the rural Saga district of Kyoto on a moonlit spring night, in search of her lover. When she finds him they exchange poems and a gift of a branch of blossom, Usuyuki abandons her male disguise and the couple are joyfully reunited.[16] This is a reworking of the famous episode in which Minamoto no Nakakuni, on the orders of Emperor Takakura, finally tracks down the beautiful Lady Kogō in her secluded retreat in Saga by following the distinctive sound of her koto playing. This *Usuyuki* version of the scene is impersonated by the kabuki actors Tsutsui Kichijūrō as a female attendant (right), Hayakawa Hatsuse as Usuyuki Gozen (centre) and Nakamura Shichisaburō (or Nakamura

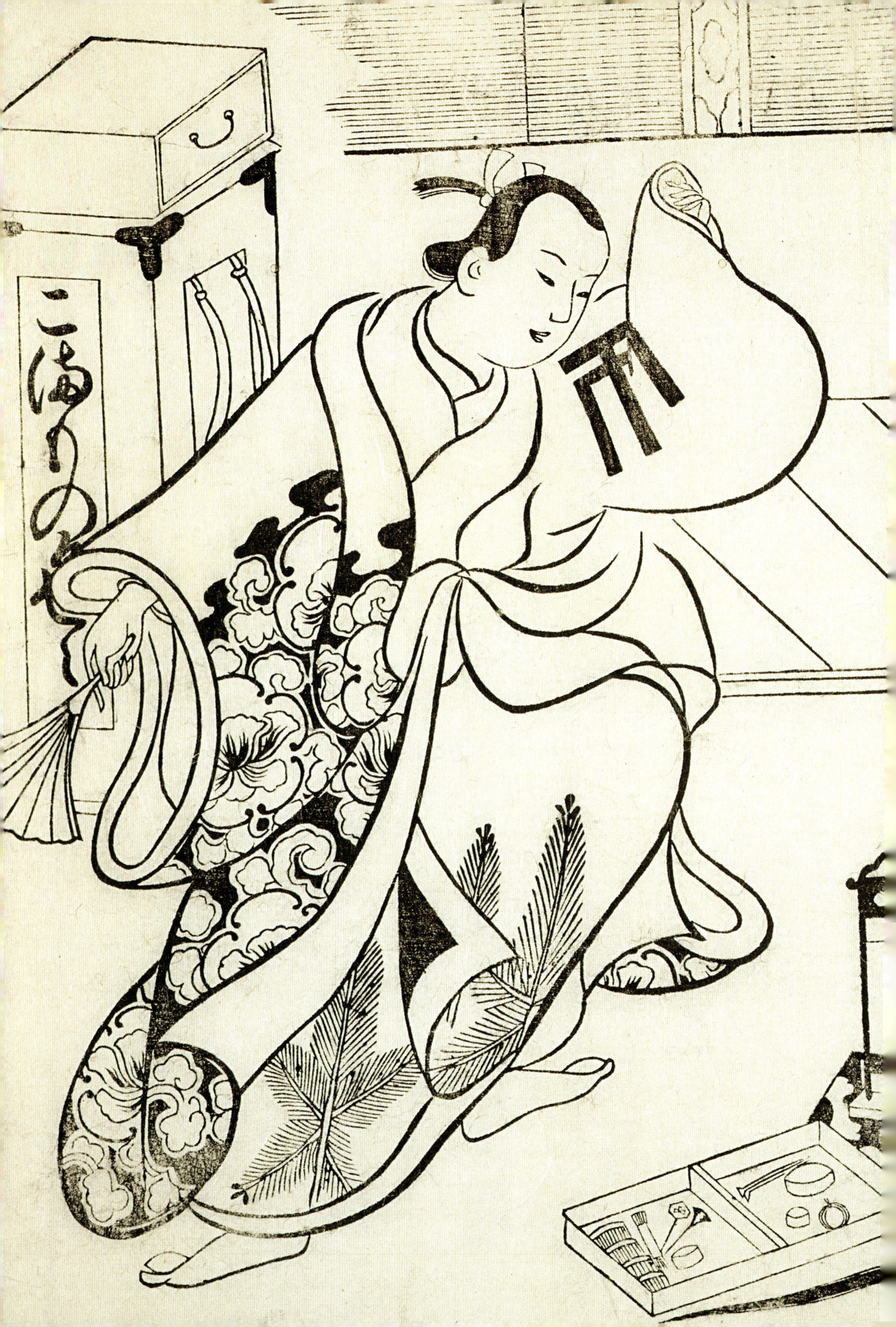

17 Torii 1989, pp. 102–3.

18 I am grateful to Mutō Junko for this suggestion (private communication).

Shinsaburō) as Sonobe no Uemon Kiyoharu (left). Following Kichijūrō's arrival in Edo in 1704/11, the three actors performed together at the Nakamura Theatre until 1706/11, when Hatsuse switched to the Ichimura.

56

A scene from Act II of *Taishi-den*, the *jōruri* version of the life of Shōtoku Taishi (574–622), the statesman and early promoter of Buddhism in Japan. Nichira Shōnin, a Buddhist monk from China, receives Imperial sanction to establish a temple and promulgate the new religion. In Act I he is opposed by Minister Moriya, who sends his henchmen to steal the statute of the Buddhist deity Amida. The deity Ida-ten intervenes to protect the statue. In Act II Moriya feigns illness and persuades Nichira to pray for his recovery, whereupon Moriya's henchmen seize the statue again. Nichira takes the form of a hawk and flies off. Moriya tries to burn the statute but it will not melt, so he throws it into a stormy sea.[17] The hero trampling the villains in Masanobu's picture looks like Soga no Gorō, so the Soga story would seem to have been superimposed on the Taishi legend. Gorō's robes bear the prominent *mimasu* crest of the Ichikawa family of actors. After the traumatic murder of Ichikawa Danjūrō I during a performance in the second month, 1704 (see p. 26), the most prominent male lead (*tachi-yaku*) actors to use the *mimasu* crest were the middle-aged Ichikawa Danshirō and the young Danjūrō II. It is not clear which of these three Ichikawa actors is depicted here, but it is most likely the deceased Danjūrō I.

57

This print would seem to depict not a *jōruri* scene, but a kabuki actor in a comic role. He is parodying the warrior Minamoto no Yorimasa, who defeated a mythical beast, the *nue*, as recounted in the medieval nō play of that name. The title appears to pun 'shikata nee' (can't be helped) with 'nue'. The actor wears a long *haori* jacket back-to-front, like armour, and brandishes a broom and two pipes like bow and arrows. The upturned tobacco pouch on his head has become a helmet. Many actors used the *katabami* (oxalis) crest seen on the jacket. The most prominent at this time were Bandō Matakurō II (Morita Kan'ya II, *d.* 1734) and his younger brother Bandō Matakurō III (Morita Kan'ya III, *d.* 1722), both of whom combined their acting with the position of manager (*za-nushi*) of the Morita Theatre. However, the face of the actor depicted looks like the second puppet on the first sheet of this series: either Saikoku Hyōgorō or Saikoku Hyōsuke, his pupil, both of whom specialised in comic roles. Hyōgorō was acting at the Yamamura Theatre in the year leading up to his death on 1705/12/9. Hyōsuke was at the Morita Theatre from 1704/11 to 1705/11. Perhaps, then, one of these two actors has borrowed Bandō Matakurō's jacket to add to the comedy of the performance.[18] TTC

58

Okumura Masanobu

A Courtesan as Fei Zhangfang (Hi Chōbō)

c. 1706–8

PUBLISHER: 'Motohama-chō Iga-ya hanmoto' (Iga-ya, publisher at Motohama-chō)

woodblock, horizontal *ōban*, *sumizuri-e*, 28.9 × 40 cm

OTHER IMPRESSION: Worcester Art Museum, Mass. (Chicago 1971, p. 95, no. 132)

Gift of Mrs Jared K. Morse, 1953

53.2923

Masanobu was not only an enterprising artist and businessman, but also a well-known *bon vivant* in the cultural circles of Edo. He was fond of reading classical Japanese and Chinese literature and, under the tutelage of Tachiba Fukaku (1662–1753),[1] learned to compose humorous and riddle-like *hiyu haikai* (metaphor *haikai*) and to link poems with playful twists (*mitate*). By ingeniously combining literary knowledge with close observation of daily life and fashion, Masanobu became a trendsetter famous for creating modern, witty scenes. In the first scene of a series of 'parody pictures' (*mitate-e*)[2] Masanobu depicted himself writing an inscription on a screen for a young couple, a samurai and a woman holding a love letter. The inscription highlights Masanobu's talent for quoting, reinterpreting and popularising classical subjects in a manner that appealed to the fashionable people of the 'floating world'.[3]

Masanobu had clearly read publications about Chinese immortals (*sennin*) – for example, *Ehon hōkan* (*Treasure Book of Pictures*, 1688, illustrated by Hasegawa Toun).[4] This Japanese woodblock-printed book includes a detailed description of the tale of Fei Zhangfang and shows the *sennin* seated on a flying crane. In some early Chinese lore Fei Zhangfang was rewarded by his teacher with a magical bamboo rod and a charm consisting of a written poem (about the rod), tools that enabled him to fly for great distances in a short amount of time.[5] Perhaps alluding to such a version of the legend, Masanobu shows the courtesan in this early *sumizuri* print holding a sheet of paper inscribed with what may be an excerpt from a classical Chinese-style poem and wearing a surcoat (*uchikake*) patterned with bamboo leaves.

Like other contemporary Japanese authors and artists, Masanobu preferred to imagine Fei Zhangfang flying on a bird: in Japan, Fei Zhangfang was known as Hi Chōbō (or Hichōbō), the first two syllables of which, when written with a different choice of *hi-chō* characters, mean 'flying bird'. The choice of a crane was natural, since it is a symbol of longevity in China and Japan and has been associated both with the ability to navigate between heaven and earth and with sensual delight.[6]

The poem, which conjures up the image of soaring high above the seas, may be translated as follows:

> The seas stretch out and island peaks soar,
> as the sun shines brightly in spring skies
> over billowing waves of clouds...[7]

As indicated by the distinctive title cartouche, the print is from a series depicting Chinese immortals.[8] Masanobu appears to have been especially interested in Fei Zhangfang/Hi Chōbō, since he developed and perfected the *mitate* theme, transforming the Chinese immortal into a courtesan who could take her admirers to a magical realm of sensual delight. An image in *Ehon Edo-e*

1 Fukaku was a prominent bookshop owner and author of erotic novels as well as a poetry judge. His verses often included eccentric wordplay, riddles and conversational flair.

2 For a discussion of *mitate* and the use of the word *mitate-e* by modern art historians, see Clark 1997.

3 The print belongs to a series dating from *c.* 1707–9. The artist is depicted writing an inscription of his own as if the words were those of the publisher. For a translation of the inscription, see p. 29. Chicago 1955, p. 121, no. 14; Vergez 1983, p. 46, fig. 4; and Clark 2000. The print is also reproduced in Shibui 1929, I-1.

4 Chicago 1931, p. 82; London 1993, pp. 666–7, nos. 611–12. Another notable publication of which Masanobu may have been aware was *Igyō sennin zukushi* (*A Collection of Chinese Immortals of Strange Appearance*, 1689), illustrated by Moronobu. Chicago 1931, pp. 108–9. He may even have known *Yūshō ressen zenden* (*Complete Illustrated Lives of the Sennin*), published in Kyoto in 1650. Chicago 1931, pp. 32–4.

5 Fei Zhangfang was a 3rd-century market official from Runan (mentioned in *Hou hanshu*, ch. 112). One day he noticed an old man, the magician Hu Kung (*Jap.* Kokō), hidden in a large jar and became his student. In Chinese lore it is traditionally the sage Wang Ziqiao (*Jap.* Ō Shikyō or Ōkyo) who ascended to heaven on a white crane playing Chinese panpipes. Waterhouse 1997, pp. 41–42; Edmunds n.d., pp. 121–2; Joly 1967, p. 201; Chicago 1931, pp. 108–9.

6 Baird 2001, p. 104; Waterhouse 1997, p. 42 and n. 21.

7 Trans. John Carpenter.

8 Two further designs from the series are in the John Chandler Bancroft Collection at the Worcester Art Museum.

sudare byōbu (*Edo Designs of Blinds and Screens*, n.d.) depicts 'the female immortal Hi Chōbō' holding a knotted love letter (*musubi-bumi*) as the crane flies over an unspecified sea and landscape.[9] An album print also shows a courtesan reading a letter as she is flown over water – a symbol of the 'floating world' – that is bordered by 'three harbours', i.e. the three most famous Japanese pleasure quarters, Shimabara in Kyoto, Shinmachi in Osaka and Yoshiwara in Edo.[10]

The most descriptive Hi Chōbō *mitate-e* is found in *Ukiyo ehon nukume-dori* (n.d.). The double-page illustration shows a courtesan pouring sake for a client on the back of a crane as they fly towards Yoshiwara, with Asakusa Kannon Temple and Mount Fuji in the distance. The accompanying verse playfully suggests that when 'intoxicated one will soar to the skies, transported on the crane'.[11] LEV

9 Waterhouse 1997, p. 43, fig. 15.

10 Kikuchi 1969, fig. 37. This print is also included in a folding album preserved in the Museum of Fine Arts, Boston, with the handwritten title *Masanobu e-dehon* (*[Okumura] Masanobu Model Picture Book*, 1 vol., 20 illus.).

11 'Sui nomi wa / kokū ni nobori / watari-tsuru', which includes a pun on 'watari-tsuru' (transport) and 'tsuru' (crane). Tokyo 1990, no. 209. Once the *mitate* of Hi Chōbō as courtesan had become part of ukiyo-e vocabulary, similar designs were produced by other artists, including Masanobu's pupil Okumura Toshinobu (active *c.* 1716–51) and Suzuki Harunobu (*d.* 1770). Kikuchi 1969, no. 94 (Toshinobu); Waterhouse 1997, p. 41, fig. 13; Machida 1987, no. 361.

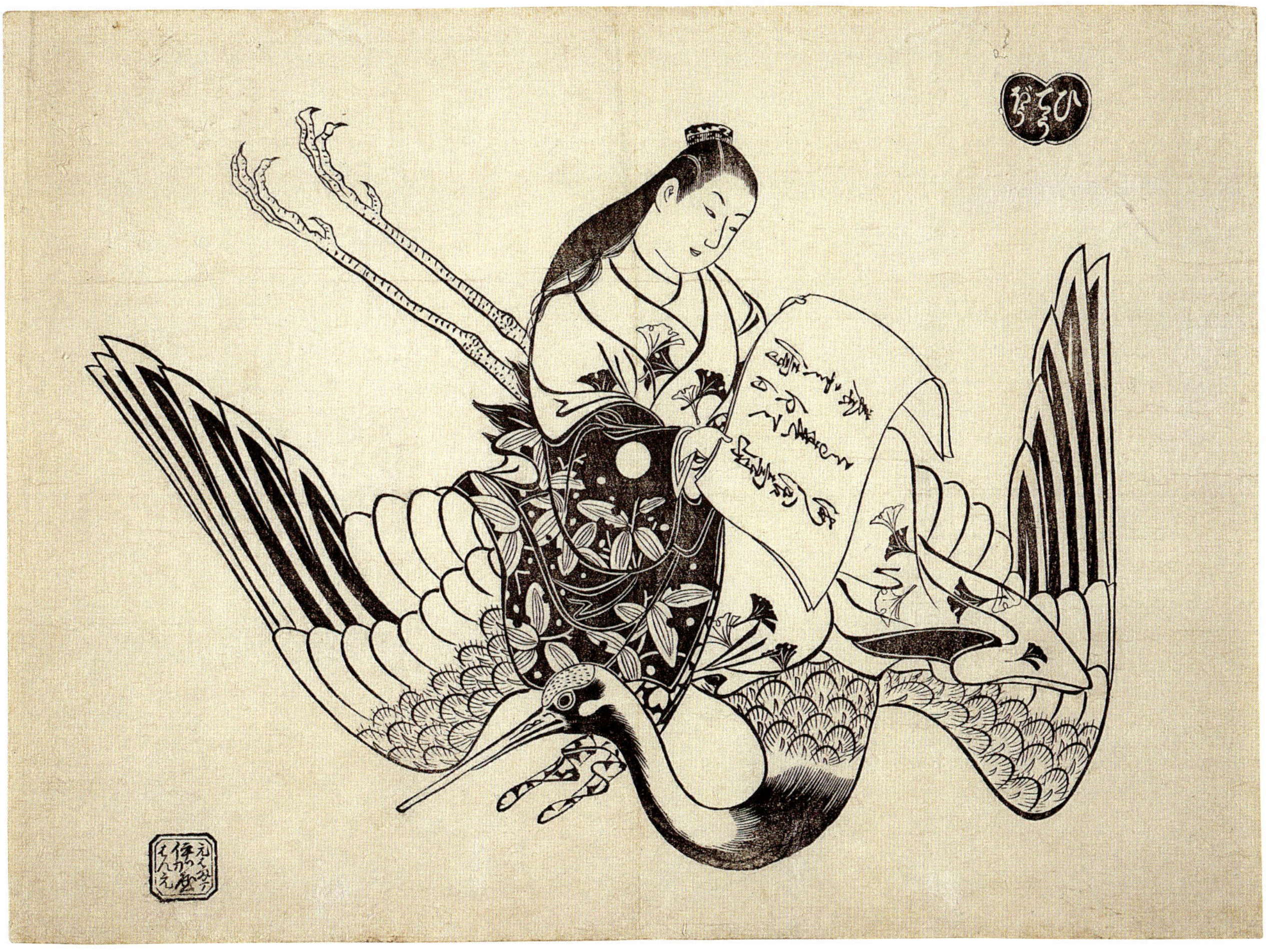

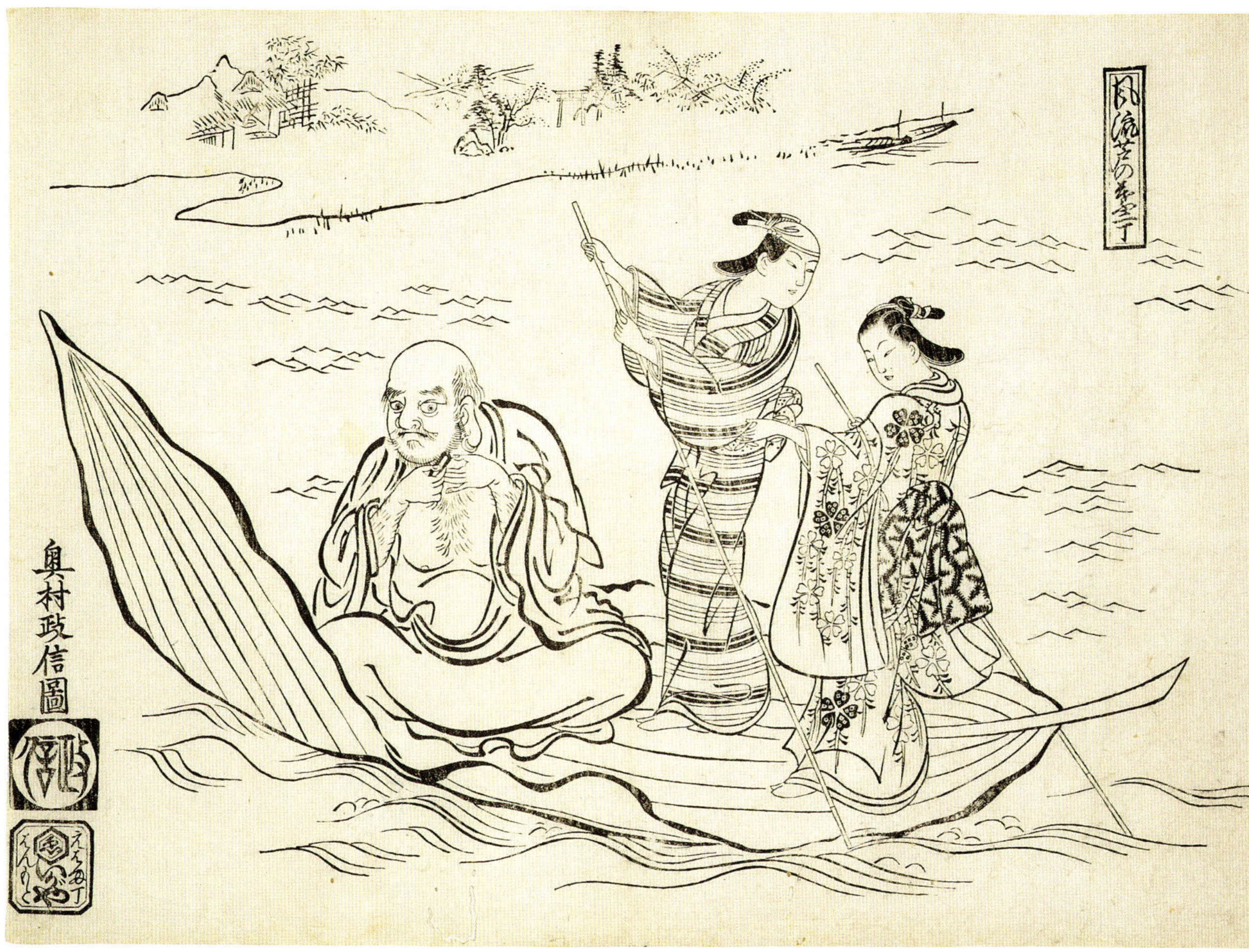
奥村政信圖

59
Okumura Masanobu
'Two Elegant Reed Leaves' (*Fūryū ashi no ha nichō*)

c. 1710

ARTIST'S SIGNATURE: 'Okumura Masanobu zu' (Drawn by Okumura Masanobu)

PUBLISHER: 'Motohama-chō Iga-ya hanmoto' (Iga-ya, publisher at Motohama-chō)

woodblock, horizontal *ōban*, *sumizuri-e*, 28.8 × 40.1 cm

OTHER IMPRESSION: Worcester Art Museum, Mass. (*Nihon bijutsu zenshū*, p. 139, fig. 67)

Gift of Mrs Jared K. Morse, 1953

53.2922

The Zen patriarch Bodhidharma (*Jap.* Daruma), who according to Japanese legend crossed from China to Japan on a reed leaf (or stalk), appears in a variety of *mitate-e* designed by Masanobu. The fun-loving dandy Hanabusa Itchō (1652–1724), greatly admired by Masanobu, is recorded as the first artist to portray Bodhidharma as a woman. Itchō's painting immediately became famous and was frequently quoted in image and word. It even became a decorative motif on *kosode* and fans and was mentioned in poems.

Itchō, it is recorded, was inspired to paint his 'female Daruma' (*Onna-Daruma*) when he heard the comment made by a former Yoshiwara courtesan about Bodhidharma's ordeal of facing a wall for nine years. Her sharp reasoning was that, as a prostitute, she had endured the hard discipline of staying put in the latticed display cage (*harimise*) day and night for ten years and should therefore be more enlightened than Bodhidharma.[1] This witticism was instantly admired, since it expressed the essence of *mitate* – the discovery of similarities between seemingly dissimilar things.

Masanobu often designed Daruma *mitate* that showed a courtesan and Daruma exchanging garments and roles.[2] This print poses a similar riddle: it questions and blurs distinctions between the spiritual and the worldly, the urbane (*ga*) and the vulgar (*zoku*). Unlike in traditional Buddhist paintings, Daruma is not depicted crossing the ocean standing regally on a reed leaf (or stalk) and dressed in a wind-blown robe; instead, the hairy-armed patriarch is shown seated and engaged in a mundane activity – pruning his beard with tweezers. It is rather the beautiful young woman and the young man who appear refined and god-like. Dressed in elegant *furisode* and *kosode*, they effortlessly punt the reed-leaf boat, ferrying even Daruma over the waves of the 'floating world' towards bliss.

The title emphasises the paradox by alluding to the option of 'two elegant reed leaves'. In other words, there are two ways to salvation, that offered by Daruma and that offered by the young guides of the pleasure world. The latter path leads to a choice between a young woman and a young man, yet both the *shinzō* (young trainee courtesan) and the *iro-ko* or *kabuki wakashu* (adolescent combining the professions of acting and male prostitution) have unblemished faces, blurring the distinction between the sexes. For a series of prints dated *c.* 1707–9, Masanobu designed a scene showing Daruma reclining on the reed-leaf punted by a young woman and Arashi Kiyosaburō I, a *wakaonna-gata* kabuki actor known for his skill in love scenes and in the roles of young courtesans.[3]

As *mitate* of Daruma became popular during the 18th century, the word *daruma* became a general slang term for prostitutes. Referring to the legless and roly-poly *daruma* toy dolls, people sometimes joked that prostitutes would bounce up just as quickly after lying down with their clients.[4] LEV

1 *Ukiyo-e jiten*, vol. 1, pp. 212–13; Waterhouse 1997, p. 36.

2 Shibui 1929, I-12; Chicago 1955, p. 124; Clark 1997, p. 25, fig. 18. See also Tokyo 1990, no. 209.

3 Oberlin 1984, pp. 129–30, no. 13; Chicago 1955, p. 123, no. 30. Arashi Kiyosaburō I acted in Edo for about two years, *c.* 1707–9; he died in spring 1713. One *ō-ōban tan-e* example of the *ashi-no-ha* Daruma theme shows a courtesan punting a reed stalk with the seated Daruma. *Genshoku ukiyo-e*, vol. 6, fig. 119.

4 Christie's 1998, p. 132.

60, 61
Okumura Masanobu
From the series *Theatre Pictures (Shibai-e)*

c. 1711

ARTIST'S SIGNATURE (last sheet): 'Tōbu Yamato eshi / Okumura Masanobu zu' (Drawn by Okumura Masanobu, Yamato picture master of Edo)

ARTIST'S SEAL: 'Okumura Masanobu'

woodblock, 2 from a set of 12 album leaves, horizontal *ōban, sumizuri-e*

OTHER IMPRESSIONS: (Shibui 1929, D-1, 10)

William Sturgis Bigelow Collection, 1911

11.13365, 11.13364

1 Shibui 1929, pp. 18–23.

2 Aoki 1999, p. 21.

3 *Kabuki nenpyō*, vol. 1, p. 380.

4 I am grateful to Mutō Junko for her assistance with these identifications.

5 The three sheets not in the Boston collection have been identified from illustrations in Shibui's 1929 article as follows: [D-5] Takii Hanshirō as Nitta Yoshisada (right), Kirinami Takie as Minase-no-mae (left), Ichimura Theatre, *Shusse Taiheiki*, 1710/11; [D-7] Katsuyama Matagorō as Nagoya Sanza (right), Tsutsui Kichijūrō as Katsuragi (left), Nakamura Theatre, *Hoshi-ai Nagoya*, 1710/7; [D-11] Asao Jūjirō (?) as a pillow-seller (right), Ikushima Shingorō (?) (left), together at Yamamura Theatre, 1709/11 – 1712.

The Boston collection includes nine from what was originally a set of twelve horizontal *ōban sumizuri-e* showing pairs of kabuki actors in scenes from recent performances. The only known complete set was reproduced by Shibui Kiyoshi in 1929 and given by him the title *Theatre Pictures (Shibai-e)*.[1] It has been possible to identify six of the twelve subjects with reasonable certainty. The dates of the performances depicted range from the seventh month, 1709, to the eleventh month, 1710. Thus, if all the prints were first issued at the same time, this is likely to have been at the New Year, 1711. At this early stage in his career Masanobu was clearly concerned that his actor prints should include *aragoto* scenes to rival the activities of the Torii school artists Kiyonobu I and Kiyomasu I. The album contains no information about the publisher. Masanobu is thought to have begun his own print-publishing business some time between 1711, the year this set may have been issued, and 1719.[2]

In cat. 60, Ichikawa Danjūrō II appears as Kume no Hachirō (left) in the guise of a seller of moxa (*mogusa*) in the play *Keisei Hibariyama*, performed at the Nakamura Theatre in the seventh month, 1709. Moxa was burnt on the skin as a traditional therapy for many illnesses and Danjūrō II's lines as a travelling salesman of the cure were a great hit, even giving rise to a popular song sung throughout the city by children.[3] Opposite him appears Nakamura Gentarō as Chūjō-hime, apparently in the guise of a courtesan.

The identification of the two actors in cat. 61 is tentative and the warrior roles have not been ascertained. Tomizawa Hanzaburō (right) and Bandō Matakurō II (left) appeared together at the Morita Theatre from 1708 to 1710 and at the Nakamura Theatre beginning in 1710/11.

The other seven sheets in the Boston collection, listed here in the order in which they appear in Shibui's article of 1929, have been identified as follows (some of the actor identifications are provisional):[4] [D-2] Matsumoto Koshirō as I no Hayata (right), Hayakawa Dengorō as Takakura no Miya (left), Ichimura Theatre, *Genpuku nue Yorimasa*, 1709/11 (11.13368); [D-3] Mizuki Takejūrō (?) as a young woman travelling (right), Ichimura Takenojō as a puppeteer (*kairai-shi*) (left), Ichimura Theatre, *Kaikei Sumidagawa*, 1710/1 (*ni no kawari*) (11.13362); [D-4] Ōtani Hiroemon (right), Nakamura Denkurō (left), together at Nakamura Theatre, 1709/11 (11.13366); [D-6] Fujimura Handayū II (?) as a courtesan and Ōtani Hiroemon as a *yakko*, together at Nakamura Theatre, 1709/11–1710/1 (11.13367); [D-8] Murayama Jūheiji (?) (right), Nakajima Kanzaemon (?) (left), together at Nakamura Theatre, 1708/11–1711 (11.13363); [D-9] Nakamura Denpachi (?) (right), Yamashita Kamenojō (?) (left), together at Nakamura Theatre, 1710/11 (11.13361); [D-12] Nakamura Denkurō as Asahina Saburō (right), Nakajima Kanzaemon as Soga no Gorō (left), Nakamura Theatre, *Senrei homare Soga*, 1710/1 (11.13369).[5]

TTC

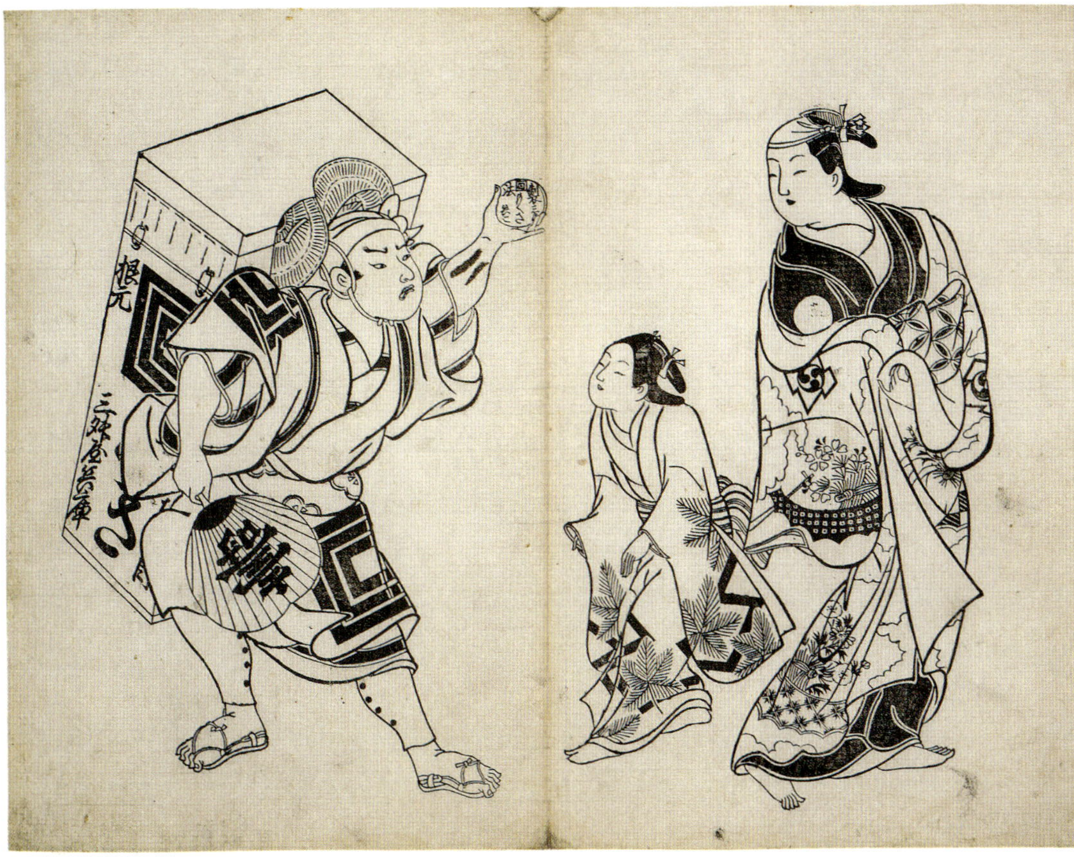

60 *Nakamura Gentarō as a Courtesan and Ichikawa Danjurō II as a Moxa-seller*
27.5 × 36.2 cm
11.13365

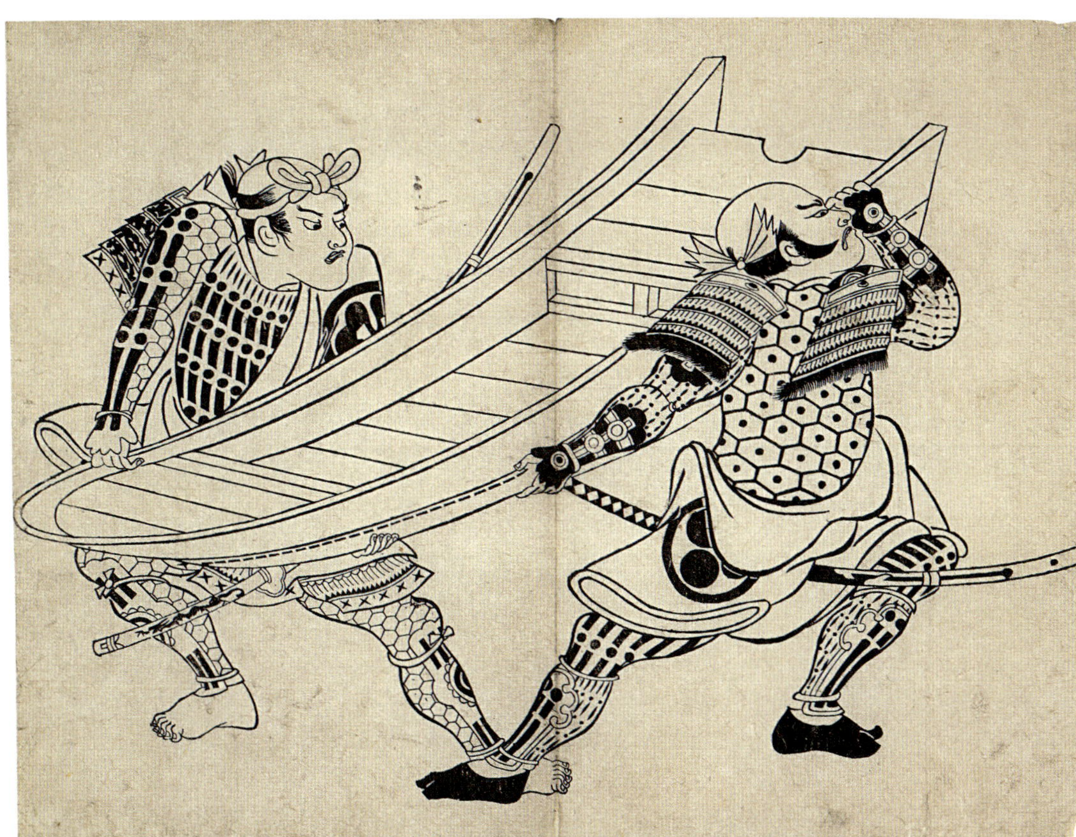

61 *Tomizawa Hanzaburō and Bandō Matakurō as Warriors*
27.4 × 36.4 cm
11.13364

62

Okumura Masanobu

Courtesan in a Furisode Decorated with Poetry Cards

c. 1708–10

ARTIST'S SIGNATURE: 'Tōbu Yamato eshi Okumura Masanobu zu' (Drawn by the Yamato picture master Okumura Masanobu of Musashi Province [Edo])

ARTIST'S SEAL: 'Masanobu'

PUBLISHER: 'Komagome Nishimura'

COLLECTOR'S SEALS: '[Sekine] Shisei zō' (Property of [Sekine] Shisei), 'Jakuso Bunko' (Jakuso Library)

woodblock, *ō-ōban, sumizuri-e*, 56.3 × 29.3 cm (two joined sheets)

OTHER IMPRESSION: M.G. Moreau Collection (formerly Hayashi Tadamasa and Wakai Kenzaburō Collection) (Vigner and Inada 1909, no.110; *Ukiyo-e taisei*, vol. 2, no. 50, *tan-e*)

William Sturgis Bigelow Collection, 1911

11.13342

Masanobu's tall courtesan stops and poses to display her beautifully patterned robes tied with an obi in a crisp bow. While her under-robe is decorated with a bamboo pattern, the fabric of her outer robe is adorned with poetry cards (*uta-garuta*) based on the classic poetry anthology *One Hundred Poems by One Hundred Poets* (*Hyakunin isshu*, compiled *c.* 1235–41 by Fujiwara no Teika). The anthology had been popularised by woodblock-printed books illustrated by Hishikawa Moronobu (for example, cat. 13). The famous Rinpa-style artist Ogata Kōrin (1658–1716) is also known to have designed an elegant card set in the early 18th century.[1]

While men were usually trained in the Chinese classics, *One Hundred Poems* was used as a text for women's education.[2] Women, including courtesans of the pleasure quarters, were fond of playing the *One Hundred Poems* card game.[3] Two hundred cards are used for the game: 100 represent a male or female poet and the first three lines (17 syllables) of his or her poem; the other 100 show the two closing lines (14 syllables). One of the players reads the opening line of a poem from a card in the first set of cards, kept in a pile, while the other players try to pick out the closing line from the set spread on the floor. The player who assembles the most pairs is the winner.

The poem cards decorating the courtesan's robe can be identified. The pair of cards placed highest, near the bow of the courtesan's obi, shows the portrait of Emperor Tenji (626–71) and his verse, a poem that is listed first in *One Hundred Poems*. The cards near the hem represent Tenji's daughter Empress Jitō (645–702) and her poem, listed second in the anthology. The *tanka* by these two poets are quoted below with the visible syllables highlighted in bold type:

Aki no ta no	***In the autumn fields***
kariho no io no	***the hut, the temporary hut***
toma o arami	***its thatch is rough***
waga koromode wa	*and so the sleeves of my robe*
tsuyu ni nuretsutsu	*are dampened night after night with dew.*
	EMPEROR TENJI (no. 1)[4]
Haru sugite	*Spring has passed, and*
natsu kinikerashi	*summer has arrived, it seems*
shirotae no	*Heavenly Mount Kagu*
koromo hosu chō	*where,* ***it is said, they dry robes***
ama no Kagu-yama	***of the whitest mulberry!***
	EMPRESS JITŌ (no. 2)[5]

The card glimpsed under the courtesan's left hand shows words from a poem by Ono no Komachi (active *c.* 833–50). Komachi, the subject of many ukiyo-e, literary works and nō plays, was known for her passionate verses as well as her wit and elegance (see also cat. 13, 39, 52, 104–6, 131). According to legend, she had many lovers, but also proudly turned down several suitors, especially after having been the mistress of Emperor Ninmyō (*reg.* 833–850).

1 Nakamachi 1979.

2 Dore 1992, pp. 66, 126.

3 Women are shown playing the game in a print by Kiyomitsu. *Ukiyo-e taikei*, no. 62.

4 Mostow 1996, pp. 28–39, 124, 131–2, 141–3.

5 Ibid., pp. 24–5, 145–7.

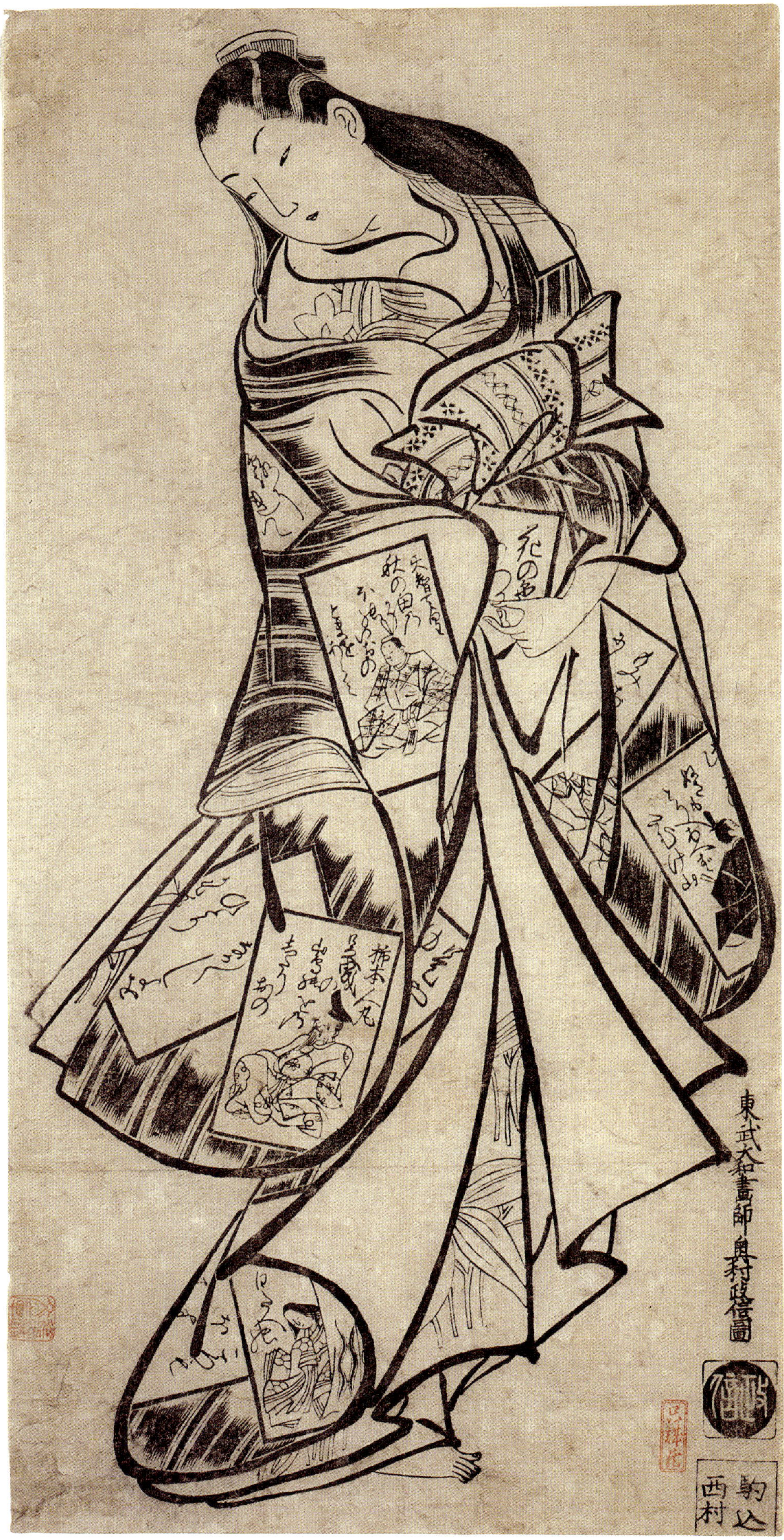
東武大和畫師奥村政信圖
駒込
西村

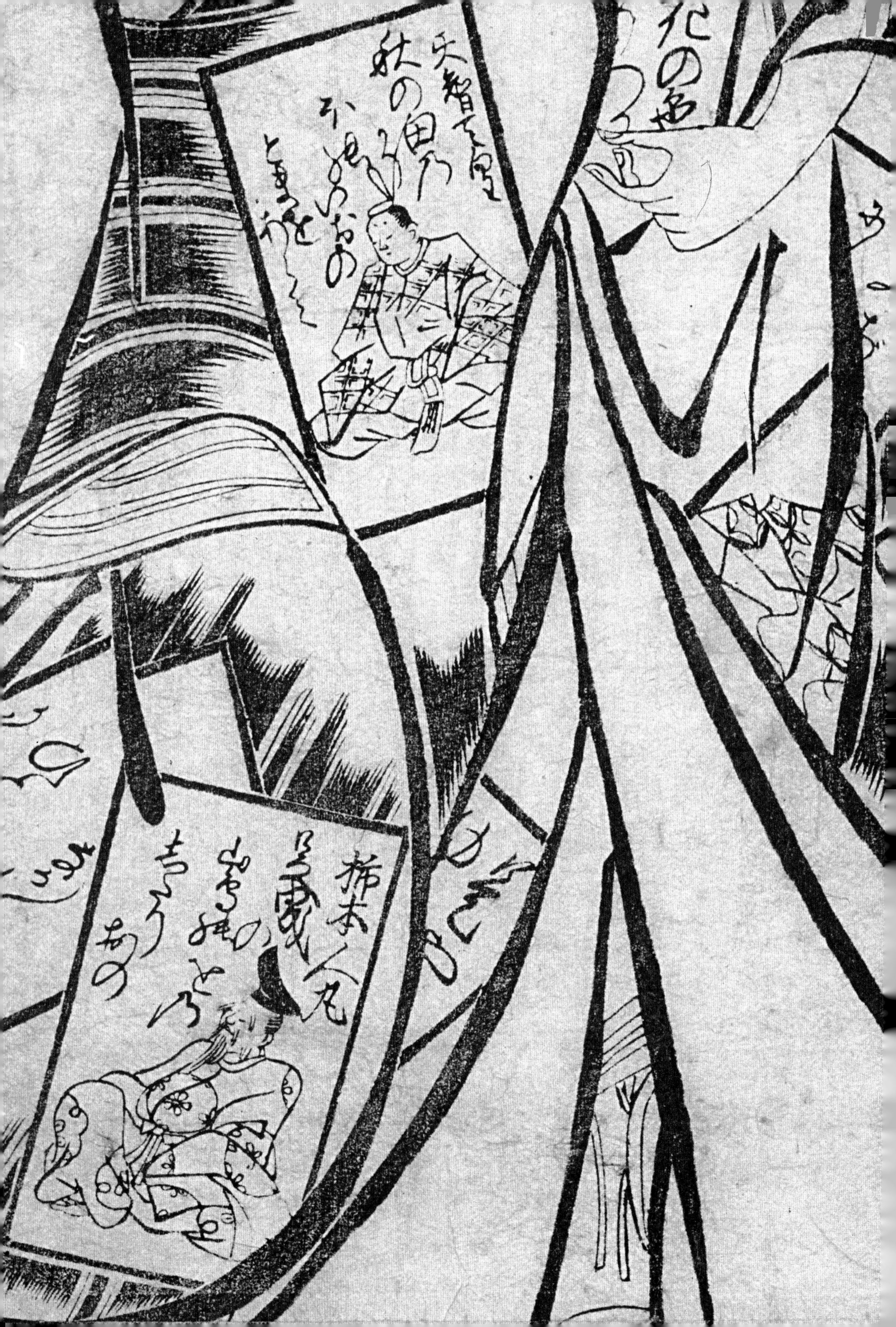
天智天皇
秋の田乃
柿本人丸

6 Ibid., pp. 168–70. For a discussion of the numerous English translations of Komachi's poem, see ibid., pp. 58–86. See also Moronobu's depiction of Komachi in cat. 13.

7 The fiction writer Ihara Saikaku (1642–93) made reference to Komachi's poem in 'The Almanac Maker's Tale' in the *kōshoku-bon* entitled *Five Women Who Loved Love* (*Kōshoku gonin onna*, published 1686). Saikaku 1963, pp. 82; 307–8, nos. 108–9; 327, n. 270; 353, n. 498.

8 Mostow 1996, pp. 54, 149–51. The poet depicted on the left sleeve with his back to the viewer is Kanke (Sugawara no Michizane, 845–903). Philadelphia 2000, p. 197, no. 61 (trans. Edwin Cranston): 'Kono tabi wa / **nusa mo toriaezu / tamuke-yama / momiji** no **ni**shiki / kami no mani-mani' (On this journey, **we could bring no votive silk: – Mount of offering,** – May the **bro**cade of your **autumnal leaves** be pleasing to the gods'; no. 24). Sugawara Michizane is venerated as the god of learning and the patron of poets and calligraphers. See cat. 77.

In the *One Hundred Poems* verse Komachi laments that her beauty and passion ('hana no iro': 'the colour of the flower[s]') have faded and come to nothing, since she has squandered her days lost in melancholy reveries:

Hana no iro wa	***The colour of the flowers***
utsurinikeri *na*	***has faded*** *indeed*
itazura ni	*in vain*
waga mi yo ni furu	*have I passed through the world*
nagameseshi ma ni	*while gazing at the falling rains.*
	ONO NO KOMACHI (no. 9)[6]

In ukiyo-e circles the key words of the poem had double meanings. The word *yo* signified both 'the world outside' and 'relations between man and woman', and *itazura,* which in the Heian period had meant 'idle,' 'vain' or 'aimless', gained the added significance of 'wanton or amorous doings'.[7]

Komachi's words, along with the poem by the court poet and 'patron saint of poetry' Kakinomoto no Hitomaru (*d.* 707 or 708) quoted on the courtesan's right sleeve, imbue the print with romantic overtones. This is conveyed as the courtesan, her hair falling loose in classic fashion, pensively inclines her head to glance at the poetic lines and her trailing skirts:

Ashibiki no	***Must I sleep alone***
yamadori no o no	***through the long autumn nights,***
shidari o no	***long like the dragging tail***
naganagashi yo o	***of the mountain pheasant***
hitori kamo *nen*	***separated from his dove?***
	KAKINOMOTO NO HITOMARU (no. 3)[8]

LEV

63
Okumura Masanobu
Courtesan with Toy Doll Representing Ōtani Hiroji I as a Fish-seller

c. 1715

ARTIST'S SIGNATURE: 'Okumura Masanobu zu' (Drawn by Okumura Masanobu)

ARTIST'S SEAL: 'Masanobu'

PUBLISHER: 'Motohama-chō Iga-ya hanmoto' (Iga-ya, publisher at Motohama-chō)

woodblock, *ō-ōban*, hand-colouring (*tan-e*), 56.7 × 32.4 cm (two joined sheets)

OTHER IMPRESSION: William S. and John T. Spaulding Collection, Museum of Fine Arts, Boston (21.5737)

Gift of Miss Ellen Starkey Bates, 1928

28.197

The young woman depicted in this print has arranged her hair in the Katsuyama style and decorated it with a gingko-leaf-shaped pin and a comb made of tortoise shell. An early impression in pristine condition of this Masanobu print is in the William S. and John T. Spaulding Collection at the Boston Museum. The yellow in this slightly later impression has faded, while the *tan* (red lead) has oxidised to give the pigment a special, crusty effect admired by many collectors.

Several clues suggest a date early in 1715. The names of Soga Jūrō Sukenari and his beautiful, loyal courtesan–mistress Ōiso no Tora are included in the calligraphic design of the woman's sleeve and bring to mind the play *Bandō-ichi kotobuki Soga* about the Soga brothers' revenge (see cat. 21). Performances of this were given at the Nakamura Theatre from the first to the seventh month, 1715. Kiyomasu I depicted the actor Fujimura Handayū II in the role of Ōiso no Tora, dressed in a *furisode* decorated with a similar design of larger characters superimposed on smaller cursive script (cat. 32).[1]

Masanobu shows the woman holding up a small toy doll in the form of the actor Ōtani Hiroji I (1699–1777) as a fish-seller, a comic role that, according to the critique *Yakusha hangon kō* (published in 1715/1), Hiroji must have performed in 1714.[2] A *sumizuri-e* by Kiyomasu I in the Chester Beatty Collection, Dublin, depicts the actor performing this role sporting a similar *itobin* hairstyle, striped leggings and a fan with crest, as well as carrying a pole over his shoulder balancing two baskets of fish.[3] LEV

1 *Ukiyo-e shūka*, vol. 1, no. 8; Mutō 1992, p. 19. The practice of incorporating calligraphy in textile patterns began in the Heian period but did not become popular until the Edo era. Many *hiinagata-bon*, paintings and prints (by Moronobu, Kiyomasu I, Masanobu and the Kaigetsudō school artists) from the 17th to the mid-18th century show beautiful women or actors wearing *kosode* or *furisode* with such cursive script designs. Takeda 1992, pp. 155–79.

2 *Kabuki hyoban-ki I*, vol. 5, p. 608.

3 Takeda 1992, p. 18, no. 21.

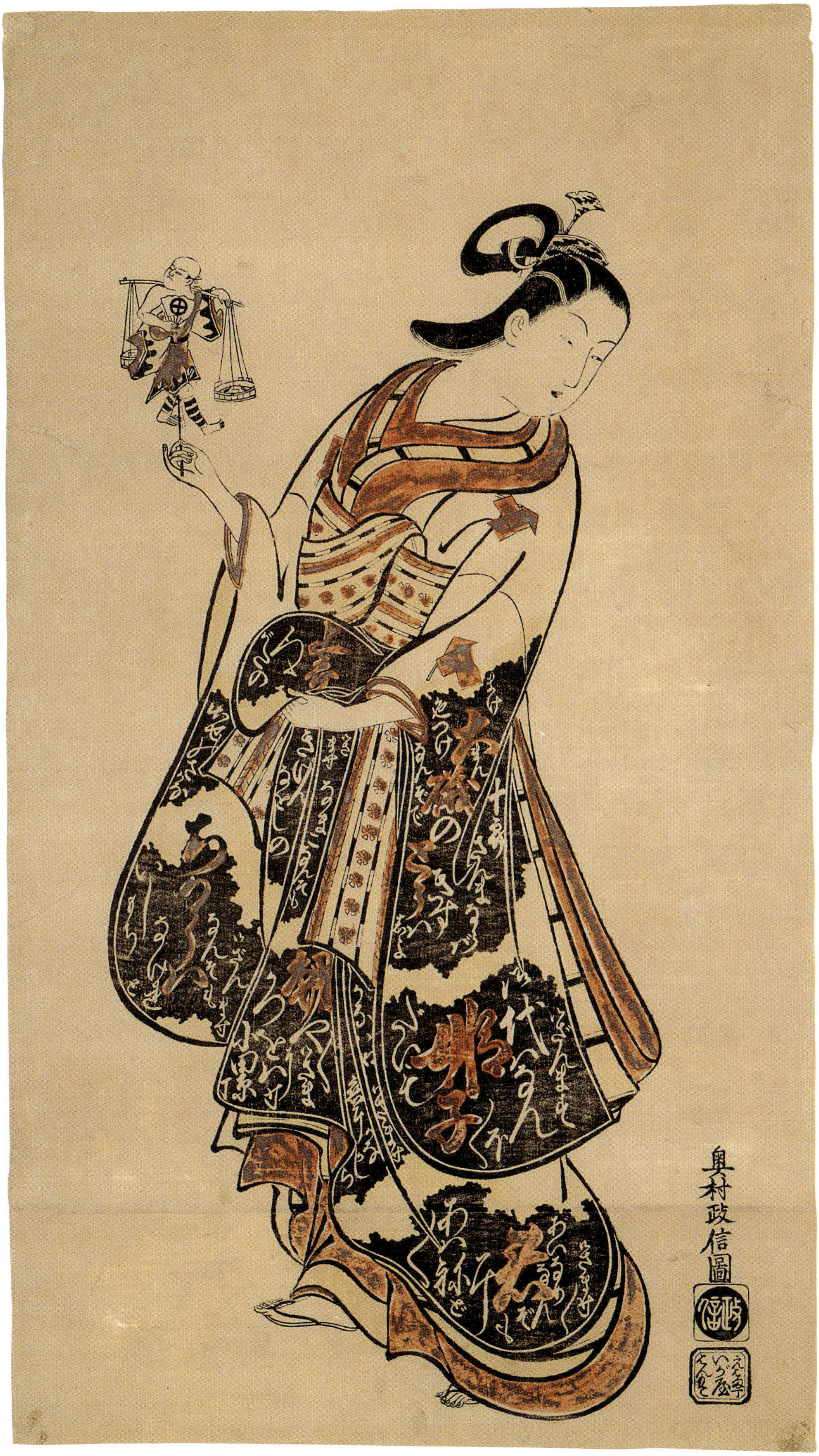
奥村政信圖

64

Okumura Masanobu

'Perspective Picture: Triptych of "The Three Evening Poems"' *(Uki-e sanseki sanpuku-tsui)*

c. 1742–4

ARTIST'S SIGNATURE: 'Watakushi-kata [no] e shita ni magirawashiki na-jirushi o tsuke, nise-jūhan horidashi-sōrō oshirase-mōshi-sōrō / shōmei Hōgetsudō Okumura Bunkaku Masanobu... [damaged]' (I beg to inform you that my pictures are being carved in fake re-cut editions, with suspicious signatures added at the bottom / genuine brush of Hōgetsudō authentic name Okumura Masanobu... [damaged])

PUBLISHER: 'Benizuri narabi [ni] uki-e kongen shōmei / Tōrishio-chō akaki (hyōtan) [no] shirushi Okumura-ya Genroku hanmoto' (The publisher Okumura-ya Genroku at the sign of the red gourd at Tōrishio-chō, authentic originator of *benizuri*[-*e*] and *uki-e*)

woodblock, horizontal *ōban*, hand-colouring (including *tan* and *beni*) and brass filings, 31.3 × 43.9 cm

OTHER IMPRESSIONS: Kobe City Museum (Machida 1999, p. 26, no. 4); Royal Ontario Museum, Toronto (Toronto 1975, pp. 70–1, no. 32)

William Sturgis Bigelow Collection, 1911

11.13344

Many *uki-e* (perspective pictures) by Masanobu show the bustling life of famous places in Edo,[1] but this woodblock print is more reminiscent of a votive image. A dramatic repoussoir view of wooden beams and tatami, flanked by quiet gardens and hallways, is used as a frame and a way of directing the eye of the viewer to a handsome male prostitute, lost in melancholy thought. Standing in the centre of the spacious teahouse room, the graceful young man, wrapped in elegant robes and plaid *haori*, inclines his head to listen to a verse read by a child attendant (*kamuro*) from a poem slip. Two seated female courtesans, facing the man on either side, enhance the quiet, poetic mood. The woman on the right reads the love letters she has written; the one on the left plays the shamisen, accompanied by an attendant with a *kokyū*.[2]

Behind the elegant trio are three framed plaques hanging from a transom, each inscribed with one of the classic 'three evening poems'. Listed together (as nos. 361–3) in the anthology *New Collection of Ancient and Modern Japanese Poems* (*Shin kokin waka-shū*; SKKS, compiled *c.* 1210), each ends with the words 'aki no yūgure' (autumn dusk/twilight). From left to right they read:

Sabishisa wa
sono iro to shi mo
nakarikeri
maki tatsu yama no
aki no yūgure

Loneliness –
the essential colour of a beauty
not to be defined:
over the dark evergreens, the dusk
that gathers on far autumn hills.
JAKUREN HŌSHI (*d.* 1202); SKKS, no. 361

Kokoro naki
mi ni mo aware wa
shirarekeri
shigi tatsu sawa no
aki no yūgure

While denying his heart
even a monk feels his body aware
of the depths of a sad beauty:
by the marsh at autumn twilight,
snipe rise to wing away.
SAIGYŌ HŌSHI (1118–90); SKKS, no. 362

Miwataseba
hana mo momiji mo
nakarikeri
ura no tomaya no
aki no yūgure

I gaze afar
and ask for neither cherry flowers
nor crimson leaves:
the inlet with its grass-thatched huts
clustered in the growing autumn dusk.[3]
FUJIWARA NO TEIKA (1162–1241); SKKS, no. 363

These verses were written by the three poets portrayed in the *kakemono* hanging scroll triptych hung in the formal alcove (*tokonoma*) at the far end of the room. The poets are depicted in three-quarter view in the landscapes they evoke in their poems: the courtier Teika stands by the inlet gazing at the huts, the monk Saigyō looks out at the marsh and the monk Jakuren gazes towards the hills with Chinese black pine (*maki*). A bamboo vase with chrysanthemums, hung on the wall near the alcove, contributes to the autumnal mood of both the paintings and the teahouse scene.

1 See cat. 62, 65 and Masanobu's *uki-e* scenes from Yoshiwara in Vergez 1983, nos. 17–19.

2 The *kokyū* (spike box lute or spike guitar) is a three or four-stringed instrument played with a bow.

3 Translations, with a few minor changes to that of Saigyō's poem, quoted from Bower and Miner 1962, pp. 261, 295, 307. The calligraphy of the three poems stresses *ura* (inlet), *shigi* (snipe) and *maki* (Chinese black pine) by making these characters larger and darker than the others.

While each of the main figures, like the poets, seems lost in the mood of 'his' evening poem, the atmosphere in the room is about to change. Two attendants arriving on the right are bringing a screen and a small wooden stand (*sanbō*) to prepare for livelier evening events. The couple behind them are perhaps a courtesan with the first client. Further, while the poems evoke a monochromatic, withered beauty, the print is alive with colours, including orpiment yellow, *tan* orange and *beni* red. The person who hand-coloured the print, possibly an apprentice, even used his fingertips to enliven the image with dabs of *nikawa* glue and brass filings.

A few clues help date the print *c.* 1742–4. The text in the right margin mentions that it was published by 'Okumura-ya Genroku at the sign of the red gourd, authentic originator of *benizuri*[*-e*] and of *uki-e*'. Masanobu is known to have designed *uki-e* from *c.* 1739 and to have started creating *benizuri-e* (two-colour prints) *c.* 1742.[4] Moreover, the actor Sanogawa Ichimatsu I started a fashion on his arrival in Edo in 1741 when he wore a chequered pattern popularly known as *ichimatsu moyō* (or *ichimatsu-zome*, *ichimatsu-gata*) while performing at the Nakamura Theatre.[5] This pattern is seen on the obi worn by the young woman playing the *kokyū*. The young man also wears a tartan-patterned *haori* similar to those worn by Ichimatsu in several prints dating from *c.* 1742.[6] On a technical level, the use of *tan* – for example, on the chrysanthemums and on the frame of the screen – makes this print an 'old-fashioned' *tan-e* and suggests a date in the first half of the 1740s.

Masanobu later 'quoted', with only minor changes, the three figures from this 'Three Evening' *uki-e* composition in a *hosoban benizuri-e* triptych entitled *Yoshiwara keisei sanseki* (*Yoshiwara Courtesans of the Three Evenings*, *c.* 1750).[7] LEV

4 The earliest *benizuri-e* known by Masanobu is a picture calendar (*e-goyomi*) from 1742. Toronto 1975, no. 33; Aoki 1999, fig. 8. It is believed that Masanobu handed over the running of his publishing business to Okumura-ya Genroku in the early 1740s. Aoki 1999, p. 22.

5 *Genshoku ukiyo-e*, vol. 5, p. 88; Leiter 1997, p. 552.

6 A print by Masanobu shows Ichimatsu as Kichisaburō, the lover of Yaoya Oshichi, standing in a very similar pose and wearing a tartan-patterned *haori*. The play was entitled *Musume Soga gaijin Yashima* and was performed in the second month, 1742, at the Nakamura Theatre. Paine 1959, cover illus.; Kikuchi 1969, no. 88.

7 An impression of the centre sheet (with a courtesan replacing the young man) is in the Boston Museum (1911.13195); an impression of the right-hand sheet is reproduced in Chicago 1955, p. 172, no. 114.

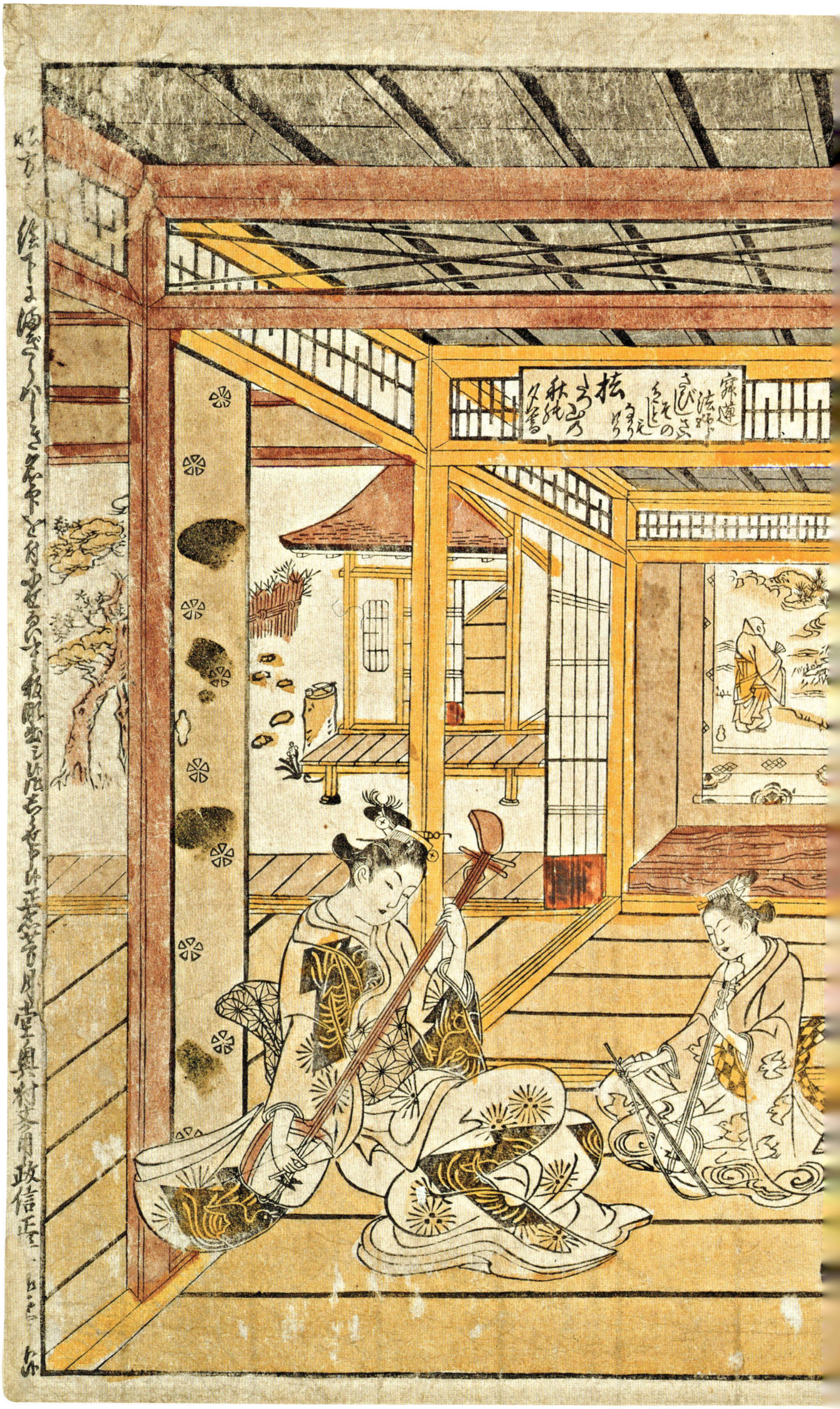

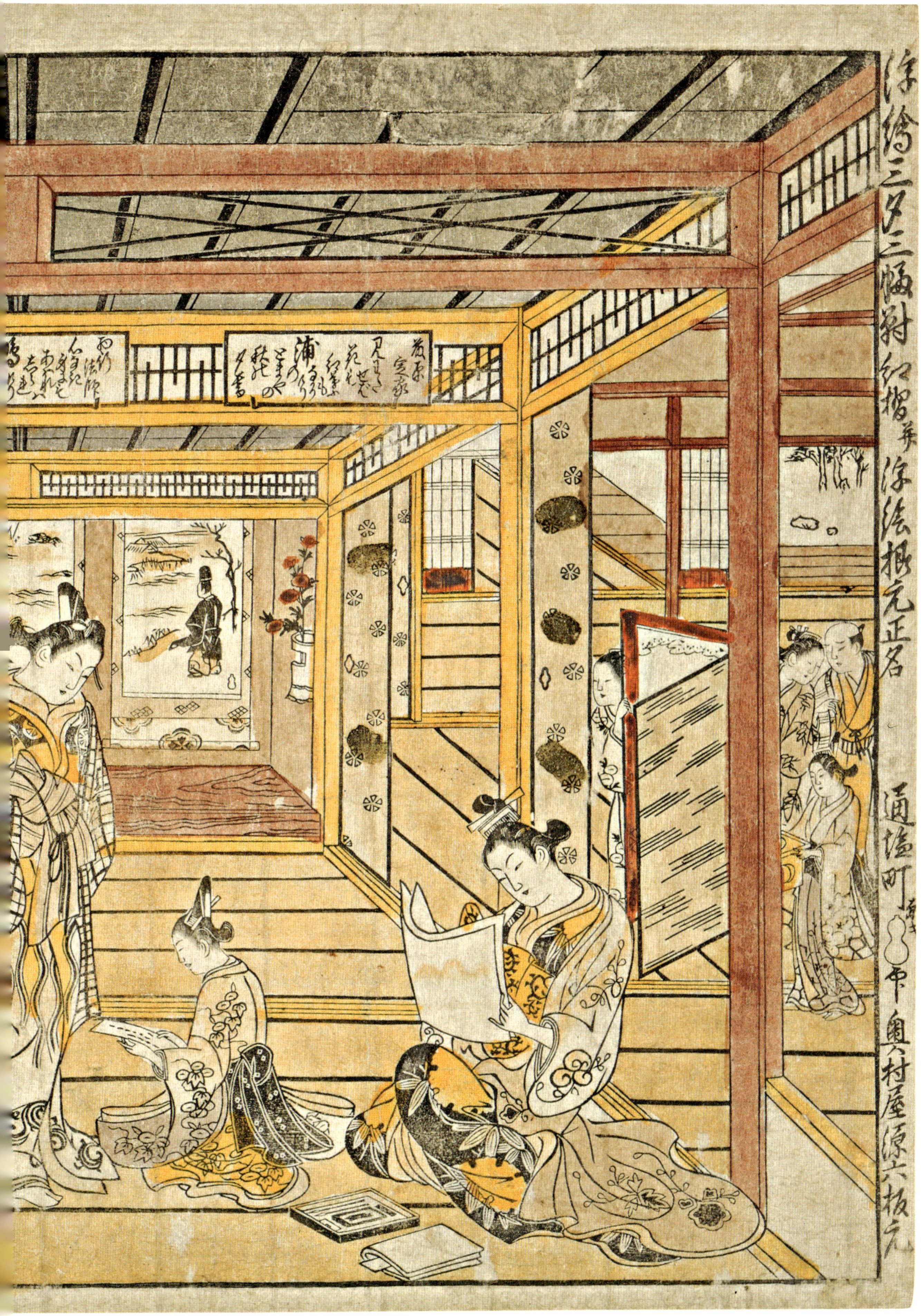
通塩町
奥村屋源六板元

65

Okumura Masanobu

'Large Perspective Picture of the Interior of Echigo-ya at Suruga-chō' (*Suruga-chō Echigo-ya gofukuten ō-uki-e*)

c. 1745

PUBLISHER: 'Tōrishio-chō Okumura-ya Genroku hanmoto akaki hyōtan no shirushi' (The publisher Okumura-ya Genroku at Tōrishio-chō at the sign of the red gourd)

woodblock, extra-large size (*toku-ōban*), hand-colouring (*urushi-e*), 47.7 × 66.9 cm

REPRODUCED: *Ukiyo-e shūka*, vol. 1, no. 32

OTHER IMPRESSIONS: Schindler Collection, Biel, Switzerland (Tokyo 1985, fig. 6); Mitsukoshi Shiryōkan (Research Institute), Tokyo; William S. and John T. Spaulding Collection, Musem of Fine Arts, Boston, 21.5775

William Sturgis Bigelow Collection, 1911

11.13343

The earliest purveyors of fashion in Japan were itinerant cloth pedlars who travelled the country with bolts of cloth stacked in boxes carried on their backs.[1] As the wealthy merchant class demanded fabrics of superior craftsmanship, drapers' shops were established in the major cities. Echigo-ya (the precursor of the present-day Mitsukoshi department store) was the most famous drapery and haberdashery store in Edo. Mitsui Takatoshi (1622–94), the founder of the shop, could offer fabrics at lower prices than his competitors because the Mitsui family owned a wholesale business, with its main office in Kyoto. The family established branch stores in Kyoto and Osaka, money exchanges and a network of expert spinners, weavers, dyers and embroiderers in Kyoto, Osaka and Edo.[2]

When Takatoshi moved Echigo-ya from Hon-chō to Suruga-chō in the Nihonbashi district of Edo in 1683 he pioneered a policy of cash sales at low, fixed prices to avoid haggling and displayed the prices next to his goods. He also instituted a system for the division of labour (*bungyō*) and offered productivity bonuses. As a result of his business acumen, the store soon became famous for its efficient customer service, fashionable fabrics sold at desired lengths, elegant accessories and creative marketing (handbills, lending clothing to famous actors and so forth), gaining loyal customers from both merchant and daimyo households.

Masanobu's print of Echigo-ya is thought to be from a series of large perspective views (*ō-uki-e*, 'large floating pictures') of the most notable places in Edo (including the theatre district; see cat. 66). The series is believed to have been published *c.* 1745, the year in which the Echigo-ya, according to its archives, enjoyed record sales.[3] This impression of the Echigo-ya *uki-e* is valued especially highly since it retains much of its original colour and the margins are intact.

Masanobu's view of Echigo-ya tells us much about business practices and daily activities in the store. The name Echigo-ya is clearly marked in white reserve on the black curtain on the far left. Boards attached to the pillars mention that this is the main branch of Echigo-ya drapery and haberdashery shop, which also sells accessories; smaller signs quote prices and give the names of the clerks on duty. A notice hanging from the ceiling lists the store rules of 'genkin kakene nashi' (cash payments and set prices).[4] Signs hanging at the back, near the latticed partition on the right, indicate where cloth could be bought by the piece from a sales clerk called Jisuke and where evening garments could be obtained.[5]

Masanobu made a few compositional adjustments in order to combine a clear view of the grand interior with a depiction of the shopfront. The four hangings on the right, marked with the Mitsui family crest (a circle with the character for 'three' boxed within the character meaning 'well'), actually hung in the foreground facing Suruga-chō, which ran from west to east. In the

1 Tokyo 1960–3, vol. 1, fig. 287.

2 For the Mitsui family businesses, see Nakane and Ōishi 1990, pp. 155–6; *Edo-gaku jiten*, pp. 231–2; Guth 1993, pp. 26–7; *Ukiyo-e jiten*, vol. 1, p. 142; and *Kodansha Encyclopedia*, vol. 5, pp. 212–13. The Echigo-ya branch in Kyoto was established in 1687, that in Osaka in 1691.

3 For a discussion of Masanobu's six known large perspective prints of famous views in Edo, including Echigo-ya, see Kishi 1994, pp. 13–36.

4 The 'rule against selling retail wares on credit' is mentioned in Saikaku's novel *The Life of an Amorous Woman* (*Kōshoku ichidai onna*, published 1686). Saikaku 1963, p. 181.

5 Jisuke is mentioned in the Echigo-ya employment records. Kishi 1994, p. 265, n. 38.

print, however, the street is depicted on the right, running south to north behind the samurai entering the store. Flying birds, and the cotton shop then opposite Echigo-ya, are visible in the background.[6]

Customers entering Echigo-ya would indeed first have seen the niche-like *fumikomi* that Masanobu depicts in the foreground of the print. A pedlar with shaven head, probably a young monk, is shown standing on his toes in this space. In the hope of selling one of the plain calendar prints he holds in his left hand (see cat. 113) he is trying to catch the attention of a sales clerk passing on the raised shop floor. The salesman, carrying rolls of fabric in his arms, notices the pedlar but walks towards his important customer, a beautiful courtesan with hair arranged in the Katsuyama style. She is seated on the left smoking a pipe and using a tobacco tray provided by the store for its customers. A very young male clerk[7] is trying to interest her in a bamboo textile design, but she glances over her shoulder at the older man kneeling behind the latticed partition. He is watching over a bundle wrapped in a *furoshiki*, perhaps fabrics that the courtesan has already purchased.

The fashionable courtesan is probably a fan of the handsome kabuki actor Sanogawa Ichimatsu I (1722–62), known for both *wakashu-gata* and *wakaonna-gata* roles, for her *kosode* with a pine tree (*matsu*) motif is tied with an obi decorated with a fashionable pattern, popularly called *ichimatsu-zome* or *ichimatsu moyō*. This chequered pattern became all the rage when Ichimatsu wore the design on his *hakama* and obi while playing the role of the youth Kumenosuke in 1741 at the Nakamura Theatre, and the actor continued to incorporate it in many of his costumes.[8] Masanobu includes a figure wearing a head covering (*birari bōshi*) and a *kosode* displaying the crest of Sanogawa Ichimatsu, shown arriving at the shop in the right background. Another ardent fan – or perhaps it is the actor himself – is dressed as a woman.

In the right foreground guests have left their straw hats and outer garments on the *tatami* floor in a pile near the brazier (*hibachi*) used by a young apprentice (*kozō*) serving tea. A servant (*yakko*) whose master is probably still shopping has been treated to a cup. A sign at the base of the right-hand pillar urges customers to be prudent with their footwear ('o-hakimono go-yōjin') so as to avoid mixing up pairs of shoes, but someone has carelessly left theirs in disarray.

In the left half of the room, behind the courtesan, clerks are seated in a row, each in front of the cloth they are responsible for selling. A few clerks show textiles to female customers; others use an abacus to add up purchases made by clients. In the distance, behind a sliding door, is the cashier's room, occupied by three men. Even further back lies the storeroom and a veranda, which face a small, quiet garden. Masanobu's attention to detail is also evident in the inclusion of the swallow's nest resting on a small ledge attached to the crowning beam. LEV

6 The floor plan of Echigo-ya from 1745 to 1762 is shown ibid., p. 34.

7 Employees were hired between the ages of eleven and thirteen and were promoted to head clerk after serving for ten to fifteen years. It usually took twelve to eighteen years to advance to the rank of group foreman. Nakane and Ōishi 1990, pp. 159–60.

8 He appeared in Act III ('Takaya Shinjū') of the play *Na-no-hana akebono Soga* (1741/2). Leiter 1997, p. 552; *Kabuki nenpyō*, vol. 2, pp. 338–9; Honolulu 1980, p. 63, no. 14; *Ukiyo-e jiten*, vol. 1, p. 54. Since ancient times the pattern had also be known as *ishi-datami* or *arare-moyō*. *Genshoku ukiyo-e*, vol. 5, p. 88. Sanogawa Ichimatsu I arrived in Edo for the spring performances of 1741. For prints by Masanobu, Toyonobu and Shigenaga depicting the actor wearing garments decorated with variations in chequered and tartan patterns, see Chicago 1955, p. 158, no. 89; p. 205, no. 15; pp. 207–8, nos. 19–20; p. 194, no. 20.

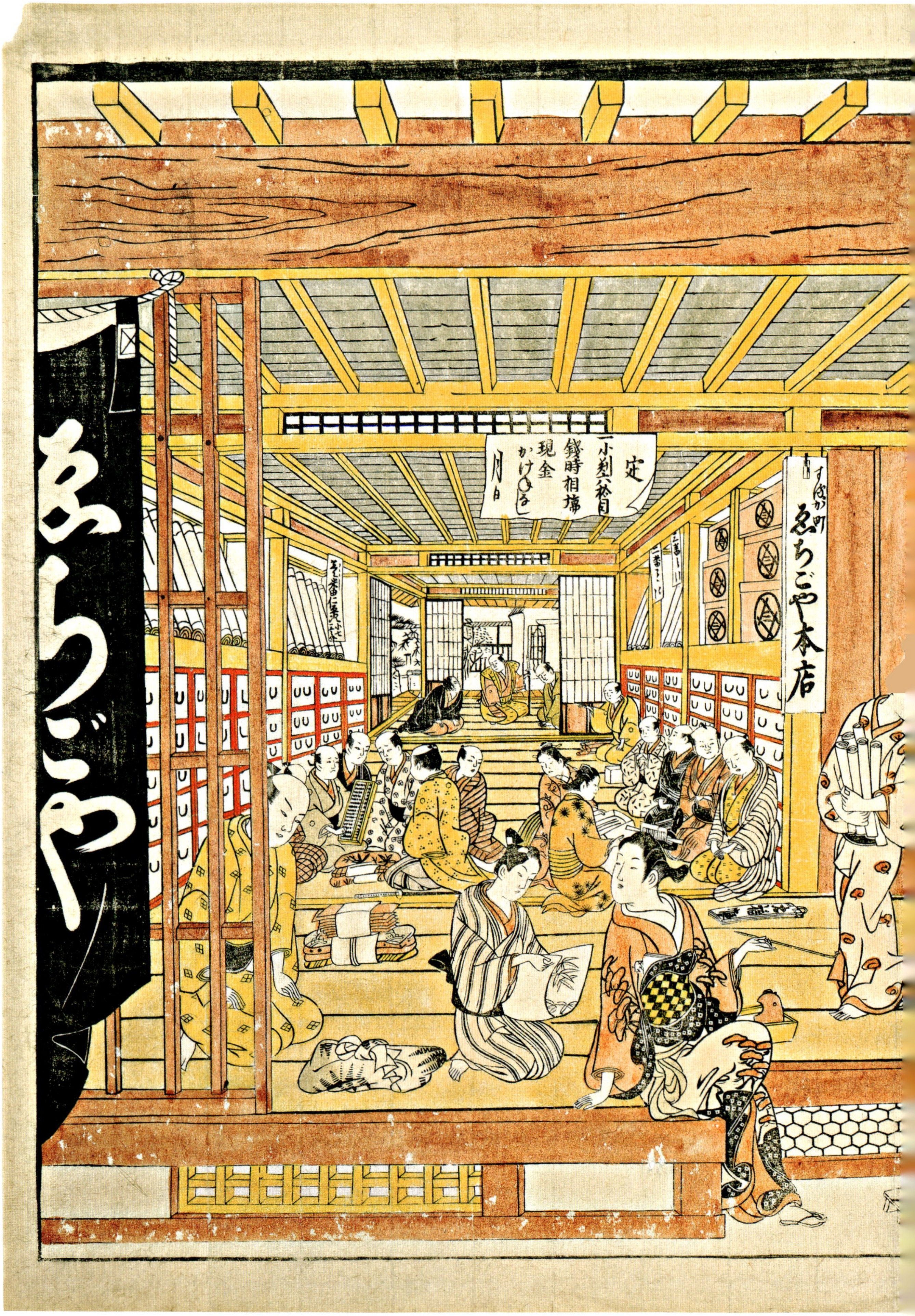
定
現金
ゑちごや本店

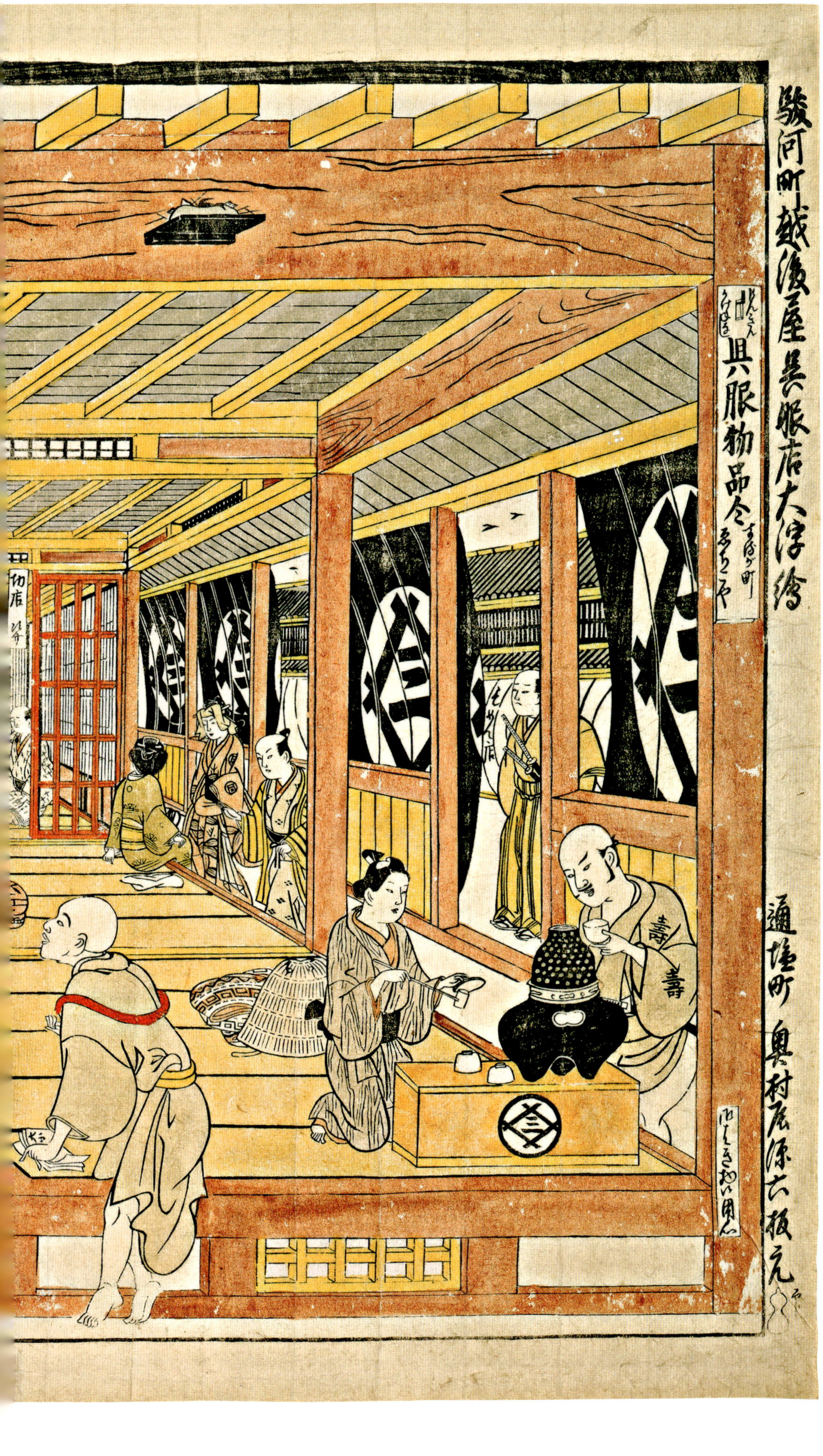
駿河町越後屋呉服店大浮絵
呉服物品々
通塩町 奥村屋源六板元

66

Attributed to Okumura Masanobu

Large Perspective View of the Theatre District in Sakai-chō and Fukiya-chō (Sakai-chō Fukiya-chō shibai-machi ō-uki-e)

New Year, 1745

ARTIST'S SIGNATURE: [trimmed]

PUBLISHER: [trimmed]

woodblock, extra-large size (*toku-ōban*), *beni-e*, 43.8 × 64.5 cm

REPRODUCED: *Ukiyo-e shūka*, vol. 1, no. 121

OTHER IMPRESSION: Pulverer Collection, Cologne (Osaka 1990, no. 1-12)

William Sturgis Bigelow Collection, 1911

11.19687

Like *Large Perspective View of the Interior of Echigo-ya on Suruga-chō* (cat. 65), this is thought to be one of a group of six extra-large perspective pictures (*uki-e*) designed by Okumura Masanobu in 1745 showing famous places in Edo. The title, artist's signature and publisher's name have been trimmed off both known impressions of this design. The title is thus not original.[1]

After the demolition of the Yamamura Theatre as a result of the Lady Ejima scandal of 1714 (see p. 26), the three remaining government-licensed kabuki theatres were the Nakamura at Sakai-chō, the Ichimura at Fukiya-chō and the Morita at Kobiki-chō. The first two appear in this print, the Nakamura in the middle of the right side of the street, and the Ichimura in the distance on the same side. The three curtained 'turrets' (*yagura*) on the left are licensed puppet theatres (from front to back): the Hizen, Geki and Tatsumatsu theatres.[2]

The Nakamura Theatre is advertising on its main title signboard the play *Hagoromo kotobuki Soga*, which was performed at the New Year, 1745. This is corroborated by the signboards that appear just below the turret to the left, which give the names of the three actors who performed on that occasion: Segawa Kikunojō, Saruwaka Kanzaburō (Nakamura Kanzaburō VI, the manager of the theatre) and Segawa Kikujirō. Below the turret to the right are four tall picture signboards (*e-kanban*) and another title board, which reads 'Waki kyōgen – Shuden-tōshi [Shuten-dōji]'. The *waki-kyōgen* was an auspicious, ceremonial performance added to the New Year programme after the solemn opening dances *Sanbasō* and *Okina*: at the Nakamura a version of the Shuten-dōji (The Sake-drinking Boy) legend was customarily performed.

At the Ichimura further down the street the main title signboard advertises *Hatsu-goyomi kotobuki Soga*, also known to have been performed at the New Year, 1745. The three actors named are Onoe Kikugorō, Ichimura Uzaemon [VIII] (manager) and Ichimura (Wakadayū?). A large oblong picture signboard appears to the right of this.

The writing on the signboards of the first two puppet theatres is impossible to make out through the lattice beside the left gatepost in the foreground. The name-board of the puppet theatre in the distance on the left side is Tatsumatsa Hachirobei, and the name of the performance *Fujiwara*... probably refers to *Fujiwara no Hidesato Tawara no keizu* (Gidayū-style *jōruri*).[3]

Also in the neighbourhood, surrounding the theatres, are a variety of theatre teahouses (*shibai-jaya*), restaurants and shops, many of them named on their advertising curtains and lanterns. Behind the street vendor of fish (right), for instance, is a restaurant called Ise-ya, specialising in boiled beancurd with toppings (*furi-kake yu-dōfu*), and just inside the gate on the right, before you reach the Nakamura Theatre, stand two theatre teahouses called Takasu-ya and Nakaya. Such teahouses arranged tickets for theatre boxes as well as serving refreshments. Leaning over the upstairs balcony and

1 Kishi 1994a, pp. 76–7, no. 2-2.

2 Ibid., p. 85, no. 22

3 I am grateful to Satō Satoru for his assistance with this identification.

4 Kishi 1994a.

looking down into the street is a young actor with a purple head-cloth, indicating that he is a player of women's roles or an adolescent trainee. Theatre teahouses were also a convenient meeting place for comely young actors and their (generally male) admirers and in the same neighbourhood were male brothels (*kagema-jaya*) where any liaisons initiated in the teahouse might be followed through. Shops on the other side of the Nakamura would appear to be called Nishimura and Fukuyama. At the far end of the street on the left is the Daikoku-ya (a teahouse?). The shop on the left in the foreground, Nakamura- ya, seems to be selling toys and/or stage props.

The bustling pre-theatre crowds are warmed up by costumed 'door entertainers' (*kido geisha*), employed by the theatres to perform mock skits from the plays on raised platforms at the side of the entrance. In the centre foreground, wearing a deep sedge hat to hide his face, is a figure sporting the twin swords of a samurai. It was considered bad form for serious warriors to take an interest in such a plebeian amusement as kabuki and many samurai patrons of the theatre preferred to attend semi-incognito. The auspicious view of distant Mount Fuji and the New Year kite is not in the same perspective as the view of the street, with its converging architectural lines. It is a common feature of Masanobu's large perspective pictures that the views at the back of the composition revert to a more traditional system of parallel perspective (see p. 30).[4] TTC

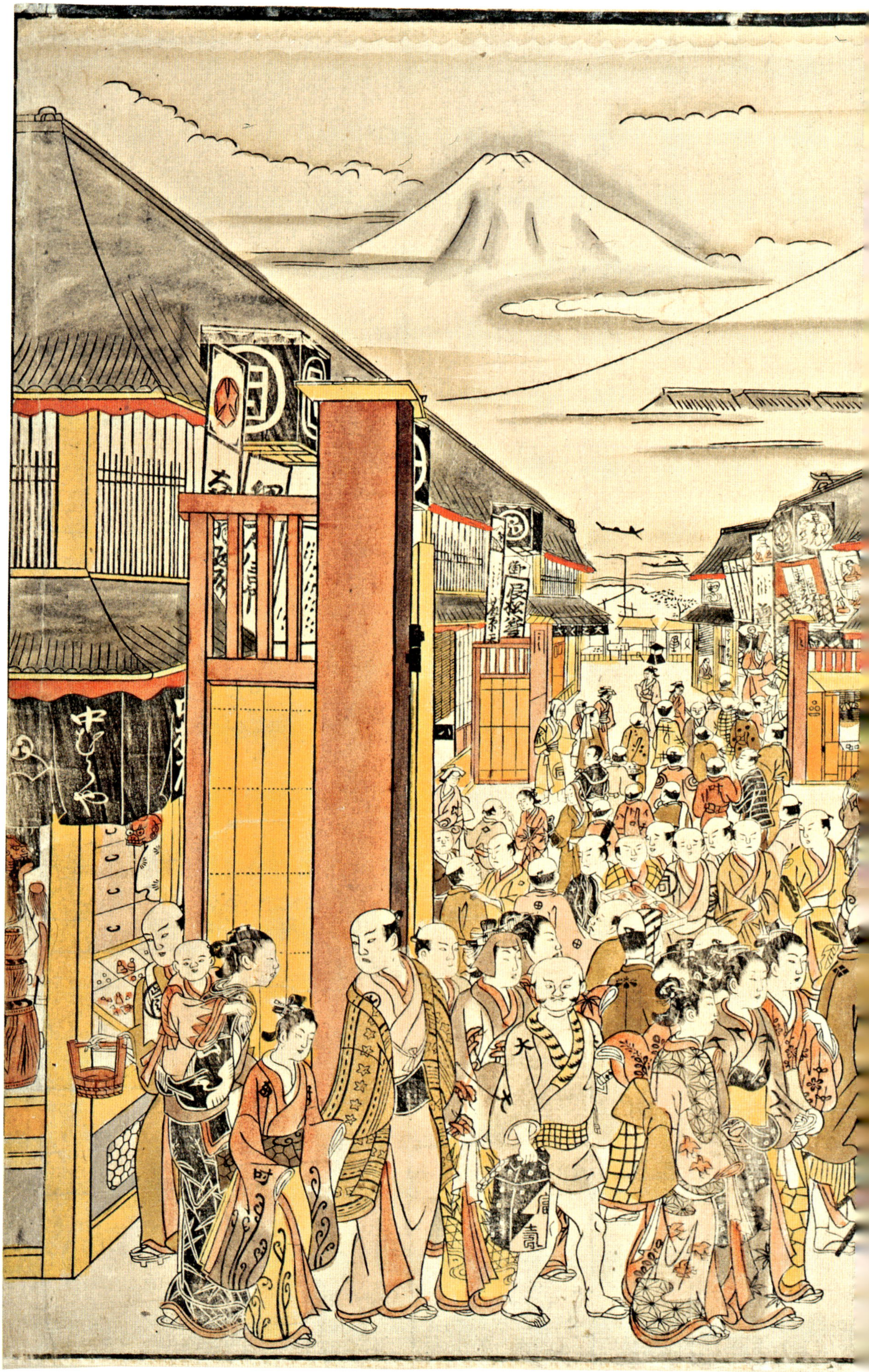

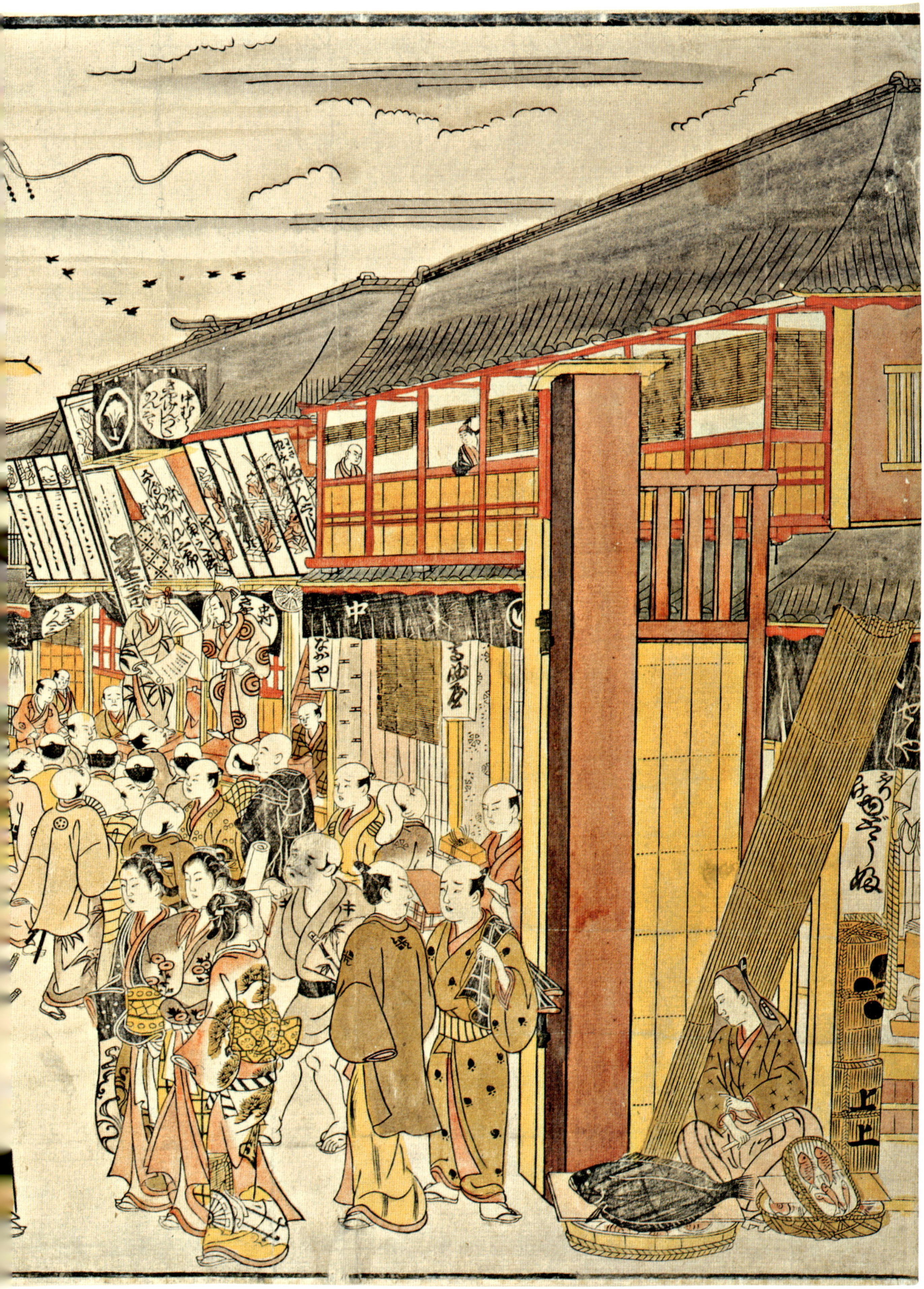

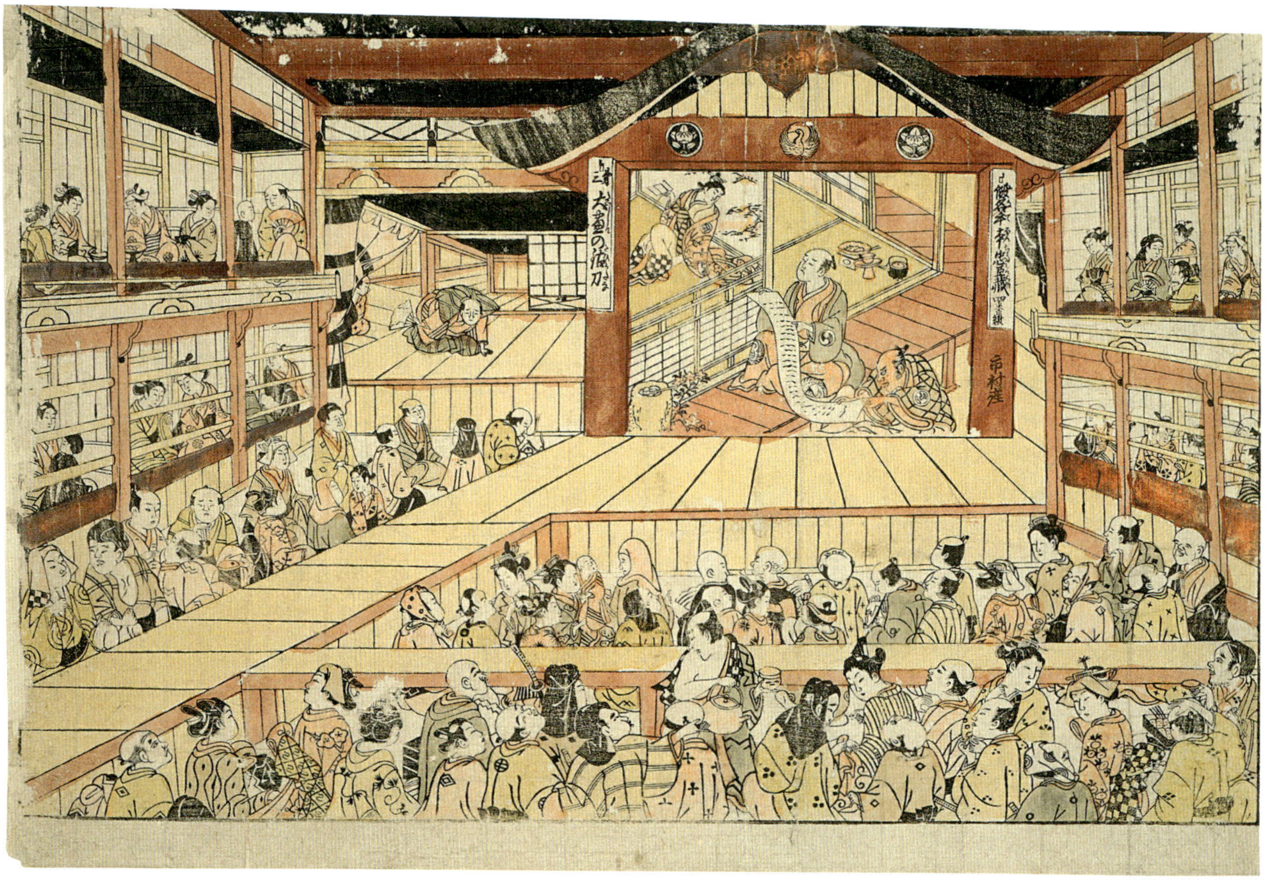
市村座

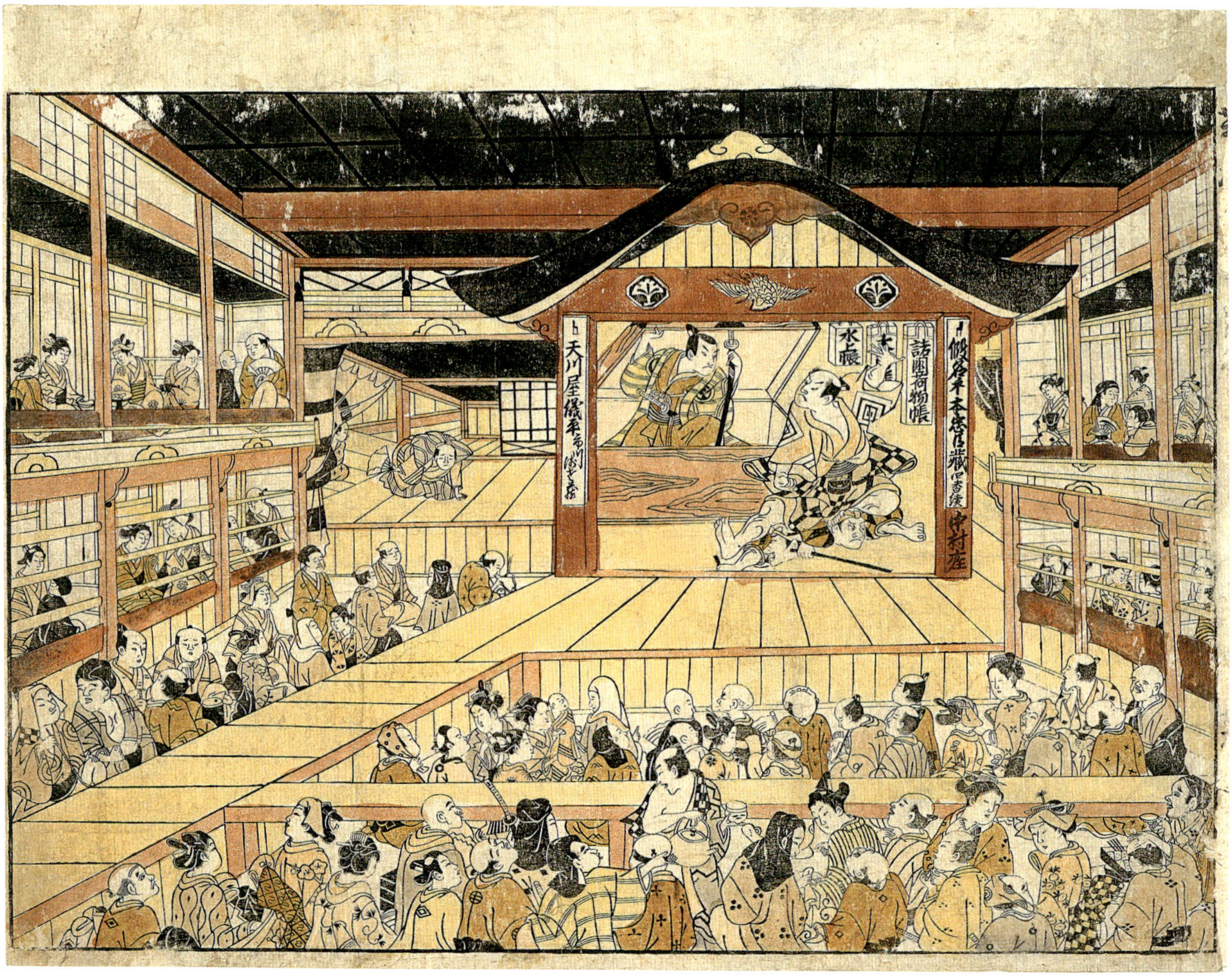
天川屋儀平
水上帳
中村座

67, 68

Attributed to Okumura Masanobu

Scene from the Play 'Kana-dehon Chūshingura' at the Ichimura Theatre

Scene from the Play 'Kana-dehon Chūshingura' at the Nakamura Theatre

67

5th month, 1749

ARTIST'S SIGNATURE: [trimmed]

PUBLISHER: [trimmed]

woodblock, horizontal *ōban*, *beni-e*, *urushi-e*, 28.4 × 42.8 cm

William Sturgis Bigelow Collection, 1911

11.19627

68

6th month, 1749

ARTIST'S SIGNATURE: [trimmed]

PUBLISHER: [trimmed]

woodblock, horizontal *ōban*, *beni-e*, *urushi-e*, 32.7 × 43 cm

REPRODUCED: *Ukiyo-e shūka*, vol. 1, no. 33

William Sturgis Bigelow Collection, 1911

11.19665

The grandest print by Okumura Masanobu showing a kabuki performance inside a theatre is *Large Perspective Picture of an Opening-of-the-Season Play on the Stage* (*Shibai kyōgen butai kaomise ō-uki-e*, Art Institute of Chicago), thought to be one of a group of six extra-large perspective pictures issued in 1745 showing famous places in Edo (see also cat. 65, 66).[1] Although the titles and signatures have been trimmed off these two prints – slightly smaller in format, but still unusually large – they too are attributed to Masanobu. His perspective pictures of kabuki performances seem to have been issued between *c.* 1743 and 1756, and in at least three cases, including cat. 68, the blocks were reused by plugging the onstage area and signboards with a section of block cut to depict a different performance. The audience remained the same.[2]

Chūshingura (*The Treasury of Loyal Retainers*) was the popular name given to plays based on a vendetta carried out by samurai of the Akō fief on their enemy Kira Yoshinaka, sensational historical events of 1701–2 that were immediately adapted in many versions for both the puppet and the kabuki stage. By far the most enduring variant has proved to be *Kana-dehon Chūshingura*, first staged as a puppet play in 1748 and then transferred to all three kabuki theatres in Edo for smash-hit runs in the spring and summer of 1749.[3] These two prints must therefore be the earliest depictions of *Kana-dehon Chūshingura*, the title of the play announced in each case on the signboards hanging on the right pillar of the stage. Cat. 67 shows the famous scene from Act VII, set in the Ichiriki-ya Teahouse, Kyoto, in which the hero Ōboshi Kuranosuke (played here by Bandō Hikosaburō) goes onto the veranda to read a secret letter, unaware that he is being spied on from the balcony above by the courtesan Okaru (Sanogawa Ichimatsu) and from under the floorboards by the villain Kudayū (Nakamura Sukegorō). This was the performance staged at the Ichimura Theatre from the fifth day of the fifth month, 1749.

Cat. 68 shows a scene from Act X, when the hero Ōboshi Yuranosuke (played by Sawamura Chōjūrō) climbs out from the large box in which he has been hiding – supposedly containing a secret shipment of arms for the loyal retainers – to reveal to the faithful merchant Amakawa-ya Gihei (Ichikawa Ebizō, the name used by Danjūrō II after 1735) the ruse that has just been played on him to test his loyalty. In typical *aragoto* style Gihei crushes underfoot two of the policemen who have tried unsuccessfully to restrain him. This was the rival performance of *Chūshingura* that commenced at the Nakamura Theatre on the sixth day of the sixth month, 1749.

As with many perspective pictures by Masanobu, the scenes onstage are drawn in a different perspective from the rest of the theatre: the figures are larger and the ground plane has been tilted more steeply, to reveal more emphatically what is going on. The audience chat with one another, drink and eat, not always attentive to what is happening in the play. TTC

1 *Ukiyo-e shūka*, vol. 4, no. 28; Kishi 1994a, pp. 75–6, no. 2-1.

2 The three cases of reuse are mentioned in Mutō 1999, p. 7.

3 For a synopsis of the eleven acts of *Kana-dehon Chūshingura*, see Halford 1956, pp. 138–65.

69

Okumura Masanobu

Young Woman with a Hand Mirror Applying Lip Rouge

c. 1743–46

ARTIST'S SIGNATURE: 'Hōgetsudō shōmei Okumura Bunkaku Masanobu shōhitsu' (Genuine brush of Hōgetsudō authentic name Okumura Bunkaku Masanobu)

ARTIST'S SEAL: 'Tanchōsai'

woodblock, *hahahiro hashira-e*, hand-colouring (*beni-e*), 71.3 × 25.2 cm

OTHER IMPRESSIONS: Honolulu Academy of Arts (Honolulu 1980, p. 112, no. 23; Michener 1959, p. 52, no. 37); Art Institute of Chicago (Chicago 1955, p. 161, no. 98); Allen Memorial Museum, Oberlin (*tan-e*) (Oberlin 1984, no. 22; *Ukiyo-e shūka*, vol. 9, no. 119)

William Sturgis Bigelow Collection, 1911

11.13337

To avoid tripping, the young woman has tucked up her skirt slightly under a narrow sash. The long sleeves and the obi tied at the back in a bow show that she is unmarried. Masanobu's image evokes her youthful sensuality. Holding a folding pocket mirror in her left hand, the woman applies lip rouge (*kuchi-beni*) with her right, enhancing the pink glow of her lips. As she contemplates her appearance, the wavering edges of the light pink under-robe, within the small openings of the sleeves, become suggestively visible. The textile patterns, in faded light green, red, purple and blue, also serve to enhance the young woman's blossoming, 'late spring' beauty. Bundles of sticks decorated with peach-blossom branches are scattered over the broad zigzag pattern of her sleeves and large peach blossoms embellish the upper part of her *furisode*. On the skirt of the *furisode*, arrowheads (*omodaka*) in bud seemingly rise from marsh waters, brought to life by the rippling hem.

The two carved blocks joined to create this wide *hashira-e* had begun to separate when this impression and those in Honolulu and Oberlin were printed. The block lines are broken along a vertical line that runs from the woman's shoulder through the middle of her sleeve to the hem. The Chicago impression is from a very early edition and shows only the beginning of a break on one block line. The design was printed in two *hashira-e* sizes; Paine also reproduces an impression of the narrower *hashira-e* version using only a third of the width of a *takenaga-bōsho* sheet.[1] LEV

1 Paine 1959, p. 44, fig. 8.

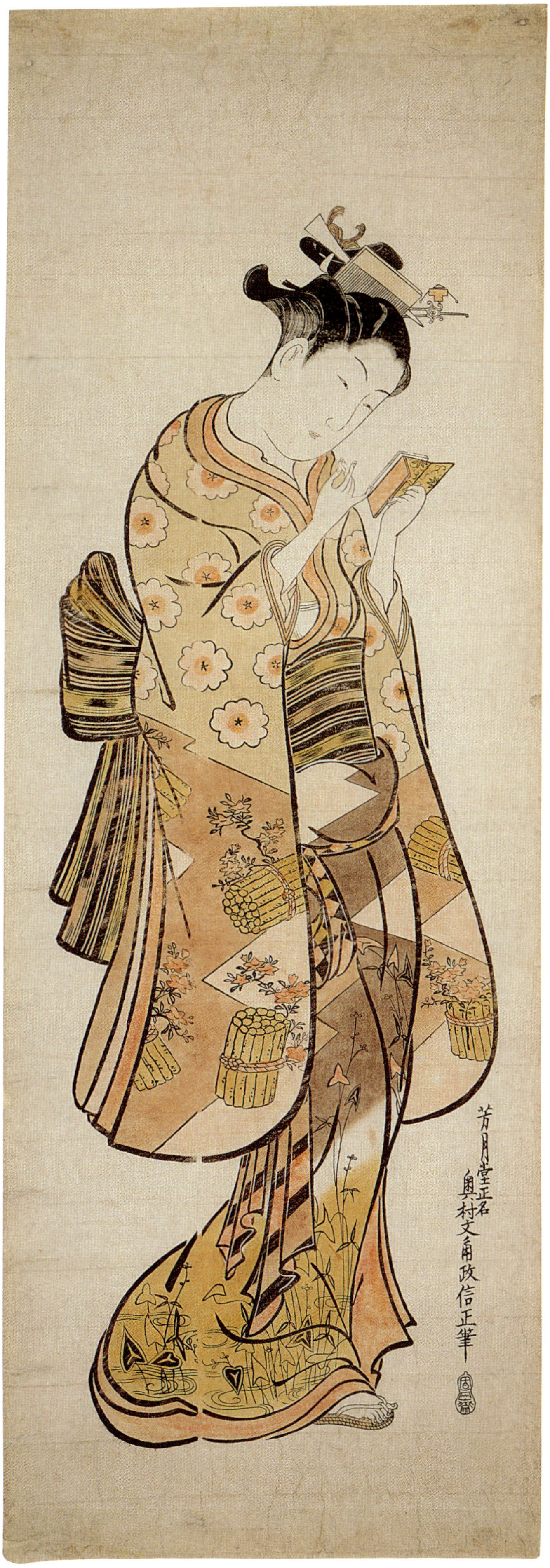
芳月堂正名
奥村文角政信正筆

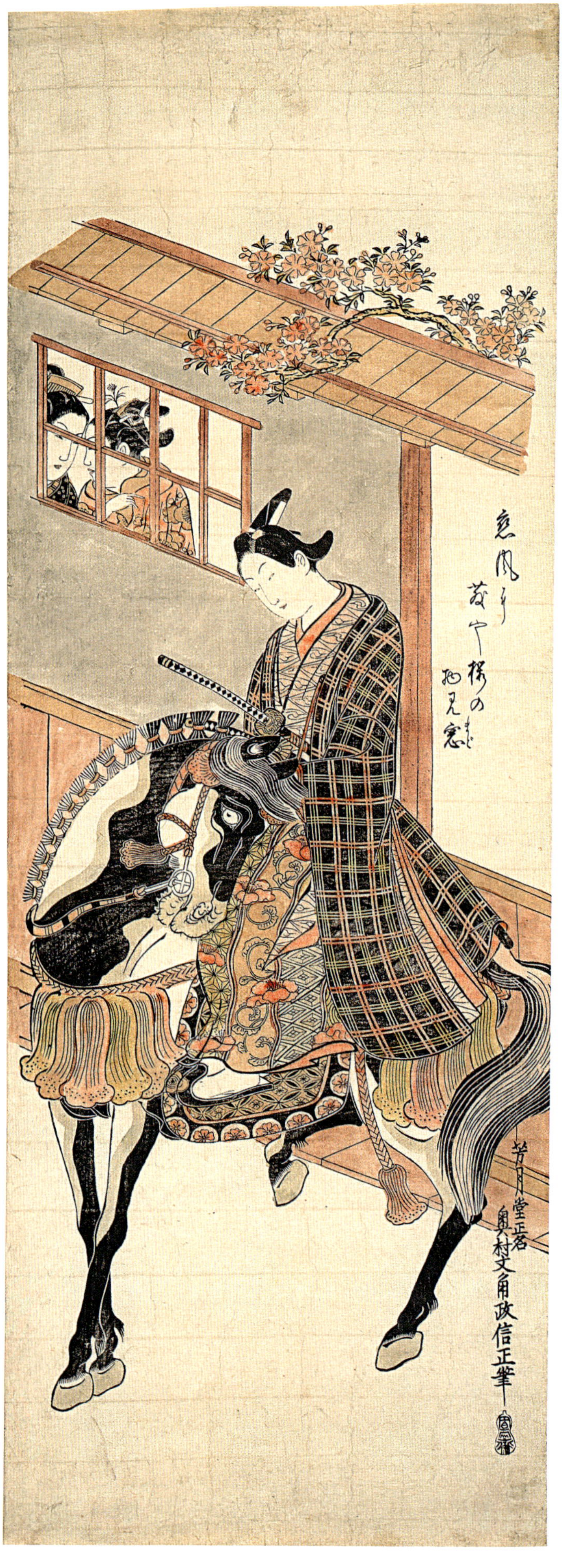
芳月堂正名
奥村文角政信正筆

70
Okumura Masanobu
Young Samurai on Horseback

c. 1743–7

ARTIST'S SIGNATURE: 'Hōgetsudō shōmei Okumura Bunkaku Masanobu shōhitsu' (Genuine brush of Hōgetsudō authentic name Okumura Bunkaku Masanobu)

ARTIST'S SEAL: 'Tanchōsai'

woodblock, *hahahiro hashira-e*, hand-colouring (*beni-e*), 69.5 × 25.2 cm

OTHER IMPRESSIONS: Honolulu Academy of Arts (Honolulu 1980, p. 115, no. 25; Michener 1959, colour pl. 33); William S. and John T. Spaulding Collection, Museum of Fine Arts, Boston, 21.5750; Tokyo National Museum (Kobayashi 1982b, colour pl. 5; Tokyo 1960–3, vol. 1, no. 265)

William Sturgis Bigelow Collection, 1911

11.13341

Recalling classical tales, a stylish young samurai on a stallion is depicted approaching a house. His arrival has caused a stir: two women have approached the window to catch a glimpse of him. A branch with delicate cherry blossoms hangs over the scene, creating a sense of intimacy. The flowers are echoed both in the plum-blossom pattern of the *kosode* worn by the younger woman and in the decorative cherry-blossom edge pattern of the saddle blanket.

Expressing the enchantment of the moment, the poem plays with the expression *koi-kaze*, which means 'winds of love' but can also be used as a metaphor of 'falling in love':

Koi-kaze ni	Stirred by the winds of love,
chiru ya sakura no	cherry blossoms scatter
monomi mado	by the viewing window.[1]

Masanobu and other ukiyo-e artists occasionally depicted warriors on horseback in prints and paintings;[2] the horse and rider in this print are especially elegant. In addition to wearing the familiar braided cords and big tassels, the mane of the dappled horse is decoratively cut and tied. The young man of fashion (*wakashu*) wears three tastefully coordinated layers: an inner robe of *beni*-coloured silk, a middle robe with a linear, decorative pattern of flying cranes and a dark outer robe with a fashionable tartan pattern. The young man's formal divided skirt (*hakama*) also displays a refined array of patterns, ranging from geometric designs to floral vines – a blending of patterns found in prints by Masanobu from the mid to late 1740s.[3]

There is a romantic, almost androgynous beauty about the young warrior *wakashu*, exemplified in the contrast between the hilt of the long samurai sword, a masculine symbol, and the flowing sleeves, traditionally worn only by courtesans, unwed young women or by *wakashu-gata*. This is not a theatre scene – no actor crests are included – but the elegant appearance of the samurai brings to mind the trendsetting kabuki actors Onoe Kikugorō (1717–83) and Sanogawa Ichimatsu I (1722–62) in the roles of handsome youths. Ichimatsu was the son of a samurai and the adopted son of a theatre assistant (*dekata*). He was famous for wearing the plain, checkered pattern popularly called *ichimatsu moyō*. However, several designs by Masanobu, Toyonobu and Shigenaga issued in the 1740s show him in *haori* with tartan variations such as that seen in this print. It is most likely that the image was intended to appeal to fans of both actors.[4] LEV

1 Trans. in consultation with John Carpenter

2 See cat. 19 or Cologne 1991, nos. 1–10.

3 Early examples are *Onoe Kikugorō I as Yoshino in the Play 'Haru no akebono kuruwa Soga'* (1743/1, Ichimura Theatre), reproduced in *Ukiyo-e taisei*, vol. 1, no. 42, and *Onoe Kikugorō I as Soga no Gorō in the Play 'Nana-kusa wakayagi Soga'* (1744/1, Ichimura Theatre), reproduced in Vergez 1983, no. 27.

4 Ichimatsu wears a very similar tartan-style *haori* in another print, made *c.* 1744–7, by Masanobu. *Genshoku ukiyo-e*, vol. 6, fig. 128. There, he is shown wearing an obi with the chequered *ichimatsu moyō* pattern and Sanogawa crest. The poem above mentions 'arare' (hail); another, more old-fashioned name for the chequered pattern is *arare moyō*. *Genshoku ukiyo-e*, vol. 5, p. 88. Bolder tartan variations are often seen worn by Ichimatsu in the earlier roles of Kichisaburō (1742/2) or Hisamatsu (1745/9). Paine 1959, cover illus.; Kikuchi 1969, no. 88; Oberlin 1984, no. 40, fig. 159; Stern n.d., p. 96, no. 40. However, Masanobu also showed Kikugorō wearing a tartan-design *haori* in *Nana-kusa wakayagi Soga* (1744). Honolulu 1980, p. 108, no. 19.

71
Okumura Masanobu
The Actor Onoe Kikugorō as Soga no Gorō

c. 1747–50

ARTIST'S SIGNATURE: 'Hōgetsudō shōmei Okumura Bunkaku Masanobu shōhitsu' (Genuine brush of Hōgetsudō authentic name Okumura Bunkaku Masanobu)

ARTIST'S SEAL: 'Tanchōsai'

woodblock, *hababiro hashira-e, beni-e,* 69.3 × 26 cm

OTHER IMPRESSIONS: Art Institute of Chicago (Chicago 1955, p. 160, Masanobu no. 95); (Higuchi 1977, Masanobu no. 76 [formerly Hirose Kinosuke Collection])

William Sturgis Bigelow Collection, 1911

11.13339

Onoe Kikugorō is depicted as Soga no Gorō in the guise of a foppish mendicant monk (*komusō*), a gentle reinterpretation of the previously *aragoto* role of Gorō introduced by Ichikawa Danjūrō II in 1715 (cat. 21). Kikugorō carries the customary deep sedge hat (*tengai*) and bamboo flute and wears a black monk's stole across his shoulder. Among various elaborately patterned sections of the robe, delicately picked out in hand-colouring of red, yellow and pink, are butterflies and plovers for the role of Gorō, a carp ascending a waterfall by a pine tree and, at the knee, Kikugorō's crest of two stylised oak leaves. A hint of dynamism comes from the pose, with one knee bent and the other foot pointing, the body turned and the back slightly arched as the actor glances coyly over his shoulder. Inscribed above is a *hokku* poem that includes a connection between the actor's family name, Onoe, and the tail of the cuckoo and likens his flute-playing to the cry of that bird. There is also a play on the word '*renbo*', which can mean both 'love' and the *komusō* style of *shakuhachi* flute-playing. Finally, '*hototogisu*' (cuckoo) is a season word for the fifth month, the time of year when the Soga brothers carried out their famous vendetta:

Ono ga ne no	Like the sound of Onoe
renbo no yami ya	playing a tune of blind love –
hototogisu	cry of the cuckoo.[1]

A *benizuri-e* by Masanobu printed in two colours in the *hosoban* format shows the same actor in similar pose, quotes the same poem, has an almost identical form of the signature and confirms the role.[2] Kikugorō is known to have played the role of Gorō at least three times, in 1744, 1747 and 1748. Mutō Junko has argued that in his *hababiro hashira-e* and *hashira-e* prints Masanobu probably attempted to invent designs not specifically linked to a single performance, thus granting the prints a longer commercial life. On the basis of similar signature forms on more precisely dateable prints she proposes a date of 1747–50 for the present design.[3]

The Boston impression was evidently taken from a block made from two pieces of cherrywood joined vertically, just right of centre. Obviously, a gap between the blocks (or a difference in the level of their surfaces), visible most clearly in the area of the hat, had developed. Similar printing flaws are found on other *hababiro hashira-e* (for example, cat. 69, 73), suggesting (i) that their blocks were constructed in a similar way and (ii) that they were used for a period long enough for such shifting or warping to take place. Comparison with an impression of the same design in the Art Institute of Chicago indicates that it must have been taken earlier than the Boston impression, because the evidence of a gap between the two sections of the blocks is not as pronounced. The Art Institute of Chicago possesses yet another impression of the same design. In this, the right section of the block is missing completely, converting the image into a normal pillar picture (*hashira-e*).[4] TTC

1 I am grateful to John Carpenter for his assistance with this translation.

2 *Ukiyo-e taika shūsei*, vol. 3, no. 106 (present whereabouts unknown). The signature reads 'Shōmei Hōgetsudō…' rather than 'Hōgetsudō shōmei', but is otherwise identical to that found here.

3 Mutō 1999, pp. 5–6.

4 Chicago 1955, Masanobu no. 96, where the impression is described as having been taken from a re-cut block. This does not seem to be the case, however, for no. 96 would appear to have been printed from the left side of the block used for no. 95 in the Chicago catalogue.

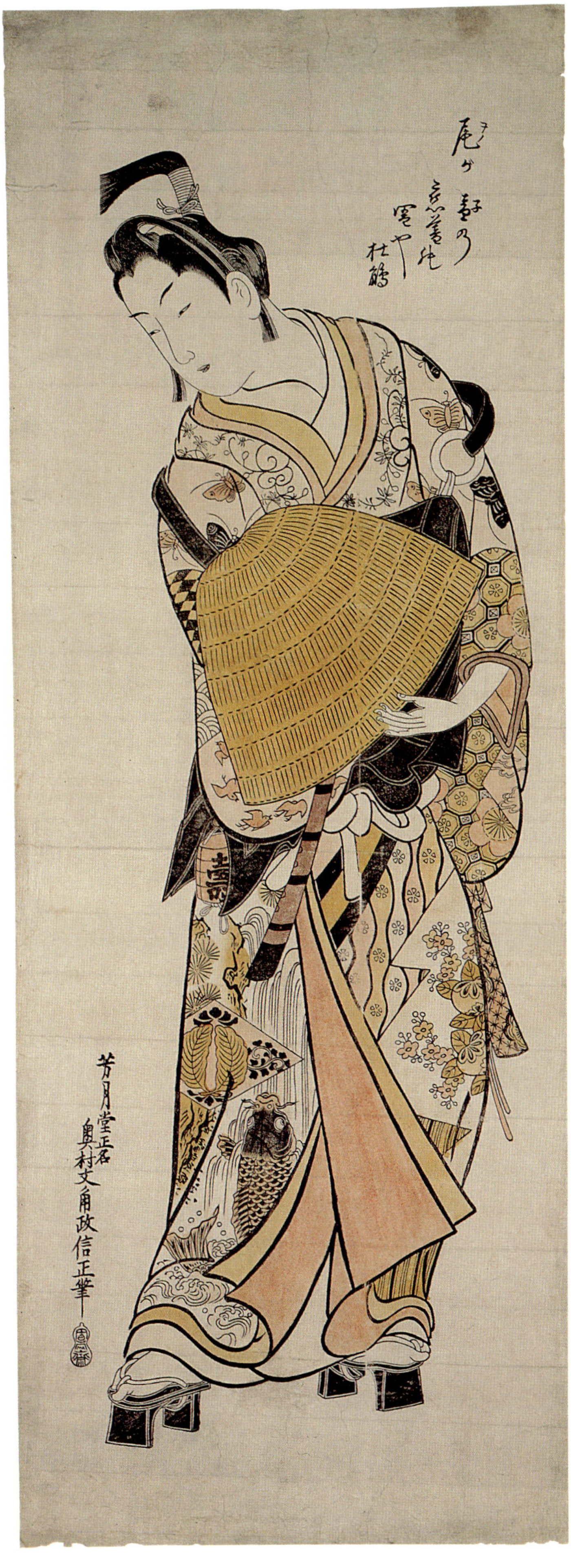
芳月堂正名
奥村文角政信正筆

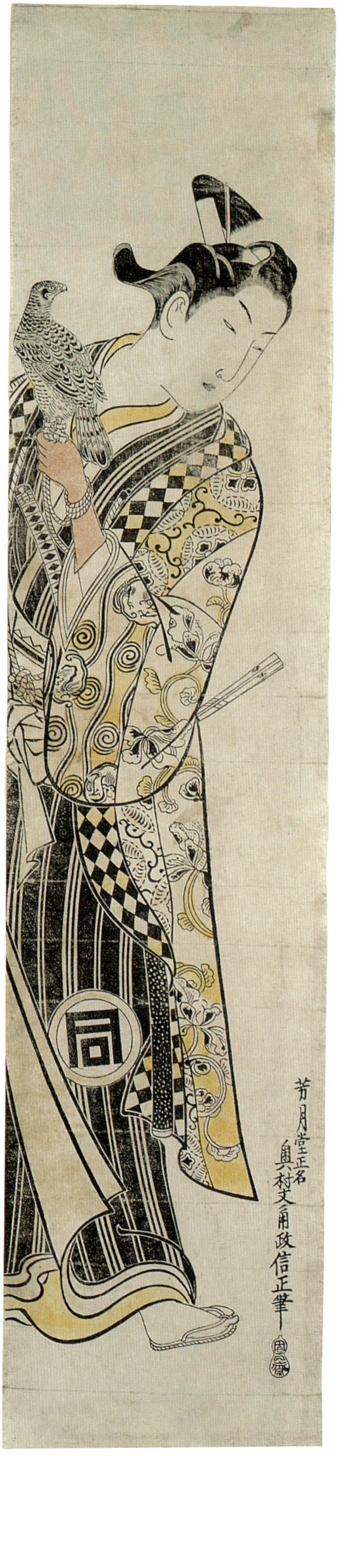
芳月堂正名
奥村文角政信正筆

72

Okumura Masanobu

The Actor Sanogawa Ichimatsu as a Hunter with Hawk

c. 1747–50

ARTIST'S SIGNATURE: 'Hōgetsudō shōmei Okumura Bunkaku Masanobu shōhitsu' (Genuine brush of Hōgetsudō authentic name Okumura Bunkaku Masanobu)

ARTIST'S SEAL: 'Tanchōsai'

woodblock, *hashira-e, beni-e,* 67.8 × 15.5 cm

OTHER IMPRESSION: British Museum, London

William Sturgis Bigelow Collection, 1911

11.26822

1 Mutō 1999, pp. 12–13.

Sanogawa Ichimatsu was a Kyoto actor who first visited Edo in 1741, immediately scoring a success in the second month of that year in the role of the ill-fated temple page-boy Kumenosuke. The black and white chequered pattern on the *hakama* trousers he wore on that occasion became all the rage in Edo, acquiring the name 'Ichimatsu pattern'. Apart from a stay in Kyoto for a few months in 1744, Ichimatsu remained the heart-throb actor of young male (*wakashu-gata*) roles in Edo, sometimes also playing young women, until his premature death in 1762, when he had just turned 40.

Here the young actor, his forelock still unshaved in the manner of an adolescent, is dressed in an extremely stylish outfit, supposedly for a hawk hunt, as indicated by the bird of prey tethered to his leather-gloved hand. Over the black and white striped *kosode* is a fashionably long *haori* jacket edged with the chequered Ichimatsu pattern and decorated with intertwining plant arabesques. A single long sword is worn almost vertically through the sash under the jacket; a folded fan is inserted in the sash at the back. One foot is slightly raised, giving a hint of animation. If a particular role is depicted, rather than an imaginary scene of Ichimatsu hawk hunting in real life, it has not yet been identified.

The dramatic cropping of the figure on the left suggests that it may have been issued not only in this 'pillar picture' (*hashira-e*) format, but also in the wider *hababiro hashira-e* format (see cat. 71). The forms of the signature and the seal are identical those on cat. 71 and the two prints must be close in date. Mutō Junko has identified approximately a dozen *hosoban* actor prints bearing signatures with this combination of names and all can be dated *c.* 1747–50.[1]

TTC

73
Okumura Masanobu
Woman with an Umbrella and a Dog

c. 1744–8

ARTIST'S SIGNATURE: 'Hōgetsudō shōmei Okumura Bunkaku Masanobu shōhitsu' (Genuine brush of Hōgetsudō authentic name Okumura Bunkaku Masanobu)

ARTIST'S SEAL: 'Tanchōsai'

woodblock, *hababiro hashira-e*, hand-colouring (*beni-e*), 72.2 × 25.2 cm

OTHER IMPRESSIONS: Private collection, Hyōgo (Machida 1987, p. 276, no. 312; Mainichi 1993, p. 20, no. 9); William S. and John T. Spaulding Collection, Museum of Fine Arts, Boston, 21. 5728

William Sturgis Bigelow Collection, 1911

11.13338

Several outstanding *beni-e* pillar pictures (*hashira-e*) from the early 1740s to the early 1750s by Masanobu, Toyonobu and Shigenaga depict beautiful young women and youths (*wakashu*) dressed in fashionable *sode-gappa* coats.[1] These long garments were fastened with varied clasps at the right shoulder and hip and endowed with high collars and wide sleeves tied with small bows. This print shows a young woman (perhaps a courtesan) about to fasten such a coat after passing through a gate with her pet dog and setting off in expectation, perhaps, of a romantic encounter.

The descending zigzag formation of geese and withered *susuki* grass, depicted on the wooden panel in the background, suggests the rain the woman anticipates – *shigure*, the chilling, sporadic showers of late autumn or early winter in the tenth lunar month. Masanobu has added a *hokku* verse hinting that she should not use an umbrella, for she will then have a greater chance of falling in love ('become wet'):

Nureru nara	Even if dripping wet,
kasa o tanomade	don't use the umbrella –
shigurekeri	in late autumn showers.[2]

The fashion among townsmen and women for wearing *sode-gappa* may have received added impetus from the trendsetter Sanogawa Ichimatsu I, who wore such a garment in a play performed in spring 1741.[3] The woman's *sode-gappa* is also decorated with 'exotic' Chinese-style patterns: phoenixes in white reserve on a black ground, clouds by the hem and a scattered floral-and-vine design.

The craze in the mid- to late 1740s for 'continental' patterns, fashions, hairstyles and 'alien customs' was stimulated by the eagerly awaited arrival of a very large embassy from Korea.[4] During this celebrated visit in the fifth and sixth months of 1748, the town magistrate forbade public dancing in Korean-style clothing.[5] The fashion of wearing luxurious silk outer coats was also so prevalent in 1748 that, on the twentieth day of the third month, the government placed a ban on 'young townswomen wearing *haori*'.[6]

The *saki-kōgai* comb set perched on the woman's coiffure further reveals her sense of style: the pin is decorated with a miniature *yajirōbei*[7] and the comb bears the crest of the actor Segawa Kikunojō I (see cat. 122). The umbrella was particularly fashionable in the late 1740s and early 1750s, a vogue fuelled by two plays, performed in 1746 and 1749, that featured the dashing romantic hero Sukeroku sporting a *janome* (snake's-eye) umbrella.[8]

This image, like many other wide pillar pictures by the artist from the 1740s, was printed on a single sheet of paper using a carved block made from two joined pieces of wood. When this impression was made, the sections had separated slightly or warped to uneven levels: the *sumi* at the top of the larger block did not register fully. Judging by the placement of the join, just below the poem, it is possible that Masanobu had envisaged the possibility of offering customers images with or without the suggestive verse.[9] LEV

1 *Genshoku ukiyo-e*, vol. 5, p. 88.

2 Trans. in consultation with John Carpenter. A pillar print showing a young man similarly setting out for a rendez-vous is reproduced in New York 1993, p. 73, no. 12, and Stern n.d., pp. 92–3. The accompanying poem reads: ' A young man still residing in his parents' home, in autumn showers contrives opportunities'. According to Julia Meech, umbrellas had come to have sexual connotations in the *ukiyo* world, Edo men pointing an umbrella upwards to open it, women, courtesans and young actor–prostitutes downwards. New York 1993.

3 In scene xii of Act III ('Takaya Shinjū') in the play *Na-no-hana akebono Soga*.

4 *Genshoku ukiyo-e*, vol. 6, p. 72, fig. 161.

5 The ban probably had little effect, since a further edict was issued in 1750 in an attempt to prevent citizens from adopting too many foreign ways. Toby 1987, pp. 448–9.

6 *Edo Tokyo nenpyō*, p. 88.

7 See cat. 37, 42, 63, 69, 124.

8 In spring 1746 Onoe Kikugorō I (1717–83) performed the role of Sukeroku (symbolised by the peony crest) as a *wakashu* at the Morita Theatre. In a powerful print of the actor, Masanobu included a poem with a suggestive mention of a 'wet young man' ('nureta wakashu', a man in love): 'Under the *shigure* umbrella, a young man in love – intertwining peony'. Honolulu 1980, p. 118, no. 28.

9 The break in the block is also seen clearly in the other impressions of this print. For another probable instance of the optional inclusion of a poem, see cat. 75 and the Chicago impression of that print.

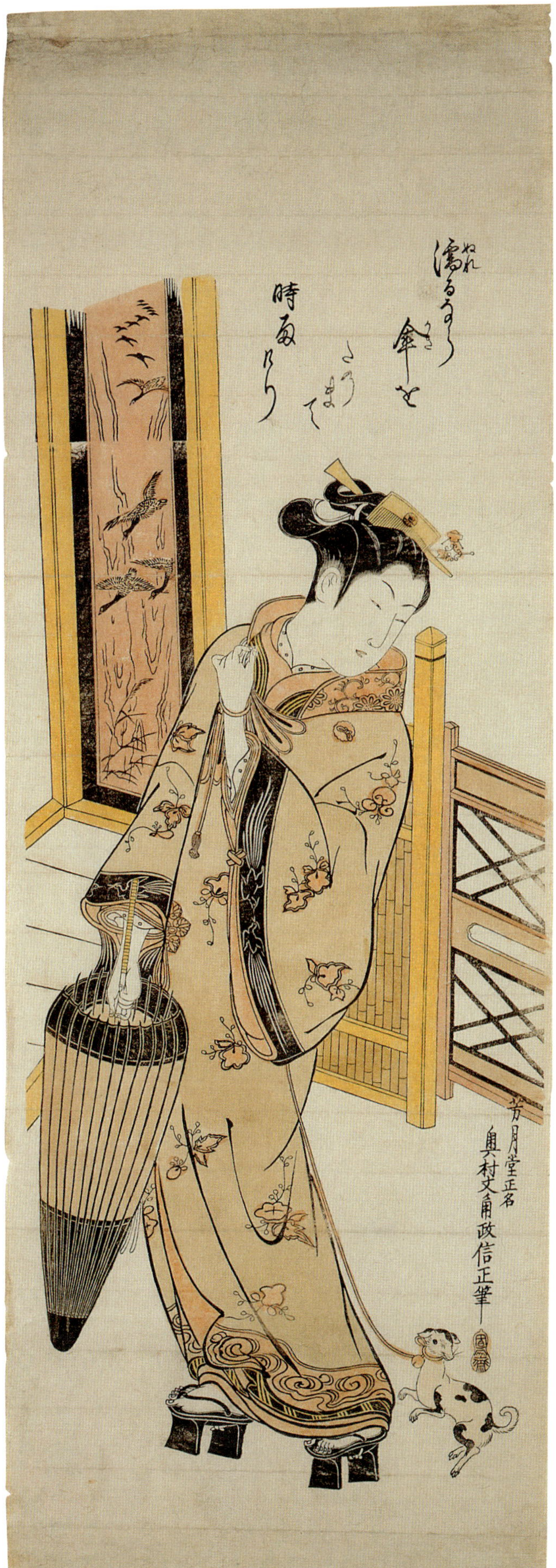
芳月堂正名
奥村文角政信正筆

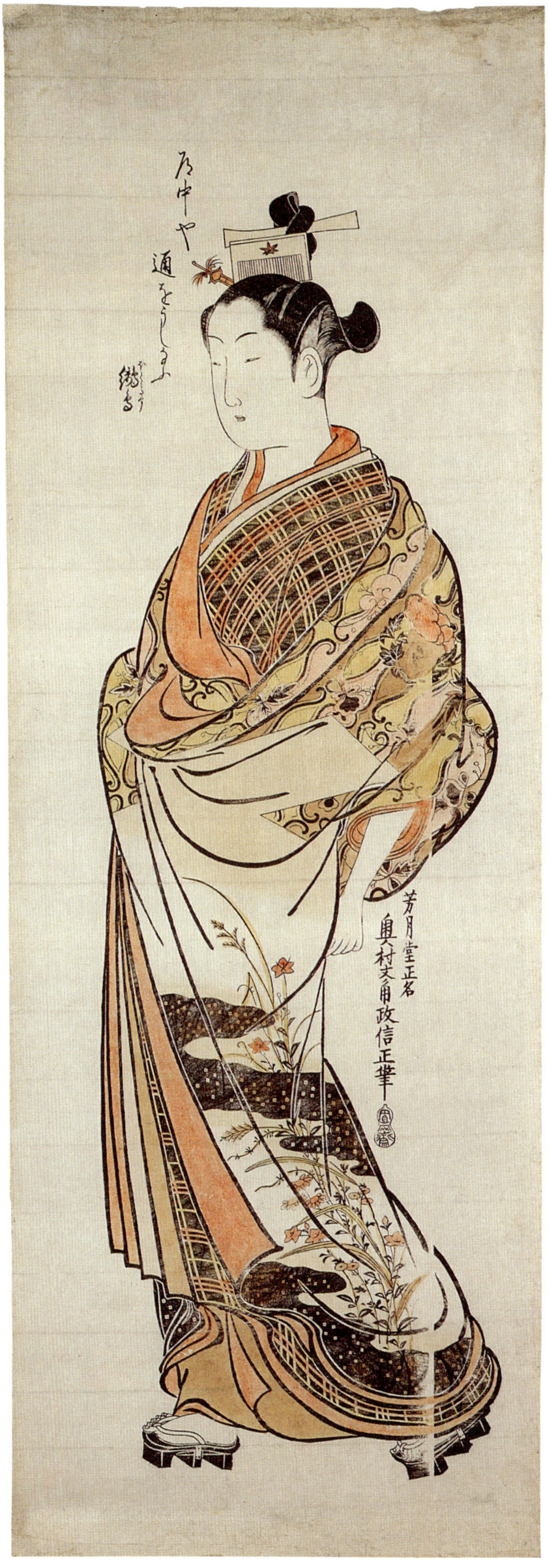
芳月堂正名
奥村文角政信正筆

74

Okumura Masanobu

Courtesan Walking

c. 1745–9

ARTIST'S SIGNATURE: 'Hōgetsudō shōmei Okumura Bunkaku Masanobu hitsu' (Genuine brush of Hōgetsudō authentic name Okumura Bunkaku Masanobu)

ARTIST'S SEAL: 'Tanchōsai'

woodblock, *hahahiro hashira-e*, hand-colouring (*beni-e*), 72 × 25.5 cm

OTHER IMPRESSIONS: Honolulu Academy of Arts (Honolulu 1980, no. 29); Tokyo National Museum (Kikuchi 1969, no. 87)

William Sturgis Bigelow Collection, 1911

11.13336

Displaying a high degree of poise and pluck, the courtesan holds her head high and walks with a self-assured stride. The very essence of spirited Edo-style *hari* (dash and independent spirit) and *iki* (chic sex appeal), the courtesan appears unaware of her long *haori* slipping off her shoulder, and yet she gathers the skirts in her right hand and lets them hang in a grand spread of *kosode* hems.[1] Active yet relaxed, her gesture, combined with the tantalising exposure of her arm, resembles the confident style developed by the *onnagata* Segawa Kikunojō I (1693?–1749). The same feminine flair, expressed in a different pose, is seen in a print of the actor dated 1745 (cat. 122). The courtesan's elegant outer robe patterned with a stylish blend of delicate organic, tartan and abstract patterns places the print, like cat. 70, in the mid to late 1740s.

The *hokku* poem playfully refers to the legend of Kume no Sennin, a Japanese sage said to have fallen from the skies after he lost his magical powers (*tsū*) as a result of being distracted by the reflection of a beautiful young woman in a stream (see cat. 128). It also hints at the spectacular sight of the courtesan, suggesting that even a sophisticated man would lose his elegant deportment (*tsū*):[2]

Dōchū ya	Seeing the courtesan on parade
tsū o ushinau	one loses power to resist –
hototogisu.	like a cuckoo falling in mid-flight.[3]

The copies and variations made of this image during the late 1740s and early 1750s testify to its great impact. A print by Ishikawa Toyonobu (1711–85), an artist likely to have followed Masanobu's lead in his own design, represents a courtesan with the same draped *haori*, gait and hairstyle. The comparatively unconvincing line work and excessive patterning weakens this print. The cartouche states that the courtesan represents the beauty from 'Edo Yoshiwara' in a set of 'Courtesans of the Three Cities', a subject invented and explored by Masanobu in the 1720s and 1730s (see also cat. 121).[4] The Boston print may therefore also once have been part of a triptych. A more inspired painting by Ishikawa Furunobu (dates unknown)[5] unquestionably shows the artist's knowledge of both the slender figure of the courtesan in Masanobu's print and of the *kosode* patterns in Toyonobu's work.[6]

The decorative peony crest on the woman's *kosode* may refer to the crest belonging to Sukeroku, a popular *otokodate* from the kabuki stage. Two plays about this hero were performed in the first month of 1746 and the third of 1749.[7] Considering the strength of the image and the growing popularity of *benizuri-e* by 1749, it is possible that this classic *beni-e* was printed *c.* 1746–7.

LEV

1 The confident attitude and the stride resemble courtesans in some prints from the late 1740s – for example, a *benizuri-e* by Ishikawa Toyonobu dated 1749. Chicago 1955, p. 214, no. 31.

2 Seigle 1993, p. 131. *Tsū* indicated connoisseurship and the person who embodied it.

3 Trans. in consultation with John Carpenter. The word 'hototogisu' (cuckoo) also refers to the fourth lunar month, i.e. the early summer.

4 Chicago 1955, p. 204, no. 19. The courtesan representing Osaka Shinmachi in the set can be seen in Kikuchi 1969, fig. 211.

5 *Ukiyo-e taisei*, vol. 3, no. 201.

6 Another close but stiff and uninspired *benizuri* copy of the courtesan (with a slightly different hairstyle), produced by Toyonobu *c.* 1752, represents Nakamura Tomijūrō (1719–86) in a female role. Chicago 1955, p. 222, no. 41. The walking figure was also used to depict courtesans or *onnagata* striding under parasols in *benizuri-e* prints, such as Chicago 1955, pp. 169 (Masanobu no. 110), 213 (Toyonobu no. 31).

7 Honolulu 1980, pp. 117–19, nos. 27–9. See also the puppets of Sukeroku and Agemaki held by Sanogawa Ichimatsu I and Onoe Kikugorō I in a print dated 1749/1. Michener 1959, pp. 77–8, no. 81.

75
Okumura Masanobu
Courtesan Holding a Pipe

mid-1740s

ARTIST'S SIGNATURE: 'Hōgetsudō Tanchōsai hashira-e kongen Okumura Bunkaku Masanobu shōhitsu' (Genuine brush of Hōgetsudō Tanchōsai originator of the pillar picture Okumura Bunkaku Masanobu)

ARTIST'S SEAL: 'Tanchōsai'

woodblock, extra tall *hashira-e*, hand-colouring (including *tan* and *beni*), 128.2 × 16 cm (two joined sheets)

OTHER IMPRESSIONS: Art Institute of Chicago (Chicago 1955, p. 158, no. 90); Tokyo National Museum (*Ukiyo-e taisei*, vol. 3, no. 155)

William Sturgis Bigelow Collection, 1911

11.13335

Masanobu designed some of his finest and most daring prints in the 1740s, and in his inscriptions he proudly declared himself to be the true originator of many novelties, among them *uki-e*, *benizuri-e* and *hashira-e*. While Masanobu was not the sole pioneer of new ideas, many scholars believe that he was the originator of *hashira-e* (pillar pictures).[1] Pillar prints were ideally formatted for hanging as painting substitutes in *tokonoma* alcoves or on house pillars. Masanobu's designs were printed in a range of widths, from half to a third or a quarter of a sheet of strong, thick *tatenaga-bōsho*.[2] Extra-tall *hashira-e* designs consisting, like this print, of two vertically joined sheets are extremely rare.

The design exists in three impressions. That in the Boston museum is unique in including a poem.[3] Probably composed by Masanobu himself, who was a student of *haikai* verse, the poem praises both the 'amorous allure' ('hana no iro': 'the colour of the flower') and the bright, hand-painted colours – yellow, blue, *tan* and *beni* – of the figure in the image:

Sugata-e no	Brilliantly reflected
utsurinikeri na	in a portrait,
hana no iro	the colours of flowers![4]

The courtesan appears very sensual, slender and relaxed, her body forming an S-curve from her inclined head to her rippled hems. Her outer robe has slipped from her shoulders and the hanging sash is tied at an angle, in a half bow above the waist that echoes the line of the long pipe.

Previously, courtesans and male prostitutes had set the styles for *onnagata* and *wakashu-gata* fashions, but in the 1740s actors took over this role. Such charismatic personalities as Sanogawa Ichimatsu I (1722–62), Onoe Kikugorō I (1717–83) and Segawa Kikunojō I (1693? –1749) began many trends by wearing certain *kosode* patterns, garments and coiffures or by making certain movements on stage. Many of the fashions were copied; courtesans and wealthy members of the 'townsmen' class (*chōnin*) could find similar fabrics and accessories at drapery and haberdashery stores like Echigo-ya (cat. 65).

The courtesan is a model of the very latest in Edo fashion. She wears a hair comb with the crest of Kikugorō, an actor who, after great success in Osaka, returned to Edo in 1743 to perform at the Ichimura Theatre. The elegant *kosode* design is decorated with bold crane medallions, highlighted with *tan* colour. While not unfamiliar from earlier textiles, the pattern is reminiscent of the crest of the Osaka *tachiyaku* actor Bandō Hikosaburō (1693–1751). The black and white striped *haori* is similar to that worn by Ichimatsu in some prints (see cat. 72).[5] The courtesan wears her hair in the *tate-hyōgomage* style with an upright, twisted topknot decorated with a comb and a large, horizontally placed pin. This was especially popular from the mid to the late 1740s, worn, for example, by Kikunojō in a print datable to 1745 (cat. 122).[6]

1 Vergez 1983, p. 38. See cat. 64 for Masanobu's claim to have invented *hashira-e*. If he did, it must have been before 1742, the date of an actor *hashira-e* by Torii Kiyoshige. Chicago 1955, p. 110.

2 A *tatenaga-bōshō* sheet of paper measured approximately 72 × 53 cm. Cologne 1991, p. 214. Proof that Masanobu also designed prints in the wide, large format as *hashira-e* can be found in his inscription on a print reproduced in Honolulu 1980, p. 117, no. 27.

3 Masanobu may have offered customers prints with or without the poem: see cat. 73.

4 Trans. in consultation with John Carpenter. The poem reads from left to right, which may be a play on its 'reflection' theme. The colours of the print were originally far brighter. The blue of one of the undergarments and of the stripes of the pipe stem has faded.

5 Kikuchi 1969, no. 88; Chicago 1955, p. 162, no. 93. See also an obi of the same striped fabric, decorated with the round crane medallions. Chicago 1955, p. 162, no. 97.

6 See also the courtesan on the right in cat. 64 and prints dated *c.* 1745 in Chicago 1955, pp. 163–4, nos. 100–1.

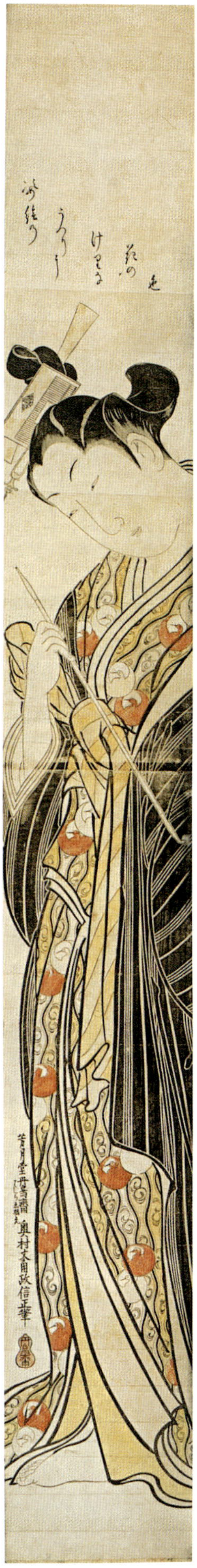

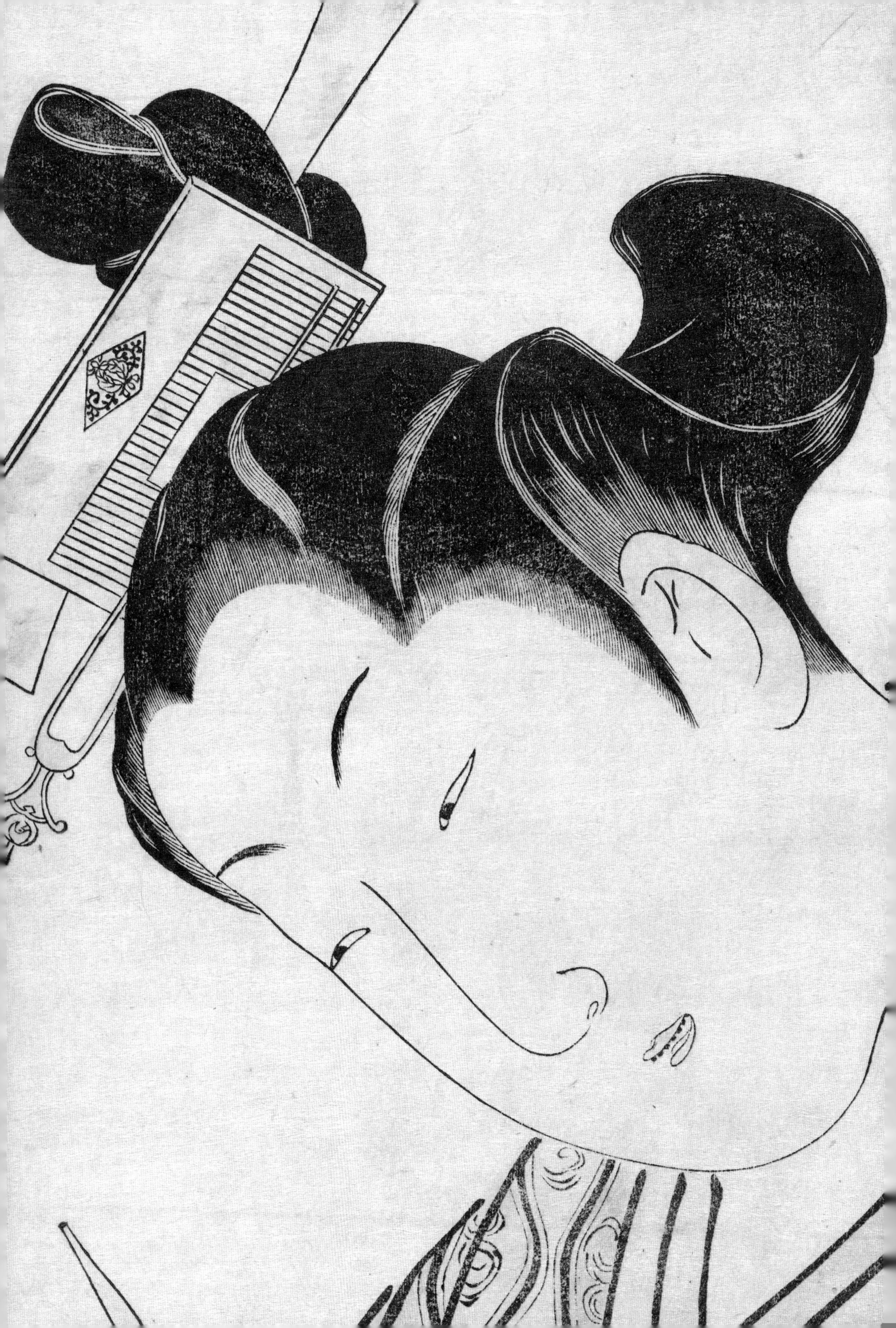

A matching extra tall *hashira-e* print in the Art Institute of Chicago shows a *wakashu* setting out for a visit: he is walking towards the right carrying a sword at his side and holding an Odawara lantern embellished with Sanogawa Ichimatsu's crest.[7] The young man wears a *haori*, with a Chinese-style cloud-and-dragon pattern and lined with Ichimatsu's characteristic chequered pattern, and a *kosode* with exotic floral vines, familiar from a print of *c.* 1746–8 (see also cat. 72).[8] The courtesan and the *wakashu* represent the pinnacle not only of sensual Edo stylishness (*iki*) but also of Masanobu's creative endeavours in the mid to late 1740s.

Only three extra-tall *hashira-e* designs by Masanobu are known, the two discussed above and a print depicting the eccentric writer and storyteller Fukai Shidōken (see cat. 126) gesturing dramatically with his left arm while banging a wooden phallus, shaped like a *matsu-take* mushroom, on his desk.[9] An impression of this third design is in the William S. and John T. Spaulding Collection at the Boston Museum (21.5753).[10] Shidōken appears together with a young couple in several prints by Masanobu and his students from the mid to late 1740s, among them one of 1747 by Mangetsudō. Masanobu himself depicted Shidōken with Oshichi and Kichisaburō (the actor Sanogawa Ichimatsu) in a print datable to about 1747.[11]

It is thus possible that the three extra-tall *hashira-e* were intended to form a triptych. The seated storyteller would then have been placed in the centre, flanked by Sanogawa Ichimatsu I and Onoe Kikugorō I in the roles of a *wakashu* and a courtesan – or, conversely, by two denizens of the Yoshiwara pleasure quarter who brought to mind those famous kabuki actors. LEV

7 Ibid., p. 158, no. 89, and, for a colour illus., Vergez 1983, no. 21.

8 Vergez 1983, contents page. The renewed interest in 'continental' patterns in the mid-1740s was stimulated by the keenly anticipated arrival of a large delegation from Korea, which visited Edo in the fifth and sixth months, 1748. See cat. 73, also *Edo Tokyo nenpyō*, p. 88, and Toby 1987, pp. 448–9. Ichimatsu first wore his chequered pattern (*ichimatsu moyō*) in 1741 and it remained popular in the 1740s and 1750s.

9 For Shidōken, see cat. 126; Binyon and Sexton 1978, pp. 46–7; *Ukiyo-e shūka*, vol. 1, no. 47; Honolulu 1980, p. 116; *Ukiyo-e taikei*, p. 102, no. 158; *Ukiyo-e jiten*, vol. 2, p. 25; and Chicago 1955, p. 159, no. 91.

10 Another (slightly trimmed) impression is reproduced in Noguchi 1933, no. 62. Its poem alludes to both sexual fulfilment and enlightenment: 'Ōguchi ni / hōbaru imo no / tsukimi kana' (A potato stuffed into the open mouth [main entrance] – moon-viewing!).

11 Mangetsudō's print is reproduced in Tokyo 1960–3, vol. 1, fig. 320. Masanobu's print is reproduced in Kikuchi 1969, fig. 78. Ichimatsu and Kumetarō performed the roles in the second month, 1751, at the Nakamura Theatre in a play called *Izu-kosode shōbai kagami*. *Kabuki nendai-ki*, p. 229. Chicago 1955, p. 218, no. 37, shows the two actors in their roles in a lovely *benizuri-e* by Toyonobu.

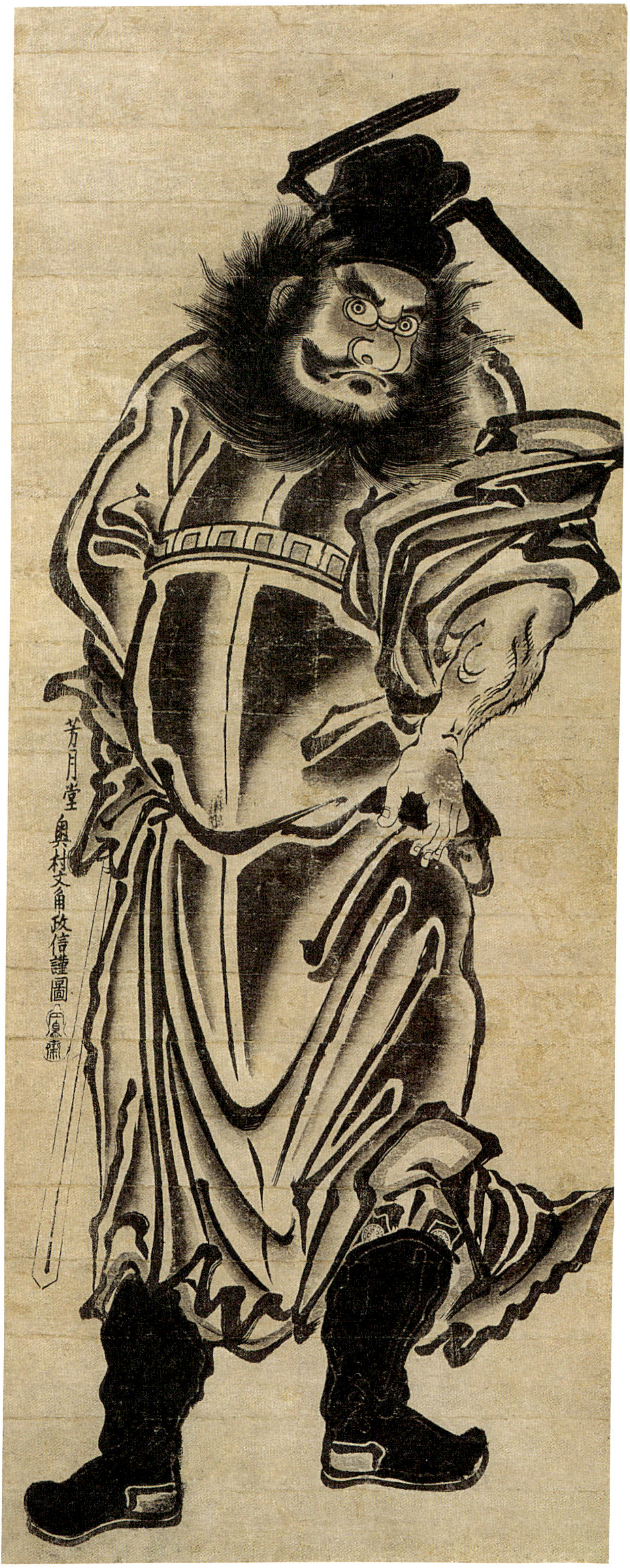
芳月堂奥村文角政信謹圖

76

Okumura Masanobu

Zhong Kui the Demon-queller (Shō Ki)

c. 1745

ARTIST'S SIGNATURE: 'Hōgetsudō Okumura Bunkaku Masanobu kin zu' (Respectfully drawn by Hōgetsudō Okumura Bunkaku Masanobu)

woodblock, *habahiro hashira-e*, hand-colouring (*urushi-e*), 60.7 × 24.4 cm

OTHER IMPRESSIONS: Honolulu Academy of Arts (2) (Honolulu 1980, pp. 113–14, nos. 24–5); William S. and John T. Spaulding Collection, Museum of Fine Arts, Boston 21.5744; Art Institute of Chicago (Chicago 1955, p. 166, no. 104); Fitzwilliam Museum, Cambridge (Cambridge 1997, pp. 26–7, no. 2); Fine Arts Museum of San Francisco (Keyes 1989, p. 77, no. 109)

Gift of Mr and Mrs Robert G. Henderson and Mr and Mrs Gregory Henderson in memory of Robert T. Paine, 1965

65.1034

Zhong Kui is a Chinese mythical figure, recognisable by his bulging eyes, active stance, bushy beard, Chinese military robe, sword, black boots and scholar's hat. He became known as a 'demon-queller' when he appeared as a spirit to drive away the demons that had infested the feverish dreams of the Tang Emperor Xuanzong (*reg.* 847–59). When the Emperor recovered his health, Zhong Kui explained that he had been a scholar–recluse who committed suicide from shame at not passing the difficult state examinations. He further said that, since the Imperial Household had given him a respectful burial, he had vowed to repay the honour by expelling demons and diseases wherever they appeared in the Empire.

Zhong Kui was seldom depicted in Chinese art after the Song period (960–1279), but he gained the status of a folk deity in Japan as Shō Ki, protector against supernatural beings, evil and ailments, particularly smallpox. The demon-queller made his first appearance in the 12th-century *Scrolls of Hell* (*Jigoku-zōshi*), was later painted by famous Muromachi period ink painters, such as Sesshū Tōyō, Kenkō Shōkei and Yamada Dōan, and then became a favourite motif of Kano school artists of the Edo era. Craftsmen and artists, including netsuke carvers, fan painters and textile designers, along with the general public, could soon see images of Shō Ki depicted in the Kano style in woodblock-printed books or single-sheet prints by major artists. The German physician and historian Engelbert Kaempfer, who visited Japan in the years 1690–2, described how many Japanese pasted images of the sword-wielding and hairy Shō Ki on their doors to ward off 'all sorts of distempers and misfortunes endeavouring to enter into the house'.[1] To assure future health, vertical banners (*nobori*) with the figure of Shō Ki became an integral part of the celebration of Boys' Day Festival (*tango no sekku*) on the fifth day of the fifth month.

To satisfy popular demand, most early 18th-century artists were commissioned by publishers to depict Shō Ki.[2] The enterprising artist–publisher Masanobu portrayed the demon-queller in many different ways and print formats – sharpening his sword, chasing demons (*oni*) and in humorous *mitate*.[3] Quite a few impressions of the present design have survived, attesting to its popularity. The Boston impression has suffered some damage, while that in the Fitzwilliam Museum, Cambridge, is a very early impression in superb condition. All impressions are shaded in the same areas, but there are slight variations in the brushstrokes and tonalities. The hand-applied shading of Shō Ki's costume is generally executed in grey *sumi*, whereas his arms and face are tinted brown with a blend of *sumi* and *beni*.

LEV

1 Cambridge 1997, p. 26; Toronto 1975, p. 187 (based on Kaempfer 1727, vol. 2, p. 418).

2 A spectacular early example of Shō Ki in *aragoto* style is reproduced in Chicago 1971, p. 67, no. 73.

3 For other Masanobu prints of Shō Ki, see Honolulu 1980, p. 132, no. 42 (*hashira-e*); Chicago 1955, p. 149, no. 72 (*hosoban*), and p. 166, no. 103 (*hashira-e*); *Genshoku ukiyo-e*, vol. 6, p. 61, fig. 127; and Oberlin 1984, p. 82, no. 23, fig. 114. For prints of Shō Ki by Shigenaga, see Oberlin 1984, no. 43, fig. 115, and Honolulu 1980, p. 164, no. 11, and p. 167, no. 14.

77

Okumura Masanobu

Portrait of Sugawara no Michizane

c. 1741–7

ARTIST'S SIGNATURE (trimmed): '[Hōgetsudō Tanchōsai] Okumura Shinmyō Bunkaku Masanobu kin zu' (Respectfully drawn by [Hōgetsudō Tanchōsai] Okumura Shinmyō Bunkaku Masanobu)

ARTIST'S SEAL: 'Tanchōsai'

woodblock, *hahahiro hashira-e* , hand-colouring (*urushi-e*), 65.7 × 23.5 cm

OTHER IMPRESSIONS: Royal Ontario Museum, Toronto (Toronto 1975, pp. 66–7); William S. and John T. Spaulding Collection, Museum of Fine Arts, Boston, 21.5774; British Museum, London; German private collection (New York 1991a, pp. 74–5)

Gift of Miss Lucy T. Aldrich, 1947

47.16

Paintings or prints of Sugawara Michizane (845–903), a patron deity of calligraphy, literature and scholarship, were often hung in the *tokonoma* alcove during poetry or other literary gatherings. This print by Masanobu, with its brocaded fabric remnants at the top and bottom edges, was clearly once treasured, for it was mounted as a hanging scroll.

Michizane, a courtier, poet and calligrapher proficient in both Chinese and Japanese classics, served for two years (899–901) as Minister of the Right (*u-daijin*).[1] His equally powerful rival Fujiwara no Tokihira (871–909), Minister of the Left, falsely accused him of plotting against Emperor Daigo. Disgraced, Michizane was demoted to head of the administrative office at Dazaifu on the island of Kyūshū. He died there two years later, after writing a number of heart-rending poems professing his sorrow and innocence.

Many of Michizane's most famous *tanka* express his love of plum trees. One such poem is said to have caused his favourite plum tree (the 'tobi-ume': 'jumping plum tree') on his estate to uproot itself and follow him to Kyūshū.

Soon after Michizane's death, natural catastrophes and mysterious illnesses befell Kyoto and members of the Imperial Household, including Tokihira and his accomplice. Believing that Michizane's angry spirit must be appeased, the Imperial Household posthumously pardoned him (in 923) and gave him the honorary title of Prime Minister (in 993). Michizane was also deified as '(Karai) Tenjin'[2] and honoured in Kitano Shrine in Kyoto (built in 947), Dazaifu Shrine and a number of other Shintō shrines throughout the country dedicated to him (Tenman-gū). Many colourful legends surrounding his life were illustrated in hand-painted scrolls, most notably the *Kitano Tenjin Engi* (1278), and described in *Genpei jōsui-ki* (or *seisui-ki*) (*An Account of the Genpei Wars*, late 12th century). They also became the subject of the nō play *Oimatsu* and of a play called *Sugawara te-narai kagami* (1746). The latter was performed, both on the puppet and the kabuki stage, in Kamigata and Edo in 1746–7, when its enormous success gave rise to a Sugawara 'boom'.[3]

A number of ukiyo-e prints show that images of Michizane were popular during the 18th century. A design by Kondō Kiyoharu (active 1705–30s)[4] became the model for works by other artists, showing the scholar–statesman wearing Chinese-style robes and standing under a pine tree with a plum-blossom branch in his arms.[5] Other prints depict Michizane standing beside or riding into exile on a royal ox.[6] In the third type, as here, Michizane is shown seated on a dais, dressed in a Japanese courtier's attire.

Michizane's court costume is decorated both with his plum-blossom crest and a pine-seedling design, patterns that harmonise with the plum and pine trees sheltering him. One of these is Michizane's favourite plum tree with red blossoms (the 'kōbai-dono'). The old, evergreen pine (*oi-matsu*), another tree loved by Michizane, helps to symbolise the courtier's virtue and steadfastness in his 'wait' (*matsu*) for a pardon that he never experienced. LEV

1 From 645 to 1885 the *u-daijin* was ranked third among the three ministers who shared the principal administrative duties.

2 Also known as Tenjin, Tenjin-sama, Tenma-tenjin, Tenman-gū or Kan Shōjō.

3 Leiter 1997, pp. 615–16. The play is described in detail in Halford 1956, pp. 306–21. At the height of the Sugawara Michizane theatre craze, Ichimatsu played Michizane's retainer Sakura-maru in *Onna Kan Shōjō utsutsu Narukami*, performed from the eleventh day of the fifth month, 1747, at the Ichimura Theatre. *Kabuki nendai-ki*, p. 204; *Kabuki nenpyō*, vol. 2, p. 528; Leiter 1997, p. 552. Michizane was said to have had triplet retainers, whom he named after his favourite trees – pine, cherry and plum (Matsuō-maru, Sakura-maru and Umeō-maru).

4 Kiyoharu's print may be based on an earlier book illustration. Oberlin 1984, p. 85; Chicago 1955, p. 70, no. 2.

5 See, for example, the works by Kiyoshige and Shigenaga in Oberlin 1984, p. 85, nos. 76, 42, fig. 120–1, and Tokyo 1960–3, vol. 1, no. 339.

6 Chicago 1955, p. 262, Torii Kiyomitsu no. 44.

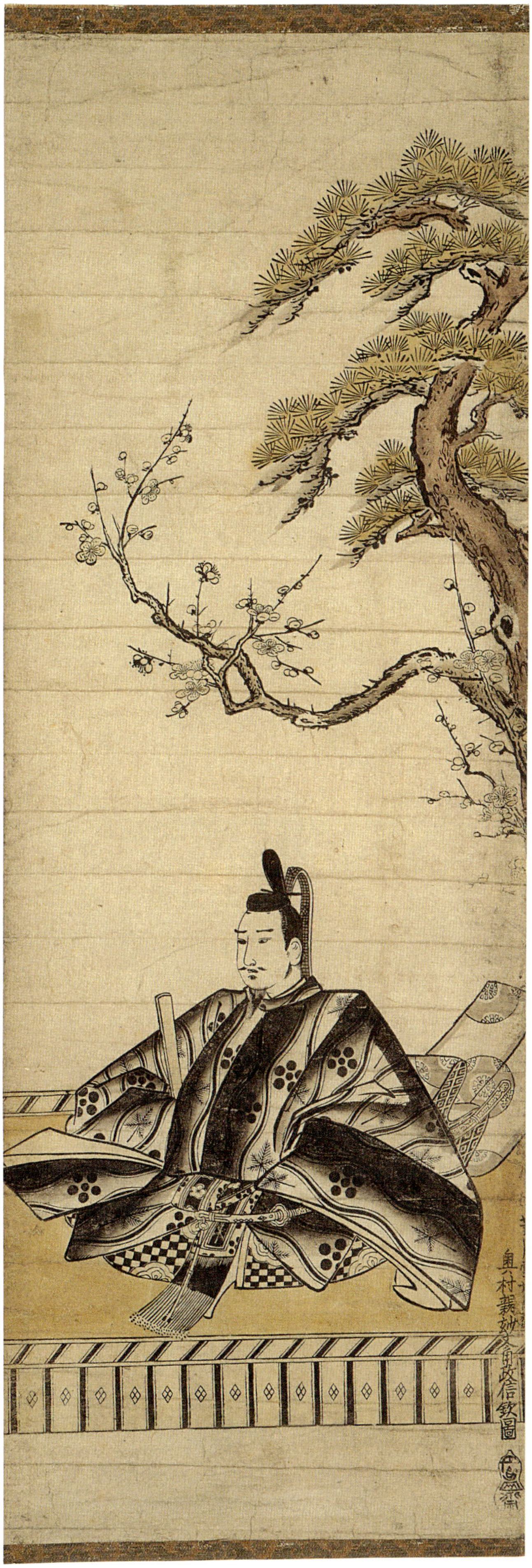
奥村親妙文角政信欽圖

78
Yoshida Hanbei
Illustrated Encyclopaedia for Use by Women (*Onna-yō kinmō zui*)

probably 1687

PUBLISHER: 'Okuda Shōhakuken'

woodblock-printed book, *fukuro-toji, sumizuri,* vol. 4 of 5, incomplete, preface, sheets numbered 1-21, 21.1 × 15 cm (covers)

source unknown, 2000

2000.1261

1 For the full quotation, see p. 10; Lane 1978, p. 11; and Shively 1991, p. 730.

Yoshida Hanbei, the primary artist of ukiyo-e subjects in the Kyoto–Osaka (Kamigata) region, was a prolific producer of illustrated books of various genres. He is best known for his illustrations to the novels of Ihara Saikaku (1642–93), the famed chronicler of urban life in the 17th century.

In *Illustrated Encyclopaedia for Use by Women* Hanbei concentrates on intricacies of dress. The fourth volume presents patterns for *furisode,* the robes with long, pendant sleeves that came into vogue for young women and entertainers in the late 17th century. The motifs encompass everyday articles and themes from classical literature. In the pages shown here the artist depicts two designs for robes in the Genroku style – a style popular during the late 1680s and the 1690s in which the motifs are boldly arranged across the back of the garment. Catering to contemporary sophisticates wishing to display their wit and erudition, Hanbei includes designs with literary allusions. On the right a cart of the type traditionally reserved for use by the aristocracy dominates the *furisode.* The pairing of this classical motif with a fan and stems of evening glories makes specific reference to the 'Yūgao' chapter in the 11th-century romantic novel *Tale of Genji* (*Genji monogatari*). On the left the artist presents the swirling waters of the Yoshino River, the banks of which were a favourite place for enjoying cherry blossoms. The addition of the sake cup and the gourd recalls the well-known words of Asai Ryōi in *Ukiyo monogatari* (*Tale of the Floating World*): 'Living only for the moment…singing songs, drinking wine, and diverting ourselves…like a gourd floating along with the river current: this is what we call *ukiyo*'.[1] ANM

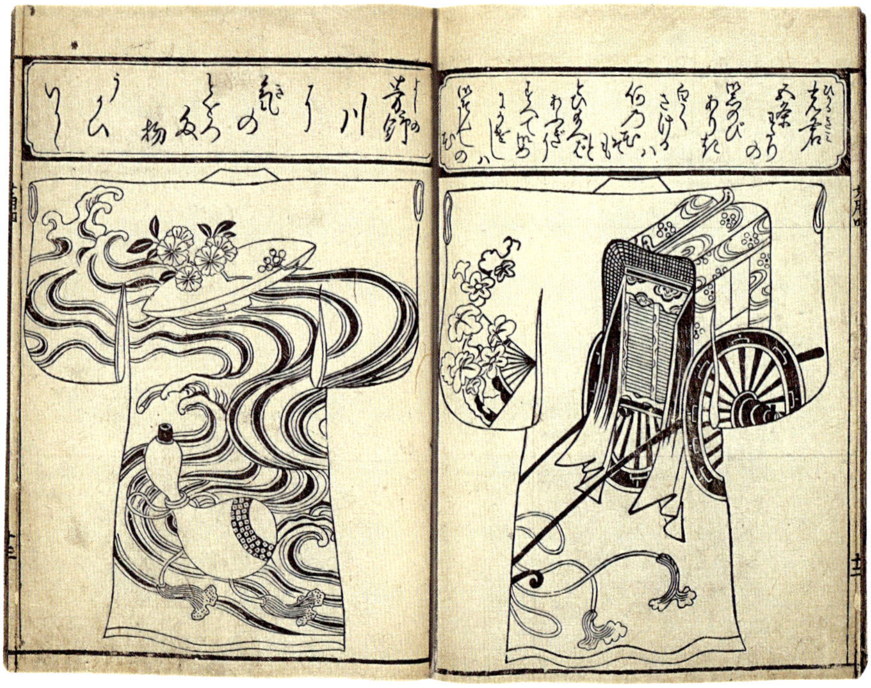

79
Nishikawa Sukenobu
Kosode Patterns of the Shōtoku Era (*Shōtoku hiinagata*)

spring 1713

ARTIST'S SIGNATURE:
'Yamato eshi Nishikawa Sukenobu kin jo' (Respectful preface by the Yamato picture master Nishikawa Sukenobu)

woodblock-printed book, *fukuro-toji*, vols. 1 and 2 of 5 bound together, incomplete, vol. 1 preface unnumbered, sheets numbered 3–15, vol. 2 sheets numbered 3–15, hand-colouring, 21.6 × 15.8 cm (covers)

William Sturgis Bigelow Collection, 2000

2000.1262

During the Edo period Japan's military rulers tried to impose sumptuary legislation to make clear the elevated social standing of the aristocracy. Frequently, the regulations were circumvented, but they did increase awareness of social distinctions in dress. *Kosode Patterns of the Shōtoku Era*, which consists of five volumes, provides an invaluable resource for studying the clothing styles of women (and young men) from different stations. The first of these is devoted to the fashions of the upper classes, women from the traditional aristocracy and the military elite. In the second, shown here, the artist turns to the dress of the wealthy merchant class and taste-setting courtesans.[1]

Many of the textile designs featured in the book would have been executed in the newly popular paste-resist *yūzen* technique. Relying on subtlety of design rather than on a display of sumptuous materials, *yūzen* expressed a new sense of understated elegance in the Edo period. In the spread illustrated here Sukenobu shows two *kosode* considered appropriate for high-level courtesans. The inscriptions state that the robe on the right should be dyed purple with the motif of folding screens in yellow and ink for the individual paintings, while the upper section of the garment on the left should also be dyed purple with the lower body reserved in white. The form of the plum-blossom motif derives from designs by the celebrated Ogata Kōrin(1658–1716), a master painter known for his simplified but sumptuous compositions in painting, ceramics and textiles.[2] ANM

1 The third volume details the dress of lower-ranked prostitutes, the fourth the style of young men and rogues, and the fifth crests. Kyoto 1999, no. 117.

2 In *Hyakunin jorō shina-sadame* (*One Hundred Women Classified According to their Rank*, 1723), Sukenobu depicts a young trainee courtesan (*hikime*) from the Shimabara district of Kyoto wearing a robe patterned with these same Kōrin-style plum blossoms.

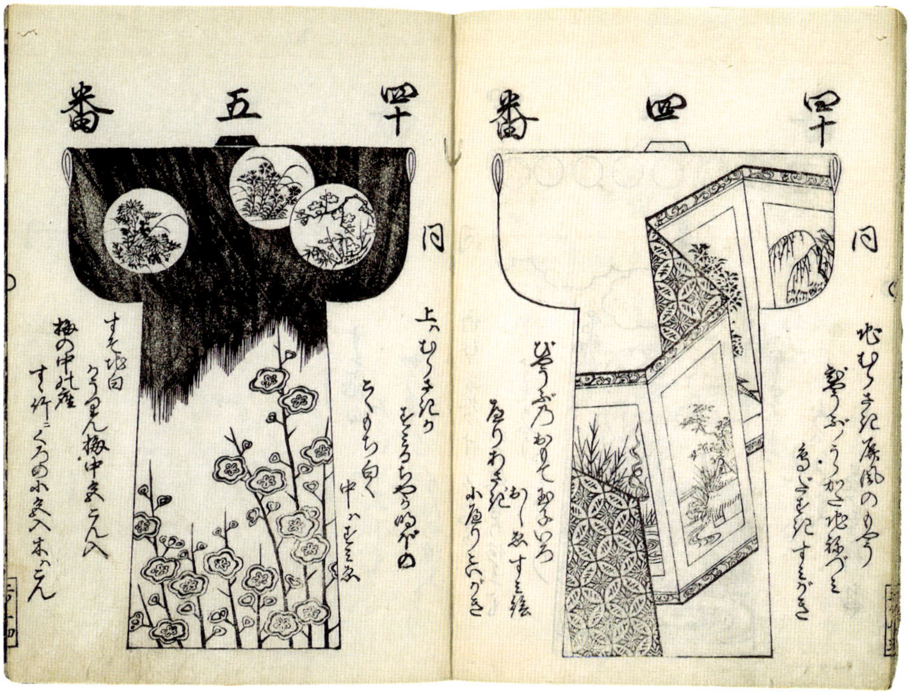

80

Nishikawa Sukenobu

Genre Scenes in the Four Seasons

c. 1716–36

ARTIST'S SIGNATURE: 'Nishikawa Ukyō Sukenobu kore [o] egaku' (This was painted by Nishikawa Ukyō Sukenobu)

ARTIST'S SEALS: 'Nishikawa-uji', 'Sukenobu kore [o] zu[su]' (This was painted by Sukenobu)

handscroll, ink, colour and silver on paper, 32.6 × 545.2 cm

REPRODUCED: Boston 2000, vol. 2, no. 20

William Sturgis Bigelow Collection, 1911

11.7794

1 Shively 1991, p. 712.

During the early Edo period the population of Kyoto, where Sukenobu resided, was more varied than in the new military capital. As the seat of the Emperor, Kyoto remained the home of the traditional aristocracy, but it also contained a small number of samurai, in residence at Nijō Castle as representatives of the military government. Merchants – many of whom had gained social standing prior to the establishment of the Tokugawa government – were certainly among Kyoto's acknowledged cultural leaders.[1]

From the early decades of the 18th century, when Sukenobu first designed pattern books, including the five-volume *Kosode Patterns of the Shōtoku Era* (1713, cat. 79) and *Kosode Patterns of Nishikawa* (*Nishikawa hiinagata*, 1718), the artist explored this richly varied society by examining the city's women and their dress. In later books, such as *Hyakunin jorō shina-sadame* (*One Hundred Women Classified According to their Rank*, 1723), he devoted two volumes to women of every class, one to women from the Empress down to peasants threshing rice, one to courtesans from the 'three cities', Kyoto, Edo and Osaka.

Genre Scenes in the Four Seasons, depicting eight scenes, two for each season, is a work of particular significance, not simply because of the high quality of its conception and execution, but also because it is the only known handscroll by Sukenobu with non-erotic subject matter. It is populated by beautiful women of the samurai and townsman classes, joined in three scenes by adolescent youths. No mature males impinge on the refined, delicate world of the customs shown here. The eight scenes depict the following:

SPRING

1. New Year celebrations in a samurai mansion. A young samurai enters a room where three women play cards, surrounded by ceremonial New Year arrangements of food and drink. A six-panel screen in the background depicts pine trees and a river in the mountains, in Kano *suiboku* style.
2. A party admiring cherry blossoms. Five young women feast and play the shamisen in a curtained enclosure beneath a blossoming tree.

SUMMER

1. A country outing. A married woman and her daughter, accompanied by two female servants, walk past a flowering deutzia bush (*unohana*). The daughter points to a cuckoo (*hototogisu*) that calls as it flies above.

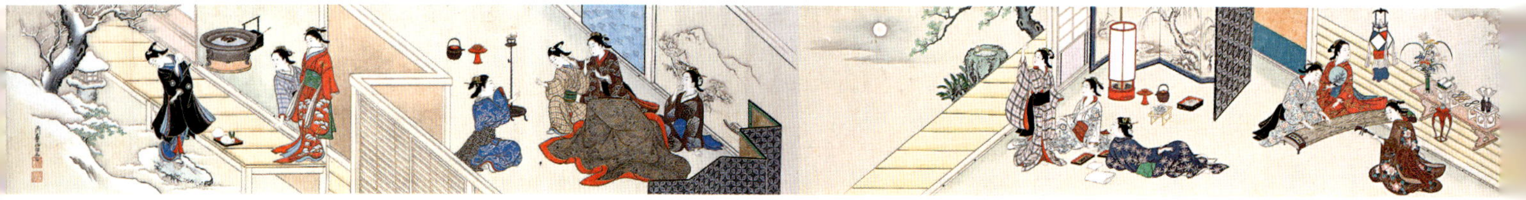

2. Enjoying the cool of evening. Two women wearing thin, semi-transparent summer *kosode* are seated beside a river on a bench beneath a willow. They are watching a small firework that burns in the brazier of their smoking set.

AUTUMN

1. Tanabata Festival. Three young women sit close by an open veranda, two of them playing the koto and the shamisen. Decorated offerings for the Tanabata Festival are placed on a low table and a festival lantern hangs from the eaves.
2. Moon viewing. Three young women admire the full moon from a veranda; writing equipment lies ready for their poems. Behind is a six-panel screen with a Kano-style *suiboku* composition of egrets on a willow beside a river.

WINTER

1. Telling ghost tales (*hyaku monogatari*). Three young women and a youth are seated around a *kotatsu*. The youth holds a taper from the lamp and is having his ear pulled by one of the women. (As more and more of the tapers in the lamp are extinguished, the room gets darker and darker, adding to the scariness of the ghost tales.) Pasted to the wall is a large *suiboku* painting of a snow-covered landscape in Kano style.
2. Snow-covered garden. A youth brings a snowball from the garden, watched by a young woman, who stands at the end of the veranda, and a maid. On a tray is a snow rabbit and in the room behind a large brazier and smoking set.

The final two scenes can be read as a continuous composition, if the inclusion of a stone lantern in the garden is taken to imply that this is night.

The chronology of Sukenobu's paintings has yet to be established. Most are dated to the Kyōhō era (1716–36). The artist's figure style developed little during his maturity, and variation either in his signature or in his use of paired seals or in the degree of their wear is slight. One hanging scroll, *Standing Beauty* (*Tachi bijin zu*; formerly Azabu Museum of Arts and Crafts), bears an inscription dating it to the Genbun era (1736–41) and this suggests that Sukenobu painted in virtually the same style until he died. Similarities between this scroll and *Ehon Tokiwa-gusa* (*Picture Book: The Pine Tree*, 1731) may indicate that both works date from about the same time. ANM, TTC

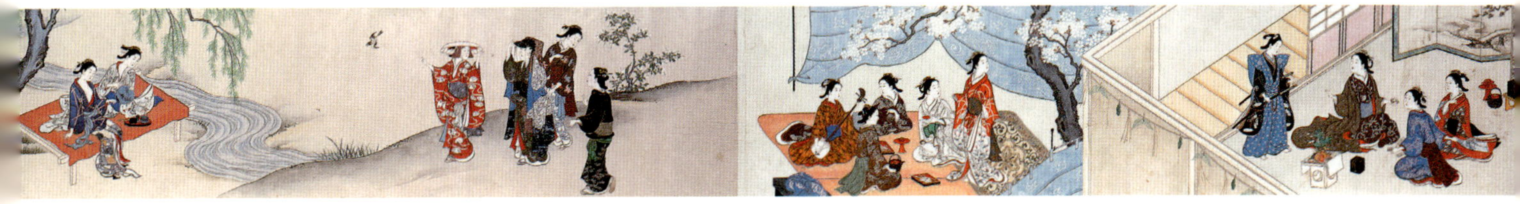

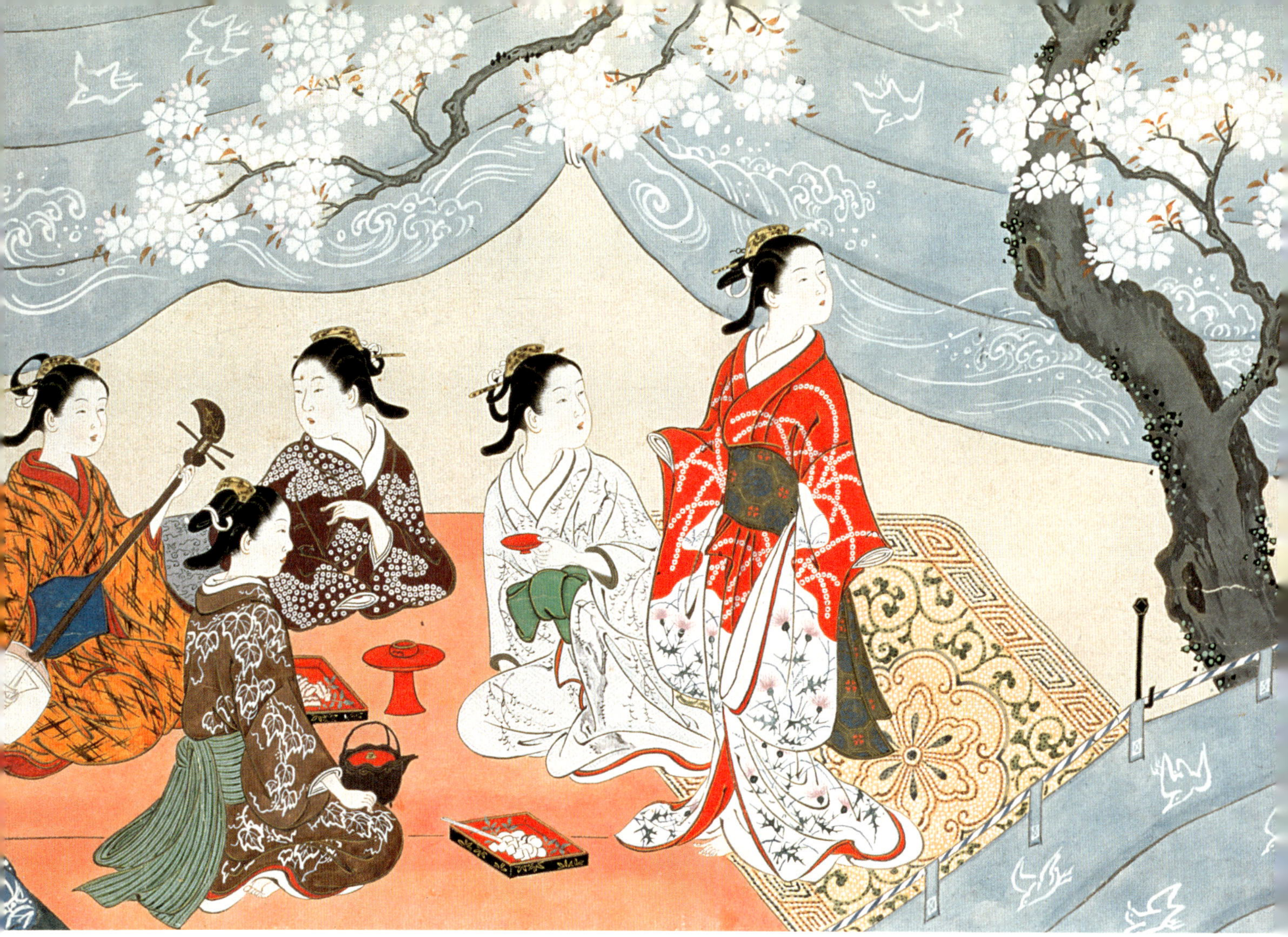

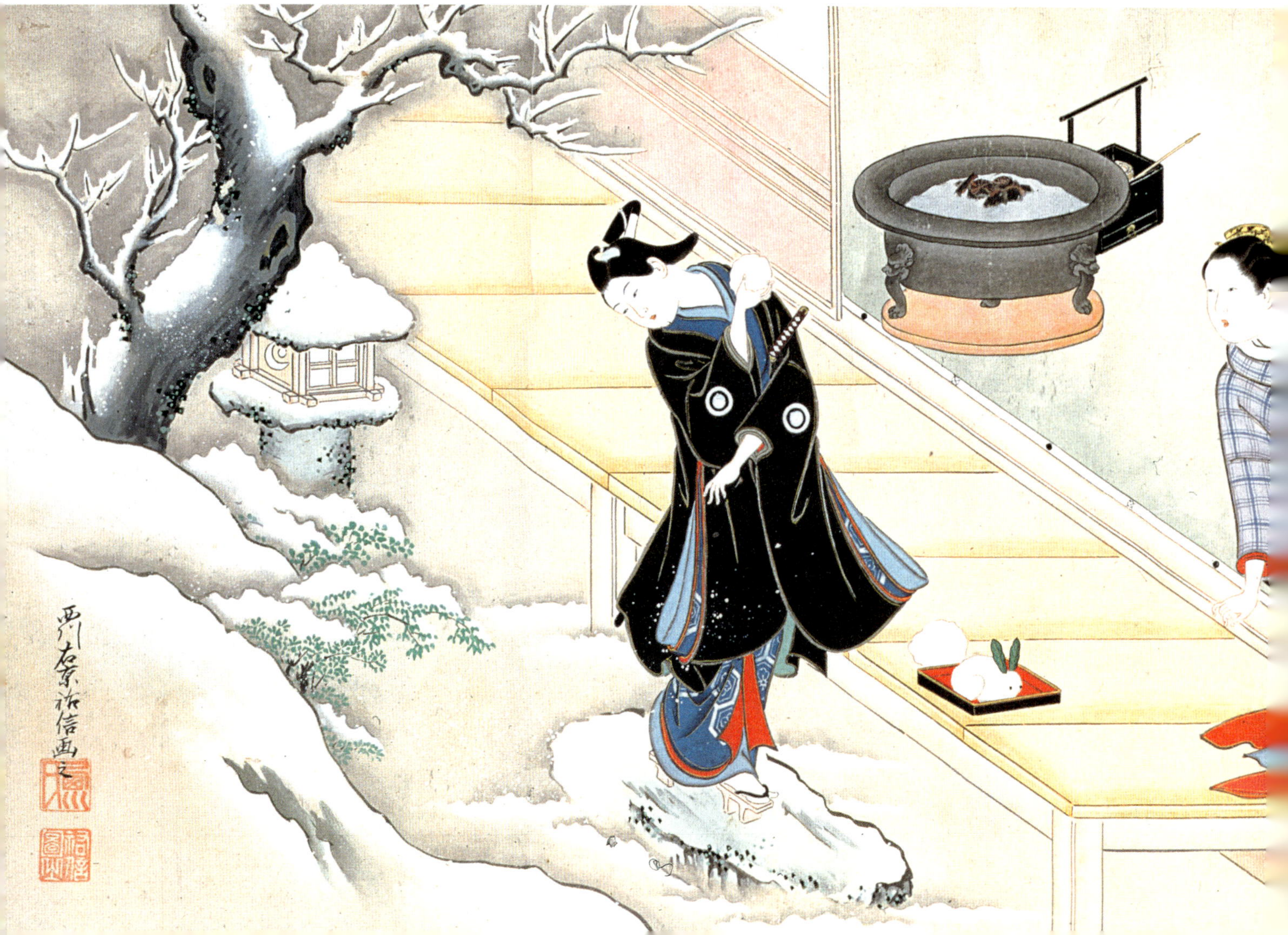
西川右京祐信画之

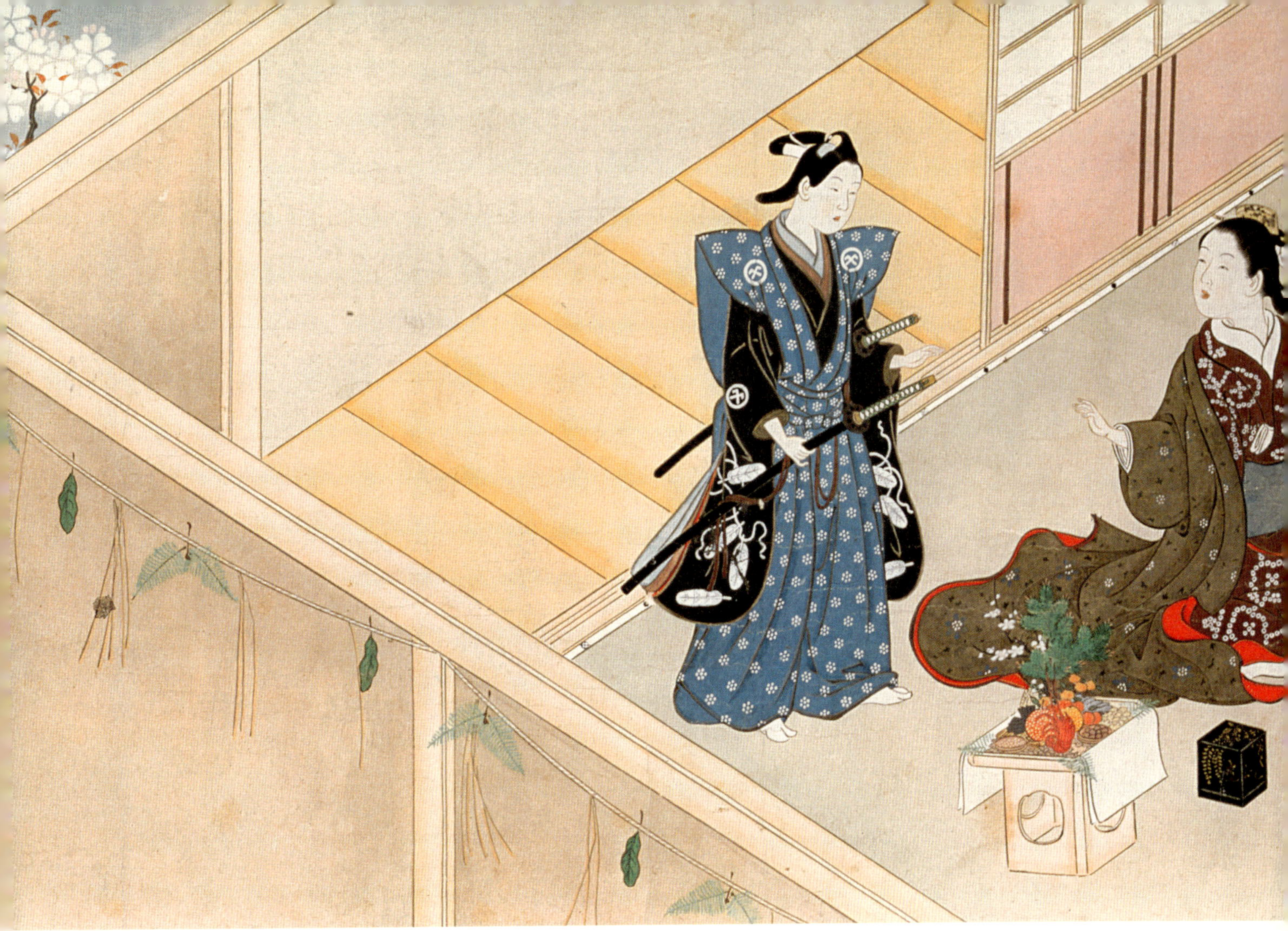

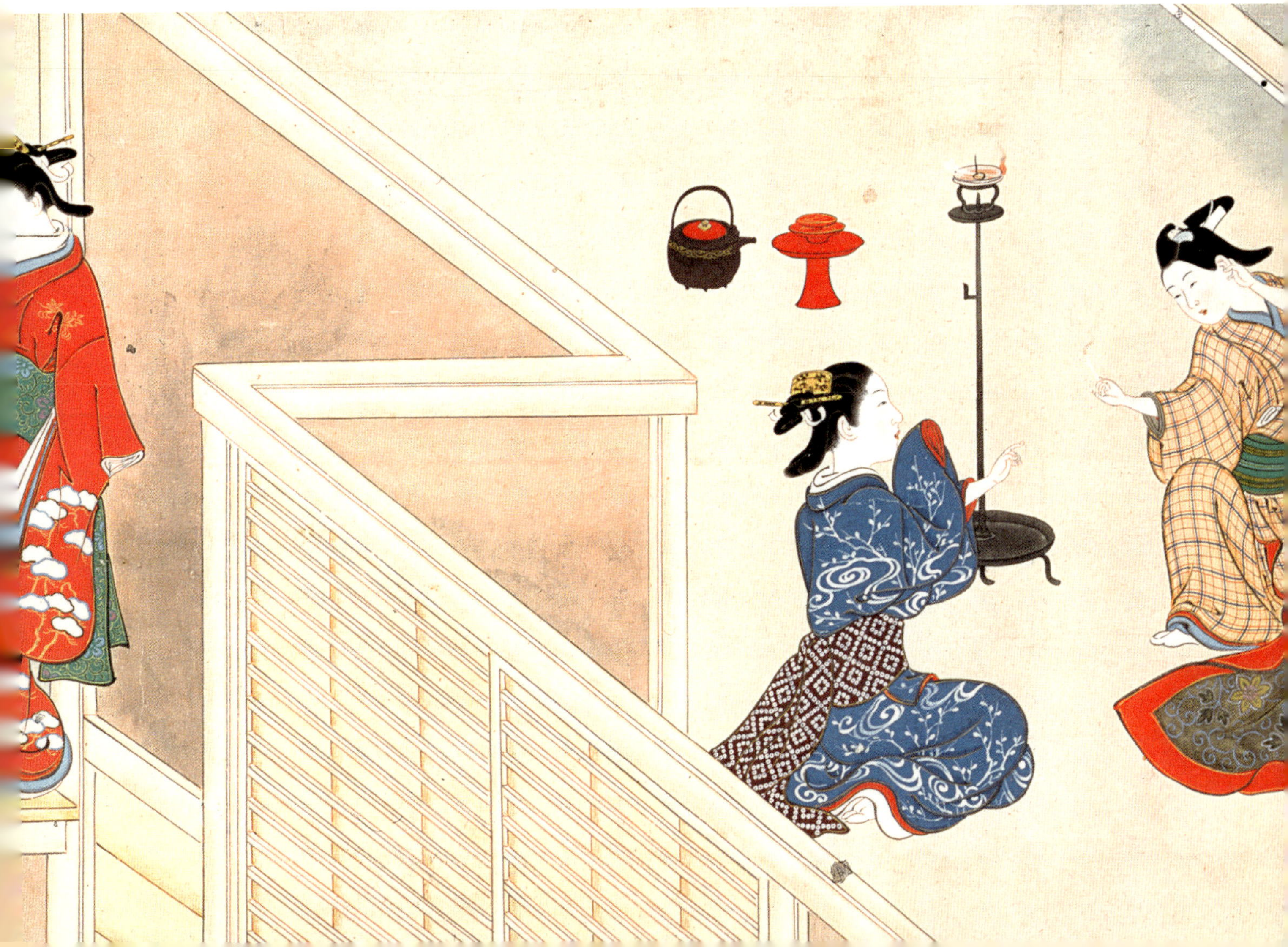

81
Nishikawa Sukenobu
Picture Book of Mount Asaka (Ehon Asaka-yama)

1739

ARTIST'S SIGNATURE: 'Karaku Bunkadō Nishikawa Sukenobu' (Bunkadō Nishikawa Sukenobu of Kyoto)

ARTIST'S SEAL: 'Sukenobu'

PUBLISHER: 'Kikuya Kihei; Kyoto, Teramachi-dōri, Matsubara sagaru-chō' (Kikuya Kihei, at Matsubara sagaru-chō, Teramachi-dōri in Kyoto)

woodblock-printed book, *fukuro-toji, sumizuri*, 1 vol., sheets numbered *i, ro, ha, ni* and 1–11; 6 single-page forming 3 double-page illus., 24 single-page compositions, 26 × 18.4 (covers)

OTHER COPIES: Rijksmuseum voor Volkenkunde, Leiden (Kerlen 1996, p. 91, no. 232); New York Public Library (New York 1978, p. 102); British Museum, London (London 1980, pp. 56–7, no. 23); Edoardo Chiossone Museum, Genoa (Genoa 1980, pp. 63–4, no. 53)

Gift of Mrs Jared K. Morse, 2000

2000.1251

1 For discussion of Sukenobu's illustrated books, see Hillier 1987, pp. 158–73; Matsudaira 1977, pp. 3–13; and Matsudaira 1988.

2 Chicago 1931, pp. 129–30.

3 *Picture Book of Mount Asaka* is reproduced in full in *Nihon-fūzoku zue*, vol. 3.

4 Waterhouse 1964, pp. 78–9, no. 19.

5 *Waka-bungaku*, p. 14.

Sukenobu was an extremely talented and highly esteemed painter, but he was also a very inventive and prolific book illustrator. It is believed that he illustrated over 200 volumes from 1708 to the close of his career. Kyoto publishers vied or collaborated with one another to publish *ehon* illustrated by this artist, but it was Kikuya Kihei, the publisher of this book, who eventually became Sukenobu's greatest sponsor. Kikuya published 21 *ehon* by him between 1729 and Sukenobu's death in 1750 and later, buying the copyright of further books of his from other publishers, he continued to reprint Sukenobu's works.[1]

Having studied the female figure and textile patterns in available *hiinagata-bon* (textile pattern books), Sukenobu developed a female ideal with rounded faces, far gentler and more frail than the women seen in, say, Masanobu's Edo prints. Quiet and refined, the women populating Sukenobu's world had the greatest impact on the depiction of the female figure in ukiyo-e during the third quarter of the 18th century. Suzuki Harunobu (*d.* 1770), who pioneered the breakthrough of 'brocade pictures' (*nishiki-e*) in Edo, fell under the spell of Sukenobu's style and later developed his own sweet and slender ideal.

Sukenobu's standing as a book illustrator was established by *Hyakunin jorō shina-sadame* (*One Hundred Women Classified According to their Rank*, 1723), a work containing masterly illustrations of women in various vocations, ranging from the Empress and her ladies to courtesans, weavers and pedlars.[2] Ever fresh and consistent in the quality of his work, Sukenobu went on to explore a wide variety of subjects that appealed to numerous Kamigata residents and increasingly also to customers in Edo. His illustrated works on *kosode* patterns, ethics or moral fables, children's games, life in Kyoto, women's calligraphy and letter writing, classical poetry and literature were all in great demand.

Sukenobu's special interest in the *fūzoku* (manners and customs) of women imbued many of his finest *ehon* with a natural, lifelike quality that made them irresistible. In *Picture Book of Mount Asaka* women drawn with thin, even, flowing lines and dressed in delicately patterned *kosode* are silhouetted against plain backgrounds.[3] Some of the women are shown with an object of daily use – for example, a mirror, lamp, flower arrangement, a battledore, ball, koto, cricket cage, water bucket, letter or fan. Other prints are enlivened by the presence of a playful cat or spritely children.

The double-page spread shown here is an instance of what Sukenobu did with apparent ease, capturing charming gestures or poses as well as intimate moments of interaction familiar to and clearly understood by all. The young woman on the right, as was the fashion, has covered her head with her outer robe. By holding up the edge of the chrysanthemum pattern above her forehead, and walking with sleeves flapping and black hem flowing, she resembles a *tanchō* crane (red-crowned Japanese crane) with its beak, eye, white plumage and black-tipped feathers. The older of the two women on the left is a married woman with her obi tied in front and a crest at her shoulder. She is speaking to her younger companion and points to the left, perhaps asking her to run an errand. The younger girl, dressed in a *kosode* with a swirling marsh and water plantain motif, gracefully turns to face her mistress, offering us a glimpse of her elegant obi and coiffure. Suzuki Harunobu (*d.* 1770), who was deeply influenced by Sukenobu's work, clearly had this design in mind when creating a *mitate* on the Kiyomizu Komachi theme for a 1766 calendar print.[4] There are two editions of *Picture Book of Mount Asaka*, both dated 1739. That containing 24 illustrations is believed to be the earlier. The later edition, to which this copy belongs, was expanded by six illustrated pages (forming three double-page illustrations), which were numbered separately and, along with a preface, placed before the other pages. The title of the book evokes the name of a mountain first mentioned in the 8th-century poetry compilation *Collection of Ten Thousand Leaves* (*Man'yō-shū*), which over the centuries had became synonymous with beauty and, above all, with the beauty and skill of women.[5] LEV

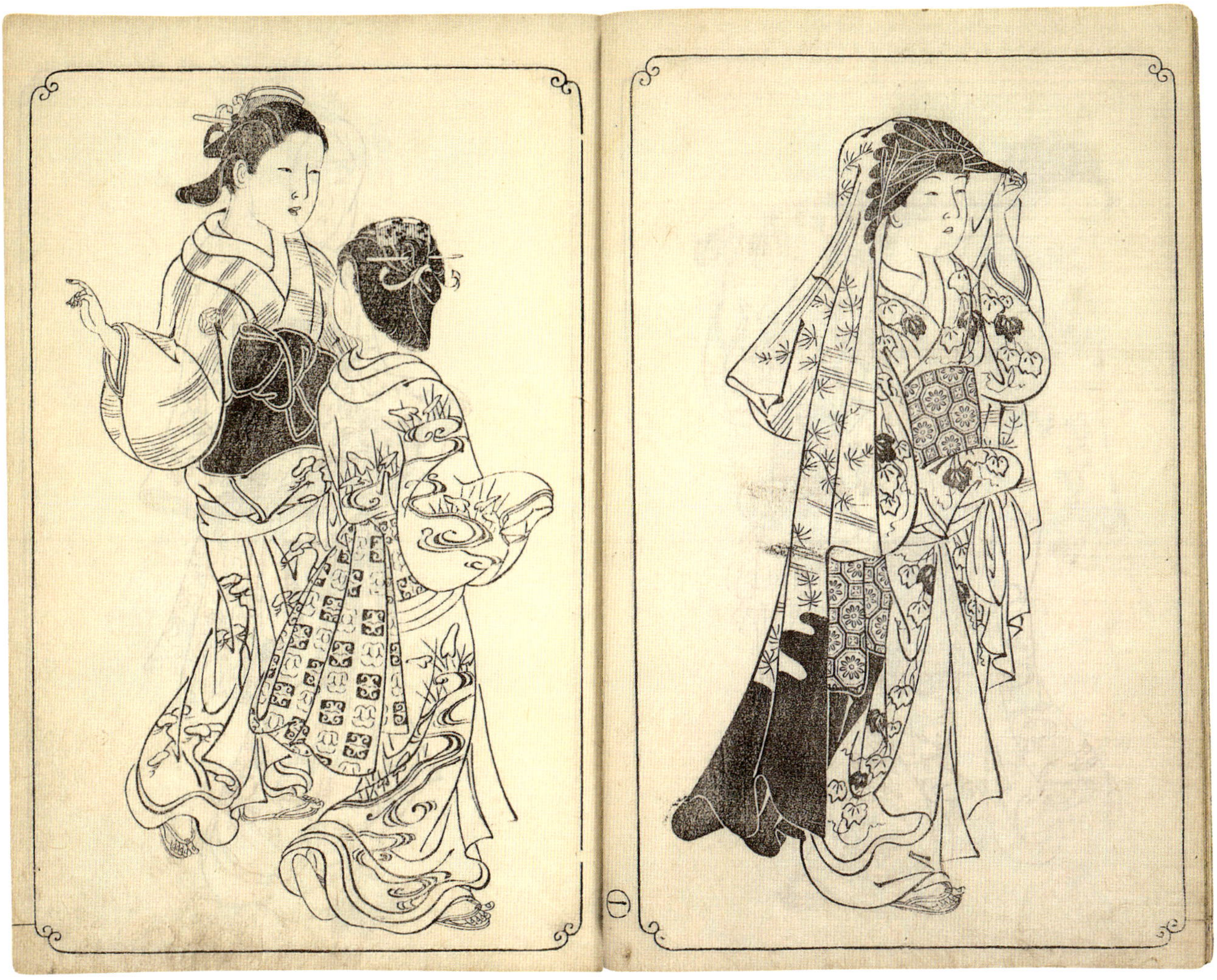

82
Kaigetsudō Ando
Standing Courtesan

c. 1704–16

ARTIST'S SIGNATURE: 'Yamato giga Kaigetsudō kore [o] zu[su]' (Light-hearted Yamato painting; this picture was done by Kaigetsudō)

ARTIST'S SEALS: 'Kan'unshi', 'Giga Ando' (Light-hearted painting by Ando)

panel, ink, colour and gold on paper, 103.9 × 44.2 cm

REPRODUCED: Boston 2000, vol. 1, no. 54

William Sturgis Bigelow Collection, 1911

11.7993

Considered by some to embody perfectly the spirit of ukiyo-e, monochrome Kaigetsudō school prints of unidentified courtesans standing statuesquely in boldly ornamented robes are among the most treasured images from early 18th-century Japan. The limited number of such designs by the followers of Kaigetsudō Ando – Anchi, Dohan and Doshin – and the elusive yet scandal-touched biography of the artist have added to the prints' desirability.[1] Yet Ando himself produced no prints: his patrons were more than willing to pay for the more expensive images of feminine allure he provided in the hanging scroll and handscroll formats. Scholars now confidently attribute some 28 signed paintings to Ando.[2] Asano Shūgō believes that most of these, whether by Ando himself or his disciples, were executed before the artist's banishment to Izu Oshima following his involvement in the Lady Ejima scandal in 1714 (see p. 26).[3] Certainly, the treatment of the figures, with their small heads, triangulated or S-shaped poses, voluminous robes and arrested walk, became a hallmark of Kaigetsudō imagery.[4]

Since the mid-17th century pictures of beautiful women had been prized by wealthy men as mementos of their visits to a pleasure quarter and by those less privileged as objects of fantasy. In Saikaku's novel *The Life of an Amorous Woman* (*Kōshoku ichidai onna*) an older man trying to procure a concubine for his lord states his requirements by producing from 'a scroll box of straight-grained paulownia wood the painting of a beautiful woman. "I'd like to engage one about like this", he said, to make clear his preference... "First of all her age should be from fifteen to eighteen, and she should have the most up-to-date good looks – that is, the face slightly rounded, the complexion of a pale cherry-blossom, the four features all perfectly regular. Narrow eyes are not wanted; the eyebrows should be thick and spaced well apart on either side of the nose, which ought to stand fairly high".'[5]

Among the first paintings to isolate beautiful women against a neutral background were the 'Kanbun Beauties' (p. 18, fig. 5), so called because they were mostly created during the Kanbun era (1661–73). Like the Kaigetsudō works, these contained careful detailing of the textile designs worn by the idealised models, but the expressions and poses of the figures were coyer. The women depicted by Ando and his followers both projected an aura of accessibility through the rounded contours of their bodies and preserved a fascinating sense of psychological distance through their placid expressions. The effect was intentional. A woman similar in pose to the present one, and likewise wearing a narcissus-decorated outer-robe, occurs in a section of a handscroll by Ando of miscellaneous subjects (Museum of Fine Arts, Boston, 11.7498). She stands apart from a group of people at her feet who engage in conversation. These figures gesticulate to each other, their emotions clearly expressed on their faces. The woman, on the other hand, is an aloof icon of beauty in the manner of Ando's pictures of individual women. ANM

1 Ando had three other disciples, Doshu, Doshū and Dochi, but these executed only paintings.

2 Lane 1959.

3 Asano 1994, p. 24. Roger Keyes, too, has stated that the prints may date from before the scandal, pointing to similarities between them and works by Okumura Masanobu and Torii Kiyomasu from around the first decade of the 18th century. Oberlin 1984, p. 22.

4 Kobayashi 1982a provides an excellent survey of the defining features of Kaigetsudō images of beautiful women.

5 The description even stipulates that the 'length of the feet [be] fixed at size eight and three-tenths – the big toe curved so that you can see its underside'. Hibbet 1959, p. 166.

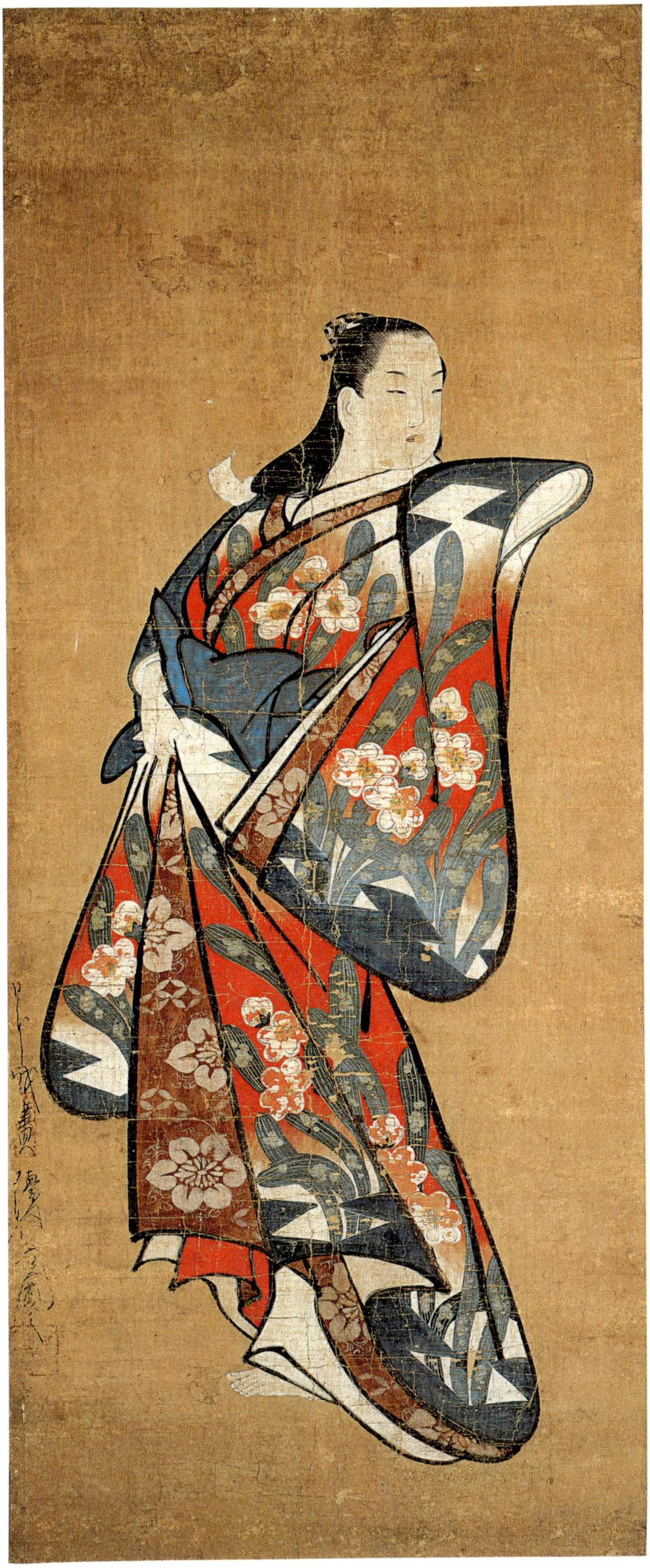

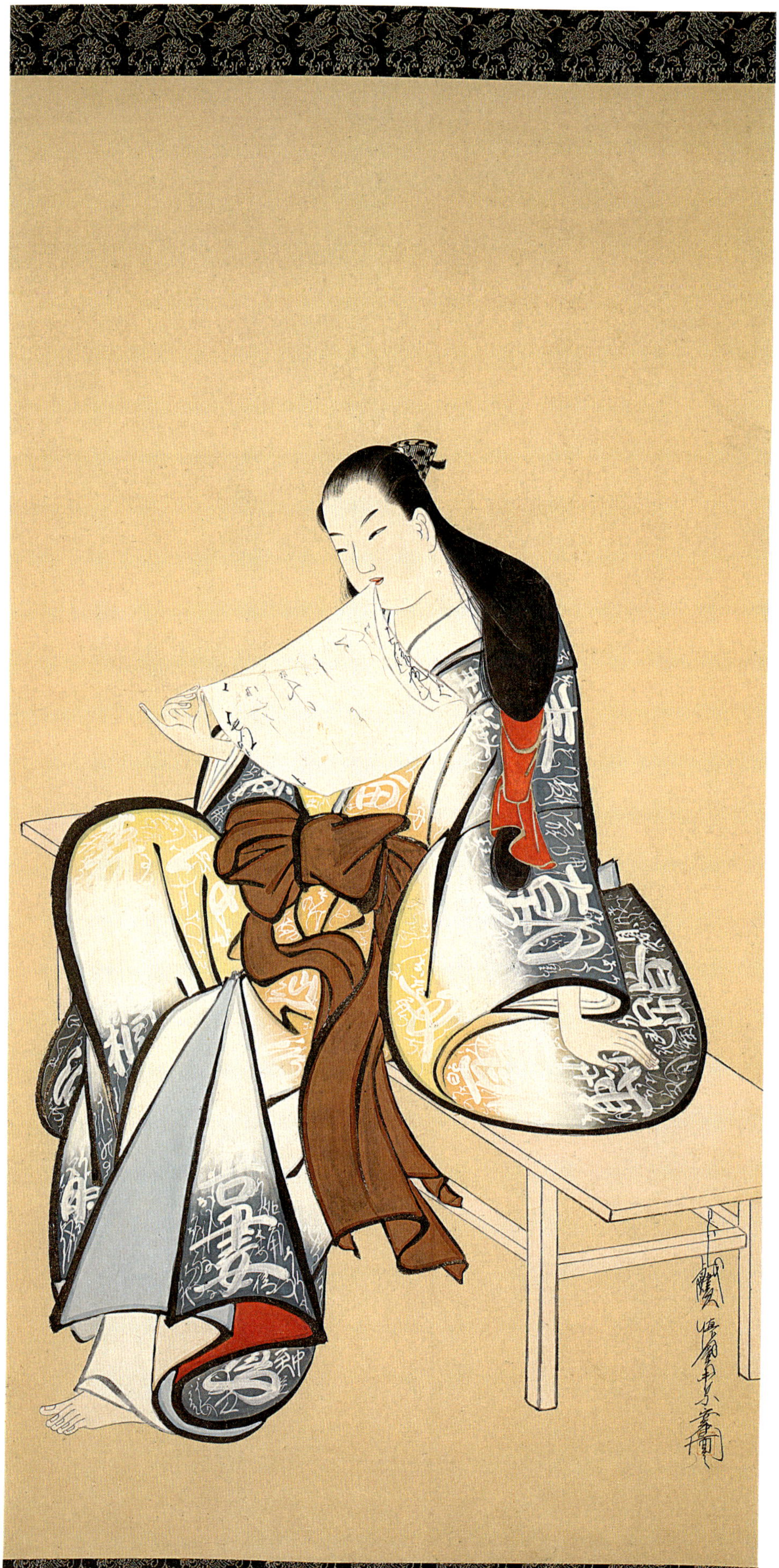

83

Kaigetsudō Anchi

Courtesan Seated on a Bench

c. 1704–16

ARTIST'S SIGNATURE: 'Yamato giga Kaigetsudō matsuyō Anchi kore [o] zu[su]' (Light-hearted Yamato painting; this picture was done by the Kaigetsu follower Anchi)

SEALS: [both illegible]

hanging scroll, ink and colour on paper, 96.8 × 51 cm

REPRODUCED: Tokyo 1983, no. 67; Boston 2000, vol. 1, no. 56

William Sturgis Bigelow Collection, 1911

11.7495

Kaigetsudō Ando explored several different themes in his paintings, including the bloody tale of Ōeyama, a portrait of a kabuki actor, still lifes and a youthful image of the Japanese Buddhist patriarch Shōtoku Taishi.[1] However, Anchi and other disciples of Ando largely confined themselves to producing images of beautiful women isolated against a plain paper ground in the manner popularised by their teacher.

Scholars have been able to identify eight print designs and some seventeen paintings by Anchi.[2] This painting is unusual in that the courtesan, rather than being shown standing, is portrayed seated on a wooden bench. She holds a letter in her mouth, which generally signifies emotional turmoil but is here made almost seductive.[3] Teasingly, she offers glimpses of the text along the edges and through the paper. Her long, slender left hand helps to support her body, which is enveloped in voluminous robes enlivened with bold characters written in white against bands of deep blue, white and yellow. Discernible among the Chinese characters are those for 'Asabune' (the name of a boat that transported passengers across Lake Biwa) and 'Azuma' (Eastern provinces).[4]

The textile design, suggestive of paste resist dyeing, is distinctive, but no early 18th-cebtury *kosode* of this type is known to have survived. This has led Sharon Takeda to wonder whether the Kaigetsudō painters were creating designs from their own imagination rather than recording actual textiles.[5] What is certain is that several Kaigetsudō-influenced artists active in the Hōei and Shōtoku eras, particularly Baiyūken Katsunobu, delighted in dressing their female subjects in such robes ornamented with scattered writing.[6] ANM

1 *Ōeyama*, 18th century, handscroll, Ōta Memorial Art Museum; *Sakata Oginojō*, 18th century, hanging scroll, Cleveland Museum of Art (both reproduced in *Nikuhitsu ukiyo-e*, vol. 2, pl. 31–3); *Miscellaneous subjects* (*Zatsuga-kan*), *c.* 1704–11, handscroll, William Sturgis Bigelow Collection, 1911, Boston Museum of Fine Arts, 11.7498 (reproduced in Boston 2000, vol. 1, no. 55, monochrome pl. 9); and *Prince Shōtoku* (*Shōtoku Taishi*), 18th century, hanging scroll, private collection (reproduced in Asano 1994).

2 The number of prints is taken from Naitō Masato's entry in Boston 2000, vol. 1, no. 56. A catalogue raisonné of Kaigetsudō painting has not been published; Richard Lane gave the number of attributable works as 'around seventeen' over forty years ago. Lane 1959, p. 74.

3 London 1992, no. 14.

4 Conversation with Asano Shūgō, 21 May 2001. Asano believes that the characters do not have any specific poetic reference.

5 Takeda 1992, pp. 168–9.

6 Examples include *Courtesan Seated on a Bench*, hanging scroll, British Museum, London (reproduced in London 1992, p. 77, no. 26), and *Standing Woman*, hanging scroll, Asian Art Museum of San Francisco, The Avery Brundage Collection (reproduced in Takeda 1992, p. 169).

84

Kaigetsudō Anchi

Courtesan with a Cloth Wrapper

early to mid-1710s

ARTIST'S SIGNATURE: 'Yamato giga Kaigetsu matsuyō Anchi zu' (Light-hearted Yamato depiction drawn by the Kaigetsu follower Anchi)

ARTIST'S SEAL: 'Anchi'

PUBLISHER'S SEAL: 'Ōdenma-chō ni-chōme Higashi Yoko-chō Maruya' (Maruya, at Higashi Yoko-chō, Ōdenma-chō ni-chōme)

woodblock, *ō-ōban*, *sumizuri-e*, two joined sheets, 62.4 × 30.6 cm

REPRODUCED: *Ukiyo-e shūka*, vol. 1, no. 163

OTHER IMPRESSION: Allen Memorial Museum, Oberlin (Oberlin 1984, p. 23, no. 10, *tan-e*)

William Sturgis Bigelow Collection, 1911

11.13158

Scholars now generally believe that Kaigetsudō Ando, along with six followers, worked at the Kaigetsudō (Yearning for the Moon Studio) in the Suwa-chō district of Asakusa near Edo's pleasure quarter, Yoshiwara. Capitalising on their location, the artists sold paintings of aloof, elegantly dressed courtesans executed in a boldly drawn and coloured style reminiscent of the votive plaques (*ema*) donated to temples. Typical clients were the Edo townsmen or provincial visitors on their way to and from the pleasure quarter – men who either dreamed of an evening with a high-class courtesan or who wanted mementos of such an experience. In an enterprising and complementary venture, three Kaigetsudō artists designed woodblock prints of similar courtesans in the vertical *ō-ōban* format suitable for mounting as hanging scrolls.

At least 23 Kaigetsudō woodblock print designs have been identified in private collections and museums; twelve are signed 'Dohan', three 'Doshin' and eight 'Anchi'.[1] Several exist in only one impression. Most include publishers' seals, and these show the prints to have been issued by three publishers: Dohan's and Doshin's by Iga-ya and Nakaya respectively, Anchi's usually by Maruya.[2] The prints may have been published as a collaborative effort to alleviate Ando's financial plight at the time of his banishment to Ōshima Island off the coast of Izu as a result of his involvement in the Lady Ejima scandal (see p. 26). On the other hand, Ando was a businessman and aware of the large-format images of courtesans and actors beginning to be designed by, among others, Masanobu, Kiyonobu I and Kiyomasu I: many poses and textile patterns found in works of *c.* 1710–15 by these artists recur in Kaigetsudō designs. It is therefore equally possible that the prints were published shortly before Ando was forced to leave Edo in 1714.

The Boston Museum possesses five representative examples of Kaigetsudō school prints.[3] These works by Anchi and Doshin present anonymous courtesans, majestically silhouetted against plain, timeless backgrounds; forceful, calligraphic lines describe the drapery and its folds, while more delicate lines depict the facial features, hair, hands and bare feet. The poses are familiar from Kaigetsudō paintings.

The courtesan in Doshin's print (cat. 85) resembles the figure in a painting by the same artist in the British Museum.[4] The courtesans in both works stand with heads tilted forward, stomachs pushed outwards and sleeves raised diagonally across the body to display the textile patterns. The courtesan depicted in Anchi's print (cat. 84) stands in a pronounced S-shaped pose, coquettishly holding the corner of a *fukusa* in her mouth. She recalls the figure in a painting by the same artist in the Tokyo National Museum.[5]

1 London 1992, p. 72.

2 One of Anchi's prints was published by Iga-ya. Ficke 1923, p. 114. According to Keyes, two prints by Dohan and one by Anchi do not bear publishers' marks. Oberlin 1984, p. 22.

3 In addition to cat. 84 and 85, the William S. and John T. Spaulding Collection at the Museum includes one print by Dohan (reproduced in *Ukiyo-e shūka*, vol. 1, no. 165) and two by Anchi (ibid., no. 164).

4 London 1992, p. 74, no. 23

5 Tokyo 1993, no. 12.

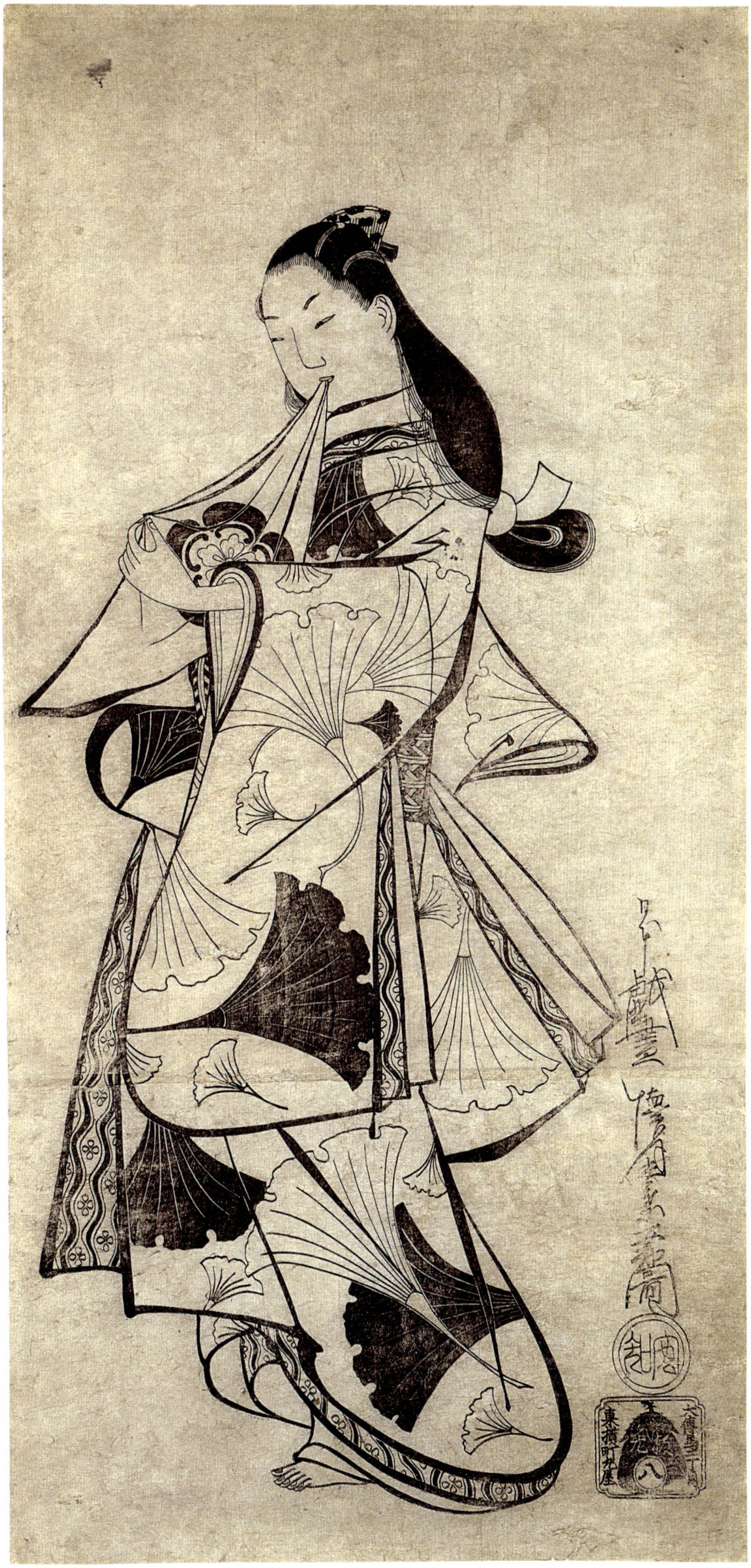

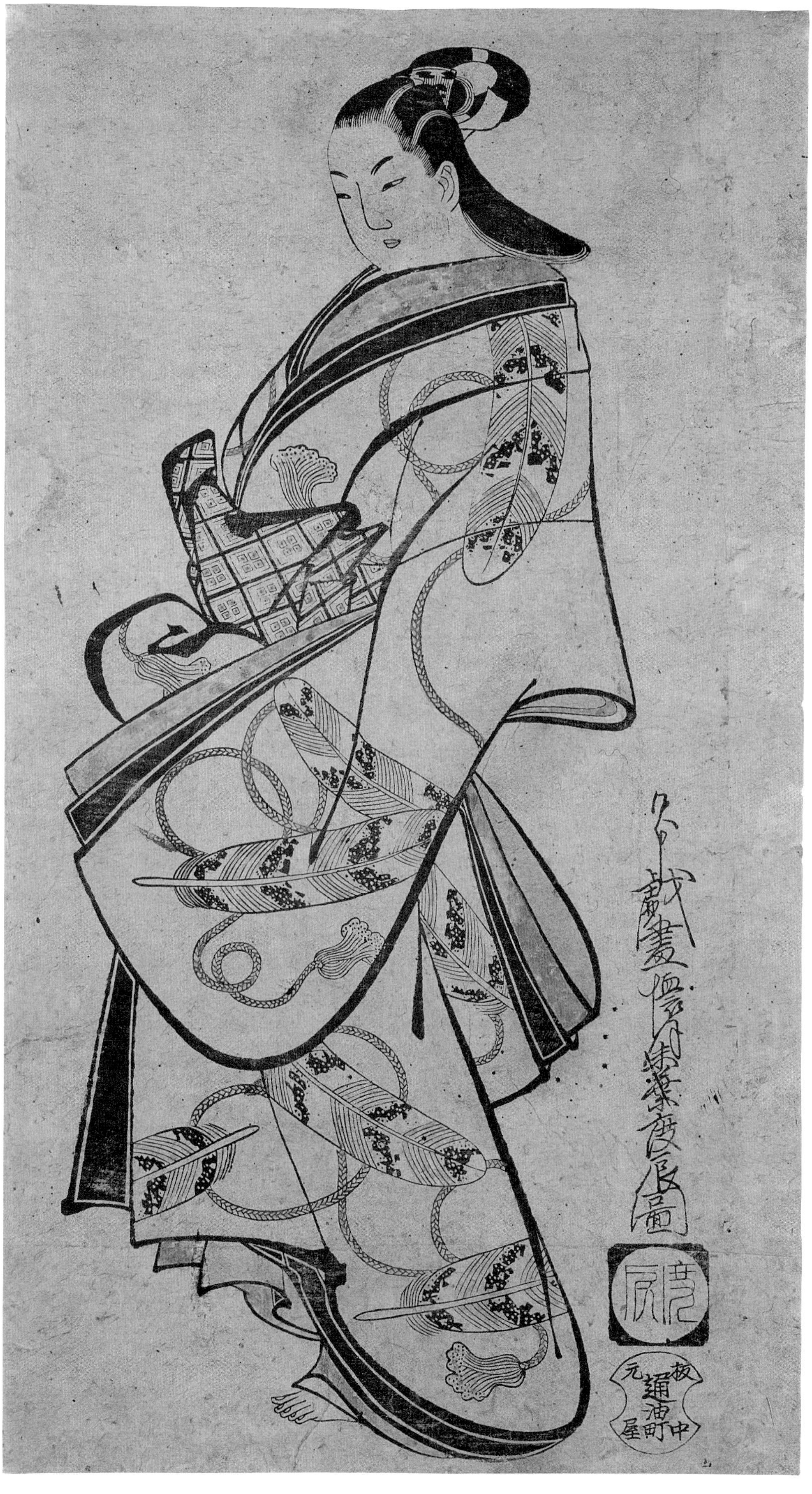
板元
通油町
中屋

85
Kaigetsudō Doshin
Standing Courtesan

early to mid-1710s

ARTIST'S SIGNATURE: 'Yamato giga Kaigetsu matsuyō Doshin zu' (Light-hearted Yamato depiction drawn by the Kaigetsu follower Doshin)

ARTIST'S SEAL: 'Doshin'

PUBLISHER'S SEAL: 'hanmoto, Tōriabura-chō, Nakaya' (The publisher Nakaya at Tōriabura-chō)

woodblock, *ō-ōban, sumizuri-e*, hand-coloured (*tan-e*), 55.5 × 31.1 cm (two joined sheets, trimmed along bottom edge)

REPRODUCED: *Ukiyo-e shūka*, vol. 1, no. 1

OTHER IMPRESSION: Metropolitan Museum of Art, Dick Fund, 1949 (formerly Ledoux Collection; Stern n.d., pp. 32–3, without *tan*)

James Fund, 1902

02.846

As both 'bodhisattvas of the world of sensual pleasures' and models for the latest fashions, the Kaigetsudō courtesans have impassive, youthful faces and are wrapped in luxurious *furisode* or *kosode*.[6] Their inclined heads, their coiffures and hips gently balance sweeping hems and swinging sleeves. Whereas the textile patterns in Kaigetsudō paintings are enriched with a tasteful combination of colours, it is the contrast of lights and darks and the dynamic line work that enliven the prints. The *furisode* worn by Anchi's courtesan (cat. 84), for example, is decorated with a bold pattern of scattered gingko leaves. Doshin's courtesan wears a *furisode* with a pattern of unravelling, braided and tasselled cords and falling falcon feathers.[7] To sustain the liveliness of the designs, the patterns are left uninterrupted by the drapery folds. In addition, Doshin's print, which shows signs along the edges of having been mounted as a hanging scroll, is brightened with *tan*.

Because Kaigetsudō paintings and prints are so similar in artistic style and calligraphic signatures, and since some paintings by Ando's followers include the master's seal, early art historians speculated that Ando may have used pseudonyms after his embroilment in the Lady Ejima scandal.[8] Most scholars now believe that several artists were involved, defining the word 'matsuyō' (literally, 'last leaf') in the signatures as 'follower' or 'student' and occasionally pointing to differences in skill and technique among the works of Anchi, Doshin, Dohan, Doshu, Doshū and Dochi.[9] Examining the prints by Anchi and Doshin in the Boston collection, one notices Doshin's tendency to dress his courtesans in voluminous, loose-fitting robes, obscuring any tiny hands that might have distracted attention from the fabric pattern. By comparison, Anchi's courtesans appear younger, slimmer and more vivacious.

The tall, unattainable Kaigetsudō courtesans influenced many artists during the first half of the 18th century. Their 'aristocratic' charm and allure made them symbols of the spirit of ukiyo-e and of ideal feminine beauty. The prints were probably sold very inexpensively, but the mystery surrounding their production and their present rarity have contributed to making them some of the most sought-after of all Japanese prints. LEV

6 In the Edo period *sei* (sexuality) had popularly come to be equated with *sei* (spirituality). Clark 1997, p. 22.

7 A similar gingko pattern is seen on the *kosode* worn by the courtesan in cat. 59, and a similar hawk and tasselled rope design on that worn by a woman in a print by Masanobu. Chicago 1955, p. 129, no. 35.

8 Binyon and Sexton 1978, pp. 162–5.

9 Lane 1978, pp. 70–3; Kobayashi 1996, pp. 51–4.

86

Kaigetsudō Dohan

Standing Courtesan

c. 1704–16

ARTIST'S SIGNATURE: 'Yamato giga Kaigetsu matsuyō Dohan kore [o] zu[su]' (Light-hearted Yamato painting; this picture was done by the Kaigetsu follower Dohan)

ARTIST'S SEAL: 'Ando'

hanging scroll, ink and colour on paper, 94.3 × 41.6 cm

REPRODUCED: Boston 2000, vol. 1, no. 57

William Sturgis Bigelow Collection, 1911

11.7499

Of the few extant works by the six artists identified as followers of Kaigetsudo Ando, the largest number belongs to Dohan. Twelve prints and approximately ten paintings have been attributed to him.[1]

In this scroll Dohan presents a courtesan with her long, glossy black hair pulled back with a tortoise-shell comb and secured at the ends with a red cloth. She assumes a contrived, graceful pose with her head looking over her shoulder, her stomach thrust slightly forward and her bare right foot shown in profile.[2] The young woman hides her right arm in the full sleeve of the three-layered robes typically worn by courtesans of the time and grasps their skirts just below the wide yellow sash.[3] The prototype of this pose is to be found in Ando's hanging scroll *Standing Beauty* (*Tachi bijin zu, c.* 1704–11), which the master artist imbued with more movement by exaggerating the curve of the courtesan's back and by extending the long sleeves to the left and right.[4] Dohan's courtesan appears a little stiff in comparison.

Other Ando pupils used the same model. A work by Doshū in the Boston Museum, and one by Doshin in the Idemitsu Museum of Arts, Tokyo, vary the figure but slightly.[5] The greatest distinguishing factors are the hairstyles and the designs of the textiles. In Dohan's scroll the courtesan wears an unusual combination of robes. The blue and white outer garment bears a pattern of clematis, a flower generally associated with summer, while the second, red robe is decorated with blue chrysanthemums, blossoms typically identified with autumn. ANM

1 Lane 1959, p. 82.

2 In *The Life of an Amorous Woman* (*Kōshoku ichidai onna*) Ihara Saikaku commented: 'A courtesan, also, has many special ways of walking. When she sallies forth, she usually wears no socks and adopts a floating walk.' Saikaku 1963, p. 138.

3 Saikaku noted: 'Her long hanging sleeves are cut in the modern fashion, measuring two and half feet at the bottom; no padding is used at the hips and the bottom of her skirt is wide. The courtesan's butt should look flat as an open fan. A wide, unpadded sash is tied loosely around her and artlessly secures her three layers of clothing'. Ibid.

4 Chiba City Museum of Art; reproduced in *Nikuhitsu ukiyo-e*, vol. 10, no. 17.

5 Kaigetsudō Doshū, *Standing Courtesan* (*Risshi yūjo zu*), *c.* 1704–16, hanging scroll, ink and colour on paper, 118.1 × 49.3 cm, William Sturgis Bigelow Collection, 1911 (11.7500); reproduced in Boston 2000, vol. 1, no. 59, where Naitō Masato points out the similarities between the two Boston paintings. Kaigetsudō Doshin, *Standing Beauty* (*Risshi bijin zu*), *c.* 1704–11, hanging scroll, ink and colour on paper, 103 × 47.4 cm; reproduced in *Nikuhitsu ukiyo-e*, vol. 3, no. 25.

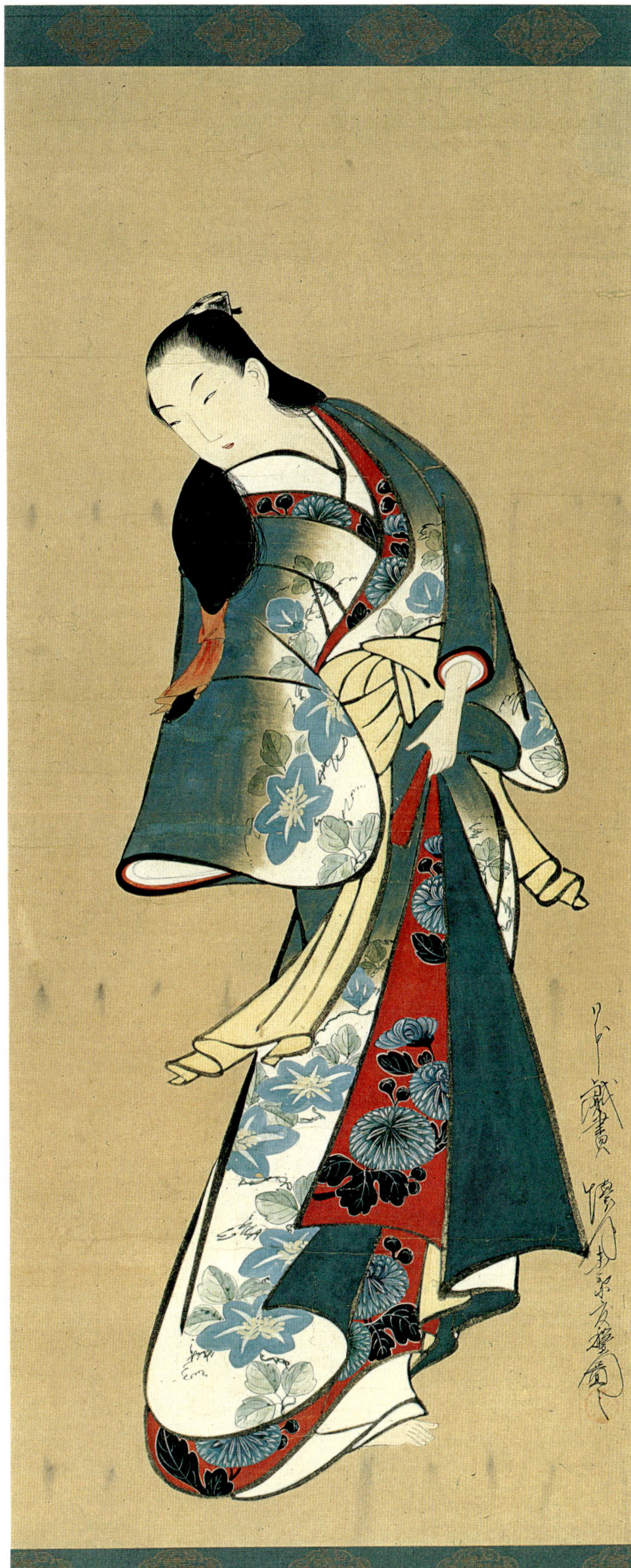

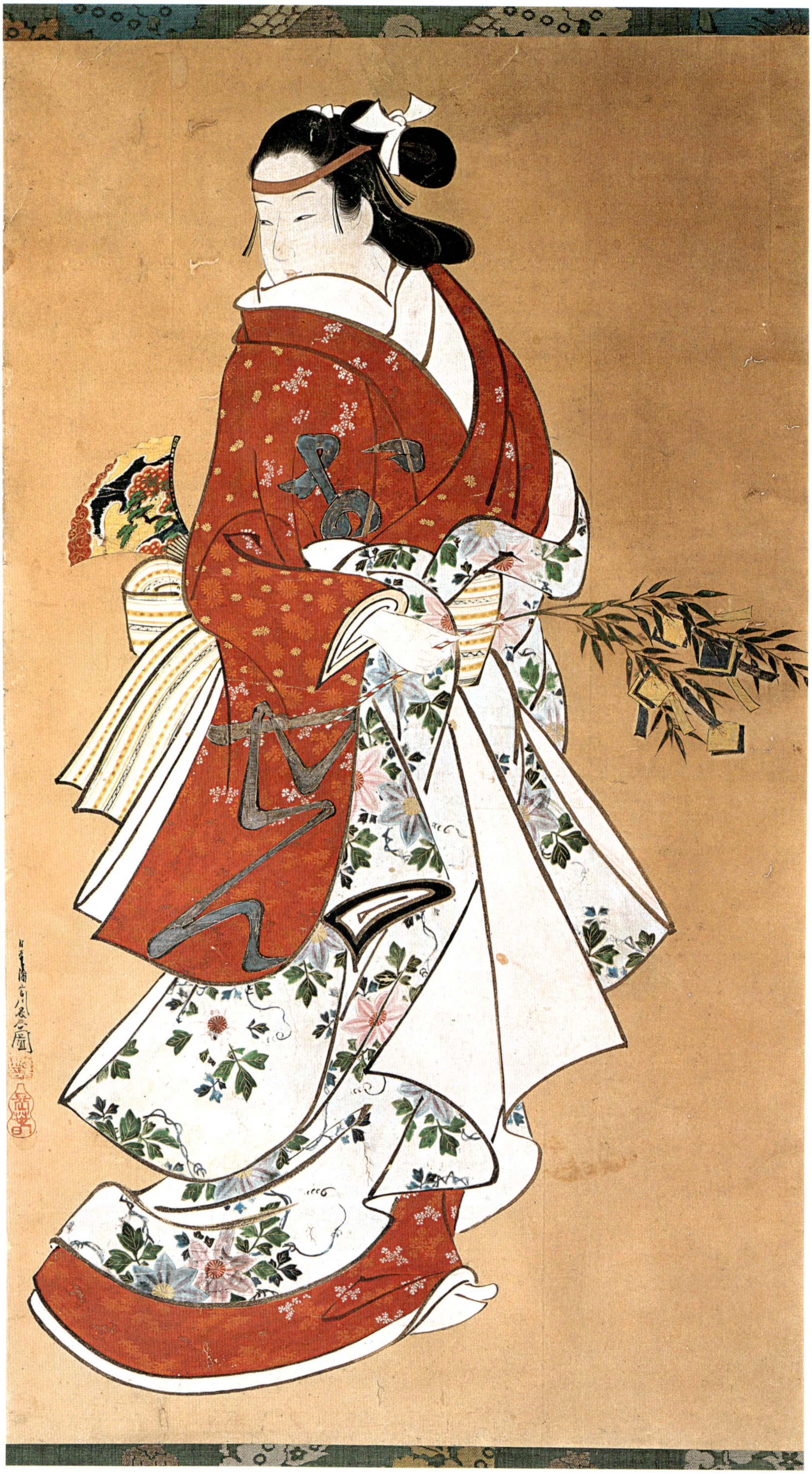

87
Miyagawa Chōshun
Female Dancer

c. 1704–25

ARTIST'S SIGNATURE: 'Yamato-e Miyagawa Chōshun zu' (Yamato picture drawn by Miyagawa Chōshun)

ARTIST'S SEALS: 'Chōshun no in' (seal of Chōshun), 'Chōshun'

hanging scroll, ink, colour, gold and silver on paper, 94.5 × 55.4 cm

REPRODUCED: Boston 2000, vol. 2, no. 8

William Sturgis Bigelow Collection, 1911

11.7662

Chōshun's dancer assumes a pose made popular during the late 17th century by paintings of 'Kanbun Beauties' (p. 18, fig. 5). Isolated against a plain paper background, the figure strides forward with her lower skirt and right foot shown in profile. Her upper torso twists slightly to her right so as to bring her into closer communication with the viewer, but she precludes direct contact by averting her eyes. This 'turning back' (*mikaeri*) position was adopted by members of the Hishikawa school and became something of a formula in paintings of standing courtesans by artists of the Kaigetsudō school – for example, two scrolls by Kaigetsudō Doshin and Kaigetsudō Doshu from the Hōei or the early Shōtoku era in the Tokyo National Museum.[1]

Chōshun himself was to use the pose for displaying the charms of women of varying types. In *Standing Beauty* (*Risshi bijin zu*) in the Idemitsu Museum of Arts, Toyko, for instance, a work slightly later than the present scroll, he portrays a high-ranked courtesan.[2] In the Boston painting he enlivens the staid pose of the dancer by boldly juxtaposing a light blue outer robe figured with pastel clematis blossoms and an inner robe of deep cherry red embellished in silver with the phonetic characters for Osen – the name of the woman, who remains unidentified.[3] The spray of bamboo with silver and gold streamers, and the fan ornamented with a landscape of pine-clad islands and gold cloud bands, add to the visual excitement.[4] ANM

1 Both entitled *Standing Courtesan* (*Yūjo risshi zu*), they are reproduced in *Nikuhitsu ukiyo-e*, vol. 1, nos. 29, 30.

2 This hanging scroll of *c.* 1716–36 (reproduced in *Nikuhitsu ukiyo-e*, vol. 3, no. 35) shows a mirror image of the courtesan in the Boston painting scroll.

3 The Osen of this painting differs from the teahouse waitress later made famous by prints designed by Suzuki Harunobu.

4 Kobayashi Tadashi identifies the bamboo with streamers as a *kurisasa*, an implement used in Shinto rituals and in nō performances when the principal actor assumed the role of someone possessed. Boston 2000, vol. 1, no. 8

88
Miyagawa Chōshun
Courtesan Seated on a Bench

c. 1716–36

ARTIST'S SIGNATURE: 'Yamato-e Miyagawa Chōshun zu' (Yamato picture by Miyagawa Chōshun)

ARTIST'S SEAL: 'Chōshun no in' (seal of Chōshun)

hanging scroll, ink, colour, gold, and silver on silk, 85 × 35.8 cm

REPRODUCED: Tokyo 1983, no. 69; Boston 2000, vol. 2, no. 2

William Sturgis Bigelow Collection, 1911

11.7659

Arranging a tortoise-shell comb in her luxurious, long black hair, a courtesan is seated on a wooden bench that extends diagonally across the lower half of the painting. She is dressed in a *kosode* of restrained elegance embellished with snow-covered dwarf bamboo (*sasa*) juxtaposed with climbing clematis in gold leaf and oxidised silver. The lines of the *ikat*-woven sash, loosely secured in the front, and the bright red under-robe are reinforced in gold.

In the upper left of the composition is a poem signed by Gengensai Kūdō Dōjin, about whom nothing is known. In a Chinese poem consisting of a quatrain of seven-syllable lines the poet describes his response to the painting. John Carpenter has commented: 'In his imagination the woman has just emerged from a bath, shaken out her robes to freshen them, and is now combing her hair in the light of the moon. Her unearthly beauty is likened to the mythical rabbit in the moon of East Asian folklore':

Mokuyoku keijin	Her body, cleansed by a bath,
mi o saran to hossu	is free of all manner of worldly dust.
Henpentaru shūseki	Layers of brocade, fluttering in the wind,
i o furuutte arata nari	are shaken clean and freshened.
Haun sogetsu	Moonlight, breaking through clouds,
hikari kami ni mitsu	fully illumines her hair as she combs.
Izure ka kore kōto	Such an alluring maiden, who is she?
izure ka bijin	Glistening white as the rabbit of the moon.
	GENGENSAI KŪDŌ DŌJIN[1]

Chōshun took the pose of the courtesan arranging the comb in her tresses from Kaigetsudō school painting, as is evident from a comparison with a hanging scroll of *c.* 1704–16 by Ando entitled *Standing Beauty* (*Risshi bijin zu*) in the Idemitsu Museum of Arts, Tokyo.[2] The positioning of the woman on a bench is likewise indebted to Kaigetsudō precedents, for a number of early 18th-century scrolls with a similar composition were clearly inspired by Kaigetsudō paintings.[3] Despite these resemblances, Chōshun has created an entirely different mood in his painting – one of intimacy. He achieves this through the delicate handling of the courtesan's facial features and the subtle selection of the textile patterns. ANM

1 Comments on and translation of the poem provided by John Carpenter in correspondence with the author, 21 May 2001.

2 Reproduced in *Nikuhitsu ukiyo-e*, vol. 3, no. 20. Donald Jenkins notes that the pose also appears in a print by Anchi (formerly Ledoux Collection) and a painting by Doshin in the Joe and Etsuko Price Collection. Chicago 1971, no. 113.

3 They include the hanging scrolls *Courtesan Seated on a Bench* by Baiyūken Katsunobu (active *c.* 1704–16) in the British Museum, London, and *Beauty on a Bench* (*Endai bijin zu*) by Takizawa Shigenobu (active *c.* 1716–36) in the Idemitsu Museum of Arts, Tokyo; reproduced respectively in London 1992, no. 26, and *Nikuhitsu ukiyo-e*, vol. 3, monochrome pl. 32.

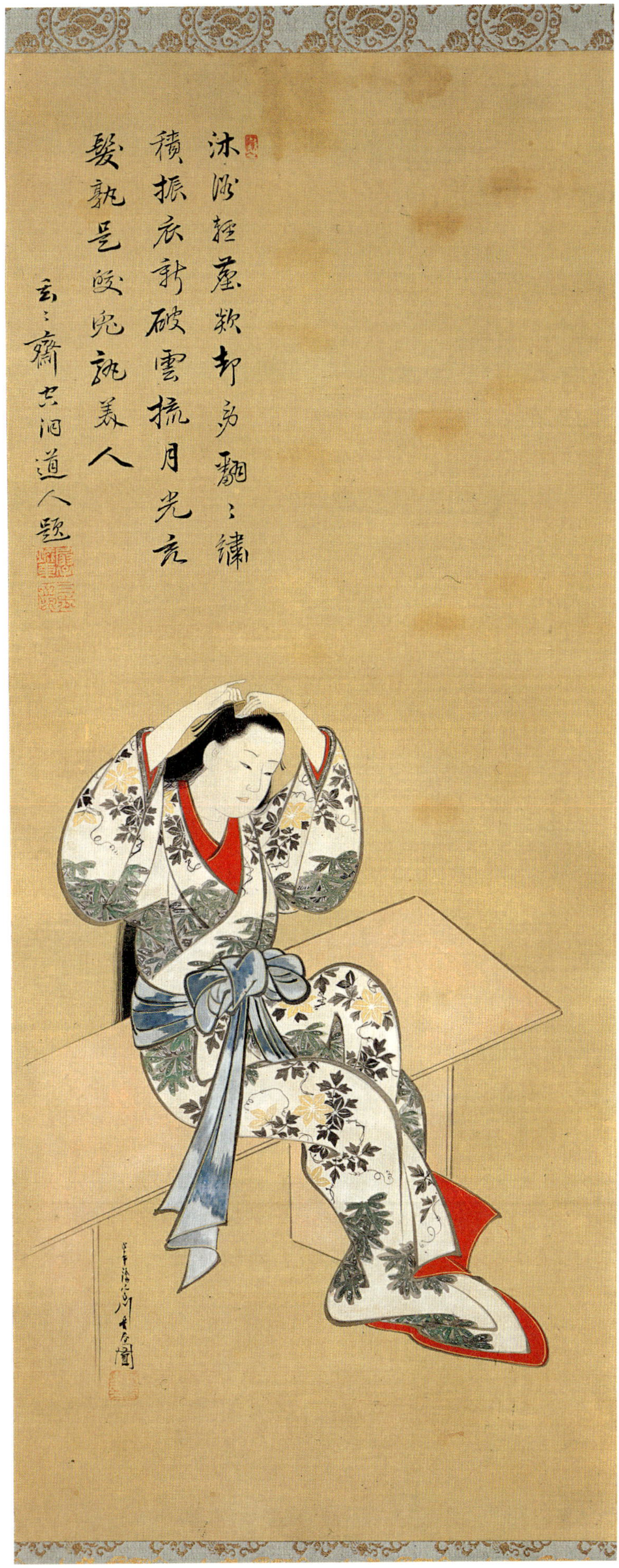

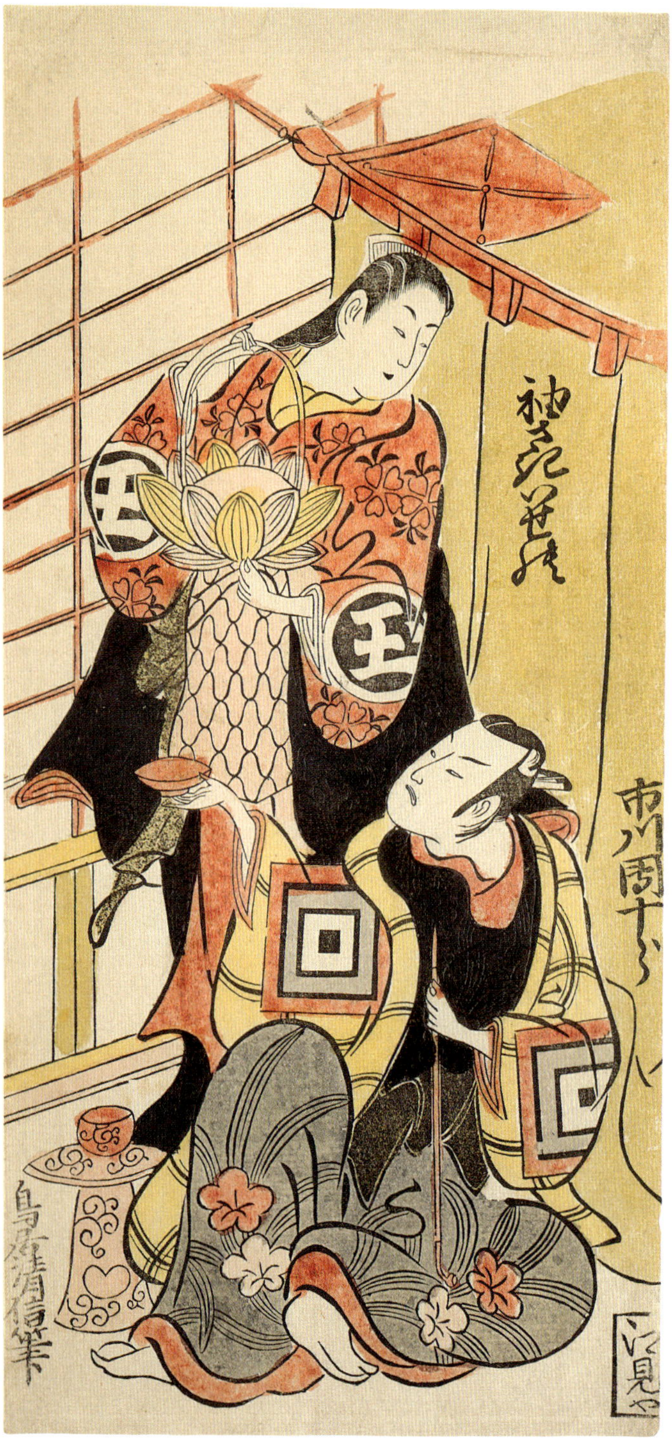
鳥居清信筆

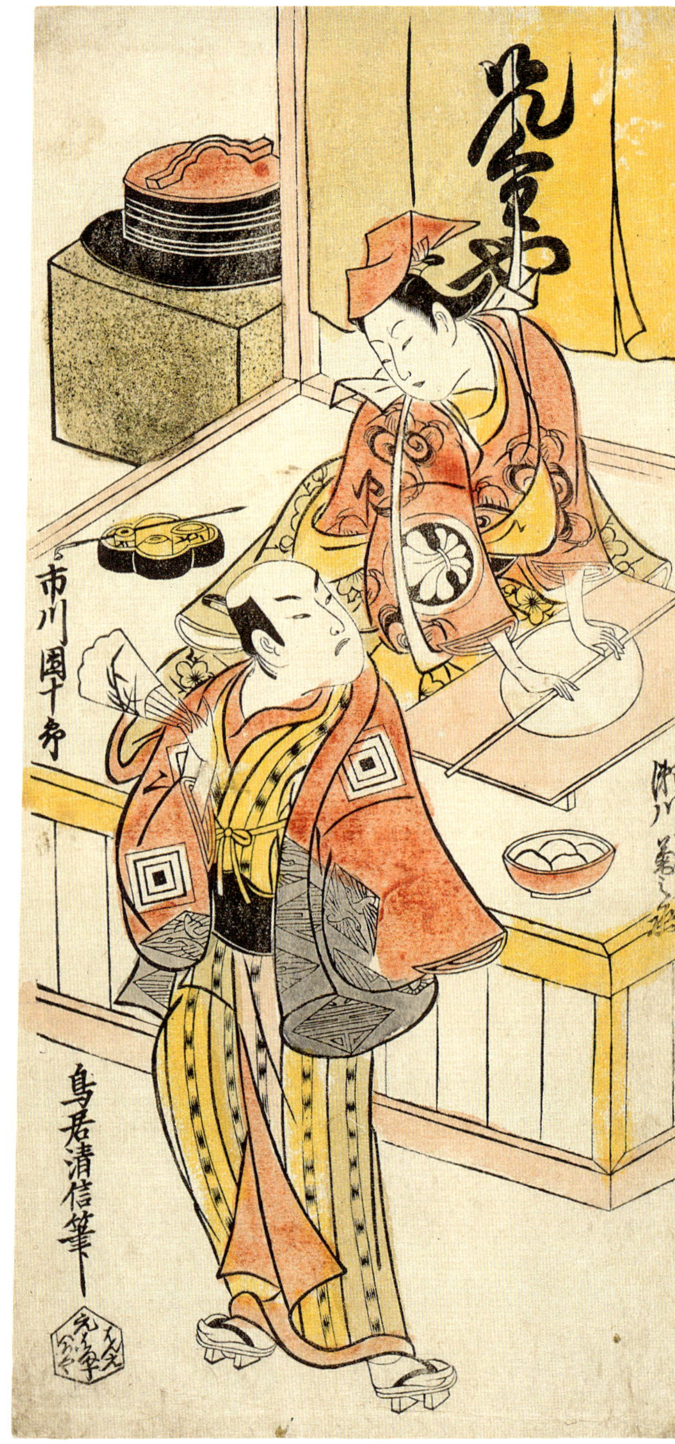
鳥居清信筆

89

Torii Kiyonobu II

The Actors Ichikawa Danjūrō II and Sodesaki Iseno

5th month (?), 1729

ARTIST'S SIGNATURE: 'Torii Kiyonobu hitsu' (Brush of Torii Kiyonobu)

PUBLISHER: 'Emi-ya'

woodblock, *hosoban, beni-e, urushi-e* with brass filings, 32.2 × 15.4 cm

William Sturgis Bigelow Collection, 1911

11.13206

1 *Kabuki hyōban-ki I*, vol. 9, p. 610. I am grateful to Mutō Junko for confirming which roles are probably depicted.

The shape of Danjūrō II's wig suggests the role of Soga no Gorō. Sodesaki Iseno did not graduate to young female roles until the opening of the season at the Nakamura Theatre in the eleventh month, 1726, and was then in the same troupe as Danjūrō II for four years. Danjūrō II played Gorō at every New Year during these years. Iseno was particularly praised for his interpretation of Kewai-zaka no Shōshō in a love scene with Danjūrō II as Gorō Shigebei in the play *Suehiro ehō Soga*, performed at the Nakamura Theatre from the New Year, 1729, and this is likely the scene depicted here.[1] This was also when Danjūrō II first performed what was to become one of his most celebrated roles, 'Arrow-sharpening Gorō' (Ya-no-ne Gorō), to *jōruri* musical accompaniment by Ōzatsuma Shuzen-dayū. The play was such a success that performances continued until the fifth month. The props here, with Danjūrō II holding a wine cup, suggest a scene in a pleasure quarter. The mosquito net, and Sodesaki's basket in the form of a lotus, suggest a summer performance and it may well be that the print was produced towards the end of the run of the play, around the fifth month (i.e. mid-summer). TTC

90

Torii Kiyonobu II

The Actors Ichikawa Danjūrō II as Kenka-ya Goroemon and Segawa Kikunojō as Osen

New Year, 1732

ARTIST'S SIGNATURE: 'Torii Kiyonobu'

PUBLISHER: 'Motohama-chō Iga-ya hanmoto' (Iga-ya, publisher at Motohama-chō)

woodblock, *hosoban, beni-e* with brass filings, 32.6 × 15.6 cm

William Sturgis Bigelow Collection, 1911

11.13203

1 *Kabuki nenpyō*, vol. 2, p. 175.

2 Another *hosoban* print, designed by Kiyomasu II, appears to show the same actors in the same roles (Art Institute of Chicago). Chicago 1955, p. 98, Kiyomasu II no. 23.

This is from the play *Hatsu-goyomi akinai Soga*, performed at the Nakamura Theatre from the New Year, 1732. The first part of the programme was the customary New Year play about the Soga brothers (see cat. 33). In the second part, set in the contemporary world, Danjūrō II is recorded as playing the role of Kenka-ya Goroemon and Segawa Kikunojō that of Osen, his wife.[1] Kikunojō had moved to Edo from Kansai in 1730 and in an actor critique of the following year was already ranked joint top performer of young female roles. The scene depicted here shows Kikunojō as a typical tradesman's wife, wearing a head-cloth to protect her hair and a cord round her neck to pull back her sleeves from her work. She rolls out dough to make cakes, and in the background is a large metal cauldron above a hearth for cooking rice. The name of the business, 'Kenka-ya' (Fight Shop), appears on the curtain behind her. Details of the roles are not known, but Danjūrō II cuts a dandyish figure in striped kimono and elegant *haori* jacket. Bearing in mind the name of his business, we may surmise that his character was a blunt, combative Edo tradesman.[2] TTC

91
Torii Kiyonobu II
The Actor Ichikawa Ebizō II as Shinozuka Gorō

11th month, 1742

ARTIST'S SIGNATURE: 'Torii Kiyonobu hitsu' (Brush of Torii Kiyonobu)

PUBLISHER: 'Hanmoto Murata-ya' (Murata-ya, publisher) with publisher's mark

woodblock, *hosoban, beni-e, urushi-e* with brass filings, 31.7 × 15.2 cm

REPRODUCED: *Ukiyo-e shūka*, vol. 1, no. 83

William Sturgis Bigelow Collection, 1911

11.13217

As the inscription at the top right records, this print was issued to mark the return to Edo of Ichikawa Ebizō II (the former Danjūrō II) in the eleventh month, 1742, after a year spent in Osaka. This was Ebizō II's only trip to Kamigata. His triple roles of Kumedera Danjō, Narukami and Fudō, performed at the Sadoshima Theatre from the first to the seventh month, 1742, were a triumph and he was paid the unprecedented salary of 2,000 *ryō* for the season's work.[1] His son Danjūrō III (1721–42) was sent home early to Edo because of illness. Ebizō II was acting onstage on the sixth day of the third month, 1742, when he heard the tragic news that Danjūrō III had died. Cancelling performances for only one day, he continued to act in Osaka until the ninth month.

The opening-of-the-season (*kaomise*) performance at Edo's Kawarazaki Theatre in the eleventh month, 1742, was entitled *Gaijin Taihei-ki*. In the first part of the programme Ebizō II played Hata Rokurōzaemon in a version of *Chronicle of the Great Peace* (*Taihei-ki*), a famous historical military tale set in the 14th century. In the second part he played Shinozuka no Gorō. An actor critique of the following spring described how he wore a *sumi-kazura* wig and performed in *aragoto* style, crushing an entire enemy host with a giant anchor.[2] An illustration in the critique shows a ship with a large anchor coming onstage: its sail displays the combined triple rice-measure (*mimasu*) and lobster crests of Ebizō II.[3]

Two-colour woodblock printing in red and green (*benizuri-e*) had been used in a picture calendar by Okumura Masanobu for the New Year of 1742 (Royal Ontario Museum, Toronto)[4] and in *hosoban* actor prints by Kiyomasu II and Kiyonobu II from, respectively, the fourth and seventh months of that year.[5] The present print must therefore be one of the last done in what had become the old-fashioned techniques of hand-applied colours (*beni-e*), glue on areas of black in imitation of lacquer (*urushi-e*) and sprinkled brass filings. TTC

1 Kominz 1997, p. 104.

2 *Kabuki hyōban-ki II*, vol. 2, p. 232.

3 Ibid., p. 239.

4 Toronto 1975, no. 33.

5 Mutō 1999, p. 18, n. 18.

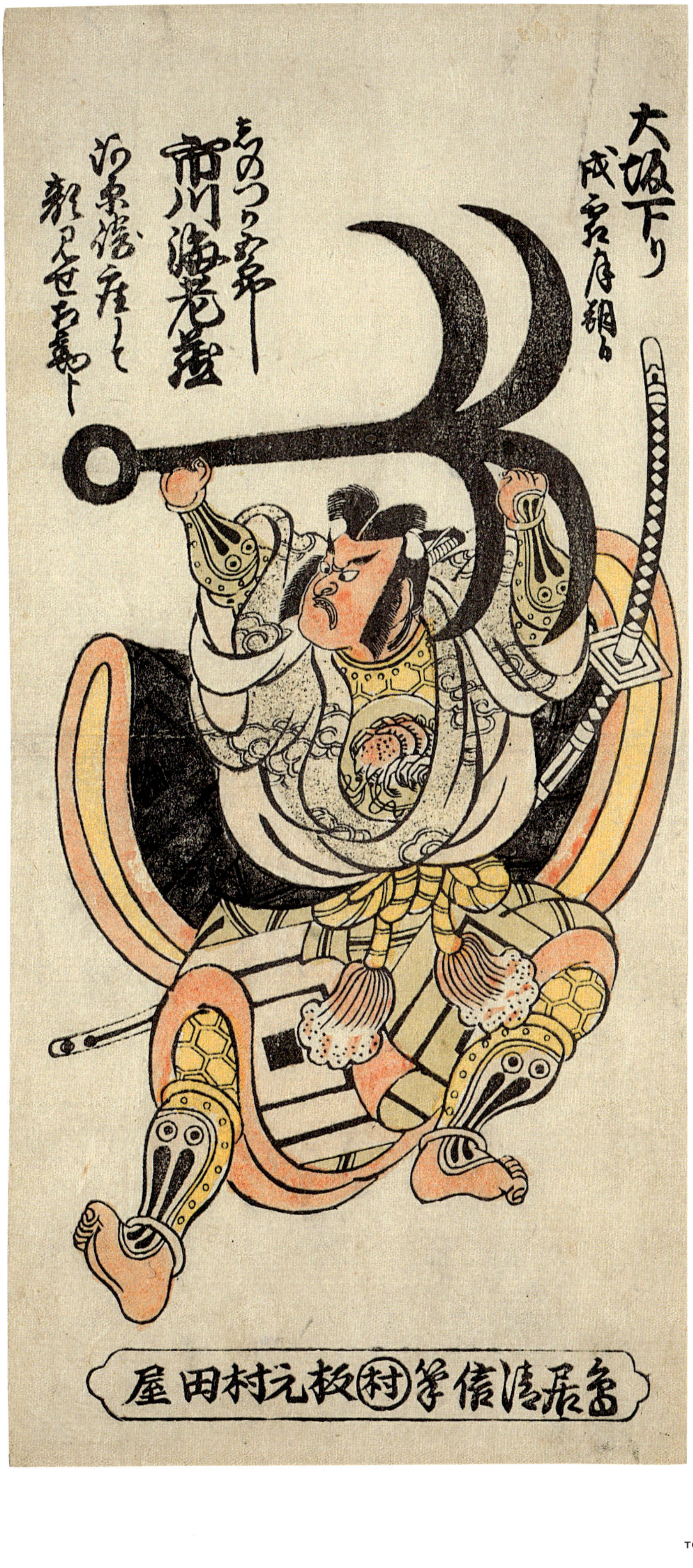
大坂下り
市川海老蔵
鳥居清信筆 村 板元村田屋

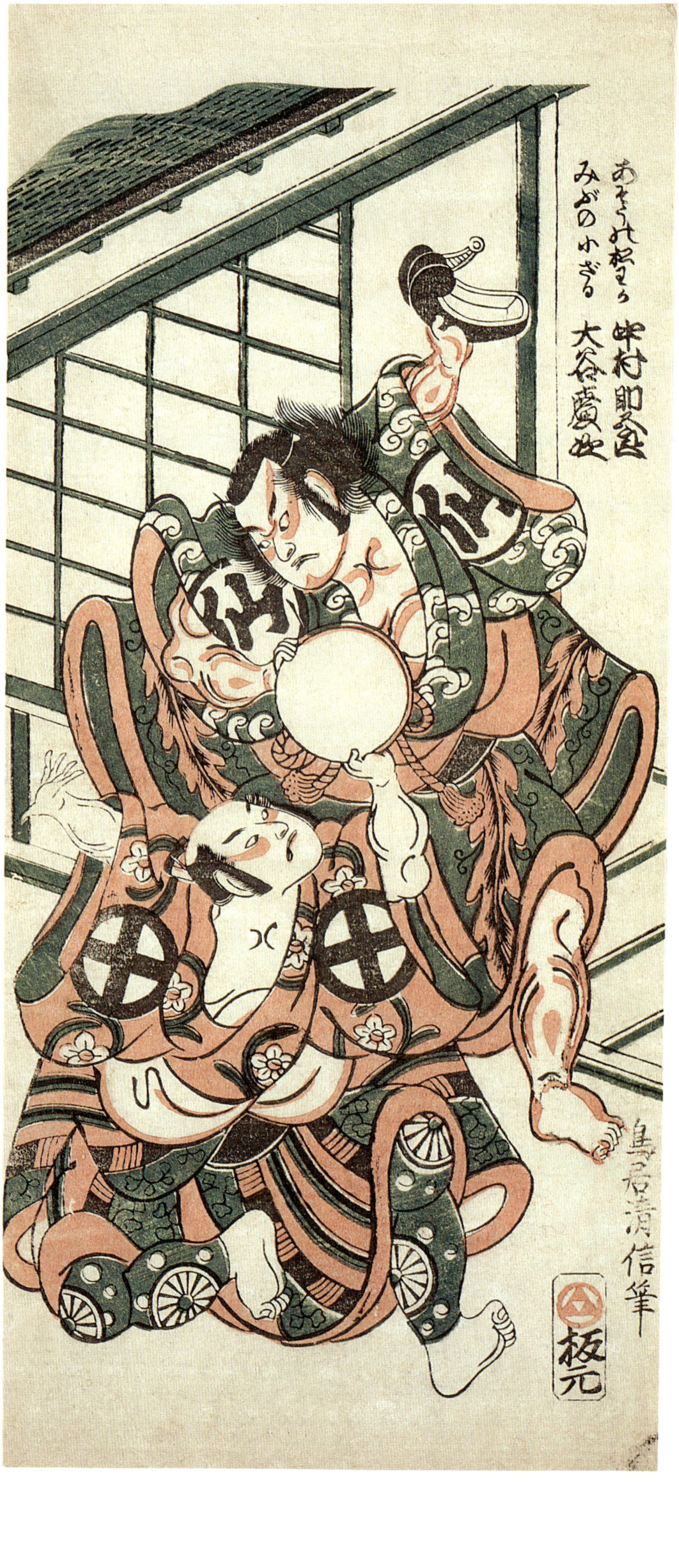

中村助五郎
大谷廣次
鳥居清信筆
板元

92
Torii Kiyonobu II
The Actors Nakamura Sukegorō as Asō no Matsuwaka and Ōtani Hiroji II as Mibu no Kozaru

early 1750s

ARTIST'S SIGNATURE: 'Torii Kiyonobu hitsu' (Brush of Torii Kiyonobu)

PUBLISHER: mark of Urokogata-ya, 'hanmoto' (publisher)

woodblock, *hosoban, benizuri-e* (2-colour), 31.5 × 14.5 cm

William Sturgis Bigelow Collection, 1911

11.13241

Nakamura Sukegorō as Asō no Matsuwaka (right) brandishes a metal stirrup in the air and engages in a tug-of-war with Ōtani Hiroji II as Mibu no Kozaru (left) for possession of a mirror. This muscular *aragoto* scene of confrontation takes place in the corner of a room that opens onto a veranda. Both men have shrugged off the top part of their outer robes, the sleeves of which hang down behind them, lending bulk to their stage presence. Sukegorō's robes are decorated with patterns of waves and phoenix tails (?), Hiroji's with narcissus and decorative blinds (?). Although the roles are named on the print, known theatrical records do not permit the play to be identified.[1]

After Hiroji II succeeded to that name in 1748 the two actors frequently played opposite one another at the Nakamura and Ichimura Theatres until Hiroji II retired in 1757. The print may have been issued in advance of a performance, before the roles had been fixed.

The two printed colours are notably well preserved, their freshness unimpaired by fading. TTC

1 A note in pencil on the old mount gives the play as *Hatsu-hana Sumida-gawa*, performed at the Ichimura Theatre from the second month, 1751. However, on that occasion Hiroji II is recorded as playing the *tachi-yaku* role of Yamada Minbuzaemon to Nakamura Sukegorō's villainous Shihei, an entertainer (*taiko-mochi*).

93

Torii Kiyonobu II

The Actor Nakamura Sukegorō as Katō Arajirō

11th month, 1754

ARTIST'S SIGNATURE: 'Torii Kiyonobu hitsu' (Brush of Torii Kiyonobu)

PUBLISHER: mark of Urokogata-ya, 'hanmoto' (publisher)

woodblock, *hosoban, benizuri-e* (2-colour), 30.4 × 14.4 cm

William Sturgis Bigelow Collection, 1911

11.13242

The *kaomise* play at the Nakamura Theatre in the eleventh month, 1754, was *Miura no Ōsuke bumon no kotobuki*, which, as was the custom, began as a historical piece, set in the world of the late 12th-century Genpei wars. This play was a vehicle to launch the new Ichikawa Danjūrō IV: on this occasion Matsumoto Kōshirō II acceded to the Danjūrō name, which had been in abeyance since the premature death of 21-year-old Danjūrō III in 1742 (see cat. 91). Danjūrō III's father, Ebizō II (formerly Danjūrō II), also appeared, to oversee the transition to his adopted successor.

The actor critique published at the following New Year, *Yakusha kezuri kake*, describes the scene depicted here. Sukegorō, in the role of Katō Arajirō, sets out in the snow to collect bamboo shoots for his mother.[1] This is a reworking of one of the classical Chinese 'Twenty-four Paragons of Filial Piety' in which Meng Zong (*Jap.* Mōsō) went out in the dead of winter to dig succulent bamboo shoots to delight his aged parents. Such a parallel would not have been lost on the audience and provided the pretext for a seasonal snow scene. What Katō Arajirō actually dug up was not bamboo shoots but, to his extreme delight, a white flag. The white flag was the battle standard of the Genji (Minamoto) clan, and the loss, theft or discovery of such precious military heirlooms was one of the main plot mechanisms of historical kabuki plays. Here, the flag has apparently been safely preserved in a luxurious lacquer box, and the actor, wearing a straw raincoat over his kimono, strikes a wonderfully stylised pose of surprise. Casting aside his spade, he simultaneously readies his sword against any possible threat associated with the mystery box, clamps a fist to his jaw, bends one muscular leg while stretching out the other and glares resolutely at the box.

The red and green of the two-colour print are remarkably fresh and set off to good advantage by the snow on the ground and on the leaves of the bamboo grove. TTC

1 *Kabuki hyōban-ki II*, vol. 5, p. 216.

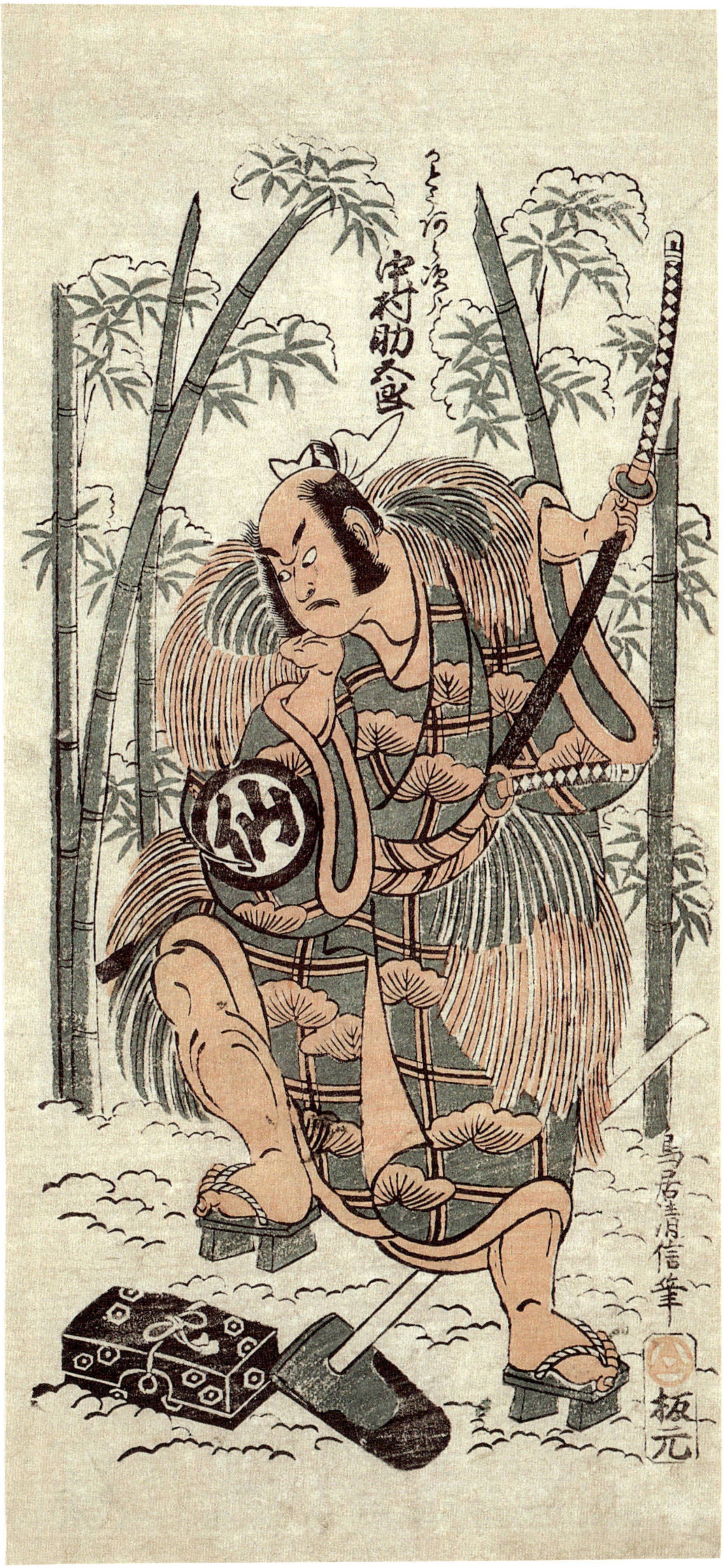
中村助五郎
鳥居清信筆
板元

94
Torii Kiyomasu II
The Actor Matsushima Hyōtarō

1724–5 (11th month, 1724?)

ARTIST'S SIGNATURE: 'Torii Kiyomasu hitsu' (Brush of Torii Kiyomasu)

PUBLISHER: 'Ise-ya'

woodblock, *hosoban*, *beni-e* with brass filings, 30.1 × 16.4 cm

REPRODUCED: *Ukiyo-e shūka*, vol. 1, no. 86

William Sturgis Bigelow Collection, 1911

11.13262

Matsushima Hyōtarō was a leading actor of young female roles in Osaka who in 1723–4 became a leader of his own troupe (*zamoto*). Just after this, in the eleventh month, 1724, he made his only visit to Edo, staying for less than one year. The role shown here has not been identified conclusively, but the print was most probably issued to celebrate Hyōtarō's arrival in Edo. The *kaomise* performance at the Ichimura Theatre in the eleventh month, 1724, was *Bankoku Taihei-ki*, one of many plays based on the military struggles of the 14th century as first recorded in *Chronicle of the Great Peace* (*Taihei-ki*). In this, his Edo debut, Hyōtarō played first Shima no Senzai, probably a courtesan role (cat. 116), then an 'imposter' Kōtō no Naishi. (The real Kōtō no Naishi, played by Sodesaki Miwano, was the wife of the warrior Nitta no Yoshisada.) The depiction of Hyōtarō here, holding aloft a helmet in front of a screen painted with plum and bamboo, is certainly consistent with the role of a samurai woman of rank: the hair is worn down the back in a single ponytail tied at the end with a red scarf and the surcoat (*uchikake*) bears a design of court blinds and trailing leaves. During the performance Hyōtarō is recorded as wielding a halberd (*naginata*) to scatter a gang of enemy forces.[1] TTC

1 *Kabuki hyōban-ki I*, vol. 9, p. 52, reproduced p. 53.

95
Torii Kiyomasu II
The Actors Yamashita Kamematsu as Ono no Komachi and Ogino Isaburō as Hannya Gorō

1733 (?)

ARTIST'S SIGNATURE: 'Torii Kiyomasu hitsu' (Brush of Torii Kiyomasu)

PUBLISHER: 'Ningyōchō-dōri Hirano-ya hanmoto' (Hirano-ya, publisher at Nigyōchō-dōri) with publisher's mark

woodblock, *hosoban*, *beni-e*, *urushi-e* with brass filings, 32 × 15.2 cm

William Sturgis Bigelow Collection, 1911

11.13300

The actor Yamashita Kamematsu poses in voluminous, multi-coloured 'twelve-layered court robes' (*jūni-hitoe*) as the great 9th-century female poet Ono no Komachi holding a poem-card. Behind Komachi, next to her court carriage, appears Ogino Isaburō as Hannya Gorō, wearing a large travelling hat of woven straw and a straw raincoat (*mino*). The red face makeup and *sumi-maegami* wig, with long bands at the front, indicate a young male lead (*waka-tachiyaku*). Many plays were set in the world (*sekai*) of Komachi and her fellow Six Poet Immortals (*rokkasen*), but the plot illustrated here is not known.

The actors appeared together at the Nakamura Theatre from 1732/11 until some time in mid-1735, when Kamematsu left Edo to tour the provinces. The crest worn here by Kamematsu – a plum blossom under crossed canes of bamboo – is recorded only in the actor critique *Yakusha jiguchi-guruma* (1733/2)[1] and was probably used by him only for a short time. The play is most likely *Ura-wakami iroha Komachi*, performed at the Nakamura Theatre in 1733.[2] TTC

1 *Kabuki hyōban-ki I*, vol. 10, p. 458.

2 The month of the performance is not known; the correct title derives from the playbill (*banzuke*). Private communication from Mutō Junko.

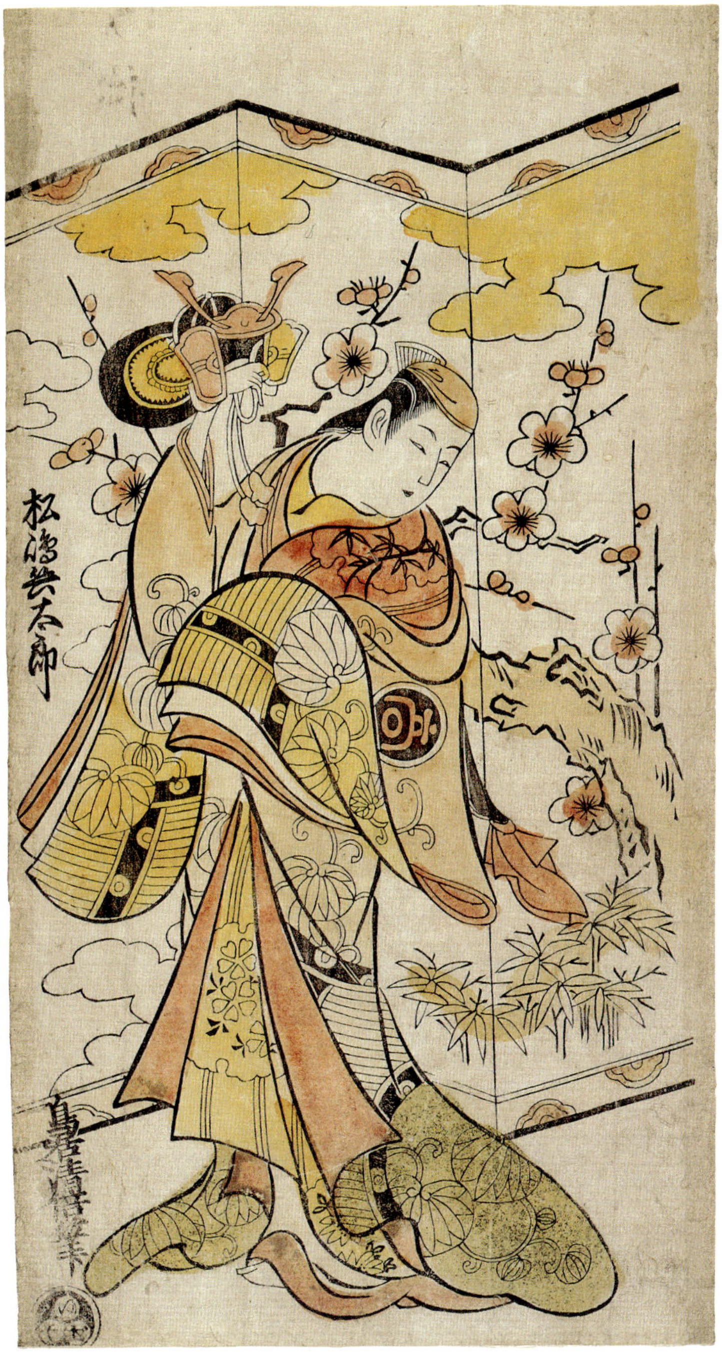

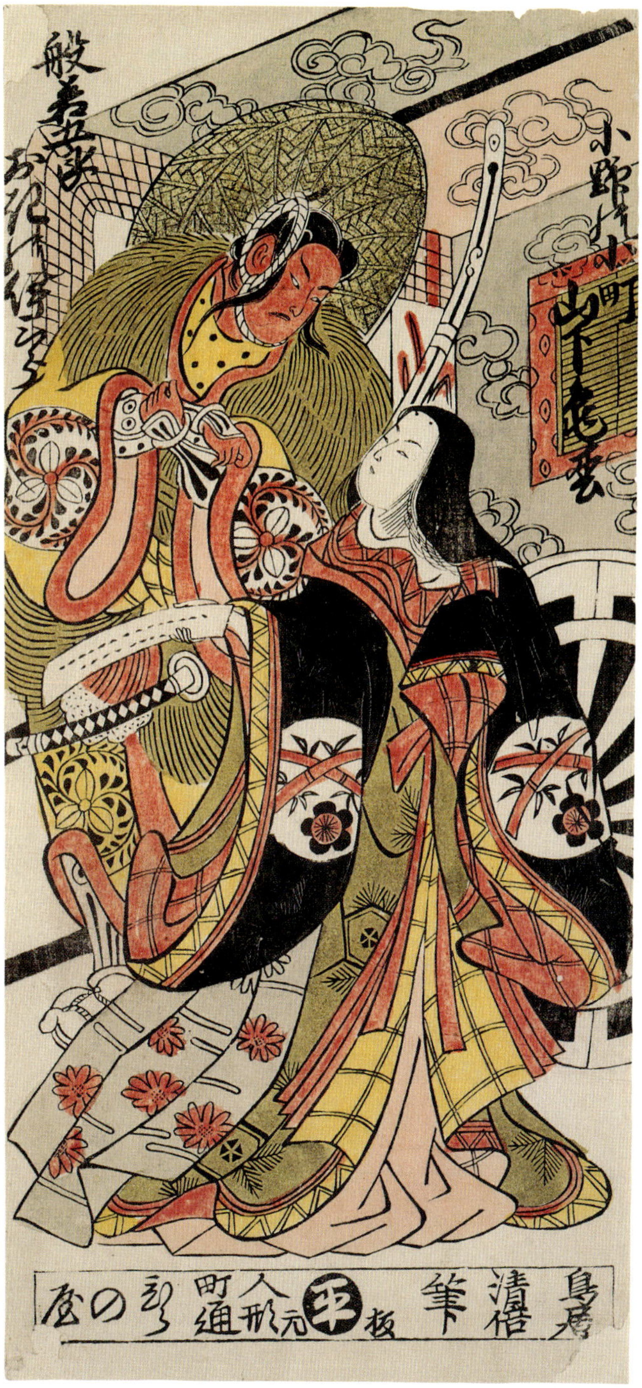

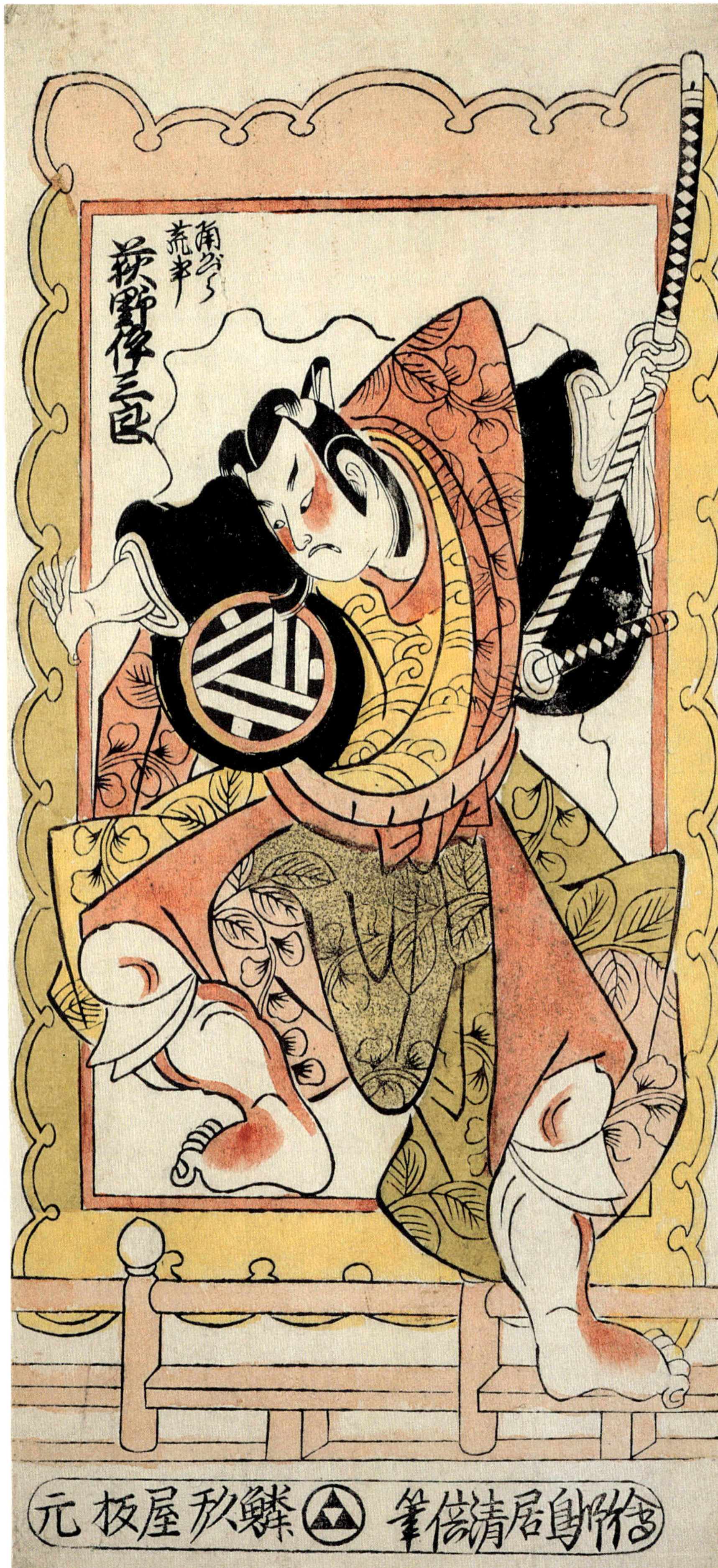

96
Torii Kiyomasu II
The Actor Ogino Isaburō as Yamagami Gennai

11th month, 1734

ARTIST'S SIGNATURE: 'Eshi Torii Kiyomasu hitsu' (Brush of the picture master Torii Kiyomasu)

PUBLISHER: 'Urokogata-ya hanmoto' (Urokogata-ya, publisher) with publisher's mark

woodblock, *hosoban*, *beni-e*, *urushi-e* with brass filings, 32 × 15 cm

William Sturgis Bigelow Collection, 1911

11.13297

1 *Kabuki hyōban-ki I*, vol. 10, p. 620.

Kyō-ganoko setchū no tama-tori, performed at the Nakamura Theatre as the *kaomise* play in the eleventh month, 1734, was a version of the struggle between Fujiwara no Kamatari and Minister Iruka, a story based on historical events of the 7th century. This print records the first time that 31-year-old Ogino Isaburō acted a role in the 'rough' style (*aragoto* – he had previously played young male [*wakashu-gata*] parts). He is shown in the *sumi-kazura* wig typical of *aragoto* roles, which included Soga no Gorō as made famous by Danjūrō II, and a critique of the following year praised Isaburō's success in imitating the style of that actor. It also noted that this marked only a 'partial' coming-of-age (*han-genpuku*, i.e. a half switch to male-lead roles), and in fact Isaburō continued to play young male and even young female roles for the rest of his career.

The critique describes the scene depicted here, in which Isaburō took the role of Yamagami Gennai. Apparently, he burst out of a framed picture (probably a votive plaque at a shrine) to rescue the courtesan Kitsuji no Wakamurasaki (played by Sanjō Kantarō II) who, pretending blindness, was about to be cast off a high building into a vat of fire.[1] Grasping the hilt of his sword, Yamagami Gennai has indeed leapt from within a large picture frame – where he must have been feigning a painted figure – and stands with one foot on the railing of the (shrine?) building and the other on the frame while looking down fiercely and splaying his fingers in anger.

The remarkably well preserved hand-colouring consists of fresh pink, red, yellow and lime green, the front of the *hakama* trousers enlivened with brass filings and the sleeves of the black kimono painted over with glue in imitation of the appearance of black lacquer (*urushi-e*). TTC

97
Torii Kiyomasu II
The Actor Sawamura Sōjūrō as Ōgishi Kunai

3rd month, 1735

ARTIST'S SIGNATURE: 'Eshi Torii Kiyomasu hitsu' (Brush of the picture master Torii Kiyomasu)

PUBLISHER: 'Urokogata-ya hanmoto' (Urokogata-ya, publisher) with publisher's mark

woodblock, *hosoban, beni-e, urushi-e* with brass filings, 32.2 × 15.1 cm

William Sturgis Bigelow Collection, 1911

11.13302

Sawamura Sōjūrō is seated on a bench beneath a willow. He wears the mop cap of a patron visiting pleasure quarters and holds an open fan over his head. On the bench beside him is a small hand drum and drumsticks. His stylish *kosode* is decorated with a bold design of banana leaves, his long *haori* jacket with plovers and waves. Three other characters peer over the wall behind, which is topped with bamboo spikes. Sōjūrō's role has been identified as that of Ōgishi Kunai in the play *Yoroi-zakura kokyō no nishiki*, performed at the Nakamura Theatre in the third month, 1735.[1] This was a version of the famous 'Akō Vendetta' (*Chūshingura*) and Sōjūrō's role corresponded to the hero of the historical incident, Ōboshi Yuranosuke. (The role was also called Ōgishi Kurando or Ōboshi Kuranosuke in later kabuki versions.) This was apparently the first time Sōjūrō interpreted the role. The scene likely takes place in the Gion pleasure quarter in Kyoto, where Ōgishi is feigning a life of dissolute pleasure-seeking in order to lull his enemies into a false sense of security. The three actors looking over the wall, and their probable roles, are, from right to left: Ōtani Fukutarō (later Ryūzaemon II) as the *yakko* Tomohachi, Nakamura Katsujūrō as O-chō, daughter of Kōno Kurozaemon, and Nakamura Kichizō as Tōtarō, son of Ōgishi Kunai. Kichizō and Fukutarō played child roles at the Nakamura Theatre from 1732/11 and 1733/11, respectively; Katsujūrō joined them in young woman roles from 1733/11.

Mutō Junko has discussed the use of the so-called 'sash-shaped' cartouche (*obi-gata hyōki*) that often appears across the bottom of *hosoban* prints from *c.* 1723 onwards.[2] Urokogata-ya, the publisher in the present instance, does not seem to have begun employing this device until *c.* 1728. Around this time he also appears to have established a special relationship with the up-and-coming artist Kiyomasu II. Mutō has identified four different kinds of sash-shaped cartouche on prints issued by Urokogata-ya and dated the use of each one. The form seen here, in which some of the characters are written in a slightly abbreviated style, was employed *c.* 1728–35. TTC

1 I am grateful to Mutō Junko for suggesting this identification (private correspondence).

2 Mutō 1997, esp. pp. 12, 16.

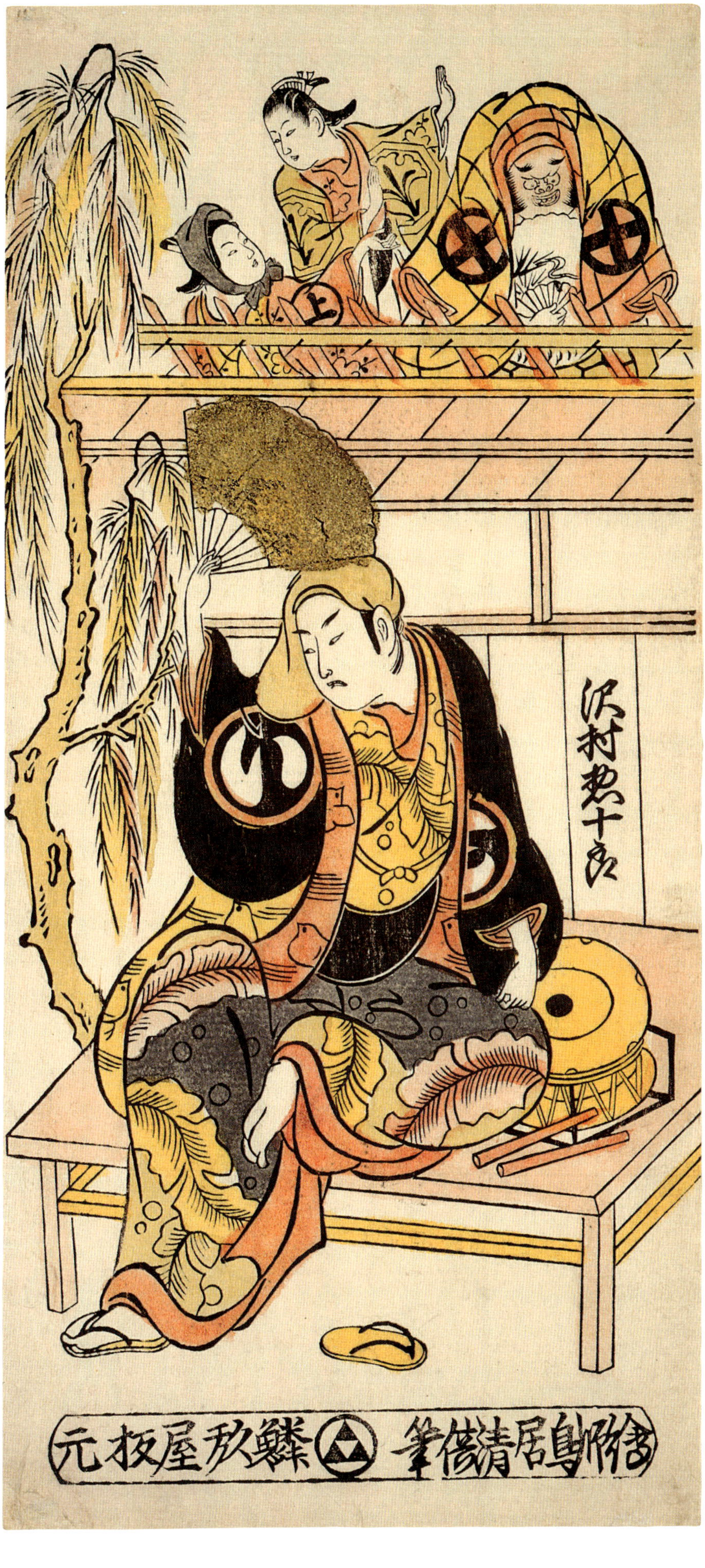

98
Torii Kiyomasu II
The Actor Ichimura Uzaemon VIII, 'Dandyish Street-tough Style' (Tanzen-fū)

c. 1737–42 (?)

ARTIST'S SIGNATURE: 'Eshi Torii Kiyomasu hitsu' (Brush of the picture master Torii Kiyomasu)

ARTIST'S SEAL: 'Kiyomasu'

PUBLISHER: 'Motohama-chō Iga-ya han' (Published by Iga-ya at Motohama-chō) with publisher's mark

woodblock, *hosoban, beni-e*, 29.9 × 15.5 cm

REPRODUCED: *Ukiyo-e shūka*, vol. 1, no. 106

William Sturgis Bigelow Collection, 1911

11.13276

The word *tanzen* in the title derives from the swagger and fashions of dandyish 17th-century street toughs who visited bathhouse girls. The style was taken into kabuki and used by male leads for ostentatious entries and in certain dance skits. Uzaemon VIII's hairstyle here, with unshaven pate, and his double swords worn high under the arm are appropriate to this style. Uzaemon VIII (1698–1762) was about 40 at the time this print was issued. He had acceded to the name Ichimura Takenojō IV, manager of the troupe (*zamoto* or *tayū-moto*), at the age of four – even before his first stage appearance, at the New Year, 1705. For many years he combined his responsibilities as *zamoto* of the Ichimura Theatre with acting in a wide variety of young man (*wakashu-gata*), young woman (*wakaonna-gata*) and male lead (*tachi-yaku*) roles. He took the name Uzaemon VIII in the eleventh month, 1736.

Mutō Junko has indicated that this form of the publisher Iga-ya's 'sash-shaped' cartouche (*obi-gata hyōki*), which includes the name of the artist, was used until about the Genbun era (1736–41).[1] Money Hickman has noted that Uzaemon VIII performed a dance skit in *tanzen* style to great acclaim in the seventh month, 1739, suggesting that this might be the performance recorded here.[2] Uzaemon VIII will have performed many *tanzen* roles, however, and it is perhaps preferable not to date the present design so precisely until it has been established whether it belongs to a series of similar bust portraits in fan-shaped borders. Whatever the role depicted, this is a particularly early instance of a close-up portrait of a kabuki actor, a form that was eventually to lead to more mimetic actor portraits (*nigao-e*).

Kiyomasu II designed a half-length portrait of another, as yet unidentified *onnagata* actor inside a fan shape at around this time,[3] as well as a half-length portrait (not inside a fan) of Ichikawa Danjūrō II performing 'Arrow-sharpening Gorō' (Ya-no-ne Gorō).[4] An unsigned half-length portrait in a fan border, titled *'Style of a Male Prostitute of Today' (Ima no kagema fū)*, shows an unidentified young trainee kabuki actor.[5] A calendar print for 1737 designed by Nishimura Shigenaga displays a half-length portrait of the Chinese hero Kan U (not an actor) inside a fan shape.[6] Apparently, the Boston collection also contains a half-length portrait in a fan-shaped border by Kiyonobu II of Segawa Kikunojō I in his hit role of Katsuragi in the play *Muken no kane*, performed at the Ichimura Theatre in the spring of 1742.[7] Only the last two of these provide precise dates for determining the parameters of the period during which half-length portraits inside fan shapes were in vogue, i.e. *c.* 1737–42. TTC

1 Private communication.

2 *Ukiyo-e shūka*, vol. 1, no. 106 (commentary by Money Hickman); *Kabuki nenpyō*, vol. 2, p. 303.

3 Philadelphia 1983, no. 12. The print, published by Ise-ya, has a sash-shaped cartouche. Mutō Junko has found a sash-shaped cartouche on Ise-ya prints only in the year 1745. Mutō 1997, p. 12.

4 *Ukiyo-e taisei*, vol. 2, no. 98.

5 Honolulu 1980, p. 306, unsigned no. 40.

6 Pulverer Collection, Cologne; Osaka 1990, no. 1-16.

7 *Ukiyo-e shūka*, vol. 1, no. 106 (commentary by Money Hickman).

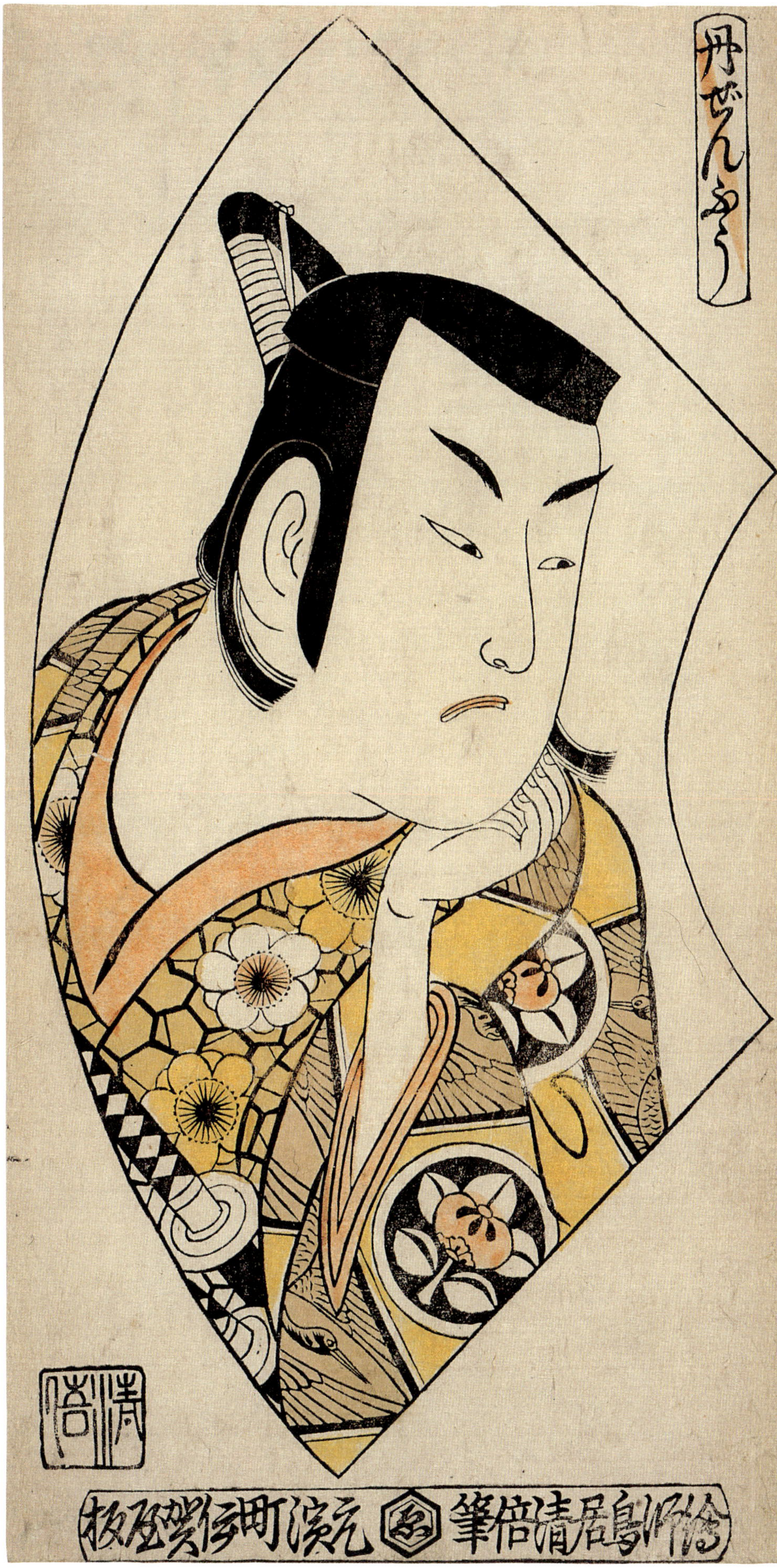

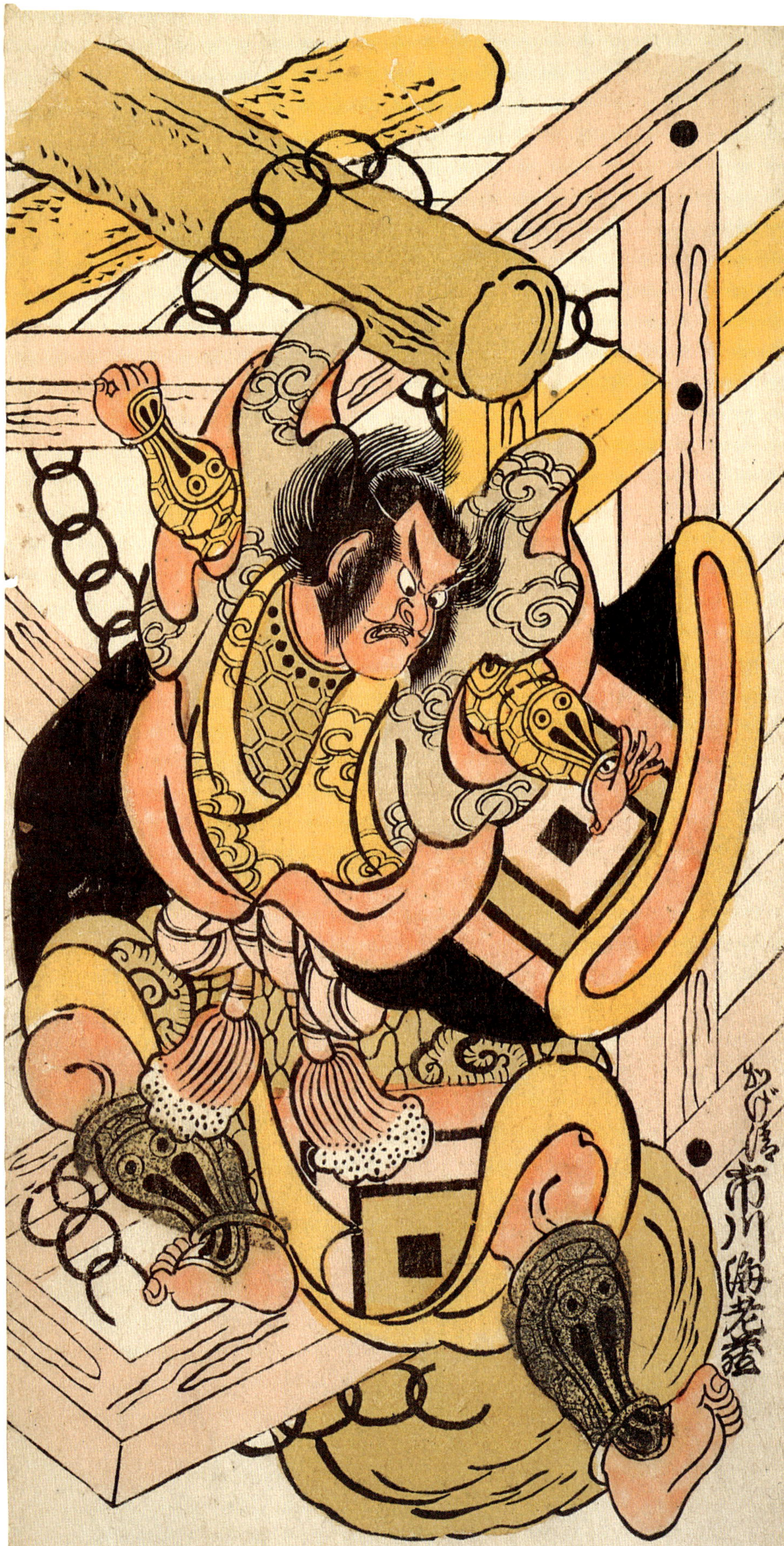
かげ清
市川海老蔵

99
Torii Kiyomasu II
The Actor Ichikawa Ebizō II as Kagekiyo

7th–10th month, 1739 (?)

ARTIST'S SIGNATURE: 'Eshi Torii Kiyomasu hitsu' (Brush of the picture master Torii Kiyomasu)

PUBLISHER: 'Urokogata-ya hanmoto' (Urokogata-ya, publisher) with publisher's mark

woodblock, *hosoban, beni-e, urushi-e* with brass filings, 29.9 × 15.1 cm

William Sturgis Bigelow Collection, 1911

11.13296

1 Iizuka 1926, p. 87.

2 Mutō 1997, p. 16.

3 *Kabuki hyōban-ki II*, vol. 1, p. 399.

Ebizō II appears as 'Jail-break Kagekiyo' (*rō-yaburi no Kagekiyo*), a quintessentially 'rough' (*aragoto*) role. Shrugging off both sleeves of his padded outer robe and stretching his arms and legs, the actor strikes a fierce stage pose (*mie*) having smashed his way out of the wooden bars and chains – presumably with the large rock that now lies under his feet. This scene was the origin of the later play *Kagekiyo*, still performed today as one of the 'Eighteen Great Hits' (*kabuki jūhachi-ban*) associated with the Ichikawa Danjūrō lineage. Kagekiyo, a surviving retainer of the Taira clan, has been imprisoned in Kamakura by the enemy Minamoto clan. When the Minamoto General Shigetada also captures Kagekiyo's wife, Akoya, and daughter Hitomaru and subjects them to torture, he breaks out of his prison in fury.[1]

The publisher Urokogata-ya is thought to have used a 'sash-shaped cartouche' (*obi-gata hyōki*) in this style from 1737 to 1742.[2] During these years Ebizō II performed Kagekiyo at least four times, sometimes for periods of many months. The four performances were:

1. *Uruu-zuki ninin Kagekiyo*, Kawarazaki Theatre, 1737/11. Danzō and Ebizō played both Kagekiyo and Hatakeyama Shōji Shigetada, hence the play title 'Two Kagekiyos'.

2. *Hatsu motoyui kayou Soga*, Ichimura Theatre, 1739/1. Ebizō II continued to play Kagekiyo almost all year, to 1739/10.

3. *Kasane gedatsu no hachisuba*, Ichimura Theatre, 1739/7. An actor critique of the following year, *Yakusha ehō mairi* (1740/1), described the success: 'He [Ebizō II] was Kagekiyo, but took the guise of Yoemon of Hanyū Village. He was captured alive by Nitan no Shirō and his subsequent jail-break was a great hit. The full houses continued until the 11th day of the tenth month and this is probably the best-received performance he has given in the last twenty-five years'.[3]

4. *Na-no-hana akebono Soga*, Nakamura Theatre, 1741/1.

In view of the specific reference to the jail-break scene and the great hit that it scored, it seems very likely that Kiyomasu II's print was issued during the three-month run of *Kasane gedatsu no hachisuba*. TTC

100

Torii Kiyomasu II

The Actor Ichikawa Ebizō II as Raigō Ajari of Mii Temple

8th month, 1741

ARTIST'S SIGNATURE: 'Eshi Torii Kiyomasu hitsu' (Brush of the picture master Torii Kiyomasu)

PUBLISHER: 'Urokogata-ya hanmoto' (Urokogata-ya, publisher) with publisher's mark

woodblock, *hosoban, beni-e, urushi-e*, 29.8 × 14.3 cm

REPRODUCED: *Ukiyo-e shūka*, vol. 1, no. 28

William Sturgis Bigelow Collection, 1911

11.13298

In the tenth month, 1741, Ichikawa Ebizō II left Edo for Osaka, where he was to stay for a triumphal year-long tour, tragically marred by the premature death of his son Danjūrō III (see cat. 91). His farewell performance in Edo was *Uruoi Seiwa Genji*, staged at the Nakamura Theatre in the eighth month, when the actor performed many different roles. A playbill (*banzuke*) issued at the time lists these as: Raigō Ajari, Ghost of Taira no Masakado, Abe no Kiyoaki, Aunt of [Watanabe no] Tsuna, and Hirai Yasumasa.[1]

Ebizō II's role is given on the print as 'Raigō Ajari of Mii Temple' (Ajari [Sanskrit *ācārya*] is an ecclesiastical title used by monks, particularly of the Tendai sect of Buddhism). Raigō (1004–84) was a historical figure, a Tendai monk at Onjō-ji (Mii-dera) whose prayers are said to have resulted in the birth of a son to Retired Emperor Shirakawa.[2] Yet when the Emperor, fearing the reaction of the monks of the existing ordination temple of Enryaku-ji, refused Raigō's request to establish an ordination platform at Onjō-ji, the monk cast a curse on Shirakawa, locked himself in the Buddha Hall of Onjō-ji and began to fast in protest.[3]

Here Raigō sits before a free-standing screen (*tsuitate*), painted with a landscape of flowing water and autumn grasses, and gazes up at a hanging scroll. The hair growing on what would normally be the shaven head of a monk suggests, perhaps, that he has locked himself away for a considerable time. The hanging scroll shows the actor Tamasawa Saijirō dressed in female court robes and is inscribed 'Kōkiden no e-sugata' (painted portrait of Kōkiden). Two black rats scurry along the top of the screen towards this painting. The exact plot of the performance of 1741/8 is not known, but in a play of 1770 that also featured Raigō he drank poisoned sake, died in agony and was transformed into a horde of rats.[4] This was elaborated from versions included in historical tales such as *Heike mongatari* (Enkyō version), which described how Raigō's spirit was transformed into a giant rat that ate the Buddhist sculptures and sutras of rival Enryaku-ji.[5] In kabuki the female character portrayed in the painting, Kōkiden, is the deceased concubine of Emperor Kazan in plays relating to the legend of 'Shuten-dōji' (The Sake-drinking Boy) and to the world of the four retainers of Minamoto no Yorimasa (Raikō), the Shitennō.[6] *Uruoi Seiwa Genji* seems, in fact, to have been a version of 'Shuten-dōji'.[7] Although the actor Tamasawa Saijirō's role is apparently not recorded on this occasion, he is known to have been performing in the same troupe as Ebizō II at the Nakamura Theatre. TTC

1 Information kindly supplied by Mutō Junko. These roles do not correspond to those given in *Kabuki nenpyō*.

2 Emperors were said to be 'retired' or 'cloistered' (*in*) when they withdrew in favour of one of their offspring in order to exercise power more effectively from behind the throne.

3 *Nihon denki*, s.v. 'Raigō'.

4 Chicago 1994, pp. 144–7, nos. 47–8.

5 *Nihon denki*, s.v. 'Raigō'.

6 Iizuka 1926, pp. 45–6.

7 *Kabuki nenpyō*, vol. 2, p. 342.

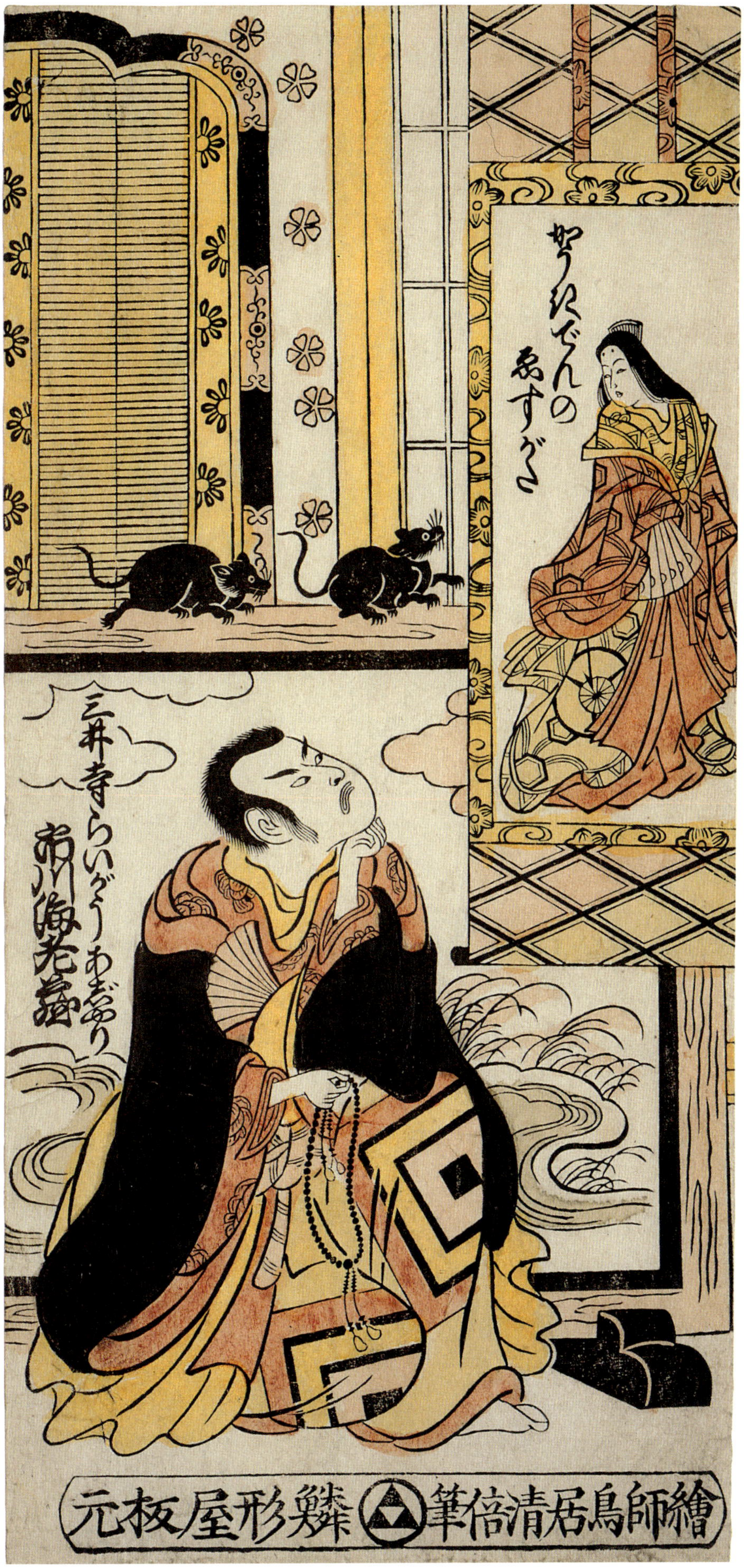
繪師鳥居清倍筆
鱗形屋板元

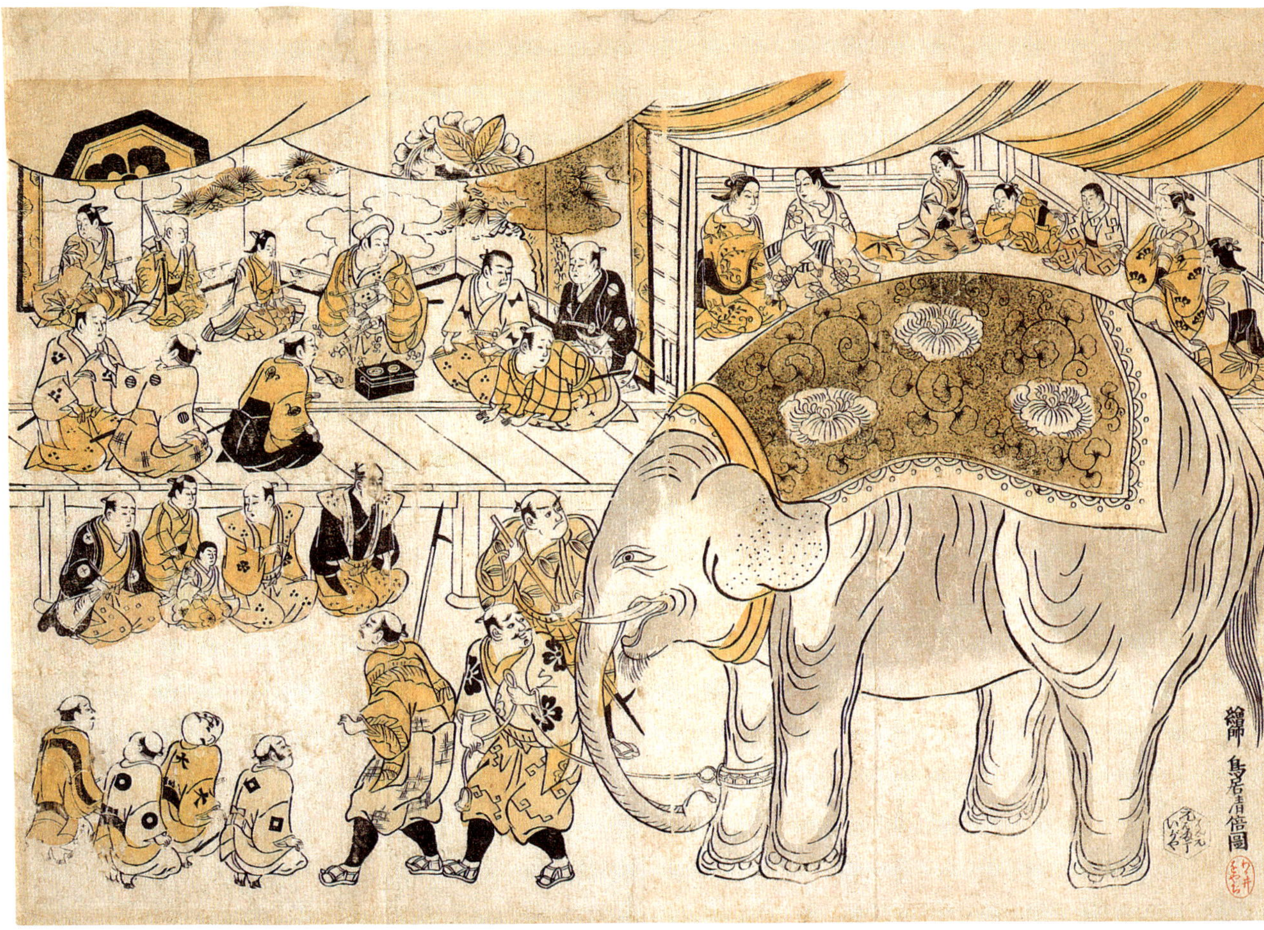
繪師 鳥居清倍圖

101

Torii Kiyomasu II

The Arrival of the Elephant

1729

ARTIST'S SIGNATURE: 'Eshi Torii Kiyomasu zu' (Drawn by the picture master Torii Kiyomasu)

PUBLISHER: 'hanmoto Motohama-chō Iga-ya' (The publisher Iga-ya, at Motohama-chō)

COLLECTOR'S SEAL: 'Wakai oyaji' (Wakai Kenzaburō)

woodblock, horizontal *ōban*, hand-colouring, *urushi-e* with brass filings, 32.8 × 47 cm

OTHER IMPRESSION: (*Ukiyo-e taisei*, vol. 2, no. 303)

Asiatic Curator's Fund, 1958

58.343

In 1728 two elephants, a male and a female, were brought to Nagasaki by a Vietnamese ship captain.[1] In the fourth month of 1729 the male was taken to Emperor Nakamikado in Kyoto and, in the following month, to Edo, where it was paraded through the streets and led to Shogun Tokugawa Yoshimune. Like many of his contemporaries, Yoshimune had studied a Dutch edition of an old zoological treatise titled *Truthful Description of Quadrupeds* (published 1660) and become interested in exotic animals.[2] He encouraged the Dutch in Nagasaki to import a great variety of rare animals and birds, as well as Western horses and dogs for hunting and breeding.

The audience looking at the elephant is seated on raised platforms decorated with hangings. The platform is divided into two sections, one for men, one for women and young children. Most of the men wear swords and are seated in front of a folding screen with a pine and cloud motif; one man wears a cap and smokes a pipe. Minor officials and attendants are seated below the platform and a few footmen kneel in the foreground. Three elephant handlers, two with goads, lead the elephant by a chain attached to a ring around its leg. Details make the scene appear credible: two of the men hold fans indicating that it may have been a hot summer's day, and the elephant is covered with a decorated cloth, perhaps from South-east Asia or China. A print by Okumura Masanobu of *c.* 1729 shows a keeper riding the elephant, seated on a similarly patterned cloth.[3]

The elephant became a popular public spectacle. Another print by Kiyomasu II shows it engaging with a bear in a tug of war over a pole. This print, and that by Masanobu just mentioned, catered to public interest by including the measurements of the elephant, Kiyomasu also stating that it was six years old.[4] The enterprising caretaker of the stables in the riding grounds of Uneme-ga-hara noticed that government officials found it difficult to take care of the elephant. He therefore applied for and was granted permission to build a number of shops by means of which he could raise funds to feed and house the elephant. The riding grounds soon flourished as an entertainment area.[5]

The elephant proved fascinating to the public and inspired craftsmen to depict it on furnishings, toys and bags. Most people living in 18th-century Japan had never seen an elephant. They knew of these animals' existence from paintings of Fugen (Samantabhadra), the Bodhisattva of Universal Virtue, who was shown seated on a white elephant. However, in such images the elephant was strangely proportioned and endowed with a very short trunk, long lashes and claw-like feet.[6] By comparison, Kiyomasu and Masanobu rendered the elephant more realistically. Although the elephant died sometime in the Kan'en era (1748–51), a picture calendar print (*e-goyomi*) for the year 1765 conceived by and signed 'Minamoto Kaishitsu' (dates unknown) showed the famous animal with its exotic covering.[7] LEV

1 They arrived in the sixth month. *Edo Tokyo nenpyō*, pp. 77–8; *Ukiyo-e jiten*, vol. 2, p. 147.

2 The book was written by a Polish naturalist of Scottish descent called John Jonston (1603–75) and illustrated by Matthieu Merian (1593–1650). Goodman 2000, pp. 36, 59–60; Blussé et al. 2000, p. 64.

3 Higuchi 1977, no. 33.

4 Ibid.; Honolulu 1980, p. 55; Machida 1987, p. 244, no. 262.

5 *Edo-gaku jiten*, p. 45.

6 See, for example, a *sumizuri-e* of *c.* 1715 in Chicago 1955, p. 135, no. 53.

7 Private collection, reproduced in *Genshoku ukiyo-e*, vol. 3, fig. 427; Machida 1999, p. 271, no. 101; and Tokyo 1996, p. 61.

102, 103

Two prints from the series *'Fifty-four Chapters from Tale of Genji'* *(Genji gojūyon-mai no uchi)*

c. 1735

102

ARTIST'S SIGNATURE: 'Yamato gakō Nishimura Shigenaga' (The Yamato painting artisan Nishimura Shigenaga)

ARTIST'S SEAL: 'Shigenaga'

PUBLISHER: 'Beni-e kongen haribako-e rui nashi hanmoto Asakusa mitsuke-mae Ryōgoku-bashi-dōri Dōbō-chō Izumi-ya Gonshirō' (The peerless publisher and originator of *beni-e* and 'needle-box' pictures Izumi-ya Gonshirō, at Dōbō-chō near Ryōgoku at the approach to Asakusa) with publisher's mark

woodblock, horizontal *hosoban*, hand-colouring, metallic filings, colour sprayed over stencils (*fuki-bokashi*) to form decorative designs of the 'long life' (*kotobuki*) character, hand drums and maple leaves, 16.3 × 33.9 cm

William Sturgis Bigelow Collection, 1911

11.19132

103

ARTIST'S SIGNATURE: 'Torii Kiyomasu hitsu' (Brush of Torii Kiyomasu)

PUBLISHER: 'On-haribako byōbu-e fusuma-e – Yamato beni-e kongen hanmoto rui nashi e-zōshi toiya Asakusa mitsuke-mae, Dōbō-chō Izumi-ya Gonshirō' (Elegant designs for [pasting on] 'needle boxes', screens and sliding doors. Izumi-ya Gonshirō of Dōbō-chō, at the approach to Asakusa, inventor of Yamato *beni-e* and peerless wholesale dealer in illustrated books) with publisher's mark

woodblock, horizontal *hosoban*, hand-colouring, metallic filings, colour sprayed over stencils (*fuki-bokashi*) to form decorative designs of opened picnic box and cherry blossom and the *mimasu* (three rice measures) crest, 16.5 × 33.8 cm

William Sturgis Bigelow Collection, 1911

11.13334

Fifty-four Chapters from Tale of Genji was conceived as a series of woodblock prints illustrating each chapter of the classic novel written by Lady Murasaki Shikibu during the Heian period.[1] Each reniform (*suhama*), or folding-fan-shaped, scene was named with a chapter title and corresponding Genji crest.[2] The set was a collaborative work by Nishimura Shigenaga and Torii Kiyomasu II: Shigenaga designed the first 26 prints, Kiyomasu the remaining 28. Although the two artists had slightly different styles when depicting classic subjects (see cat. 104–6), they clearly harmonised their modes of expression for this series. Only 23 of the designs are known, seventeen by Shigenaga, six by Kiyomasu.[3] In commissioning and marketing the series the publisher Izumi-ya may have been competing with the artist–publisher Okumura Masanobu, who *c.* 1730 had issued a similar series in the vertical *hosoban* format.[4] The series was marketed with an inscribed suggestion that the scenes, in a manner widespread with painted fans since the late 16th century, should be cut out and pasted on screens or sliding doors. Another suggestion was to glue the prints on 'needle boxes' (*haribako*), i.e. on the sewing or workboxes that were popular among women and children in the Kyōhō era (1716–36).[5]

Two distinct opinions of *Tale of Genji* existed in the early 18th century. On the one hand, it was viewed as an essential part of a gracious education, the recognised authority on everything courtly and elegant in deportment and poetic sensibility. On the other hand, the tale was condemned as a dangerous, immoral book, suitable as a guide for rakes frequenting pleasure quarters.[6] From 1707 to 1710 Okumura Masanobu, a notable designer of 'parody pictures' (*mitate-e*), wrote and illustrated colloquial versions (*zokuyaku*) of the first eight chapters of *Tale of Genji* in four separate works that were reprinted several times during the first half of the century.[7] These publications, which included courtesan critiques, *kōshoku-bon* and *sharebon* by several other famous writers,[8] served to link courtesans and their accomplishments with the courtly world of Genji.

Many authors and artists were inspired by *Tale of Genji* as an erotic casebook, but Izumi-ya Gonshirō issued a Genji print series that catered to educated townsmen and women wanting renditions of favourite passages. The scenes by Shigenaga and Kiyomasu II are depicted in the traditional Tosa school style, including choice *waka* in stylised clouds. The text of *Tale of Genji* had become accessible to all citizens with the requisite financial means from the second half of the 17th century. Commentaries on the novel, especially *Kogetsushō* (*Lake Moon*, 1675) by Kitamura Kigin (1624–1705), and synopsis books (*kōgai-sho*) written in clear, simple language, such as *Osana Genji* (*Genji for Young People*, 1666) by Nonoguchi Ryūho (1595–1669), which appeared in four editions and a number of pirated versions, had helped fire enthusiasm for the classic.

102
Nishimura Shigenaga
'The Wind in the Pines' (Chapter 18)
(*Matsukaze*)

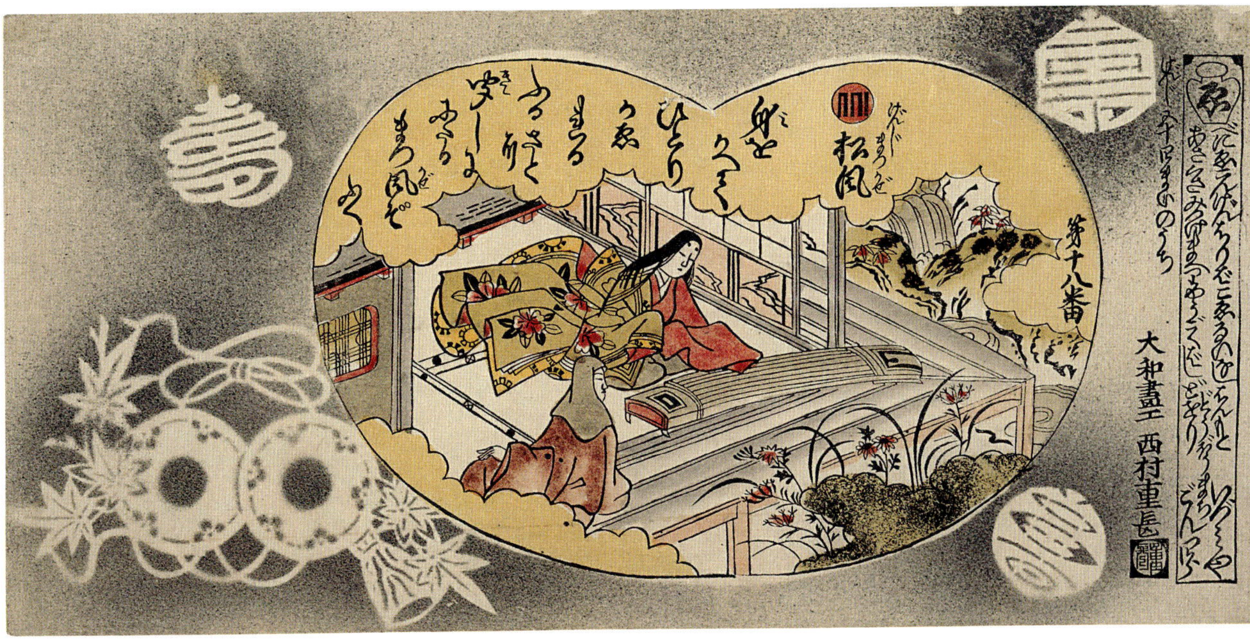

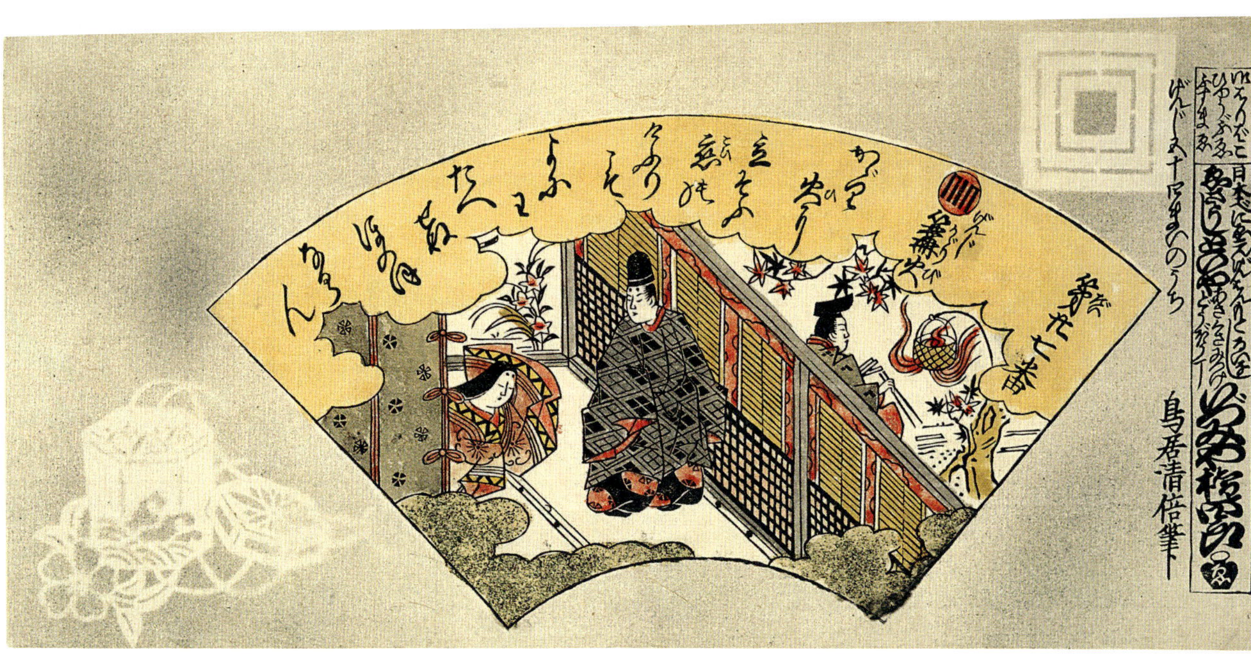

103
Torii Kiyomasu II
'The Flares' (Chapter 27)
(*Kagaribi*)

Nishimura Shigenaga's print (cat. 102) illustrates Chapter 18. When Genji was in exile at the seaside village of Akashi, he had met and courted the so-called Akashi Lady (Akashi-no-ue). Later, after Genji had been reinstated at the Imperial court, the Akashi Lady moved to a family residence in Ōi (Katsura) in the countryside outside Kyoto. The scene in the fan shows the homesick Akashi Lady playing a koto that Genji had given her, accompanied by the wind in the pines. Her mother, who had been resting, comes out to join her daughter and, while looking at the scenery, recites a poem:

Mi o kaete	I returned,
hitori kaereru	as if back alone
furusato ni	in the old village
kikishi ni nitaru	to hear the wind
matsukaze zo fuku	still blowing in the pines.

The Akashi Lady responds:

Furusato ni	I long
mishi yo no tomo o	for those familiar
koiwabite	with the country sounds
saezuru koto o	who listen to my koto,
tare ka wakuran	and understand.[9]

Torii Kiyomasu II's print (cat. 103) illustrates Chapter 27, during which Prince Genji, on a dark, late summer night, gives a koto lesson to Tamakazura, the long-lost daughter of his close friend and rival Tō-no-Chūjō and Lady Yūgao. Guards had lit flares in an iron basket hanging from a tree in the garden but, as Genji prepares to leave, he notices that the flames are low and sends an officer to stir the fires. Feeling paternal as well as romantic feelings towards Tamakazura, Genji tells her that an unlit garden on a moonless night can be frightening. He then composes a poem (quoted in the print) comparing his love to a flame that would never be extinguished:

Kagaribi ni	Flares rise
tachisou koi no	and drift as smoke
keburi koso	in this world my love
yo ni wa taesenu	a flame
honō naruran	that will not be dispersed.

Tamakazura, puzzled by what she finds a strange statement, replies:

Yukue naki	If flares
sora ni kechite yo	and flames of love are linked
kagaribi no	then one might guess
tayori ni taguu	the smoke alike,
keburi to naraba	should vanish in the heavens.[10]

LEV

1 Written in the early 11th century, *Tale of Genji* describes the life and love affairs of Prince Genji. The earliest surviving texts are from the late Heian period (794–1185). There are two famous English translations, by Arthur Waley and Edward G. Seidensticker (Murasaki 1935 and 1980).

2 The Genji crests (Genji *mon*), listed in Lane 1978, p. 224, consist of five short vertical strokes, some connected at the top by crossbars. They were originally used for keeping score in the incense game (*kō-awase*).

3 Cologne 1991, p. 181; Toronto 1975, pp. 34–7, 81–7; Dresden 1995, pp. 26–7; Chicago 1955, p. 191, no. 16; *Ukiyo-e jiten*, vol. 1, p. 344. The Boston Museum possesses seven prints from the series. The other chapters represented are 'Kiritsubo' (1), 'Hahakigi' (2), 'Utsusemi' (3), 'Aoi' (9) and 'Sekiya' (16), all five illustrated by Shigenaga.

4 Toronto 1975, pp. 61–3, nos. 27–8. Examples from another Genji series by Masanobu , in the *yotsugiri* format, are reproduced in Machida 1999, p. 117, nos. 88.1–5.

5 Such prints (*haribako-e*), much in vogue in the Kyōhō era, were designed by Masanobu, Toshinobu, Kiyomasu II, Shigenaga and others. See *Ukiyo-e jiten*, vol. 3, p. 41. Ukiyo-e prints made to be mounted and used as fans had been produced since the end of the 17th century, but few have survived.

6 Explicitly erotic prints became illegal after the enactment of the Kyōhō publishing reforms proclaimed in 1722/11, and the ban was effective for fifteen to twenty years.

7 Masanobu's *mitate-e* series *Genji Monogatari* is reproduced in Chicago 1955, pp. 127–30, nos. 28–39. Under the pseudonym Baiō, Masanobu wrote: *Kōhaku Genji monogatari* (*Red and White Genji Monogatari*, 1707), soon reissued as *Wakagusa Genji monogatari* (*Young Grasses Genji Monogatari*, repr. 1721 and 1738); *Hinazuru Genji* (*Fledgling Crane Genji*, 1708, repr. 1720, 1721, 1727); *Kōhaku Genji* (*Red and White Genji*, 1709); and *Zokkai Genji monogatari* (*The Tale of Genji in Vernacular Interpretation*, 1710).

8 For example, Ihara Saikaku (1642–93). See also *Yoshiwara Genji gojūshi-kun* (*Fifty-four Ladies of a Yoshiwara Genji*, 1687), written by the *haikai* poet Kikaku (1661–1707) under the alias Azuma Tarō, and *Yoshiwara Genji rokujitchō hyōban-ki* (*Critique of a Yoshiwara Genji*, 60 vols., 1737) by the unknown author Genjaku.

9 Translations adapted by the author from Waley's and Seidensticker's, for which see Murasaki 1935, p. 349, and 1980, p. 323, respectively. See also Murasaki 1975, p. 363.

10 Translations adapted by the author from Waley's and Seidensticker's, for which see Murasaki 1935, p. 525, and 1980, pp. 455–6, respectively. See also Murasaki 1975, p. 522.

104–6

Torii Kiyomasu II

From the series *'Seven Aspects of Ono no Komachi'* (*Nana Komachi*)

c. 1735–40

ARTIST'S SIGNATURE: 'Eshi Torii Kiyomasu hitsu' (Brush of the picture master Torii Kiyomasu)

PUBLISHER: 'Motohama-chō Iga-ya hanmoto' (The publisher Iga-ya at Motohama-chō) with publisher's mark

woodblock, *hosoban*, *urushi-e*, colour sprayed over stencils (*fuki-bokashi*), hand-colouring

William Sturgis Bigelow Collection, 1911

Landscapes and courtly scenes incorporating episodes from classical literature and depicted in a style reminiscent of works by artists of the Tosa and Kano schools became fashionable in woodblock prints of the 1720s and 1730s. The trend towards reinterpreting subjects rooted in the Yamato tradition in a modern way was inspired by a steady output of publications reproducing famous artists' paintings and by Nishikawa Sukenobu's popular illustrated books.

In striving to produce fresh images of traditional literary and artistic subjects for the general public, enterprising printmakers such as Masanobu (also a publisher), Toshinobu, Shigenaga and Kiyomasu II used the increasingly popular *hosoban* format for both vertical or horizontal images. They also enlivened the prints with novel *urushi* and stencil-printing techniques. Besides 'Fifty-four Chapters from Tale of Genji' (cat. 102, 103) and 'Seven Aspects of Ono no Komachi', the subjects featured included 'Eight Views of Ōmi' (*Ōmi hakkei*), 'Six Tama Rivers' (*Mu Tamagawa*) and 'Four Seasons of the Countryman' (*Shiki no hyakushō*).[1] In addition, the repertoire was expanded to encompass series devoted to eight views of Edo, Kanazawa and Yoshiwara, classical poets and their poems and the pleasures of the four seasons.[2]

Shigenaga and Kiyomasu II collaborated on *Fifty-four Chapters from Tale of Genji*, but less extensive series were generally produced by a single artist. Shigenaga and Kiyomasu II, for example, created separate series dedicated to the Heian period woman poet Ono no Komachi. Although there are clear artistic similarities between the two, certain differences indicate that Kiyomasu II's technically more polished prints, with their greater *ukiyo* flair, are likely to have been based on Shigenaga's innovative designs of *c.* 1727–30. That the two series were issued in such rapid succession testifies to the popularity of the subject.

Komachi, who served as a lady-in-waiting at the Imperial court from 850 to 869, is believed to have been brilliant and beautiful and to have had several lovers. Many of her poems speak nevertheless of unhappy and unrequited love, and she ended her days in poverty and loneliness. It appears that she left the capital by 873; thereafter, according to legend, she lived in a hovel, haunted by regret and guilt over her cruel treatment of a former lover. The romantic tales and tragic fate associated with Komachi inspired numerous plays and works of art. Kan'ami Kiyotsugu (1338–84) and his son Zeami Motokiyo (1363–1443) wrote seven nō plays on the subject. Five of these plays have survived in their entirety, while only the plot of one, *Amagoi Komachi*, and the general content of another, *Kiyomizu Komachi*, are known. Together, they were to form the basis of the 'Seven Aspects [i.e. episodes from the life] of Ono no Komachi'.[3] The episodes are: 1. 'Komachi Washing the Manuscript' (*Sōshi-arai Komachi*; cat. 39), 2. 'Komachi at Sekidera' (*Sekidera*

1 'Eight Views of Ōmi': (by Masanobu) Vergez 1983, fig. 24; New York 1991a, pp. 68–9; Noguchi 1933, nos. 54–5; (by Shigenaga) Honolulu 1980, pp. 155–7, nos. 2–4; *Genshoku ukiyo-e*, vol. 6, p. 70, fig. 155; *Ukiyo-e taikei*, vol. 1, no. 52; Chicago 1955, p. 187, nos. 2–6; New York 1991a, pp. 120–5; Toronto 1975, p. 80, no. 39; (by Kiyomasu II) Chicago 1955, p. 93, no. 11; Stern n.d., pp. 64–5, no. 24. 'Six Tama Rivers': (by Kiyomasu II) Kikuchi 1969, fig. 168. 'Four Seasons': (by Kiyomasu II) New York 1991a, pp. 98–9; Chicago 1955, p. 94, nos. 12–14.

2 'Eight Views of Edo': (by Shigenaga) Chicago 1955, p. 188, no. 7. 'Eight Views of Kanazawa': (by Shigenaga) Honolulu 1980, p. 158, no. 5. 'Eight Views of Yoshiwara': (by Kiyomasu II) Kikuchi 1969, fig. 169. 'Classical Poets': (by Shigenaga) *Genshoku ukiyo-e*, vol. 6, p. 70, fig. 154. 'Pleasures of the Four Seasons': (by Toshinobu) Chicago 1955, p. 181, no. 19, and *Genshoku ukiyo-e*, vol. 6, p. 68, no. 149.

3 The episodes are discussed in Waterhouse 1964, pp. 297–302, and Fiorillo 1999, pp. 17–30.

106

'Parrot Komachi' (No. 6) (*Ōmu Komachi*)

34 × 16.2 cm

11.13328

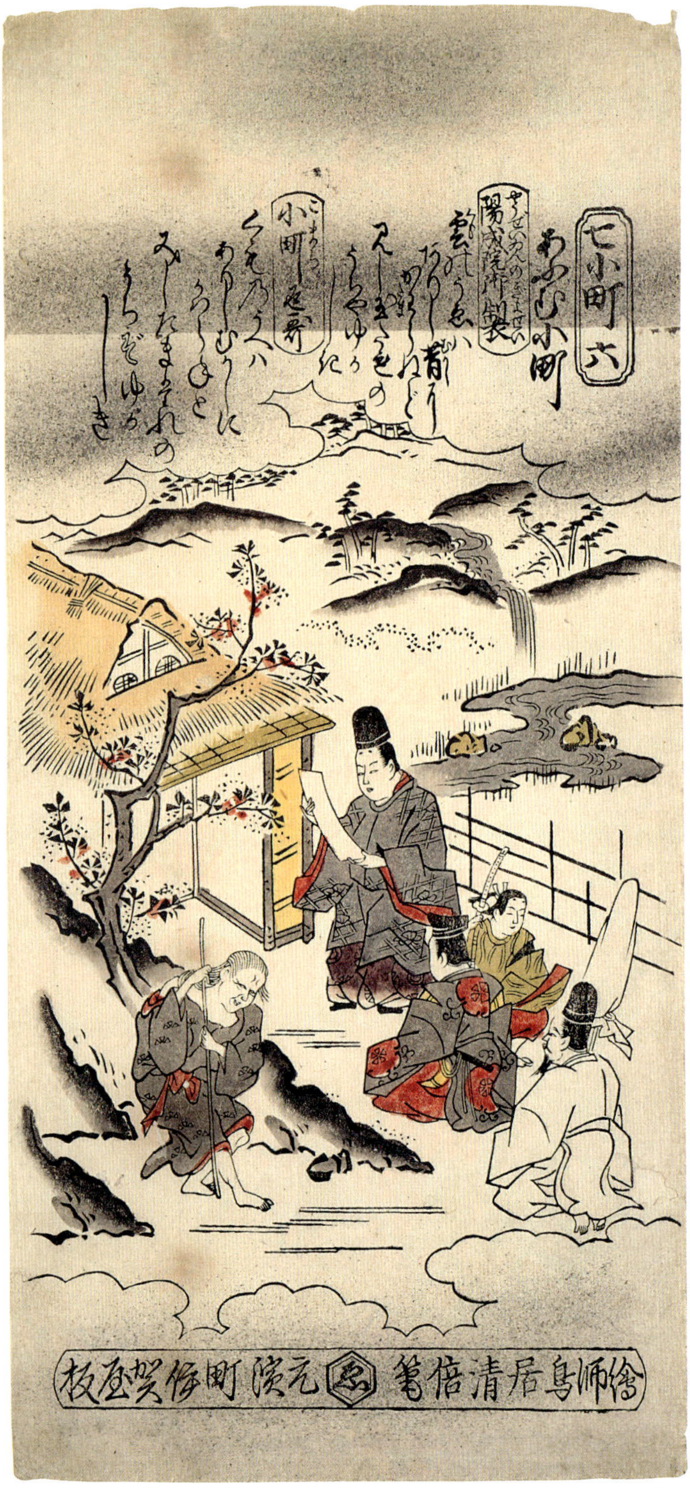

105

'Komachi and the Suitor' (No. 4) (*Kayoi Komachi*)

34.4 × 16.2 cm

OTHER IMPRESSION: Royal Ontario Museum, Toronto (Toronto 1975, p. 40, no. 12)

11.13327

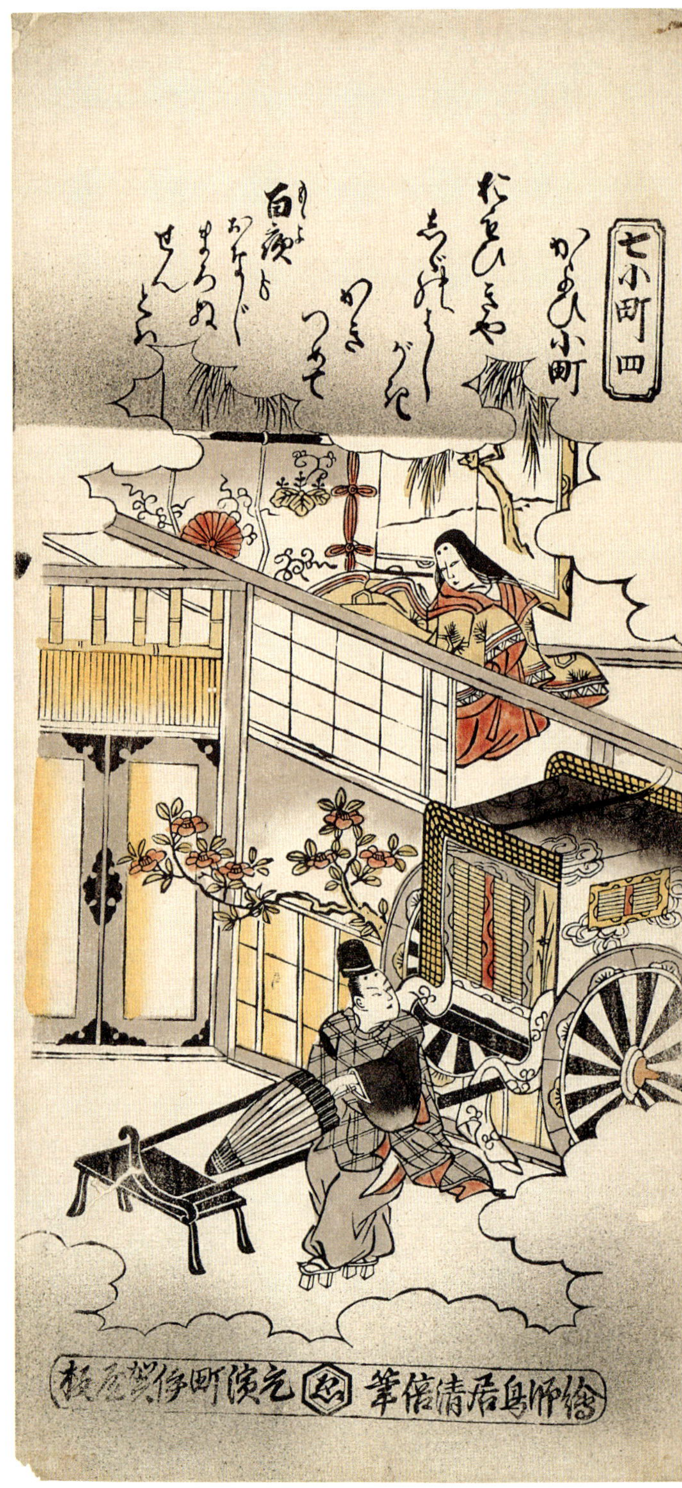

104

'Komachi at Kiyomizu' (No. 3) (*Kiyomizu Komachi*)

33.7 × 15.8 cm

11.13326

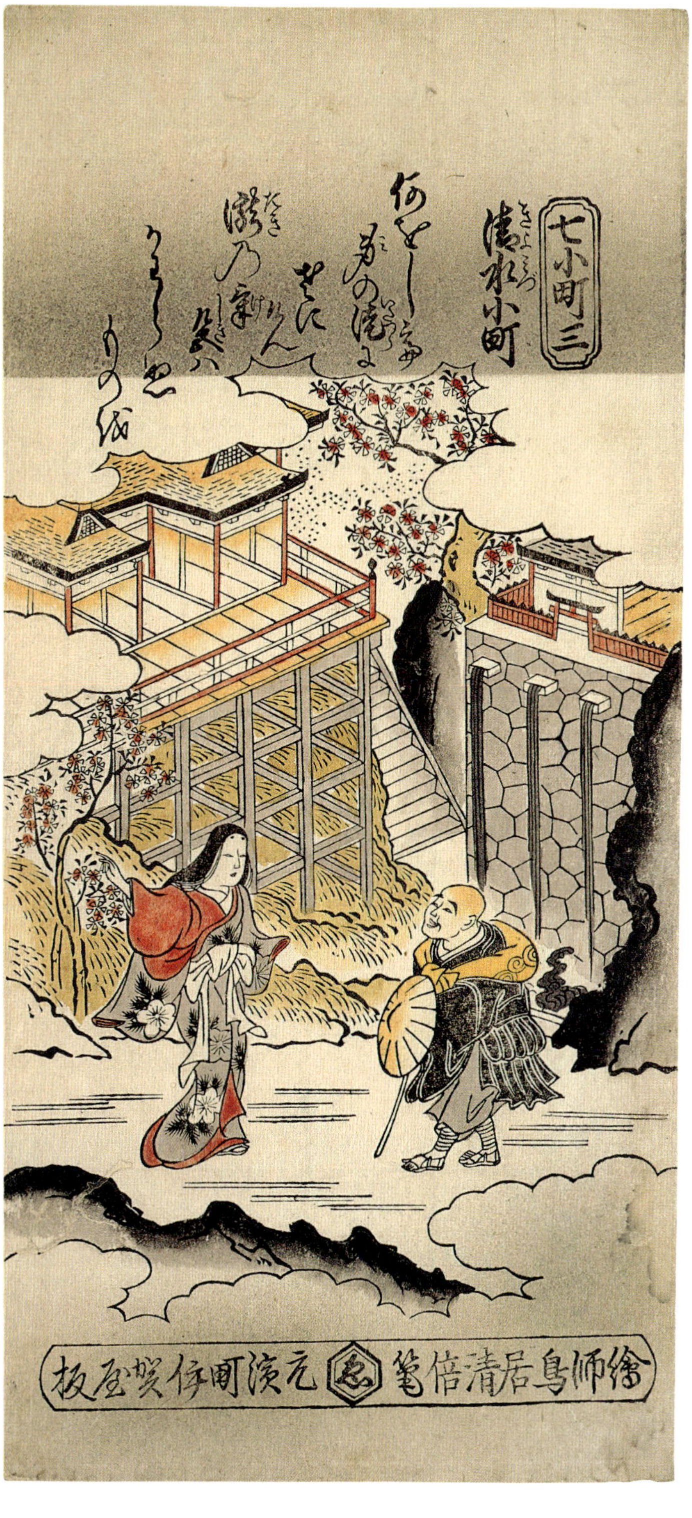

Komachi), 3. 'Komachi at Kiyomizu Temple' (*Kiyomizu Komachi*), 4. 'Courting Komachi' (*Kayoi Komachi*; cat. 52), 5. 'Praying for Rain Komachi' (*Amagoi Komachi*), 6. 'Parrot Komachi' (*Ōmu Komachi*), 7. 'Grave-marker Komachi' (*Sotoba Komachi*).[4]

The setting depicted in cat. 104 is Kiyomizu-dera (Temple of Clear Water) in Kyoto, dedicated to Eleven-headed Kannon. The main hall of the temple was placed on stilts close to a steep slope near the Otawa-no-taki waterfall, where the founders of the temple had first met.[5] A monk on a pilgrimage is shown arriving at the temple and sees a votive painting with a poem written by Komachi lamenting the ravages of time:

Nani o shite	Despite all I do
mi no itazura ni	it is of no avail –
oiniken	my body has grown old;
taki no keshiki wa	while the waterfall remains
kawaranu mono o	unchanged in its appearance.[6]

A beautiful woman, who has overheard the monk's prayers on behalf of Komachi's soul, points to the nearby village of Ichiharano, where Komachi still lives, and subsequently leads him there.

Shigenaga's version of this episode had been comparatively free of extraneous detail and 'classical' in its bird's-eye view of the tilted roof and isolated figures.[7] Its painterly rendering of the rocks resembled Kano-style brushwork. Kiyomasu II's scene was more evenly balanced, decoratively detailed and realistically drawn. It also revealed the artist's delight in the *beni* rose colour. While Shigenaga had focused on the woman's gesture, Kiyomasu II (in the spirit of ukiyo-e) evinced greater interest in the interaction between the figures: they look at each other as they approach one another on what the horizontal lines show to be the same level. Moreover, the figures' garments hang more naturally, with a livelier, more fashion-conscious swing that hints at *ukiyo* fashion. The same respective stylistic traits are apparent in the two artists' versions of both the following episodes.

Like the others in the series, the scene depicted in cat. 105 is shown as if glimpsed between clouds, an artistic device derived from classical hand scrolls. Legend had it that at the end of her life Komachi was haunted by the ghost of a former suitor, Captain Fukakusa no Shōshō. Distrusting Fukakusa'a ardent love, Komachi had tested his fidelity by demanding that he visit her for 100 consecutive nights before they consummated their relationship. Fukakusa came to her gate, night after night, and almost succeeded in his task. On the 99th night – according to the print, in the early spring season of flowering camellias – he felt the wind tugging at his hems and opened his umbrella. He was soon enveloped by a sudden blizzard and froze to death.

4 For the Ōno no Komachi legends and translations of the nō plays, see Teele 1993. Beginning in the late 1720s (and reaching a peak in the late 1740s), puppet plays about literary and historical personalities were written by groups of playwrights. The 'Seven Aspects of Komachi', for instance, were the subject of a *jōruri* by the playwright–manager Takeda Izumo I (*d.* 1747) and others, first performed in Osaka in 1727. The episodes not illustrated here are reproduced as follows: 1. (by Kiyomasu II) Chicago 1955 p. 93, no. 10; Honolulu 1980, p. 58, no. 9; Toronto 1975, pp. 38–8, no. 11; 2. (by Shigenaga) Toronto 1975, p. 78, no. 37; (by Kiyomasu II) Toronto 1975, p. 41, no. 13; Dresden 1995, pp. 24–5; 5. (by Shigenaga) *Genshoku ukiyo-e*, vol. 6, p. 56, fig. 113.

5 The main hall was originally a private mansion donated by Lady Miyoshi in 807. A monk named Enchin lived near the waterfall. When General Kanoue no Tamuramaro (758–811) heard Enchin's lecture on the evils of killing he became a convert and offered the monk support in founding the temple in 798.

6 Although this is not among the 80 poems firmly attributed to Komachi, and indeed is thought to have been written later than the Heian period, it is believed that it may have been part of the lost nō play. The words 'Nani o shite mi o itazura ni oi' refer to a *waka* in the early 10th-century poetry anthology *Collection of Ancient and Modern Japanese Poems* (*Kokin waka-shū*, no. 1063).

7 Reproduced in Toronto 1975, p. 79, no. 38.

8 Toronto 1975, p. 40, no. 12. The poem chosen to complement the image is by Fujiwara Shunzei and is included in the anthology *Collection of [Japanese Poems] of a Thousand Years* (*Senzai-shū*, XII:778), completed in 1187–8. Shunzei's verses may allude to a poem from *Collection of Ancient and Modern Japanese Poems* (*Kokin waka-shū*, XV:761). Shigenaga's print of this scene is reproduced in Machida 1999, p. 62, no. 36.

9 The poem and translations are quoted from Toronto 1975, pp. 42–3, no. 14. Although Komachi died in obscurity, her fame grew and she became known as one of the Six Poet Immortals (*rokkasen*) and as one of the Thirty-six Poet Immortals (*sanjū-rokkasen*).

A poem by Fujiwara Shunzei (1114–1204) conveys the mood of the frustrated lover:

Omoiki ya	I should have realised! –
shiji no hashigaki	having scored up all those marks
kakitsumete	on your mounting-block,
momo yo mo onaji	the 100th night is the same:
marone sen to wa	I see I must sleep alone.[8]

According to the nō play *Ōmu Komachi*, Komachi was a nun and very old when she received a visit from Yukiie, councillor of the retired Emperor Yōzei (*reg.* 877–884). Yukiie brought a poem from the Emperor, which asked whether Komachi still remembered him and her life in the palace. Komachi lamented that her humble existence did not inspire replies in lofty poetry but, in her desire and need to respond, she suddenly thought of a solution. She returned the poem to Yukiie with only one syllable changed; by substituting the character *ya* for *zo* she had transformed the Emperor's question into an affirmation:

'Emperor Yōzei's poem' ('Yōzei-in no gyosei'):

Kumo no ue wa	The cloud-capped palace
arishi mukashi ni	where you lived long ago
kawaranedo	has not changed at all:
mishi tamadare no	but you saw through my bead curtains –
uchi ya yukashiki	do you think fondly of that?

'Komachi's reply poem' ('Komachi no henka'):

Kumo no ue wa	The cloud-capped palace
arishi mukashi ni	where I lived long ago
kawaranedo	has not changed at all:
mishi tamadare no	but I saw through my bead curtains –
uchi zo yukashiki	Yes, I think fondly of that!

The scene depicted (cat. 106) takes place in a rural landscape near Komachi's straw-thatched hut. Komachi, seen leaning on a staff under a blossoming cherry tree, smiles as the amazed Yukiie reads her reply. When he asks her whether the poem truly conforms to poetic tradition, Komachi – showing her innate brilliance and knowledge of poetry – reassures him that it is a form of *tanka* called *ōmu-gaeshi* ('parrot reply'). She tells him that 'in China there is a bird called the parrot, which takes in the words people say and turns them into their own chatter. If you say something to it, it answers with its own words. So when an answering poem is just like this parrot bird, we call it the "Parrot Reply".'[9] LEV

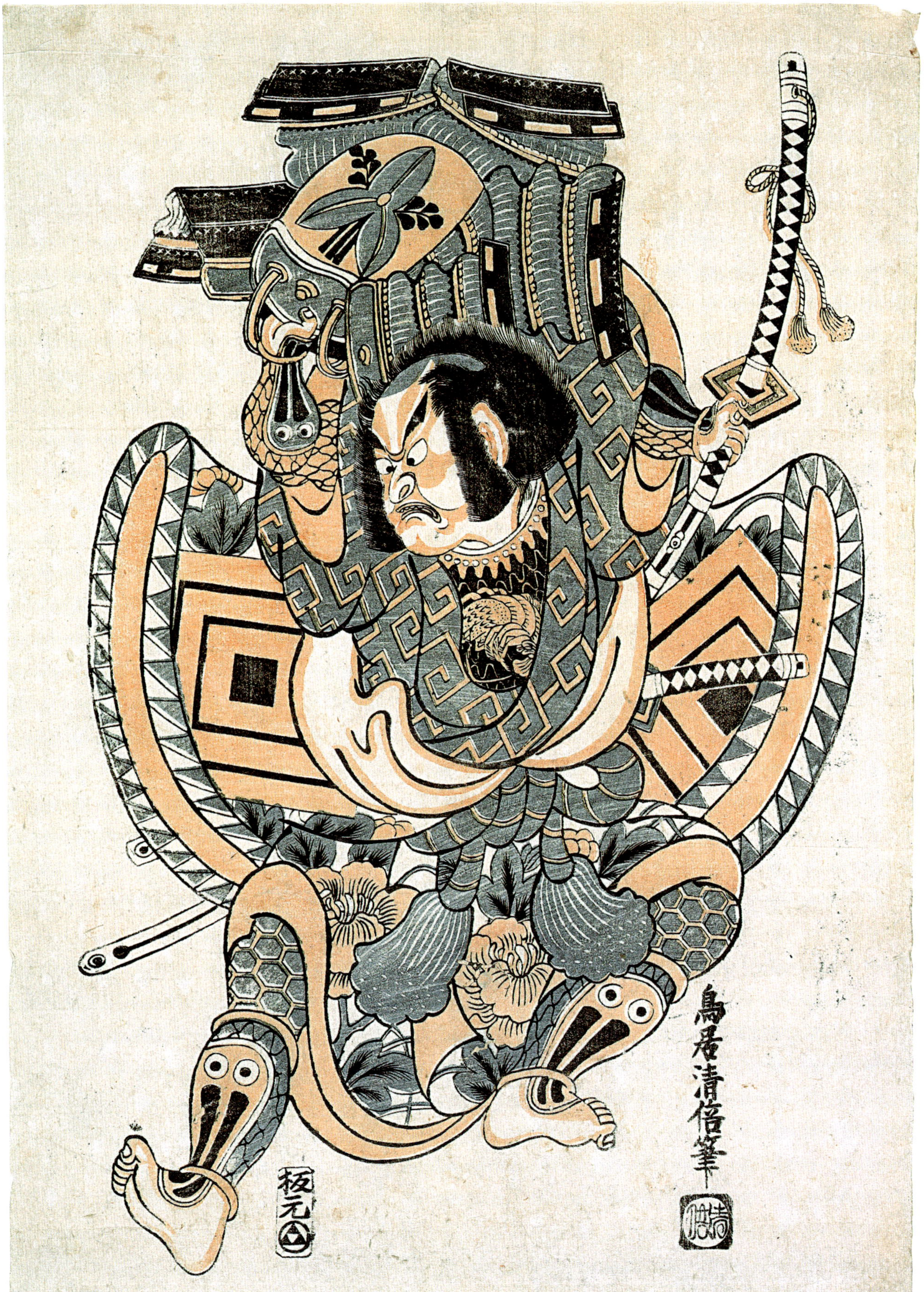
鳥居清倍筆
板元

107

Torii Kiyomasu II

The Actor Ichikawa Ebizō II as Kagekiyo (Nise Gorō)

1st month, 1752 (?)

ARTIST'S SIGNATURE: 'Torii Kiyomasu hitsu' (Brush of Torii Kiyomasu)

ARTIST'S SEAL: 'Kiyomasu'

PUBLISHER: 'hanmoto' (publisher) with mark of Urokogata-ya

woodblock, *ōban*, *benizuri-e* (2-colour), 43.1 × 31 cm

REPRODUCED: *Ukiyo-e shūka*, vol. 1, no. 29

John Ware Willard Fund, 1947

47.231

This dynamic design bristles with the energy generated by the classic *aragoto* roles as interpreted by the great Ichikawa Ebizō II (formerly Danjūrō II). Both sleeves of his padded outer robe are shrugged off and spread out behind him like great wings, revealing the stylised lightning pattern on the middle robe and his lobster crest on the under-shirt. The outer robe is emblazoned with two great *mimasu* (triple rice measure) crests surrounded by trailing peonies. With one hand the actor hoists a whole suit of body armour above his head, while resolutely gripping the hilt of his preternaturally long sword with the other. His legs are splayed powerfully, one bent, the other stretched out straight. His explosion of rage is accompanied by a scowling cross-eyed glare (*nirami*), a forte of the Danjūrō lineage.

Larger, *ōban*-sized prints with *benizuri-e*-style printed colours seem to have appeared from about 1750.[1] It has been suggested that the present design shows Ebizō II as Kagekiyo posing as 'Imposter Gorō' (Nise Gorō) in the play *Yuzuri wa sugata-mi Soga*, performed at the Ichimura Theatre at the New Year, 1752.[2] This identification accords well with a mention of armour in the actor critique *Yakusha hitori-annai*, published two months later, in 1752/3: 'He revealed himself to Kudō as Kagekiyo, they exchanged [his] armour with the upside-down water plantain [crest] for the jewel that was the gift from the gods (*shinji*), and parted ways'.[3]

The role of Kagekiyo – in history a retainer of the Taira who vowed revenge on the Minamoto clan after the destruction of the Taira at the Battle of Dannoura in 1185 – seems first to have been performed in kabuki by Danjūrō II in the play *Ō-itchō sakae Soga* at the Nakamura Theatre in the autumn of 1732. Beginning with a performance of *Uruu-zuki ninin Kagekiyo* at the Kawarazaki Theatre in the eleventh month, 1737, Kagekiyo regularly impersonated other characters in the Soga world, as here, and they impersonated him. In the autumn of 1739 Danjūrō II scored a further triumph with his scene of 'Jail-break Kagekiyo' (*rō-yaburi no Kagekiyo*; cat. 99). In his various guises Kagekiyo indisputably belonged among the actor's greatest creations.

During the few years before his death in the ninth month, 1758, ill heath sometimes prevented Ebizō II from performing for months at a time: he was absent from the stage from the autumn of 1752 until the eleventh month, 1753, and from the spring of 1757 until one final performance in the fourth month, 1758. Nevertheless he seems to have been determined to repeat his famous *aragoto* roles. The forceful style of the figure in this print and the way it fills the sheet may be compared to Kiyonobu II's votive plaque (*ema*) painting *The Actor Ichikawa Ebizō II in the 'Arrow-sharpening' Scene* (p. 24, fig. 12) of 1754. TTC

1 Mutō 1999, p. 9, proposes this date for the earliest *ōban* actor prints by Okumura Masanobu.

2 *Ukiyo-e shūka*, vol. 1, no. 29 (commentary by Money Hickman).

3 *Kabuki hyōban-ki II*, vol. 4, p. 349.

108
Torii Kiyotada
The Actors Sanjō Kantarō II and Ichimura Takenojō IV

c. 1721–2

ARTIST'S SIGNATURE: 'Torii Kiyotada hitsu' (Brush of Torii Kiyotada)

ARTIST'S SEAL: 'Kiyotada'

PUBLISHER: 'Komatsu-ya'

woodblock, *hosoban*, *beni-e* with brass filings, 31.1 × 15.6 cm

REPRODUCED: *Ukiyo-e shūka*, vol. 1, no. 27

William Sturgis Bigelow Collection, 1911

11.13273

Identified by their crests – a butterfly and a branch of mandarin orange – and by the names written on the print, Sanjō Kantarō II, sheltering the couple with an umbrella, is borne piggyback in the rain by Ichimura Takenojō IV, who wears trailing *naga-bakama* trousers and carries a long sword. Seen elsewhere in this volume in their 1718 hit roles of Oshichi and Kichisaburō (cat. 37), the pair continued to act frequently together at the Ichimura Theatre for much of the 1720s. The roles and play illustrated here have not been identified, but a woman carried piggyback by her lover may relate in some way to the well-known 'Akutagawa' scene of elopement from the 10th-century *Tales of Ise* (*Ise monogatari*).[1] The fact that Kantarō II plays a young woman role, the form of the publisher's mark and the absence of a 'sash-style publisher's cartouche' (*obi-gata hyōki*) suggest a date of *c.* 1721–2.[2]

Kiyotada is thought to have been a pupil of Torii Kiyonobu I and is known for a small number of *hosoban* designs decorated in the *urushi-e* technique and for perspective views (see cat. 109). The hand-applied colours of this print have faded severely, but this is apparently the only extant impression of this charmingly romantic design. TTC

1 For a recent discussion of ukiyo-e parodies of the Akutagawa episode and related themes, see Nakamachi 2000, esp. pp. 70–4.

2 I am grateful to Mutō Junko for her assistance with this dating.

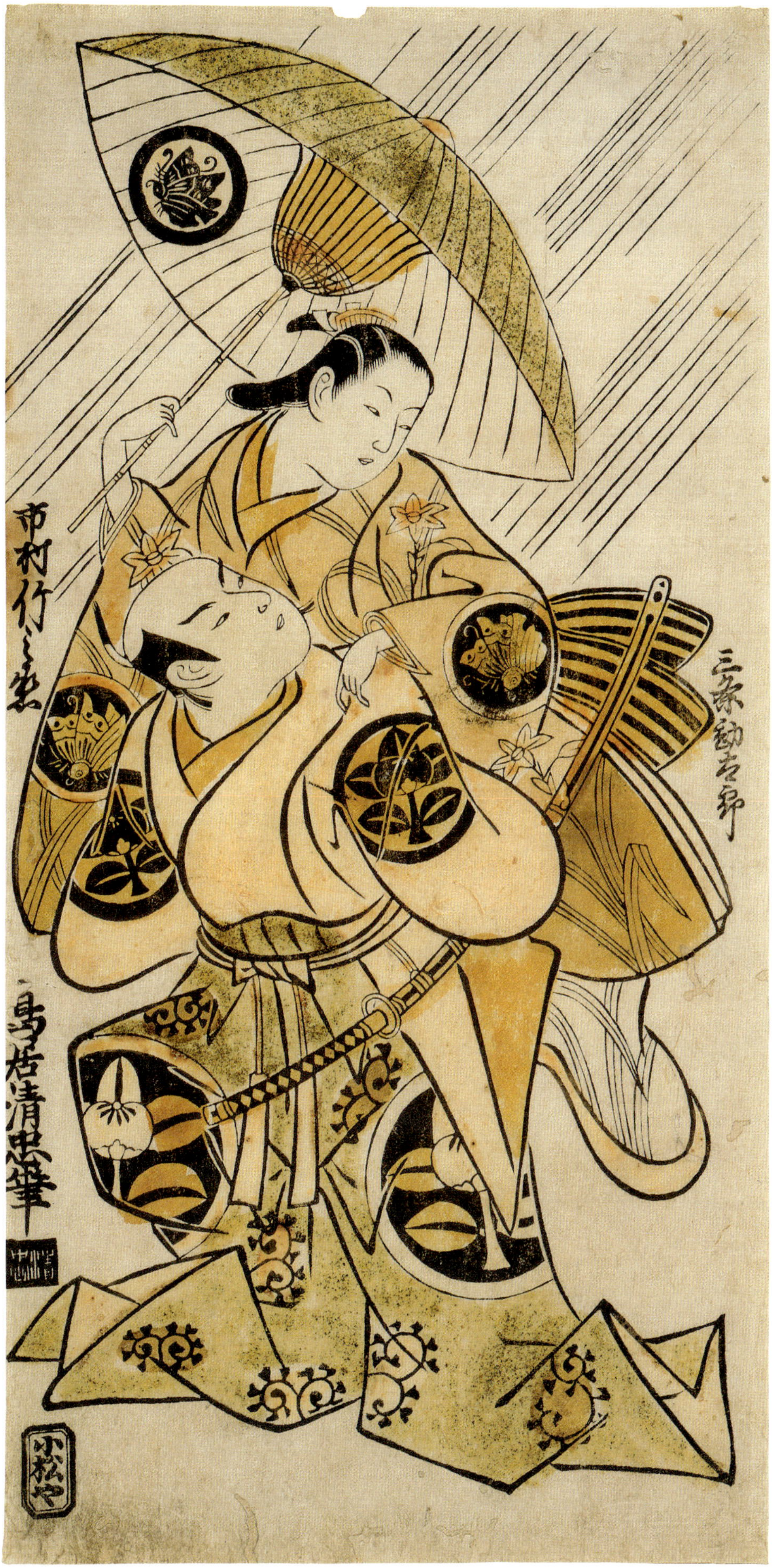
市村竹之丞
三条勘太郎
鳥居清忠筆
小松や

109

Torii Kiyotada

'The Main Gate, New Yoshiwara' *(Shin-Yoshiwara Ōmon-guchi)*

c. 1745

ARTIST'S SIGNATURE: 'Eshi Torii Kiyotada hitsu' (Brush of the picture master Torii Kiyotada)

PUBLISHER: mark of Urokogata-ya Magobei

BLOCK CUTTER: 'Sekine Shintarō'

woodblock, extra-large size (*toku-ōban*), *beni-e*, 47.7 × 64 cm (trimmed)

OTHER IMPRESSIONS: Art Institute of Chicago (Chicago 1955, Kiyotada no. 2; *Ukiyo-e shūka*, vol. 4, no. 33); Museum of Fine Arts, Boston, 21. 5677; (*Ukiyo-e taisei* vol. 3, no. 168)

Special Funds, 1954

54.181

The view is through the Main Gate (Ōmon-guchi) of Yoshiwara, the single government-licensed pleasure quarter, re-located amid fields on the northern outskirts of the city of Edo after the conflagration of 1657. We are looking down the central boulevard, Nakano-chō, lined on either side with assignation teahouses (*ageya*), where clients had to apply if they sought an appointment with a top-ranked courtesan. The teahouse names can be read on the short curtains hanging from the eaves: Masuya, Tsutaya and Owari-ya on the right side of the street, Tamaya, Wakata-ya and Nagasaki-ya on the left. Framed by the far end of the street is an auspicious view of distant Mount Fuji. The frieze of figures across the front shows a courtesan and her two child attendants (*kamuro*) on the left and a potential client being importuned by another child attendant and male entertainer (*hōkan* or *taiko-mochi*) on the right. Behind them are various pedlars and tradesmen selling fish, (possibly) books, cakes and, in the case of the pedlar dressed in a chequered costume in the centre, moxa (burned on the skin as a medical treatment).[1]

At the time when this print is thought to have been issued, in the mid-1740s, the ranking system for courtesans in Yoshiwara was in transition. Traditionally, it was the highest ranked *tayū* and second ranked *kōshi* who proceeded with a spectacular retinue from the brothels on the side streets to meet their wealthy patron in the teahouse, after the teahouse had negotiated on his behalf. But by the mid-18th century the *tayū* had all but priced themselves out of existence: 'between 1740 and 1760, *tayū* numbered scarcely more than two or three at a time. Consequently, the *ageya* whose business depended on *tayū* disappeared also, leaving only the Owari-ya'.[2] The *ageya* transformed themselves into *hikite-jaya* (assignation teahouses), serving a similar function to the *ageya* but in a less expensive manner and catering for the new highest grade, the *yobidashi*, which came into existence *c.* 1761.[3] A 1752 guide to the quarter includes teahouse names that accord with those in Kiyotada's print – Masuya Shichi'emon (fourth on the right), Tsutaya Jinshirō (seventh on the right), Owari-ya Shichibei (fourteenth on the right) – although the artist naturally had to limit the number severely in the interests of pictorial legibility. The *ageya* were lavish: 'Owari-ya and Izumi-ya typically had large, finely appointed rooms surrounding a magnificent garden including a pond, shapely trees and shrubbery, a bridge crossing over to a little island, tastefully placed rocks , and cascading water'.[4] Moronobu's book *A Guide to Love in Yoshiwara* (cat. 11) of 1678 had included at the end four double-page illustrations of the customs surrounding the entertainments of the *ageya*.

If, as appears likely, the perspective pictures (*uki-e*) by Okumura Masanobu in this particularly large format (see cat. 65, 66)[5] should be dated *c.* 1745, then it seems logical to suggest that Kiyotada's design was created at

1 The trade name on his box of wares could be read 'Kyū-Dai' or possible 'Kyū-Shiro'. The chequered pattern became popular after it was used on the *hakama* worn by the actor Sanogawa Ichimatsu I in the role of Kumenosuke in a performance of *Kōya shinjū* at the Nakamura Theatre during the second month, 1741. Nojima 1988, p. 282. It may be significant that the *kume* character used to write Kumenosuke is very similar to the character *kyū* (moxa) used here in the pedlar's trade name.

2 Seigle 1993, p. 126.

3 Ibid., pp. 229–31.

4 Ibid., p. 64.

5 Termed most precisely the *take-naga hōsho zenban* format, which uses the whole of the largest sheets of paper customarily used for ukiyo-e prints. Sometimes called the *toku-ōban*, or the horizontal *ō-ōban*, this format is known to have been used for eleven large perspective views during this period. Kishi 1994a, pp. 73–4.

6 See also the commentaries to cat. 65, 66 and Kishi 1994a.

7 *Ukiyo-e shūka*, vol. 4, 1979, no. 135.

8 See Asano's comments in Tokyo 1985a, no. 46.

9 Kishi 1994a, p. 84, n. 10.

around the same time.[6] Indeed, Masanobu himself designed a very similar view through the Main Gate of Yoshiwara (Art Institute of Chicago),[7] except that the vantage point is slightly further outside the gate. If we accept that Masanobu was the originator of perspective pictures, then Kiyotada's view may have been derived from Masanobu's. A further large perspective view from this period, *Parlour of the Daimonji-ya, Shin-Yoshiwara Nakano-chō* (*Shin-Yoshiwara Nakano-chō Daimonji-ya zashiki*, British Museum), bears the printed signature of Kiyotada and the name of the publisher Okumura-ya in the margins. However, this print, which has apparently been skilfully re-margined on all sides, has been attributed tentatively by Asano Shūgō to Okumura Masanobu.[8] The other three large perspective prints by Kiyotada, including the present design, were published by Urokogata-ya.[9] TTC

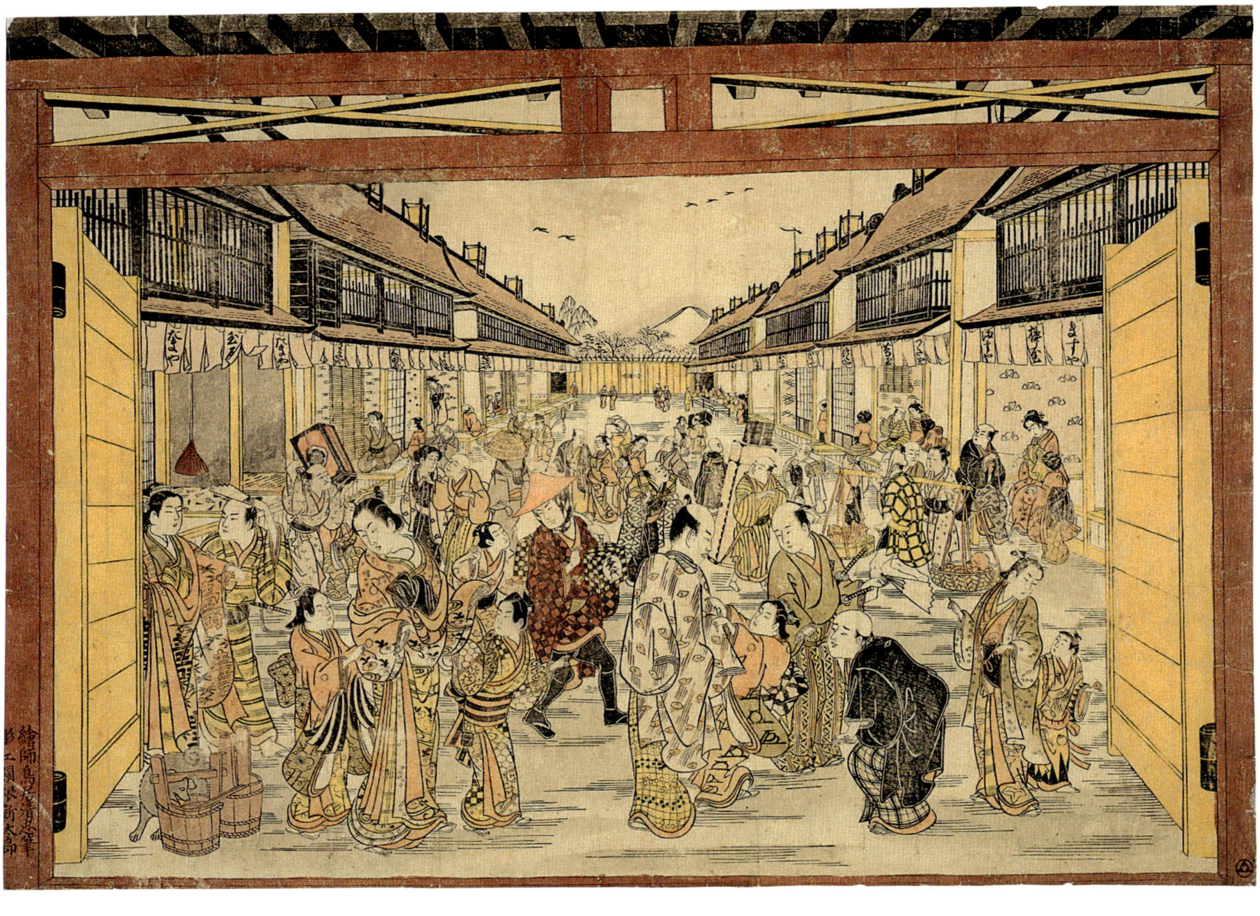

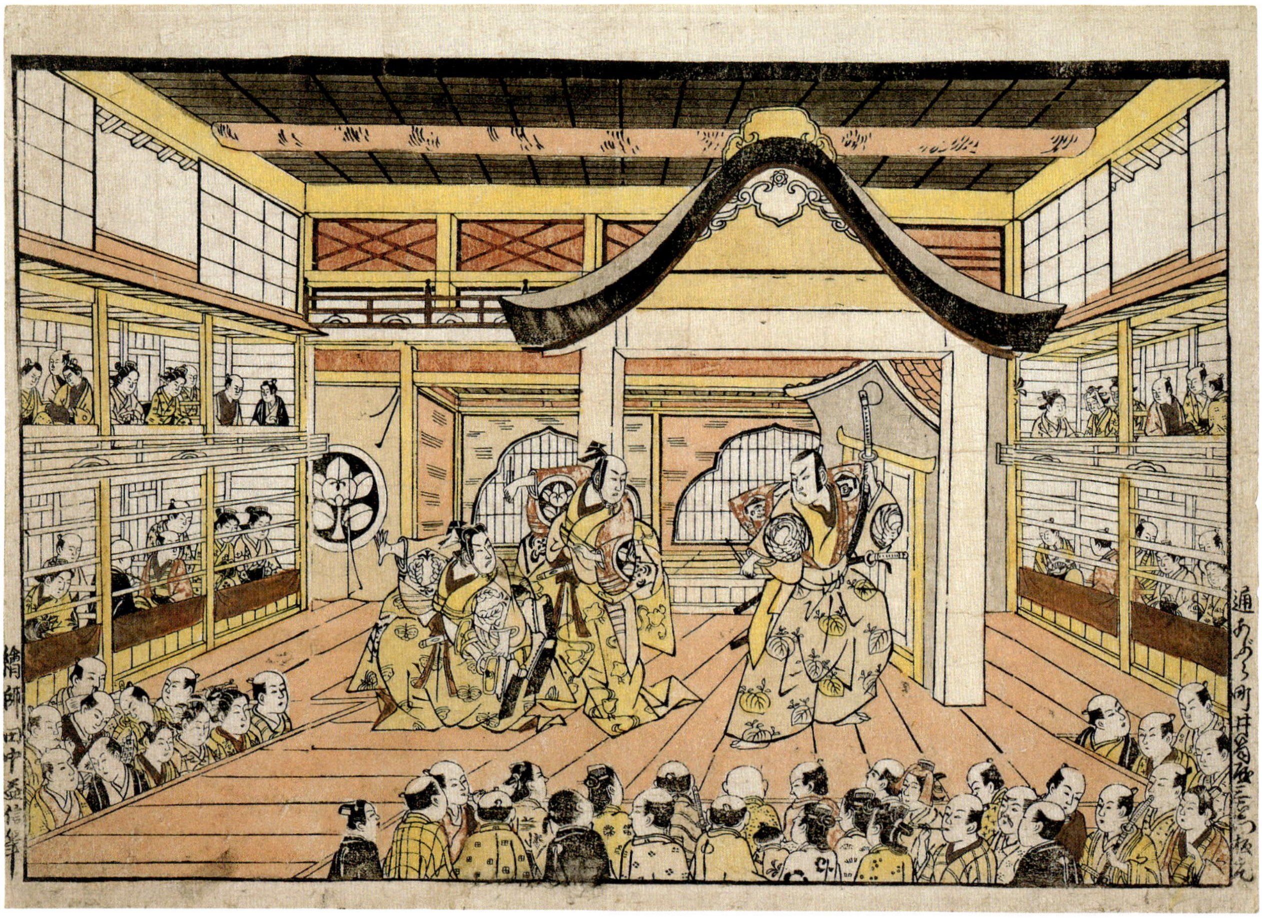
繪師田中益信筆

110

Tanaka Masunobu

Scene from the Play 'Nana-kusa wakayagi Soga' at the Ichimura Theatre

New Year, 1744

ARTIST'S SIGNATURE: 'Eshi Tanaka Masunobu hitsu' (Brush of the picture master Tanaka Masunobu)

PUBLISHER: 'Tōriabura-chō Izutsu-ya San'emon hanmoto' (Izutsu-ya San'emon, publisher at Tōriabura-chō)

woodblock, horizontal *ōban*, *beni-e*, 31.5 × 44.9 cm

REPRODUCED: *Ukiyo-e shūka*, vol. 1, no. 45

William Sturgis Bigelow Collection, 1911

11.19686

1 *Ukiyo-e shūka*, vol. 1, no. 45 (commentary by Money Hickman). The three Shigenaga prints are reproduced in Yamamura and Machida 1919, nos. 52–4.

2 *Ukiyo-e zenshū*, vol. 1, fig. 113.

Although Okumura Masanobu is generally held to be the originator in Edo of perspective pictures (see cat. 65, 66), other artists, both major and minor, also designed examples. Commercially, scenes in the interiors of kabuki theatres were particularly advantageous because the same block could be reused several times. Costs could be cut by plugging with wood and re-cutting the scene onstage so as to depict a new performance; the surrounding architecture and audience remained the same. One instance is known of a design by Nishimura Shigenaga that was reused no less than three times to depict successive performances of 1747, 1749 and 1752 (see also cat. 68).[1]

The performance in progress here is *Nana-kusa wakayagi Soga* at the Ichimura Theatre at the New Year, 1744. Bandō Hikosaburō as the villain Kudō Suketsune (right) faces off the brothers Soga no Jūrō (played by Ichimura Manzō, centre) and Soga no Gorō (Onoe Kikugorō, left). Small breaks visible in the lines make it clear that the key block has been plugged in a large rectangular area in the centre that extends to below the actors' feet, to the edge of the boxes right and left, and up to the bottom of the cusped roof over part of the stage. Since this area includes the curtain leading backstage at the left, which bears a branch of mandarin orange, the emblem of the Ichimura Theatre, it is quite likely that the block was first used to depict a performance in a different theatre. As one would expect, the lines of the faces of the audience are noticeably more worn than those of the actors, suggesting that hundreds, if not several thousand, impressions were taken from the key block. The date of the block's first use is not known, however; nor have any earlier impressions taken from it been identified. A different view of the interior of the Ichimura Theatre by Tanaka Masunobu, also published by Izutsu-ya, depicts a performance during the eleventh month, 1745 (Tokyo National Museum).[2] From breaks in the key block, this shows every evidence of having been reused in the same way as the present example. Clearly, perspective pictures of theatre interiors enjoyed a tremendous vogue in the mid-1740s.

The cusped roof is similar in construction to those found above nō stages from the medieval period onwards. To lessen the risk of fire, night-time kabuki performances, which would have required the use of candles, were prohibited. The stage is lit for the most part by daylight from the large open widows above the boxes and just under the roof on either side. TTC

111

Torii Kiyoshige

The Actors Sodesaki Kikutarō as a Woman Bathing and Ichikawa Masugorō as Yonosuke

1731 (?)

ARTIST'S SIGNATURE: 'Torii Kiyoshige hitsu' (Brush of Torii Kiyoshige)

PUBLISHER: 'Ningyō-chō Hirano-ya' (Hirano-ya, at Ningyō-chō) with publisher's mark

woodblock, *hosoban, beni-e, urushi-e* with brass filings, 32.5 × 15.5 cm

William Sturgis Bigelow Collection, 1911

11.19192

1 Kobayashi 1996a, no. 37 (Keiō Gijuku University, Tokyo).

A well-known scene from floating-world fiction: at the tender age of nine, Yonosuke, precocious hero of Saikaku's erotic novel *The Life of an Amorous Man* (*Kōshoku ichidai otoko*, 1682; see pp. 15–16), uses a telescope to spy on a young female neighbour as she bathes. A print of similar composition by Toshinobu confirms the name of the role as Yonosuke.[1]

Ichikawa Masugorō was the son of Danjūrō II. He took this name as a child actor in the winter of 1725 and used it until he progressed to become Danjūrō III in 1735/11 (when Danjūrō II acceded to the name Ebizō II). Masugorō and Kikutarō appeared together at the Nakamura Theatre from 1727/11, and Kikutarō began to be featured in actor critiques in 1731/1. Masugorō's robe bears the crests of other leading actors, all working at the Nakamura Theatre from 1730/11 until 1731/11, when Hiroji moved to the Ichimura Theatre. These are (from the top, clockwise): Sodesaki Kikutarō; *mimasu* crest (used by both Masugorō and his father, Danjūrō II); Ōtani Hiroji; Sodesaki Miwano; Nakajima Miura'emon; Segawa Kikunojō; Sawamura Sōjūrō; *mimasu* crest again. Although records do not permit a precise identification of the play, from the above information the print was most likely issued some time in 1731. TTC

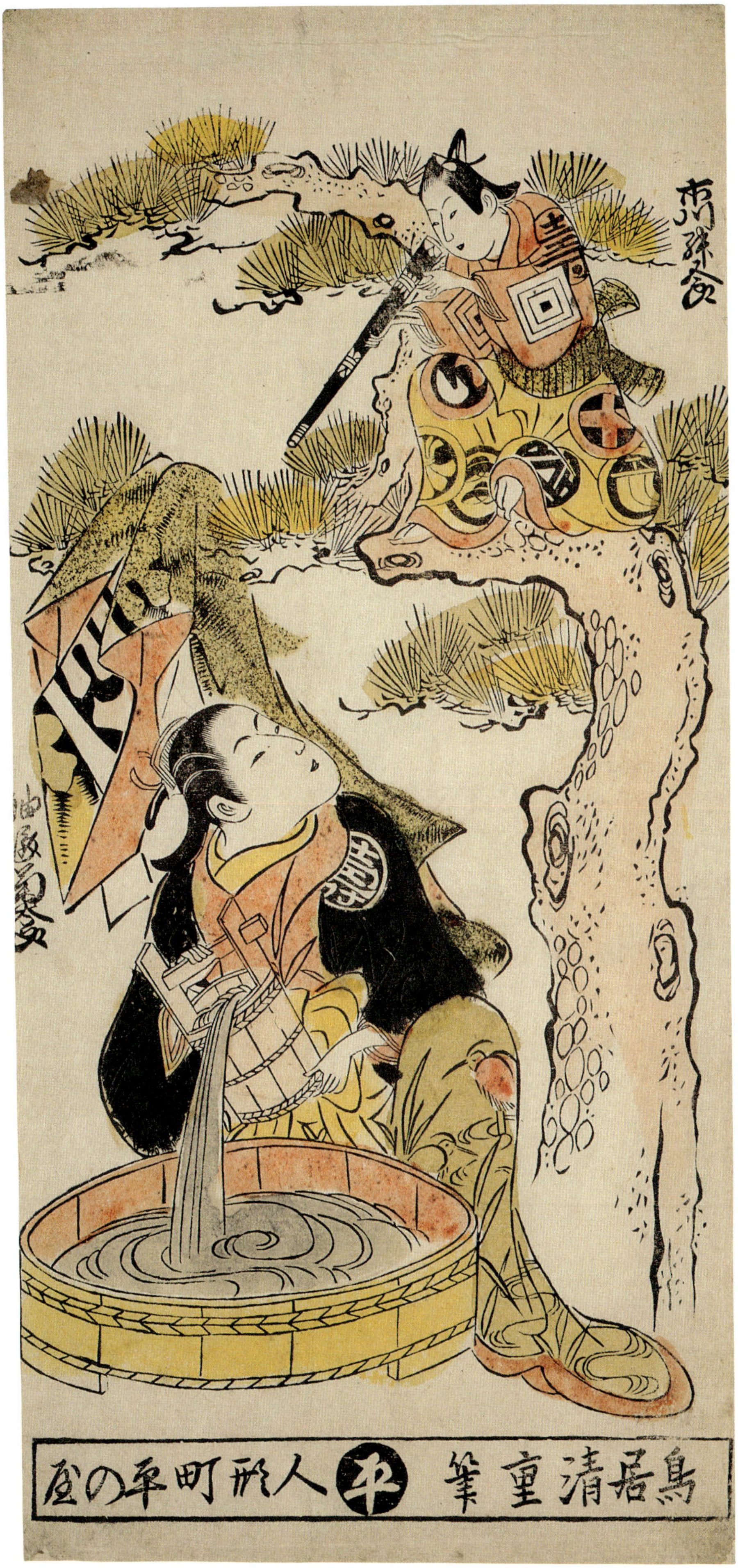
鳥居清重筆
平
人形町平の屋

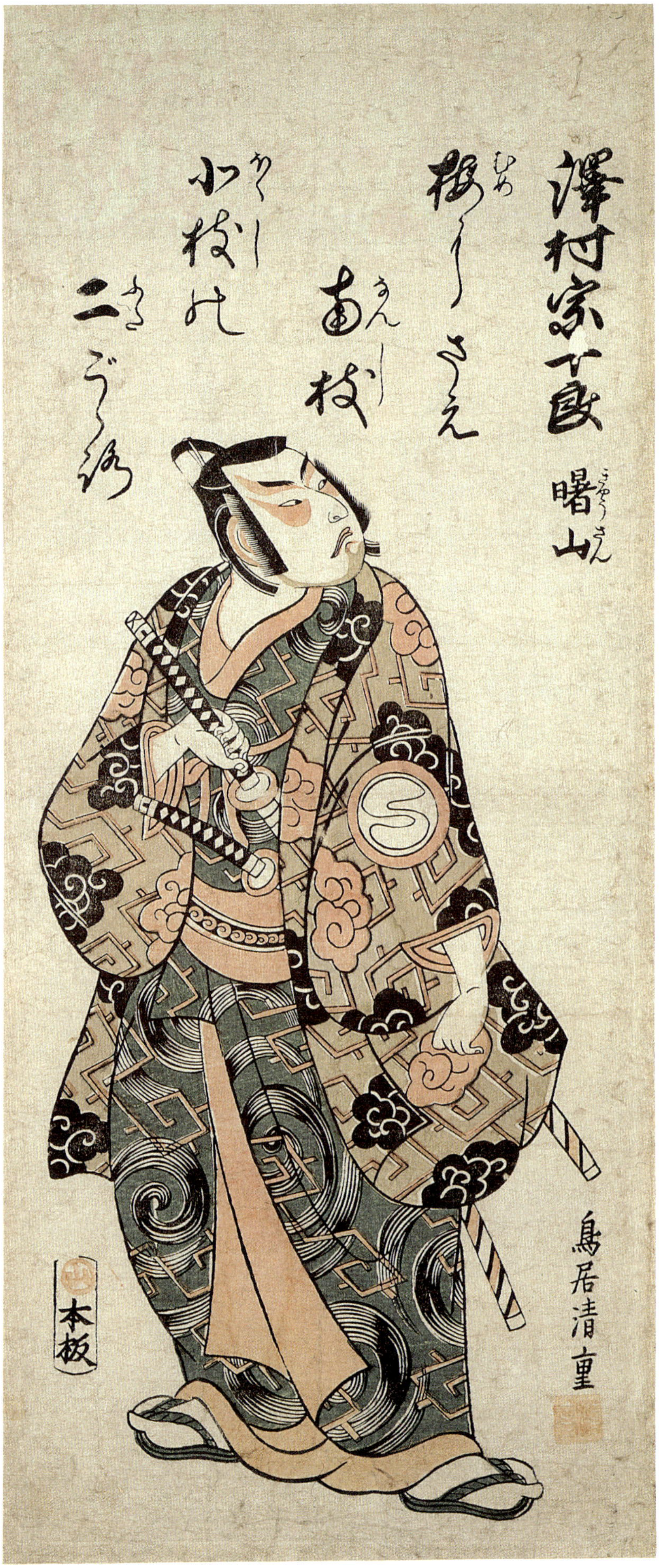
澤村宗十郎
曙山
鳥居清重
本板

112

Torii Kiyoshige

The Actor Sawamura Sōjūrō as Fuwa Banzaemon

1st month, 1757

ARTIST'S SIGNATURE: 'Torii Kiyoshige'

ARTIST'S SEAL: 'Kiyoshige'

PUBLISHER: 'Yamamoto han' (Published by Yamamoto) with mark of Maruya Kohei

woodblock, *ō-hosoban, benizuri-e* (3-colour), 38.9 × 16.7 cm

OTHER IMPRESSION: (*Ukiyo-e taisei*, vol. 3, no. 52)

William Sturgis Bigelow Collection, 1911

11.19697

The lightning and cloud pattern covering the *kosode* and *haori* jacket identifies the role as Fuwa Banzaemon, rival with Nagoya Sanzaburō for the affections of the courtesan Katsuragi in one of the oldest kabuki plays. The pattern was adopted by Danjūrō I for the role from the first time he performed it, aged twenty, in 1680 (see also cat. 23).[1] Fuwa poses resolutely, grasping the hilt of one of his twin swords. Sawamura Sōjūrō appeared at the Morita Theatre from the New Year, 1757, in a succession of six roles in various *jōruri* scenes. The final role was Fuwa Banzaemon.[2]

This has been identified as one of a group of large *hosoban* format portraits of actors by Kiyoshige dating from around the Hōreki era (1751–64), each inscribed with a *hokku* poem composed by the actor himself. The eleven designs from the group currently known are exclusively of male roles, often with the villainous appearance that was Kiyoshige's speciality.[3] Mutō Junko has demonstrated that the combination of actor portrait and poem was a popular novelty of the 1750s, produced by many artists, and has suggested that several of the groups designed by Kiyoshige show the beginnings of depicting the individual likenesses (*nigao-e*) of the actors concerned. The inclusion of poetry reflects the increasing popularity of Edo-style *haikai* (*Edo-za haikai*) in these years and the participation of kabuki actors in this literary movement. Here the poem is signed with Sōjūrō's pen-name, Shōsan, and mixes the seasonal motif of plum with an allusion to Katsuragi's prevarication about her choice of lover:

Ume ni sae *nan-shi hoku-shi no* *futa-gokoro*	Even the plum is of two minds – a branch to the south or a branch to the north?

TTC

1 Iizuka 1926, p. 677, states that Danjūrō was 30 at the time, but this must be a mistake.

2 *Kabuki nenpyō*, vol. 3, p. 292.

3 Listed in Mutō 1999a, pp. 75–6, 83. Mutō also links these to seven other, similar designs in the smaller *hosoban* format ('group C').

113

Hanekawa Chinchō

The Monk Saigyō on a Pilgrimage

1724

ARTIST'S SIGNATURE: 'Hanekawa Motonobu hitsu' (Brush of Hanekawa Motonobu) with artist's *kakihan* (handwritten seal)

PUBLISHER: 'Jinmei-mae Emi-ya' (Emi-ya at Jinmei-mae)

woodblock, *hosoban*, *urushi-e* with hand-colouring and brass filings, 32.3 × 15.8 cm

William Sturgis Bigelow Collection, 1911

11.13261

Images composed of calligraphic characters (*moji-e*), often with a humorous twist, have a long history in Japan and reached their most creative form in the 18th century, in print designs and book illustrations[1] and especially in picture calendars. The present, complex *moji-e* calendar print includes characters referring to the 'dai' (long) months of the lunar year, incorporated in the dress and staff of the wandering monk. The character for 'dai' is shown on the hat and the year 'kinoe tatsu' (1724) in the vine-like cursive characters clinging to the staff. Characters for the 'shō' (short) months, including the 'interposed' *urūzuki* ('intercalary month'), are incorporated in the mnemonic poem above.[2]

The clever concealment of numbers in poems and pictures to indicate long and short months in the *e-goyomi* was adopted as a means of circumventing the law: after 1716 it was forbidden for anyone except the eleven publishers licensed by the Tokugawa government to produce calendars. This edict was repeated in 1744, but commercially produced *urushi-e* and *benizuri-e* picture calendars continued to be made until *c.* 1750.[3]

Although depicted in a cursive manner, the figure can easily be recognised as Saigyō, a Buddhist monk of the Shingon sect and a brilliant *waka* poet.[4] The emphasis here is on the riddle-like wordplay of a 31-syllable poem:

Kokoro naki	Even one who no longer cares about things
mi ni mo urū ha	May want to know the long and SHORT of it:
shirarekeri	The THIRD, SECOND, and FOURTH LEAP months;
samidare sugite	Then, once FIFTH-month rains have passed
kasasagi no shimo.	Come Tanabata magpies in the SEVENTH,
	And finally frost in the ELEVENTH.[5]

The opening words of the poem, 'kokoro naki mi ni mo' ('one who has no feelings of attachment' – a Buddhist monk, for example), are quoted from the famous autumn evening poem by Saigyō (see cat. 64, 141). The first syllable of 'kokoro' has been written with the character 'small' to indicate that the numbers of the short months have been woven into the verse. The second line, 'mi ni mo urū ha', refers with its characters to the second ('ni') and third ('mi') months as well as the intercalated ('urū') month, inserted after the fourth. The fourth line refers to the 'fifth month rains' ('samidare'). The fifth and final line refers to both the seventh and the eleventh month. The seventh is indicated by the word 'Tanabata' (written with the characters for 'seven' and 'night'), the name of a festival that took place on the seventh night of the seventh month. The *furigana* next to the characters indicate that they should be read as 'kasasagi' – 'magpies'. Magpies have come to symbolise Tanabata, since it is believed that on that day they line up to form a bridge so that the two star lovers, the Ox Herder (Altair in the constellation of Aquila) and the Weaver Maid (Vega in the constellation of Lyra), can meet on the Milky Way. Similarly, *furigana* indicate that the characters for 'eleven' should be read as 'shimo', meaning 'frost' – associated with the eleventh month. LEV

1 Masanobu designed a *kosode* pattern with *moji-e* designs of poets (*kasen-e*) (cat. 43). See also his portrait of a courtesan drawn with the characters of phrases used by women in letters. Chicago 1955, p. 136, no. 55. *Moji-e* of famous contemporary actors, or persons in various professions, became the subject of book illustrations datable to the Kyōhō era (1716–36). *Kabuki zusetsu*, no. 107; Tokyo 1990, no. 133.

2 Calendars of this type were known as *dai-shō-ryaku-reki* (abbreviated calendars showing the long and short months), *dai-shō* for short, and those with images were often called (*dai-shō*) *e-goyomi*. The long months in 1724 were one, four, six, eight, nine, ten and twelve, the short ones two, three, intercalary four, five, seven and eleven.

3 Mnemonic poems and rebus-like pictures were produced from the 1680s; *e-goyomi* appeared in the Kyōhō era. An unsigned calendar print shows Ebisu, one of the Seven Lucky Gods, stepping on an account book dated 1706; the characters outlining his costume spell out a poem. Honolulu 1980, p. 280, no. 14. A few rare *e-goyomi* date from *c.* 1723–4. *Ukiyo-e shūka*, vol. 1, no. 168 (Kiyomasu II, 1724); New York 1991, p. 14, fig. 3 (Tsunekawa Shigenobu, 1729); Oberlin 1984, p. 92, fig. 142–3 (Kiyomasu II, 1727; Kiyoharu, 1731); Chicago 1955, p. 76, no. 6 (Kiyonobu II, 1731). The lunar calendar was used in Japan until 1873. The first day of each of the twelve months coincided with the new moon, the fourteenth or fifteenth day with the full moon. Each month had either 30 days (long) or 29 (short). Approximately every three years an extra month (*urūzuki*) would be inserted, or 'intercalated'.

4 Born into a samurai household, Saigyō travelled widely in search of beauty, unconcerned about social strife or court intrigue, translating his experiences and ideals into moving verses. For a brief summary of his career, see Miner et al. 1985, pp. 222–3.

5 Trans. John Carpenter.

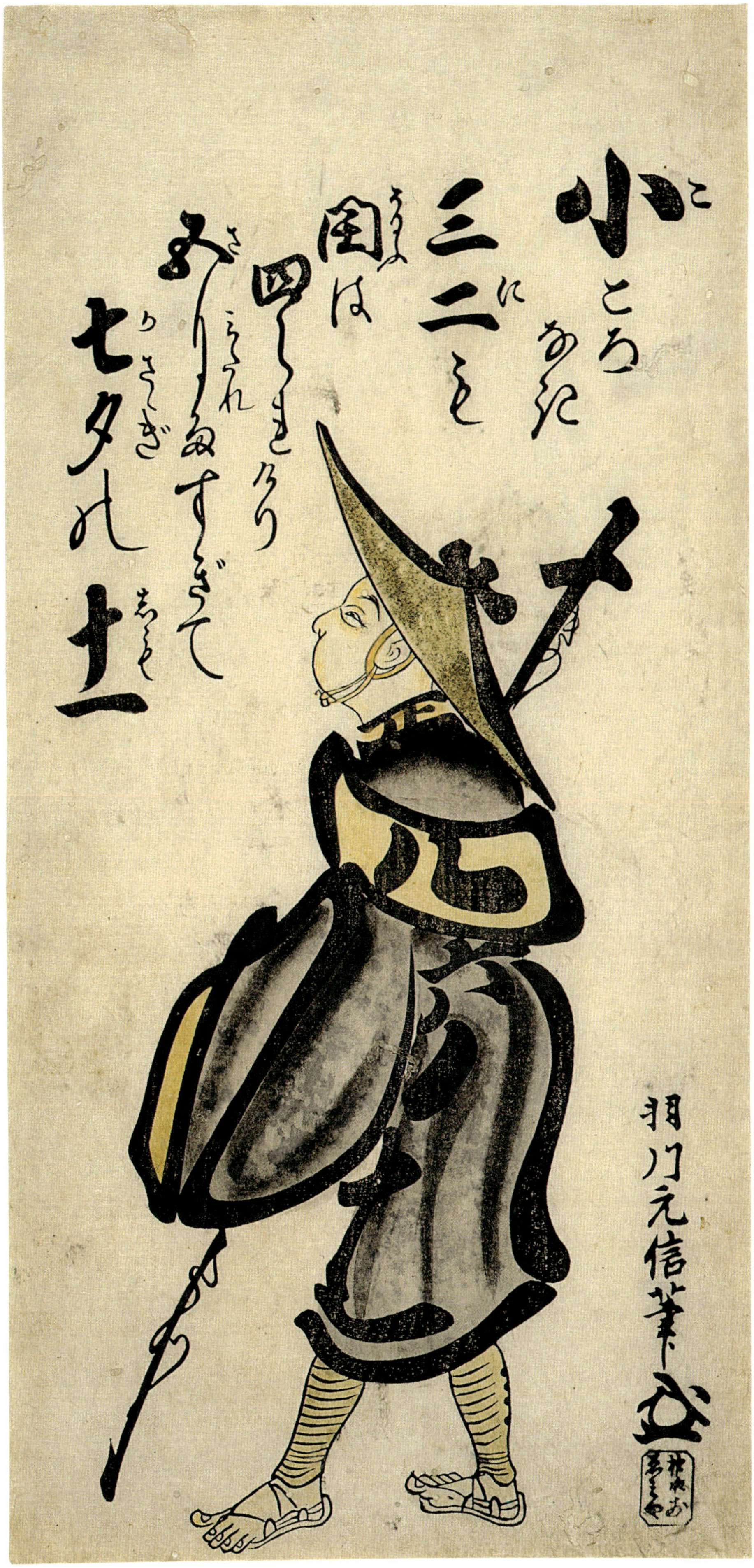

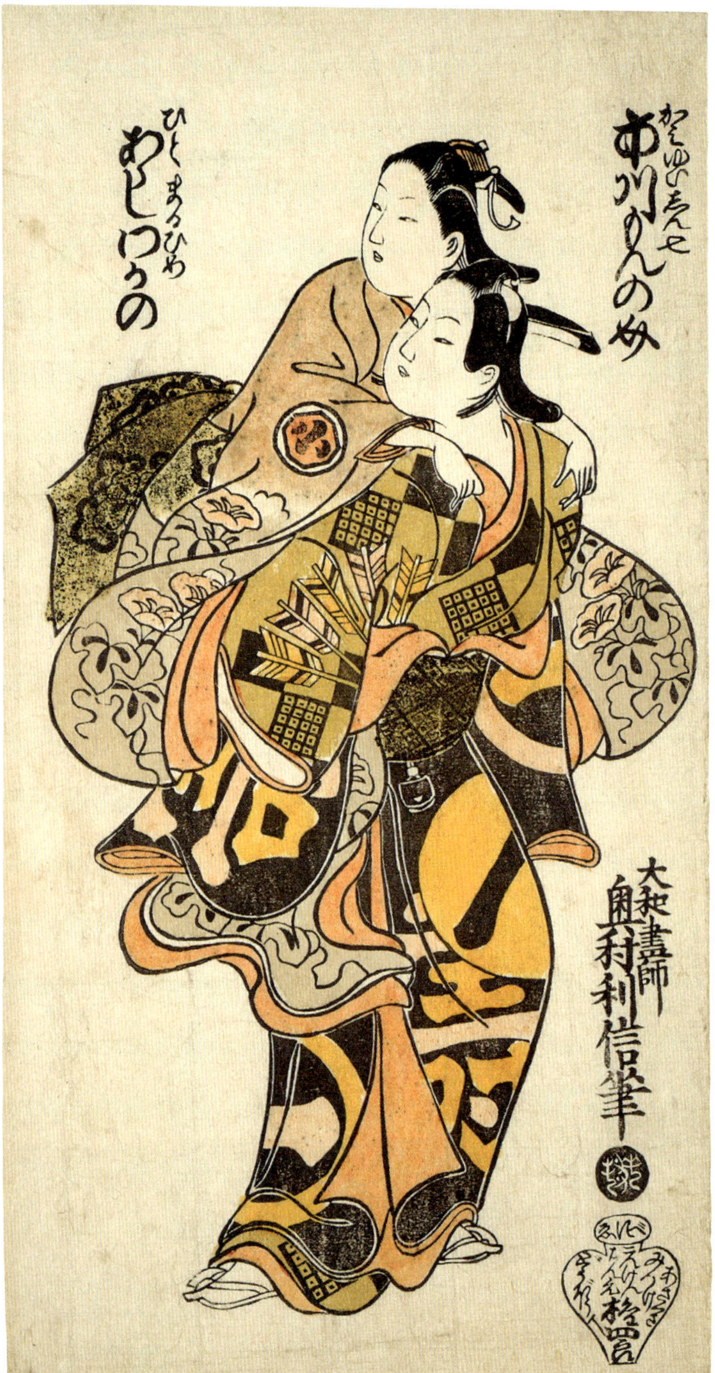
大和畫師
奥村利信筆

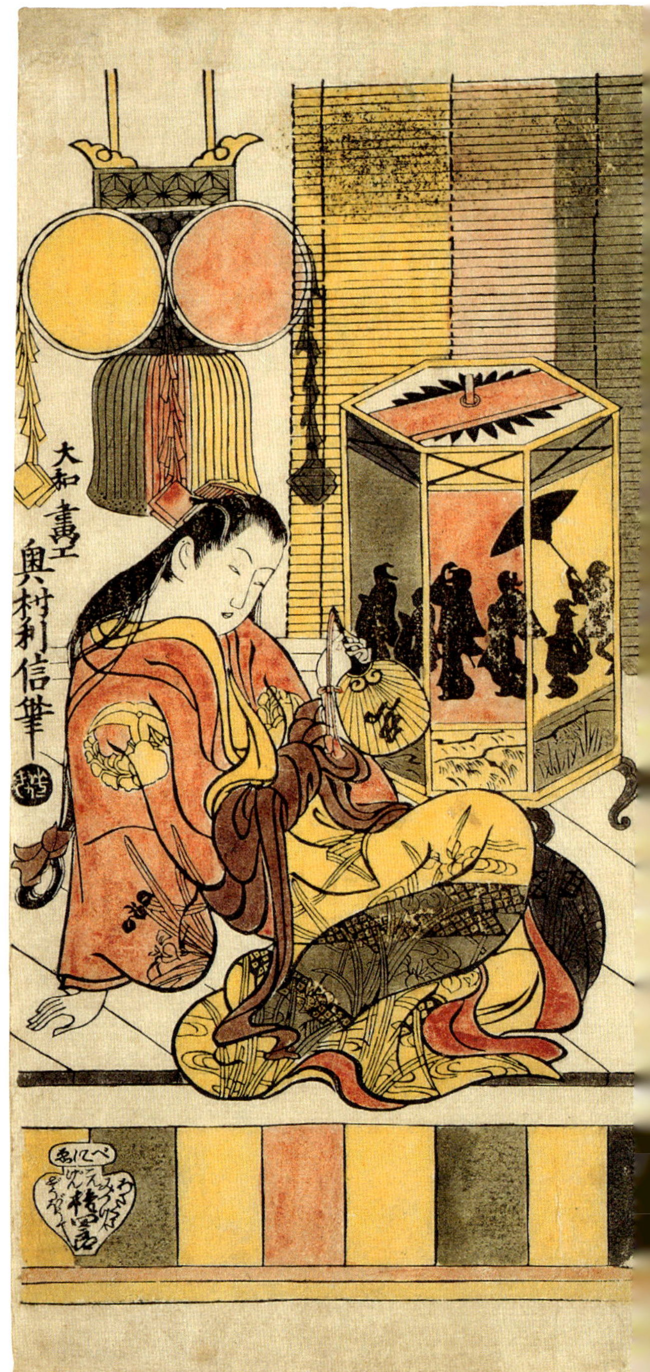
大和畫工
奥村利信筆

114
Okumura Toshinobu
The Actors Ichikawa Monnosuke as Shinshichi the Barber and Arashi Wakano as Princess Hitomaru

c. 1723 (?)

ARTIST'S SIGNATURE: 'Yamato eshi Okumura Toshinobu hitsu' (Brush of the Yamato picture master Okumura Toshinobu)

ARTIST'S SEAL: 'Okumura [?]'

PUBLISHER: 'Asakusa Mitsuke Dōbō-chō beni-e kongen hanmoto Gonshirō' (The publisher [Izumi-ya] Gonshirō, originator of *beni-e*, at Dōbō-chō, Asakusa Mitsuke)

woodblock, *hosoban, beni-e* with brass filings, 30 × 15.7 cm

William Sturgis Bigelow Collection, 1911

11.19119

Ichikawa Monnosuke as Kamiyui Shinshichi (Shinshichi the Barber) carries on his back Arashi Wakano as Hitomaru-hime (Princess Hitomaru). The young woman huddles close to her lover for protection; her long, hanging sleeves billow around him, their morning glory design seeming to cling around the more masculine motif of arrow flights on his under-robe. His black outer robe is decorated with a bold alternating pattern that combines the written character *kotobuki* (long life) with the actor's crest, a single horizontal line inside a circle. The sleeves of the outer robes have been shrugged off to free him for his exertions.

Although the roles are named on the print, known theatrical records do not permit a precise identification of the play. The piggyback pose and anxious expressions of the lovers suggest a scene of elopement (see also cat. 108). Monnosuke and Wakano performed together at the Nakamura Theatre from 1722/11 to 1726. Other examples of Toshinobu designs published by Izumi-ya Gonshirō have already been dated to the period 1718/11 to 1722, so a tentative date of *c.* 1723 is proposed here for the Boston print.[1] TTC

1 I am grateful to Mutō Junko for her assistance with this dating.

115
Okumura Toshinobu
Courtesan Admiring a Shadow Lantern

c. 1720s

ARTIST'S SIGNATURE: 'Yamato gakō Okumura Toshinobu hitsu' (Brush of the Yamato painting artisan Okumura Toshinobu)

PUBLISHER: 'Asakusa Mitsuke Dōbō-chō beni-e kongen hanmoto Gonshirō' (The publisher [Izumi-ya] Gonshirō, originator of *beni-e*, at Dōbō-chō, Asakusa Mitsuke)

woodblock, *hosoban, beni-e, urushi-e* with brass filings, 33.7 × 15.8 cm

William Sturgis Bigelow Collection, 1911

11.19112

It is an evening in early autumn and still very hot. A courtesan sits in a relaxed, seductive pose on an open veranda – perhaps at an assignation teahouse (*ageya*) – hoping to cool herself in any passing breeze. Prospective clients will be passing as well, of course. She leans back, admiring the shadow show on the rotating mechanical lantern (*mawari-dōrō*) beside her, which shows the retinue of a grand courtesan (*oiran dōchū*) in procession beneath a large parasol. The winding path amid reeds along the bottom of the lantern must represent Nihon-tsutsumi (Japan Embankment), the route to the Yoshiwara pleasure quarter. Hanging behind her to the left of the reed blind is a large decorative *bon* lantern (*bon-dōrō*) for the *ura-bon* festival, held in veneration of dead ancestors around the fifteenth day of the seventh month.

Prominent on the courtesan's sleeve is a crest of combined wisteria and water plantain (*fuji-omodaka*). Not the crest of a kabuki actor, it is probably the personal crest of the courtesan. This is thus a genre scene, not a theatrical print. The character *shinobu* written on the courtesan's fan may be her name. TTC

1 The Tokyo National Museum collection includes another, similar print by Toshinobu, published by Emi-ya, in which a courtesan with a fan is seated on a veranda beneath a *bon* lantern. Tokyo 1960–3, vol. 1, no. 306.

116

Okumura Toshinobu

The Actors Matsushima Hyōtarō as a Courtesan and Nakamura Ujūrō and Tsuruya Nanboku [?] as Samurai

11th month, 1724

ARTIST'S SIGNATURE:
'Yamato gakō Okumura Toshinobu hitsu' (Brush of the Yamato painting artisan Okumura Toshinobu)

PUBLISHER:
'Sakai-chō hanmoto Nakajima-ya' (Nakajima-ya, publisher at Sakai-chō)

woodblock, *hosoban*, *beni-e* with brass filings, 30.2 × 16 cm

REPRODUCED: *Ukiyo-e shūka*, vol.1, no. 36

William Sturgis Bigelow Collection, 1911

11.13225

Matsushima Hyōtarō, a Kamigata actor who specialised in female roles, worked in Edo for only one year, beginning in the eleventh month, 1724. This print seems to depict a scene from his very first performance in the eastern capital, in *Bankoku Taihei-ki*, the *kaomise* play at the Ichimura Theatre (see cat. 94). Although precise details of the plot are not known, the actor critique *Yakusha miya-suzume*, published at the following New Year, makes reference to Hyōtarō's role as a courtesan: 'Hyōtarō took the role of the courtesan Shima no Senzai and, with a child attendant [*kamuro*] and an umbrella, acted a scene of a courtesan's procession and entry into the assignation teahouse [*ageya-iri*]'.[1] In the present print the courtesan is shown in her upstairs apartments in a Yoshiwara brothel, dressing her hair as she kneels in front of a mirror. Both the mirror stand and her robe are emblazoned prominently with Hyōtarō's crest – the character *akinai* (trade) inside a circle – which will have been unfamiliar to Edo audiences. The winding path on a raised embankment in the background is Nihon-tsutsumi, which leads through open fields to the Main Gate (Ōmon-guchi) of the pleasure quarter, clearly sign-posted. Two samurai pleasure-seekers and their manservant would seem to be walking away from Yoshiwara along the embankment. Carrying twin swords, both samurai sport stylish outfits for wooing. The critique indicates that in this play Nakamura Ujūrō (right) played the role of Ōyodo Heima and Tsuruya Nanboku (left) that of Shinozuka: Ujūrō is listed among the actors of villain roles and Nanboku among comic actors.[2] After this performance references to Ujūrō disappear from known theatrical records.

The roof of the brothel in the print has been thickly coated with brass filings. Although the safflower red (*beni*) and other hand-applied colours have faded considerably, this is apparently the only surviving impression of this attractive design. TTC

1 *Kabuki hyōban-ki I*, vol. 9, p. 52.

2 The identity of the actor playing the samurai on the left, who wears a wide sedge hat and is described on the print simply as 'Nanboku', remains open to doubt. In 1719/11 Nanboku Magotarō I took the name Tsuruya Nanboku I, and his son Tsuruya Genzō become Nanboku Magotarō II. The crest drawn on his jacket in the print, the character *dai* (big), is given as Magotarō II's in the actor critique of 1725/1. Beginning with the critique of 1726/1, however, this same crest is said to be Nanboku's. Since Nakamura Ujūrō is described on the print simply as 'Ujūrō', on balance it seems likely that the 'Nanboku' named on the print refers to Tsuruya Nanboku rather than to his son Nanboku Magotarō II. Both father and son specialised in comic roles. (I am grateful to Mutō Junko for her opinion on this matter.)

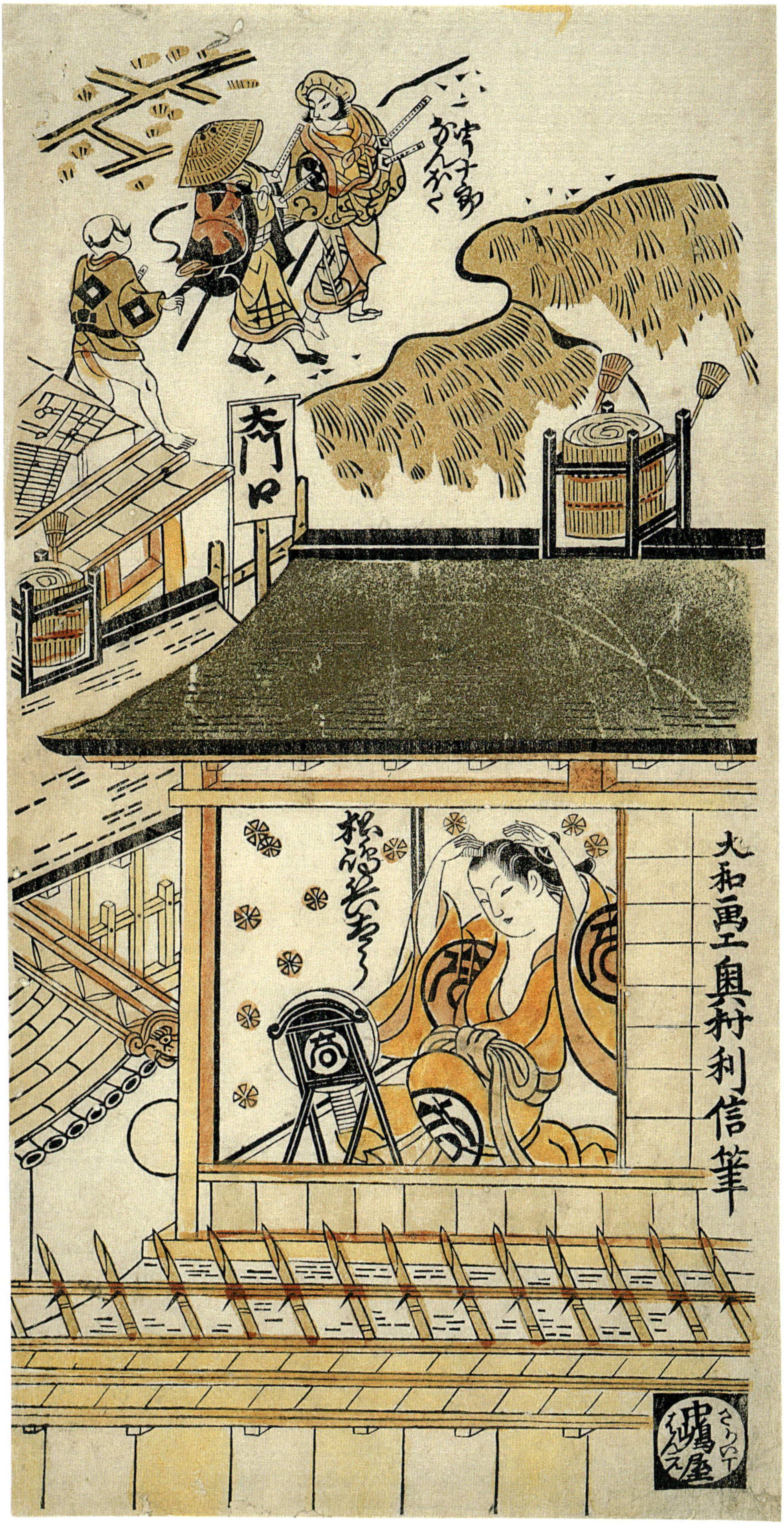
大門口
大和画工奥村利信筆

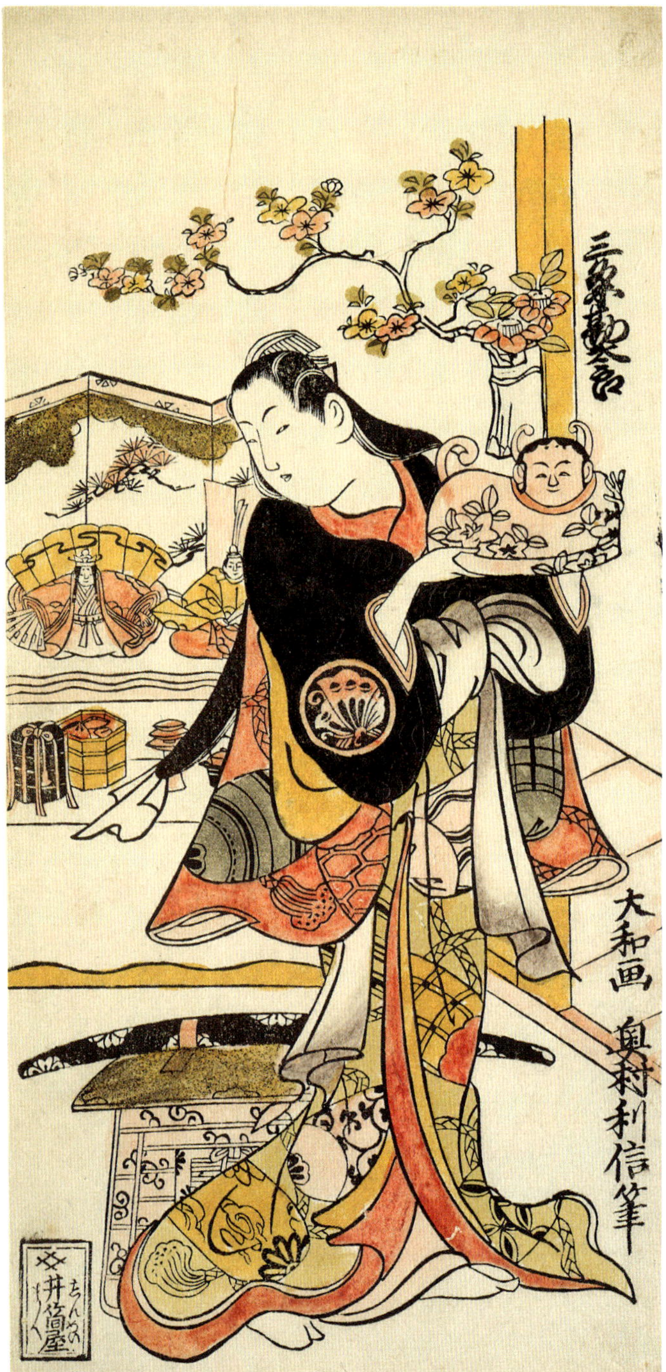
大和画
奥村利信筆

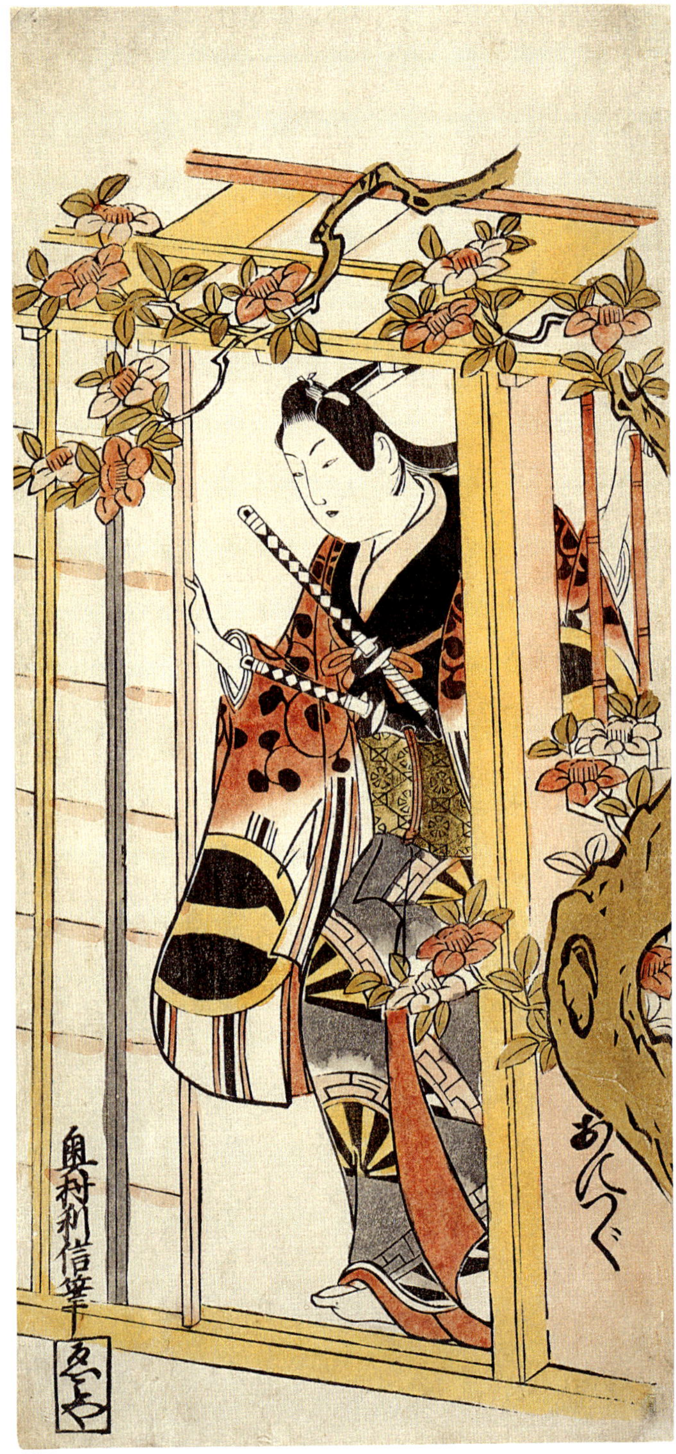
奥村利信筆

117
Okumura Toshinobu
The Actor Sanjō Kantarō II

c. 1724–5 (?)

ARTIST'S SIGNATURE: 'Yamato-e Okumura Toshinobu hitsu' (Yamato picture, brush of Okumura Toshinobu)

PUBLISHER: 'Shinmei-mae Izutsu-ya' (Izutsu-ya [Chūzaemon] at Shinmei-mae)

woodblock, *hosoban, beni-e, urushi-e* with brass filings, 32.8 × 15.4 cm

William Sturgis Bigelow Collection, 1911

11.19123

The performance here has not been precisely identified, but Sanjō Kantarō II's role looks to be that of a woman from an aristocratic household. She holds a papier mâché dog (*inu-hariko*), and behind her, on a tiered platform in the formal *tokonoma* alcove, are Emperor and Empress dolls arranged in front of a small folding screen, and a miniature lacquer sake set for the Dolls Festival (*hina matsuri*) held on the third day of the third month. In the vase hanging from the pillar of the alcove are seasonal sprigs of cherry and camellia. The woman's hair is combed out at the back and tied with a ribbon at the end of the ponytail. She has shrugged off the sleeves of her *kosode*, which is decorated with a pattern of large tasselled pillows.

The delicate hand-colouring features gradated purple on the sash and pink on the butterfly crest on Kantarō II's under-robe. This bears an embossed design of eddying water and has glue painted over the black in imitation of the appearance of lacquer (*urushi-e*). The form of the publisher's mark and the existence of related designs by Okumura Masanobu and Okumura Toshinobu suggest a date of *c.* 1724–5 for the print.[1] TTC

1 Another print with this type of Izutsu-ya mark can be dated *c.* 1722. Designs are also known by Okumura Masanobu (published by Okumura-ya; British Museum, London, 1921.11-15.01) and Okumura Toshinobu (published by Ōmi-ya at Yokoyama-chō) that show Sanjō Kantarō II holding a toy palanquin similar to that placed here on the floor behind her. The publisher's seals point to dates of *c.* 1723–7 and *c.* 1725 respectively for these designs, which most likely relate to the same play as the Boston print (private communication from Mutō Junko).

118
Okumura Toshinobu
The Actor Ichikawa Monnosuke as Onitsugu

11th month, 1725

ARTIST'S SIGNATURE: 'Okumura Toshinobu hitsu' (Brush of Okumura Toshinobu)

PUBLISHER: 'Emi-ya'

woodblock, hosoban, *beni-e, urushi-e* with brass filings, 32.7 × 15.3 cm

William Sturgis Bigelow Collection, 1911

11.19124

Ichikawa Monnosuke appears at a gate, framed by a camellia tree. The *furisode* – with patterns of vine leaves and the wheels of court carriages – the twin swords and the unshaven forelock suggest the role of an adolescent samurai. The name of the role, Onitsugu, is written unobtrusively in the bottom right corner of the print. Monnosuke played Onitsugu, the young tutor (*menoto*) of Terute (performed by Yamamoto Hanazato), in *Oguri chōsei-den*, given at the Nakamura Theatre in 1725/11.

Monnosuke assumed that name in 1713/11. His nickname was Maruichi (a circle and a line after his crest) and, much admired for his good looks and clear voice, he was in many ways regarded as the founder of the *wakashu* (delicate young man) aesthetic among Edo actors. The actor critique *Yakusha shōgatsu kotoba*, published at the New Year, 1726, following the performance depicted here, proclaimed: 'Never mind the three cities [Edo, Kyoto, Osaka], there cannot be such an illustrious *wakashu* performing even in the theatres of China and India....May he keep these looks for 580 years'.[1] TTC

1 Meaning 'for ever and a day'. *Kabuki hyōban-ki I*, vol. 9, p. 135.

119

Nishimura Shigenobu

The Actors Ōtani Hiroji as Arajishi Otokonosuke and Segawa Kikujirō as Izumo no Okuni

11th month, 1731

ARTIST'S SIGNATURE: 'Nishimura Shigenobu hitsu' (Brush of Nishimura Shigenobu)

PUBLISHER: 'Shiba Shinmei Izutsu-ya' (Izutsu-ya [Chūzaemon] at Shiba Shinmei)

woodblock, *hosoban, beni-e, urushi-e* with brass filings, 33.3 × 15.5 cm

William Sturgis Bigelow Collection, 1911

11.19155

1 *Kabuki hyoban-ki I*, vol. 10, pp. 292, 303, critiques of Ōtani Hiroji and Segawa Kikujirō. A similar chicken coop is shown in the illustration in the actor critique, with Ichimura Takenojō as Yoshimasa inside it.

A scene from the play *Higashiyama-dono eiga butai*, performed at the Ichimura Theatre in the eleventh month, 1731. Ōtani Hiroji appears as Arajishi Otokonosuke, cradling a small child on his lap, with Segawa Kikujirō as Izumo no Okuni standing behind him holding his *haori* jacket with its 'otoko' crest for Otokonosuke. The cage behind them is a chicken coop. Ostensibly, the play was set in the world of the Higashiyama court of Shogun Ashikaga Yoshimasa (1436–90). For part of the story Otonosuke took the name Mibu no Yoshitora and became the guardian of Yoshimasa (Lord Higashiyama).

The actor critique of the following spring, *Yakusha haru-goma*, described the scene: 'He [Hiroji as Otokonosuke] put Yoshimasa [played by Ichimura Takenojō] into a chicken coop (*toya*) and had him crow like a bird. . . .He wrapped the child of O-Kuni and. . . Yoshimasa in a *haori* and exchanged it for a golden pheasant, which was then killed. . . .She [Kikujirō] really thought it was her baby when Hiroji showed her he was killing the child – although he had substituted a bird – and her grief was well portrayed. Wanting to take one last look at the face of her dead child, she unwrapped the *haori* jacket. When she found it was a bird and not the child she had to apologise to Hiroji'.[1] TTC

120

Nishimura Shigenobu

The Actor Sawamura Sōjūrō as Kyō no Jirō

spring 1734

ARTIST'S SIGNATURE: 'Eshi Nishimura Shigenobu hitsu' (Brush of the picture master Nishimura Shigenobu)

PUBLISHER: 'Shiba Shinmei-mae Yoko-chō Izutsu-ya, Seisuidō' (Seisuidō, Izutsu-ya [Chūzaemon] at Shinmei-mae Yoko-chō, Shiba)

woodblock, *hosoban, beni-e, urushi-e* with brass filings, 33 × 15 cm

William Sturgis Bigelow Collection, 1911

11.19158

1 *Kabuki hyoban-ki I*, suppl. vol., pp. 216–17, reproduced p. 218.

Sawamura Sōjūrō appears as Kyō no Jirō in the play *Jūhakkō imayō Soga*, performed at the Nakamura Theatre in spring 1734. An untitled actor critique (Cambridge University Library, *c.* 1734/3) describes Sōjūrō's performance in this, the second part of the plot: 'in the guise of a big spender [*daijin*] called Kurosuke. Came on tipsy. He hated dogs, so he cut the paw off the Pekinese kept by the brothel madam and said: "this looks like a fox's paw".' Kyō no Jirō's mission seems to have been to prevent the Soga brothers frequenting the pleasure quarter. He mixed sake with ash in a teacup and used the dog's paw to make footprints leading to the courtesan Tora's room. He then quizzed the mysterious 'fox-courtesan'. This was a 'great, great hit' (*ō-ō-atari*).[1]

Big spender Kurosuke's robe is decorated with the characters *kandō* (disinheritance), presumably relevant to the plot. Behind him is a 'gate pine' (*kadomatsu*) New Year decoration and ceremonial sake kettle and cup ready for the holiday celebrations. The hapless pup curls up on his discarded *haori* jacket. TTC

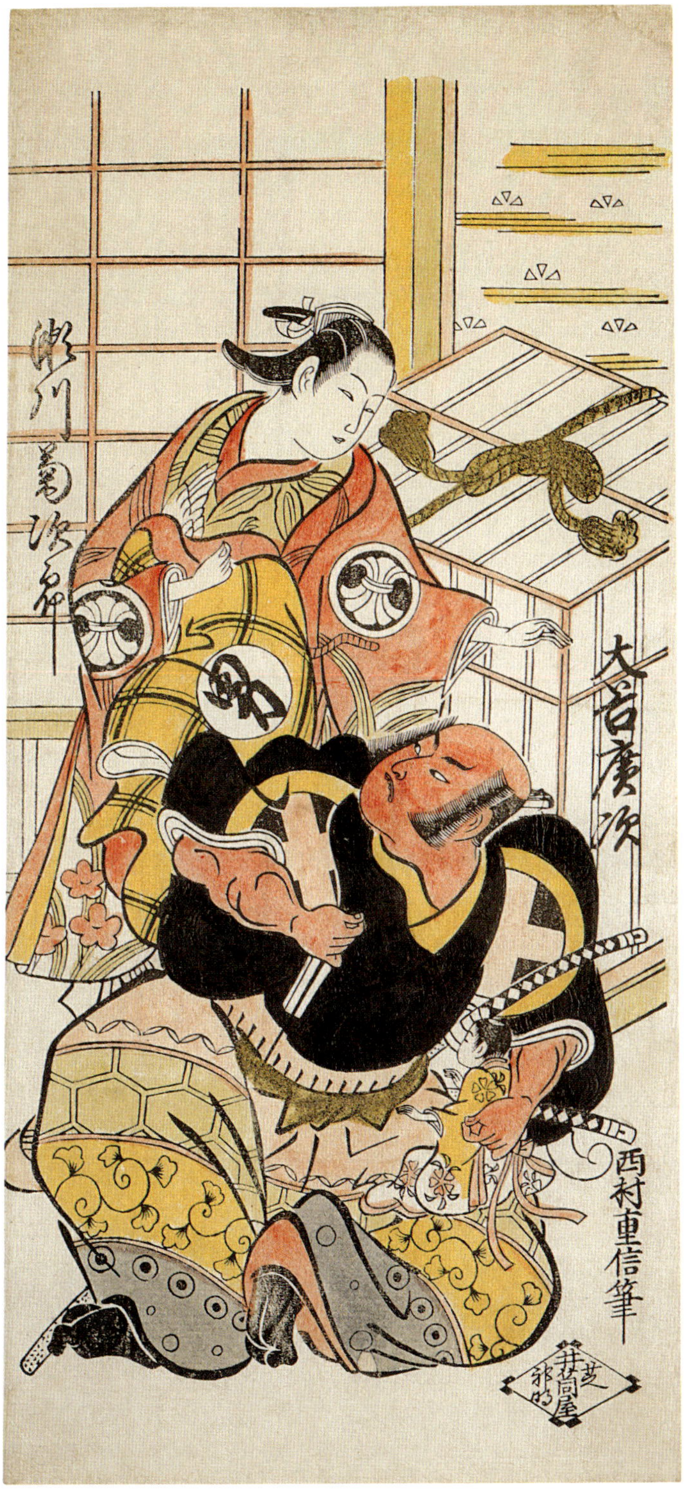

大谷廣次
西村重信筆

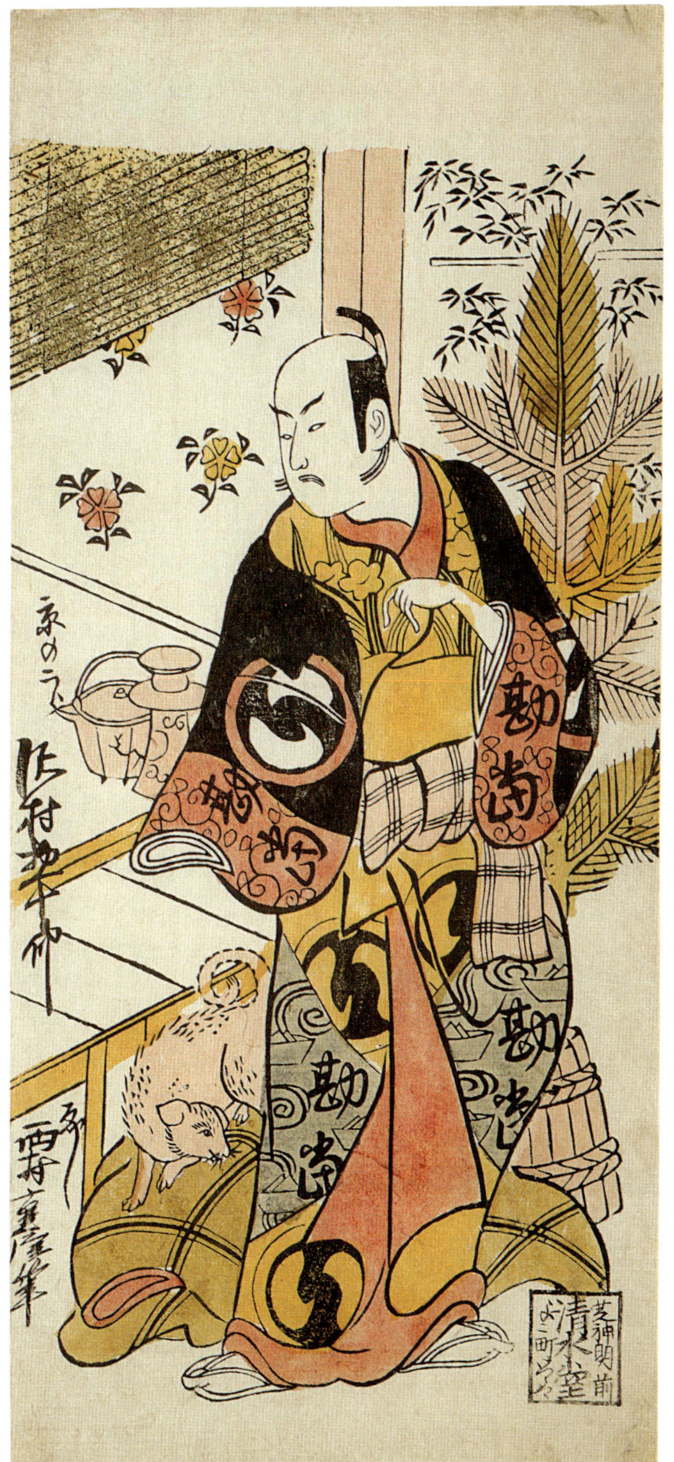

121

Ishikawa Toyonobu

'A Triptych of Beauties of the Three Capitals: Left, Osaka' (*Sanpuku-tsui; Osaka hidari*)

c. 1745

ARTIST'S SIGNATURE: 'Tanjōdō Ishikawa Shūha zu' (Picture by Tanjōdō Ishikawa Shūha)

ARTIST'S SEALS: 'Ishikawa-uji' (Ishikawa family), 'Toyonobu'

PUBLISHER: 'hanmoto Urokogata-ya' (Urokogata-ya, publisher) with publisher's mark

woodblock, *hahahiro hashira-e, beni-e,* left sheet of a triptych, 64 × 23.8 cm

OTHER IMPRESSIONS: William S. and John T. Spaulding Collection, Museum of Fine Arts, Boston, 21.6273; Art Institute of Chicago (Chicago 1955, p. 208); Worcester Art Museum, Mass. (Worcester 1996, p. 66)

William Sturgis Bigelow Collection, 1911

11.19681

This large hand-coloured wide pillar picture depicts an Osaka courtesan reading a love letter. Her assistant-in-training (*kamuro*) walks beside her carrying a tea set. The small cartouche in the upper left corner indicates that this is the left panel of a set of three (*sanpuku-tsui*) and shows an Osaka courtesan. The complete triptych, of which only one set is known, features a Kyoto courtesan in the middle and an Edo courtesan on the right. Collectively, they depict a theme referred to as the 'Courtesans of the Three Cities', which reflects a long-standing cultural rivalry between Kyoto, Japan's traditional capital, Osaka, its largest mercantile centre, and Edo, the seat of the shogunal government.

Okumura Masanobu invented the *sanpuku-tsui* idea and the three courtesans theme in the late 1710s. The earliest versions featured all three courtesans on a single sheet with the Edo courtesan above and the Kyoto and Osaka courtesans below. A little later Masanobu reconfigured the composition for the *ōban yoko-e* format, arranging the courtesans in a horizontal row.[1] This type of image became increasingly popular in the 1730s and several artists produced variations on it, even extending it to subjects other than courtesans. Wide pillar picture versions, including this example by Toyonobu, are rare, however. The large format, with each courtesan on a single sheet, suggests that such sets were specialised products, perhaps intended for clients who could afford to have them mounted as hanging scrolls.

Toyonobu's treatment of the *kamuro* in this design is especially noteworthy. Print artists generally depicted women's faces in profile or three-quarter view, partly because of artistic convention, partly because Yoshiwara protocols trained courtesans to submit demurely to the gaze of their male clients. The *kamuro* in this design transgresses these protocols by directly engaging the viewer's gaze. Toyonobu may have wanted to capture the precocity and curiosity of the *kamuro*, most of whom were younger than ten. Perhaps he simply welcomed the challenge of depicting a face in full frontal view. AH

1 Paine 1963a discusses and reproduces several examples by Masanobu and others.

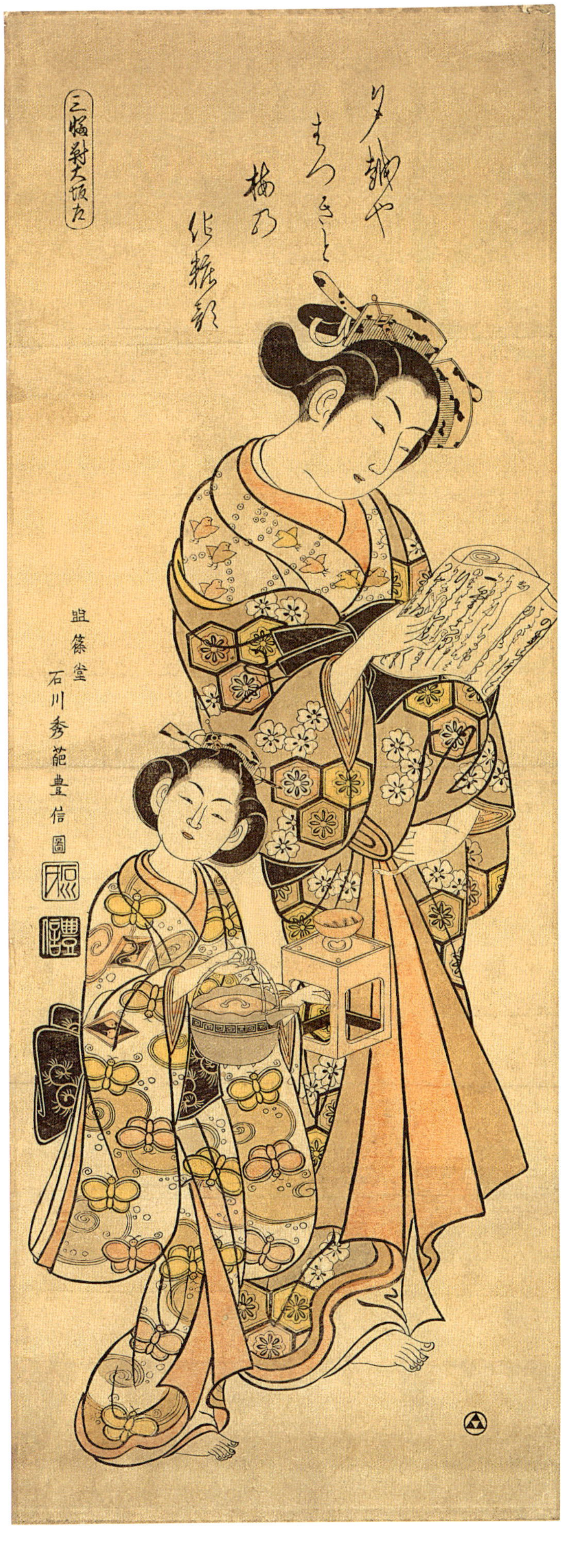
明篠堂
石川秀範豊信圖

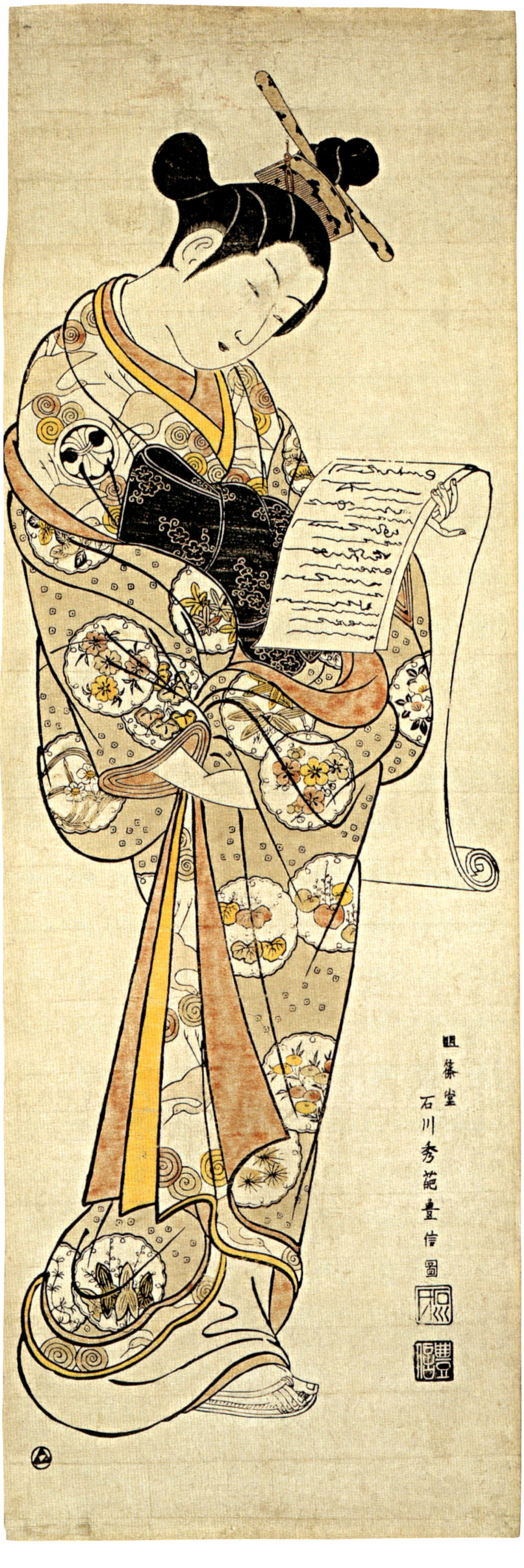
石川秀葩豊信圖

122

Ishikawa Toyonobu

The Actor Segawa Kikunojō as a Courtesan Reading a Letter

late 1740s

ARTIST'S SIGNATURE: 'Tanjōdō Ishikawa Shūha Toyonobu zu' (Picture by Tanjōdō Ishikawa Shūha Toyonobu)

ARTIST'S SEALS: 'Ishikawa-uji', 'Toyonobu'

PUBLISHER: mark of Urokogata-ya

woodblock, *hahahiro hashira-e, beni-e*, 65.5 × 22.8 cm

OTHER IMPRESSION: Art Institute of Chicago (Chicago 1955, p. 209, [Toyonobu] no. 26)

William Sturgis Bigelow Collection, 1911

11.19680

1 In the critique *Yakusha nezumi-zan* (1744/1) he was awarded the supreme rank 'extremely upper, upper felicitous' (*kyoku jō jō kichi*). *Kabuki hyōban-ki II*, vol. 2, pp. 385–6. For recent accounts of the career of Segawa Kikunojō, see Satō 1997 and Satō 1998.

2 *Ukiyo-e taikei*, vol. 1, no. 55 (Art Institute of Chicago impression, commentary by Narazaki Muneshige).

3 Chicago 1955, [Toyonobu] no. 26.

4 Satō 1998, p. 186.

The great impersonator of women Segawa Kikunojō (1693–1749), identified by his crest – a bundle of cotton floss (*yui-wata*) – and by the snowflake-shaped roundels (*yuki-wa*) on his surcoat (*uchikake*), appears in the role of a courtesan who stands engrossed in reading a letter. Like all the great early impersonators of women (*onnagata*) in kabuki, the actor was a native of the Kamigata region. He took the name Kikunojō in 1712. In 1728/2 he scored a major hit at the Ichiyama Theatre in Kyoto with the 'Muken no kane' (Bell of Eternity) scene and, after visiting Edo for the first time in the winter of 1730, repeated the role to great acclaim at the Nakamura Theatre from the second to the fifth month, 1731. Other great dance roles interpreted by him were Shakkyō and Dōjō-ji. By 1744 he was being hailed as the greatest *onnagata* in all 'the three cities' (Kyoto, Edo, Osaka).[1]

It is difficult to pinpoint the courtesan role depicted here, if indeed the print does record a particular performance. The hairstyle, combed tightly back from the forehead and with a single tortoiseshell bodkin (*kōgai*) passed through the twisted topknot and a single comb, is certainly typical of the later 1740s. Yoshida Teruji apparently suggested that the role may be that of the courtesan Kayoiji in the play *Hagoromo kotobuki Soga*, performed at the Nakamura Theatre at the New Year, 1745.[2] Another proposal has been the courtesan Nishikigi in *Izu gunzei sumō nishiki*, given at the Nakamura Theatre in the eleventh month, 1747.[3] Kikunojō's final illness forced him to cease performing around the middle of the third month, 1748, and although his name was included in several playbills after this date, he does not appear to have been well enough to perform. He died on the second day of the ninth month, 1749.[4]

The palette of the careful hand-colouring in the Boston print is almost identical to that in the only other known impression (Art Institute of Chicago), except that the Boston colours have faded far more. The Chicago impression also has a pink blush painted on the cheek, while the eye in the Boston impression has been repaired and the sheet trimmed close to the figure on the left side. TTC

123
Ishikawa Toyonobu
Kan U with a Courtesan

late 1740s

ARTIST'S SIGNATURE: 'Tanjōdō Ishikawa Shūha Toyonobu zu' (Picture by Tanjōdō Ishikawa Shūha Toyonobu)

ARTIST'S SEALS: 'Ishikawa-uji', 'Toyonobu'

PUBLISHER: mark of Urokogata-ya

woodblock, *hashira-e*, *beni-e*, 60.9 × 15.8 cm

OTHER IMPRESSIONS: Royal Ontario Museum, Toronto (Toronto 1975, no. 49); (formerly K. Kawaura Collection); (Jacob Pins Collection)[1]

William Sturgis Bigelow Collection, 1911

11.19679

Kan U (*Chin.* Guan Yu), worshipped in China as the god of war, is depicted in Japan in the same way as in China, with an imposing build, a full beard and a ruddy complexion, and carrying his 'blue dragon lance' (*seiryū-tō*). He swore blood brotherhood with Liu Bei (*Jap.* Ryū Bi) and Zhang Fei (*Jap.* Chō Hi) in a peach garden, and together the three fought successfully to establish Liu Bei as the first Emperor of the Shu kingdom, in AD 221, events later much embroidered in the novel *Romance of the Three Kingdoms* (*Sanguozhi yanyi, Jap. Sangoku-shi engi*) and in Chinese drama. In this print Kan U is shown in the unlikely situation of holding one end of a love letter read by a courtesan – probably a parody of a traditional scene in which Liu Bei is depicted standing guard with his lance behind a table at which Kan U sits reading a scroll of military strategy. The courtesan, wearing a surcoat (*uchikake*) with a design of egrets flying among snow-covered willow branches, is all but dwarfed by Kan U's bulky form and flowing brocade robes towering behind her.

Kan U seems to have entered Japanese literature and art in the early 18th century.[2] In the eleventh month, 1737, the kabuki actor Ichikawa Ebizō II first played the role of Kan U in the play *Uruu-zuki ninin Kagekiyo* at the Kawarazaki Theatre, in a plot in which the identities of the Chinese heroes were temporarily adopted in an otherwise Japanese setting. Ichikawa Danzō as Kagekiyo took on the guise of Chō Hi in order to steal secretly into the mansion of Noriyori. Thereupon Ebizō II as Shigetada took on the guise of Kan U and exposed Kagekiyo's true identity. Ebizō performed Kan U three more times in his career – at the Ichimura Theatre in 1739/11, at the Sadoshima Theatre in 1742/9 while on tour in Osaka, and at the Ichimura Theatre in 1756/11, one of the actor's last appearances before his final illness. The success of these performances alone suffices to explain the adoption of Kan U into the repertoire of ukiyo-e subject matter.

Another pillar print by Toyonobu dating from about the same time (Art Institute of Chicago) pairs a young woman with one of the gods of good fortune, Hotei, in a similar manner.[3] This print was issued by a different publisher, Murata-ya Jirobei. The fashions worn by the women in both designs suggest a date in the late 1740s.

The hand-colouring of the Boston impression has faded considerably, the colours of the Toronto impression less so. TTC

1 The last two are mentioned in Pins 1982, no. 49.

2 David Waterhouse mentions an *aka-hon* of 1721 on the *Sangoku-shi* theme with illustrations by Hanekawa Chinchō, along with later works on the same subject. Toronto 1975, no. 49. There is also a *hosoban* print of *c.* 1723–9 by Shigenaga that includes *Sangoku-shi* among the volumes being sold by Yamashita Kinsaku I playing a book-pedlar (p. 20, fig. 8).

3 Pins 1982, no. 50; Chicago 1955, p. 204, [Toyonobu] no. 12.

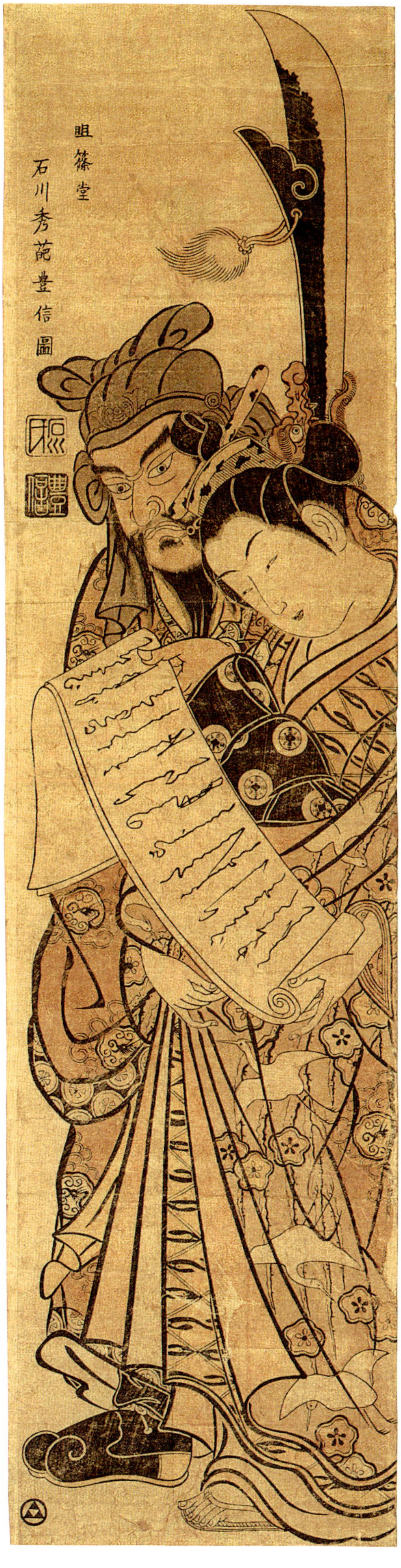
眀篠堂
石川秀葩豊信圖

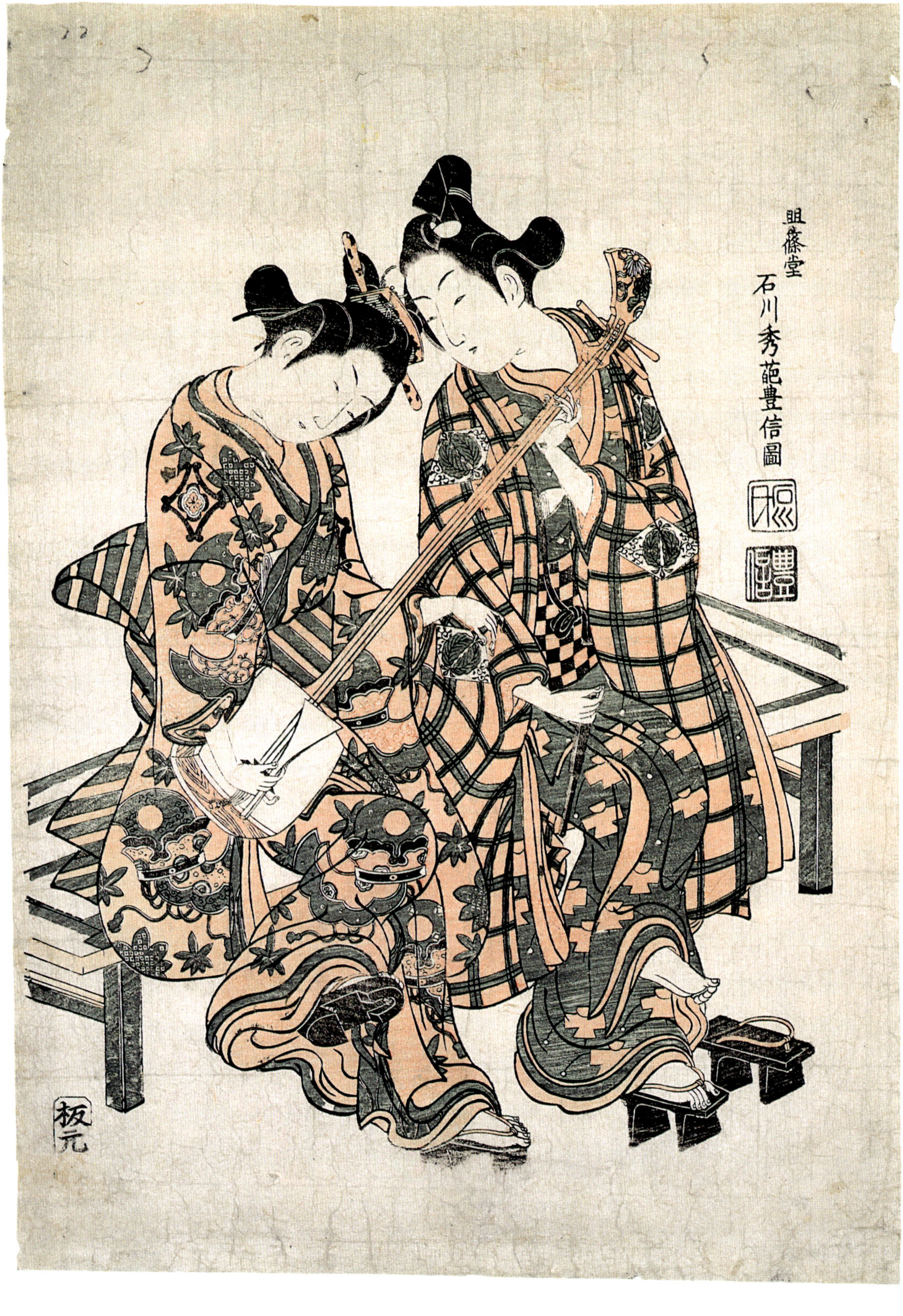
旦條堂
石川秀葩豊信圖
板元

124

Ishikawa Toyonobu

The Actors Onoe Kikugorō and Nakamura Kiyosaburō Playing a Shamisen Together

c. 1750–2 (?)

ARTIST'S SIGNATURE: 'Tanjōdō Ishikawa Shūha Toyonobu zu' (Picture by Tanjōdō Ishikawa Shūha Toyonobu)

ARTIST'S SEALS: 'Ishikawa-uji', 'Toyonobu'

PUBLISHER: 'hanmoto' (publisher) with mark of Urokogata-ya

woodblock, *ōban, benizuri-e* (2-colour), 43.2 × 30.7 cm

OTHER IMPRESSIONS: Tokyo National Museum (Tokyo 1960–3, vol. 1, no. 378); Grunwald Graphic Arts Foundation, University of California, Los Angeles (Stern n.d., no. 37)

William Sturgis Bigelow Collection, 1911

11.19674

In the early 1750s there was a vogue for *ōban*-format *benizuri-e* prints showing imaginary desirable pairings (*mitate-e*) of popular actors. Here the pair sits on a bench, Nakamura Kiyosaburō (left) in female guise strumming the strings of a shamisen with a plectrum, while Onoe Kikugorō (right), as a young man dressed in a feminine *furisode*, obliges with the fingering on the neck of the same instrument. With his free hand the young impersonator of women delicately touches Kikugorō's arm, while Kikugorō toys with a folded fan. Kiyosaburō bows his head shyly and half-crosses his legs to provide support for the body of the shamisen. Kikugorō crosses his legs more nonchalantly and looks smilingly at his companion. Lovers shown playing a single musical instrument together would immediately have evoked the story of the Chinese Emperor Xuanzong (685–762) of the Tang dynasty playing a single flute with his beautiful concubine Yang Guifei.

Nakamura Kiyosaburō first visited Edo in 1749/11, when he performed at the Ichimura Theatre. The crest he used on that occasion was rather different from that shown here, which is first recorded in an actor critique of 1751/1.[1] In 1752/11 he returned to Osaka, appearing again in Edo from 1754/11 to 1758/11. After 1752/11 Kikugorō switched from female (*onnagata*) to male lead (*tachi-yaku*) roles. Another attractive print of the same kind by Toyonobu is known (Hiraki Ukiyo-e Museum, Yokohama). This shows Kikugorō and Kiyosaburō as *tori-oi* ('bird-catchers', itinerant street musicians), with *kokyū* and shamisen respectively, and must date from about the same time as the present print.[2] TTC

1 *Yakusha makura kotoba*, in *Kabuki hyōban-ki II*, vol. 4, p. 146.

2 *Ukiyo-e taikei*, vol. 1, no. 58; also published by Urokogata-ya, with the same forms of the actors' crests.

125
Ishikawa Toyonobu
'Courtesans of the Three Cities'
(Edo, Kyō, Ōsaka keisei sanpuku-tsui)

late 1750s

ARTIST'S SIGNATURE: 'Ishikawa Toyonobu hitsu' (Brush of Ishikawa Toyonobu)

PUBLISHER: 'hanmoto Urokogata-ya' (Urokogata-ya, publisher) with publisher's mark

woodblock, horizontal *ōban, benizuri-e,* 29.5 × 43.3 cm

REPRODUCED: *Ukiyo-e shūka,* vol. 1, nos. 157–9

OTHER IMPRESSION: William S. and John T. Spaulding Collection, Museum of Fine Arts, Boston, 21.6860

William Sturgis Bigelow Collection, 1911

11.19672

Comparison of the left panel of this print with cat. 121 illustrates a practice common among ukiyo-e artists: successful ideas developed in one format were often reworked and reissued in commercially more viable forms. The wide pillar picture prototypes from which this design was derived were painstakingly hand-coloured. This reworked version was colour-printed and Toyonobu collapsed the three wide pillar pictures of the original triptych into a single *ōban* sheet. Elaborate backgrounds were a common feature of single-sheet depictions of this theme, but in conventional examples they usually consist of the latticed parlours that fronted most brothels. In this case Toyonobu gives us a glimpse of the luxurious interiors associated with high-ranked courtesans.

The blue in this print has a noticeably mottled quality. This effect was deliberate. The printer allowed the pigment to dry a little on the block before taking an impression, causing the pigment to coalesce into small patches between the laid and chain lines of the paper. Such techniques, which required considerable skill, demonstrate how attentive printers were to the possibilities afforded by the production process. In another impression of this design, also in the Boston Museum, the printer replaced the blue with a rich green, producing a remarkably different, but no less effective image. AH

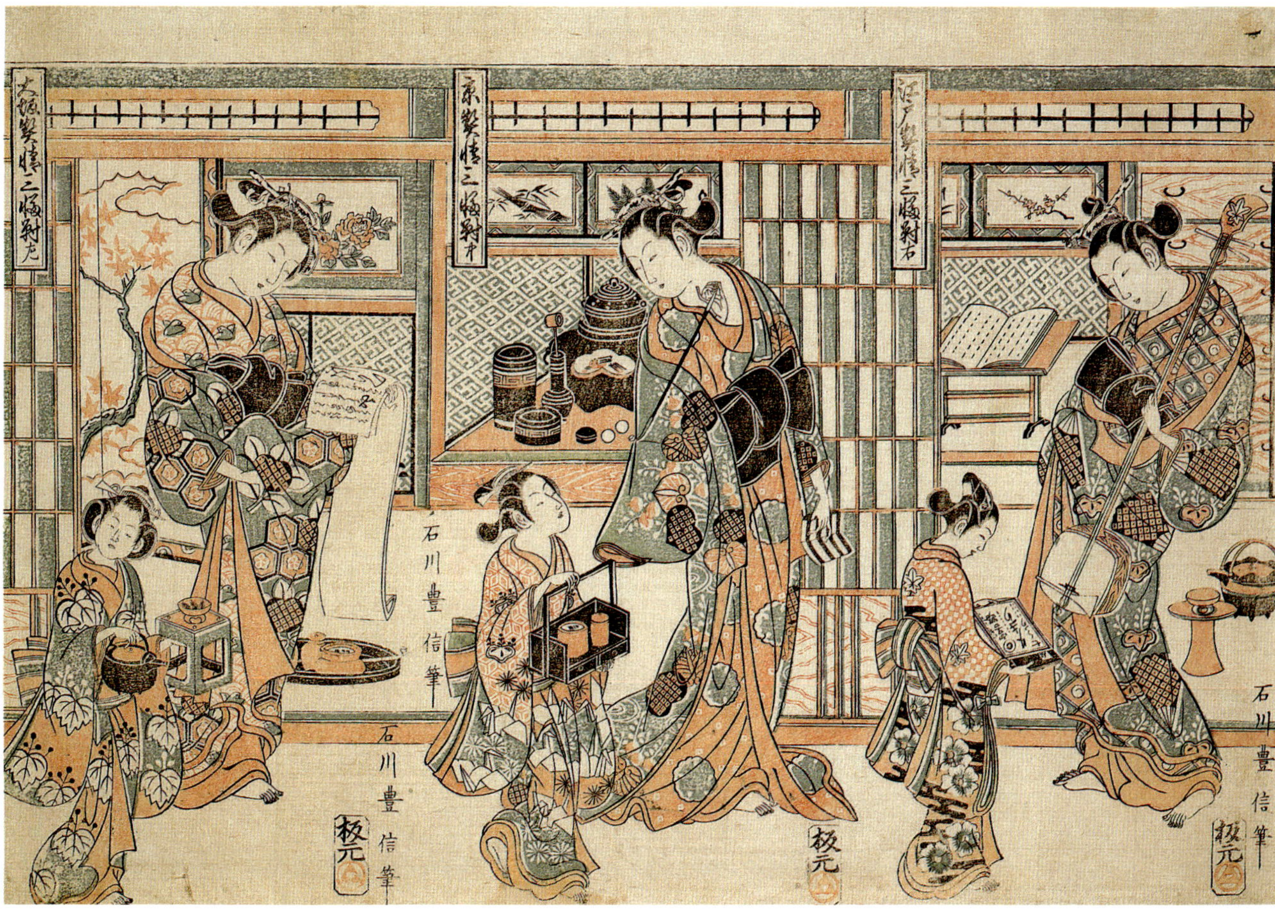
石川豊信筆
板元
石川豊信筆
板元
石川豊信筆
板元

126
Ishikawa Toyonobu
Fukai Shidōken Lecturing

1750s

ARTIST'S SIGNATURE: 'Ishikawa Toyonobu hitsu' (Brush of Ishikawa Toyonobu)

PUBLISHER: 'Hanmoto' (publisher) with mark of Urokogata-ya

woodblock, horizontal *ōban*, *benizuri-e* (2-colour), 29.4 × 43.3 cm

REPRODUCED: *Ukiyo-e shūka*, vol. 1, no. 47

OTHER IMPRESSIONS: (*Ukiyo-e taisei*, vol. 3, no. 26); (Higuchi 1977, pl. 69, no. 53) (both same impression?)

William Sturgis Bigelow Collection, 1911

11.19631

By the time this print was issued in the 1750s, Fukai Shidōken (?1680–1765) had become something of a celebrity in Edo. He gave highly eccentric public lectures from a temporary platform surrounded by reed blinds, erected next to the main worship hall of Asakusa Kannon Temple. One modern scholar has described the contents and performance style of the lectures as follows: 'as the alternative names for his performances suggest – "obscene sermons" (*bare-kōshaku*), "crazy lectures" (*kyō-kō*) and so on – his unique appeal lay in his revelations, with a stick in the shape of a phallus in his hand, that the three creeds of Shintō, Confucianism and Buddhism were all intimately bound up with intercourse between men and women; this and the fact that he imitated the body actions himself.'[1]

This was a far cry from Shidōken's earlier career, when had been an assistant to the influential neo-Shingon prelate Ryūkō (1642–1724), much patronised by Shogun Tsunayoshi (1646–1709) because he preached in favour of the protection of animals. With Tsunayoshi's death and Ryūkō's fall from grace, Shidōken was forced to take up begging for a while, before reinventing himself early in the Kyōhō era (1716–36), at about the age of 40, as the popular lecturer of Asakusa. As his notoriety spread, several ukiyo-e artists did portraits of him: pillar prints exist of Shidōken by Masanobu and one Seigyū Gyōchin; a *hosoban* print by Mangetsudō dated 1747 shows him counselling a young couple; and in a large horizontal *ōban* (similar in size and date to the present Toyonobu print), again by Masanobu, he gives advice to none other than Oshichi and Kichisaburō, the protagonists of a famous love-suicide play (see cat. 37).[2] In this last print Shidōken holds a copy of a pamphlet published by him in 1748, *Motonashi-gusa*, which propounded the familiar theory that the source of all creation was to be sought in the conjugation of man and wife.[3] The grandest print of Shidōken is an extra-tall pillar print, which Louise Virgin has suggested forms a triptych with pillar prints showing Sanogawa Ichimatsu I and Onoe Kikugorō I (see cat. 75).

In 1753 Shidōken was catapulted to the forefront of avant-garde literature when he featured as the protagonist of *Fūryū Shidōken* (*Shidōken the Elegant*), a humorous story by Hiraga Gennai (1728–79). Given a huge feathered fan by the mythological winged *tengu* beast, Shidōken's fictional alter ego embarks on a voyage of sexual discovery in Yoshiwara, in the unlicensed brothel districts of Edo and in all the mythical lands of the world – such as Borneo and Holland – before finally awaking in the precincts of the Asakusa temple. Here he attracts a crowd by telling war tales (the sign behind him on the left in the present print reads 'Tales of Old Battles, lecturer Shidōken' [*Kosen monogatari, kōshi Shidōken*]): 'Beating time with his funny stick shaped like a *matsutake* mushroom, he has everyone splitting their sides....It has to be said that he is amazingly good at doing the styles of impersonators of women [*onnagata*], imitating their movements and their voices.'[4] Not everyone shared

1 *Nihon koten*, vol. 3, s.v. 'Shidōken' (commentary by Nakano Mitsutoshi).

2 Chicago 1955, p. 159, Masanobu no. 91; London 1988, no. 60; *Ukiyo-e zenshū*, fig. 165, pl. 54.

3 *Nihon koten* (note 1).

4 Quoted in *Ukiyo-e shūka*, vol. 1, no. 47 (commentary by Money Hickman).

5 Baba Bunkō, 'Tōdai Edo hyaku bakemono', in *Nihon zuihitsu taisei*, pp. 405–6.

6 Bunkō was arrested and executed in the ninth month, 1758, ostensibly for having contravened the censorship laws by referring in a public performance to the factional fighting (*sōdō*) within the Kanemori family of Mino Province. *Nihon koten*, vol. 5, s.v. 'Baba Bunkō' (commentary by Nobuhiro Shinji).

7 By the Genroku era (1688–1704) *hangon-tan* was being made and sold nationwide by the Toyama fief. By the Kyōhō era (1716–36) the pills were apparently being manufactured in Edo at Shingyō-in Temple at Dōbō-chō and sold from a business called Sakai-ya at Tamachi in Shiba. *Nihon kokugo dai-jiten*, vol. 8, s.v. 'Hangon-tan'.

8 *Edo-gaku jiten*, pp. 536–7, s.v. 'Misemono'.

9 Ibid., p. 542, s.v. 'Dai-dōgei'.

this enthusiasm. Another, perhaps rival, public lecturer (*kōsaku-shi*), Baba Bunkō (?1718–58), was known for his outspokenness and his criticism of people as far up the social hierarchy as the daimyo and the shogun himself. Bunkō's *Tōdai Edo hyaku bakemono* (*One Hundred Frights of Edo Today*), published in the autumn of 1758, included a stinging criticism of Shidōken, denouncing his views as heretical with regard to all the precious truths of the three creeds, admired only by fools and certainly not fit to be voiced in front of women and children: 'He leads the world astray, destroying the bonds of affection between parent and child, older and younger brother. He is a criminal of the very worst order.' Bunkō further wrote that people of his parents' generation born in the Jōkyō era (1684–8) knew Shidōken when he was a young acolyte at Goji-in Temple (where he had studied with Ryūkō) and that he was 'ignorant of letters and short on brains' (*monmō tansai*).[5] In the event, it was Bunkō, not Shidōken, who was judged the criminal by the authorities for daring to comment too openly on the feudal establishment.[6]

Shidōken is shown in mid-performance, with a knowing leer on his face as he holds the wooden phallus upright. No children are present, but two young women sightseers wearing *furisode* appear on the right, apparently as embarrassed as they are fascinated: one raises a sleeve to her mouth, the other fiddles nervously with her hair comb. The other seven customers are male, at least two of them samurai bearing double swords. The elderly man and youth in the foreground may be teacher and pupil: the younger man leans attentively towards the older. The woman in the bottom left corner is a waitress preparing to serve tea to the (paying) guests. Indeed, the setting looks to be the second-floor rooms of a permanent teahouse, with a view onto blossoming cherry trees, rather than Shidōken's temporary enclosure.

The sign behind Shidōken on the right offers a clue as to the location of the teahouse. The sign reads 'Secret Family Formula: *Hangon-tan*' (*Kaden hangon-tan*). *Hangon-tan* was an ancient patent medicine, originally from China and mostly used to treat stomach ailments.[7] One of the popular sideshows at Okuyama in Asakusa during the Meiwa era (1764–72) is described by Ōta Nanpo in his *Hannichi kanwa* (*Half-day's Idle Chat*) as '*Hangon-tan* sword-duelling' (*Hangon-tan no iai-nuki*).[8] This seems to have consisted of duelling with extra-long swords between two toothpaste-selling firms, Matsui and Nagai, who claimed they had been granted their patents for Toyama *hangon-tan* by the great warrior Takeda Shingen.[9] Hence, the teahouse depicted in the print may well have been located in Shidōken's familiar Asakusa neighbourhood and the sign simply advertises a local product. TTC

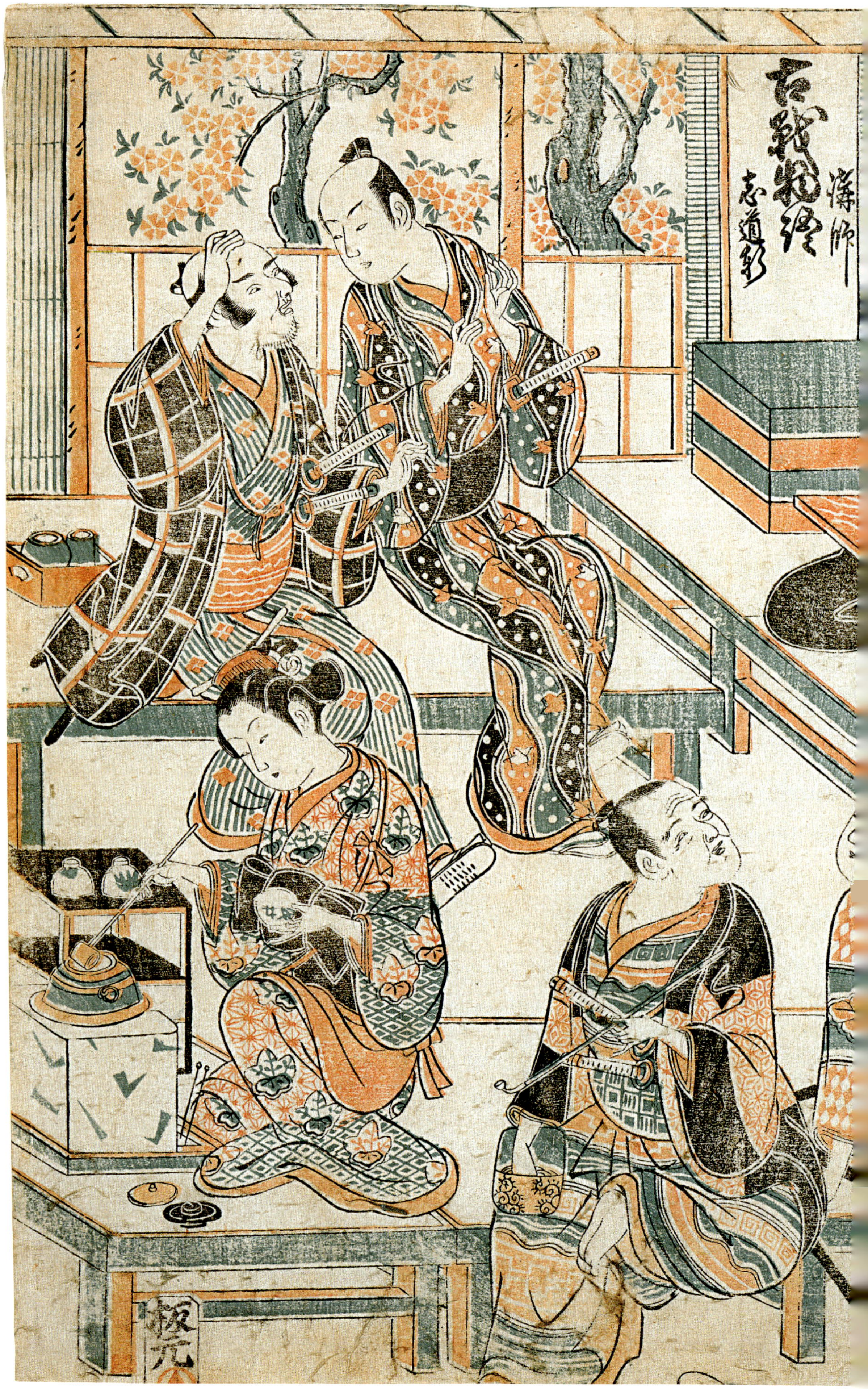
板元

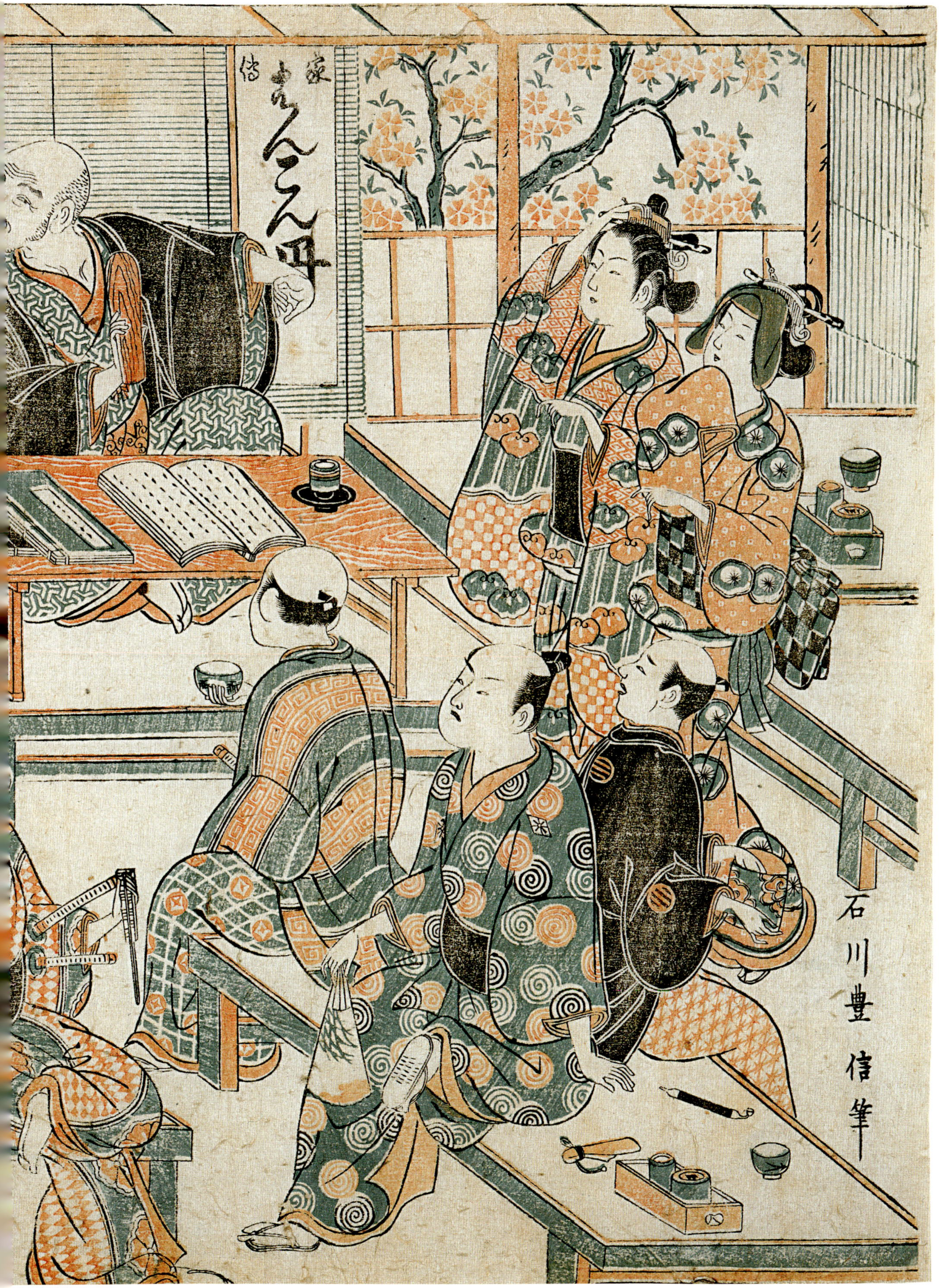
石川豊信筆

127

Ishikawa Toyonobu

Young Woman Entering a Bath

early 1760s

ARTIST'S SIGNATURE: 'Ishikawa Toyonobu zu' (Picture by Ishikawa Toyonobu)

ARTIST'S SEAL: 'Toyonobu'

woodblock, *hashira-e, benizuri-e*, 69.6 × 10.5 cm

REPRODUCED: *Ukiyo-e taisei*, vol. 3, no. 33

William Sturgis Bigelow Collection, 1911

11.21280

Although print artists frequently designed sexually explicit images (see cat. 22), the Western tradition of the nude had no direct counterpart in Japanese art. *Abuna-e* (risqué pictures), which came into fashion after a government crackdown on erotic images in the early 1720s, are perhaps the closest approximation in that they deliberately put a woman's body on display for male viewers. Typically, *abuna-e* capture a private moment in which the subject is in a state of partial undress. The narrow *hashira-e* (pillar picture) format of the present design further enhances the illicit view Toyonobu offers us. The narrow format crops the woman's body in a manner that suggests we are peering through a partly opened *shōji* (sliding screen) or a latticed fence to observe her as she prepares to enter the bath.

The poem inscribed on the print draws attention to the whiteness of the woman's skin as she slips out of her garment:

Shitahimo no	As the tie cords
tandan tokete	gradually unravel,
yuki no hada	skin like snow.

Toyonobu's design responds accordingly. The smooth whiteness of the woman's skin contrasts strikingly with the rich textures suggested by the elaborate printing of the garment, especially noticeable in the *kiri* (paulownia) design it bears. Some of the *kiri* are printed in *beni*, others are green. One below the woman's right leg has a purple-brown hue, the one above is *beni* overprinted with green. Yet another, near her right hand, is left uncoloured. AH

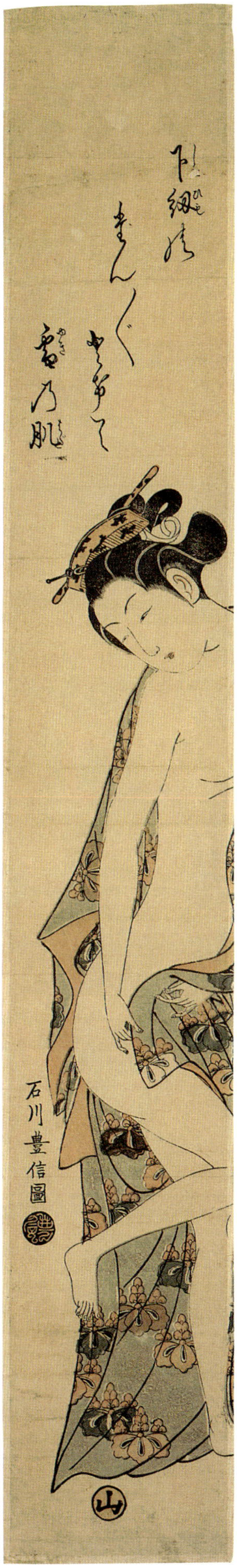
石川豊信圖

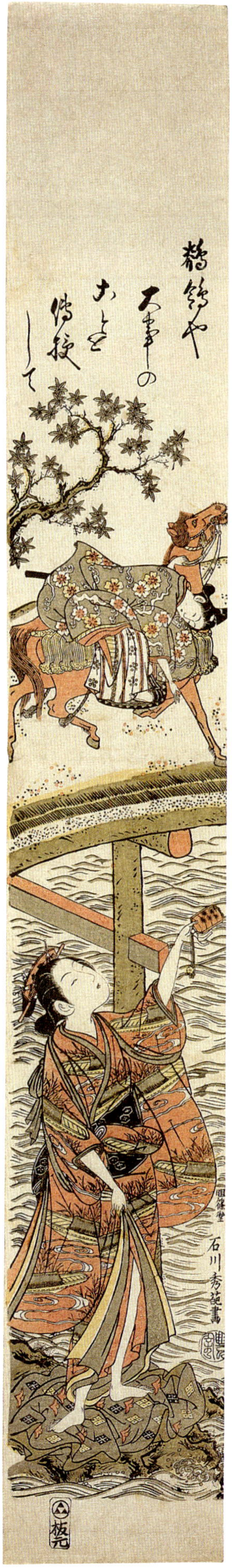

128

Ishikawa Toyonobu

Parody of Zhang Liang and Huangshi Gong

c. 1765

ARTIST'S SIGNATURE: 'Tanjōdō Ishikawa Shūha ga' (Drawn by Tanjōdō Ishikawa Shūha)

ARTIST'S SEAL: 'Toyonobu'

PUBLISHER: 'hanmoto' (publisher) with mark of Urokogata-ya

woodblock, *hashira-e*, *benizuri-e* (3-colour), 70.5 × 10.2 cm

William Sturgis Bigelow Collection, 1911

11.19678

A young man crossing a country bridge on horseback is shown leaning down to retrieve an elegant lacquer medicine case (*inrō*) he has dropped, which is offered back to him by a young woman who is cleaning washing by trampling the clothes underfoot on the bank of the river. That the attractive young man and young woman are both extremely fashionably dressed subverts this seemingly simple bucolic scene, alerting us to other layers of meaning.

Zhang Liang (*Jap.* Chō Ryō) went into hiding in Xiapei in Jiangsu Province after his failed attempt to assassinate the Qin Emperor Shi Huangdi in 218 BC. The sage Huangshi Gong (Kōseki Kō) sought him out to persuade him to continue the campaign against the Qin tyrant. To test Zhang's character, Huangshi Gong contrived to let fall his shoe as he crossed a small bridge on horseback. Zhang returned the shoe with such perfect courtesy that Huangshi Gong presented him with a precious scroll of military secrets.

Kume no Sennin was an eremite of Yoshino who practised the 'methods of the immortals' (Daoism) and gained the power of flight: 'As Kume was flying along, he passed over the Yoshino River, where a young woman stood at the riverbank, laundering her clothes. As she washed, she raised the hem of her kimono to keep it dry, inadvertently exposing her legs. When Kume looked down at the white flesh of her thighs, carnal thoughts clouded his mind, and he came tumbling down right in front of her and took her as his wife.'[1] One of the key pictorial clues to this second allusion is the pose of the young man, which suggests Kume tumbling out of the sky as much as Huangshi Gong reaching down to retrieve his shoe.

Finally, the *hokku* poem alludes to the creation myths of Japan in which the male and female *kami* Izanagi and Izanami learned the techniques of lovemaking by imitating mating wagtails and conjoined to form the islands of Onokoro-jima (Japan) and procreate a string of other deities:

Sekirei ya	Yes, indeed, wagtails
daiji no koto o	transmitted the secrets
denju shite	of what matters most.[2]

The military secrets transmitted by Huangshi Gong are thus likened to the sex education provided by the wagtails.

Five more similar designs are known by Toyonobu; it is likely that they form a set.[3] Whether such pictures, loosely termed 'parody pictures' in English, should be called *mitate-e* or *yatsushi-e* has been hotly debated.[4] Of particular interest in the present case is the clear double parody – or triple parody, if one counts the allusion in the poem. The sophistication of the three-colour printing (with yellow printed over blue to produce a fourth, lime greenish shade) and the delicacy of the figure style are certainly close to the *chūban* prints of Harunobu that began to be issued in 1765 (cat. 142), many of which likewise contain playful up-to-date allusions to classical tales. TTC

1 The passage comes from the collection *Konjaku monogatari* (*Ancient and Modern Tales*), compiled in the early 12th century. Hickman 1981 (p. 21 for Hickman's translation, quoted here).

2 I am grateful to John Carpenter for suggesting this translation.

3 Pins 1982, nos. 66–9 and (possibly) 74. David Waterhouse has written a detailed commentary on *Ariwara no Narihira Eloping with the Future Empress Nijō* (Royal Ontario Museum, Toronto), for which he suggests a date of *c.* 1765. Toronto 1975, no. 51.

4 The case for *yatsushi-e* rather than *mitate-e* is convincingly put in Iwata 1993. Some of the arguments have been summarised in English in Clark 1997.

129

Torii Kiyohiro

The Actor Ōtani Hiroji II as Ume no Yoshihei

New Year 1753

ARTIST'S SIGNATURE: 'Torii Kiyohiro hitsu' (Brush of Torii Kiyohiro)

PUBLISHER: 'hanmoto' (publisher) with mark of Urokogata-ya

woodblock, *hosoban*, *benizuri-e* (2-colour) with embossing, 31.5 × 14.6 cm

William Sturgis Bigelow Collection, 1911

11.19066

In *Otokodate hatsukai Soga*, performed at the Nakamura Theatre at the New Year of 1753, Ōtani Hiroji II played two roles: Oniō in the first part, Ume no Yoshihei in the second. Here he poses in the snow, protecting himself against the inclement weather with a sleeved outer-jacket (*sode-gappa*; see also cat. 73) worn over a *kosode* decorated with a plum (*ume*) pattern after his name. Hiroji II's crest, a cross inside a circle, appears at the top of the umbrella. The actor critique *Yakusha iro-banjō* of 1753/3 praised his confrontation with Nakamura Sukegorō as Uba no Genpei in a scene set in the pleasure quarter in which both men played street toughs (*otoko-date*), and this may be the guise depicted here.[1]

This is among the earliest known actor prints by Kiyohiro.[2] TTC

1 *Kabuki hyōban-ki II*, vol. 4, pp. 481–2.

2 Mutō Junko has commented that Kiyohiro's dateable actor prints all fall in the period 1753–7. Mutō 1999a, p. 85.

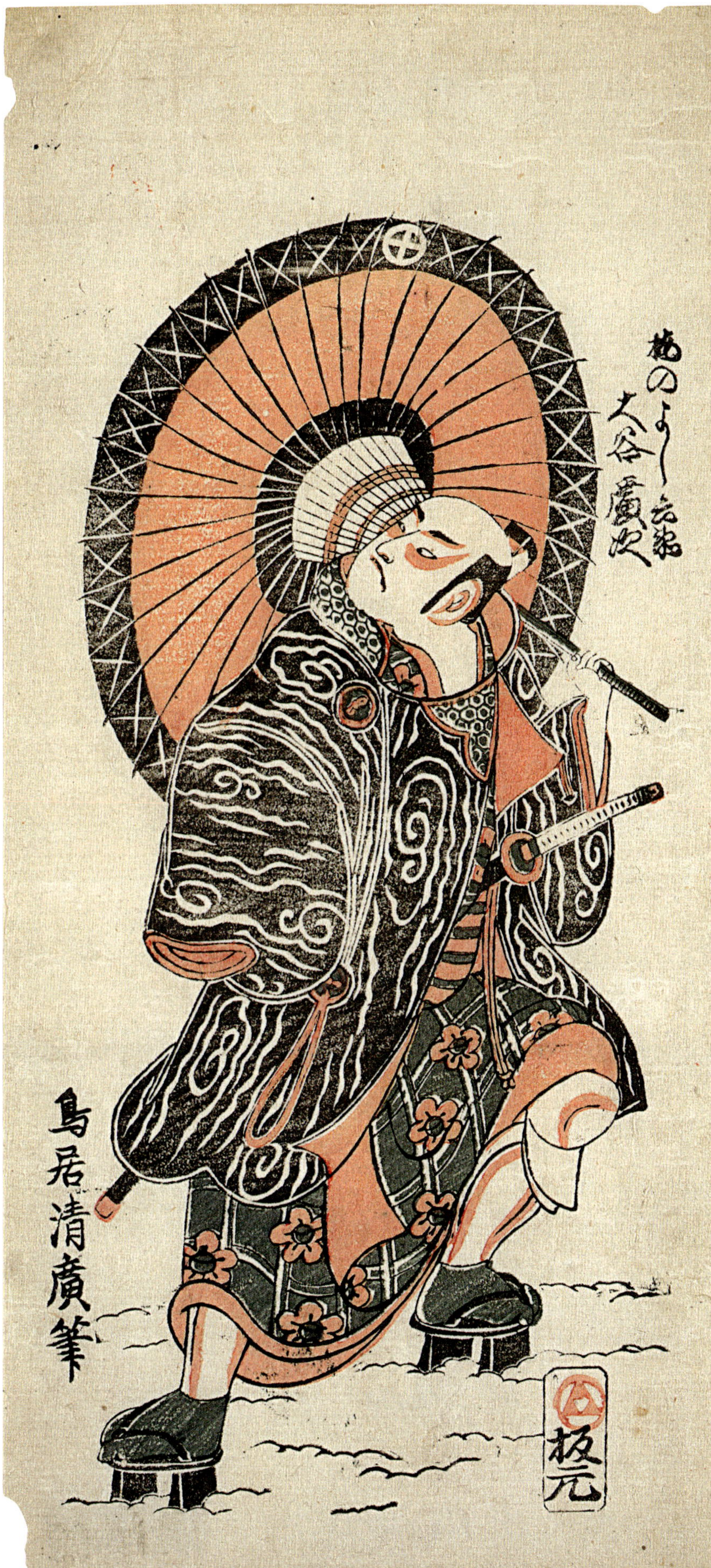
大谷廣次
鳥居清廣筆
板元

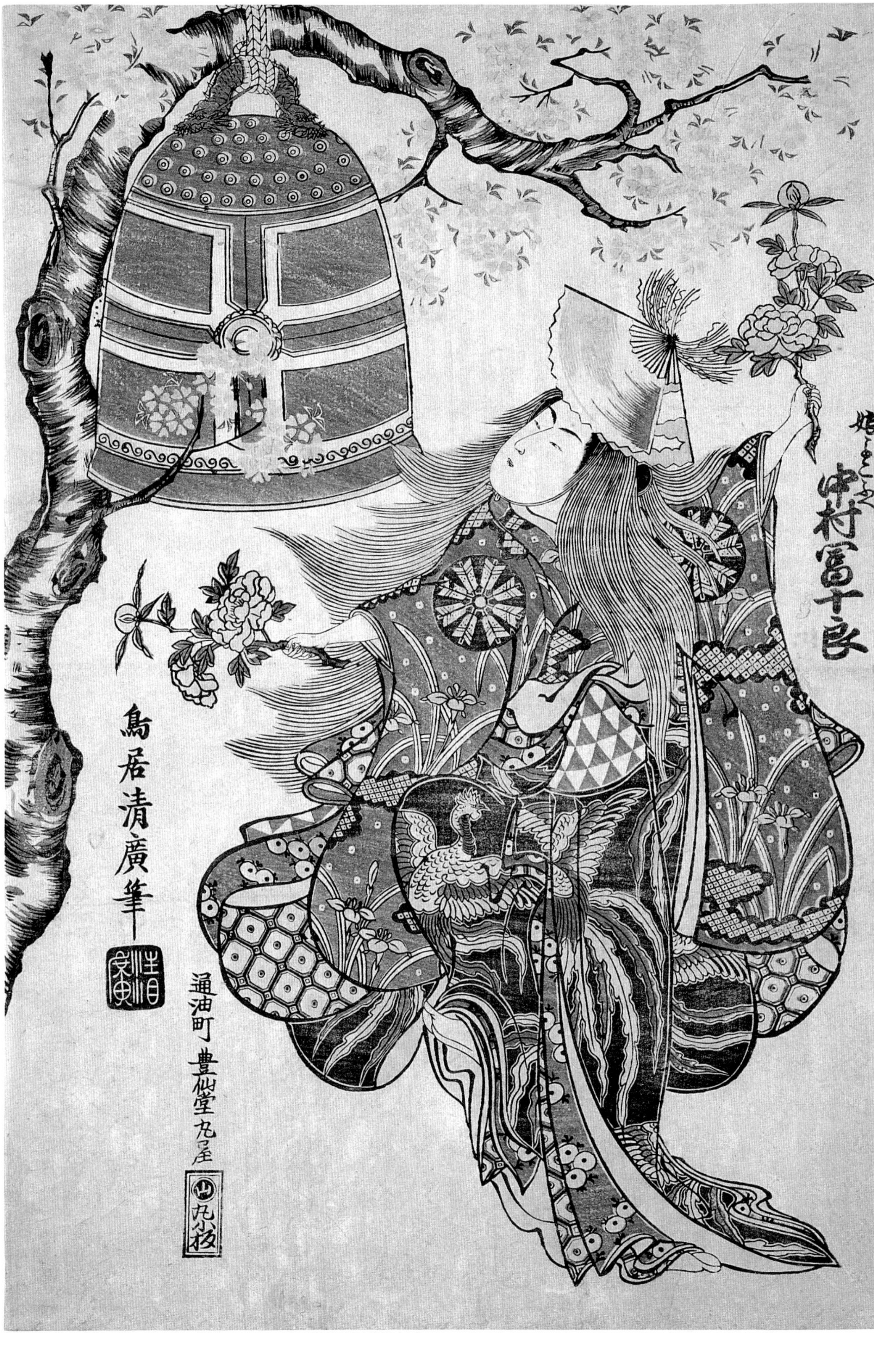
中村富十郎
鳥居清廣筆
通油町 豊仙堂 丸屋

130
Torii Kiyohiro
The Actor Nakamura Tomijūrō as Musume Yokobue

3rd month, 1753

ARTIST'S SIGNATURE: 'Torii Kiyohiro hitsu' (Brush of Torii Kiyohiro)

ARTIST'S SEAL: 'Kiyohiro'

PUBLISHER: 'Tōriabura-chō Hōsendō Maruya' (Hōsendō Maruya at Tōriabura-chō) with publisher's mark and 'Maru-Ko han' (Published by Maru-Ko)

woodblock, *ōban*, *benizuri-e* (2-colour), 42.1 × 28.6 cm

OTHER IMPRESSIONS: Nelson-Atkins Gallery, Kansas City (Stern n.d., no. 42); (*Genshoku ukiyo-e*, vol. 6, p. 84, no. 194); Chiba City Museum of Art

William Sturgis Bigelow Collection, 1911

11.19702

The legend of Dōjō-ji Temple in Kii Province was first told in the early 12th-century collection *Konjaku monogatari* (*Ancient and Modern Tales*) and later adapted as a nō play. Kiyohime, the daughter of an estate manager at Manago in Hidaka, developed an all-consuming passion for the young monk Anchin of Dōjō-ji Temple. Faithful to his vow of celibacy, Anchin rejected her advances and fled to the temple, hiding under its large bronze bell. Crazed with desire, Kiyohime took the form of a large snake, coiled herself seven-and-a-half times around the bell and incinerated it, with the unfortunate Anchin inside.

From the earliest period of kabuki, the nō version of the story was adapted for dance. In the second month, 1723, a fully fledged kabuki version, *Keisei Dōjō-ji*, was performed by Ogino Yaegiri, and subsequently *onnagata* actors vied with one another to produce new interpretations of the story. By the Hōreki era (1751–64) some twelve different versions had been devised.[1] It was in the third month, 1753, at the Nakamura Theatre, that Nakamura Tomijūrō first performed what became the classic form of the play, *Kyō-ganoko musume Dōjō-ji*, which has survived to the present day. So successful was it that the run continued for a remarkable 125 days. Yokobue, daughter of Saemon, the estate manager of Manago village, develops a passion for a certain Takiguchi Koshirō. Her love unrequited, she goes mad and is killed. Her spirit turns into a *shirabyōshi* dancer and appears at Dōjō-ji Temple for the ceremony held to dedicate a new bell.[2] This follows quite closely the plot of the nō play, in which the mysterious female pilgrim dances closer and closer to the bell, finally disappearing under it and then revealing herself as the serpent she-devil. In addition, the story of Takiguchi and Yokobue has been entwined with that of Dōjō-ji.

Here Tomijūrō appears as Yokobue, dancing vigorously under the bell, which is suspended from a blossoming cherry branch. His costume is that used at the end of the *nagauta* chanted sequence, in which the performer wears the red wig of a lion dancer (*Shakkyō*), with two fans as a hat, and carries peonies in each hand. He will eventually leap under the bell.

Tomijūrō peformed *Dōjō-ji* on two occasions in the 1750s. In the third month, 1753, at the Ichimura Theatre he danced it as part of seven quick-change roles.[3] In the ninth month, 1759, as part of his farewell performance in Edo before returning to Osaka, he again performed it at the Ichimura Theatre.[4]

The printed pink of this impression has faded considerably, but the complex cutting of the robe patterns is none the less remarkable. An outer robe decorated with phoenixes has been shrugged off both arms to reveal another *furisode*, with long, hanging sleeves and a pattern of iris and tie-dyed clouds. In the Boston print the sash has a chequered triangular 'snake scale' (*urokogata*) pattern not seen in other impressions.[5] TTC

1 Iizuka 1926, pp. 459–60.

2 Synopsis from *Genshoku ukiyo-e*, vol. 6, p. 84, no. 194, with additional information from Mutō Junko (private communication).

3 *Kabuki nenpyō*, vol. 3, p. 340.

4 Ibid., p. 377.

5 For example, *Genshoku ukiyo-e*, vol. 6, p. 84, no. 194 (unnamed collection).

131

Anonymous (Attributed to the Torii school)

Theatre Signboard Depicting Scenes from the Play 'Nishiki-gi sakae Komachi'

1758

panel, ink, colour and gold on paper, 177.6 × 97.2 cm

REPRODUCED: Boston 2000, vol. 2, no. 94

William Sturgis Bigelow Collection, 1911

11.7529

Much like the movie posters of today, signboards (*kanban*) served as an effective means of drawing in passers-by to pay to attend a kabuki performance. As can be seen in a print attributed to Okumura Masanobu (cat. 66), these framed paper advertisements projected from the eaves of the individual theatres so as to be visible to pedestrians in the narrow streets below. The signboards featured the lead actors – their crests prominently displayed – in selected dramatic moments.

Identifying particular roles by the poem slip (*tanzaku*) and umbrella depicted, and correlating the actors' crests with their descriptions in the *Gekidai-shū*, an early 18th-century compilation belonging to Tokyo University, Asano Shūgō recently determined that this signboard was designed for the play *Nishiki-gi sakae Komachi*. This was performed at the Nakamura Theatre from the first day of the eighth month, 1758.[1] The precise contents of the play are unknown, but the division of the signboard into an interior scene above and a riverbank view below suggests that two scenes have been highlighted. Performing in the first were Ichikawa Yaozō as Kanja no Tarō Sadakage (left), Onoe Kikugorō as Godai Saburō (centre) and the *onnagata* Arashi Tominosuke as Gion no Kaji (left). In the second Ichikawa Masuzō as the raincoat-garbed Hannya no Gorō Terukage (left), Segawa Kikunojō II as the unfairly maligned poet Ono no Komachi (centre) and Ichikawa Danjūrō IV as the villainous Ōtomo no Kuronushi (right) re-enact the electrifying moment in the play when Komachi establishes her innocence by washing away the lines added by Kuronushi to an earlier manuscript. The scene will have been well-known to contemporary audiences for it was a popular subject of prints and paintings (for example, cat. 39) and was central to plays about the 9th-century court lady.

Although signboards were once produced in great numbers, like most advertisements for ephemeral events they were disposed of after the run of performances. Asano's identification of the play has established this signboard as the earliest in existence.[2] Typically, it is unsigned, yet it was almost certainly executed by a member of the Torii school, which from the time of Torii Kiyonobu I's father, Kiyomoto (1645–1702), had been associated with *kanban* painting. Asano suggests that it could be the work of Kiyonobu II, Kiyomasu II or Kiyomitsu I. Although members of the Torii school adhered to more or less the same set of conventions when depicting actors, comparison of this signboard with a print of the same year by Kiyomitsu I showing two of the same actors[3] suggests that he may have created the Boston work. ANM

1 This commentary is greatly indebted to Asano Shūgō in Boston 2000, vol. 1, no. 94.

2 The Museum of Fine Arts has five *kanban* in its collection. The present example, another depicting scenes from *Nue Shigedō sakiwake yūsha* (1767), one for the play *Shusse Taihei-ki* (1775) and a fourth with Osagawa Tsuneyo II as Tora and Bandō Matatarō IV as Asahina in *Harukoma* (*c.* 1781–9) predate those previously known. Reproduced in Boston 2000, vol. 2, nos. 94–8 (commentaries by Asano Shūgō).

3 *Ichikawa Danjūrō IV as Abura-ya Kuheiji and Onoe Kikugorō as Hirano-ya Tokubei*, James A. Michener Collection, Honolulu Academy of Arts. Reproduced in Honolulu 1980, p. 216.

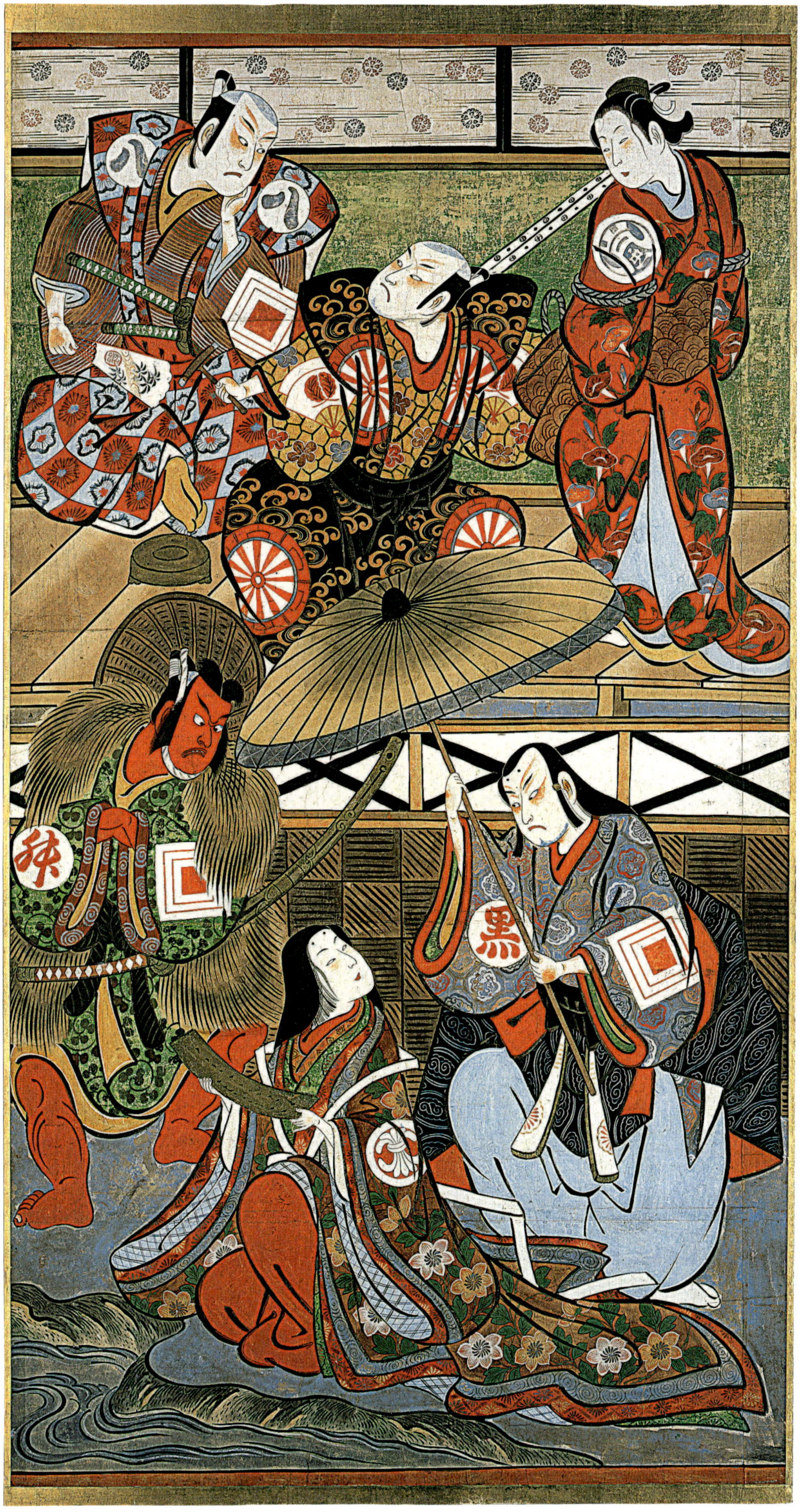

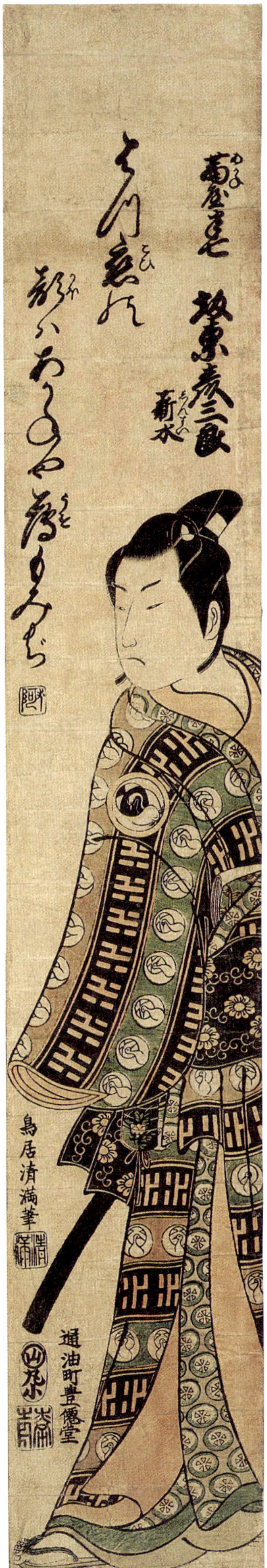
坂東彦三郎
鳥居清満筆

132
Torii Kiyomitsu
The Actor Bandō Hikosaburō II as Akaneya Hanshichi

6th month, 1760

ARTIST'S SIGNATURE: 'Torii Kiyomitsu hitsu' (Brush of Torii Kiyomitsu)

ARTIST'S SEAL: 'Kiyomitsu'

INSCRIPTION SEAL: 'Jōa'

PUBLISHER: 'Tōriabura-chō Hōsendō' (Hōsendō at Tōriabura-chō) with marks of Maruya Kohei

woodblock, *hashira-e*, *benizuri-e* (3-colour), 60.7 × 10.2 cm

Special Funds, 1954

54.366

Bandō Hikosaburō II appears as an adolescent youth with his forelock still unshaven, wearing a kimono that alternates bands of his 'dancing crane' crest with ones of another pattern. A more precise identification of this and the following pillar print (cat. 133) raises some problems. The actor, role and poetry name of the actor – Bandō Hikosaburō [II], Akaneya Hanshichi and Shinsui – are given in the printed inscription. Hanshichi and the courtesan Sankatsu were the doomed young couple in a popular love-suicide play based on a double suicide that had occurred in Osaka in 1695. The *hokku* poem above, which is followed by the Jōa seal of the popular writer Kansuidō Jōa (1686 – ?after 1767),[1] puns the name of the Akaneya business with the red colour *akane* (madder):

Hatsu-koi no	The face of young love
kao wa akane ya	blushes madder
usu-momiji.	or pale maple.

A different edition of this design (formerly Carl Schraubstadter Collection)[2] bears the name, address and seal of another publisher at the bottom, below the scabbard: Yamashiro-ya (Shōkakudō) at Bakuro-chō Itchōme. Its printed inscription at the top, which gives the role as Hachiman Tarō Yoshiie, contains a completely different poem.[3] It would appear that the top and bottom sections of the block were plugged and re-cut, leaving the figure and the artist's signature and seal the same as in the previous edition. The actor took the name Hikosaburō II in 1751/11. He began performing male lead (*tachi-yaku*) roles in 1756/11, mainly at the Ichimura Theatre. He is known to have taken the role of Akaneya Hanshichi in the second part of the play *Soga mannen-bashira* at that theatre in the sixth month, 1760, after it had been rebuilt following a fire.[4] In the eleventh month of that year, also at the Ichimura, he played the role of Hachiman Tarō Yoshiie in the *kaomise* play *Mume-momiji Date ō-kido*. The Maruya edition would therefore seem to pre-date Yamshiro-ya's, suggesting that one publisher sold the blocks to the other. The costume depicted here is not particularly appropriate for either role and it may well be that Hikosaburō II, a very popular actor at the time, was drawn in a generalised outfit so as to facilitate reuse in this manner.

At least two pillar print designs have survived in versions by both Kiyohiro and Kiyomitsu (see cat. 133).[5] If an unsigned pillar print of a woman with a battledore,[6] previously attributed to Masanobu, is ascribed to Kiyohiro – and its style makes this a much more plausible attribution – then three examples of this phenomenon are known to have survived. In each case the same, or a very similar, design exists in a version by Kiyohiro with an anonymous inscription (published by Yamashiro-ya) and in a version by Kiyomitsu with a different Jōa inscription (published by Maruya). In all three instances the blocks appear to have been completely re-cut between the

1 For more on Jōa, see Satō 1990, who lists approximately 50 examples of Jōa inscriptions on ukiyo-e prints, most of which are actor prints by Torii school artists, particularly Kiyomitsu. The actor prints for which Satō is able to suggest fairly firm dates of performance range from 1753 to 1763.

2 Parke-Bernet 1948, no. 186; also reproduced in Pins 1982, no. 81.

3 'Michinoku no / homare naru-beshi / tō-jibai'.

4 *Kabuki nenpyō* dates the performance of *Soga mannen-bashira* to the third month, 1760, and gives Hikosaburō II's role in the first part of the play only – Senji-bō. The printed *banzuke* for the performance, probably far more reliable, gives the date as 1760/6 and includes Hikosaburō II as Hanshichi among the roles in the second part. I am grateful to Mutō Junko for informing me of the contents of the *banzuke*.

5 This phenomenon is commented on in Toronto 1975, p. 31, no. 6, pp. 44–5, no. 15; Honolulu 1980, p. 212, Kiyomitsu no. 13; Pins 1982, nos. 86/133, 115/132.

6 *Ukiyo-e taisei*, vol. 3, no. 156.

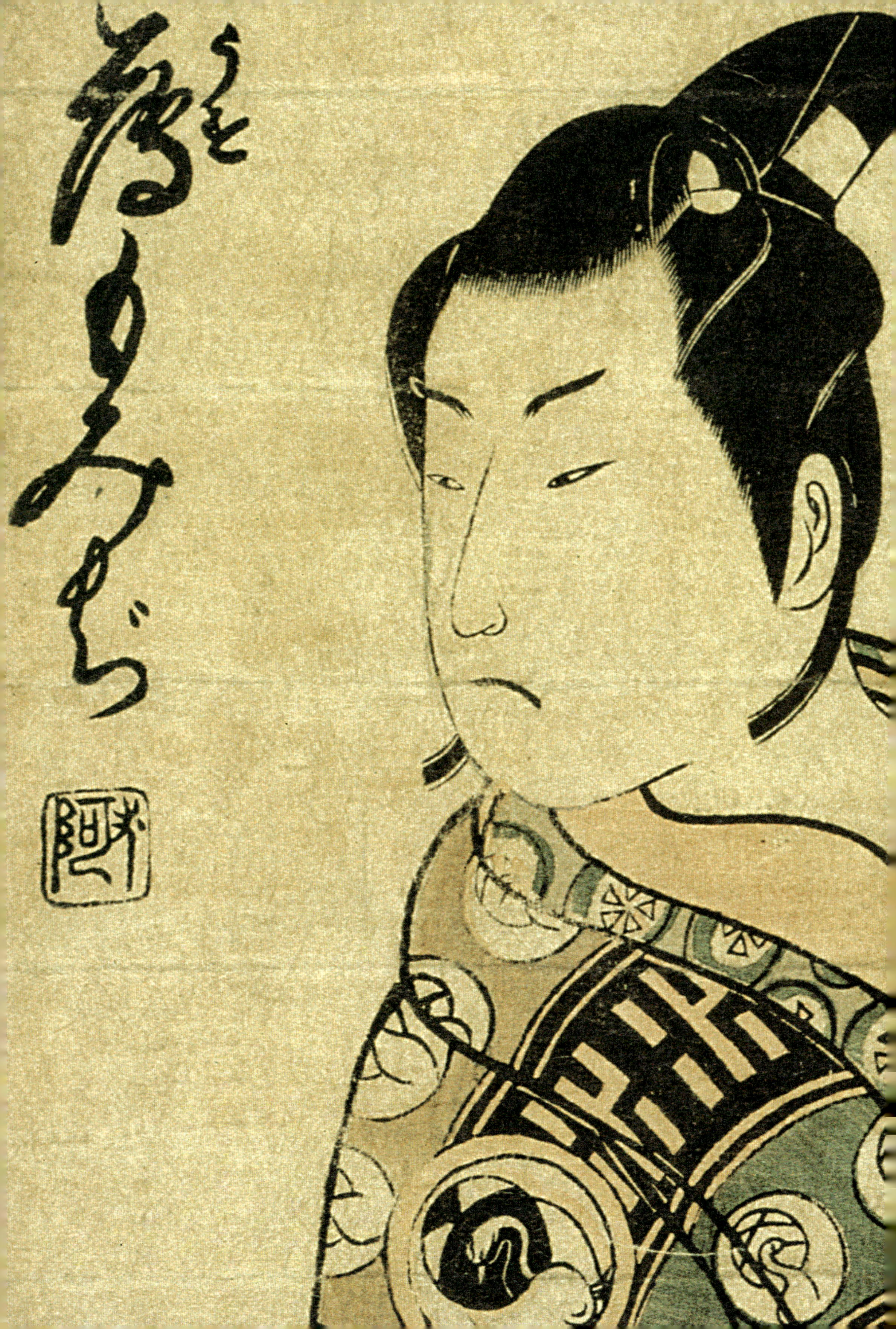

7 Toronto 1975, pp. 44–5, no. 15.

8 Such conclusions are best arrived at by carefully observing the comparative wear to the printing block evinced by each impression. Unfortunately, the present location of the Schraubstadter impression is unknown.

editions. A square seal reading 'fuji' is used by both Yamashiro-ya and Maruya on these designs, perhaps suggesting some special relationship between the two firms. All previous commentators have thought the Kiyohiro editions probably earlier than Kiyomitsu's. From the actor's crest on the figure's robes and the content of Jōa's poem, one of the Kiyomitsu pillar prints published by Maruya has been identified as a performance by Segawa Kikunojō II of the role of Osome at the Nakamura Theatre at the New Year, 1758.[7]

The two editions of the present print of Hikosaburō were issued by the same two publishers as the Kiyohiro/Kiyomitsu editions described above, but the block seems to have been re-cut only partly. Both bear Kiyomitsu signatures. In the case of cat. 133, no less than three editions are known: Kiyohiro (Yamashiro-ya), Kiyomitsu (Maruya) and Kiyomitsu (Enami). Without drawing premature conclusions about the relative dates of these editions,[8] two general observations may be made concerning pillar prints of this period in relation to other, smaller designs: they seem to have been sold over a greater length of time, perhaps to defray the higher cost of their production; and they appear to have been more frequently re-cut and re-issued by different publishers. TTC

133

Torii Kiyomitsu

The Actor Segawa Kikunojō II

c. 1758–60 (?)

ARTIST'S SIGNATURE: 'Torii Kiyomitsu ga' (Drawn by Torii Kiyomitsu)

ARTIST'S SEALS: 'Kiyomitsu', 'Tsūsen'

INSCRIPTION SEAL: 'Jōa'

PUBLISHER: 'Tōriabura-chō Hōsendō' (Hōsendō at Tōriabura-chō) with marks of Maruya Kohei

woodblock, *hashira-e, benizuri-e* (3-colour), 66 × 10 cm

REPRODUCED: Stern n.d., no. 46

Special Funds, 1954

54.367

The actor Segawa Kikunojō II, who succeeded to that name in 1756/11, is depicted wearing a type of padded cap he made famous (*Segawa bōshi* or *Segawa wata*) and robes decorated all over with his personal emblem, a chrysanthemum, and his crest, a bundle of silk wadding (*yui-wata*).[1] Although the female role is not named on the print, the twin swords worn prominently through the sash make it clear that the character is acting in place of a male samurai relative. Above the figure appear the actor's name and poetry name, Rokō, and a *hokku* poem with the 'Jōa' seal of the popular writer Kansuidō Jōa (1686 – ?after 1767)[2] which puns on his name and crest:

Fure ya yuki	Snowflakes flutter
tsumoru omoi no	while thoughts of love pile high
Segawa wata	as a padded Segawa cap.[3]

An almost identical design (Honolulu Academy of Arts), bearing a Kiyohiro signature, possibly printed from re-cut blocks and published by Yamashiro-ya, has another, unsigned poem and partly different patterns on the robe. Howard Link has suggested that the role may be Enju, avenging daughter of Numada Shōji, in the play *Ume-no-hana aoi hachinoki*, which was performed at the Nakamura Theatre in the eleventh month, 1758.[4]

A third edition of the design (Art Institute of Chicago) looks to have been printed from the same block as the Honolulu 'Kiyohiro' print and shows the same unsigned poem, but replaces the signature of the Honolulu impression with 'Torii Kiyomitsu hitsu' (From the brush of Torii Kiyomitsu) and the publisher's seal with 'Enami'.[5] The Chicago signature is written in a more delicate style, not at all like the bold calligraphic writing seen on the Boston impression and most other prints by Kiyomitsu.

That three similar pillar print designs by Kiyohiro and Kiyomitsu exist in different editions issued by Yamashiro-ya and Maruya has been discussed in the commentary to cat. 132. As mentioned there, most authorities have assumed the Kiyohiro designs to be earlier than Kiyomitsu's, yet the existence in the present case of a third edition, apparently by Kiyomitsu, but published by Yamashiro-ya, complicates matters still further. Any attempt to establish the chronology of the editions will have to involve careful examination of the Honolulu 'Kiyohiro' and the Chicago 'Kiyomitsu' prints for relative block wear. TTC

1 For three other pillar prints by Kiyomitsu of Kikunojō II from this period, see Chicago 1955, p. 249, Kiyomitsu nos. 17–19.

2 See cat. 132, note 1.

3 I am grateful to John Carpenter for his assistance with this translation.

4 Honolulu 1980, p. 212, Kiyomitsu no. 13. The poem reads: 'Kangiku ya / musume katagi no / saki-gokoro' (Winter chrysanthemum / like the revenge blooming / in a daughter's heart). The role of Ko-Shizuka, performed by Kikunojō II at the Nakamura Theatre in 1757/11, also seems to have been that of an avenging daughter.

5 Chicago 1955, p. 271, Kiyomitsu no. 62; also reproduced in Pins 1982, no. 86.

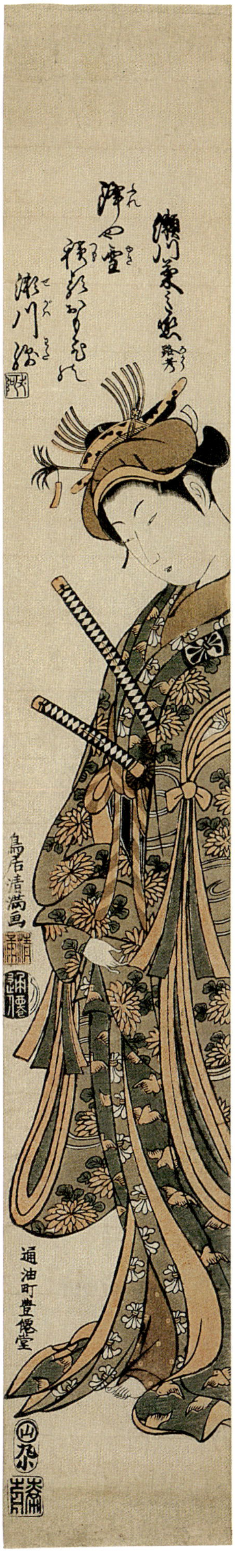
鳥居清満画
通油町

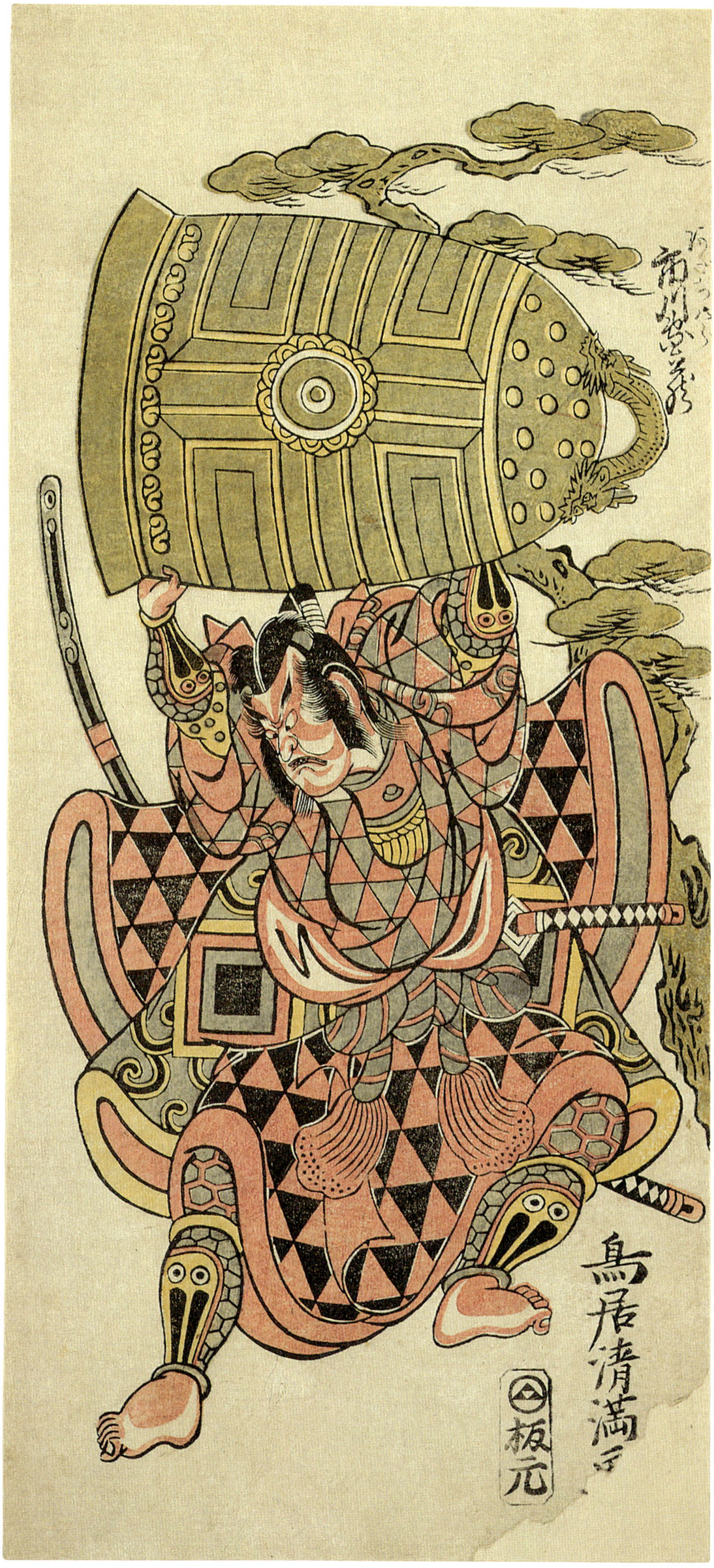
鳥居清満
板元

134
Torii Kiyomitsu
The Actor Ichikawa Danzō III as Adachi Hachirō

11th month, 1762

ARTIST'S SIGNATURE: 'Torii Kiyomitsu ga' (Drawn by Torii Kiyomitsu)

PUBLISHER: mark of Urokogata-ya, 'hanmoto' (publisher)

woodblock, *hosoban*, *benizuri-e* (3-colour), 30.6 × 14.2 cm

William Sturgis Bigelow Collection, 1911

11.19030

Kisoe-uta sakae Komachi, the *kaomise* performance at the Ichimura Theatre in the eleventh month, 1762, seems to have combined the world of the female poet Ono no Komachi with a *jōruri* dance skit on the theme of the love of the salt maidens Matsukaze and Murasame for the courtier Yukihira. Ichikawa Danzō III is recorded as having taken the part of one Adachi Hachirō, the name of the role written on the print here. The actor is depicted in the *aragoto* costume, make-up, wig and pose more customary for Soga no Gorō (see, for example, cat. 107) as he lifts above his head a massive bronze temple bell – which he is doubtless about to hurl at a gang of hapless foes. His costume features a repeating triangular 'snake-scale' (*urokogata*) pattern. There is no mention of the bell in the brief accounts contained in the following year's actor critiques, which simply record Danzō III as the actor of the *shibaraku* (Stop one moment!) role, which would require a quite different costume. In the critique's single illustration he is shown in the costume of a court servant watching for the result of a contest between two fighting cocks, an aspect of the role mentioned in the critique.[1]

Ichikawa Danzō III had succeeded to that acting name in 1740/11 after the deaths earlier the same year of his adoptive father and brother, Danzō I and Danzō II. In 1744 he went to work in Kamigata, not returning to Edo until 1761/11. After that, apart from one brief visit to Kamigata during the 1765–6 season, he acted in Edo until his retirement in 1772. His style resembled that of Danjūrō II (Ebizō II) and he frequently performed roles that were the speciality of the Ichikawa family,[2] as is apparent in this depiction. Yet he did not appear with Danjūrō IV until the third month, 1764, at the Nakamura Theatre.[3]

Printing in three colours, generally red, yellow and blue, was in regular use by the early 1760s. Yellow could be printed over the blue, as here, to produce a fourth colour, green. TTC

1 *Kabuki hyōban-ki II*, vol. 7, pp. 512, 516.

2 Nojima 1988, pp. 101–2.

3 *Kabuki nenpyō*, vol. 3, p. 544.

135

Torii Kiyomitsu

The Actors Segawa Kikunojō II as Keisei Katsuragi and Ichimura Uzaemon IX as Nagoya Sanza

11th month, 1766

ARTIST'S SIGNATURE: 'Torii Kiyomitsu ga' (Drawn by Torii Kiyomitsu)

ARTIST'S SEAL: 'Kiyomitsu'

PUBLISHER: 'Eijudō' with seals 'Hibino', 'Kaihan' (commencing publication) and 'Nishimura' with publisher's mark

woodblock, *ōban*, *benizuri-e* (3-colour), 42.4 × 28.9 cm

John Ware Willard Fund, 1945

45.832

The actor critique published at the New Year, 1767, gave an ironic description of reactions to the alluring performance of Segawa Kikunojō II in the second part of the *kaomise* play *Higashiyama-dono kabuki no tsuitachi*, which had been staged at the Ichimura Theatre in the eleventh month of the previous year: 'To a *jōruri* chanted by [Tokiwazu] Moji-dayū, he danced together with the theatre manager [*tayū-moto*, i.e. Ichimura Uzaemon IX], both of them dressed as mendicant monks [*komosō* or *komusō*]. Things came to a fine pass in the tear-jerking love scene: the audience down in the stalls got drenched by drool from the boxes!'[1]

Ever since Ichikawa Danjūrō II as Soga no Gorō had first taken the guise of a *komusō* monk in a performance of 1715 (cat. 34), this had become a regular theatrical device to enable characters to travel incognito or otherwise evade the rules of society. It is not clear exactly when the device was extended to a pair of lovers, here the courtesan Katsuragi and her handsome suitor Nagoya Sanza. Resembling less and less the austere robes of a destitute monk, the apparel used for the disguise became increasingly foppish, the deep sedge hat (*tengai*), monk's stole (*kesa*) and *shakuhachi* flute in an elaborate brocade bag acquiring the status of elegant fashion accessories in their own right. The kimono worn here may be patchwork, but patchwork made from combinations of very stylish fabrics – chrysanthemum pattern for Kikunojō II and plovers and stylised waves for Uzaemon IX. Katsuragi seems shyly and hesitantly to finger a tune, while Sanza strikes a stylish pose and gazes into her eyes. The *hokku* poem printed above contains imagery of secret refuge, weaving in a reference to Kikunojō II's emblem flower and to the name of a famous *shakuhachi* tune, 'The Crane in its Nest' (*Tsuru no su-gomori*):[2]

Tsuru no su ni *kiku saku kado ya* *fuyu-gomori*	A crane's nest and blooming chrysanthemums at the gate – settling in for the winter.

In the 1760s Nishimura-ya was an up-and-coming publishing firm, trying hard to secure a strong presence on the market with new types of print. Several large *ōban*-sized designs by Kiyomitsu of pairs of young actors in similar, carefully composed complimentary poses can be dated *c.* 1764–5.[2] These display the actors' crests prominently above the figures, but do not include a poem. Evidently, Nishimura-ya was continually experimenting with innovations that would enable him to compete with the new full-colour 'brocade prints' (*nishiki-e*; see cat. 142) designed by Harunobu. TTC

1 *Kabuki hyōban-ki II*, vol. 8, p. 597.

2 See, for example, *Hizō ukiyo-e*, vol. 2, no. 8 (Nakamura Matsue as Hanshichi and Segawa Kikunojō II as Ohana), which Asano Shūgō dates to the 1st month, 1765, and ibid., no. 9 (Arashi Hinaji and Bandō Hikosaburō II), which he dates *c.* 1764–5.

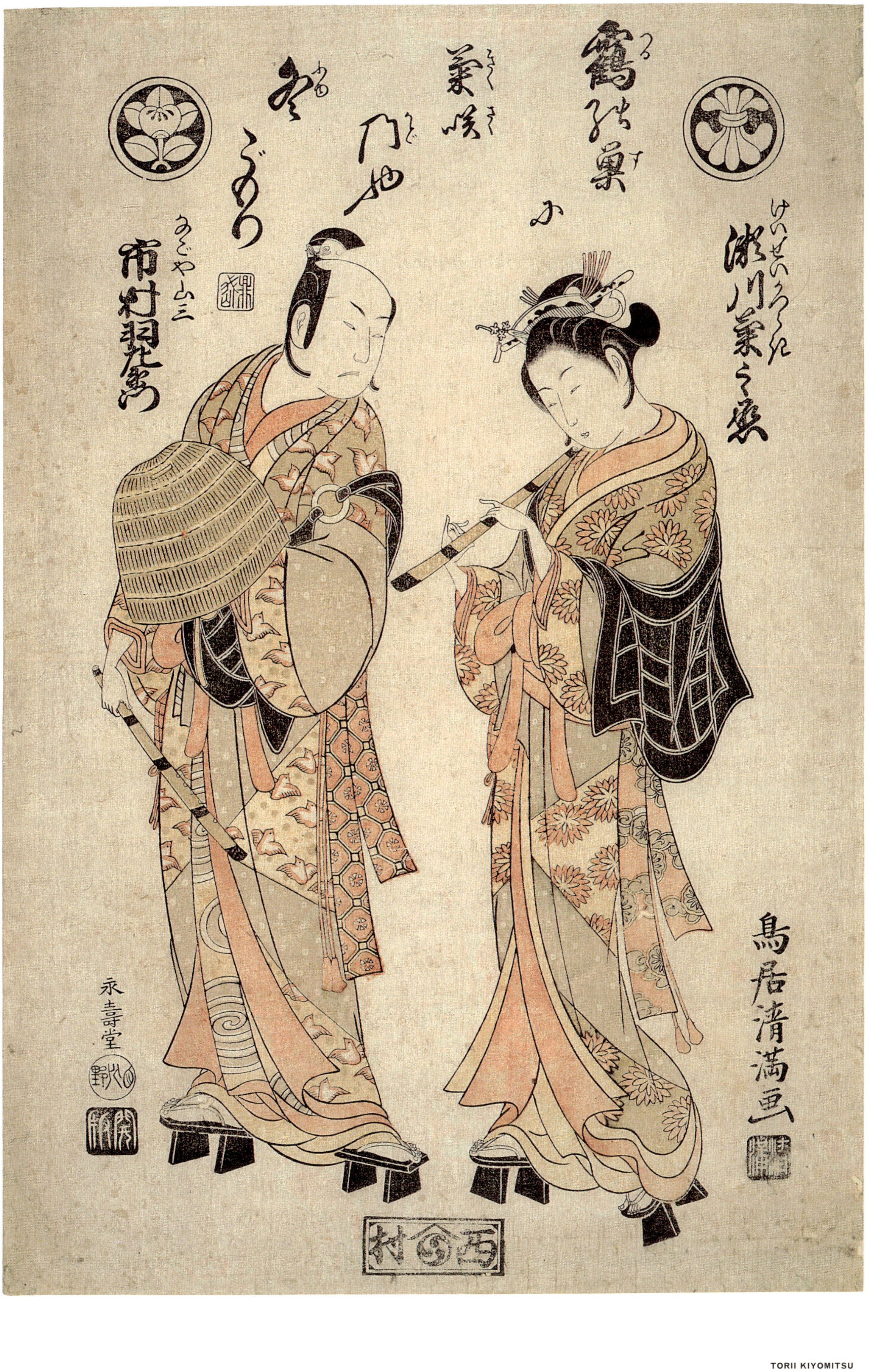
鳥居清満画
永寿堂
西村

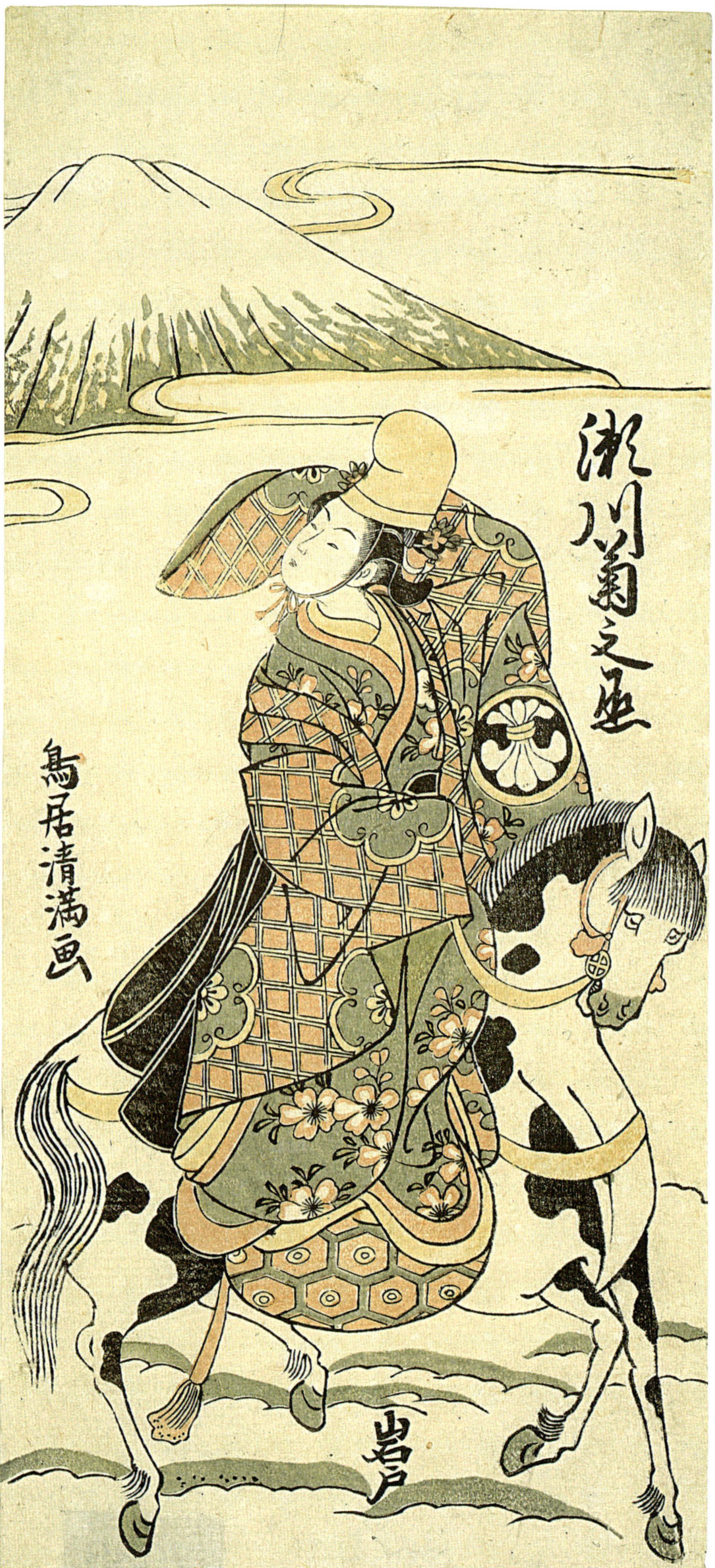
瀬川菊之丞
鳥居清満画
岩戸

136
Torii Kiyomitsu
The Actor Segawa Kikunojō II as Itsuki

11th month, 1767

ARTIST'S SIGNATURE: 'Torii Kiyomitsu ga' (Drawn by Torii Kiyomitsu)

PUBLISHER: 'Iwato' [Iwato-ya Genpachi?]

woodblock, *hosoban*, *benizuri-e* (3-colour), 31.1 × 14 cm

William Sturgis Bigelow Collection, 1911

11.19020

For *Tales of Ise* and the episode from it depicted here, see the commentary to cat. 14. A three-colour horizontal *ōban* of the scene acted out by figures in contemporary dress, designed by Kiyomitsu, published by Iwato-ya and quoting the *Tales of Ise* poem, was issued *c.* 1764 (Art Institute of Chicago).[1] Several famous episodes from *Tales of Ise* served as material for a wide range of reinterpretations – literary, theatrical and artistic – in later times, particularly in Edo popular culture, as has recently been demonstrated by Nakamachi Keiko.[2] The Boston print brings together some of the complex strands of these reinterpretations.

The play *Taihei-ki shizunome furisode*, performed at the Nakamura Theatre in the eleventh month, 1767, included the scene '"Narihira's Journey to the East" played by actors in contemporary guise', in which Segawa Kikunojō II performed the role of Itsuki, younger sister of Kuri'u Saemon, and made an entrance via a rising trapdoor in the stage (*seri-dashi*).[3] The costume, including the golden court cap, and the pose, with the sleeve of the court cloak drawn up behind the head in appreciation of the view, are familiar from many classical paintings of Narihira's journey. The kabuki version is set in the snow, *de rigueur* for a mid-winter *kaomise* performance in the eleventh month, even though this contradicts the letter and the spirit of Narihira's mid-summer poem.

Another three-colour *hosoban* print by Kiyomitsu (Museum für Ostasiatische Kunst, Cologne) shows Kikunojō II in the same scene on horseback, but with the additional figure of Bandō Hikosaburō II as Oyamada Tarō and without Mount Fuji.[4] A grand three-colour *ōban* print (formerly Henri Vever Collection) by Kitao Shigemasa (1739–1820) again shows Kikunojō II on horseback, but this time with Ichikawa Komazō as Yoshisada and with Fuji,[5] while a three-colour *hosoban* print by Shigemasa (Art Institute of Chicago) includes Kikunojō II, Hikosaburō II and Fuji.[6] Clearly this was a particularly picture-worthy performance. TTC

1 Chicago 1955, p. 261, [Kiyomitsu] no. 41.

2 Nakamachi 2000, esp. pp. 61–70.

3 *Kabuki hyōban-ki II*, vol. 9, p. 109; Nakamachi 2000, p. 66.

4 Cologne 1991, no 116.

5 Hillier 1976, vol. 1, no. 212.

6 Chicago 1965, p. 279, [Shigemasa] no. 12.

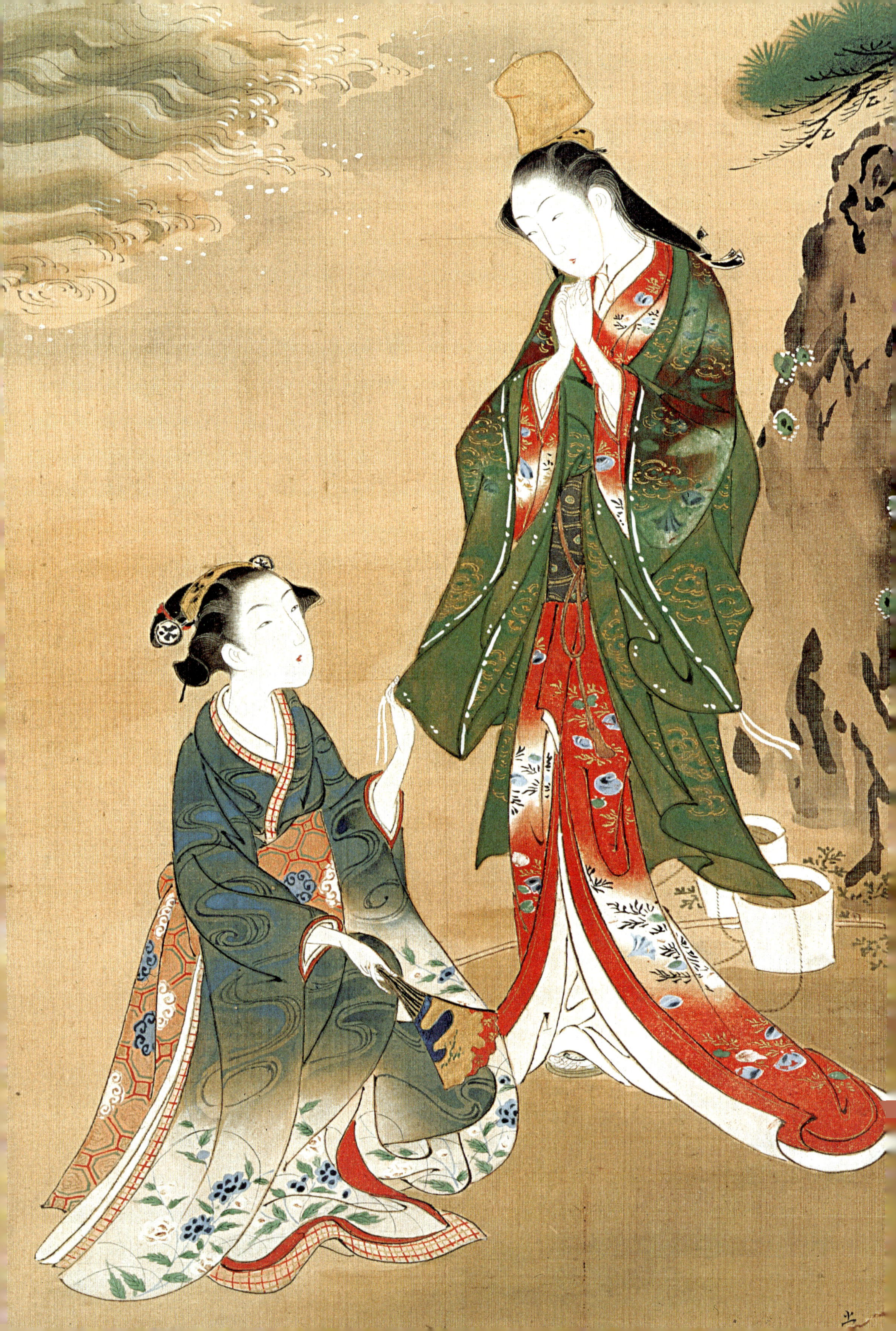

137–9
Kawamata Tsunemasa
Parodies of Historical Figure Subjects of China and Japan

c. 1744–51

ARTIST'S SIGNATURE: 'Tsunemasa ga' (Painted by Tsunemasa)

ARTIST'S SEAL: 'Tsunemasa'

triptych of hanging scrolls, ink, colour and gold on silk, 85.1 × 27.2 cm

REPRODUCED: Boston 2000, vol. 1, nos. 72–4

William Sturgis Bigelow Collection, 1911
11.7896–8

In these three paintings Kawamata Tsunemasa presents elegant contemporary interpretations of well-known themes from Chinese and Japanese legend and literature. In the scroll on the right a young attendant holds up a round silvered mirror on an elaborate lacquer stand for the courtesan to adjust her hair. The painting makes reference to the celebrated Chinese beauty Wang Zhaogun (*Jap.* Ōshōkun). Said to be a member of the household of Emperor Yuandi, Wang was reputedly of impeccable character. When the Emperor ordered that a portrait be made of his concubines so that one woman could be sent to appease a much-feared 'barbarian', Wang refused to bribe the court painter. Thus spurned, the duplicitous artist sent an extremely unattractive portrait of the lady, leading the Emperor to select her as the sacrificial bride. Much to his horror, he later discovered that he had dispatched the most beautiful woman at his court.

In the centre scroll Tsunemasa explores a story made famous for its enactment in nō performances – that of the sisters Matsukaze and Murasame. Fleeing from a cruel stepmother, they took refuge with a fisherman, who gave them employment transporting buckets of brine to be turned into salt. For a while the sisters were visited by Ariwara no Yukihira, the Minister of State, who gave them his gauze jacket (*kariginu*) and court hat as emblems of his affection. Fickle in his attentions, he never returned, leaving the two women to pine after him.

In the left scroll an extremely elegant youth standing beneath a cherry tree looks down to read a poem just penned by his kneeling female companion. Naitō Masato has concluded that the young man is Prince Genji, protagonist of *Tale of Genji* (see cat. 102, 103), an identification based on the mention of this subject in the writing on the box that houses the triptych.[1]

In the three paintings Tsunemasa has transformed the appearance of his Chinese and Japanese subjects in accordance with 18th-century fashions, especially noticeable in the *au courant* textiles and hairdos. Comparison of the slender, almost fragile figures and their small, fine-boned faces with those in a print of the same subject by Suzuki Harunobu, *The Autumn Moon of Matsukaze* (*Matsukaze no shūgetsu*) from the series 'Fashionable Eight Views of Nō Plays' (*Fūryū utai hakkei*),[2] suggests that Tsunemasa was an important source of inspiration for Harunobu. ANM

1 Boston 2000, vol. 1, nos. 72–4 (commentary by Naitō Masato).

2 Collection of Mr and Mrs Richard P. Gale; reproduced in Hillier 1970, vol. 1, no. 94.

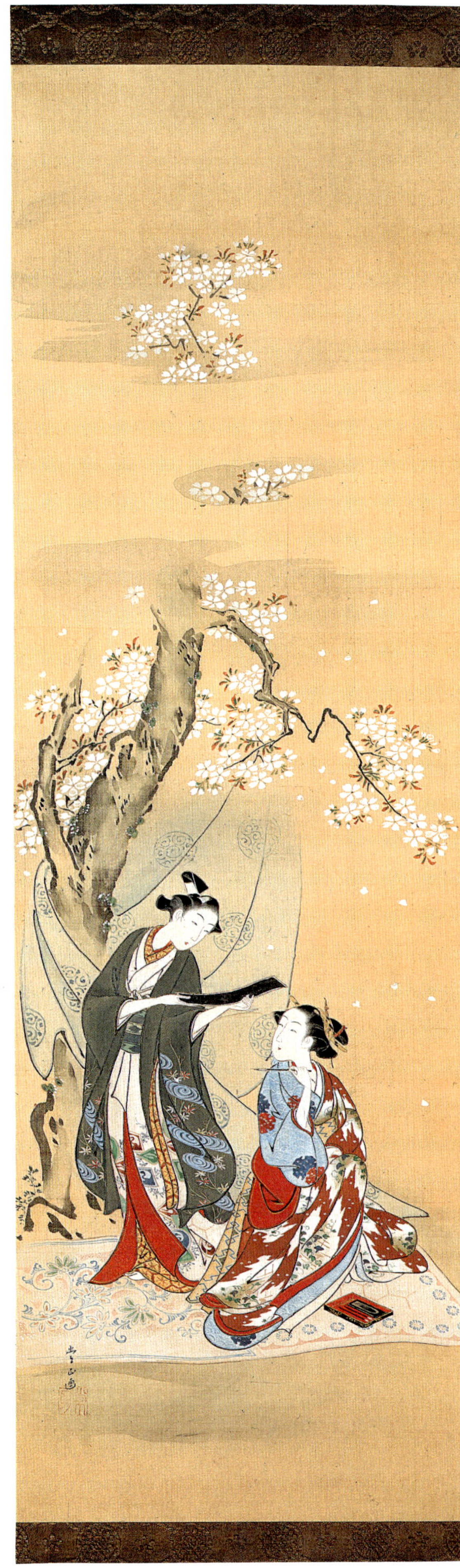

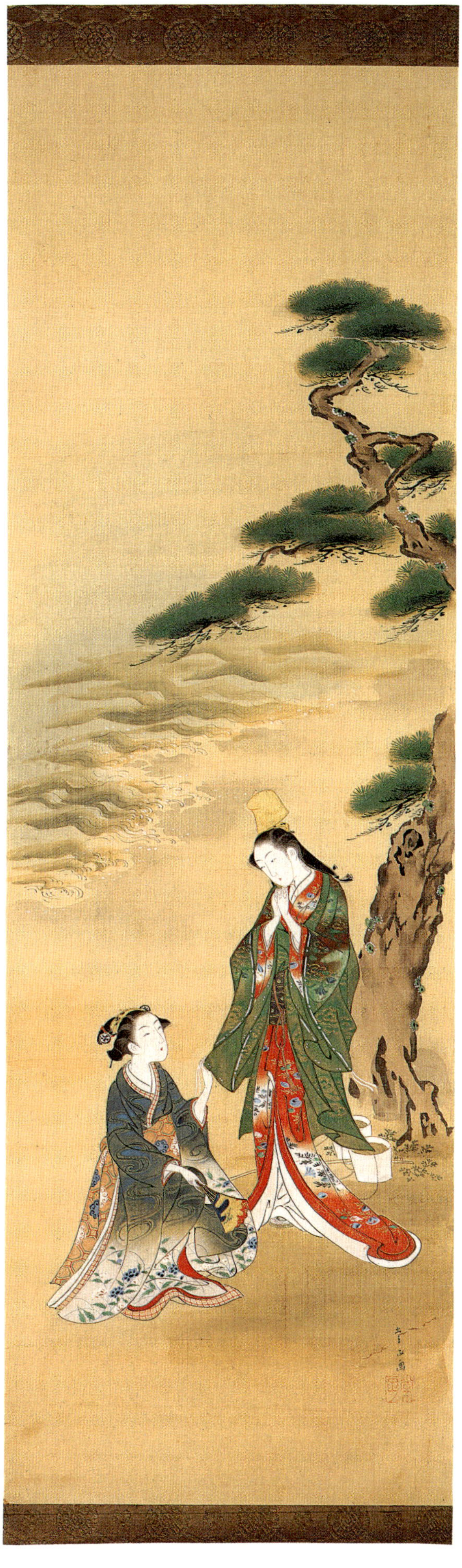

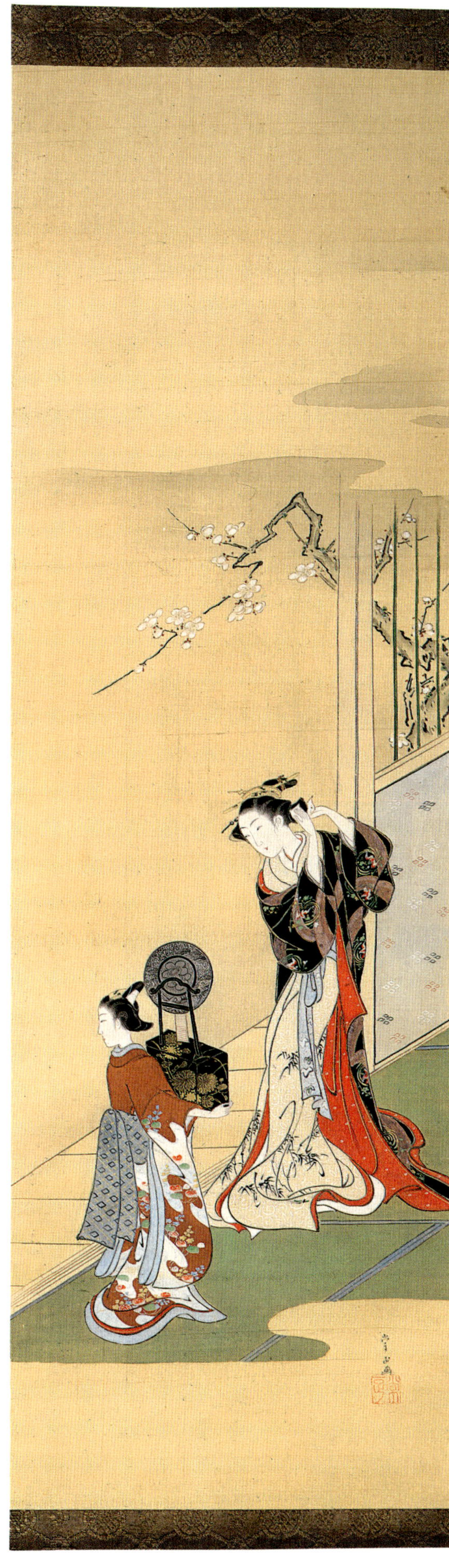

140
Suzuki Harunobu
The Warrior Kojima Bingo no Saburō Takanori

c. 1762–4

ARTIST'S SIGNATURE: 'Suzuki Harunobu hitsu' (Brush of Suzuki Harunobu)

PUBLISHER: 'Sakai-ya'

woodblock, *ōban*, *benizuri-e*, 39.3 × 27.6 cm

REPRODUCED: *Ukiyo-e shūka*, suppl. vol. 1, p. 143, no. 71

William Sturgis Bigelow Collection, 1911

11.19633

1 *Ukiyo-e shūka*, suppl. vol. 1, p. 143, no. 71 (commentary by David Waterhouse)

2 McCullough 1959, p. 108.

This print depicts an incident recorded in the *Chronicle of the Great Peace* (*Taiheiki*), a medieval warrior epic documenting Emperor Go-Daigo's attempts to overthrow the Kamukura shogunate and re-establish Imperial rule. Samurai clans across Japan took sides in the conflict. Kojima Bingo no Saburō Takanori, the warrior depicted in this print, was an adherent of Go-Daigo. While Takanori was on his way to meet the Emperor and pledge his support, Go-Daigo's forces suffered a setback and the Emperor was exiled. He carved the following poem in the bark of a cherry tree on the road that the Emperor was to travel along:

Ten Kōsen o munashū suru koto nakare	Heaven will not destroy Goujian;
Toki ni Hanrei naki ni shi mo arazu[1]	a Fan Li is not lacking today.[2]

Members of the Emperor's escort could not understand the poem, but Go-Daigo recognised the reference to a famous episode in Chinese history in which the loyalty and cunning of Fan Li, a minister at the court of Goujian, brought victory to his lord, who had suffered defeat and humiliation at the hands of his enemies. Fan Li's dedication was such that he refused any reward for his efforts.

Although many 18th-century ukiyo-e artists designed warrior prints (*musha-e*), most were issued as book illustrations. Single-sheet designs in the *ōban* format, such as that shown here, were extremely rare until *musha-e* emerged as a major print genre in the 19th century.

Suzuki Harunobu is known especially for his production in 1765 of the first full-colour prints in Japan. His earlier work generally receives less attention, but the present design suggests that it is undervalued. This is a sophisticated example of the *benizuri-e* technique just prior to the introduction of full-colour printing. The *sumi*, *beni*, blue and yellow were printed from separate blocks, while the green was produced by overprinting some of the yellow with blue. AH

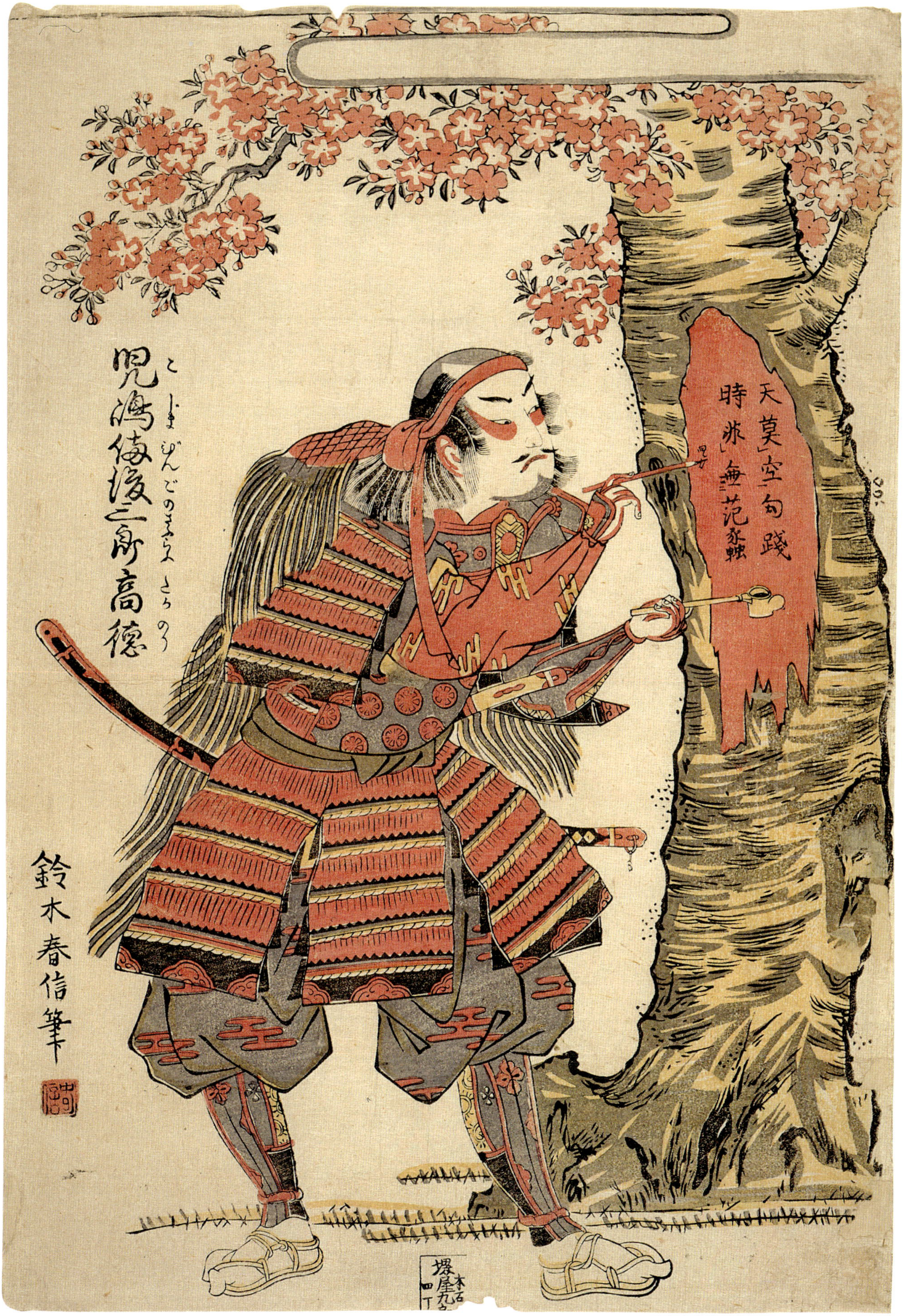

児嶋備後三郎高徳
天莫空勾践
時非無范蠡
鈴木春信筆

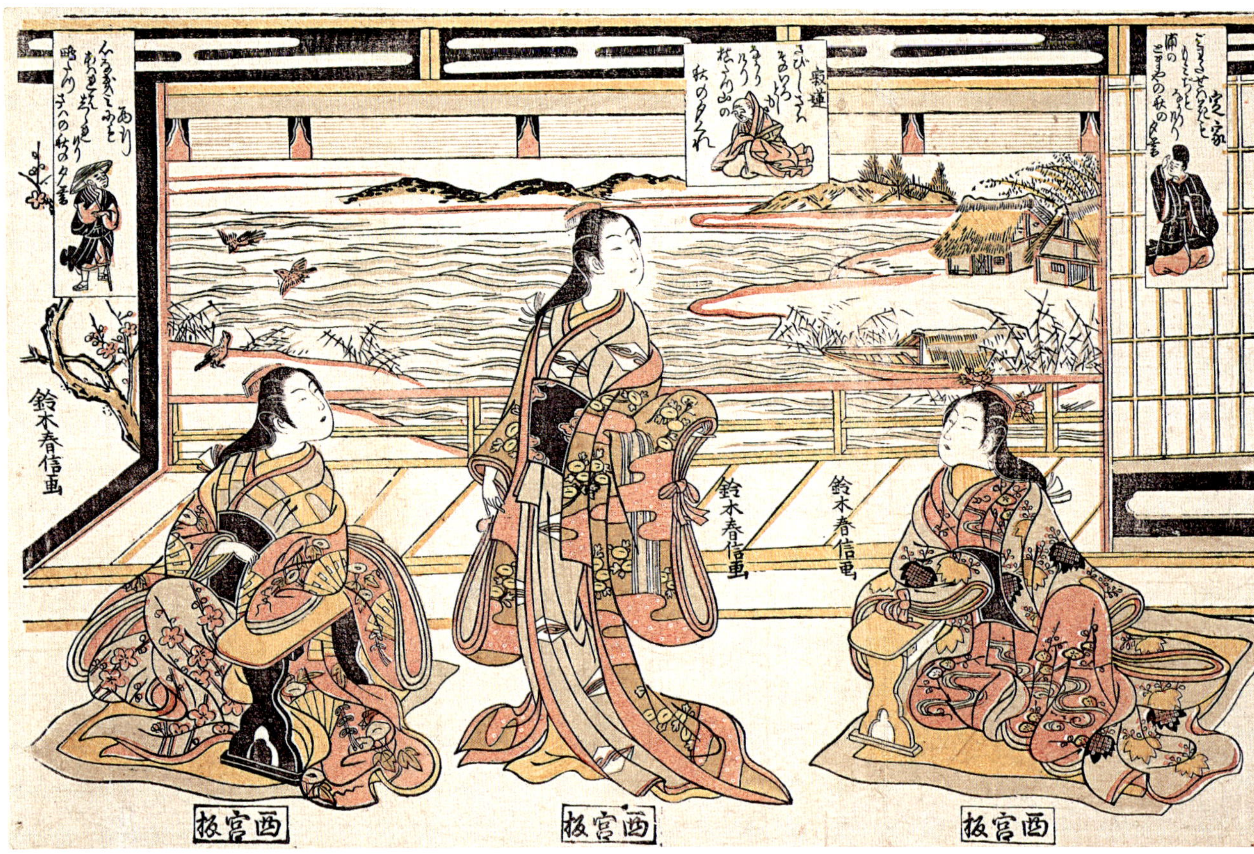
寂蓮
定家
鈴木春信画
鈴木春信画
鈴木春信画
西宮板
西宮板
西宮板

141
Suzuki Harunobu
Parody of the Three Evening Poems: Teika, Jakuren and Saigyō

1763–4

ARTIST'S SIGNATURE: 'Suzuki Harunobu ga' (Drawn by Suzuki Harunobu)

PUBLISHER: 'Nishinomiya [Shinroku]'

woodblock, horizontal *ōban*, *benizuri-e*, 27 × 41.3 cm

REPRODUCED: *Ukiyo-e shūka*, suppl. vol. 1, p. 31, no. 10

William Sturgis Bigelow Collection, 1911

11.19703

1 Philadelphia 1970, pp. 93–8.

2 See ibid. for a discussion and reproductions of all these prints.

Harunobu's treatment of the 'Three Evening Poems' weaves together straightforward and *mitate-e* expressions of the theme while exploiting the two traditions of Japanese poem painting. The three women depicted in the foreground constitute a *mitate* of the poets Saigyō, Teika and Jakuren, depicted in the insets arranged across the top of the design. Harunobu's composition enhances this relationship. Supporting themselves on arm rests, the two seated women look towards the third, who stands in between them. Saigyō and Teika are shown standing in the left and right inserts respectively – rather than sitting, like their *mitate-e* counterparts – but they also gaze at Jakuren in between them, represented on the middle panel. The insets follow the *kasen-e* mode of poem painting, which depicts the poets who wrote the poems inscribed on the painting or print. *Uta-e*, on the other hand, render some aspect of the poem. The landscape in this design, which Harunobu borrowed from an illustration in the first volume of Nishikawa Sukenobu's *Ehon Yamato hiji* (published 1735–42),[1] draws on this tradition. It consists of a compilation of the views described in the three poems (quoted in full at cat. 64): 'a thatched hut by the shore' from Teika's poem, 'the marsh where snipe start up' from Saigyō's and 'black firs growing on the hills' from Jakuren's.

Harunobu reused elements of the background landscape in a sequence of 'parodies of the Three Evening Poems' (*mitate sanseki*) prints. In 1766 he designed a set of three *chūban* prints that bore the seals of Kyosen, the *haikai* poet who played a prominent role in the early development of *nishiki-e*. These prints were reissued in 1767 without Kyosen's seals. A third version, also in the *chūban* format but with poems added to each design, was issued in 1768. In 1770 Harunobu reworked the theme in a triple *hosoban* design that again used the same landscape features.[2] AH

142
Suzuki Harunobu
A Kamuro Uses a Mirror to Penetrate a 'Komusō's' Disguise

1766

ARTIST'S SIGNATURE: 'Suzuki Harunobu ga' (Drawn by Suzuki Harunobu)

BLOCK CUTTER'S SEALS: 'Sekine', 'Kaei'

woodblock, *chūban, nishiki-e*, 28.1 × 21 cm

REPRODUCED: *Ukiyo-e shūka*, suppl. vol. 2, p. 44, no. 17

OTHER IMPRESSIONS: William Sturgis Bigelow Collection, Museum of Fine Arts, Boston, 11.19428; Art Institute of Chicago (Chicago 1965, p. 33); (Yoshida 1942, no. 73)

John Ware Willard Fund, 1945

45.833

Komusō were itinerant monks of the Fuke sect of Zen Buddhism, easily recognisable by the accoutrements associated with their order. These included a *kesa*, a black stole that hung round their neck and shoulders, a *shakuhachi*, which they played as a form of meditation, and a bamboo hat known as a *tengai* that covered their head and face, presumably to screen them from temptation. *Komusō* attire, especially the hat, became the preferred disguise in kabuki narratives in which the hero needed to travel incognito (see cat. 135). As this print suggests, it was also a convenient disguise for an illicit visit to Yoshiwara. Using a mirror, the courtesan's attendant (*kamuro*) reveals the identity of the young man masquerading as a *komusō*. Perhaps she had become suspicious because of the expensive *inrō* with a zoomorphic design (possibly a dragon face) hanging from the *komusō*'s sash.

This is an *e-goyomi* (picture calendar), a product closely associated with the development of *nishiki-e*. The 'era date' (*nengō*), Meiwa 3, and the zodiacal (*kanshi*) designation, *hinoe inu*, both of which refer to the year 1766, appear in the pattern of the courtesan's obi. Early calendar prints, especially Harunobu's, frequently drew on book illustrations by other artists. Guessing the source of the illustration was part of the elaborate play associated with the exchange of *e-goyomi* during gatherings of Edo's *haikai* poetry clubs in 1765 and 1766. In the present case, Harunobu borrowed the *kamuro* and *komusō* from an image in the third volume of Okumura Masanobu's picture book *Ukiyo ehon nukume-dori* of *c.* 1745.

As with most *e-goyomi*, this design had a complex afterlife. The second state, a specimen of which is also in the Boston Museum, lacks the seals and the silver lines on the *komusō*'s *kesa*. This has led some scholars to suggest that these lines may have been calendrical markings, perhaps a list of the long or short months of the year.[1] For the third state, a specimen of which is in the Art Institute of Chicago, the calendrical markings on the courtesan's obi were eliminated. The heads of the courtesan and *kamuro* were also re-cut for this edition because the block had become extremely worn. The fourth state has further alterations to the garments of all three figures. AH

1 For the Japanese lunar calendar, see cat. 113, note 3.

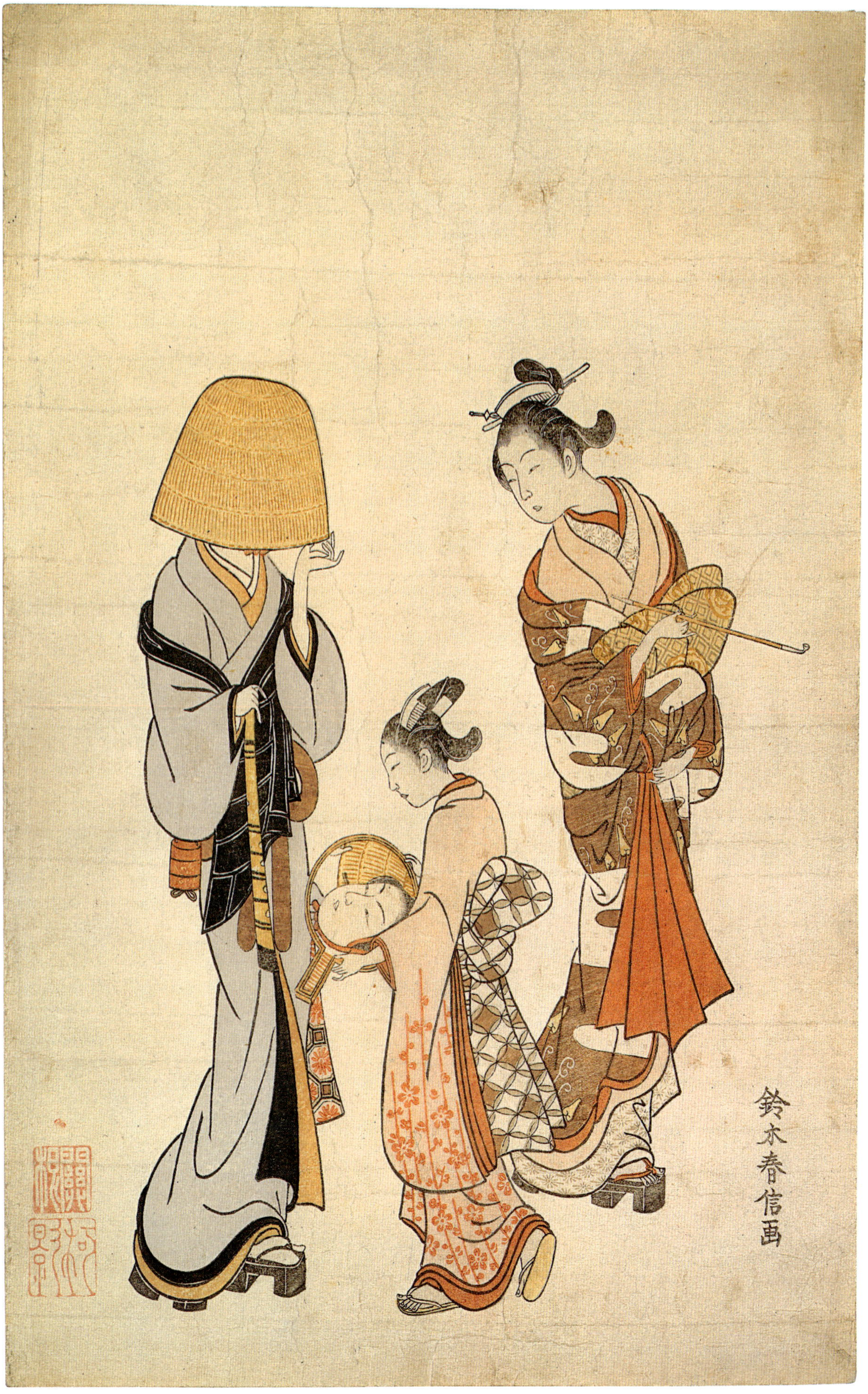
鈴木春信画

Bibliography

AKAMA 1994
Akama Ryō, 'Edo kabuki no e-kanban to Torii-ha no katsudō–tsuketari e-kanban to kusa-zōshi no e-daisen ni tsuite', *Kabuki: kenkyū to hihyō* 14, Dec. 1994, pp. 3–15.

AOKI 1999
Aoki Takayuki, 'Okumura Masanobu: rakkan, hanmoto-in kara saguru sōsaku katsudō', *Ukiyo-e geijutsu* 133, Oct. 1999, pp. 20–33.

AOKI 2000
Aoki Takayuki, 'Chūgoku ichimai-zuri hanga', *Ukiyo-e geijutsu* 136, July 2000, pp. 26–9.

ASANO 1984
Asano Shūgō, 'Hishikawa Moronobu no mago-musume Osan', *Denki (Sanko-kai)* 7, Sept. 1984, pp. 25–6.

ASANO 1987
Asano Shūgō, 'Kanbun kara Hōreki-ki no nikuhitsu ukiyo-e', in Narazaki Muneshige, ed., *Nikuhitsu ukiyo-e I*, Nihon no bijutsu 248, Tokyo 1987, pp. 20–80.

ASANO 1994
Asano Shūgō, 'Kaigetsudō Ando hitsu *Tachi bijin zu*', *Kokka* 1183, June 1994, pp. 24–8.

ASANO 1995
Asano Shūgō, ed., *Ukiyo-e soroimono makura-e (ge)*, Tokyo 1995.

ASANO 1999
Asano Shūgō, 'Shunga-shi gaisetsu', *Bungaku* 10, no. 3, July 1999, pp. 38–42.

ASANO 2001
Asano Shūgō, 'Hishikawa-ha no hanga, hanpon no seisaku to ryūtsū', paper delivered at the Hotei Publishing Ukiyo-e Conference, Leiden, Jan. 2001.

BAIRD 2001
Merrily Baird, *Symbols of Japan: Thematic Motifs in Art and Design*, New York 2001.

BINYON AND SEXTON 1978
Laurence Binyon and J. J. O'Brien Sexton, *Japanese Colour Prints*, London 1923, repr. 1978.

BLUSSÉ ET AL. 2000
Leonard Blussé, Willem Remmelink and Ivo Smits, eds., *Bridging the Divide: 400 Years, The Netherlands–Japan*, Leiden 2000.

BOSTON 1894
Boston, Museum of Fine Arts, *Japanese Engravings: Old Prints in Color Collected by S. Bing, Paris*, by Siegfried Bing, exh. cat., New York 1894.

BOSTON 2000
Boston, Museum of Fine Arts, *Bosuton Bijitsukan nikuhitsu ukiyo-e / Ukiyo-e Paintings: Museum of Fine Arts, Boston*, 3 vols., Boston and Tokyo 2000.

BOSTON 2001
Boston, Museum of Fine Arts, *Bosuton Bijitsukan nikuhitsu ukiyo-e / Ukiyo-e Paintings: Museum of Fine Arts, Boston*, suppl. vol: *Shunga meihin sen*, Boston and Tokyo 2001.

BOWER AND MINER 1962
Robert H. Bower and Earl Miner, *Japanese Court Poetry*, London 1962.

BOWRING 1992
Richard Bowring, 'The Ise Monogatari: A Short Cultural History', *Harvard Journal of Asiatic Studies* 50, no. 2, Dec. 1992, pp. 401–80.

CAMBRIDGE 1997
Cambridge, Fitzwilliam Museum, *Prints of the Floating World: Japanese Woodblock Prints from the Fitzwilliam Museum, Cambridge*, by Craig Hartley, London 1997.

CHALFIN 1904
Paul Chalfin, 'Report of the Curator of the Chinese and Japanese Department', *Annual Report* [of the Museum of Fine Arts, Boston], 1904, pp. 65–9.

CHIBA 2000
Chiba City Museum of Art, *Hishikawa Moronobu ten*, by Asano Shūgō, exh. cat., Chiba 2000.

CHICAGO 1931
Art Institute of Chicago, *Descriptive Catalogue of the Japanese and Chinese Illustrated Books in the Ryerson Library of the Art Institute of Chicago*, by Toda Kenji, Chicago 1931.

CHICAGO 1955
Art Institute of Chicago, *The Clarence Buckingham Collection of Japanese Prints*, vol. 1, *The Primitives*, by Helen C. Gunsaulus, Chicago 1955.

CHICAGO 1965
Art Institute of Chicago, *The Clarence Buckingham Collection of Japanese Prints*, vol. 2, *Harunobu et al.*, by Margaret Gentles, Chicago 1965.

CHICAGO 1971
Art Institute of Chicago, *Ukiyo-e Prints and Paintings: The Primitive Period, 1680–1745*, by Donald Jenkins, exh. cat., Chicago 1971.

CHICAGO 1994
Art Institute of Chicago, *The Actor's Image: The Print Makers of the Katsukawa School*, by Timothy Clark and Osamu Ueda, Chicago 1994.

CHRISTIE'S 1988
The Donald and Mary Hyde Collection of Japanese Books and Manuscripts, auction cat., Christie's, New York, 7 Oct. 1988.

CHRISTIE'S 1998
An Important Collection of Japanese Ukiyo-e Paintings, auction cat., Christie's, New York, 28 Oct. 1998.

CLARK 1992
Timothy Clark, 'Kunisada and Decadence: The Critical Reception of Nineteenth Century Japanese Figure Prints in the West', in *Modern Japanese Art and the West*, Meiji Bijutsu Gakkai, Tokyo 1992, pp. 89–100.

CLARK 1997
Timothy Clark, 'Mitate-e: Some Thoughts, and a Summary of Recent Writings', *Impressions* 19, 1997, pp. 6–27.

CLARK 2000
Timothy Clark, 'Prostitute as Bodhisattva: The Eguchi Theme in Ukiyo-e', *Impressions* 22, 2000, pp. 36–53.

COALDRAKE 1981
William H. Coaldrake, 'Edo Architecture and Tokugawa Law', *Monumenta Nipponica* 36, no. 3, autumn 1981, pp. 235–84.

COLOGNE 1991
Cologne, Museum für Ostasiatische Kunst, *Heiteres Treiben in der vergänglichen Welt: Japanische Holzschnitte des 17. bis 19. Jahrhunderts*, by Asano Shūgō, exh. cat., Cologne 1991.

CORTAZZI 1991
Sir Hugh Cortazzi, 'The British in Japan in the Nineteenth Century', in London 1991, pp. 55–65.

DE BECKER 1971
J.E. De Becker, *The Nightless City, or the History of the Yoshiwara*, Tokyo 1971.

DITTRICH 1977
Edith Dittrich, *Das Westzimmer: Hsi-hsiang chi – Chinesische Farbholzschnitte von Min Ch'i-chi*, Cologne 1977.

DORE 1992
Ronald Philip Dore, *Education in Tokugawa Japan* (1965), Michigan Classics in Japanese Studies 8, Ann Arbor 1992.

DRESDEN 1995
Dresden, Kupferstich-Kabinett, *Gems of the Floating World: Ukiyo-e Prints from the Kupferstich-Kabinett Dresden*, by Rose Hempel, exh. cat., Dresden and New York 1995.

DUNN AND TORIGOE
Charles Dunn and Bunzō Torigoe, eds., *The Actors' Analects*, New York 1969.

EDMUNDS n.d.
William H. Edmunds, *Pointers and Clues to the Subjects of Chinese and Japanese Art*, London n.d. [1934].

EDO JIDAI
Edo jidai bungei shiryō, vol. 2, Tokyo 1916.

EDO TOKYO NENPYŌ
Edo Tokyo nenpyō, ed. Ōhama Tetsuya and Yoshiwara Ken'ichirō, Tokyo 1993.

EDO-GAKU JITEN
Edo-gaku jiten, Tokyo 1994.

FENOLLOSA 1884
Ernest Francisco Fenellosa, 'Review of the Chapter on Painting in L'Art Japonais by L. Gonse', *The Japan Weekly Mail* 2, no. 2, 12 July 1884, pp. 37–46.

FENOLLOSA 1912
Ernest Francisco Fenollosa, *Epochs of Chinese and Japanese Art*, 2 vols., New York 1912.

FICKE 1923
Arthur Davison Ficke, 'The Prints of Kwaigetsudo', *The Arts* 4, no. 2, Aug. 1923, pp. 95–119.

FIORILLO 1999
John Fiorillo, 'Refashioning the Legends of Komachi in mitate-e', *Andon* 63, 1999, pp. 17–30.

FISCHER 1992
Felice Fischer, 'Meiji Painting from the Fenollosa Collection', *Philadelphia Museum of Art Bulletin* 88, no. 375, autumn 1992, pp. 2–23.

FUJIKAKE 1943
Fujikake Shizuya, *Ukiyo-e no kenkyū*, 3 vols., Tokyo 1943.

GENOA 1980
Genoa, Edoardo Chiossone Civic Museum of Oriental Art, *Ukiyo-Prints and Painting from the Early Masters to Shunshō*, by Luigi Bernabò Brea and Eiko Kondo, Genoa 1980.

GENSHOKU UKIYO-E
Genshoku ukiyo-e dai hyakka jiten, vol. 3, *Yōshiki, hori-suri, hanmoto*, by Kikuchi Sadao, Kobayashi Tadashi and Murakami Seizō; vol. 5, *Fūzoku*, by Endō Takeshi; vol. 6, *Sakuhin 1, Moronobu, Harunobu*, by Yamaguchi Keizaburō and Asano Shūgō, Tokyo 1982.

GENTLES 1964
Margaret Gentles, *Masters of the Japanese Print: Moronobu to Utamaro*, exh. cat., New York 1964.

GERHART 1999
Karen M. Gerhart, *The Eyes of Power: Art and Early Tokugawa Authority*, Honolulu 1999.

GERSTLE 1989
C. Andrew Gerstle, ed., *18th Century Japan: Culture and Society*, Sydney 1989.

GERSTLE 2001
C. Andrew Gerstle, *Chikamatsu: 5 Late Plays*, New York 2001.

GOODMAN 2000
Grant K. Goodman, *Japan and the Dutch 1600–1853*, Richmond 2000.

GUTH 1993
Christine Guth, *Art, Tea and Industry: Masuda Takashi and the Mitsui Circle*, Princeton 1993.

HALFORD 1956
Aubrey S. Halford and Giovanna M. Halford, *The Kabuki Handbook*, Rutland, VT, and Tokyo 1956.

HALL 1991
John Whitney Hall, ed., *Early Modern Japan*, Cambridge History of Japan 4, Cambridge 1991.

HATTORI 1983
Hattori Yukio et al., eds., *Kabuki jiten*, Tokyo 1983.

HAYASHI 1964
Hayashi Yoshikazu, *Enpon kenkyū: Harunobu*, Tokyo 1964.

HAYASHI 1986
Hayashi Kyōhei, 'Torii Kiyoshige no *Kusazuri-biki zu* ema', *Azabu Bijutsukan kenkyū kiyō* 2, autumn 1986, pp. 44–6.

HEMPEL 1997
Rose Hempel, *Meisterwerke des japanischen Farbholzschnitts*, Munich and New York 1997

HIBBETT 1959
Howard Hibbett, *The Floating World in Japanese Fiction*, London 1959.

HICKMAN 1978
Money L. Hickman, 'Views of the Floating World', *Bulletin of the Museum of Fine Arts, Boston* 76, 1978, pp. 4–33.

HICKMAN 1981
Money L. Hickman, 'On the Trail of Kume the Transcendant', *Bulletin of the Museum of Fine Arts, Boston* 79, 1981, pp. 20–43.

HIGUCHI 1977
Higuchi Hiroshi, *Shoki ukiyo-e*, Tokyo 1977.

HILLIER 1959
Jack Hillier, 'Sugimura Jihei', *Oriental Art* 1, 1959, pp. 2–10.

HILLIER 1970
Jack Hillier, *Catalogue of the Japanese Paintings and Prints in the Collection of Mr. & Mrs. Richard P. Gale*, 2 vols., London 1970.

HILLIER 1976
Jack Hillier, *Japanese Prints and Drawings from the Vever Collection*, 3 vols., London 1976.

HILLIER 1987
Jack Hillier, *The Art of the Japanese Book*, 2 vols., London 1987.

HIZŌ UKIYO-E
Hizō ukiyo-e taikan, ed. Narazaki Muneshige, 13 vols., Tokyo 1987–90.

HOCKLEY 2000
Allen Hockley, 'Shunga: Function, Context, Methodology', *Monumenta Nipponica* 55, no. 2, Spring 2000, pp. 257–69.

HOCKLEY n.d.
Allen Hockley, *The Prints of Isoda Koryūsai*, Seattle n.d. [forthcoming].

HONOLULU 1977
Honolulu Academy of Arts, *The Theatrical Prints of the Torii Masters: A Selection of Seventeenth and Eighteenth Century Ukiyo-e*, by Howard A. Link, exh. cat., Honolulu 1977.

HONOLULU 1980
Honolulu Academy of Arts, *Primitive Ukiyo-e from the James A. Michener Collection in the Honolulu Academy of Arts*, by Howard A. Link, Honolulu 1980.

HONOUR AND FLEMING 1982
Hugh Honour and John Fleming, *A World History of Art*, London 1982.

HORIOKA 1974
Horioka Chimyō, 'Sugimura Jihei ron', *Ukiyo-e geijutsu* 40, May 1974, pp. 5–33.

IIZUKA 1926
Iizuka Tomoichirō, *Kabuki saiken*, Tokyo 1926.

INOUE 1920
Inoue Kazuo, 'Ishikawa Toyonobu no sakuga nendai, jō, chū, ge', *Ukiyo-e* 53, April 1920, pp. 16–20; 54, June 1920, pp. 1–5; 55, Aug. 1920, pp. 1–5.

INOUE 1923
Inoue Kazuo, 'Torii Kiyonobu to Kiyomasu, Torii-ke no daidai', *Ukiyo-e no kenkyū* 3, nos. 3–4, July 1923, pp. 13–27.

INOUE 1929
Inoue Kazuo, 'Okumura Masanobu ni kansuru sensaku', *Ukiyo-e no kenkyū* 5, no. 3, Dec. 1926, pp. 2–10.

ITŌ 1984
Itō Toshiko, *Ise monogatari-e*, Tokyo 1984.

IWATA 1992
Iwata Kōtarō, 'Toshi keizai no tenkan', in Yoshida 1992, pp. 263–302.

IWATA 1993
Iwata Hideyuki, 'Mitate-e ni kansuru gimon', in *Edo bungaku kenkyū*, Tokyo 1993, pp. 568–81.

JENKINS 1972
Donald Jenkins, 'A Comparison of the Ryerson Shidare Yanagi and Kiyonobu's Keisei ehon', *Ukiyo-e geijutsu* 36, 1972, pp. ii–vii.

JOLY 1967
Henri L. Joly, *Legend in Japanese Art*, Rutland, VT, and Tokyo 1967.

KABUKI HYŌBAN-KI I
Kabuki hyōban-ki shūsei, 1st series, 11 vols., Tokyo 1972–7.

KABUKI HYŌBAN-KI II
Kabuki hyōban-ki shūsei: Daini-ki, 2nd series, 11 vols., Tokyo 1987–95.

KABUKI NENDAI-KI
Kabuki nendai-ki, by Tatekawa Enba, rev. Yoshida Teruji, Tokyo 1926.

KABUKI NENPYŌ
Kabuki nenpyō, ed. Ihara Tōshirō, 8 vols., Tokyo 1956–63.

KABUKI ZUSETSU
Kabuki zusetsu, ed. Shuzui Kenji and Akiba Yoshimi, Tokyo 1931.

KAEMPFER 1727
Engelbert Kaempfer, *The History of Japan, Together with a Description of the Kingdom of Siam*, trans. J.G. Scheuchzer, 2 vols., London 1727.

KATAGIRI 1996
Katagiri Yōichi, ed., *Ise monogatari: Keichō jusannen kan Saga-bon dai isshu*, Osaka 1996.

KAWASE 1932
Kawase Kazuma, *Saga-bon zukō*, Tokyo 1932.

KEENE 1976
Donald Keene, *World Within Walls: Japanese Literature of the Pre-Modern Era, 1600–1867*, New York 1976.

KERLEN 1996
H. Kerlen, *Catalogue of Pre-Meiji Japanese Books and Maps in Public Collections in the Netherlands*, Amsterdam 1996.

KEYES 1972
Roger Keyes, 'Suzuki Harunobu hanga zen-sakuhin mokuroku', in *Zaigai hihō (Harunobu)*, Tokyo 1972, pp. 84–94.

KEYES 1989
Roger Keyes, *The Male Journey in Japanese Prints*, Berkeley and Los Angeles 1989.

KIKUCHI 1969
Sadao Kikuchi, *A Treasury of Japanese Woodblock Prints*, trans. Don Kenny, Tokyo and New York 1969.

KINSEI FŪZOKU
Kinsei fūzoku zufu, vol. 6, *Yūri*, Tokyo 1982.

KISHI 1994
Kishi Fumikazu, *Edo enkin-hō: ukiyo no shikaku*, Tokyo 1994.

KISHI 1994A
Kishi Fumikazu, 'The Perspective System of Early Uki-e: Okumura Masanobu's Series of Ō uki e', *Aesthetics* (Japanese Society for Aesthetics) 6, March 1994, pp. 73–86.

KISHO FUKUSEIKAI
Kisho fukuseikai sōsho, vols. 25, 27, 28, ed. Nakamura Yukihiko and Hino Tatsuo, Tokyo 1990.

KITA 1999
Sandy Kita, *The Last Tosa: Iwasa Katsumochi Matabei, Bridge to Ukiyo-e*, Honolulu 1999.

KOBAYASHI 1970
Kobayashi Tadashi, *Harunobu*, Tōyō bijutsu sensho, Tokyo 1970.

KOBAYASHI 1977
Kobayashi Tadashi, 'Akusho-zu toshite no kabuki-zu: Hishikawa Moronobu no byōbu o chūshin ni', in *Nihon byōbu-e shūsei*, vol. 13, Tokyo 1977, pp. 130–4.

KOBAYASHI 1982
Kobayashi Tadashi, *Edo no bijinga*, Tokyo 1982.

KOBAYASHI 1982A
Kobayashi Tadashi, 'Kaigetsudō Ando to sono bijin-ga', in *Nikuhitsu ukiyo-e 2: Moronobu*, Tokyo 1982, pp. 130–4.

KOBAYASHI 1982B
Kobayashi Tadashi, *Ukiyo-e: An Introduction to Japanese Woodblock Prints*, Tokyo 1982; 1st paperback edn, 1997.

KOBAYASHI 1985
Kobayashi Tadashi, *Harunobu*, Nihon no bijutsu 228, Tokyo 1985.

KOBAYASHI 1986
Kobayashi Tadashi, 'Shinshutsu no nikuhitsu ukiyo-e sansaku ni tsuite, *Ukiyo-e geijutsu* 87, July 1986, frontispieces, pp. 3–4.

KOBAYASHI 1988
Kobayashi Tadashi, *Hanabusa Itchō*, Nihon no bijutsu 260, Tokyo, 1988.

KOBAYASHI 1995
Kobayashi Tadashi, ed., *Ukiyo-e soroimono makura-e (jō)*, Tokyo 1995.

KOBAYASHI 1996
Kobayashi Tadashi, 'Hishikawa Moronobu no Yoshiwara fūzoku-zu ni tsuite', in *Nikuhitsu ukiyo-e taikan* 7, Tokyo 1996, pp. 214–17.

KOBAYASHI 1996A
Kobayashi Tadashi, *Moronobu to shoki ukiyo-e*, Nihon no bijutsu 363, Tokyo 1996.

KOBAYASHI AND ŌKUBO 1994
Kobayashi Todashi and Ōkubo Jun'ichirō, *Ukiyo-e no kanshō kiso chishiki*, Tokyo 1994.

KODANSHA ENCYCLOPEDIA
Kodansha Encyclopedia of Japan, 9 vols., Tokyo 1983.

KOKUSHO SŌ-MOKUROKU
Kokusho sō-mokuroku, 9 vols., Tokyo 1996–7.

KOMINZ 1995
Laurence R. Kominz, *Avatars of Vengeance: Japanese Drama and the Soga Literary Tradition*, Ann Arbor 1995.

KOMINZ 1997
Laurence R. Kominz, *The Stars Who Created Kabuki: Their Lives, Loves and Legacies*, Tokyo 1997.

KORNICKI 1998
Peter Kornicki, *The Book in Japan: A Cultural History from the Beginnings to the Nineteenth Century*, Leiden 1998, repr. Honolulu, 2001.

KUROKI 1987
Kuroki Takashi, 'Meireki no taika-go no machi-zukuri', and 'Meireki no taika', in *Edo Tokyo gaku jiten*, Tokyo 1987, pp. 343–4, 880–1.

KYOTO 1991
Kyoto Bunka Hakubutsukan, *Kyō no kabuki ten*, exh. cat., Kyoto 1991.

KYOTO 1999
Kyoto National Museum, *Hana miyako no mōdo*, exh. cat., Kyoto 1999.

LANE 1957
Richard Lane, 'The Beginnings of the Modern Japanese Novel: *Kana-zōshi*, 1600–1682', *Harvard Journal of Asiatic Studies* 20, nos. 3–4, Dec. 1957, pp. 644–701.

LANE 1957A
Richard Lane, 'The Clarence Buckingham Collection of Japanese Prints: The Primitives', *Harvard Journal of Asiatic Studies*, 1957, pp. 346–57.

LANE 1959
Richard Lane, *Kaigetsudo (circa 1700–1750)*, ed. Takahashi Seiichirō, Rutland, VT, and Tokyo 1959.

LANE 1962
Richard Lane, *Masters of the Japanese Print: Their World and their Work*, New York 1962.

LANE 1963
Richard Lane, 'Some Japanese Bans on Art and Literature', in *Felix Tikotin zum Siebsigsten Geburtstag*, Basle 1963, not paginated.

LANE 1973–6
Richard Lane, *Shunga Books of the Ukiyo-e School*, 3 vols., Tokyo 1973–6.

LANE 1978
Richard Lane, *Images from the Floating World*, Oxford 1978.

LANE 1979
Richard Lane, *The Early Shunga Scroll*, Tokyo 1979.

LANE 1980
Richard Lane, 'Sugimura Jihei no sashi-e', *(Kikan) Ukiyo-e* 81, April 1980, pp. 1–8, 29–36.

LANE 1981
Richard Lane, 'Sugimura Jihei no ō-ōban', *(Kikan) Ukiyo-e* 84, Jan. 1981, pp. 28–46.

LANE 1981A
Richard Lane, 'Sugimura's Heike Prints', *Andon* 3, 1981, pp. 1–8.

LANE 1985
Richard Lane, 'Eros Crosses the Seas: Ming Erotica in Edo Japan', *Andon* 5, no. 20, 1985, pp. 75–80.

LANE 1995
Richard Lane, *Shinpen shoki hanga: Makura-e*, Tokyo 1995.

LEE 1977
Julian Jinn Lee, 'The Origin and Development of Japanese Landscape Prints: A Study in the Synthesis of Eastern and Western Art', Ph.D. thesis, University of Washington, 1977.

LEITER 1997
Samuel L. Leiter, *New Kabuki Encyclopedia: A Revised Adaptation of Kabuki Jiten*, Westport, CT, and London 1997.

LONDON 1980
London, British Museum, *Japanese Prints: 300 Years of Albums and Books*, by Jack Hillier and Lawrence Smith, exh. cat., London 1980.

LONDON 1988
London, British Museum, *Ukiyo-e: Images of Unknown Japan*, ed. Lawrence Smith, exh. cat., London 1988.

LONDON 1991
London, Barbican Art Gallery, *Japan and Britain: An Aesthetic Dialogue 1850–1930*, ed. Tomoko Sato and Toshio Watanabe, exh. cat., London 1991.

LONDON 1992
London, British Museum, *Ukiyo-e Paintings in the British Museum*, by Timothy Clark, London 1992.

LONDON 1993
London, British Library, *Descriptive Catalogue of Japanese Books in the British Library Printed before 1700*, by Kenneth B. Gardner, London 1993.

LOS ANGELES 1992
Los Angeles Country Museum of Art, *When Art Became Fashion: Kosode in Edo-Period Japan*, by Dale Carolyn Gluckman and Sharon Sadako Takeda, exh. cat., Los Angeles 1992.

McARTHUR 1999
Meher McArthur, *Gods and Goblins: Japanese Folk Paintings from Otsu*, exh. cat., Pasadena 1999.

MCCULLOUGH 1959
Helen Craig Mc Cullough, trans., *The Taiheiki: A Chronicle of Medieval Japan*, New York 1959.

MCCULLOUGH 1968
Helen Craig McCullough, trans., *Tales of Ise: Lyrical Episodes from Tenth-Century Japan*, Stanford 1968.

MACHIDA 1987
Machida City Museum of Graphic Arts, *Meisaku ni miru Nihon hanga*, exh. cat., Machida 1987.

MACHIDA 1999
Machida City Museum of Graphic Arts, *Edo no hana ukiyo-e ten: Nishiki-e no seiritsu katei*, exh. cat., Machida 1999.

MAINICHI 1993
Mainichi Shinbun, Tokyo, *Edo no some: Ukiyo-e meihin-ten*, exh. cat., Tokyo 1993.

MATSUDAIRA 1977
Matsudaira Susumu, 'Sukenobu ehon no hankō to fukyū', *Ukiyo-e geijutsu* 53, 1977, pp. 3–13.

MATSUDAIRA 1981
Matsudaira Susumu, 'Koten no taishū-ka to Sukenobu ehon', *Bungaku* 49, Nov. 1981, pp. 55–70.

MATSUDAIRA 1988
Matsudaira Susumu, *Moronobu Sukenobu ehon shoshi*, Nihon shoshigaku taikei 57, Tokyo 1988.

MICHENER 1959
James A. Michener, *Japanese Prints from the Early Masters to the Modern*, Rutland, VT, and Tokyo 1959.

MINER ET AL. 1985
Earl Miner, Hiroko Odagiri and Robert Morell, *The Princeton Companion to Classical Literature*, Princeton 1985.

MIYATAKE 1909
Miyatake Gaikotsu, *Hishikawa Moronobu gafu*, Osaka 1909.

MIYATAKE 1910
Miyatake Gaikotsu, *Okumura Masanobu gafu*, Osaka 1910.

MIYATAKE 1911
Miyatake Gaikotsu, *Nishikawa Sukenobu gafu*, Osaka 1911.

MIZUTANI 1935
Mizutani Yumihiko, *Kohan shōsetsu sōga shi*, Tokyo 1935.

MORI 1981
Mori Tōru, *Kasen-e: Hyakunin isshu-e*, Tokyo 1981.

MORSE 2000
Anne Nishimura Morse, 'Miyagawa Chōsun hitsu Yoshiwara fūzoku zu byōbu', *Kokka*, 1261, Nov. 2000, pp. 19–23.

MOSTOW 1996
Joshua S. Mostow, *Pictures of the Heart: The Hyakunin Isshu in Word and Image*, Honolulu 1996.

MURAKATA 1971
Akiko Murakata, 'Selected Letters of Dr. William Sturgis Bigelow', Ph.D. thesis, George Washington University, Washington 1971.

MURASAKI 1935
Murasaki Shikibu, *The Tale of Genji: A Novel in Six Parts by Lady Murasaki*, trans. Arthur Waley, London 1935.

MURASAKI 1975
Murasaki Shikibu, *Genji Monogatari*, ed. Imaizumi Tadayoshi, Mori Shōichi and Okazaki Masatsugu, Tokyo 1975.

MURASAKI 1980
Murasaki Shikibu, *The Tale of Genji*, trans. and intro. Edward G. Seidensticker, New York 1980.

MURRAY 1972
Peter and Linda Murray, *A Dictionary of Art and Artists*, 3rd edn, Harmondsworth 1972.

MUTŌ 1992
Mutō Junko, 'Shosei Torii Kiyomasu kō: yakusha-e o tōshite no ichi-kōsatsu', *Ukiyo-e geijutsu* 106, Nov. 1992, pp. 11–34.

MUTŌ 1994
Mutō Junko, '(Fūryū ehon) Shihō byōbu kō', *Ukiyo-e geijutsu* 112, July 1994, pp. 5–12.

MUTŌ 1996
Mutō Junko, 'Edo kabuki no e-kanban: Shōtoku-ki o chūmoku shite', *Kabuki: kenkyū to hihyō* 17, June 1996, pp. 97–110.

MUTŌ 1997
Mutō Junko, 'Shoki Torii-ha to Kyōhō nana-nen no shuppan rei: Kiyonobu, Kiyomasu o chūshin ni', *Ukiyo-e geijutsu* 123, March 1997, pp. 3–20.

MUTŌ 1999
Mutō Junko, 'Okumura Masanobu no yakusha-e: sakuga jiki to seisaku jōkyō o chūshin ni', *Ukiyo-e geijutsu* 133, Oct. 1999, pp. 3–19.

MUTŌ 1999A
Mutō Junko, 'Torii-ha no yakusha nigao: Torii Kiyoshige ni chūmoku shite', in Yamaguchi Keizaburō, ed., *Ukiyo-e no genzai*, Tokyo 1999, pp. 71–97.

NAGASAKI 1992
Nagasaki Iwao, 'Designs for a Thousand Ages: Printed Pattern Books and Kosode', in Los Angeles 1992, pp. 95–113.

NAGATA 1989
Helen Mitsu Nagata, 'Images of the Tale of Ise', in *Word in Flower: The Visualization of Classical Literature in Seventeenth Century Japan*, exh. cat., Yale University Art Gallery, 1989, pp. 54–83.

NAKADA 1950
Nakada Katsunosuke, *Ehon no kenkyū*, Tokyo 1950.

NAKAMACHI 1979
Nakamachi Keiko, 'Ogata Kōrin no zōkei ni kansuru ichi-kōsatsu: Hyakunin isshu-e karuta o chūshin to shite', *Kokka* 1027, 1979, pp. 9–36.

NAKAMACHI 2000
Nakamachi Keiko, 'Ukiyo-e Memories of Ise Monogatari', *Impressions* 22, 2000, pp. 54–85.

NAKANE AND ŌISHI 1990
Chie Nakane and Shinzaburō Ōishi, *Tokugawa Japan: The Social and Economic Antecedents of Modern Japan*, trans. and ed. Conrad Totman, Tokyo 1990.

NAKANO 1993
Nakano Mitsutoshi, 'Kyōhō kaikaku no bunka-teki igi', in *Nihon no kinsei*, vol. 12, Tokyo 1993, pp. 48–57.

NARA 1972
Nara, Yamato Bunkakan, *Chūgoku no Min-Shin jidai no hanga*, exh. cat., Nara 1972.

NEW YORK 1978
New York Public Library, *Catalogue of Japanese Illustrated Books and Manuscripts in the Spencer Collection of the New York Public Library*, by Shigeo Sorimachi, Tokyo 1978.

NEW YORK 1986
New York Public Library, *Tales of Japan: Scrolls and Prints from the New York Public Library*, by Miyeko Murase, New York and Oxford 1986.

NEW YORK 1991
New York, Asia Society Galleries, *Undercurrents in the Floating World: Censorship and Japanese Prints*, by Sarah E. Thompson and H.D. Harootunian, exh. cat., New York 1991.

NEW YORK 1991A
New York, Japan Society Gallery, *Early Masters: Ukiyo-e Prints and Paintings from 1680 to 1750*, by Gunhild Avitabile, exh. cat., New York 1991.

NEW YORK 1993
New York, Japan Society, *Rain and Snow: The Umbrella in Japanese Art*, by Julia Meech, exh. cat., New York 1993.

NIHON BIJUTSU ZENSHŪ
Nihon bijutsu zenshū, vol. 22, *Edo shomin no kaiga: Fūzoku-ga to ukiyo-e*, Tokyo 1979.

NIHON DENKI
Nihon denki densetsu dai-jiten, ed. Inui Katsumi et al., Tokyo 1986.

NIHON FŪZOKU ZUE
Nihon fūzoku zue, ed. Kurokawa Mamichi, 12 vols., Tokyo 1914–5.

NIHON KOKUGO DAI-JITEN
Nihon kokugo dai-jiten (Shōgakkan), 10 vols., Tokyo 1981.

NIHON KOTEN
Nihon koten bungaku dai-jiten, 6 vols., Tokyo 1985.

NIHON KOTEN BUNGAKU
Nihon koten bungaku taikei, vol. 91, *Ukiyo-zōshi shū*, Tokyo 1966.

NIHON ZUIHITSU TAISEI
Nihon zuihitsu taisei, dai-niki, vol. 2, Hayakawa Junsaburō, ed., Tokyo 1916.

NIKUHITSU UKIYO-E
Nikuhitsu ukiyo-e, 10 vols., Tokyo 1980–2.

NIKUHITSU UKIYO-E TAIKAN
Nikuhitsu ukiyo-e taikan, 10 vols., Tokyo 1994–6.

NISHIZAKA 1992
Nishizaka Yasushi, 'Kinsei toshi to ō-dana', in Yoshida 1992, pp. 173–220.

NOGUCHI 1933
Yone Noguchi, *The Ukiyo-e Primitives*, Tokyo 1933.

NOJIMA 1988
Nojima Jusaburō, ed., *Kabuki jinmei jiten*, Tokyo 1988.

OBERLIN 1984
Oberlin, OH, Oberlin College, Allen Memorial Art Museum, *Japanese Woodblock Prints: A Catalogue of the Mary A. Ainsworth Collection*, by Roger Keyes, Oberlin 1984.

OKANO 1999
Okano Tomoko, 'Edo meisho zu no tanjō: Hosomi bijutsukan bon *Edo meisho yūraku zu byōbu* o chūshin ni', *Bijutsu-shi* 48, no. 2, March 1999, pp. 268–83.

ORII 2000
Orii Takae, 'Bugi zu byōbu no seiritsu to tenkai ni kansuru ichi-kōsatsu', *Kokka* 1260, Oct. 2000, pp. 5–18.

OSAKA 1990
Osaka, Matsuzaka-ya, *Doitsu Puruberaa korekushon ukiyo-e hanga meihin ten zuroku*, exh. cat., Osaka 1990.

OSAKA 1998
Osaka, Osaka Municipal Museum, *Wa no ishō*, exh. cat., Osaka 1998.

PAINE 1959
Robert Treat Paine, Jr., 'Some Pillar Prints by Masanobu', *Bulletin of the Museum of Fine Arts, Boston* 53, no. 308, 1959, pp. 41–7.

PAINE 1963
Robert Treat Paine, Jr., 'Japanese Prints of Birds and Flowers by Masanobu and Shigenaga', *Oriental Art* 9, no. 1, 1963, pp. 22–34.

PAINE 1963A
Robert Treat Paine, Jr., 'The Masanobu Tradition of Courtesans of the Three Cities', *Ars Orientalis* 5, 1963, pp. 273–81.

PARIS 1909
Paris, Musée des Arts Décoratifs, *Estampes Japonaises Primitives*, by Charles Vignier and Hogitarō Inada, exh. cat., Paris 1909, repr. Geneva 1973.

PARKE-BERNET 1948
Fine Japanese Color Prints...Collection of the Late Carl Schraubstadter (Part Two), auction cat., Parke-Bernet, New York, 8–9 March 1948.

PHILADELPHIA 1970
Philadelphia Museum of Art, *Suzuki Harunobu*, by Jack Hillier, exh. cat., Philadelphia 1970.

PHILADELPHIA 1983
Early Japanese Prints in the Philadelphia Museum of Art, by David Waterhouse, Toronto 1983.

PHILADELPHIA 2000
Philadelphia Museum of Art, *The Arts of Hon'ami Kōetsu, Japanese Renaissance Master*, by Felice Fischer, exh. cat., Philadelphia 2000.

PHILLIPS 1996
Quitman Eugene Phillips, 'The Price Shuten Dōji Screens: A Study of Visual Narrative', *Ars Orientalis* 26, 1996, pp. 1–21.

PINS 1982
Jacob Pins, *The Japanese Pillar Print: Hashira-e*, London 1982.

REIZEI 1996
Reizei Tamehito, 'Shiki kōsaku-zu no genryū', in *Mizuho no kuni Nihon: Shiki kōsaku-zu no sekai*, Kyoto 1996, pp. 4–7.

RUMPF 1932
Fritz Rumpf, *Das Ise Monogatari von 1608 und sein Einfluss auf die Buchillustration des XVII. Jahrhunderts in Japan*, Berlin 1932.

SAIKAKU 1956
Ihara Saikaku, *Five Women who Loved Love*, trans. Wm. Theodore de Bary, Rutland, VT, and Tokyo 1956; repr. 1982.

SAIKAKU 1963
Ihara Saikaku, *The Life of an Amorous Woman and Other Writings*, trans. and ed. Ivan Morris, New York 1963.

SAIKAKU 1969
Ihara Saikaku, *The Japanese Family Storehouse*, trans. G.W. Sargent, Cambridge 1969.

SAIKAKU 1984
Ihara Saikaku, *The Life of an Amorous Man*, trans. Kengi Hamada, Rutland, VT, 1984.

SAKAKIBARA 1984
Sakakibara Satoru, 'Santorii Bijutsukan-bon *Shuten-dōji emaki* o megutte (jō, ge)', *Kokka* 1076, Sept. 1984, pp. 7–26; 1077, Oct. 1984, pp. 33–56.

SATŌ 1986
Satō Satoru, '(*Hishikawa*) *Tsukinami no asobi* shohan-bon no hakken to hōkoku: Moronobu ehon e no gimon', *Shoshigaku geppō* 25, 1986, pp. 11–8.

SATŌ 1990
Satō Satoru, 'Jōa oboegaki', *Jissen Joshi Daigaku Bungaku-bu kiyō* 32, March 1990, pp. 1–9.

SATŌ 1991
Satō Satoru, 'Hishikawa Moronobu no sai-kentō', *Tabako to Shio no Hakubutsukan kenkyū kiyō* 4, March 1991, pp. 41–9.

SATŌ 1992
Satō Satoru, 'Hanpon shōkai 1: Kokon yakusha monogatari', *Ukiyo-e geijutsu* 103, Jan. 1992, pp. 14–37.

SATŌ 1997
Satō Chino, 'Gensō Segawa Kikunojō no geifū: Kyōhō no onnagata', *Kokugo to koku-bungaku* 74, no. 4, April 1997, pp. 41–55.

SATŌ 1998
Satō Chino, 'Gensō Segawa Kikunojō shukkin nempu', *Kabuki: kenkyū to hihyō* 22, Dec. 1998, pp. 163–87.

SATŌ 2001
Satō Satoru, 'Okumura Masanobu ga *Okumura furu-e*', *Jissen koku-bungaku* 59, March 2001, pp. 26–52.

SAYRE 1979
Charles Franklin Sayre, 'Illustrations of the Ise monogatari: Survival and Revival of Heian Court Culture', 3 vols., unpublished Ph.D. thesis, Yale University, 1979.

SCREECH 1999
Timon Screech, *Sex and the Floating World: Erotic Images in Japan 1700–1820*, London 1999.

SEIGLE 1993
Cecilia Segawa Seigle, *Yoshiwara: The Glittering World of the Yoshiwara Courtesan*, Honolulu 1993.

SHIBUI 1926–8
Shibui Kiyoshi, *Genroku ko-hanga shūei / Estampes Erotiques Primitives du Japon*, 2 vols., Tokyo 1926–8.

SHIBUI 1927
Shibui Kiyoshi, 'Ukiyo-e no kigen', *Ukiyo-e no kenkyū*, extra edition, June 1927, pp. 1–78.

SHIBUI 1929
Shibui Kiyoshi, 'Masanobu no sumi-e', *Ukiyo-e no kenkyū* 6, no. 2, March 1929, pp. 1–66.

SHIBUI 1954
Shibui Kiyoshi, *Shoki hanga*, Tokyo 1954.

SHIBUI AND KIKUCHI 1964
Shibui Kiyoshi and Kikuchi Sadao, *Sugimura*, Ukiyo-e hanga 7, Tokyo 1964.

SHIMAZU 1969
Shimazu Tadao, ed., *Hyakunin isshu*, Tokyo 1969.

SHINODA 1991
Shinoda Jun'ichi, ed., *Ningyō jōruri butai shi*, Tokyo 1991.

SHINODA 1995
Shinoda Jun'ichi, *Nise monogatari-e: e to bun, bun to e*, Tokyo 1995.

SHIVELY 1955
Donald H. Shively, 'Bakufu versus kabuki', *Harvard Journal of Asiatic Studies* 18, Dec. 1955, pp. 326–56.

SHIVELY 1964–5
Donald H. Shively, 'Sumptuary Regulation and Status in Early Tokugawa Japan', *Harvard Journal of Asiatic Studies* 25, 1964–5, pp. 123–64.

SHIVELY 1991
Donald H. Shively, 'Popular Culture', in Hall 1991, pp. 706–9.

STERN n.d.
Harold P. Stern, *Master Prints of Japan: Ukiyo-e Hanga*, New York n.d.

STRAUSS AND BRONZE 1979
Walter L. Strauss and Carol Bronze, eds., *Seventeenth Century Monogatari Fiction*, Japanese Woodcut Book Illustrations, vol. 1, New York 1979.

SUWA 1994
Suwa Haruo, 'Kamigata yakusha-e no genryū', *Kokka* 1186, Sept. 1994, pp. 21–30.

SUWA 1996
Suwa Haruo, 'Kenkyū shiryō: Ukiyo-e no mitate', *Kokka* 1213, Dec. 1996, pp. 28–33.

SUZUKI 1975
Suzuki Jūzō, 'Uki-e no tenkai to henbō', in *Uki-e*, exh. cat., Tokyo, Riccar Bijutsukan, Tokyo 1975, not paginated.

SUZUKI 1979
Suzuki Jūzō, 'Ukiyo-e shoki hanga no seisaku shisei', in *Ukiyo-e shūka*, vol. 4, *The Art Institute of Chicago I*, Tokyo 1979, pp. 229–35.

SUZUKI 1979A
Suzuki Jūzō, ed., *Kinsei Nihon fūzoku ehon shūsei*, vol. 5: *Yoshiwara koi no michibiki*, Kyoto 1979.

TAKEDA 1977
Takeda Tsuneo, ed., *Fūzoku: Sairei, kabuki*, Nihon byōbu-e shūsei 13, Tokyo 1977.

TAKEDA 1992
Sharon Sadako Takeda, 'Clothed in Words: Calligraphic Design on Kosode', in Los Angeles 1992, pp. 155–69.

TAKEMURA 1991
Takemura Akihiko, *Fukusa: Japanese Gift Covers*, Tokyo 1991.

TAKIZAWA 1998
Takizawa Maya, 'Shūsaku-ki no Harunobu: Yakusha-e sakuhin o chūshin ni', *Ukiyo-e geijutsu* 127, March 1998, frontispiece, pp. 3–14.

TANABE 1990
Tanabe Masako, 'Suzuki Harunobu no zugara shakuyō: Mitate no shukō toshite no sai-hyōka', *Bijutsu shi* 39, no. 1, Feb. 1990, pp. 66–86.

TEELE 1993
Ono no Komachi: Poems, Stories, Nō Plays, trans. Roy E. Teele, Nicholas J. Teele and H. Rebecca Teele, New York and London 1993.

TENRI 1973
Tenri University, eds., *Yūjo hyōban-ki shū*, Tenri Toshokan zenpon sōsho 11, Tokyo 1973.

TENRI 1983
Tenri University, eds., *Moronobu Masanobu ehon shū*, Tenri Toshokan zenpon sōsho 67, Tokyo 1983.

TOBY 1987
Ronald P. Toby, 'Carnival of Aliens: Korean Embassies in Edo-Period Art and Popular Culture', *Monumenta Nipponica* 42, no. 1, spring 1987, pp. 415–56.

TOKYO 1960–3
Tokyo National Museum, *Tokyo Kokuritsu Hakubutsukan zuhan mokuroku: Ukiyo-e hanga*, 3 vols., Tokyo 1960–3.

TOKYO 1975
Tokyo, Gotoh Art Museum, *Genroku no ukiyo-e: Moronobu to Itchō o chūshin toshite*, exh. cat., Tokyo 1975.

TOKYO 1977
Tokyo, Riccar Bijutsukan, *Torii-ha no yakusha-e*, by Howard A. Link, exh. cat., Tokyo 1977 [Japanese edn of Honolulu 1977].

TOKYO 1983
Tokyo National Museum, *Bosuton Bijutsukan shozō Nihon kaiga meihin ten*, exh. cat., Tokyo 1983.

TOKYO 1985
Tokyo, Matsuya Ginza et al., *Shindora korekushon ukiyo-e meihinten / Masterpieces of Ukiyo-e Prints from the Schindler Collection*, exh. cat., Tokyo 1985.

TOKYO 1985A
Tokyo, Ueno no Mori Bijutsukan, *Daiei Hakubutsukan shozō ukiyo-e meisaku ten / Masterpieces of Ukiyo-e from the British Museum*, exh. cat., Tokyo 1985.

TOKYO 1986
Tokyo, Kokuritsu Bunkazai Kenkyū-jo, eds., 'Shibai ema no hozon shūfuku shochi no kenkyū', *Azabu Bijutsukan kenkyū kiyō* 2, autumn 1986, pp. vi–xi.

TOKYO 1988
Tokyo, Idemitsu Bijutsukan, *Nikuhitsu ukiyo-e*, by Naitō Masato, Tokyo 1988.

TOKYO 1990
Tokyo, Tabako to Shio no Hakubutsukan, *Hanpon*, Tokyo 1990.

TOKYO 1993
Tokyo National Museum, *Tokyo Kokuritsu Hakubutsukan-zō: Nikuhitsu ukiyo-e*, exh. cat., Tokyo 1993.

TOKYO 1994
Tokyo, Suntory Museum of Art, *Kinsei kimono no banka-kyō*, exh. cat., Toyko, 1994.

TOKYO 1994A
Tokyo, Suntory Museum of Art, *Ukiyo-e tanjō: Hishikawa Moronobu ten*, exh. cat., Tokyo 1994.

TOKYO 1996
Tokyo, Edo-Tokyo Museum, *Nishiki-e no tanjō: Edo shomin bunka no kaika*, exh. cat., Tokyo 1996.

TOKYO 1998
Tokyo, Koishikawa Ukiyo-e Museum, *Matsui Korekushon: Ippin ni miru ukiyo-e 250 nen / Ukiyo-e Arts Spanning 250 Years: Introducing the Matsui Collection*, exh. cat., Tokyo 1998.

TOKYO 1999
Tokyo National Museum, *Edo mōdo taizukan: Kosode moyō ni miru bi no keifu*, exh. cat., Tokyo 1999.

TOKYO 1999A
Tokyo, Edo-Tokyo Hakubutsukan, *Genroku ryōran ten*, exh. cat., Tokyo 1999.

TORII 1972–7
Torii Fumiko, ed., *Tosa jōruri shōhon shū*, 3 vols., Tokyo 1972–7.

TORII 1989
Torii Fumiko, *Kinsei geinō no kenkyū: Tosa jōruri no sekai*, Tokyo 1989.

TORII 1996
Torii Fumiko, 'Tosa jōruri no hanmoto', *Tokyo Joshi Daigaku ronshū* 46, no. 2, March 1996, pp. 640–55.

TORONTO 1975
Toronto, Royal Ontario Museum, *Images of Eighteenth Century Japan: Ukiyoe Prints from the Sir Edmund Walker Collection*, by David Waterhouse, Toronto 1975.

TSCHICHOLD 1972
Jan Tschichold, *Chinese Colour Prints from the Ten Bamboo Studio*, London 1972.

TSIEN 1985
Tsien Tsuen-Hsuin, 'Development of Multi-colour Printing', in Joseph Needham, ed., *Science and Civilization in China 5/1, Paper and Printing*, Cambridge 1985, pp. 277–87.

TSUJI 1987
Tsuji Nobuo, *Iwasa Matabei*, Nihon no Bijutsu 259, Tokyo 1987.

TSUJI 2000
Tsuji Nobuo, 'Hishikawa Moronobu hitsu shibaimachi yūri zu byōbu', *Kokka* 1261, Nov. 2000, pp. 31–3.

TSUJI ET AL. 1968
Tsuji Nobuo, Kobayashi Tadashi and Kōno Motoaki, 'Miyake, Mikura, Nii-jima santō ni nokoru Hanabusa Itchō no gaseki: Miyagawa Isshō, Kaigetsudō Ando no shiryō nado mo awasete', *Kokka* 920, Nov. 1968, pp. 36–46.

UCHIDA 2000
Uchida Kinzō, 'Hishikawa-ha *Hanami zu byōbu* kenkyū: Hishikawa-ha sai-makki no yōsō', *Ukiyo-e geijutsu* 134, Jan. 2000, pp. 3–20.

UKIYO-E JITEN
Ukiyo-e jiten, ed. Yoshida Teruji, 3 vols., Tokyo 1965.

UKIYO-E SHŪKA
Ukiyo-e shūka, vol. 1, *Museum of Fine Arts, Boston I: Early Ukiyo-e*, by Money Hickman, Tokyo 1983; vol. 4, *The Art Institute of Chicago I*, by Suzuki Jūzō and Yamaguchi Keizaburō, Tokyo 1979; vol. 9, *Minneapolis Institute of Arts, Portland Art Museum, Allen Memorial Art Museum (Oberlin College), Achenbach Foundation for Graphic Arts, Cleveland Museum of Art*, Tokyo 1981; suppl. vols. 1 and 2, *Boston Museum of Fine Arts: Harunobu I and II*, by David Waterhouse, Tokyo 1987.

UKIYO-E TAIKEI
Ukiyo-e taikei, vol. 1, *Moronobu*, by Narazaki Muneshige, Tokyo 1976.

UKIYO-E TAIKA SHŪSEI
Ukiyo-e taika shūsei, vol. 2, Kiyonobu, Kiyomasu, Masanobu, by Sasakawa Rinpū, Tokyo 1932; vol. 3, Kaigetsudō, Chōshun, by Sasakawa Rinpū and Yoshida Teruji, Tokyo 1932.

UKIYO-E TAISEI
Ukiyo-e taisei, vol. 2, *Hanga sōji jidai I*, by Yoshida Teruji, Tokyo 1931; vol. 3, *Hanga sōji jidai II*, by Yoshida Teruji, Tokyo 1931; vol. 4, *Nishiki-e shoki jidai I*, Tokyo 1930.

UKIYO-E ZENSHŪ
Ukiyo-e zenshū, vol. 1, *Shoki hanga*, ed. Shibui Kiyoshi, Tokyo 1957.

VAN GULIK 1951
R. H. van Gulik, *Erotic Prints of the Ming Period*, Tokyo 1951.

VERGEZ 1975
Robert Vergez, 'Okumura Genroku, Artist and Publisher', *Ukiyo-e geijutsu* 49, Oct. 1975, pp. i–v.

VERGEZ 1983
Robert Vergez, *Early Ukiyo-e Master: Okumura Masanobu*, Tokyo 1983.

VON SEIDLITZ 1910
W. von Seidlitz, *A History of Japanese Colour-Prints*, London 1910.

WAKA BUNGAKU
Waka bungaku daijiten, Tokyo 1962.

WASHINGTON 1973
Washington DC, Freer Gallery of Art, *Ukiyo-e Painting*, by Harold P. Stern, Washington 1973.

WASHINGTON 1998
Washington DC, National Gallery, *Edo: Art in Japan 1615–1868*, by Robert T. Singer with John T. Carpenter et al., exh. cat., Washington 1998.

WATERHOUSE 1964
David Waterhouse, *Harunobu and his Age: The Development of Colour Printing in Japan*, London 1964.

WATERHOUSE 1981
David Waterhouse, 'New Light on the Life and Work of Suzuki Harunobu', *Impressions* 5, Spring 1981, pp. 1–6.

WATERHOUSE 1991
David Waterhouse, 'The Heirs of Harunobu: Shiba Kōkan and Others', *Impressions* 16, Summer 1991, not paginated.

WATERHOUSE 1997
David Waterhouse, 'Some Confucian, Buddhist, and Taoist Mitate-e by Harunobu', *Impressions* 19, 1997, pp. 29–47.

WELCH 1994
Matthew Welch, *Otsu-e: Japanese Folk Paintings from the Harriet and Edson Spencer Collection*, exh. cat., Minneapolis 1994.

WILSON 1991
Richard Wilson, *The Art of Ogata Kenzan: Persona and Production in Japanese Ceramics*, New York 1991.

WORCESTER 1996
Worcester Art Museum (Mass.), *The Women of the Pleasure Quarter: Japanese Paintings and Prints of the Floating World*, by Elizabeth de Sabato Swinton, exh. cat., New York 1996.

YAMAMURA AND MACHIDA 1919
Yamamura Kōka and Machida Hakuzō, eds., *Shibai nishiki-e shūsei*, Tokyo 1919.

YAMANE ET AL. 1998
Yūzō Yamane, Masato Naitō and Timothy Clark, *Rimpa Art from the Idemitsu Collection, Tokyo*, London 1998.

YOSHIDA 1942
Yoshida Teruji, *Harunobu zenshū*, Tokyo 1942.

YOSHIDA 1984
Kogorō Yoshida, *Tanrokubon: Rare Books of Seventeenth-Century Japan*, Tokyo 1984.

YOSHIDA 1992
Yoshida Nobuyuki, ed., *Nihon no kinsei*, vol. 9, *Toshi no jidai*, Tokyo 1992.

YURA 1979
Yura Tetsuji, ed., *Sōkō Nihon ukiyo-e ruikō*, Tokyo 1979.

Glossary

COMPILED BY ALFRED HAFT

ageya
House of assignation in Shin-Yoshiwara featuring large, richly decorated rooms and expensive cuisine. The place where a *tayū* entertained her clients.

aka-hon
Literally 'red books', illustrated works of children's literature issued *c.* 1675–1735, consisting of approximately five *chō* and bound in red covers.

ao-hon
Literally 'pale blue books', mid-18th-century illustrated editions of popular works of literature on themes relating to kabuki, *jōruri*, history and legend, consisting of approximately five *chō* and bound in pale blue covers.

aragoto
Distinctively masculine ('rough') style of kabuki acting and production developed in Edo by Ichikawa Danjūrō I. It employed a formalised vocabulary of gestures, poses, vocalisations, make-up and costumes to create the image of a hero possessing superhuman strength and valour. The style became the hallmark of the Danjūrō line of actors.

beni-e
Sumizuri print hand-coloured in orange or safflower red (*beni*), yellow, blue and green.

benizuri-e
Colour print in safflower red (*beni*) and green, sometimes also containing yellow, blue or grey, in which each colour is printed from a separate block.

chō
A page or (folded) sheet in a Japanese book. The *recto* and *verso* of a folded sheet are counted as one *chō*.

chūban
Small print format, approximately 26 × 19 cm.

e
General term denoting a picture, used as a prefix or suffix.

e-goyomi
Literally 'picture calendar', a print in which the symbols for the long and short months of the year are concealed in the design.

ehon
Picture book.

eshi
Literally 'picture master', often used in signatures of early ukiyo-e painters and print artists.

fukuro-toji
Literally 'bag-binding'. Traditional method of bookbinding: pages are folded on outside edge and sewn together along spine.

furigana
Literally 'attached *kana*', Japanese phonetic writing (*kana*) inscribed vertically to the right of a Chinese character to indicate the intended reading.

furisode
see *kosode*

furoshiki
Square wrapping cloth.

ga
'Painting' (or 'picture') often used in signatures to mean 'drawn by' or 'painted by'.

gōkan
Multi-volume illustrated novels and romances popular in the 19th century.

hahahiro hashira-e
Wide-format pillar picture, either 69–75 × 17 cm or 69–75 × 26 cm. Common in the 1740s and 50s. See also *hashira-e*.

haikai
Form of linked verse featuring long stanzas of seventeen syllables alternating with short stanzas of fourteen syllables. A sequence always begins with a long stanza, known as the *hokku* (issuing verse), which set the tone of rest of the sequence. In the late 19th century the *hokku* came to be treated as an independent verse form and was called the *haiku*.

hikimaku
Curtain pulled across stage between scenes in kabuki.

hanamichi
In kabuki, a raised passageway leading through the auditorium to the side of the stage on the audience's left. It serves not only for entrances and exits, but also as an extension of the stage on which many important moments are enacted. It became an established feature of theatre architecture during the first quarter of the 18th century.

haori
Outer garment of varying length worn over the *kosode*. The front edges do not overlap but hang parallel to each other. The robe is secured by tying a pair of braided silk cords attached to the front.

hashira-e
Literally 'pillar picture', a narrow, upright print format, approximately 69–75 × 13 cm, made by pasting two sheets together vertically.

hiinagata-bon
Book of *kosode* patterns.

hitsu
Literally, 'brush of' or 'brushed by', a term used in artists' signatures.

hokku
see *haikai*

hosoban
Small print format, approximately 33 × 15 cm.

jōruri
A general term, introduced in the late 17th century, for plays with musical narration, but referring more particularly to the repertoire of the puppet theatre (now called *bunraku*). Takemoto Gidayū developed the dominant style of *jōruri* musical accompaniment in the mid-1680s for the plays of Chikamatsu Monzaemon. The principal instrument is the shamisen. The plays tend to be either five-act history dramas based on events in epic poetry or three-act contemporary-life dramas based on local topical events.

kakemono-e
Large upright print measuring approximately 76 × 23 cm.

kaomise
Literally 'face-showing', the premier theatrical event of the year, at which a kabuki theatre announced its newly engaged company of actors, who then performed together for the first time. In Edo it was held between the first day of the eleventh month and the tenth day of the twelfth month. At this time the front of the theatre would be piled with gifts of rice and sake from supporting organisations. Actors had two weeks to rehearse from casting to the first *kaomise* performance.

kasha-gata
see *onnagata*

kōshoku-bon
Books with erotic or amatory interest, often associated with the author Saikaku and his followers in the late 17th century.

kosode
Type of kimono with a small wrist opening and either short or long hanging sleeves. Long-sleeved *kosode* are called *furisode*.

koto
Thirteen-stringed, plucked zither, made of paulownia wood and with movable bridges for each string. A classical stringed instrument.

kuro-hon
Literally 'black books', illustrated editions of popular literary works on themes similar to those of *ao-hon*, issued in black covers in the early to mid-18th century (particularly the 1740s), consisting of approximately five *chō*. Often illustrated by Torii artists.

michiyuki
In kabuki a kind of dance signifying that the characters are travelling, often accompanied by a recitation of the places being passed and their historical associations. The playwright Chikamatsu Monzaemon (1653–1724) gave the device a dramatic twist in his play *Sonezaki shinjū* (1703) by using it to depict a pair of lovers journeying to commit double suicide.

mimasu
Literally, 'three rice measures': crest of the Ichikawa line of actors, formed by three concentric squares.

mitate-e
The meaning of the term varied in the Edo period, but current usage favours a definition as an ukiyo-e image in which a classical incident is re-enacted by modern (i.e. Edo period) men and women.

monogatari
General term for an extended narrative.

nagauta
In kabuki a type of lyrical song accompanied by the shamisen.

nigao-e
Printed portrait capturing aspects of an individual's real facial appearance. Generally applied to actor prints, particularly after the late 1760s.

nishiki-e
Literally 'brocade picture', the full-colour woodblock print, devised in 1764–5 and often employing advanced printing techniques, such as embossing (*karazuri*).

ōban
Print format, approximately 46 × 33 cm or 39 × 27 cm, depending on the period.

obi
Waist wrapper or sash worn with the *kosode* to keep it closed. In the early 17th century the *obi* was a narrow string or twisted cord, but by the end of the century a wider *obi* of 15 cm had become fashionable.

onnagata
Actors who play female roles; also the roles themselves. The art form began its major phase of development in the mid-17th century, following a ban on young men's kabuki. By the 1690s it was fully established, with actors specialising either in young female roles (*wakaonna-gata*) – princesses and courtesans – or older female roles (*kasha-gata*) – teahouse proprietresses and samurais' wives, skilled in martial arts.

ō-ōban
Large *ōban*, approximately 58 × 32 cm.

otogi-zōshi
Short prose narratives of the medieval period, ranging in subject matter from the lives and loves of the nobility to didactic Buddhist stories, which provided material for many literary genres of the Edo period.

otokodate
In kabuki and *jōruri* plays the chivalrous commoner siding with the townsman class against oppressive samurai in the service of the shogun.

roppō
In plays, a swaggering exit down the *hanamichi*, used to demonstrate the hero's power and boldness. Derived by kabuki actors from the movements of the *otokodate* on the streets of Edo.

Sanseki no waka
'Three Evening Poems', three famous *waka* sharing the same concluding line, 'Evening in autumn' (*aki no yūgure*), and forming part of the anthology *Shin kokin waka-shū* (*c.* 1200).

satsu
Volume forming part of a larger book.

shakuhachi
Recorder-like wind instrument made of bamboo.

shamisen
Literally 'three strings', this instrument with a long neck and square sound box has been the principal provider of musical accompaniment in kabuki and puppet plays since the 17th century. It is an adaptation of a larger and louder instrument thought to have come from China via the islands south of Kyūshū in the 1560s.

sharebon
Short novels about life in the licensed pleasure quarters, popular in the mid to late 18th century.

shibaraku
Literally 'Stop one moment!', an *aragoto*-style

set-piece scene in kabuki first performed by Ichikawa Danjūrō I in 1697 and thereafter proprietary to actors in the Ichikawa line.

Shin-Yoshiwara
Literally 'New Yoshiwara', this was the name given to Edo's licensed courtesan district when it was rebuilt north of the city following the Meireki Fire of 1657. The term continued in use throughout the Edo period.

shirabyōshi
Female performer in the medieval period who danced wearing the high lacquered hat and the long swords of a man's court costume.

sumizuri
Printing with *sumi* ink on paper.

tachi-yaku
Leading male roles and the actors who specialise in them. The term covers a variety of types, including the romantic young man, but is associated particularly with characters who remain dignified, wise and capable even in tragic circumstances.

tanka
Early term for the poetic form now generally known as *waka*.

tayū
First rank of courtesan, who met clients only at an *ageya*. A Yoshiwara directory of the mid-17th century listed 75 *tayū*, but a century later this had dwindled to one or two and the term subsequently disappeared from official use. Nevertheless, the image of a *tayū* and her entourage on parade from the brothel to the *ageya* remained a symbol of the Yoshiwara and a favourite subject of ukiyo-e artists.

tobira-e
Frontispiece.

uchikake
Garment worn unbelted over all other robes on formal or ceremonial occasions. It originated with upper-class samurai women of the Kamakura period (1185–1333). In the 18th century padding was added to the hem.

ukiyo-zōshi
In the late 17th century a general term for floating-world novels, which became popular after the publication of Saikaku's *The Life of an Amorous Man* (*Kōshoku ichidai otoko*) in 1682.

urushi-e
Literally 'lacquer picture', a *beni-e* with glue spread over areas of black pigment to produce a lustrous effect reminiscent of lacquer (*urushi*). Metal filings (usually of brass or bronze) were sometimes sprinkled on the pigments for further effect.

wagoto
Delicate acting style associated with certain romantic male characters usually preoccupied with a lover's problems. Speech and movement are performed in a soft and refined manner. Developed in the late 17th century in connection with contemporary-life dramas written for theatres in Kyoto and Osaka.

waka
Classical Japanese verse form of 31 syllables arranged in five metrical units of 5, 7, 5, 7 and 7 syllables each.

wakaonna-gata
see *onnagata*

wakashu-gata
In kabuki, delicate young male roles.

yatsushi
In kabuki the condition of the scion of a wealthy family forced by circumstances (such as disinheritance or a usurped fortune) to make his way in the world as a craftsman or labourer. In ukiyo-e, *yatsushi-e* is the depiction of a scene from classical literature in an elegant, up-to-date manner.

zu
'Picture'. Often used in signatures to mean 'drawn by' or 'painted by'.

Index

All references are to page numbers; those in **bold** type indicate catalogue entries, and those in *italic* type indicate essay illustrations

L

M

N

O

P

Royal Academy Trust

MAJOR BENEFACTORS

The Trustees of the Royal Academy Trust would like to thank all those who have been exceedingly generous over a number of years in support of the galleries, the exhibitions, the conservation of the Permanent Collection, the Library, the Royal Academy Schools and the education programme:

HM The Queen
The 29th May 1961 Charitable Trust
The Annie Laurie Aitken Charitable Trust
American Associates of the Royal Academy Trust
The Honorable and Mrs Walter H Annenberg
Barclays Bank
Mr and Mrs Sid R Bass
B.A.T. Industries plc
Tom Bendhem
Brenda M Benwell-Lejeune
John Frye Bourne
British Telecom
The Brown Foundation Inc
Mr Raymond M Burton CBE
Sir Trevor Chinn CVO and Lady Chinn
The Trustees of the Clore Foundation
The John S Cohen Foundation
Mr Edwin L Cox
Sir Harry and Lady Djanogly
The Dulverton Trust
Alfred Dunhill Limited
The John Ellerman Foundation
The Eranda Foundation
Ernst and Young
Esso UK plc
Esmée Fairbairn Charitable Trust
Mr and Mrs Eugene V Fife
Walter Fitch III
Mrs Henry Ford II
The Honorable Amalia Lacroze de Fortabat
The Foundation for Sport and the Arts
Friends of the Royal Academy
The Getty Grant Program
Glaxo Holdings plc
Diane and Guilford Glazer
Jack and Grete Goldhill
Maurice and Laurence Goldman
The Horace W Goldsmith Foundation
The late Dr Armand Hammer
Mr and Mrs Jocelin Harris
The Philip and Pauline Harris Charitable Trust
The Hayward Foundation
The Hearst Corporation
Drue Heinz Trust
Henry J & Drue Heinz Foundation
Heritage Lottery Fund
IBM United Kingdom Limited
The Idlewild Trust
The JP Jacobs Charitable Trust
Lord and Lady Jacobs
The Japan Foundation
Gabrielle Jungels-Winkler Foundation
Mr and Mrs Donald P Kahn
The Kresge Foundation
The Kresse Foundation
The Lankelly Foundation
Mr John S Latsis
Mrs Katherine L Lawrence
The Leverhulme Trust
Lex Service plc
The Linbury Trust
Sir Sydney Lipworth QC and Lady Lipworth
The Henry Luce Foundation
John Madejski
Her Majesty's Government
The Manifold Trust
Mr and Mrs John L Marion
Marks and Spencer
Mr and Mrs Jack C Massey
Mr Hamish Maxwell
Ronald and Rita McAulay
Mrs John P McGrath
McKinsey and Company Inc
The Estate of Paul Mellon KBE
The Mercers' Company
The Monument Trust
The Henry Moore Foundation
The Moorgate Trust Fund
Robin Moss
Museums and Galleries Improvement Fund
National Westminster Bank
Mrs Nancy B Negley
New Opportunities Fund
Stavros S Niarchos
Diane A Nixon
The Otemae College
The Peacock Trust
The Pennycress Trust
PF Charitable Trust
The Pilgrim Trust
Leon B Polsky and Cynthia Hazen Polsky
The Edith and Ferdinand Porjes Trust
Rio Tinto plc
John A Roberts FRIBA
The Ronson Foundation
The Rose Foundation
Rothmans International plc
Mrs Arthur M Sackler
Mrs Jean Sainsbury
The Saison Foundation
The Basil Samuel Charitable Trust
Mrs Louisa S Sarofim
Sea Containers Ltd
Shell UK Limited
Miss Dasha Shenkman
William and Maureen Shenkman
The Archie Sherman Charitable Trust
Ms Kathleen D Smith
The Starr Foundation
Mr and Mrs Robert L Sterling Jr
Sir Hugh Sykes DL
Alfred Taubman
Mr and Mrs Vernon Taylor Jr
Sir Anthony and Lady Tennant
Eugene & Clare Thaw Charitable Trust
Ware and Edythe Travelstead
The Trusthouse Charitable Foundation
The Douglas Turner Trust
Unilever plc
The Weldon UK Charitable Trust
The Welton Foundation
Garry H Weston and the Weston family
The Honorable and Mrs John C Whitehead
Mr and Mrs Frederick B Whittemore
The Maurice Wohl Charitable Foundation
The Wolfson Foundation
and others who wish to remain anonymous

BENEFACTORS

The Trustees of the Royal Academy Trust would like to thank all those who have recently supported the galleries, the exhibitions, the conservation of the Permanent Collection, the Library, the Royal Academy Schools or the education programme:

BENJAMIN WEST GROUP DONORS

Patron
The Hon Raymond G H Seitz
Chairman
The Hon Barbara S Thomas
Donors
Lady Adamson
Mr and Mrs Rudolph Agnew
Michael and Barbara Anderson
Mrs Charlotte Artus
Mr and Mrs D Bader
Mr and Mrs Thomas Berger
Mr and Mrs Mark Booth
Mrs Adrian Bowden
Mr and Mrs Charles Brocklebank
A Chilcott Fawcett
Mr and Mrs Paul Collins
Mrs Joan Curci
Mr and Mrs C R Dammers
Mrs Sheryl Daniels Young
Mr and Mrs Domenico De Sole
Mr and Mrs David Diwik
Mr and Mrs Robert L Forbes
The David Gill Memorial Fund
Mr and Mrs John Gore
Mr and Mrs Abel Halpern
Mrs M R Hambro
Mrs Susan Hayden
Mr Paul Josefowitz
Mr and Mrs Richard Kaufman
Rona and Robert Kiley
Mr Charles G Lubar
Ms Claudine B Malone
Mr and Mrs Bruce McLaren
Mr and Mrs Philip Mengel
Mr and Mrs Edward Miller
Mr and Mrs Donald Moore
Robin Heller Moss
Mr Neil Osborn and Ms Holly Smith
Sir William and Lady Purves
Mr and Mrs Nicolas Rohatyn
Albert and Marjorie Scardino
Mrs Sylvia B Scheuer
Mr and Mrs Stuart L Scott
Mr and Mrs Paul Shang
Mrs Tara Stack
Barbara and Allen Thomas
Mrs Kathryn Uhde
Michael and Yvonne Uva
Mr and Mrs Jeffrey Weingarten
Mr Randall J Willette
Mr John D Winter
and others who wish to remain anonymous

COLLECTION PATRONS GROUP

Miss B A Battersby
The Lesley David Trust
Mrs Helena Frost
David and Maggi Gordon
The Idlewild Trust
The Leche Trust
The Leverhulme Trust
Mr Lowell J Libson
Pamela Littman JP
Sir Kit and Lady McMahon
The Henry Moore Foundation
Robin Heller Moss
New Opportunities Fund
Mrs Graham Reddish
Joseph Strong Frazer Trust
and others who wish to remain anonymous

EDUCATION PATRONS GROUP

Mr Tom Bendhem
David and Janice Blackburn
The Goldsmiths' Company Charities
J P Morgan Fleming Foundation
The Kobler Trust
John Lyon's Charity
The Mercers' Company
The Merrell Foundation
The Millichope Foundation
The Austin and Hope Pilkington Trust
Mr and Mrs J A Pye's Charitable Settlement
Mrs Jean Sainsbury
The Save and Prosper Foundation
The Peter Storrs Trust
The Walcot Educational Foundation
The Woo Charitable Foundation
and others who wish to remain anonymous

EXHIBITIONS PATRONS GROUP

President
Mr Garry Weston
Co-Chairmen
Mrs John Burns
Sir Trevor Chinn CVO
The Hon Mrs Anne Collins
The Lady Lever of Manchester

Gold Patrons
The 29th May 1961 Charitable Trust
Lord and Lady Attenborough
Ivor Braka
Dr Christopher Brown
Mr and Mrs John Burns
Mr Raymond M Burton CBE
C H K Charities Limited
Sir Trevor and Lady Chinn
The Hon Mrs Anne Collins
Mr and Mrs David Diwik
EFG Private Bank Limited
Mrs Helena Frost
The Robert Gavron Charitable Trust
Jacqueline and Michael Gee
David and Maggi Gordon
The Gosling Foundation
Mrs Sue Hammerson
Mrs Gabrielle Jungels-Winkler
Mr and Mrs Donald P Kahn
Mr and Mrs Joseph Karaviotis
The Kreitman Foundation
The Kirby Laing Foundation
The Lady Lever of Manchester
Sir Sydney Lipworth QC and Lady Lipworth
Mr and Mrs Ronald Lubner
Sir Kit and Lady McMahon
Mr and Mrs Edward Miller
Paul and Alison Myners
The P F Charitable Trust
The Rayne Foundation
Mr John A Roberts FRIBA
Mr and Mrs Nicolas Rohatyn
Mrs Coral Samuel CBE
Ms Pierrette Schlettwein
Mrs Stella Shawzin
Mr and Mrs Richard Simmons
Mrs Roama Spears
Mr and Mrs Nicholas Stanley
Sir Anthony and Lady Tennant
Eugene V and Clare E Thaw Charitable Trust
Roger and Jennifer Wingate
Mr and Mrs Ronald W Zeghibe
Mr and Mrs Michael Zilkha

Silver Patrons
Mr and Mrs Paul Baines
Tom Bendhem
The Peter Boizot Foundation
Alain and Marie Boublil
Mrs Adrian Bowden
Mrs Elie R Brihi
Lady Brown
Jim and Margaret Butler
Mr and Mrs P H G Cadbury
A Chilcott Fawcett
Mr and Mrs G L Collins
Mr and Mrs Paul Collins
Mr and Mrs Patrick Doherty
Mr and Mrs Maurice Dwek
Mr and Mrs Gerald Fogel
Mr and Mrs James Gourlay of Kincraig
Charles and Kaaren Hale
Mr and Mrs Abel Halpern
Mr and Mrs Jocelin Harris
Mrs Susan Hayden
Mr and Mrs Alan Hobart
Mr and Mrs Jon Hunt
Mr Jonathon E Lyons
Fiona Mactaggart
Sir William and Lady Purves
Mrs Jean Redman-Brown
Mr and Mrs Robert E Rhea
Mr and Mrs Gerry Robinson
Sophie and David Shalit
Mr and Mrs Clive Sherling
James and Alyson Spooner
Mrs Tara Stack
Mr and the Hon Mrs Richard Szpiro
Barbara and Allen Thomas
Mr and Mrs Anthony Weldon
Mrs Linda M Williams

Bronze Patrons
Mr and Mrs Gerald Acher
Lady Adamson
Mrs Denise Adeane
Mrs Annabel Agace
Mr and Mrs Rudolph Agnew
Mr and Mrs V Alaghband
Dr M Al-Ali
Mr and the Hon Mrs Michael Alen-Buckley
Mr Peter Allinson
The Earl and Countess of Ancram
Michael and Barbara Anderson
Mr Zeev Aram
Mrs Charlotte Artus
Mr and Mrs D Bader
Mr Stephen Bampfylde
Jane Barker
James M Bartos
The Duke of Beaufort
Mrs Wendy Becker Payton
Dr Sheilah D Bell
Mr and Mrs Simon Bentley
Mr and Mrs Thomas J Berger
Mrs Vanessa Bernstein
Mr Mark Birley
Sir Victor and Lady Blank
Mr and Mrs George Bloch
Mr and Mrs K E Boas
Mr and Mrs Mark Booth
Mr Peter Bowring CBE
Mr and Mrs Michael Bradley
The Britto Foundation
Mr and Mrs Charles Brocklebank
Jeremy Brown
Mrs Ian Buckley-Sharp
Mrs Richard Burton
Marlene Burston
Mr and Mrs P H G Cadbury
Mrs Lily Cantor
Mr F A A Carnwath CBE
Jean and Eric Cass
The Marquise de Cérenville
Mrs Rivka Chenevix-Trench
John Chiene
Mr and Mrs T E Childs
Mrs Nicola Clark
Mrs Denise Cohen
Mr Ed Cohen
Carlo Colombotti
Mrs Douglas Connor
Neville and Carole Conrad Charitable Trust
David J and Jennifer A Cooke
Corona Extra Beer
Tom Corrigan
Mr John Cox
Mrs Joan Curci
Mr and Mrs C R Dammers
Mrs Sheryl Daniels Young
Mr and Mrs Hans de Gier
Peter and Kate De Haan
The de Laszlo Foundation
Mr and Mrs Domenico de Sole
Mrs Ellsworth Donnell
Sir Philip Dowson PPRA and Lady Dowson
John Drummond FCSD HON DES RCA
Mrs Alyce Faye Eichelberger Cleese
Mr and Mrs Peter Ellis
John and Tawna Farmer
Mary Fedden RA
Mrs Juliet Fenton
Mr and Mrs Bryan Ferry
Mrs Kaye Finegold
Mrs Donatella Flick
Flying Colours Gallery
Mr and Mrs George Fokschaner
Mr and Mrs Robert L Forbes
Mrs Edwin Fox
Cyril Freedman
Mr Monty Freedman
Michael and Clara Freeman
A Fulton Company Limited
Jacqueline and Jonathan Gestetner
The David Gill Memorial Fund
Mme Michel Goldet
Sir Nicholas and Lady Goodison's Charitable Settlement
Mr and Mrs John Gore
Lady Gosling
Nicholas Gould and Rachel Selzer
Mrs Michael Green
Mr and Mrs Clifford J Gundle
Mrs M R Hambro
David and Lella Harris
The Harris Family
David and Lesley Haynes
Michael and Morven Heller
Robin Heller Moss
Matthew and Rachel Hockley Smith
Mr and Mrs J Hodkinson
Anne Holmes-Drewry
Dr and Mrs Allan J Horan
Mr and Mrs Ken Howard
Mrs Sue Howes and Mr Greg Dyke
Mr and Mrs Allan Hughes
Mrs Pauline Hyde
Simone Hyman
Mr Oliver Iny
Sir Martin and Lady Jacomb
Mr and Mrs Ian Jay
Mr and Mrs Harold Joels
Mr and Mrs David Josefowitz
Paul Josefowitz Esq
Sir Paul Judge
Mr and Mrs Richard Kaufman
Mr and Mrs Laurence Kelly
Rona and Robert Kiley
Mr D H Killick
Mr and Mrs James Kirkman
Tom Larsen, Holt Value Associates
Mr George Lengvari
Colette and Peter Levy
Sir Christopher and Lady Lewinton
Susan Linaker
Miss R Lomax-Simpson
Mr and Mrs Mark Loveday
Mr Charles G Lubar
Mrs Gertie Lurie
Mr and Mrs Eskandar Maleki
Ms Claudine B Malone
Mr and Mrs Michael (RA) and José Manser
Dr Abraham Marcus
Mr and Mrs Aldo Mareuse
Mr and Mrs M Margulies
Marsh Christian Trust
R C Martin
Mr and Mrs Stephen Mather
Mrs Jack Maxwell
Mrs M C W McCann
Mr and Mrs Bruce McLaren
Mr and Mrs Philip Mengel
The Mercers' Company
Lt Col L S Michael OBE
Mr and Mrs Donald Moore
Mr and Mrs Peter Morgan
Mr and Mrs I Morrison
Mr and Mrs Carl Anton Muller
John Nickson and Simon Rew
Mr Bruce Oldfield OBE
Mr Neil Osborn and Ms Holly Smith
Sir Peter Osborne
Mr Michael Palin
Mr and Mrs Vincenzo Palladino
Mr and Mrs Gerald Parkes
John Pattisson
The Pennycress Trust

Miss Karen Phillipps
Mr Godfrey Pilkington
George and Carolyn Pincus
Mr and Mrs William A Plapinger
David and Linda Pohs-Supino
John Porter Charitable Trust
Miss Victoria Provis
The Quercus Trust
Mr and Mrs J V Radford
Mr and Mrs P V Radford
Barbara Rae RA
John and Anne Raisman
Sir David and Lady Ramsbotham
Mrs Pauline Recanati
Mr T H Reitman
Sir John and Lady Riddell
The Roland Group of Companies Plc
Mr and Mrs Ian Rosenberg
Alastair and Sarah Ross Goobey
Mr and Mrs Kerry Rubie
Mr John J Ryan III
The Audrey Sacher Charitable Trust
Dr P B St Leger
Mr and Mrs Victor Sandelson
Mr and Mrs Nicholas Sassow
Albert and Marjorie Scardino
Mrs Sylvia B Scheuer
Mr and Mrs Stuart L Scott
Dr Lewis Sevitt
The Countess of Shaftesbury
Mr and Mrs Paul Shang
Mr Christopher and Lady Mary Gaye Shaw
Mr and Mrs Clive Sherling
Mr and Mrs Richard Sherrington
Mrs Lois Sieff OBE
Mr Peter Simon
Mr and Mrs John Sorrell
Mrs Jack Steinberg
Mr and Mrs David Stileman
Dr Miriam Stoppard and Sir Christopher Hogg
Mr and Mrs R W Strang
The Swan Trust
Mr and Mrs David Swift
Mr and Mrs John D Taylor
Mr and Mrs Julian Treger
Mrs Kathryn Uhde
Michael and Yvonne Uva
Mr and Mrs Tim Vignoles
Visa Lloyds Bank Monte Carlo
Mrs Catherine Vlasto
Mrs Claire Vyner
The Walter Guinness Charitable Trust
John B Watton
Mr and Mrs Jeffrey M Weingarten
Edna and Willard Weiss
Mrs Gerald Westbury
Mr Randall J Willette
Mr Jeremy Willoughby
Mr and Mrs Ami Wine
Mr John D Winter
The Rt Hon Lord and Lady Young of Graffham
and others who wish to remain anonymous

SCHOOLS PATRONS GROUP
Arts and Humanities Research Board
The Lord Aldington
The Charlotte Bonham-Carter Charitable Trust
Mrs Stephen Boyd
The Candide Charitable Trust
Mr Raymond Cazalet
Smadar and David Cohen
The Ernest Cook Trust
Mr Simon Copsey
Mr and Mrs Keith Dawson
Debenhams Retail plc
The Delfont Foundation
The D'Oyly Carte Charitable Trust
The Marchioness of Dufferin and Ava
The Gilbert & Eileen Edgar Foundation
The Eranda Foundation
Jack and Greta Goldhill
P H Holt Charitable Trust
The Lark Trust
The Leverhulme Trust
The Loughborough Fellowship in Fine Art
Stuart and Ellen Lyons Charitable Trust
The Mercers' Company
The Henry Moore Foundation
Robin Heller Moss
Newby Trust Limited
The Worshipful Company of Painter-Stainers
The Stanley Picker Trust
Pickett Fine Leather Ltd
Edith and Ferdinand Porjes Charitable Trust
The Radcliffe Trust
Rio Tinto plc
Mr Charles Saatchi
Mr and Mrs Anthony Salz
Pauline Denyer Smith and Paul Smith CBE
The South Square Trust
Mr and Mrs Michele Sportelli
The Starr Foundation
The Steel Charitable Trust
Mr and Mrs Robert Lee Sterling Jr
The Peter Storrs Trust
Mr and Mrs Denis Tinsley
The Celia Walker Art Foundation
The Harold Hyam Wingate Foundation
and others who wish to remain anonymous

GENERAL DONORS
Mr Charles Akle
Mr Keith Bromley
Miss Jayne Edwardes
Lady Sainsbury
The Schneer Foundation Inc
The Rt Hon Lord and Lady Young of Graffham
and others who wish to remain anonymous

American Associates

Benefactors
American Express
Mrs Deborah Loeb Brice
Mr D Francis Finlay
Mrs Melville Wakeman Hall
Ms Frances S Hayward
Ms Brenda Neubauer Straus
WPP Group

Sponsors
Mrs Jan Cowles
Lady Mary Fairfax
Mrs Katherine D W Findlay
Mr and Mrs Lewis P Grinnan, Jr
Mr Edward H Harte
Mr and Mrs Stephen M Kellen
Mr James Kemper Jr
Mrs Linda Noe Laine
Mrs Edmond J Safra
Mr Peter Schoenfeld
Ms Muriel Siebert
Virgin Atlantic

Patrons
Ms Helen Harting Abell
Mr and Mrs Steven Ausnit
Mr and Mrs Stephen D Bechtel, Jr
Mrs William J Benedict
Mr and Mrs James Benson
Mr Donald A Best
Mr and Mrs Henry W Breyer III
Mrs Mildred C Brinn
Dr and Mrs Robert Carroll
Mr William L Clark
Ms Elaine T Cooper
Ms Anne S Davidson
Ms Zita Davisson
Mr and Mrs Charles Diker
Mrs June Dyson
Mrs John W Embry
Mrs A Barlow Ferguson
Mrs Robert Ferst
Mr Ralph A Fields
Mr Richard E Ford
Mrs William Fox, Jr
Mr and Mrs Lawrence S Friedland
Goldman, Sachs & Co
Mrs Betty N Gordon
Mr and Mrs Martin D Gruss
Mrs Richard L Harris
Mr O D Harrison, Jr
Mr and Mrs Gurnee F Hart
Mr and Mrs Gustave M Hauser
Mr and Mrs John R Hupper
Mr Robert J Irwin
Ms Betty Wold Johnson and Mr Douglas Bushnell
The Honorable & Mrs W Eugene Johnston III
Mr William W Karatz
Mr and Mrs Gary A Kraut
The Nathan Manilow Foundation
Mrs John P McGrath
Mrs Mark Millard
Mrs Barbara T Missett
Mr Paul D Myers
Mrs Richard D O'Connor
Mr and Mrs Jeffrey Pettit
Mr Robert S Pirie
Mrs Nanette Ross
Mr and Mrs Derald H Ruttenberg
Mrs Frances G Scaife
Ms Jan Blaustein Scholes
Mr and Mrs Stanley D Scott
Ms Georgia Shreve
Mr James Sollins
Mrs Frederick M Stafford
Mr and Mrs Stephen Stamas
Ms Brenda Neubauer Straus
Mr Arthur O Sulzberger and Ms Allison S Cowles
Mrs Royce Deane Tate
Mrs Britt Tidelius
Ms Sue E Van de Bovenkamp
Mrs Vincent S Villard, Jr
Mr and Mrs Stanford Warshawsky
Mrs Sara E White
Dr and Mrs Robert D Wickham
Mr Robert W Wilson
Mr and Mrs Kenneth Woodcock
and others who wish to remain anonymou

Friends of the Royal Academy

PATRON FRIENDS
Mrs Meg Allen
Mrs Elizabeth S Alston
Mr Brian Bailey
Mr Paul Baines
Mrs Yvonne Barlow
Mr P F J Bennett
Mrs V Bondarenko
Mr and Mrs Sidney Corob
Mrs S Dawson
Mr David Duncan
Mr Michael Godbee
Ms Katrin Henkel
Mr S Isern-Feliu
Mr and Mrs S D Kahan
Mr David Ker
Mrs Joyce Lacerte
Dr C McFadden
Mrs Maureen D Metcalfe
Mr R J Mullis
Mr and Mrs Derald H Ruttenberg
Mrs C A Sellars
Mr Alan K Simpson
Mr Robin Symes
Mr J A Tackaberry
Mrs K L Troughton
Mrs Cynthia H Walton
Mrs Roger Waters
The Hon Mrs Simon Weinstock
Mrs I Wolstenholme
and others who wish to remain anonymous

SUPPORTING FRIENDS
Mr Richard B Allan
Mr Ian Anstruther
Mr Keith G Bennett
Mrs Susan Besser
Mrs C W T Blackwell
Mr C Boddington and Ms R Naylor
Mrs J M Bracegirdle
Mr Cornelius Broere
Mrs Jean Burton
Mrs Anne Cadbury OBE JP DL
Miss E M Cassin
Mr R A Cernis
Mr S Chapman
Mr and Mrs John Cleese
Mrs D H Costopoulos
Mr and Mrs Chris Cotton
Mrs M F Coward
Anthea Craigmyle
Mrs Nadine Crichton
Mrs Saeda H Dalloul
Mr Julian R Darley
Mrs Belinda Davie
Mr John Denham
Miss N J Dhanani
Miss Carol Dodds
Mr Kenneth Edwards
Jack and Irene Finkler
Mrs R H Goddard
Mrs D Goodsell
Mr R Gow
Mr Gavin Graham
Mr and Mrs Jonathan Green
Mrs Richard Grogan
Mr Malcolm P Herring
Mr R J Hoare
Mrs Manya Igel
Mrs Jane Jason
Mrs G R Jeffries
Mr Roger A Jennings
Mr Harold Joels
Mrs P Keely
Mr and Mrs J Kessler
Mr N R Killick
Mrs L Kosta
Mrs Carol Kroch
Mrs Joan Lavender
Mr and Mrs David Leathers
Mr Owen Luder CBE PRIBA FRSA
Miss Julia MacRae
Mr Donald A Main
Lord Marks of Broughton
Mr J B H Martin
Mrs Gillian McIntosh
Mr R T Miles
Mrs A Morgan
Mrs Elizabeth M Newell
Miss Kim Nicholson
Mr Robert Linn Ottley
Mr Brian Oury
Mrs Anne Phillips
Mr Ralph Picken
Mr D B E Pike
Mrs Beatrice Prevett
Mr Benjamin Pritchett-Brown
Mr W S C Richards OBE
Mrs Elizabeth Ridley
Mr F Peter Robinson
Mr D S Rocklin
Mrs A Rodman
Mr and Mrs O Roux
Dr Susan Saga
Lady Sainsbury
The Rt Hon Sir Timothy Sainsbury
Mrs E M Sandelson
Dr I B Schulenburg
Mrs D Scott
Mrs E D Sellick
Mr and Mrs Richard Seymour
Mr R J Simmons CBE
Mr John H M Sims
Miss L M Slattery
Dr and Mrs M L Slotover
Mrs P Spanoghe
Professor Philip Stott
Mr James Stuart
Mrs J A Tapley
Mr W N Trotter
Mr and Mrs Ludovic de Walden
Miss J Waterous
Mrs Claire Weldon
Mr Frank S Wenstrom
Mrs Sheree D Whatley
Mr W M Wood
Mr R M Woodhouse
and others who wish to remain anonymous

Corporate Membership of the Royal Academy of Arts

Launched in 1988, the Royal Academy's Corporate Membership Scheme has proved highly successful. With 104 members it is now the largest membership scheme in Europe.

Corporate membership offers company benefits to staff and clients and access to the Academy's facilities and resources. Each member pays an annual subscription to be a Member (£7,000) or Patron (£20,000).

Participating companies recognise the importance of promoting the visual arts. Their support is vital to the continuing success of the Academy.

CORPORATE MEMBERSHIP SCHEME

Corporate Patrons
Arthur Andersen
Bloomberg LP
BNP Paribas
BP Amoco p.l.c.
Debenhams Retail plc
Deutsche Bank AG
The Economist Group
Ernst and Young
GE Group
GlaxoSmithKline plc
Granada Media
Merrill Lynch
Morgan Stanley International
Royal & Sun Alliance

Honorary Corporate Patron
Credit Suisse First Boston

Corporate Members
Apax Partners & Co. Ltd.
Athenaeum Hotel
Aukett Europe
AXA UK plc
Bacon and Woodrow
Bank of America
Barclays plc
Bartlett Merton Ltd
Bass PLC
Bear, Stearns International Ltd
BG plc
The Boston Consulting Group
Bovis Lend Lease Limited
British Alcan Aluminium plc
The British Land Company PLC
BT plc
Bunzl plc
Cazenove & Co
CB Hillier Parker
Chase Fleming Asset Management
Christie's
Chubb Insurance Company of Europe
CJA (Management Recruitment Consultants) Limited
Clayton Dubilier & Rice Limited
Clifford Chance
Colefax and Fowler Group
Consultivity
Cookson Group plc
Credit Agricole Indosuez
De Beers
Diageo plc
Dresdner Kleinwort Benson
Eversheds
Foreign & Colonial Management plc
Gartmore Investment Management plc
Goldman Sachs International
Heidrick & Struggles
H J Heinz Company Limited
HSBC plc
ICI
John Lewis Partnership
J Sainsbury plc
King Sturge
KPMG
Lex Service PLC
Linklaters & Alliance
Macfarlanes
Man Group plc
marchFIRST
Marconi Ltd
McKinsey & Co.
MoMart Ltd
Newton Investment Management Ltd
Old Mutual Asset Managers
Ove Arup Partnership
Pearson plc
The Peninsular and Oriental Steam Navigation Company
Pentland Group plc
Provident Financial plc
Raytheon Systems Limited
Reed Elsevier (UK) Limited
Rowe & Maw
The Royal Bank of Scotland
Schroder Salomon Smith Barney
Schroders Investment Management Limited
Sea Containers Ltd.
SG
Skanska Construction Group Limited
Slaughter and May
SmithKline Beecham
Smiths Group plc
The Smith & Williamson Group
Sotheby's
Strutt & Parker
Telegraph Group Limited
Tiffany & Co.
Travelex
Trowers & Hamlins
Unilever UK Limited
UPC Services
Whitehead Mann GKR Ltd

Honorary Corporate Members
All Nippon Airways Co. Ltd
A.T. Kearney Limited
Cantor Fitzgerald
London First
Reuters Limited
Sony Uk Limited
Yakult UK Limited

Sponsors of Past Exhibitions

The President and Council of the Royal Academy thank sponsors of past exhibitions for their support. Sponsors of major exhibitions during the last ten years have included the following:

Allied Trust Bank
- Africa: The Art of a Continent, 1995*

Anglo American Corporation of South Africa
- Africa: The Art of a Continent, 1995*

A.T. Kearney
- Summer Exhibition 1999
- Summer Exhibition 2000

The Banque Indosuez Group
- Pissarro: The Impressionist and the City, 1993

Barclays
- Ingres to Matisse: The Triumph of French Painting, 2001

BBC Radio One
- The Pop Art Show, 1991

BMW (GB) Limited
- Georges Rouault: The Early Years, 1903–1920, 1993
- David Hockney: A Drawing Retrospective, 1995*

British Airways Plc
- Africa: The Art of a Continent, 1995

BT
- Hokusai, 1991

Cantor Fitzgerald
- From Manet to Gauguin: Masterpieces from Swiss Private Collections, 1995
- 1900: Art at the Crossroads, 2000

The Capital Group Companies
- Drawings from the J Paul Getty Museum, 1993

Chase Fleming Asset Management
- The Scottish Colourists 1900–1930, 2000

Chilstone Garden Ornaments
- The Palladian Revival: Lord Burlington and His House and Garden at Chiswick, 1995

Christie's
- Frederic Leighton 1830–1896, 1996
- Sensation: Young British Artists from The Saatchi Collection, 1997

Classic FM
- Goya: Truth and Fantasy, The Small Paintings, 1994
- The Glory of Venice: Art in the Eighteenth Century, 1994

Corporation of London
- Living Bridges, 1996

Country Life
- John Soane, Architect: Master of Space and Light, 1999

Credit Suisse First Boston
- The Genius of Rome 1592–1623, 2000

The Daily Telegraph
- American Art in the 20th Century, 1993
- 1900: Art at the Crossroads, 2000

De Beers
- Africa: The Art of a Continent, 1995

Debenhams Retail plc
- Premiums and RA Schools Show, 1999
- Premiums and RA Schools Show, 2000

Deutsche Morgan Grenfell
- Africa: The Art of a Continent, 1995

Diageo plc
- 230th Summer Exhibition, 1998

The Drue Heinz Trust
- The Palladian Revival: Lord Burlington and His House and Garden at Chiswick, 1995
- Denys Lasdun, 1997
- Tadao Ando: Master of Minimalism, 1998

The Dupont Company
- American Art in the 20th Century, 1993

Elf
- Alfred Sisley, 1992

Ernst & Young
- Monet in the 20th Century, 1999

eyestorm
- Apocalypse: Beauty and Horror in Contemporary Art, 2000

Fondation Elf
- Alfred Sisley, 1992

Friends of the Royal Academy
- Victorian Fairy Painting, 1997

Game International Limited
- Forty Years in Print: The Curwen Studio and Royal Academicians, 2001

The Jacqueline and Michael Gee Charitable Trust
- LIFE? or THEATRE? The Work of Charlotte Salomon, 1999

Générale des Eaux Group
- Living Bridges, 1996

Glaxo Wellcome plc
- The Unknown Modigliani, 1994

Goldman Sachs International
- Alberto Giacometti, 1901–1966, 1996
- Picasso: Painter and Sculptor in Clay, 1998

The Guardian
- The Unknown Modigliani, 1994

Guinness Peat Aviation
- Alexander Calder, 1992

Guinness PLC (see Diageo plc)
- 223rd Summer Exhibition, 1991
- 224th Summer Exhibition, 1992
- 225th Summer Exhibition, 1993
- 226th Summer Exhibition, 1994
- 227th Summer Exhibition, 1995
- 228th Summer Exhibition, 1996
- 229th Summer Exhibition, 1997

Harpers & Queen
- Georges Rouault: The Early Years, 1903–1920, 1993
- Sandra Blow, 1994
- David Hockney: A Drawing Retrospective, 1995*
- Roger de Grey, 1996

The Headley Trust
- Denys Lasdun, 1997

The Henry Moore Foundation
- Alexander Calder, 1992
- Africa: The Art of a Continent, 1995

Ibstock Building Products Ltd
- John Soane, Architect: Master of Space and Light, 1999

The Independent
- The Pop Art Show, 1991
- Living Bridges, 1996
- Apocalypse: Beauty and Horror in Contemporary Art, 2000

Industrial Bank of Japan, Limited
- Hokusai, 1991

Donald and Jeanne Kahn
- John Hoyland, 1999

Land Securities PLC
- Denys Lasdun, 1997

The Mail on Sunday
- Royal Academy Summer Season, 1992
- Royal Academy Summer Season, 1993

Marks & Spencer
- Royal Academy Schools Premiums, 1994
- Royal Academy Schools Final Year Show, 1994*

Martini & Rossi Ltd
- The Great Age of British Watercolours, 1750–1880, 1993

Paul Mellon KBE
- The Great Age of British Watercolours, 1750–1880, 1993

Mercury Communications
- The Pop Art Show, 1991

Merrill Lynch
- American Art in the 20th Century, 1993*

Midland Bank plc
- RA Outreach Programme, 1992–1996
- Lessons in Life, 1994

Minorco
- Africa: The Art of a Continent, 1995

Natwest Group
- Nicolas Poussin 1594–1665, 1995

The Nippon Foundation
- Hiroshige: Images of Mist, Rain, Moon and Snow, 1997

Olivetti
- Andrea Mantegna, 1992

Peterborough United Football Club
- Art Treasures of England: The Regional Collections, 1997

Premiercare (National Westminster Insurance Services)
- Roger de Grey, 1996*

RA Exhibition Patrons Group
- Chagall: Love and the Stage, 1998
- Kandinsky, 1999
- Chardin 1699–1779, 2000
- Botticelli's Dante: The Drawings for The Divine Comedy, 2001

Redab (UK) Ltd
- Wisdom and Compassion: The Sacred Art of Tibet, 1992

Reed Elsevier plc
- Van Dyck 1599–1641, 1999

Republic National Bank of New York
- Sickert: Paintings, 1992

The Royal Bank of Scotland
- Braque: The Late Works, 1997*
- Premiums, 1997
- Premiums, 1998
- Premiums, 1999
- Royal Academy Schools Final Year Show, 1996
- Royal Academy Schools Final Year Show, 1997
- Royal Academy Schools Final Year Show, 1998

The Sara Lee Foundation
- Odilon Redon: Dreams and Visions, 1995

Sea Containers Ltd
- The Glory of Venice: Art in the Eighteenth Century, 1994

Silhouette Eyewear
- Wisdom and Compassion: The Sacred Art of Tibet, 1992
- Sandra Blow, 1994
- Africa: The Art of a Continent, 1995

Société Générale, UK
- Gustave Caillebotte: The Unknown Impressionist, 1996*

Société Générale de Belgique
- Impressionism to Symbolism: The Belgian Avant-Garde 1880–1900, 1994

Spero Communications
- Royal Academy Schools Final Year Show, 1992

Thames Water Plc
- Thames Water Habitable Bridge Competition, 1996

The Times
- Wisdom and Compassion: The Sacred Art of Tibet, 1992
- Drawings from the J Paul Getty Museum, 1993
- Goya: Truth and Fantasy, The Small Paintings, 1994
- Africa: The Art of a Continent, 1995

Time Out
- Sensation: Young British Artists from The Saatchi Collection, 1997
- Apocalypse: Beauty and Horror in Contemporary Art, 2000

Tractabel
- Impressionism to Symbolism: The Belgian Avant-Garde 1880–1900, 1994

Union Minière
- Impressionism to Symbolism: The Belgian Avant-Garde 1880–1900, 1994

Vistech International Ltd
- Wisdom and Compassion: The Sacred Art of Tibet, 1992

Yakult UK Ltd
- RA Outreach Programme, 1997–2000*
- *alive*: Life Drawings from the Royal Academy of Arts & Yakult Outreach Programme

* Recipients of a Pairing Scheme Award, managed by Arts + Business. Arts + Business is funded by the Arts Council of England and the Department for Culture, Media and Sport.

OTHER SPONSORS

Sponsors of events, publications and other items in the past five years:

Carlisle Group plc
Country Life
Derwent Valley plc
Fidelity Foundation
Foster and Partners
Goldman Sachs International
Gome International
Rob van Helden
IBJ International plc
John Doyle Construction
Marks & Spencer
Michael Hopkins & Partners
Morgan Stanley Dean Witter
Prada
Richard and Ruth Rogers
Strutt & Parker